# John Willis

# *Theatre World*

## 1991-1992 SEASON

### VOLUME 48

**APPLAUSE**

**THEATRE BOOK PUBLISHERS**

211 WEST 71 STREET • NEW YORK NY • 10023

# TO
# **JEROME ROBBINS**

*whose unparalleled virtuosity as dancer, choreographer, director and producer for ballet, theatre, film, opera and television has been acknowledged with numerous awards, including Donaldsons, Tonys, Oscars, Emmys, the Screen Directors Guild, Kennedy Center Honors, American Academy and Institute of Arts and Letters, and the Presidential National Medal of Art. In addition to his oeuvre in other art forms, for his 20 years of glorious musicals on Broadway, we are forever gratefully indebted.*

# CONTENTS

**EDITOR: JOHN WILLIS**
*ASSISTANT EDITOR:* TOM LYNCH
*Assistants:* Herbert Hayward, Jr., Barry Monush, Stanley Reeves, John Sala
*Staff Photographers:* Gerry Goodstein, Michael Riordan, Michael Viade, Van Williams

(center) Walter Bobbie, Nathan Lane, J.K. Simmons and the company of "Guys & Dolls,"
winner of 1992 "Tonys" for Best Revival, Best Actress-Musical (Faith Prince),
Best Director-Musical, Best Scenic Design *(Martha Swope Photo)*

The season started slowly with only 5 productions opening during the first 6 months, and 21 of 37 opening during the last 3 months. For many years the new season began in early fall, but it now seems to be shifting to February through April in order to better compete for the Tony Awards. The audience depends in great part on tourism, but very few visit during January and February. Nine members of the Tony nominating committee were replaced by the administration whose spokesman said they want "working professionals" to see ALL productions for next season's nominees. The current committee had given 9 nominations to shows that had already closed. Seemingly the administration did not want honors bestowed upon productions that were not currently running.

But Broadway had a very profitable year: more productions, more Hollywood stars, more theatregoers than in several years, and a boxoffice record was broken. According to a report from the League of American Theatres and Producers, more people attended theatre than all New York City sports events combined. Nationwide, professional theatre sells more tickets than the combined National Football League, National Basketball Association, and National Hockey League. However, in spite of boxoffice success, attendance has been on the decline for the past 10 years. 6 of Broadway's 13 musicals were selling seats for $65 each, and the cost of mounting new musicals is soaring beyond reason ($8 million and up), and long-running productions make theatres unavailable for new ones.

15 new plays arrived as did 7 new musicals (3 revivals) and last season's "Peter Pan" made a return visit for the holiday season. 10 plays were revived; the majority in non-profit houses. The hits were "A Christmas Carol," "Dancing at Lughnasa," "Death and the Maiden," "Man of La Mancha" and "Peter Pan." There were 9 failures, 11 undetermined, 11 non-profit, and 16 holdovers from the past seasons: more productions than in any of the last 5 years. 1980-1981 remains the best season, and 1972-1973 the worst, according to the League.

Tonys were awarded "Dancing at Lughnasa" (Best Play/Best Featured Actress, Brid Brennan/Director, Patrick Mason), "Crazy for You" (Best Musical/Costumes/Choreography), "Falsettos" (Best Book/Score), Judd Hirsch (Best Actor/"Conversations with My Father"). Glenn Close (Best Actress/ "Death and the Maiden"); for "Jelly's Last Jam" (Best Actor in a Musical, Gregory Hines/ Best Featured Actress in Musical, Tonya Pinkins/ Lighting Design), Laurence "Larry" Fishburne (Featured Actor in a Play/ "Two Trains Running"), Scott Waara (Featured Actor in Musical/ "The Most Happy Fella"), "Guys and Dolls" (Best Revival/ Best Actress in a Musical, Faith Prince/ Best Director, Jerry Zaks/ Best Sets/ Costumes). Special Tonys went to Chicago's Goodman Theatre, and to Off-Broadway's long-running "The Fantasticks." The uninspired televised presentations on Sunday, May 31, 1992 were the briefest on record and did not receive rave reviews. Thanks to the musicals, there were "happy dancing feet" and applause-provoking choreography. However, the New York Drama Critics Circle gave no honors for a musical, but cited Brian Friel's "Dancing at Lughnasa" as Best Foreign Play and August Wilson's "Two Trains Running" as Best New American Play. Ingmar Bergman's impressive revivals at the Brooklyn Academy of Music were unfortunately not eligible for Tonys, even though among the most deserving. "Miss Julie," "A Long Day's Journey into Night," and "A Doll's House" were performed in Swedish by Mr. Bergman's Royal Dramatic Theatre Company of Sweden. Tony Randall's National Theatre was not eligible for Tonys either, because with a $3 million deficit it could not afford to give free seats to all Tony voters. The enviable Clarence Derwent Award checks went to Tonya Pinkins ("Jelly's Last Jam") and Patrick Fitzgerald of Off-Broadway's "Grandchild of Kings."

Although Broadway was enjoying record boxoffice receipts, the over 200 Off-Broadway and small non-profit theatres were hurting and over 25 were forced to lower their final curtain. The 25-year-old Negro Ensemble Company closed, as did the 13-year-old Manhattan Punch Line. The 24-year-old AMAS Repertory Theatre suspended its operations temporarily, and other fatalities were the Double Image Company, Apple Corps Theatre, The New Theatre of Brooklyn, and Quaigh Theatre. Companies with more donors and larger subscriber lists were able to continue. La Mama was also on the verge of collapse, but was temporarily saved by fund-raising performances to supplement the enormously reduced federal, state, city and corporate funding. Fortunately, the New York Theatre Workshop (founded in 1979 by James Nicola) experienced a record breaking increase in subscribers and was able to buy its own venue. Its greatest success this year was "Mad Forest."

Notable Off-Broadway productions during the season include "The Complete Works of William Shakespeare (Abridged)" by the Reduced Shakespeare Company, "Red Scare on Sunset," "The Haunted Host/Safe Sex," "The Good Times Are Killing Me," "Mambo Mouth" (written and performed by John Leguizamo), "Beau Jest," "Distant Fires," "Ruthless!," "From the Mississippi Delta," "The Blue Man Group in Tubes," revivals of musicals "Rags" and "Chess," "Grandchild of Kings," "Marvin's Room," "Crown of Kings," "Lips Together, Teeth Apart," "Sight Unseen," "Boesman and Lena" and "Fires in the Mirror" (written and performed by Anna Deavere Smith).

Performances worth noting (in addition to those mentioned above) were given by Bruce Adler, Alan Alda, Jane Alexander, Ann-Margret, Conrad Bain, Alec Baldwin, Talia Balsam, Christine Baranski, Brian Bedford, Jodi Benson, Stephen Bogardus, Walter Bobbie, Barry Bostwick, Laura Bundy, Kate Burton, Charles Busch, Joanne Camp, Keith Carradine, Stockard Channing, Charles Cioffi, Joan Collins, Jane Connell, Michael Cristofer, Lindsay Crouse, Keith David, Mac Davis, Mary Bond Davis, Joan Diener (returned to her original 1965 role in "Man of La Mancha"), Donal Donnelly, Polly Draper, Richard Dreyfuss, Craig Dudley, Griffin Dunne, Ann Duquesnay, Sheena Easton, Donna English, Giancarlo Esposito, Laura Esterman, Harvey Fierstein, Peter Gallagher, Victor Garber, Ben Gazzara, Daniel Gerroll, Debbie Gibson, Tony Gillan, Joanna Gleason, Savion Glover, Harry Groener, Gene Hackman, Mel Harris, Sophie Hayden, Anthony Heald, Jonathan Hogan, Zeljko Ivanek, Dana Ivey, Judith Ivey, Simon Jones, Jonathan Kaplan, Judy Kuhn, Jack Klugman, Nathan Lane, Stephen Lang, Jessica Lange, Liz Larson, Lou Liberatore, Laura Linney, Dorothy Loudon, Rob Lowe, Amy Madigan, Mako, Spiro Malas, Cynthia Martells, Elizabeth McGovern, Barry Miller, Debra Mooney, Brian Murray, James Naughton, Al Pacino, Estelle Parsons, Anne Pitoniak, Maryann Plunkett, Kevin Ramsey, Tony Randall, Gordana Rashovich, Lynn Redgrave, Vivian Reed, Scott Renderer, Cathy Rigby, Jason Robards, Mark Rosenthal, Michael Rupert, Chris Sarandon, George C. Scott, Tony Shalhoub, Helen Shaver, Martin Sheen, Sheila Smith, Patrick Stewart, Eric Stoltz, Keith Szarabajka, Eugene Terry, Lynne Thigpen, Linda Thorson, Brenda Vaccaro, Joyce Van Patten, Christopher Walken, Eli Wallach, Barbara Walsh, Fritz Weaver, Jake Weber, Al White, Paxton Whitehead, Ruth Williamson, Laura Linney, Chandra Wilson, Scott Wise, Jason Workman, Teresa Wright, Michael York, Karen Ziemba, Chip Zien, Adrian Zmed, and the entire cast of "Dancing at Lughnasa."

RANDOM NOTES during the year: An increased number of foreign corporations were investing in Broadway in turn for ancillary rights...The Democratic Convention to nominate a presidential candidate failed to create as much revenue as anticipated...Variety Photo Plays Theatre (14 St. & 3rd Ave.) was rented for 25 years, refurbished, renovated, renamed Variety Arts Theatre, and re-opened as a 499 seat Off-Broadway facility with "Return to the Forbidden Planet" (A London award-winning musical) on Sept. 7 1991...Off Broadway's venerable Roundabout theatre moved to Broadway's Criterion Center and opened Jan. 1, 1992 with Jane Alexander in a memorable performance of "The Visit." It is a designated Broadway House with productions eligible for Tonys, although a non-profit theatre...Oct. 31, 1991 Joseph Papp, one of the most influential producers in American theatre history died of cancer and on Apr. 23, 1992 the landmark complex he created was re-named The Joseph Papp Public Theatre...Although "Nick & Nora" was an unqualified "flop," it was recorded... "Shimada" was the first production to provide simultaneous Japanese translation... Theatre for the Blind presented "Hamlet" Off Broadway with a cast of only 6... From Jan. 26, 1992 theatres are required to have infra-red hearing devices for the hearing impaired... New buildings on Broadway and Seventh Avenue have brought bigger and better neon signs to illuminate "The Great White Way..." A commemorative plaque was installed in the Shubert Theatre to honor the 15 year residency of "A Chorus Line" Dec. 3, 1991 was the third annual "Gypsy of the Year" competition in the St. James Theatre... "Cats" celebrated its ninth year appropriately... Former Mayor Ed Koch became a film and theatre critic for a chain of weekly papers... AEA filed a grievance against producers of "The Will Rogers Follies" for racial discrimination in hiring. Subsequently 2 black actresses were added to the cast... The 100th anniversary of Cole Porter's birth was celebrated with a concert in Carnegie Hall in conjunction with the Second International Festival of the Arts (Martin E. Segal, Chairman). The Festival ran for 16 days in June 1991 with fewer productions, but better quality than its predecessor... NYSF/Delacorte in Central Park presented a Brazilian /all-Portuguese-language "Midsummer Night's Dream" with nudity...Show Business (a theatrical paper with casting tips folded after many years... As of Jan. 1, 1992, new uniformed security and information officers were assigned to the theatre district (42nd to 52nd Sts.) from 9:30AM to 1AM daily. Uniforms are similar but not identical to police. Times Square Business Improvement District (B.I.D.) also provides sanitation crews to keep the area cleaner and safer. Parking meters (896) were installed also... A "Broadway Line" was established to provide prospective ticket buyers information about productions on and off Broadway... Sadly, the Mark Hellinger Theatre was sold to the Times Square Church, proving landmarking doesn't necessarily save a theatre... TV and radio critics were cut from several stations.. The Post Office issued stamps with Al Hirschfeld's comedians — first artist so honored... Once again Off-Broadway Passports during April offered discounts of up to 50% for some 75 production... The 6th annual Easter Bonnet Competition honoring the cast with the best hat, and also the one having collected the most funds during the year for Broadway Cares/Equity Fights Aids... Again receipts for touring companies set a record: up 11% from the previous season... The Edison Theatre was converted to the cabaret Supper Club... American Theatre Wing initiated a program to cultivate theatre audiences by allowing a number of high school students to attend Broadway productions at minimal prices: students pay half and the Wing pays half... The Department of Consumer Affairs voted to have future ads clearly disclose when a play is previewing and when it officially opens... New York City Museum desperately needs funds and help for its theatre collection that documents the New York stage from 1767 with the city's first permanent playhouse, the John Street Theatre.

# BROADWAY PRODUCTIONS

### (June 1,1991 through May 31, 1992)

## THE ODD COUPLE

By Neil Simon; Director, Harvey Medlinsky; Presented by the National Actors Theatre for one night only in the Belasco Theatre on Sunday, June 23, 1991.

### CAST

| | |
|---|---|
| Felix Unger | Tony Randall |
| Oscar Madison | Jack Klugman |
| Pigeon Sisters | Kate Nelligan, Joanna Gleason |
| Poker Players | Martin Sheen, Abe Vigoda, Cleavon Little, Jack Weston |

A benefit performance of the 1965 comedy. For original Broadway production see *Theatre World* Vol.21.

LEFT: Jack Klugman    RIGHT: Tony Randall

## GETTING MARRIED

By George Bernard Shaw; Director, Stephen Porter; Sets, James Morgan; Costumes, Holly Hynes; Lighting, Mary Jo Dondlinger; Casting, Judy Henderson, Alycia Aumuller; Company Manager, Susan Elrod; Stage Managers, Wm. Hare, Jack Gianino; Presented by Circle in the Square Theatre (Theodore Mann, Artistic Director; Robert Buckley, Managing Director; Paul Libin, Consulting Producer); Press, Maria Somma; Previewed from Friday, June 7; Opened in the Circle In The Square Uptown on Wednesday, June 26, 1991.*

### CAST

| | |
|---|---|
| Mrs. Bridgenorth | Elizabeth Franz |
| Collins | Patrick Tull |
| General | Nicolas Coster |
| Lesbia | Victoria Tennant |
| Reginald | Simon Jones |
| Leo | Madeleine Potter |
| Bishop | Lee Richardson |
| Hotchkiss | Scott Wentworth |
| Cecil | J.D. Cullum |
| Edith | Jane Fleiss |
| Soames | Walter Bobbie |
| Beadle | Guy Paul |
| Mrs. George | Linda Thorson |

**UNDERSTUDIES:** Burt Edwards (Collins/General/Beadle/Reginald/Bishop), Alexandra O'Karma (Mrs. George/Mrs. Bridgenorth/Lesbia), Alexandra Napier (Leo/Edith)

A comedy in two acts. The action takes place at The Bishop's Palace during the 1908 spring.

This new production of Shaw's 1908 work was met with a mixed critical reception. All seemed to feel the play itself was lesser Shaw, but still worthwhile. *Times* critics were split with Wilborn Hampton finding the cast "mostly able" while David Richards said "there are precious few signs of life here, independent of the playwright's." The *Post's* Clive Barnes found the evening "witty...clever". At the *Daily News* Howard Kissel found it "a long sit" while Doug Watt called it "halfway very much worthwhile." *Newsday's* Jan Stuart commented the play had "deliriously frayed ends."

*Closed August 25, 1991 after 70 performances and 22 previews.

*Martha Swope Photos*

**Top Left: Scott Wentworth, Linda Thorson**
**Above: Patrick Tull, Elizabeth Franz**

# A LITTLE NIGHT MUSIC

Music/Lyrics, Stephen Sondheim; Book, Hugh Wheeler; Based on Ingmar Bergman's film *Smiles of a Summer Night*; Director, Scott Ellis; Conductor, Paul Gemignani; Orchestrations, Jonathan Tunick; Sets, Michael Anania; Costumes, Lindsay W. Davis; Lighting, Dawn Chiang; Choreography, Susan Stroman; Sound, Abe Jacob; Musical Preparation, Douglas Stanton; Presented by the New York City Opera (Christopher Keene, General Director); Originally Produced on Broadway by Harold Prince; Press, Susan Woelzl/Dale Zeidman; Opened in the New York State Theatre on Tuesday, July 9, 1991.*

## CAST

| | |
|---|---|
| Mrs. Segstrom | Susanne Marsee |
| Mr. Lindquist | Ron Baker |
| Mrs. Nordstrom | Lisa Saffer |
| Mrs. Anderssen | Barbara Shirvis |
| Mr. Erlanson/Bertrand | Peter Blanchet |
| Fredrika Armfeldt | Danielle Ferland |
| Madame Armfeldt | Elaine Bonazzi |
| Frid | David Fuller |
| Henrik Egerman | Kevin P. Anderson |
| Anne Egerman | Beverly Lambert |
| Fredrik Egerman | George Lee Andrews |
| Petra | Joanna Glushak |
| Desiree Armfeldt | Sally Ann Howes |
| Malla | Raven Wilkinson |
| Count Carl-Magnus Malcolm | Michael Maguire |
| Countess Charlotte Malcolm | Maureen Moore |
| Osa | Judith Jarosz |
| Serving Gentlemen | Kent A. Heacock, Ronald Kelley, Jeff Kensmoe, Ian D. Klapper, Brian Michaels, Brian Quirk, John Henry Thomas, Mike Timoney |

**MUSICAL NUMBERS:** Overture, Night Waltz, Now/Later/Soon, Glamorous Life, Remember?, You Must Meet My Wife, Liaisons, In Praise of Women, Every Day a Little Death, Weekend in the Country, The Sun Won't Set, It Would Have Been Wonderful, Perpetual Anticipation, Send in the Clowns, Miller's Son, Finale

A new production of the 1973 musical in two acts. The action takes place in turn of the century Sweden. For original Broadway production see *Theatre World* Vol.29.

This production, first performed last season, was rapturously received by drama and music critics. Newsday's Jan Stuart wrote "*Night Music* is all of 18 years young. It exudes the plushy, lived-in comfort of a classic." Allan Kozinn at the *Times* felt "Mr. Sondheim has developed a sophisticated theatre style that transforms fairly easily to the opera stage..." At the *News* Doug Watt was "cheered by the company's continuing policy ...to slip revivals of major Broadway musicals into the repertoire." The *Post's* Susan Elliott agreed, calling the production "a triumph of the stage."

*Closed August 10, 1991 after 7 limited performances in repertory

*Carol Rosegg/Martha Swope Photos*

**A Little Night Music**

**ABOVE: Elizabeth Walsh, Louis Quilico**

# THE MOST HAPPY FELLA

Music/Lyrics/Book by Frank Loesser; Based on *They Knew What They Wanted* by Sidney Howard; Director/Conductor, Chris Nance; Orchestrations, Don Walker; Sets, Michael Anania; Lighting, Mark W. Stanley; Costumes, Beba Shamash; Choreography, Dan Siretta; Sound, Abe Jacob; Chorus Master, Joseph Colaneri; Musical Preparation, Douglas Stanton; Presented by the New York City Opera (Christopher Keene, General Director); Press, Susan Woelzl, Dale Zeidman; Opened in the New York State Theatre on Wednesday, September 4, 1991.*

## CAST

| | |
|---|---|
| Cashier/Postman | William Ledbetter |
| Cleo | Karen Ziemba, Joanna Glushak |
| Rosabella | Elizabeth Walsh, Michele McBride |
| Waitresses | Jean Barber, Joan Mirabella, Deidre Sheehan |
| Busboys | Dean Dufford, Michael Langlois |
| Tony | Louis Quilico, John Fiorito |
| Marie | Elaine Bonazzi, Susanne Marsee |
| Max | Ron Hilley |
| Herman | Lara Teeter, Brian Quinn |
| Clem | Gregory Moore |
| Jake | David Frye |
| Al | Jonathan Guss |
| Joe | Burke Moses, John Leslie Wolfe |
| Giuseppe | Arthur Rubin |
| Pasquale | Richard Byrne |
| Ciccio | John Lankston |
| Doctor | Peter Blanchet |
| Priest | Don Yule |
| Tessie | Alice Roberts |
| Gussie | Zachary London |
| Artie | Alexander Senchak, Jonathan Zwi |
| Neighbors | Harris Davis, Michael Langlois, Louis Perry, Phillip Sneed, William Ward, Edward Zimmerman, Lee Bellaver, Esperanza Galan, Stephanie Godino, Rita Metzger |
| Station Attendant | James Russell |

A new production of the 1956 musical in three acts with eleven scenes. The action takes place in San Francisco and Napa, California in 1953. For original Broadway production see *Theatre World* Vol.12.

Utilizing the complete original orchestrations, the show was mostly joyfully received. The *Times* found the "...split-level aspirations..." of the musical/opera mix "...uneven." while other critics didn't worry about which genre *Fella* best represents. The *News* proclaimed it "...triumphant..." and claimed "...the humongous cast didn't have a weak link." The *Post* said it was a "...guaranteed happy time..." and *Newsday* called it a "...bright, unfailingly lively revival." *Variety* summed up: "a worthwhile reminder that full-blown doesn't necessarily mean overblown."

*Closed October 18 after 10 limited performances in repertory.

*Carol Rosegg/Martha Swope Photos*

# BARRY MANILOW'S SHOWSTOPPERS

Director, Kevin Carlisle; Sets, Jim Youmans; Lighting, Don Holder; Musical Director, Kevin Bassinson; Press, Susan DuBow/Solters, Roskin, Friedman; Opened in the Paramount Theatre on Wednesday, September 25, 1992*

## CAST

### BARRY MANILOW
Kevin Brakett, Debra Byrd, Donna Cherry, Craig Meyer, Michelle Nicastro

**MUSICAL NUMBERS INCLUDED:** Give My Regards to Broadway, The Kid Inside, You Can Have the TV, Where or When, Dancing in the Dark, I Got Rhythm, Rhapsody in Blue/Trying to Get the Feeling Again, Tonight/Somewhere in the Night, Cabaret/Daybreak, Once in Love with Amy, 76 Trombones/It's a Miracle, Even Now, Fascinating Rhythm, Mandy, Read 'em and Weep, NYC Rhythm, I am Your Child, Never Met a Man I Didn't Like, Old Friends, I'll Be Seeing You

Performed with one intermission. This presentation marked the re-opening of the former Felt Forum, now the new Paramount. Mr. Manilow's previous Broadway engagements include a 1989 run at the Gershwin and in 1976 at the same theatre when it was the Uris.

*Closed September 28, 1992 after limited engagement of 4 performances.

**RIGHT: Barry Manilow**

# ON BORROWED TIME

By Paul Osborn; Based on the novel by L. E. Watkin; Director, George C. Scott; Sets, Marjorie Bradley Kellogg; Costumes, Holly Hynes; Lighting, Mary Jo Dondlinger; Casting, Judy Henderson, Alycia Aumuller; Stage Manager, Wm. Hare; Presented by Circle in the Square (Theodore Mann, Artistic Director; Managing Director, Paul Lubin, Consulting Producer); Press, Maria Somma, Patty Onagan; Previewed from Friday, September 20; Opened in the Circle in the Square Uptown on Wednesday, October 9, 1991*

## CAST

| | |
|---|---|
| Pud | Matthew Porac |
| Julian Northrup/Gramps | George C. Scott |
| Nellie/Grannie | Teresa Wright |
| Mr. Brink | Nathan Lane |
| Marcia Giles | Alice Haining |
| Demetria Riffle | Bette Henritze |
| Boy in Tree | Matt White |
| Workmen | Arnie Mazer, James Noah |
| Dr. Evans | Conrad Bain |
| Mr. Grimes | George DiCenzo |
| Mr. Pilbeam | Allen Williams |
| Sheriff | James Jamrog |
| Betty | Marilyn |

**UNDERSTUDIES:** Bill Severs (Gramps/Evans), John LaGioia (Brink), Jennie Ventriss (Granny/Demetria), Katie Finnernan (Marcia), Arnie Mazer (Mr. Pilbeam/Sheriff), James Noah (Grimes), Daniel Reifsnyder (Pud/Boy)

A new production of the 1938 fantasy performed in two acts with eight scenes. The action takes place on a late summer's day before the Great War.

George C. Scott received the lion's share of praise from the critics, who found the play dated. The *Times'* Frank Rich said Mr. Scott is "the main reason for even considering a visit." and David Richards felt ..."Mr. Scott is carrying this old chestnut on his burly shoulders." Clive Barnes in the *Post* felt "...fashion has passed by and history not quite caught up with .." the play. The *News* critics praised the play with Howard Kissel finding it "...worth reviving..whimsy and fantasy..." and Watt finding "...charm and humor..." Linda Winer in *Newsday* found Mr. Scott "...always welcome."

*Closed January 5, 1992 after 99 performances and 26 previews.

*Martha Swope Photos*

Nathan Lane (top), Matthew Porac, George C. Scott

**Carlo Olds**

# ANDRE HELLER'S WONDERHOUSE

Created/Designed/Directed by Andre Heller; Asst. Director, Ivana De Vert; Lighting, Pluesch; Rideau de Scene; Erte; Costumes, Susanne Schmoegner; Sound, T. Richard Fitzgerald; English Adaptation, Mel Howard; Music Arranger/Orchestration, Andrew Powell; Conductor, J. Leonard Oxley; Stage Managers, Jack Lorden, Jack Gianino; Company Manager, Julie Crosby; Executive Producer, Norman E. Rothstein; Press, Susan Bloch/Kevin P. McAnarney, Ellen Zeisler; Previewed from Friday October 11; Opened in the Broadhurst Theatre on Sunday, October 20, 1991*

## CAST

Igor...................................................................................................................Billy Barty
Olga.................................................................................................................Patty Maloney
Stagehand.....................................................................................................Gunilla Wingquist
Guests...............................Carlo Olds, Macao, Baroness Jeanette Lips Von Lipstrill,
Omar Pasha, Ezio Bedin, Marion & Robert Konyot,
Rao, Milo & Roger, Aroon Kalan

An entertainment performed without intermission. The action takes place in the old Wonderhouse Theatre at present.

This celebration of variety, originally titled *Andre Heller's Wunderhaus*, didn't fare well with the press. *Variety* recorded 5 favorable, 2 mixed and 8 negative notices. Mel Gussow in the *Times* proclaimed "...the only wonder is that the show managed to get to Broadway." while Richards mentioned "...it is very easy to feel superior to all this." Kissel in the *News* felt "...it may be too understated, too European..." On the upside Winer in *Newsday* found the show "...odd and gentle...occasionally quite beautiful." Barnes (*Post*) felt it "...a great deal more than the sum of its parts." *Variety* noted "...a glimpse of a theatrical tradition that has all but vanished."

*Closed October 27, 1991 after 9 performances and 11 previews.

*Daniel Cande Photo*

**Conrad Bain, George C. Scott, George DiCenzo in "On Borrowed Time"**

# DANCING AT LUGHNASA

By Brian Friel; Director, Patrick Mason; Design, Joe Vanek; Lighting, Trevor Dawson; Sound, T. Richard Fitzgerald; Prod. Supervisor, Jeremiah J. Harris; Choreography, Terry John Bates; Stage Manager, Sally J. Jacobs; Company Manager, Nancy Simmons; Presented by Noel Pearson in association with Bill Kenwright, Joseph Harris, and The Abbey Theatre; Press, Shirley Herz/Sam Rudy, Glenna Freedman; Miller Wright, Robert Larkin; Previewed from Friday, October 11; Opened in the Plymouth Theatre on Thursday, October 24, 1991*

## CAST

| | |
|---|---|
| Michael | Gerard McSorley +1 |
| Chris | Catherine Byrne +2 |
| Maggie | Dearbhla Molloy +3 |
| Agnes | Brid Brennan +4 |
| Rose | Brid Ni Neachtain +5 |
| Kate | Rosaleen Linehan +6 |
| Gerry | Robert Gwilym +7 |
| Jack | Donal Donnelly |

UNDERSTUDIES:Bernadette Quigley (Agnes/Chris), Alma Cuervo (Kate), Selena Carey-Jones (Maggie/Rose), Liam Gannon (Jack), Kenneth L. Marks (Gerry/Michael)

A drama in two acts. The action takes place in the home of the Mundy family, near Ballybeg, County Donegal, Ireland.

Most of the critics raved about this play which received its world premiere last season in Dublin. Rich (*Times*) proclaimed "...this play does exactly what theatre was born to do, carrying both its characters and audience aloft..." while Richards felt it "...flawlessly acted." Both *News* aisle watchers agreed with Kissel commenting "...a rich, deeply moving evening..." and Watt adding the play would "...linger in the mind through the years." The *Post*'s Barnes called it "...a remarkable play-a wondrous experience..." though Winer at *Newsday* found it "more ...an acting exercise than ...character study." Jeremy Gerard in *Variety* felt it "...never transcends the distant time and place that anchors it so far from Broadway audiences."

*Closed October 25, 1992 after 421 performances and 15 previews. Winner of "Tony", NY Drama Critics Circle and Outer Critics Circle awards for Best Play. Winner of "Tonys" for Best Direction of a Play and Featured Actress in a Play (Brid Brennan).

+Succeeded by:1. Kenneth L. Marks 2. Jennifer Van Dyck 3. Jacqueline Knapp 4. Jan Maxwell 5. Miriam Healy-Louie 6. Patricia Hodges 7. John Wesley Shipp

*Tom Lawlor Photos*

**Jennifer Van Dyck, John Wesley Shipp**
Top: **Catherine Byrne, Brid Brennan**                                    **Jacqueline Knapp**

Dearbhla Molloy, Catherine Byrne, Rosaleen Linehan, Brid Ni Neachtain, Brid Brennan

The Company

TOP: **Daniel Gerroll, John Horton, Reed Diamond, Jonathan Hogan, (seated) Lindsay Crouse, Roy Dotrice**

# THE HOMECOMING

By Harold Pinter; Director, Gordon Edelstein; Sets, John Arnone; Costumes, William Ivey Long; Lighting, Peter Kaczorowski; Sound, Philip Campanella; General Manager, Ellen Richard; Casting, Pat McCorkle, Richard Cole; Stage Managers, Kathy J. Faul, Matthew T. Mudinger; Fights, David Leong; Presented by Roundabout Theatre Company (Todd Haimes, Producing Director; Gene Feist, Founding Director); Press, Joshua Ellis/Susanne Tighe; Previewed from Wednesday, October 9; Opened in the Criterion Center Stage Right on Sunday, October 27, 1991*

### CAST

| | |
|---|---|
| Max | Roy Dotrice |
| Lenny | Daniel Gerroll |
| Sam | John Horton |
| Joey | Reed Diamond |
| Teddy | Jonathan Hogan |
| Ruth | Lindsay Crouse |

A new production of the 1965 play performed in two acts with five scenes. The action takes place in an old house in North London. For original 1967 Broadway production see *Theatre World* Vol.23.

The first Broadway staging since the original proved *Homecoming* still has the power to divide. Rich in the *Times* felt "...the Pinter revolution against theatrical literal-mindedness has long since been fought and won" but Richards found it an "...altogether praiseworthy production." The *News* was split with Kissel saying the play "...lacked menace" while Watt disagreed : "...retains all its wry, amusing and somewhat gamy attraction." Barnes (*Post* ) opined the play was a "...virtual classic" and *Newsday* (Winer) felt "...time and Pinter have long ago made the unfathomable seem almost logical."

*Closed December 8, 1991 after 49 performances and 21 previews.

*Martha Swope Photos*

**Lindsay Crouse, Roy Dotrice**

# MOSCOW CIRCUS CIRK VALENTIN

Artistic Director, Valentin Gneushev; Staging/Book, Bob Bejan; Music, Bobby Previte; Choreography, Pavel Briun; Design/Lighting, Stephen Bickford; Costumes, Audrey Carter; Sound, Scott Rogers, Alexei Volkov; Makeup/Haistylist, Lev Novikov; Company Manager, Brian Cooper; Prod. Supervisor, Robert Socha; Stage Manager, John Wismer; General Manager, Marvin Krauss; Executive Producer, Bill Franzblau; Presented by Steven E. Leber & Soyuzgoscirk; Press, Peter Cromarty, Diane Blackman; Previewed from Tuesday, November 5; Opened in the Gershwin Theatre on Wednesday, November 6, 1991*

## PERFORMERS

| | | |
|---|---|---|
| Alexander "Sasha Frish" | Gennady Chizhov | Pavel Boyarinov |
| Nikolai Zemskov | Yuli Babich | Igor Boitsov |
| Natalia Ioshina | Yuri Maiorov | Irina Mironova |
| Yelena Mironova | Valery Sychev | Yelena Fedotova |
| Anatoly Stykan | Yuri Borzykin | Yelena Larkina |
| Serogia Loskutov Jr. | Sergey Loskutov Sr. | Nikolai Zemskov |
| Igor Boitsov | Yuli Babich | Sergey Kuznetsov |
| Slava Lunin | Yuri Odintsov | Nina Zemskova |
| Alexander "Sasha Streltsov | Andrey Ridetsky | Sergey Rudenko |
| Sergey Shipunov | Vladimir Sizov | Valery Sychev |
| Alexei Ivanov | | |

A circus entertainment in two parts encompassing eleven acts.

The critics had a mixed response. Gussow in the *Times* felt "...the most novel aspect...is that it has no rings and takes place center stage in a Broadway theatre." The *News*(Watt) found it lacking compared to "...the astonishing variety of the truly great Moscow Circus...years back..." Commenting on an opening night mishap, *Newsday* questioned whether "...to be scared or relieved to see these guys are human after all."

*Closed December 1, 1991 after 32 performances.

**RIGHT: Yelena Fedotova, Anatoly Stykan**

# BRIGADOON

Music, Frederick Loewe; Lyrics/Book, Alan Jay Lerner; Orchestrations, Ted Royal; Conductor, Paul Gemignani; Director, Gerald Freedman; Sets, Costumes, Desmond Heeley; Lighting, Duane Schuler; Sound, Abe Jacob; Choreography, (original) Agnes de Mille, (recreation) James Jamieson; Chorus Master, Joseph Colaneri; Press, Dale Zeidman; Presented by New York City Opera (Christopher Keene, General Director); Opened in the New York State Theatre on Thursday, November 7, 1991*

## CAST

| | |
|---|---|
| Tommy Albright | John Leslie Wolfe, George Dvorsky |
| Jeff Douglas | Tony Roberts |
| Maggie Anderson | Joan Mirabella |
| Archie Beaton | William Ledbetter |
| Angus MacGuffie | Don Yule |
| Meg Brockie | Joyce Castle, Louisa Flanigam |
| Stuart Dalrymple | Richard Byrne |
| Sandy Dean | Gregory Moore |
| Harry Beaton | Scott Fowler |
| Andrew MacLaren | David Rae Smith |
| Fiona MacLaren | Michele McBride, Elizabeth Ealsh |
| Jean MacLaren | Camille de Ganon |
| Charlie Dalrymple | David Eisler, Robert Tate |
| Fish Monger | Stephanie Godino |
| Mr. Lundie | Ron Randell |
| Sword Dancers | Joe Deer, William Ward |
| Bagpiper | Stephen Fox |
| Frank | Jonathan Guss |
| Jane Ashton | Leslie Farrell |

**MUSICAL NUMBERS:** Once in the Highlands, Brigadoon, Down on MacConnachy Square, Waitin' for My Dearie, I'll Go Home with Bonnie Jean, Heather on the Hill, The Love of My Life, Jeannie's Packin' Up, Come to Me Bend to Me, Almost Like Being in Love, Wedding Dance, Sword Dance, Chase, There But for You Go I, My Mother's Weddin' Day, Funeral Dance, From This Day On

The 1947 musical in two acts. City Opera originated their *Brigadoon* in 1986. For original Broadway version see *Theatre World* Vol.3.

*Closed November 17, 1991 after 12 limited performances in repertory.

*Carol Rosegg/Martha Swope Photos*

**George Dvorsky, Elizabeth Walsh**

**Jason Robards**
RIGHT: **Judith Ivey**

# PARK YOUR CAR IN HARVARD YARD

By Israel Horovitz; Director, Zoe Caldwell; Set, Ben Edwards; Costumes, Jane Greenwood; Lighting, Thomas R. Skelton; Sound, John Gromada; Stage Managers, Jay Adler, Dianne Trulock; Company Manager, Bruce Klinger; Presented by Robert Whitehead, Roger L. Stevens, Kathy Levin, and American National Theatre and Academy; Press, Shirley Herz/Glenna Freedman, Miller Wright, Sam Rudy; Previewed from Wednesday, October 30; Opened in the Music Box Theatre on Thursday, November 7, 1991*

## CAST

Jacob Brackish..................................................................................Jason Robards
Kathleen Hogan .....................................................................................Judith Ivey

**UNDERSTUDIES:** Salem Ludwig (Jacob), Kristin Griffith (Kathleen)

A comedy performed without intermission. The action takes place in Gloucester, Massachusetts from one winter to the next.

The actors, rather than the play, were the thing. *Variety* tallied 3 favorable, 10 mixed and 5 negative reviews. The *Times*' Rich called it "...one of those one-set, two actor, odd couple contractions that periodically seduce producers." Both *News* critics praised the players with Kissel calling their work "...an illuminating example of the actors art..." and Watt finding "...two first-rate actors..." in "...not much of a play." In the *Post* Barnes said "...for admirers of Judith Ivey and Jason Robards..." while *Newsday* (Winer) felt when "...those actors happen to be of the caliber of Robards and Ivey, it is extremely likely that something will catch fire...and so it does..."

*Closed February 22, 1992 after 122 performances and 8 previews.

*Joan Marcus Photos*

**Jason Robards, Judith Ivey**

# RADIO CITY CHRISTMAS SPECTACULAR

Director/Choreography, Scott Salmon; Originally Conceived, Produced and Directed by Robert F. Jani; Sets, Charles Lisanby; Musical Director/Vocal Arrangements, Don Pippin; Lighting, Ken Billington; Costumes, Pete Menefee; Original Staging/Choreography Restaging, Violet Holmes, Linda Lemac; Stage Manager, Howard Kolins; Executive Producer, David J. Nash; New Orchestrations, Michael Gibson, Danny Troob, Jonathan Tunick, Jim Tyler, Bob Wheeler; Original Songs, Stan Lebowsky, Fred Tobias, Billy But; Press, Kevin M. Brockman; Opened in Radio City Music Hall on Friday, November 15, 1991*

## CAST

Charles Edward Hall (Santa/Scrooge), Marty Simpson (Mrs. Santa), David Elder (Cratchit), James Darrah (Nephew), Scott Spahr (Marley's Ghost), Pascale Faye-Williams (Christmas Past), Tim Hamrick (Christmas Present), Leigh-Anne Wencker (Mrs. Cratchit), Suzanne Phillips (Belinda), Laura Bundy, Christen Tassen (Sarah), Sean Dooley, Joey Rigol (Peter), Christopher Boyce, Ari Vernon (Tiny Tim), Todd Hunter (Poultry Man), Laurie Welch, Randy Coyne, Alison Blake, Bruce Hurd (Skaters), Robert E. Lee, R. Louis Carry, John Edward Allen, Michael J. Gilden, Leslie Stump, Elena Rose Bertagnolli, Phil Fondacaro (Elves), Ellyn Arons, Leslie Bell, Michael Berglund, John Clonts, James Darrah, John Dietrich, Jack Hayes, Nanci Jennings, Keith Locke, Michelle Mallardi, Sharon Moore, Wendy Piper, Stephen Reed, Mary Jayne Waddell, Jim Weaver, David Wood (Singers), Joe Bowerman, Tina DeLeone, David Elder, Christopher Gattelli, Steve Geary, Bill Hastings, Terry Lacey, Bonnie Lynn, Marty McDonough, Joan Mirabella (Dancers), Charles Edward Hall (Narrator)

### The Rockettes

**PROGRAM:** Herald Trumpeters, We Need a Little Christmas, Overture, Nutcracker, A Christmas Carol, Christmas in New York, Ice Skating in the Plaza, Santa Claus, They Can't Start Christmas, Parade of the Wooden Soldiers, Santa's Journey, Carol of the Bells, Living Nativity, One Solitary Life, Joy to the World

The annual holiday attraction.

*Closed January 7, 1992 after 176 performances

*Mark Kozlowski Photos*

**Living Nativity**

**Bears in Toyland**

**Cathy Rigby**
Top Left: J.K. Simmons, Cathy Rigby

# PETER PAN

Music, Moose Charlap, Jule Styne; Lyrics, Carolyn Leigh, Betty Comden and Adolph Green; Adapted from the play by Sir James M. Barrie; Director, Fran Soeder; Restaging, Bill Bateman; Original Conception/Direction/Choreography, Jerome Robbins; Musical Director, Brian Tidwell; Musical Supervisor, Kevin Farrell; Orchestrations, Albert Sendrey (original), M. Michael Fauss, Mr. Farrell (new); Choreography, Marilyn Magness; Sets, Michael J. Hotopp, Paul dePass, James Leonard Joy; Costumes, Mariann Verheyen; Lighting, Natasha Katz; Sound, Peter J. Fitzgerald; Wigs, Rick Geyer; General Manager, Lonn Entertainment; Stage Managers, Frank Hartenstein, Eric Insko; Flying by Foy; Presented by Thomas P. McCoy, Keith Stava, P.P. Investments, and Jon B. Platt; Press, Shirley Herz/Glenna Freedman, Sam Rudy, Miller Wright; Opened in the Minskoff Theatre on Wednesday, November 27, 1991*

## CAST

Wendy Darling/Jane ....................................................................Cindy Robinson
John Darling ...................................................................................David Burdick
Michael Darling .....................................................................................Joey Cee
Liza ..............................................................................................Anne McVey
Nana.............................................................................................Bill Bateman
Mrs. Darling/Wendy grown ....................................................Lauren Thompson
Mr. Darling/Captain Hook ..............................................................J.K. Simmons
Peter Pan ........................................................................................Cathy Rigby
Curly ............................................................................................Alon Williams
1st Twin......................................................................................Janet Kay Higgins
2nd Twin.........................................................................................Courtney Wynn
Slightly ....................................................................................Christopher Ayres
Tootles ......................................................................................Julian Brightman
Mr. Smee .............................................................................................Don Potter
Cecco .............................................................................................Calvin Smith
Gentleman Starkey.............................................................................Carl Packard
Crocodile .......................................................................................Barry Ramsey
Tiger Lily.................................................................................Michelle Schumacher
Pirates and Indians ......................Andy Ferrara, Mr. Bateman, Ms. McVey, Charlie Marcus, Mr. Packard, Mr. Ramsey, Joseph Savant,
...........................................................Mr. Smith, David Thome, John Wilkerson

**UNDERSTUDIES:** Cindy Robinson (Pan), Carl Packard (Mr. Darling/Hook), Anne McVey (Mrs. Darling), Bill Bateman (Smee), Courtney Wynn (Wendy/Tiger Lily), Christopher Ayres (John), David Burdick (Michael), Julian Brightman (Twins), Janet Kay Higgins (Tootles/Slightly/Curly), **SWING:** Jim Alexander

**MUSICAL NUMBERS:** Tender Shepherd, I've Got to Crow, Neverland, I'm Flying, Pirate March, Princely Scheme, Indians!, Wendy, Tarantella, I Won't Grow Up, Ugg-a-Wugg, Distant Melody, Hook's Waltz, Finale

A production of the 1954 musical in three acts. The action takes place in the Darling residence, London, and in Neverland. A return engagement of last season's revival. For original Broadway production see *Theatre World* Vol 11. For last season's version, see *Theatre World* Vol. 47.

*Carol Rosegg/Martha Swope Photos*

* Closed Jan. 5, 1992 after 48 performances.

**Cindy Robinson, Cathy Rigby**
Above: Cathy Rigby

# CATSKILLS ON BROADWAY

Conception, Freddie Roman; Supervision, Larry Arrick; Set, Lawrence Miller; Lighting, Peggy Eisenhauer; Sound, Peter Fitgerald; Musical Director, Barry Levitt; Opening Musical Sequence Arrangement, Don Pippin; Design, Wendall Harrrington; Creative Consultant, Richard Vos; General Manager, Peter T. Kulok; Company Manager, Kathleen Lowe; Stage Managers, Martin Gold, David O'Brien; Associate Producer, Sandra Greenblatt; Presented by Kenneth D. Greenblatt, Stephen D. Fish, and 44 Productions; Press, Shirley Herz/Miller Wright, Sam Rudy, Glenna Freedman; Previewed from Tuesday, November 11; Opened in the Lunt-Fontanne Theatre on Thursday, December 5, 1991*

## CAST

Freddie Roman
Marilyn Michaels +1
Mal Z. Lawrence
Dick Capri

**UNDERSTUDIES:** During illness, guest performers included Julie Budd, Henny Youngman, Nipsey Russell

An evening of comedy performed without intermission.

"The title of the show ... deserves a truth-in-advertising award" commented Mel Gussow for the *Times*, adding "there is no special adaptation to the Broadway stage" but "you pay your money and you get the jokes." The *Daily News* concurred "no surprises, but a lot of fun." Clive Barnes in the *Post* felt "half ... is thoroughly entertaining - Broadway stuff, Broadway style - but the other half is more like dinner-theatre fare, with the dinner not that great and the fare not that fair." *Newsday*'s Jan Stuart observed it was "an authentic tribute to the sentimental and vulgar art of Catskills stand-up..." while *Variety* noted "the entire evening could just as easily take place at Grossingers or an Atlantic City casino." *Variety* tallied 8 favorable and 4 mixed reviews.

*Martha Swope Photo*

*Closed Jan. 3, 1993 after 452 performances and 19 previews.

+ Succeeded by : 1. Louise DuArt

CLOCKWISE FROM TOP LEFT: **Marilyn Michaels, Freddie Roman, Dick Capri, Mal Z. Lawrence**

Freddie Roman, Mal Z. Lawrence, Dick Capri, Marilyn Michaels

# NICK & NORA

Music, Charles Strouse; Lyrics, Richard Maltby, Jr.; Book/Director, Arthur Laurents; Based on characters created by Dashiell Hammett, and the *Thin Man* movies; Orchestrations, Jonathan Tunick; Musical/Vocal Director, Jack Lee; Sets, Douglas W. Schmidt; Costumes, Theoni V. Aldredge; Lighting, Jules Fisher; Choreography, Tina Paul; Dance/Incidental Arrangements, Grodon Lowry Harrell; Sound, Peter Fitgerald; Hairstylist/Makeup, Robert DiNiro; Animals, William Berloni; Casting, Stuart Howard, Amy Schecter; Production Supervisor, Janet Beroza; Technical, Jeremiah J. Harris; General Manager, Ralph Roseman; Stage Managers, Robert Bennett, Maureen F. Gibson; Press, Jeffrey Richards, David LeShay; Original Cast Recording, TER; Previewed from Tuesday, October 8; Opened in the Marquis Theatre on Sunday, December 8, 1991*

## CAST

| | |
|---|---|
| Asta | Riley |
| Nora Charles | Joanna Gleason |
| Nick Charles | Barry Bostwick |
| Tracy Gardner | Christine Baranski |
| Yukido | Thom Sesma |
| Mavis | Kathy Morath |
| Delli/Waitress | Kristen Wilson |
| Max Berheim | Remak Ramsay |
| Victor Moisa | Chris Sarandon |
| Spider Malloy | Jeff Brooks |
| Lorraine Bixby | Faith Prince |
| Edward J. Connors | Kip Niven |
| Lt. Wolfe | Michael Lombard |
| Maria Valdez | Yvette Lawrence, Josie de Guzman (previews) |
| Lily Connors | Debra Monk |
| Selznick | Hal Robinson |
| Msgr. Flaherty | John Jellison |
| Mariachi | Tim Connell, Kris Phillips |

**UNDERSTUDIES/STANDBYS:** Kay McClelland (Nora/Tracy), Richard Muenz (Nick/Victor), Hal Robinson (Max/Wolfe), Kathy Morath (Lorraine/Lily), Kristen Wilson (Maria), John Jellison (Spider/Connors), Kris Phillips (Yukido), BJ (Asta), **SWINGS:** Mark Hoebee, Cynthia Thole, **Captain:** Mr. Hoebee

**MUSICAL NUMBERS:** Is There Anything Better Than Dancing?, Everybody Wants to Do a Musical, Not Me, Swell, As Long as You're Happy, People Get Hurt, Men, May the Best Man Win, Detectiveland, Look Who's Alone Now, Class, Let's Go Home, A Busy Night at Lorraine's, Boom Chicka Boom.

**ADDITIONAL NUMBERS DURING PREVIEWS:** Now You See Me Now You Don't, Quartet in Two Bars, There's More, The Second Time We Met, It's Easy, Battlecry, Hollywood, People Like Us, Cocktails for One, A Dangerous Man, The Road to Guadalajara, See Me, Time to Go.

A musical in two acts. The action takes place in Hollywood, 1937.

The first original musical of the season was a disaster for the critics. *Variety* tallied 1 favorable, 2 mixed and 16 negative notices. The *Times*'s Rich said "the story of *Nick & Nora* in previews, should it ever be fully known, might in itself make for a riotous, 1930's-style screwball-comedy musical. But the plodding show that has emerged is...an almost instantly forgettable mediocrity...There are some pretty tunes along the way." Richards added the score "...might actually prove rather engaging..." but the show "...consistently takes one step forward and one step back..." Kissel (*News*) felt "...the mystery itself is so contrived that even if Bogart had been resuscitated to solve it, no one would care." In the *Post* Barnes found the score "...a real charmer" but found the rest "...a bad idea turned sour." *Newsday*'s Winer called it "...flat, diffuse and dull" while *Variety*'s Gerard noted the show was "...vulgar, ungainly, mean spirited and witless...Asta ain't the only dog onstage."

*Nathaniel Kramer Photos*

*Closed December 15, 1991 after 9 performances and 71 previews.

**TOP RIGHT: Christine Baranski, Joanna Gleason, Barry Bostwick**
**CENTER: Riley (Asta), Bostwick, Gleason**
**RIGHT: Gleason, Debra Monk, Bostwick**

# THE CRUCIBLE

ɣ Arthur Miller; Director, Yossi Yzraely; Sets, David Jenkins; Costumes, Patricia
ɪpprodt; Lighting, Richard Nelson; Sound, T. Richard Fitzgerald; Incidental Music,
hn Kander; Music Supervision, David Loud; Prod. Supervisor, Thomas A. Kelly;
ɪsting, Georgianne Walken, Sheila Jaffe; Executive Producer, Manny Kladitis;
esented by National Actors Theatre (Tony Randall, Founder and Artistic Director);
ɒmpany Manager, Erich Hamner; Stage Managers, Glen Gardali, Donna A. Drake;
ess, John & Gary Springer; Previewed from Tuesday, November 19; Opened in the
ɛlasco Theatre on Tuesday, December 10, 1991*

## CAST

| | |
|---|---|
| ɛtty Paris | Genia Sewell Michaela |
| ev. Samuel Parris | Brian Reddy |
| tuba | Carol Woods |
| ɒbigail Williams | Madeleine Potter |
| usanna Wallcott | Nell Balaban |
| ɪnn Putnam | Molly Regan |
| ʰomas Putnam | Peter McRobbie |
| ɪercy Lewis | Danielle Ferland |
| ɪary Warren | Jane Adams |
| ʰn Proctor | Martin Sheen |
| ɛbecca Nurse | Martha Scott |
| ɪles Corey | George N. Martin |
| ev. John Hale | Michael York |
| izabeth Proctor | Maryann Plunkett |
| ɪancis Nurse | John Beal |
| ɛzekiel Cheever | John Fiedler |
| ʰn Willard | Patrick Tull |
| ɪdge Hathorne | Bruce Katzman |
| ɛputy-Governor Danforth | Fritz Weaver |
| ɪarah Good | Priscilla Smith |
| ʰopkins | Andrew Hubatsek |

**ɴNDERSTUDIES/STANDBYS:** Doug Adair (Hopkins/Hathorne), Nell Balaban
(Mary/Abigail), Priscilla Smith (Ann/Elizabeth), Trazana Beverley (Tituba), Richard
ɛrrone (Proctor/Putnam), Melissa Joan Hart (Susanna/Betty/Sarah), Michael O'Hare
(Willard/Hale), Lucille Patton (Rebecca/Sarah), Martin Rudy
(Parris/Corey/Cheever/Danforth/Nurse), Tony Randall (for Fritz Weaver during
ɪness)

A new production of the 1953 drama in two acts. The action takes place in Salem,
ɪassachusetts, 1692. For original Broadway production see *Theatre World* Vol.9.

*Variety* tallied 7 favorable, 2 mixed and 4 negative reviews. At the *Times*, Rich
ɪll found the play "...relevant..." but "...directed as if it were written in 1692 instead
f set then." Richards found it "...dull" although praising the size of the venture. The
ɛws (Kissel) felt "...the production illustrates the problems of a star-oriented
ɒmpany." Barnes was enthusiastic in the *Post* :...a first rate staging...a great team
ʰfort...pushes the aim of a major New York acting ensemble significantly nearer
lfillment." Winer (*Newsday*) agreed: "*The Crucible*...doesn't get much better than
ʰis one."

Closed January 5, 1992 after limited run of 32 performances and 24 previews.

*Joan Marcus Photos*

**Top Right: Maryann Plunkett, Martin Sheen
Center: Martin Sheen**

**Madeleine Potter, Martin Sheen**

**Nell Balaban, Madeleine Potter, Jane Adams, Danielle Ferland**

19

# A CHRISTMAS CAROL

By Charles Dickens; Adaptation, Patrick Stewart; Lighting, Fred Allen; General Managers, Gatchell & Neufeld, Nina Lannan; Stage Manager, Kate Elliott; Presented by Timothy Childs; Press, Chris Boneau/Adrian Bryan-Brown, Jackie Green, Jim Sapp, Bob Fennell; Previewed from Tuesday, December 17; Opened in the Eugene O'Neill Theatre on Thursday, December 19, 1991*

## CAST

### PATRICK STEWART

A solo performance in two acts.

*Variety* noted 6 favorable reviews, with no mixed or negative. Mel Gussow (*Times*) stated the show "...reveals the work's full narative splendor, its humor as well as its humanity." The *News* (Harry Haun) felt "...a generous and majestic actor playing all the parts is all that's really required for a full, uplifting evening." The *Post*'s Barnes : "...unexpectedly beautiful and thrilling." *Newsday's* Stuart noted the "...listener-friendly approach..." and *Variety* (Greg Evans) felt Patrick Stewart "...warmed this seasonal chestnut into a satisfying holiday dish."

*Closed December 29, 1991 after a limited run of 14 performances and 2 previews.

*Jim Farber Photos*

**BELOW: Patrick Stewart**
**RIGHT: Victor Garber in "Two Shakespearean Actors"**
**BOTTOM RIGHT: Brian Bedford in "Two Shakespearean Actors"**

...an Brasington, LeClanche DuRand, Bill Moor, Michael Butler, Brian Bedford, Tim Macdonald, Tom Aldredge  TOP RIGHT: Graham Winton, Željko Ivanek, Victor Garber, Eric Stoltz, Laura Innes

# TWO SHAKESPEAREAN ACTORS

...Richard Nelson; Director, Jack O'Brien; Sets, David Jenkins; Costumes, Jane ...eenwood; Lighting, Jules Fisher; Sound, Jeff Ladman; Score Bob James; Fights, ...ve Rankin; Prod. Manager, Jeff Hamlin; General Manager, Steven C. Callahan; ...mpany Manager, Bruce Klinger; Stage Managers, Alan Hall, Deborah Clelland; ...esented by Lincoln Center Theatre (Gregory Mosher, Director; Bernard Gersten, ...ecutive Producer); Press, Merle Debuskey/Susan Chicoine; Previewed from ...esday, December 17; Opened in the Cort Theatre on Thursday, January 16, 1992*

## CAST

...tors at the Broadway Theatre (parts in parenthesis)
...win Forrest (Macbeth/Metamora).....................................................Victor Garber
...e Bass (1st Witch) .......................................................Jennifer Van Dyck
...len Burton (2nd Witch/Goodenough).....................................Judy Kuhn
...ne Holland (3rd Witch/Nahmeokee)........................................Hope Davis
...ton (Porter/Church)..........................................................Tom Lacy
...omas Fisher (Young Siward/Kaweshine)......................Graham Winton
...bert Jones (Banquo/Malcolm/Anrawandah).................David Andrew Macdonald
...Blakely (Duncan/Errington)..........................................Richard Clarke
...ott (Injured Macduff)..............................................Jeffrey Allan Chandler
...an Ryder (Macduff fill-in) ...............................................Željko Ivanek
...tors at the Astor Place Opera House
...lliam Charles Macready (Macbeth) ...........................................Brian Bedford
...s. Pope (Lady Macbeth) ...................................................Le Clanche Du Rand
...arles Clark (Macduff) ....................................................Alan Brasington
...orge Bradshaw (Banquo) ...............................................Michael Butler
...ederick Wemyss (Siward/Old Man) ......................................Bill Moor
...nes Bridges (Young Siward/3rd Witch/Ross) ...............Tim Macdonald
...an Sefton (1st Witch/Donalbain).....................................James Murtaugh
...Chippindale (2nd Witch)..............................................Mitchell Edmonds
...er Arnold (Malcolm)...........................................................Ben Bode
...iends and Family
...therine Forrest ........................................................Frances Conroy
...ss Wemyss ...............................................................Katie Finnneran
...on Boucicault.................................................................Eric Stoltz
...nes Robertson ..............................................................Laura Innes
...ashington Irving..............................................................Tom Aldredge
...tors/Servants ........................Katie MacNichol, Susan Pellegrino, Thomas Schall

...NDERSTUDIES: Michael Butler (Forrest), Hope Davis (Jane), Katie MacNichol ...elen/Anne/Miss Wemyss), Mitchell Edmonds (Tilton/Blakely), Ben Bode (Bridges), ...vid Andrew Macdonald (Fisher/Arnold), James Murtaugh (Scott), Alan Brasington ...yder), Jeffrey Allan Chandler (Macready), Thomas Schall ...lark/Bradshaw/Sefton/Chippindale/Jones), Susan Pellegrino (Mrs. ...pe/Catherine/Agnes), Richard Clarke (Wemyss/Irving), Graham Winton ...oucicault)

A drama in two acts. The action takes place in New York City between May 3 -10, ...49.

*Variety* tallied nine favorable reviews, four mixed and three negative. Neither ...nes critic cared much for the show with Rich finding "it never lives up to its ...omise. And a lot is promised ..." and Richards feeling it "works more for its pungent ...s and pieces than for its meandering whole. " More favorable was Kissel who found ...very witty play ... a superb production." His *News* colleague, Watt, however ...ought it too "...cliched..." The *Post*'s Barnes quoted the play : "...life's not half as ...ch fun as theatre." In *Newsday* Stuart summed up with "... a rare event for ...oadway, a big, populated show in which life, art and melodrama happily co-exist."

...losed February 9, 1992 after 29 performances and 33 previews.

*Brigitte Lacombe Photos*

Judy Kuhn, Victor Garber, Jennifer Van Dyck, Laura Innes, Željko Ivanek, Frances Conroy, Brian Bedford
CENTER: Brian Bedford, Željko Ivanek, Victor Garber

**Jane Alexander**
TOP RIGHT: **Jane Alexander and Company**

# THE VISIT

By Friedrich Durrenmatt; Adaptation, Maurice Valency; Director, Edwin Sherin; Sets, Thomas Lynch; Costumes, Frank Krenz; Lighting, Roger Morgan; Music/Sound, Douglas J. Cuomo; Masks, Michael Curry; Casting, Pat McCorkle, Richard Cole; General Manager, Ellen Richard; Stage Manager, Matthew T. Mundinger; Presented by Roundabout Theatre Company (Todd Haimes, Producing Director; Gene Feist, Founding Director); Press, Joshua Ellis/Susanne Tighe; Previewed from Wednesday, January 1; Opened in the Criterion Center Stage Right on Thursday, January 23, 1992*

## CAST

| | |
|---|---|
| 1st Man/Bobby/Cameraman | Richard Levine |
| 2nd Man/Loby/Conductor/Athlete/Truck Driver | Gordon Joseph Weiss |
| 3rd Man/Pedro/Ottilie | Timothy Britten Parker |
| 4th Man/Schultz/Mayor's Wife/Reporter | Jarlath Conroy |
| Painter/Frau Schill/1st Woman/Sacristan | Ellen Lancaster |
| Mayor | Doug Stender |
| Teacher/5th Man | Tom Tammi |
| Priest/Dr. Nusslin/Egg Man | Paul Kandel |
| Anton Schill | Harris Yulin |
| Station Master/Koby/Karl/Sound Man | Kelly Walters |
| Claire Zachanassian | Jane Alexander |
| Mike | John Jason |
| Max | Gary D. Williams |

**UNDERSTUDIES:** Ellen Lancaster (Claire), Daniel P. Donnelly (Men/Mayor/Teacher)

A new production of the 1957 adaptation of Durrenmatt's 1956 play in two acts. The action takes place in the town of Gullen. For original 1958 Broadway Broadway version see *Theatre World* Vol. 14.

*Variety* tallied seven favorable, three mixed and five negative reviews. The *Times'* Rich felt the work itself "stands as a small masterpiece" but felt the production "inconsistent..." Richards added "Jane Alexander is giving an astonishing performance..." At the *News* there was disagreement with Kissel calling the play "second-rate Brecht" and Watt submitting it "remains a classics, distinguished by Alexander's formidable presence." Barnes (*Post*) also admired the work and called the show "an evening to remember that you might want to forget...unpleasant but, for good or ill, unforgettable." *Newsday's* Winer found it a "tough, grotesque, deeply pessimistic and engaging satirical cartoon." *Variety* countered criticism that the 1958 version was too toned down by saying "a little glamour is a beguiling frame for a monstrous proposition."

* Closed Mar. 1, 1992 after limited run of 45 performances and 26 previews.

*Martha Swope Photos*

**Jane Alexander and Company**
CENTER: **Jane Alexander, Harris Yulin**

# A LITTLE HOTEL ON THE SIDE

Georges Feydeau and Maurice Desvallieres; Translated by John Mortimer from *Hotel du Libre Echange*; Director, Tom Moore; Sets, David Jenkins; Costumes, Patricia Zipprodt; Lighting, Richard Nelson; Sound, T. Richard Fitzgerald; Music, Jerry Delinger; Casting, Georgianne Walken, Sheila Jaffe; Prod. Supervisor, Glen Birdali; Company Manager, Erich Hamner; Stage Managers, Mitchell Erickson, John Handy; Executive Producer, Manny Klasitis; Presented by National Actors Theatre (Tony Randall, Founder/Artistic Director); Press, John Springer/Gary Springer; Reviewed from Wednesday, January 15; Opened in the Belasco Theatre on Sunday, January 26, 1992*

## CAST

| | |
|---|---|
| Benoit Pinglet | Tony Randall |
| Angelique Pinglet | Lynn Redgrave |
| Marcelle Paillardin | Maryann Plunkett |
| Henri Paillardin | Bruce Katzman (George N. Martin during previews) |
| Maxime | Rob Lowe |
| Victoire | Madeleine Potter |
| Mathieu | Paxton Whitehead |
| Head Porter | John Beal |
| Porters/Constables | Doug Adair, Danny Burstein, Andrew Hubatsek, Richard Ferrone |
| Violette | Siobhan Tull |
| Paquerette | Kia Graves |
| Pervenche | Danielle Ferland |
| Marguerite | Nell Balaban |
| Bastien | Patrick Tull |
| Boulot | Alec Mapa |
| Priest | Brian Reddy |
| Lady | Carol Woods |
| Chervet | Zane Lasky |
| Inspector (of Morality) Boucard | John Fiedler |
| 1 Constable | Bruce Katzman (succeeded by Danny Burstein) |
| 2nd Constable | Richard Ferrone |
| Hotel Guests | Leslie Anderson, Angela Baker, Karen Chapman, Heather Harlan, Liam Leone, Lisa Ann Li, Lucille Patton, Dennis Pressey, Brian Reddy, Steven Satta, Daisy White |

**UNDERSTUDIES:** Nell Balaban (Victoire), Andrew Hubatsek (Maxime/Boulot), Brian Reddy (Benoit), Bruce Katzman (Paillardin/Bastien/Boucard), Karen Chapman (Marcelle), Richard Ferrone (Chervet/Matieu), Lucille Patton (Lady), Martin Rudy (Head Porter), Doug Adair, Danny Burstein (Constables)

A farce in three acts performed with one intermission. The action takes place in Paris, just after the turn of the century. The 1894 comedy was previously adapted for Broadway in 1957 under the title *Hotel Paradiso* (See *Theatre World* Vol. 13)

*Variety* tallied eight favorable, three mixed and three negative reviews. The *Times'* Rich was least happy: "a complete flop..." while his colleague Richard praised the performances of Randall, Redgrave and Whitehead. Both *News* critics enjoyed the performers more than the production as a whole while Barnes (*Post*) found the classic farce a good change of pace for the new repertory company. Winer in *Newsday* wrote that Rob Lowe is likable and confident with the in-joke of the virginal philosophy student in a light night of ...inconsequential theatre..." Gerard in *Variety* had complaints, but noted "such quibbles cleary didn't matter to a cheering audience..."

Closed Mar. 1, 1992 after limited run of 41 performances and 15 previews.

*Joan Marcus Photos*

**Maryann Plunkett, Tony Randall**

**Lynn Redgrave, Tony Randall**
**TOP: Madeleine Potter, Rob Lowe**

**ABOVE & LEFT: Barry Miller, Polly Draper**

# CRAZY HE CALLS ME

By Abraham Tetenbaum; Director, John Ferraro; Sets, Loren Sherman; Costum
Jennifer von Mayrhauser; Lighting, Dennis Parichy; Sound, Raymond D. Schi
Casting, Pat McCorkle; Company Manager, Peter Bogyo; Stage Managers, Ka
Armstrong, Dan Hild; a Broadway Alliance Presentation; Presented by Weissr
Productions and Roger Alan Gindi; Press, Shirley Herz/Miller Wright, Gle
Freedman, Sam Rudy; Previewed from Tuesday, January 14; Opened in the Wa
Kerr Theatre on Monday, January 27, 1992*

### CAST

Benny ...............................................................................................Barry Miller
Yvette ...............................................................................................Polly Draper

A comedy in two acts. The action takes place in and around Brooklyn, NY, 19
40.

*Variety* tallied four mixed and ten negative reviews. In the *Times* Rich called
show "a tiny piece of nonsense" and colleague Richards added "neither touching,
funny, nor captivating, nor insightful..." The *News* agreed, with Kissel saying "inc
and Watt feeling "it is utterly unworthy..." Winer (*Newsday*) found more to
writing "this one has major pleasures in it ... the delightfully formidable Draper ..."
*Variety* also praised the acting with Gerard calling both players "talented."

*Closed Feb. 1, 1992 after 7 performances and 16 previews.

*Martha Swope Photos*

# THE MOST HAPPY FELLA

Music/Lyrics/Book by Frank Loesser; Based on Sidney Howard's play *They Knew What They Wanted*; Director, Gerald Gutierrez; Choreography, Liza Gennaro; Duo Piano Arrangements, Robert Page, under Loesser's supervision; Cast Recording, RCA Victor; Sets, John Lee Beatty; Costumes, Jess Goldstein; Lighting, Craig Miller; Musical Director, Tim Stella; Artistic Associate, Jo Sullivan; Casting, Warren Pincus; Prod. Manager, Jeff Hamlin; General Manager, Steven C. Callahan; Company Manager, Edward J. Nelson; Stage Managers, Michael Brunner, Kate Riddle; Presented by The Goodspeed Opera House Center Theatre Group/Ahmanson, Lincoln Center Theatre, The Shubert Organization, and Japan Satellite Broadcasting/Stagevision; Press, Merle Debuskey/Susan Chicoine; Previewed from Friday, January 24; Opened in the Booth Theatre on Thursday, February 13, 1992*

## CAST

| | |
|---|---|
| Casier/Postman/Doctor | Tad Ingram |
| Cleo | Liz Larson |
| Rosabella | Sophie Hayden |
| Tony | Spiro Malas |
| Herman | Scott Waara |
| Clem | Bob Freschi |
| Jake | John Soroka |
| Al | Ed Romanoff |
| Marie | Claudia Catania |
| Max/Priest | Bill Badolato |
| Joe | Charles Pistone |
| Pasquale | Mark Lotito |
| Ciccio | Buddy Crutchfield |
| Giuseppe | Bill Nabel |

Folks of San Francisco and Napa Valley ........... John Aller, Anne Allgood, Molly Brown, Mr. Badolato, Kyle Craig, Mary Helen Fisher, Mr. Reschi, Ramon Galando, T. Doyle Leverett, Ken Nady, Gail Pennington, Mr. Romanoff, Jane Smulyan, Mr. Soroka, Laura Streets, Thomas Titone, Melanie Vaughan

**UNDERSTUDIES/STANDBYS:** Jack Dabdoub (Tony standby), T. Doyle Leverett (Tony/Al), Anne Allgood (Rosabella), Melanie Vaughan, Molly Brown (Cleo), John Soroka (Herman), Ed Romanoff (Joe), Jane Smulyan (Marie), Bob Freschi (Cashier/Postman/Doctor), John Aller (Pasquale/Ciccio), Thomas Titone (Giuseppe/Clem/Jake)

**MUSICAL NUMBERS:** Ooh My Feet, Somebody Somewhere, Most Happy Fella, Standin' on the Corner, Joey Joey Joey, Rosabella, Abbondanza, Sposalizio, Benvenuta, Don't Cry, Fresno Beauties, Happy to Make Your Acquaintance, Big D, How Beautiful the Days, Young People, Warm All Over, I Like Everybody, My Heart Is So Full of You, Mamma Mamma, Song of a Summer Night, Please Let Me Tell You, I Made a Fist, Finale.

A new production of the 1956 musical in three acts, performed with one intermission. The action takes place in San Francisco and Napa, California in 1927. For original Broadway production see *Theatre World* Vol. 12. For 1979 Broadway revivial see *Theatre World* Vol. 36.

*Variety* tallied 16 favorable and 3 negative reviews. At the *Times* Rich stated "...simple poetry and unforgettable melodies ... these feelings will never go out of fashion, and neither will musicals containing them if they are as powerfully acted, sung and staged" although he did admit the pared down, two-piano arrangement left one "missing the musical colors of the haunting Don Walker orchestrations..." Colleague Richards noted "The Booth, one of Broadway's smallest theatres, couldn't be more hospitable." The *News'* Kissel felt this version had "great sensitivity and intelligence" while Watt felt the small scale "might set a trend, enabling classic American "song" musicals to return to Broadway." Barnes, in the *Post*, noted "the lack of orchestration is a serious loss" but added"for what it is (it) is perfectly fine." In *Newsday* Winer wrote "a lovingly staged reduction of an old-fashioned sweetheart of a show." Commenting on the reduced orchestration, *Variety* (Gerard) said "one had the weird sense of watching a silent movie meller..." but overall "it's a production to be cherished."

*Closed Aug. 30, 1992 after 229 performances and 23 previews.

Winner of "Tony" Award for Featured Actor in a Musical (Scott Waara)

*Martha Swope Photos*

**TOP:** Sophie Hayden, Spiro Malas
**BELOW:** Malas, Charles Pistone
**THIRD PHOTO:** Bill Nabel, Laura Streets and Company
**BOTTOM:** Liz Larson, Scott Waara

# CRAZY FOR YOU

Music, George Gershwin; Lyrics, Ira Gershwin, Gus Kahn, Desmond Carter; Book, Ken Ludwig; Conception, Mr. Ludwig and Mike Ockrent, inspired by material by Guy Bolton and John McGowan; Director, Mr. Ockrent; Choreography, Susan Stroman; Orchestrations, William D. Brohn, Sid Ramin; Musical Director, Paul Gemignani; Musical Consultant, Tommy Krasker; Dance/Incidental Arrangements, Peter Howard; Sets, Robin Wagner; Costumes, William Ivey Long; Lighting, Paul Gallo; Sound, Otts Munderloh; Casting, Julie Hughes, Barry Moss; Cast Recording, Broadway Angel; Fights, B.H. Barry; Hairstylist, Angela Gari; General Manager, Gatchell & Neufeld; Prod. Manager, Peter Fulbright; Company Manager, Abbie M. Strassler; Stage Managers, Steven Zweigbaum, John Bonanni; Associate Producers, Richard Godwin, Valerie Gordon; Presented by Roger Horchow and Elizabeth Williams; Press, Bill Evans/Jim Randolph, Susan L. Schulman, Erin Dunn; Previewed from Friday, January 31; Opened in the Shubert Theatre on Wednesday, February 19, 1992*

## CAST

| | |
|---|---|
| Tess | Beth Leavel |
| Patsy | Stacey Logan |
| Bobby Child | Harry Groener |
| Bela Zanger | Bruce Adler |
| Sheila | Judine Hawkins Richard |
| Mitzi | Paula Leggett |
| Susie | Ida Henry |
| Louise | Jean Marie |
| Betsy | Peggy Ayn Maas |
| Margie | Salome Mazard |
| Vera | Louise Ruck |
| Elaine | Pamela Everett |
| Irene Roth | Michele Pawk |
| Mother | Jane Connell |
| Perkins/Cactus | Gerry Burkhardt |
| The Manhattan Rhythm Kings { Moose | Brian M. Nalepka |
| Mingo | Tripp Hanson |
| Sam | Hal Shane |
| Junior | Casey Nicholaw |
| Pete | Fred Anderson |
| Jimmy | Michael Kubala |
| Billy | Ray Roderick |
| Wyatt | Jeffrey Lee Broadhurst |
| Harry | Joel Goodness |
| Polly Baker | Jodi Benson |
| Everett Baker | Ronn Carroll |
| Lank Hawkins | John Hillner |
| Eugene | Stephen Temperley |
| Patricia | Amelia White |

**UNDERSTUDIES:** Michael Kubala (Bobby/Lank/Bela), Beth Leavel (Polly), Jessica Molaskey (Irene/Patricia), Gerry Burkhardt (Everett), Amelia White (Mother), Paula Leggett (Tess), Casey Nicholaw (Eugene), Peggy Ayn Maas (Pastsy)

**MUSICAL NUMBERS:** Original sources follow in parentheses: K-ra-azy for You (*Treasure Girl,* 1928), I Can't Be Bothered Now (Film: *A Damsel in Distress,* 1937), Bidin' My Time (*Girl Crazy,* 1930), Things Are Looking Up ( *A Damsel in Distress,*),

Jodi Benson

(center) Jodi Benson, Harry Groener
CENTER: Penny Ayn Maas, Harry Groener, Paula Leggett
TOP: Harry Groener and Showgirls

Harry Groener

Could You Use Me (*Girl Crazy*), Shall We Dance (Film: *Shall We Dance*, 1937), Someone to Watch Over Me (*Oh Kay*, 1926), Slap That Bass (*Shall We Dance*), Embraceable You (*Girl Crazy*), Tonight's the Night (previously unused), I Got Rhythm (*Girl Crazy*), The Real American Folk Song Is a Rag (*Ladies First,* 1918), What Causes That? (*Treasure Girl*), Naughty Baby (previously unused), Stiff Upper Lip (*A Damsel in Distress*), They Can't Take That Away from Me (*Shall We Dance*), But Not for Me (*Girl Crazy*), Nice Work If You Can Get It (*A Damsel in Distress*), Finale

A musical comedy, inspired by *Girl Grazy* (1930), in two acts with 17 scenes. The action takes place in New York City and Deadrock, Nevada in the 1930's.

The critics were crazy for *Crazy For You* with *Variety* recording 19 favorable, 4 mixed and 1 negative review. Rich (*Times*) led the parade : "when future historians try to find the exact moment at which Broadway finally rose up to grab the musical back from the British, they just may conclude that the revolution began last night." Colleague Richards called the show "...not to be missed..." but was unenthusaistic about the cast. The *News* had Kissel calling it "...something scrumptious..." and Watt seconding with "...glorious..." Winer (*Newsday*) was dismayed the new book was "low vaudeville..."while Barnes (*Post*) noted "...it has more tap on tap than any Broadway show since *42nd St.*" *Variety*(Gerard) summed up : "...going to cheer up a lot of people in the Broadway vicinity..."

*Still playing May 31, 1992. Winner of "Tonys" for Best Musical, Best Choreography and Best Costumes.

*Joan Marcus Photos*

**Harry Groener, Jodi Benson**
**CENTER: Ronn Carroll, Jodi Benson**
**TOP: Harry Groener, Jane Connell**

27

# PRIVATE LIVES

By Noel Coward; Director, Arvin Brown; Sets, Loren Sherman; Costumes, Wil
Ivey Long; Lighting, Richard Nelson; Sound, Tom Morse; Choreography, Mic
Smuin; Fights, Ellen Saland; Casting, Johnson-Liff & Zerman; General Mana
Marvin A. Krauss; Company Manager, Kim Sellon; Stage Managers, Franklin Ke
Judith Binus; Presented by Charles H. Duggan by arrangement with Michael Coc
Press, Pete Sanders; Previewed from Tuesday, February 11; Opened in the Broadl
Theatre on Thursday, February 20, 1992*

## CAST

| | |
|---|---|
| Sybil Chase | Jill Taske |
| Elyot Chase | Simon Jone |
| Victor Prynne | Edward Duke |
| Amanda Prynne | Joan Collin |
| Louise | Margie Ryn |

**STANDBYS:** Mary Layne (Amanda), Guy Paul (Elyot/Victor)

A new production of the 1930 comedy in three acts. The action takes plac
France in the mid-1930s.

*Variety* tallied 8 favorable, 6 mixed and 4 negative reviews. The *Times* critics
unimpressed with Rich claiming "An ideal Amanda Prynne she is not, but she ma
the best possible Joan Collins..." while Richards recognized "...Those who are goir
seize it already know who they are and don't need me and my two cents." At the *M*
Kissel felt the play "...may not be actorproof, but its crystalline illogic rem
impressive" and Watt called it "...flat (very flat) revival..." Barnes (*Post*) was ki
saying "...any perverted snob going to the theatre hoping to see a TV super-ma
falling over the furniture that she did not actually chew up can save his money
avoid disappointment." *Variety* (Gerard) reminded "...the play is a triumph of s
over substance."

*Closed March 22, 1992 after 37 performances and 11 previews.

*T. Charles Erickson Photos*

**TOP: Joan Collins, Simon Jones**
**CENTER: Joan Collins, Edward Duke**
**BOTTOM LEFT: Edward Duke, Jill Tasker, Margie Rynn, Joan Colli**
**Simon Jones**
**BELOW: Simon Jones, Joan Collins**

TOP LEFT: Michael Hammond, Griffin Dunne
TOP RIGHT: Griffin Dunne, Keith Szarabajka, Mike Hodge
CENTER: T.G. Waites, Griffin Dunne
BOTTOM RIGHT: Keith Szarabajka, Paul Guilfoyle, Griffin Dunne

# SEARCH AND DESTROY

By Howard Korder; Director, David Chambers; Sets, Chris Barreca; Costumes, Candice Donnelly; Lighting, Chris Parry; Sound, David Budries; Casting, Judy Henderson, Alycia Aumuller; Stage Manager, Wm. Hare; Company Manager, Susan Elrod; Presented by Circle in the Square (Theodore Mann, Artistic Director; Robert A. Buckley, Managing Director; Paul Lubin, Consulting Producer); Press, Maria Somma/Patty Onagan; Previewed from Friday, February 7; Opened in the Circle in the Square Uptown on Wednesday, February 26, 1992*

### CAST

| | |
|---|---|
| Martin Mirkheim | Griffin Dunne |
| Accountant | James Noah |
| Lauren/Jackie/Radio Announcer | Jane Fleiss |
| Robert | T.G. Waites |
| Kim | Keith Szarabajka |
| Marie/Terry | Welker White |
| Roger | Gregory Simmons |
| Hotel Clerk/Carling | Michael Hammond |
| Security Guard/Nunex | Jerry Grayson |
| Dr. Waxling | Stephen McHattie |
| Bus Driver/State Trooper | Mike Hodge |
| Ron | Paul Guilfoyle |
| Pamfilo | Arnold Molina |
| Lee | Thom Sesma |

A dark comedy in two acts. The action takes place all over the United States of America at present.

*Variety* tallied 8 favorable, 5 mixed and 3 negative notices. Gussow in the *Times* found "...the sum is less than some of its parts..."but praised Griffin Dunne and the direction. Richards called the play a "...darkly compelling comedy...Bitterly funny...." Kissel (*News*) felt "...a certain vitality..." while Watt didn't like the play but called Dunne "...first rate...sharply staged and well played..." The *Post*'s Barnes felt "...a truly brilliant Griffin Dunne..." the reason to see a "...fragmentary offering..." agreeing with *Newsday*'s Winer who found it "...extremely hard to care...". *Variety*'s Gerard noted "...no less than a frightening tour of the underside of the American conscience..."

Closed April 5, 1992 after 46 performances and 22 previews.

*Martha Swope Photos*

29

# DEATH AND THE MAIDEN

By Ariel Dorfman; Director, Mike Nichols; Set, Tony Walton; Costumes, Ann Ro░
Lighting, Jules Fisher; Sound, Tom Sorce; General Manager, Leonard Solowa░
Company Manager, Ron Gubin; Stage Managers, Anne Keefe, Steven Sha░
Associate Producers, Hal Luftig, Ron Kastner, Peter Lawrence, Sue MacNa░
Presented by Roger Berlind, Gladys Nederlander, Frederick Zollo in association wi░
Thom Mount and Bonnie Timmermann; Press Bill Evans/Susan L. Schulman, Ji░
Randolph, Erin Dunn; Previewed from Tuesday, February 18; Opened in the Broo░
Atkinson Theatre on Tuesday, March 17, 1992*

## CAST

Paulina Salas....................................................................................Glenn Close +1
Gerardo Escobar ............................................................................Richard Dreyfuss
Roberto Miranda..............................................................................Gene Hackman+2

**STANDBYS:** Lizbeth Mackay (Paulina), David Goewey (Gerardo), Jimmie R░
Weeks (Roberto)

A drama in two acts. The action takes place in a country that is probably Chile, b░
could be any country that has given itself a democratic government just after a lo░
period of dictatorship. The time is the present.

*Variety* tallied 8 favorable, 4 mixed and 9 negative notices. *Times* critics were sp░
with Rich saying "Mr. Nichols has given Broadway its first escapist entertainme░
about political torture. He has also allowed three terrific actors...to produce artist░
escapism of their own." . Richards countered with "...there is nothing wrong wi░
Broadway that can't be remedied by a director and performers like these...impeccab░
acted..." *News* critics were thumbs down with Kissel finding it "...so terrib░
American..." and Watt adding "...little more than a simple thriller." "Crowd-pleasing░
effective..." trumpeted the *Post* (Barnes). *Newsday*(Winer) said the show "...is mo░
compelling as a combination of star power and political power."

*Closed August 2, 1992 after 159 performances and 33 previews. Winner of 199░
"Tony" for Best Actress (Close).

+Succeeded by: 1.Lizbeth Mackay during illness  2. Jimmie Ray Weeks durir░
absence

*Joan Marcus Photos*

**TOP: Glenn Close**
**CENTER: Gene Hackman, Richard Dreyfuss**
**BOTTOM LEFT: Richard Dreyfuss, Glenn Close**
**BELOW: Gene Hackman, Richard Dreyfuss, Glenn Close**

Gene Hackman, Richard Dreyfuss, Glenn Close

**James Naughton, Eugene Perry, Stockard Channing**
**TOP RIGHT: Stockard Channing**
**CENTER: Stockard Channing, James Naughton**

# FOUR BABOONS ADORING THE SUN

By John Guare; Director, Peter Hall; Music, Stephen Edwards; Sets, Tony Walton; Costumes, Willa Kim; Lighting, Richard Pilbrow; Sound, Paul Arditti; Projections, Wendall K. Harrington; Musical Director, Michael Barrett; Hairstylist, Angela Gari; Prod. Manager, Jeff Hamlin; General Manager, Steven C. Callahan; Company Manager, Edward J. Nelson; Stage Managers, Thomas A. Kelly, Charles Kindl, Mark Dobrow; Presented by Lincoln Center Theater (Andre Bishop and Bernard Gersten, Directors); Press, Merle Debuskey, Susan Chicoine; Previewed from Saturday, February 22; Opened in the Vivian Beaumont Theatre on Wednesday, March 18, 1992*

### CAST

| | |
|---|---|
| Eros | Eugene Perry |
| Penny McKenzie | Stockard Channing |
| Philip McKenzie | James Naughton |
| Wayne | Wil Horneff |
| Lyle | Michael Shulman |
| Sarah | Ellen Hamilton Latzen |
| Teddy | Alex Sobol |
| Halcy | Angela Goethals |
| Jane | Zoe Taleporos |
| Peter | John Ross |
| Robin | Kimberly Jean Brown |
| Roger | Zachary Phillip Solomon (succeeded by Noah Fleiss) |

**UNDERSTUDIES:** Andrew Solomon Glover (Eros), Harriet Harris (Penny), Eddie K. Thomas (Wayne), Kate Bernsohn (Jane/Sarah), Noah Fleiss (Roger/Robin/Teddy), Zoe Taleporos (Halcy), Nathew McCurley (Lyle/Peter).

A play with music performed without intermission. The action takes place in Sicily, a few years ago.

John Guare's follow up to the *Six Degrees of Separation* clearly divided it's critics and audiences. Rich in the *Times* called it "...the most contoversial play of the season...I can only speak from the perspective of someone who was deeply stirred by this play..." In the *News* Kissel mused "...It is certainly bizzare and irrational.." while Watt criticized the play but noted Guare was "...the most imaginative of contemporary playwrights..." The *Post* (Barnes) called it "...a glossy production of a glossy play..." and *Newsday*'s Winer felt it "...betrays its characters and its audience with a cruelty that would be appalling even if not from an artist of such renowned generosity of spirit." *Variety* (Gerard) summed up "...for those willing to yield to its self-conscious quirks, this play has an ineluctable emotional power..." while tallying 3 favorable, 3 mixed and 11 negative notices.

*Closed April 19, 1992 after 38 performances and 26 previews.

*Martha Swope Photos*

**Stockard Channing, James Naughton (front) , Wil Horneff, Michael Shulman, John L. Ross, Angela Goethals, Zoe Taleporos, Alex Sobol, Eugene Perry Kimberly Jean Brown, Ellen Hamilton Latzen, Zachary Phillip Soloman, (rear)**

# THE MASTER BUILDER

By Henrik Ibsen; Translation, John Fillinger; Director, Tony Randall; Sets, David Jenkins; Costumes, Patricia Zipprodt; Lighting, Richard Nelson; Sound, T. Richard Fitzgerald; Casting, Georgianne Walken, Sheila Jaffe; General Manager, Niko Associates; Company Manager, Erich Hamner; Stage Managers, Glen Gardali, Joe McGuire; Executive Producer, Manny Kladitis; Presented by National Actors Theatre (Mr. Randall, Founder/Artistic Director); Press, John Springer/Gary Springer; Previewed from Wednesday, March 11; Opened in the Belasco Theatre on Thursday, March 19, 1992*

## CAST

| | |
|---|---|
| Kaja Fosli | Maryann Plunkett |
| Knut Brovik | John Beal |
| Ragnar Brovik | Peter McRobbie |
| Halvard Solness | Earle Hyman |
| Mrs. Alvine Solness | Lynn Redgrave |
| Dr. Herdal | Patrick Tull |
| Hilde Wangel | Madeleine Potter |

**UNDERSTUDIES/STANDBYS:** Nell Balaban (Kaja), Martin Rudy (Knut), Bruce Katzman (Brovik/Herdal), Lucille Patton (Alvine), Robert Stattel (Halvard)

A drama in three acts. The action takes place in a Norwegian town about the turn of the century.

*Variety* tallied one favorable and eleven negative reviews. In the *Times*, Rich found it a "passionless recital," The *News* critics agreed, with Kissel feeling "nothing shows any great depth" and Watt saying "the three acts drag along." Barnes (*Post*) was the production's champion, countering "it is ... as good as most and better than many..." *Newsday*'s Stuart felt "you feel every one of the play's 100 years" while Evans noted, in *Variety*, "greater allowance might have been afforded had it been the troupe's initial effort."

*Closed Apr. 26, 1992 after 45 performances and 11 previews.

*Joan Marcus Photos*

**TOP RIGHT: Earle Hyman, Madeleine Potter**
**CENTER: Lynn Redgrave, Earle Hyman**

**Madeleine Potter, Lynn Redgrave**

**Lynn Redgrave, Madeleine Potter, Maryann Plunkett, Earle Hyman**

33

# JAKE'S WOMEN

By Neil Simon; Director, Gene Saks; Sets/Costumes, Santo Loquasto; Lighting, Tharon Musser; Sound, Tom Morse; Prod. Supervisor, Peter Lawrence; Casting, Jay Binder; General Manager, Leonard Soloway; Company Manager, Sammy Ledbetter; Stage Managers, John Brigleb, Greta Minsky; Press, Bill Evans/Jim Randolph, William Schelble, Susan L. Schulman, Erin Dunn; Presented by Emanuel Azenberg; Previewed from Thursday, March 12; Opened in the Neil Simon Theatre on Tuesday, March 24, 1992*

### CAST

| | |
|---|---|
| Jake | Alan Alda |
| Maggie | Helen Shaver +1 |
| Karen | Brenda Vaccaro |
| Molly (age 12) | Genia Michaela |
| Molly (age 21) | Tracy Pollan +2 |
| Edith | Joyce Van Patten |
| Julie | Kate Burton |
| Sheila | Talia Balsam |

**STANDBYS:** Munson Hicks (Jake), Marsha Waterbury (Maggie), Linda Atkinson (Karen/Edith), Beau Dakota Berdahl (Molly - 12), Maura Russo (Molly - 21), Ilana Levine (Julie/Sheila)

A comedy in two acts. The action takes place in Jake's apartment in Soho and in his mind.

Mr. Simon's 26th Broadway play was met with six favorable, four mixed and six negative notices. The *Times* critics were mixed but Rich noted "Mr. Simon does know more about playwriting and comedy than most mortals ... uniformly charming cast ..." The *News* critics were in a mood for the less serious Simon while Barnes (*Post*) called this play "a comedy of the moment, an intricately devised, bizarrely convincing portrait of the artist..." Winer wrote "a wild card in his oevre..." in *Newsday*, while *Variety*'s Gerard felt the play "never comes together..."

*Closed Oct. 25, 1992 after 245 performances and 15 previews.

Succeeded by: 1. Marsha Waterbury    2. Maura Russo

*Martha Swope Photos*

**Top Left:** (front) Joyce Van Patten, Alan Alda, Helen Shaver, Genia Michaela, (rear) Brenda Vaccaro, Talia Balsam, Tracy Pollan, Kate Burton    **Left:** Helen Shaver, Alan Alda

**Alan Alda, Joyce Van Patten**
**Above: Kate Burton, Alan Alda, Tracy Pollan**

**Alan Alda, Talia Balsam**
**Above: Alan Alda, Talia Balsam, Helen Shaver**

# CONVERSATIONS WITH MY FATHER

By Herb Gardner; Director, Daniel Sullivan; Sets, Tony Walton; Costumes, Robert Wojewodski; Lighting, Pat Collins; Sound, Michael Holten; Casting, Meg Simon; General Manager, James Walsh; Company Manager, Florie Seery; Stage Managers, Warren Crane, Anna Jo Gender; Presented by James Walsh; Press, Jeffrey Richards/David LeShay, Ben Gutkin; Previewed from Thursday, March 3; Opened in the Royale Theatre on Sunday, March 29, 1992*

## CAST

| | |
|---|---|
| Charlie | Tony Shalhoub +1 |
| Josh/Joey | Tony Gillan +2 |
| Eddie | Judd Hirsch +3 |
| Gusta | Gordana Rashovich |
| Zaretsky | David Margulies+4 |
| Young Joey | Jason Biggs +5 |
| Hannah Di Blindeh | Marilyn Sokol |
| Nick | William Biff McGuire +6 |
| Finney the Book | Peter Gerety |
| Jimmy Scalso | John Procaccino +7 |
| Blue | Richard E. Council |
| Young Charlie | David Krumholtz +8 |

**UNDERSTUDIES/STANDBYS:** Sidney Armus (Zaretsky), Robert Canaan (Josh/Joey), Richard E. Council (Scalso), Cheryl Giannini (Gusta/Hannah), John Procaccino (Charlie), Michael M. Ryan (Nick/Blue/Finney), Tristan Smith (Young Charlie/Young Joey)

A drama in two acts. The action takes place on Canal St. in New York City between 1936-76.

*Variety* tallied ten favorable, six mixed and one negative review. The *Times* critics had both praise and reservations. Rich called the work "brutally honest and clinically detached...evocatively staged and superbly acted..." and Richards said the play "rewards and frustrates..." Kissel, in the *News*, wrote "the play seldom seems focused," but in the *Post*, Barnes called it "pungent, deep-felt and very powerful..." In *Newsday*, Winer described it as a "richly convoluted family play..."

*Closed March 14, 1993 after 402 performances and 30 previews. Winner of "Tony" Award for Best Actor in a Play (Judd Hirsch).

Succeeded by: 1. James Sutorius 2. Robert Canaan 3. James Belushi 4. Richard Libertini during previews 5. Rick Faugno 6. Alan North 7. Joseph Siravo 8. Jason Woliner

*Marc Bryan-Brown Photos*

**TOP LEFT: Tony Gillan, Judd Hirsch
CENTER: David Krumholtz, Judd Hirsch
BOTTOM LEFT: William Biff McGuire, Marilyn Sokol, Peter Gerety, Judd Hirsch
BELOW: Judd Hirsch**

# HAMLET

By William Shakespeare; Director, Paul Weidner; Sets, Christopher H. Barreca; Costumes, Martin Pakledinaz; Lighting, Natasha Katz; Sound, Douglas J. Cuomo; Fights, David Leong; Literary Advisor, Isiah Sheffer; Casting, Pat McCorkle, Richard Cole; General Manager, Ellen Richard; Stage Managers, Kathy J. Faul, Matthew T. Mundinger; Presented by Roundabout Theatre Company (Todd Haimes, Producing Director; Gene Feist, Founding Director); Press, Joshua Ellis/Susanne Tighe; Previewed from Wednesday, March 11; Opened in the Criterion Center Stage Right on Thursday, April 2, 1992*

## CAST

Bernardo/Fortinbras' Captain ...............................................James Colby
Francisco/Lucianus/Sailor/Norwegian Soldier .......................Bruce Faulk
Horatio ............................................................................Michael Genet
Marcellus ..........................................................................Thomas Schall
Claudius...........................................................................Michael Cristofer
Laertes.............................................................................Bill Campbell
Polonius ...........................................................................James Cromwell
Hamlet .............................................................................Stephen Lang
Gertrude ...........................................................................Kathleen Widdoes
Ophelia ............................................................................Elizabeth McGovern
Ghost of Hamlet's Father/Player King...............................Robert Hogan
Reynaldo/Priest.................................................................Torben Brooks
Rosencrantz ......................................................................Michael Galardi
Guildenstern......................................................................Michael John McGann
Player Queen/Fortinbras .....................................................David Comstock
Gravedigger ......................................................................John Newton
Osric ................................................................................Charles E. Gerber
Lady-in-Waiting .................................................................Kathleen Christal
Courtiers/Norwegian Soldiers ...............Robert Driscoll, Joe Latimore, Tim McGee

**UNDERSTUDIES:** Torben Brooks (Horatio/Rosencrantz), Kathleen Christal (Ophelia), James Colby (Guildenstern/Gravedigger), David Comstock (Laertes), Bruce Faulk (Fortinbras), Michael Galardi (Hamlet), Tim McGee (Osric), John Newton (Polonius)

Performed with one intermission. The action takes place in and near Elsinore Castle in Denmark.

*Variety* tallied two favorable and eight negative reviews. Gussow, in the *Times*, said "Although Mr. Lang is always interesting to watch onstage, his restless energy cannot compensate for the imprecision that surrounds him." In the *News* Kissel felt it was "...an altogether enervating production." Barnes (*Post*), however, felt it was "A nihilistic Hamlet ...but powerfully impressive." *Newsday*'s Stuart found it a "..dry,businesslike staging..." and *Variety*'s Evans felt "Special mention should be made of the effective sword fight..."

*Martha Swope Photos*

*Closed May 10, 1992 after limited run of 45 performances and 26 previews.

**BELOW: Stephen Lang
TOP RIGHT: Stephen Lang, Kathleen Widdoes, Michael Cristofer, Bill Campbell
RIGHT: Stephen Lang, Elizabeth McGovern**

Milton Craig Nealy, Kevin Ramsey, Glenn Turner, Doug Eskew,
Jeffrey Sams   RIGHT: (clockwise) Doug Eskew, Jeffrey D. Sams, Glenn
Turner, Kevin Ramsey, Milton Craig Nealy

# FIVE GUYS NAMED MOE

Music/Lyrics by  Louis Jordan with Leo Hickman, Dallas Bartley, Larry Wynn, Jerry
Breslen, Morry Lasco, Dick Adams, Fleecie Moore, Claude Demetriou, Jon Hendricks,
Lora Lee, Johnny Burke, Jimmy Van Heusen, Sid Robin, Bill Davis, Don Wolf,
Johnny Lange, Hy Heath, Joe Willoughby, Dr. Walt Merrick, Ellis Walsh, Bubsy
Meyers, R. McCoy, C. Singleton, Browley Bri, Sam Theard, Spencer Lee, Joan
Whitney, Alex Kramer, Jo Greene, Vaughn Horton, Denver Darling, Milton Gabler,
Joseph Meyer, Buddy Bernier, Robert Emmerich, S. Austin; Book, Clarke Peters;
Director/Choreographer, Charles Augins; Orchestrations, Neil McArthur; Vocal
Arrangements/Musical Supervision, Chapman Roberts; Musical Director/Supervisor,
Reginald Royal; Design, Tim Goodchild; Lighting, Andrew Bridge; Costumes, Noel
Howard; Sound, Tony Meola/Autograph; Cast Recording, Columbia; Casting,
Johnson-Liff & Zerman; General Manager, Alan Wasser; Company Manager, Michael
Sanfilippo; Stage Managers, Marybeth Abel, Gwendolyn M. Gilliam, Roumel Reaux;
Executive Producer, Richard Jay Alexander; Presented by Cameron Mackintosh;
Press, Merle Frimark/Marc Thibodeau; Previewed from Friday, March 20; Opened in
the Eugene O'Neill Theatre on Wednesday, April 8, 1992*

### CAST

Nomax .................................................................................Jerry Dixon
Big Moe ..............................................................................Doug Eskew
Four-Eyed Moe ...........................................................Milton Craig Nealy
No Moe ...............................................................................Kevin Ramsey
Eat Moe ..........................................................................Jeffrey D. Sams
Little Moe............................................................................Glenn Turner

**UNDERSTUDIES:** Phillip Gilmore (Nomax/Four Eyed/Eat Moe), Michael Leon
Wooley (Big Moe/Eat Moe), W. Ellis Porter (Four-Eyed/No Moe/ Little Moe)

**MUSICAL NUMBERS:** Early in the Morning, Five Guys Named Moe, Beware
Brother Beware, I Like 'em Fat Like That, Messy Bessy, Pettin' and Pokin', Life Is So
Peculiar, I Know What I've Got, Azure Te, Safe Sane and Single, Push Ka Pi Shi Pie,
Saturday Night Fish Fry, What's the Use of Getting Sober, If I Had Any Sense, Dad
Gum Your Hide Boy, Let the Good Times Roll, Reet Petite and Gone, Caldonia, Ain't
Nobody Here But Us Chickens, Don't Let the Sun Catch You Crying, Choo Choo
Ch'boogie, Look Out Sister, Hurray Home/Is You Is or Is You Ain't My Baby?, Finale

A musical in two acts.

*Variety* reported 12 favorable, four mixed and five negative reviews. Neither *Times*
critic was too pleased; Rich: "Some Broadway musicals want to make you think...*Five
Guys* ...wants to sell you a drink." Richards: "...it seems a phony piece of goods..." In
the *News*, Kissel praised the cast: "They have rich, mellow voices, nimble feet, no
apparent joints and an infectous enthusiasm for their work." Barnes felt it had "...more
perspiration than inspiration..." in the *Post*. Winer felt "...the story actually contradicts
the lyrics..." in *Newsday* while *Variety* (Gerard) noted the show "...is bringing a
racially mixed audience to the district, which is terrific."

*Joan Marcus Photos*

*Closed May 2, 1993 after 445 performances and 19 previews.

Jeffrey Sams, Kevin Ramsey, Doug Eskew, Milton Craig Nealy,
Glenn Turner, (seated) Jerry Dixon                                    **37**

Alec Baldwin, Jessica Lange

# A STREETCAR NAMED DESIRE

By Tennessee Williams; Director, Gregory Mosher; Sets, Ben Edwards; Costumes, Jane Greenwood; Lighting, Kevin Rigdon; Music, Michael Barrett; Sound, Scott Lehrer; Casting, Billy Hopkins, Suzanne Smith, Ann Goulder; Company Manager, Lisa M. Poyer; General Manager, James Walsh; Stage Managers, Michael F. Ritchie, Sally J. Jacobs; Presented by Mr. Mosher, Mr. Walsh, Capital Cities/ABC, Suntory International, and The Shubert Organization; Press, Bill Evans/Susan L. Schulman, Jim Randolph, Erin Dunn, William Schelble; Previewed from Tuesday, March 17; Opened in the Ethel Barrymore Theatre on Sunday, April 12, 1992*

## CAST

| | |
|---|---|
| Stanley Kowalski | Alec Baldwin |
| Stella Kowalski | Amy Madigan |
| Eunice Hubbell | Aida Turturro |
| Negro Woman | Edwina Lewis |
| Blanche DuBois | Jessica Lange |
| Steve Hubbell | James Gandolfini |
| Harold Mitchell | Timothy Carhart |
| Pablo Gonzales | Lazaro Perez |
| Young Collector | Matt McGrath |
| Mexican Woman | Sol Echeverria |
| A Man | William Cain |
| A Woman | Susan Aston |

**UNDERSTUDIES:** Leslie C. Hendrix (Blanche), Deborah LaCoy (Stella/Woman), Don Yesso (Stanlet/Steve/Pablo), James Gandolfini (Harold), Susan Aston (Eunice/Mexican/Negro), Michael P. Connor (Collector), Richard Thomsen (Man)

The 1947 drama in two acts. The action takes place in New Orleans, 1947. The original Broadway Production (*Theatre World* Vol. IV) also opened at the Barrymore with Marlon Brando, Jessica Tandy and Kim Hunter.

*Variety* recorded two favorable, four mixed and thirteen negative notices. Rich reminded *Times* readers that the play "...is either the greatest or second-greatest play ever written by an American...Mr. Baldwin is simply fresh, dynamic and true to his part..." Richards found "...no chemistry between the leads." *News* men were negative; Kissel: "...crudely directed..." Watt: "...all the players seem at loose ends." Barnes (*Post*) praised Miss Lange calling her "...a new and wanly vivid Blanche..." and *Newsday*(Winer) regretted "...the passion never happens..."

*Brigitte LaCombe Photos*

*Closed August 9, 1992 after 137 performances and 31 previews.

**CLOCKWISE FROM TOP LEFT: Alec Baldwin, Jessica Lange, Timothy Carhart, Amy Madigan**

**Alec Baldwin, James J. Gandolfini, Timothy Carhart**
**ABOVE: Alec Baldwin, Amy Madigan**

**Alec Baldwin, Jessica Lange**
**ABOVE: Jessica Lange, Alec Baldwin**

39

# TWO TRAINS RUNNING

By August Wilson; Director, Lloyd Richards; Sets, Tony Fanning; Costumes, Christi Karvonides; Lighting, Geoff Korf; Casting, Meg Simon; General Manager, Laurel Ann Wilson; Company Manager, Noel Gilmore; Stage Managers, Karen L. Carpenter, Fred Seagraves; Presented by Yale Repertory Theatre (Stan Wojewodski, Artistic Director), Center Theatre Group/Ahmanson (Gordon Davidson, Producing Director), Jujamcyn Theatres (Benjamin Mordecai, Executive Producer), Huntington Theatre Co., Seattle Repertory Theatre, and Old Globe Theatre; Press, Jeffrey Richards/David LeShay; Previewed from Tuesday, April 7; Opened in the Walter Kerr Theatre on Monday, April 13, 1992*

## CAST

| | |
|---|---|
| Risa | Cynthia Martells |
| Wolf | Anthony Chisholm |
| Memphis | Al White |
| Holloway | Roscoe Lee Browne |
| Hambone | Sullivan Ealker |
| Sterling | Larry Fishburne |
| West | Chuck Patterson |

**UNDERSTUDIES/STANDBYS** Ed Cambridge (Holloway/West), Robinson Frank Adu (Memphis/Hambone)

A drama in two acts with eight scenes. The action takes place in Memphis Lee's restaurant in the Hill District of Pittsburgh, 1969.

*Variety* tallied 14 favorable, 3 mixed and 1 negative review. Both *Times* critics had praise with Rich : "...sometimes touching, often funny..." and Richards feeling it was Wilson's "...most benevolent work to date." Kissel noted "...His plays have a musical quality that give them interest..."(*News*) but Barnes (*Post*) opined "*Two Trains* has less immediacy and more padding than the cycle's earlier plays." In *Newsday*, Winer praised the "...splendid cast..." while *Variety*(Gerard) stated "...there's no better new play running..."

*Closed August 30, 1992 after 160 performances and 7 previews. Winner of "Tony" for Best Featured Actor in a Play (Larry Fishburne). New York Drama Critics Circle awarded this Best American Play of the season.

*Jay Thompson Photos*

**Larry Fishburne, Cynthia Martells**
ABOVE: **Roscoe Lee Browne, Cynthia Martells, Al White**

The Company

**Walter Bobbie, Nathan Lane, J.K. Simmons**
CENTER: (center) Scott Wise and Ensemble
TOP LEFT: Nathan Lane, Peter Gallagher

**(center) Walter Bobbie and Company**
CENTER: (center) Faith Prince and Hot Box Girls
TOP RIGHT: Faith Prince, Nathan Lane

# GUYS AND DOLLS
## A Musical Fable Of Broadway

Music/Lyrics, Frank Loesser; Book, Jo Swerling and Abe Burrows; Director, Jerry Zaks; Choreography, Christopher Chadman; Orchestrations, (original) George Bassman, Ted Royal, (new) Michael Starobin, Michael Gibson; Musical Supervision, Edward Strauss; Sets, Tony Walton; Costumes, William Ivey Long; Lighting, Paul Gallo; Dance Music, Mark Hummel; Sound, Tony Meola; Asst. Choreographer, Linda Haberman; Musical Coordinator, Seymour Red Press; Hairstylist, David H. Lawrence; Casting, Johnson-Liff & Zerman; Prod. Manager, Peter Fulbright; Company Manager, Marcia Goldberg; Stage Managers, Steven Beckler, Clifford Schwartz, Joe Deer; Cast Recording, RCA Victor; Executive Producer, David Strong Warner; Associate Producers, Playhouse Sq. Center, David B. Bode; Presented by Dodger Productions, Roger Berlind, Jujamcyn Theatres/TV ASAHI, Kardana Prod., and Kennedy Ceneter for the Performing Arts; Press, Chris Boneau/Adrian Bryan-Brown, John Barlow, Jackie Green; Previewed from Monday, March 16; Opened in the Martin Beck Theatre on Tuesday, April 14, 1992*

### CAST

| | |
|---|---|
| Nicely-Nicely Johnson | Walter Bobbie |
| Benny Southstreet | J.K. Simmons |
| Rusty Charlie/Guy | Timothy Shew |
| Sarah Brown | Josie de Guzman +1 |
| Arvide Abernathy | John Carpenter |
| Agatha | Eleanor Glockner |
| Calvin/Guy | Leslie Feagan |
| Martha | Victoria Clark |
| Harry the Horse | Ernie Sabella |
| Lt. Brannigan | Steve Ryan |
| Nathan Detroit | Nathan Lane +2 |
| Angie the Ox/Joey Biltmore/Guy | Michael Goz |
| Miss Adelaide | Faith Prince |
| Sky Masterson | Peter Gallagher +3 |
| Hot Box MC/Guy | Stan Page |
| Mimi/Doll | Denise Faye |
| Gen. Matilda B. Cartwright | Ruth Williamson |
| Big Jule | Herschel Sparber |
| Drunk/Guy | Robert Michael Baker |
| Waiter/Guy | Kenneth Kantor |
| Crapshooter Dance Lead/Guy | Scott Wise |
| Other Guys | Gary Chryst, R.F. Daley, Randy Andre Davis, David Elder, Cory English, Mark Esposito, Carlos Lopez, John MacInnis |
| Other Dolls | Tina Marie DeLeone, JoAnn M. Hunter, Nancy Lemenager, Greta Martin, Pascale Faye-Williams |

**UNDERSTUDIES:** Jeff Brooks, Larry Cahn (Nathan/Benny/Harry), Robert Michael Baker (Sky), Leslie Feagan (Harry), Michael Goz (Jule), Kenneth Kantor (Brannigan), Stan Page (Arvide), Timothy Shew (Nicely/Brannigan), Steven Sofia (Calvin), Scott Wise (Charlie), Victoria Clark (Adelaide/Agatha), Eleanor Glockner (Cartwright), Tina Marie DeLeone (Mimi), Denise Faye (Agatha), Nancy Lemenager (Martha)
**SWINGS:** Mr. Cahn, Susan Misner, Mr. Sofia

**MUSICAL NUMBERS:** Fugue for Tinhorns, Follow the Fold, The Oldest Established, I'll Know, A Bushel and a Peck, Adelaide's Lament, Guys and Dolls, Havana, If I Were a Bell, My Time of Day, I've Never Been in Love Before, Take Back Your Mink, More I Cannot Wish You, Crapshooter's Dance, Luck Be a Lady, Sue Me, Sit Down You're Rockin' the Boat, Marry the Man Today, Finale

A new production of the 1950 musical in two acts with seventeen scenes. The action takes place in "Runyonland" around Broadway and in Havana, Cuba. The original production (*Theatre World* Vol.7) opened at the Forty-Sixth St. Theatre on Nov.24, 1950 featuring Vivian Blaine, Robert Alda, Sam Levene, Isabel Bigley and Stubby Kaye , running 1200 performances.

This revival was rapturously received with *Variety* tallying 23 favorable and 1 mixed notice. The *Times* featured the opening on page 1 and inside Rich said "...The cherished Runyonland of memory is ...felt and dreamt anew by intoxicated theatre artists." Richards felt it only "...a fair to good mounting..." At the *News* Kissel called it "...a welcome reminder of the vitality of the city and its musical theatre..." while Watt added "...flawless..." Barnes(*Post*) : "...a gorgeous gem..." and Winer (*Newsday*) agreed with "brash , bright and adorable..."

*Still playing May 31, 1992. Winner of 1992 "Tonys" for Best Revival, Best Actress - Musical (Faith Prince), Best Director-Musical, Best Scenic Design

+Succeeded by: 1. Preceeded by Carolyn Mignini during previews 2. Adam Arkin  3. Tom Wopat

**TOP RIGHT: Peter Gallagher, Josi de Guzman**
**RIGHT: Faith Prince**

# METRO

Music, Janusz Stoklosa; English Lyrics, Mary Bracken Phillips; Original Book/Lyrics, Agata and Maryna Miklaszewskal; English Book, Ms. Phillips and Janusz Jozefowicz; Direction/Choreography, Mr. Jozefowicz; Musical Direction/Vocal & Orchestral Arrangements, Mr. Stoklosa; Sets, Janusz Sosnowski; Costumes, Juliet Polcsa, Marie Anne Chiment; Lighting, Ken Billington; Sound, Jaroslaw Regulski; Lasers, Mike Deissler; Technical Supervisor, Arthur Siccardi; Musical Coordinator, John Monaco; American Dance Supervisor, Cynthia Onrubia; General Manager, Leonard Soloway; Company Manager, Stanley D. Silver; Stage Managers, Beverly Randolph, Dale Kaufman, Michael Pule; Executive Producer, Donald C. Farber; Presented by Wiktor Kubiak; Press, Bill Evans/Jim Randolph, William Schelble, Susan L. Schulman, Erin Dunn; Previewed from Thursday, March 26; Opened in the Minskoff Theatre on Thursday, April 16, 1992*

## CAST

| | |
|---|---|
| Anka | Katarzyna Groniec |
| Jan | Robert Janowski |
| Edyta | Edyta Gorniak |
| Max | Mariusz Czajka |
| Philip | Olek Krupa, succeeded by Janusz Jozefowicz |
| Viola | Violetta Klimczewska |
| Iwona | Iwona Runowska |
| Anka Alternate/Standby | Roby Griggs |
| Jan Alternate/Standby | Rohn Seykell |

and Krzysztof Adamski, Monika Ambroziak, Andrew Appolonow, Jacek Badurek, Alicja Borkowska, Michal Chamera, Pawel Cheda, Magdalena Depczyk, Jaroslaw Derybowski, Wojciech Dmochowski, Malgorzata Duda, Katarzyna Galica, Katarzyna Gawel, Denisa Geislerova, Lidia Groblewska, Piotr Hajduk, Joanna Jagla, Jaroslaw Janikowski, Adam Kamien, Grzegorz Kowalczyk, Andrzej Kubicki, Katarzyna Lewandowska, Barbara Melzer, Michal Milowicz, Radoslaw Natkanski, Polina Oziernych, Marek Palucki, Beata Pawlik, Katarzyna Skarpetowska, Igor Sorine, Ewa Szawlowska, Marc Thomas, Ilona Trybula, Beata Urbanska, Kamila Zapytowska

**MUSICAL NUMBERS:** Overture, Metro, My Fairy Tale, But Not Me, Windows, That's Life (previews), Bluezwis, Love Duet, Tower of Babel, Labels (previews), Benajmin Franklin In God We Trust, Uciekali, Waiting, Pieniadze, Love Duet II, Dreams Don't Die

A musical in two acts and seventeen scenes. The action takes place somewhere in Europe in a Metro.

*Variety* tallied 1 favorable, 3 mixed and 14 negative notices. "What's the Polish word for fiasco?" asked Rich in the *Times* but Richards noted the cast "...gets A for effort." Kissel (*News*) called it "...a naive return to 1968" while Barnes (*Post*) turned thumbs down on "...the painfully conventional music..." Gerard (*Variety*) : "...subways are for sleeping, aren't they? *Metro* is."

*Closed April 26, 1992 after 13 performances and 24 previews.

*Wojciech Glinka Photos*

**Top Right: The Company**
**Right: Robert Janowski, Katarzyna Groniec**
**Below: The Company**

# THE HIGH ROLLERS SOCIAL AND PLEASURE CLUB

Director/Choreographer, Alan Weeks; Arrangements/Musical Direction/Orchestrations, Allen Toussaint; Conception, Judy Gordon; Sets, David Mitchell; Costumes, Theoni V. Aldredge; Lighting, Beverly Emmons; Sound, Peter Fitzgerald; Music Advisors, Jerry Wexler, Charles Neville; Musical Coordinator, John Miller; Associate Director, Bruce Heath; Casting, Alan Filderman; Prod. Supervisor, Mary Porter Hall; General Manager, Brent Peek Prod.; Company Manager, Kip Makkonen; Stage Manager, David H. Bosboom; Associate Producers, Nicholas Evans, Donald Tick, Mary Ellen Ashley, Irving Welzer; Presented by Ms. Gordon, Dennis Grimaldi, Allen M. Shore, Marin Markinson; Previewed from Monday, April 6; Opened in the Helen Hayes Theatre on Wednesday, April 22, 1992*

### CAST

| | |
|---|---|
| Wonder Boy #1 | Keith Robert Bennett |
| Queen | Deborah Burrell-Cleveland |
| King | Lawrence Clayton |
| Jester | Eugene Fleming |
| Sorcerer | Michael McElroy |
| Enchantress | Vivian Reed |
| Princess | Nikki Rene |
| Wonder Boy #2 | Tarik Winston |

and Allen Toussaint

**UNDERSTUDIES:** Bruce Anthony Davis (Wonder Boys/Jester), Mona Wyatt (Queen/Enchantress/Princess), Frederick J. Boothe (King/Sorcerer)

**MUSICAL NUMBERS:** Tu Way Pocky Way, Open Up, Mr. Mardi Gras, Piano Solo, Chicken Shack Boogie, Lady Marmalade, Don't You Feel My Leg, You Can Have My Husband, Fun Time, It Will Stand/Mother-in-Law/Working in a Coal Mine, Lipstick Traces/Rockin' Pneumonia/Sittin' in Ya Ya, Feet Don't Fail Me Now, Ooh Poo Pa Doo, Dance the Night/Such a Night, All These Things, Mellow Sax, Sea Cruise, Jambalaya, Bourbon Street Parade, Jelly Roll, Heebie Jeebie Dance, I Like It Like That, Fiyou on the Bayou, Marie Leveau, Walk on Gilded Splinters, Black Widow Spider, Tell It Like It Is/You're the One, Let the Good Times Roll, Challenge Dance, Mos Scoscious, We All Need Love, Injuns Here We Come, Golden Crown, Jockomo, Hey Mama, Saints Go Marchin' In

A musical revue in two acts. The action takes place in the High Rollers Social and Pleasure Club, New Orleans, with a side trip to the Bayou. The time is Mardi Gras.

*Variety* recorded two favorable, four mixed and nine negative notices. Gussow (*Times*) : "On the positive side, the show has spirit and...a fervently talented cast." The *News*(Kissel) felt that R & B and theatre music did not mix well. The *Post's* Barnes stated "...the cast is excellent." *Newsday*(Stuart) felt the show "...utterly a mess..." *Variety* mentioned the show "...just about kills itself trying to give the audience a good time."

*Closed May 2, 1992 after 14 performances and 18 previews.

*Joan Marcus Photos*

**BELOW: Michael McElroy, Vivian Reed**
**TOP RIGHT: Vivian Reed**
**RIGHT: Michael McElroy, Nikki Rene, Vivian Reed, (rear) Allen Toussaint**
**BOTTOM RIGHT: The Company**

**Ellen Burstyn, Ben Gazzara**
RIGHT: Ellen Burstyn, Estelle Parsons
CENTER: Jon Matthews, Mako, Robert Joy
BOTTOM: Robert Joy, Mako, Estelle Parsons, Ellen Burstyn, Tracy
Sallows

# SHIMADA

By Jill Shearer; Director, Simon Phillips; Sets, Tony Straiges; Costumes, Judy
Dearing; Lighting, Richard Nelson; Score, Ian McDonald; Sound, Peter Fitzgerald;
Casting, Elissa Myers, Paul Fouquet; Stage Managers, Martin Gold, John McNamara;
Company Manager, Robb Lady; General Management, Kepam Corp., Sylrich
Management; Presented by Paul B. Berkowsky, Richard Seader, Furuyama Int'l, Ellis
and Mike Weatherly in association with Sally Sears; Press, Keith Sherman/Chris Day,
Jim Byk, Joel Dein; Preveiwed from Monday, April 6; Opened in the Broadhurst
Theatre on Thursday, April 23, 1992*

## CAST

Shimada/Toshio Uchiyama ............................................................Mako
Eric Dawson ..............................................................................Ben Gazzara
Clive Beaumont/Mark Beaumont ...........................................Robert Joy
Denny ........................................................................................Estelle Parsons
Jan Harding/Wisteria Lady ......................................................Tracy Sallows
Sharyn Beaumont ....................................................................Ellen Burstyn
Billy .........................................................................................Jon Matthews

**UNDERSTUDIES/STANDBYS:** Jack Davidson (Eric), Judith Bancroft
(Sharyn/Denny), Ernest Abuba (Shimada/Toshio), Christopher Taylor
(Clive/Mark/Billy/Matsumoto/Samurai), Pamela Stewart (Jan/Wisteria Lady)

A drama in two acts. The action takes place in present-day Australia, with
flashbacks to a Japanese prisoner-of-war camp in the Burmese jungle in 1945, near the
end of World War II.

*Variety* tallied 17 negative notices. The *Times'* Rich felt the play "...moves at the
pace of bulk mail...most novel aspect..as the first Broadway show to offer a
simultaneous Japanese translation..." At the *News* Kissel criticized the plays
"...simplistic treatment of its large themes.." but praised the actors . Barnes (*Post*) also
praised the "..fine actors..." in a "...sadly inept Australian play..." *Newsday* (Winer)
added " ...a lame piece of sit-dram..." and *Variety* felt "It's the season's biggest bore."
In a letter to the *Times*, Ellen Burstyn and cast wrote "...We were shocked and stunned
that they (critics) had missed what the play was about..."

*Closed April 25, 1992 after 4 performances and 20 previews.

*T. Charles Erickson Photos*

# MAN OF LA MANCHA

Music, Mitch Leigh; Lyrics, Joe Darion; Book, Dale Wasserman; Director, Albert Marre; Orchestrations, Music Makers Inc.; Musical Director, Brian Salesky; Sets/Costumes, Howard Bay; Costumes, Patton Campbell; Lighting, Gregory Allen Hirsch; Sound, Weston; Dance Arrangements, Neil Warner; Casting, Richard Shulman; Asst. Director, Ted Forlow; Company Manager, Lynn Landis; Stage Managers, Patrick Horrigan, Betsy Nicholson; Executive Producer, Manny Kladitis; Presented by The Mitch Leigh Co.; Previewed from Tuesday, March 31; Opened in the Marquis Theatre on Friday, April 24, 1992*

## CAST

Cervantes/Don Quixote .................................................................Raul Julia +1
Aldonza/Dulcinea...............................................................Sheena Easton +2
Sancho.....................................................................................Tony Martinez
Governor/Pedro.......................................................................Chev Rodgers
Padre........................................................................................David Wasson
Dr. Carrasco................................................................................Ian Sullivan
Innkeeper................................................................................David Holliday
Antonia................................................................................Valerie De Pena
Housekeeper......................................................................Marceline Decker
Barber...........................................................................................Ted Forlow
Paco/Mule..........................................................................Hechter Ubarry
Juan/Horse.......................................................................Jean-Paul Richard
Manuel..........................................................................................Luis Perez
Tenorio.............................................................................Gregory Mitchell
Jose..........................................................................................Bill Santora
Jorge/Guard............................................................................Chet D'Elia
Maria....................................................................................Tanny McDonald
Fermina..........................................................................Joan Susswein Barber
Capt. of Inquisition..........................................................Jon Vandertholen
Guitarists .............................................Robin Polseno, David Serva
Guard .....................................................................................Darryl Ferrera

**UNDERSTUDIES:** David Holliday (Cervantes/Quixote/Gov.), Joan Susswein Barber (Aldonza/Antonio/Maria), Darryl Ferrera (Sancho/Padre/Barber), Chev Rodgers (Innkeeper), Jon Vandertholen (Carrasco), Tanny McDonald (Fermina/Dancer), Bill Santora (Mule), Jean-Paul Richard (Capt.), SWING: Rick Manning

**MUSICAL NUMBERS:** Man of La Manch (I Don Quixote), It's All the Same, Dulcinea, I'm Only Thinking of Him, I Really Like Him, What Does He Want of Me, Little Bird, Barber's Song, Golden Helmet of Mambrino, To Each His Dulcinea, The Quest (The Impossible Dream), The Combat, The Dubbing, The Abduction, Moorish Dance, Aldonza, Knight of the Mirrors, A Little Gossip, The Psalm, Finale

A new production of the 1965 musical performed without intermission. Suggested by the life and works of Miguel de Cervantes y Saavedra. The action takes place in a dungeon in Seville at the end of the sixteenth century and in the imagination of Cervantes.

The original production (*Theatre World* Vol.22) won all the best musical awards but critics were less impressed this time and *Variety* recorded one favorable, one mixed and ten negative notices. Gussow (*Times*) :"It is not a musical that is crying for another revival...to deny its popularity would be like tilting with windmills." The *News* (Kissel): "...unusually lugubrious..." while the *Post* (Barnes) added "If you have seen it before, this might recall happier memories..." Winer called it "...a road quality, paint-by-numbers re-creation..." in *Newsday*.

+Succeeded by: 1. David Holliday, Laurence Guittard 2. Joan Susswein-Barber during illness, Joan Diener (originated role in 1965)

*Closed July 26, 1992 after 108 performances and 28 previews.

*Joan Marcus Photos*

**TOP LEFT: Raul Julia**
**TOP RIGHT: Sheena Easton**
**CENTER: Antony De Vecchi, Ted Forlow, Tony Martinez, Julia, Joan Susswein Barber**
**BOTTOM: Guittard, Joan Diener**

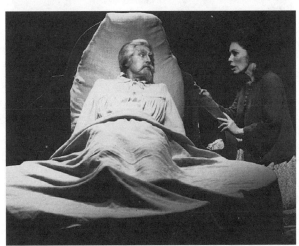

The "Hunnies" and Ensemble
Top: Savion Glover, Gregory Hines

# JELLY'S LAST JAM

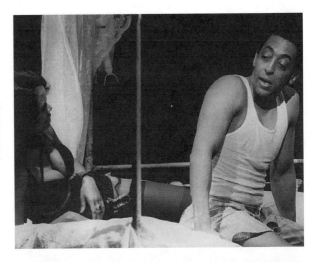

Music, Jelly Roll Morton, Luther Henderson; Lyrics, Susan Birkenhead; Book/Direction, George C. Wolfe; Choreography, Hope Clarke; Tap Choreography, Gregory Hines, Ted L. Levy; Musical Adaptation/Orchestrations/Musical Supervision, L. Henderson; Musical Director, Linda Twine; Sets, Robin Wagner; Costumes, Toni-Leslie James; Lighting, Jules Fisher; Musical Coordinator, John Miller; Sound, Otts Munderloh; Cast Recording, Mercury; Masks/Puppets, Barbara Pollitt; Hairstylist, Jeffrey Frank; Casting, Hughes/Moss & Stanley Soble; General Manager, David Strong Warner; Company Manager, Susan Gustafson; Stage Managers, Arturo E. Porazzi, Bernita Robinson, Bonnie L. Becker; Associate Producers, Peggy Hill Rosenkranz, Marilyn Hall, Dentsu Inc; Presented by Margo Lion and Pamela Koslow in association with Polygram Diversified Entertainment, 126 Second Ave. Corp., Hal Luftig, Rodger Hess, Jujamcyn Theatres, TV Asahi and Herb Alpert; Press, Richard Kornberg/Carol R. Fineman; Previewed from Tuesday, March 31; Opened in the Virginia Theatre on Sunday, April 26, 1992*

## CAST

| | |
|---|---|
| Chimney Man | Keith David |
| The Hunnies | Mamie Duncan-Gibbs, Stephanie Pope, Allison M. Williams |
| The Crowd | Ken Ard, Adrian Bailey, Sherry D. Boone, Brenda B. Braxton, Mary Bond Davis, Ralph Deaton, Melissa Haizlip, Cee-Cee Harshaw, Ted L. Levy, Stanley Wayne Mathis, Victoria Gabrielle Platt, Gil Pritchett III, Michele M. Robinson |
| Jelly Roll Morton | Gregory Hines |
| Young Jelly | Savion Glover |
| Sisters | Victoria Gabrielle Platt, Sherry D. Boone |
| Ancestors | Adrian Bailey, Mary Bond Davis, Ralph Deaton, Ann Duquesnay, Melissa Haizlip |
| Miss Mamie | Mary Bond Davis |
| Buddy Bolden | Ruben Santiago-Hudson |
| Too-Tight Nora | Brenda Braxton |
| Three Finger Jake | Gil Pritchett III |
| Gran Mimi | Ann Duquesnay |
| Jack the Bear | Stanley Wayne Mathis |
| Foot-in-Yo-Ass Sam | Ken Ard |
| Anita | Tonya Pinkins |
| Melrose Brothers | Don Johanson, Gordon Joseph Weiss |

**UNDERSTUDIES/STANDBYS:** Lawrence Hamilton (Jelly), Ken Ard (Chimney Man), Jimmy W. Tate (Young Jelly), Stephanie Pope (Anita), Ralph Deaton (Jack-the-Bear), Adrian Bailey (Buddy), Clare Bathe (Mimi/Maimie), Melissa Haizlip (Hunnies), Bill Brassea (Melrose Bros.) **SWINGS:** Ken Roberson, Janice Lorraine-Holt, La-Rose Saxon

**MUSICAL NUMBERS:** Jelly's Jam, In My Day, The Creole Way, The Whole World's Waitin' to Sing Your Song/Street Scene, Michigan Water, Get Away Boy/Lonely Boy Blues, Somethin' More, That's How You Jazz, The Chicago Stomp, Play the Music for Me, Lovin' Is a Lowdown Blues, Dr. Jazz, Good Ole New York, Too Late Daddy, That's the Way We Do Things in New Yawk, Jelly's Isolation Dance, Last Chance Blues, The Last Rites

A musical in two acts with twelve scenes. The action takes place in The Jungle Inn, a lowdown club somewhere's 'tween Heaven 'n' Hell on the eve of Jelly Roll Morton's death.

*Variety* tallied 15 favorable, 3 mixed and 1 negative review. Rich told *Times* readers "...something new and exciting is happening..." and Richards agreed: "...a breakthrough musical..." At the *News* , Kissel called it "...a glorious tribute to the musical culture of New Orleans..." while Watt questioned why more original Morton material wasn't used. The *Post* (Barnes) felt it "...the most original musical to hit Broadway in years.." and *Newsday* (Winer) described it as "...witty, confident..." *Variety* (Gerard) summed up "If Broadway has room for another big, splashy, tuneful crowd-pleaser, here it is."

Closed September 5, 1993 after 569 performances and 25 previews. Winner of "Tony" awards for Best Actor in a Musical (Gregory Hines), Best Featured Actress/Musical (Tonya Pinkins) and Best Lighting

*Martha Swope Photos*

**TOP: Tonya Pinkins, Gregory Hines**
**CENTER: Gregory Hines, Stanley Wayne Mathis**
**BOTTOM: Keith David, Gregory Hines**

# A SMALL FAMILY BUSINESS

By Alan Ayckbourn; Director, Lynne Meadow; Sets, John Lee Beatty; Costumes, Roth; Lighting, Peter Kaczorowski; Sound, Tom Sorce; Music, Jake Holmes; Fight Allen Suddeth; Hairstylist, John Quagglia; Casting, Donna Isaacson, Randy Car Company Manager, Peter Bogyo; Stage Managers, James Harker, John M. Ather General Manager, Victoria Bailey; Executive Producer, Barry Grove; Assoc Producer, Roger Alan Gindi; Presented by Weissman Productions Inc. and M Productions; Press, Helene Davis/David Roggensack; Previewed from Tuesday, Ma 31; Opened in the Music Box Theatre on Monday, April 27, 1992*

## CAST

| | |
|---|---|
| Jack McCraken | Brian Murray |
| Poppy | Jane Carr |
| Ken Ayres | Thomas Hill |
| Tina | Barbara Garrick |
| Roy Ruston | Robert Stanton |
| Samantha | Amelia Campbell |
| Cliff | Mark Arnott |
| Anita | Caroline Lagerfelt |
| Desmond | John Curless |
| Harriet | Patricia Conolly |
| Yvonne Doggett | Patricia Kilgarriff |
| Benedict Hough | Anthony Heald |
| Giorgio Rivetti/Orlando Rivetti/Vincenzo Rivetti/Lotario Rivetti/ Umberto Rivetti | Jake Weber (alternately billed as Abe Jerkew, Jere Kwabe, Jeb. E. Waker, J. Weak Beer) |

**UNDERSTUDIES:** Robin Mosely (Poppy/Anita/Harriet/Yvonne), Edmund C. Da (Roy/Cliff/Benedict/Rivettis), John Curles (Jack), Philip LeStran (Jack/Ken/Desmond), Kari McGee (Tina/Samantha)

A dark comedy in two acts. The action takes place in England at present.

*Variety* recorded 10 favorable, 5 mixed and 3 negative notices. At the *Times* R was mixed : "Some but not all of the play's humor and nastiness come through while Richards felt it "...the most bracing comedy on Broadway..." The *News* men s with Kissel finding " an admirable balance between the laughter and the disquiet reality.." but Watt saying "...Ayckbourn doesn't travel too well..." Barnes (*Post*) lik it but felt "...its appeal to American audiences...might be dubious." *Newsday*'s Wi felt it "...surprisingly mild and middling."

*Closed June 7, 1992 after 48 performances and 31 previews.

*Gerry Goodstein Photos*

**TOP:** Anthony Heald, Brian Murray
**LEFT:** Brian Murray, Jane Carr
**BOTTOM LEFT:** Amelia Campbell, Brian Murray, Robert Stanton, Ja Carr, Barbara Garrick
**BELOW:** Brian Murray

(rear) **Mark Arnott, Jake Weber, Caroline Lagerfelt, Robert Stanton, Patricia Kilgarriff, Joan Curless, Patricia Conolly,** (front) **Barbara Garrick, Brian Murray, Thomas Hill, Jane Carr, Amelia Campbell, Anthony Heald**
TOP: **John Lee Beatty's set**

Michael Rupert, Stephen Bogardus, Heather Mac Rae, Carolee Carmello
TOP: (back row) Michael Rupert, Heather Mac Rae, Carolee Carmello, (front row) Chip Zien, Barbara Walsh, Stephen Bogardus, (at bat)
Jonathan Kaplan

# FALSETTOS

sic/Lyrics, William Finn; Book, Mr. Finn, James Lapine; Director, Mr. Lapine; angements, Michael Starobin; Musical Director, Scott Frankel; Sets, Douglas Stein; stumes, Ann Hould-Ward; Lighting, Frances Aronson; Sound, Peter Fitzgerald; rstylist, Phyllis Della; Musical Contractor, John Monaco; Cast Recording, DRG e-acts); Casting, Wendy Ettinger, Susan Howard, Amy Schecter; Prod. Supervisor, ig Jacobs; General Manager, Barbara Darwall; Company Manager, Kim Sellon; ge Manager, Karen Armstrong; Produced in association with James and Maureen Sullivan Cushing and Masakazu Shibaoka Broadway Pacific; Associate Producer, cia Parker; Presented by Barry and Fran Weissler; Press, Pete Sanders; Previewed m Wednesday, April 8; Opened in the John Golden Theatre on Wednesday, April 1992*

## CAST

| | |
|---|---|
| rvin | Michael Rupert +1 |
| nizzer | Stephen Bogardus |
| ndel | Chip Zien |
| on | Jonathan Kaplan +2, Andrew Harrison Leeds (matinees) |
| na | Barbara Walsh |
| arlotte | Heather Mac Rae |
| rdelia | Carolee Carmello +3 |

**NDERSTUDIES:** Philip Hoffman, John Ruess, Maureen Moore, Susan Goodman

**USICAL NUMBERS:** Four Jews in a Room Bitching, A Tight Knit Family, Love Blind, Thrill of First Love, Marvin at the Psychiatrist, Everyone Tells Jason to See a ychiatrist, This Had Better Come to a Stop, I'm Breaking Down, Jason's Therapy, A rriage Proposal, Trini's Song, March of the Falsettos, Chess Game, Making a me, Games I Play, Marvin Goes Crazy, I Never Wanted to Love You, Father to n, Welcome to Falsettoland, Year of the Child, Miracle of Judaism, Sitting atching Jason Play Baseball, A Day in Falsettoland, Everyone Hates His Parents, at More Can I Say, Something Bad Is Happening, Holding to the Ground, Days ke This I Almost Believe in God, Cancelling the Bar Mitzvah, Unlikely Lovers, other Miracle of Judaism, You Gotta Die Sometime, Jason's Bar Mitzvah, What ould I Do ?

A musical in two acts. The action takes place in 1979 and 1981.

*Variety* tallied 14 favorable and 3 negative notices for this combination/revision of o earlier off-broadway musicals, *March of the Falsettos (Theatre World* Vol.37) and *lsettoland (Theatre World* Vol.47). The *Times* critics: Rich: "...exhilarating and artbreaking...what more perfect end to this season could there be?" Richards: artists are at work and their artistry is pure and beautiful." The *News* critics: Kissel ted "Finn's verbal and musical dexterity..." which left Watt cold: "...chattering, attering score..." Barnes (*Post*) decried the "sticky with sentiment" theme, but *wsday's* Winer said "...the only completely original, contemporary, brilliant, merican concept musical of the season...I laughed!...I cried!" *Variety*(Gerard): "...a asterly feat of comic storytelling...a visionary musical theatre work."

losed June 27, 1993 after 487 performances and 33 previews. Winner of 1992 onys" for Best Score and Best Book for a Musical.

ucceeded by:1.Adrian Zmed, Michael Rupert 2.Sivan Cotel 3.Maureen Moore, arolee Carmello

*Carol Rosegg/Martha Swope Photos*

**LEFT: Chip Zien**
**RIGHT: Michael Rupert**

(clockwise) Michael Rupert, Chip Zien, Barbara Walsh, Jonathan Kaplan, Heather Mac Rae, Carolee Carmello
**ABOVE:** Michael Rupert, Jonathan Kaplan, Barbara Walsh

(clockwise) Debra Mooney, Eli Wallach, Joe Spano, Hector Elizondo
TOP RIGHT: Joe Spano, Eli Wallach, Hector Elizondo
CENTER: Eli Wallach, Debra Mooney, Hector Elizondo
BOTTOM: Hector Elizondo, Debra Mooney, Joe Spano, (seated) Eli
Wallach

# THE PRICE

By Arthur Miller; Director, John Tillinger; Sets, John Lee Beatty; Costumes, Jane Greenwood; Lighting, Dennis Parichy; Sound, Douglas J. Cuomo; Casting, Pat McCorkle, Richard Cole; General Manager, Ellen Richard; Stage Managers, Matthew T. Mundinger, Kathy J. Faul; Press, Joshua Ellis, Susanne Tighe; Presented by Roundabout Theatre Company (Todd Haimes, Producing Director; Gene Feist, Founding Director); Previewed from Wednesday, May 20; Opened in the Criterion Center Stage Right on Wednesday, June 10, 1992*

## CAST

Victor Franz..................................................................................Hector Elizondo
Esther Franz....................................................................................Debra Mooney
Gregory Solomon ..................................................................................Eli Wallach
Walter Franz .........................................................................................Joe Spano

**STANDBYS:** Jack Davidson (Victor/Walter), Dawn Jamieson (Esther), David Kennedy (Gregory)

A new production of the 1968 drama in two acts. The action takes place in the attic floor of a Manhattan brownstone. Original Production (*Theatre World* Vol.24) featured Pat Hingle, Arthur Kennedy and Kate Reid at the Morosco Theatre.

*Variety* noted 9 favorable and 2 mixed reviews. The *Times*' Gussow called the production "...scrupulous...perceptive..." The *News* (Kissel): "...one of Miller's richest plays..." and the *Post* (Barnes) : "Long live the Broadway season!" *Newsday*'s Stuart felt the play "...immaculately suited..." to Wallach, and *Variety* (Gerard) called it "...consistent and rewarding..."

*Closed July 19, 1992 after limited run of 47 performances and 25 previews.

*Martha Swope Photos*

# SALOME

By Oscar Wilde; Director, Robert Allan Ackerman; Choreography, Lar Lubovitch; Music, Richard Peaslee, Hamza El Din; Sets/Costumes, Zack Brown; Lighting, Arden Fingerhut; Sound, Fox and Perla; Casting, Judy Henderson, Alycia Aumuller; Stage Manager, Wm. Hare; Company Manager, Susan Elrod; Presented by Circle in the Square (Theodore Mann, Artistic Director; Robert A. Buckley, Managing Director; Paul Libin, Consulting Producer); Press, Maria Somma, Patty Onagan; Previewed from Monday May 25; Opened in the Circle In The Square Uptown on Sunday, June 28, 1992*

## CAST

| | |
|---|---|
| A Soldier | Kevin Carrigan |
| Manasseh | Mark Wilson |
| Young Syrian,Capt. of Guard | Esai Morales |
| Page of Herodias | Mark Kevin Lewis |
| Soldier #1 | John Robinson |
| Soldier #2 | Neil Maffin |
| A Cappadocian | Rene Rivera |
| Naaman | Dennis P. Huggins |
| Jokanaan | Arnold Vosloo |
| Salome | Sheryl Lee |
| A Slave | Keith Randolph Smith |
| Herod Antipas | Al Pacino |
| Herodias | Suzanne Bertish |
| Tigellinus | John Joseph Freeman |
| Jew #1 | Frank Raiter |
| Jew #2 | Kermit Brown |
| Jew #3 | John Straub |
| Jew #4 | Tom Brennan |
| Nazarene #1 | Charles Cragin |
| Nazarene #2 | Alan Nebelthau |
| A Roman | Emilio Del Pozo |
| A Slave | Scott Rabinowitz |
| Attendants to Salome | Tanya M. Gibson, Molly Price |

**UNDERSTUDIES:** Emilio Del Pozo (Herod), Neil Maffin (Jokanaan), Molly Price (Salome/Herodias)

The 1892 drama, originally written for Sarah Bernhardt, takes place in the Palace of Herod. Written in French, the play was banned by the Lord Chamberlain and didn't reach the Paris stage till 1896 without Miss Bernhardt.

*Variety* tallied 3 favorable, 4 mixed and 10 negative reviews. At the *Times* , Gussow called Pacino "...daring...He is the only reason to see this..." while Richards added "...one of the reasons we go to theatre...is to watch actors act. The play doesn't always have to be the thing." Kissel (*News*) called the play "...Wilde's oddest..." but Barnes (*Post*) hailed Pacino's "...triumphant Broadway return..." Winer (*Newsday*) noted a "...truly weird, intense, goofy and mesmerizing performance by Pacino." *Variety* called the show "...utterly watchable..."

*Closed July 29, 1992 after limited run of 18 performances and 16 previews. Performed in repertory with *Chinese Coffee*.

*Anita & Steve Shevett Photos*

**Arnold Vosloo, Sheryl Lee**
**TOP: Al Pacino, Suzanne Bertish**

# CHINESE COFFEE

By Ira Lewis; Director, Arvin Brown; Sets/Costumes, Zack Brown; Lighting, Arden Fingerhut; Casting, Judy Henderson, Alycia Aumuller; Company Manager, Susan Elrod; Stage Managers, Wm. Hare, Jack Gianino, Joe Lorden; Presented by Circle in the Square (Theodore Mann, Artistic Director; Robert A. Buckley, Managing Director; Paul Libin, Consulting Producer); Press, Maria Somma, Patty Onagan; Previewed from Thursday, May 28; Opened in the Circle In The Square Uptown on Monday, June 29, 1992*

## CAST

| | |
|---|---|
| Jacob Manheim | Charles Cioffi |
| Harry Levine | Al Pacino |

A comedy performed without intermission. The action takes place in a lower Manhattan loft, late 1980s.

*Variety* recorded 5 favorable, 5 mixed and 4 negative notices. Gussow (*Times*) felt "...Mr. Pacino and Mr. Cioffi invest the show with acting panache." Kissel (*News*) complained about the the "...thinness of the writing..." while Barnes (*Post*) countered "...slight, but not weak..." *Variety* (Gerard) noted "...this is a star turn, and Pacino delivers."

*Closed August 1, 1992 after 9 performances and 14 previews. Performed in repertory with *Salome*.

**Charles Cioffi, Al Pacino**

55

# BROADWAY PRODUCTIONS FROM PAST SEASONS THAT PLAYED THROUGH THIS SEASON

## CATS

Music, Andrew Lloyd Webber; Based on *Old Possum's Book Of Practical Cats* by T.S. Eliot; Orchestrations, David Cullen, Lloyd Webber; Prod. Musical Director, David Caddick; Musical Director, Edward G. Robinson; Sound, Martin Levan; Lighting, David Hersey; Design, John Napier; Choreography/Associate Director, Gillian Lynne; Director, Trevor Nunn; Original Cast Recording, Geffen; Casting, Johnson-Liff & Zerman; General Managers, Gatchell & Neufeld; Company Manager, James G. Mennen; Stage Managers, Peggy Peterson, Tom Taylor, Suzanne Viverito; Presented by Cameron Mackintosh, The Really Useful Co., David Geffen, and The Shubert Organization; Press, Fred Nathan/Bert Fink; Previewed from September 23; Opened in the Winter Garden Theatre on Thursday, October 7, 1982*

### CAST

| | |
|---|---|
| Alonzo | Scott Taylor |
| Bustopher/Asparagus/Growltiger | Dale Hensley/Jeffrey Clonts |
| Bombalurina | Marlene Danielle |
| Cassandra | Leigh Webster/Darlene Wilson |
| Coricopat | Johnny Anzalone |
| Demeter | Brenda Braxton/Mercedes Perez |
| Grizabella | Lillias White/Laurie Beechman |
| Jellylorum/Griddlebone | Bonnie Simmons |
| Jennyanydots | Cindy Benson/Rose McGuire |
| Mistoffelees | Michael Arnold/Kevin Poe |
| Mungojerrie | Ray Roderick/Roger Kachel |
| Munkustrap | Greg Minahan/Bryan Batt |
| Old Deuteronomy | Larry Small/Ken Prymus |
| Plato/Macivity/Rumpus Cat | Randy Wojcik |
| Pouncival | John Joseph Festa/Devanand N. Janki |
| Rumpleteazer | Kristi Lynes |
| Rum Tum Tiger | Frank Mastrocola/Bradford Minkoff |
| Sillabub | Michelle Schumacher/Lisa Mayer |
| Skimbleshanks | Eric Scott Kincaid/George Smyros |
| Tantomile | Lisa Dawn Cave/Michelle Artigas |
| Tumblebrutus | Jay Poindexter |
| Victoria | Claudia Shell |
| Cat Chorus | John Briel, Jay Aubrey Jones, Susan Powers, Heidi Stallings |

**STANDBYS/UNDERSTUDIES:** Brian Andrews(Alonzo/Mungojerrie/Plato/ Macivity/Rumpus/Pouncival/Tumblebrutus), Joe Locarro (Alonzo/Growltiger/ Munkustrap/Plato/Macivity/Rumpus/Rum Tum Tiger), Jack Magredey/ Alonzo/Coricopat/Mungojerrie/Growltiger/Deuteronomy), Dawn Marie Church (Bombalurina/Cassandra/Demeter/Sillabub), Lynn Shuck (Bombalurina/ Cassandra/Demeter/Jellylorum/Griddlebone/Tantomile), Darlene Wilson (Bombalurina/ Demeter/Grizabella/Tantomile), Lilly-Lee Wong (Cassandra/Rumpleteazer/Sillabub/Tantomile/Victoria), Wade Laboissonniere (Coricopat/Mungojerrie/Pouncival/Skimbleshanks/Tumblebrutus), John Vincent Leggio (Coricopat/Mistoffelees/ Mungojerrie/Pouncival/Skimbleshanks/ Tumblebrutus), Mercedes Perez, Heidi Stallings (Grizabella), Susan Powers, Sally Ann Swarm (Jellylorum/Griddlebone/ Jennyanydots), Johnny Anzalone, Devanand N. Janki, Roger Kachel, Joey Pizza (Mistoffelees), Scott Taylor (Munkustrap/Plato/Macacavity/Rumpus/Rum Tum Tugger), Jay Aubrey Jones (Deuteronomy), Michelle Schumacher (Rumpleteazer/Sillabub/ Tantomile/Victoria), Randy Wojic (Rum Tum Tugger), Lisa Mayer (Victoria).

**MUSICAL NUMBERS:** Jellicle Songs for Jellicle Cats, Naming of Cats, Invitation to the Jellicle Ball, Old Gumbie Cat, Rum Tum Tugger,Grizabella the Glamour Cat, Bustopher Jones, Mungojerrie and Rumpleteazer, Old Deuteronomy, Aweful Battle of the Pekes and Pollicles, Memory, Moments of Happiness, Gus the Theatre Cat, Growltiger's Last Stand, Skimbleshanks, Macavity, Mr. Mistoffelees, Journey to the Heavyside Layer, Ad-dressing of Cats.

A musical in two acts with 20 scenes.

*Still playing May 31, 1992. Now performed more than 4000 times on Broadway. Winner of 1983 "Tonys" for Best Musical, Score, Book, Direction, Costumes, Lighting, and Featured Actress in a Musical (Betty Buckley as Grizabella). For original 1982 production see *Theatre World* Vol.39.

**Members of the Company**
CENTER: Laurie Beechman
TOP: John Festa, Bryan Batt, Lisa Meyer

# GRAND HOTEL

ic/Lyrics, Robert Wright and George Forrest; Additional Songs, Maury Yeston;
k, Luther Davis; Based on the novel by Vicki Baum; Director/Choreographer,
my Tune; Sets, Tony Walton; Costumes, Santo Loquasto; Lighting, Jules Fisher;
hestrations, Peter Matz; Musical/Vocal Director, Jack Lee; Musical
ervision/Additional Music, Wally Harper; Conductor, Randy Booth; 1st Associate
ductor, Sande Campbell; Associate Director, Bruce Lumpkin; Ballroom
reography, Pierre Dulaine & Yvonne Marceau; Sound, Otts Munderloh; Music
rdinator, John Monaco; Hairstylist, Werner Sherer; General Manager, Joey Parnes;
l. Associate, Kathleen Raitt; Company Managers, Jeff Capitola, Steve Winton,
n Markinson, Steven H. David; Stage Managers, Mr. Lumpkin, Robert Kellogg,
Babbitt; Original Cast Recording, RCA Victor; Presented by Martin Richards,
y Lea Johnson, Sam Crothers, Sandy Grubman, and Marvin A. Krauss; Press, Judy
sina/Julianne Waldheim; Previewed from October 17, 1989; Opened in the Martin
k Theatre on Sunday, November 12, 1989*

## CAST

| | |
|---|---|
| Doorman | George Dudley |
| Doctor Ottenschlag | John Wylie +1 |
| Countess and The Gigolo | Yvonne Marceau, Pierre Dulaine +2 |
| na, The Grand Concierge | Rex D. Hays |
| , Front Desk | Bob Stillman |
| boys : | |
| Georg Strunk | Ken Jennings |
| Kurt Kronenberg | Carlos Lopez |
| Hanns Bittner | Gerrit de Beer |
| Willibald Captain | J.J. Jepson |
| ephone Operators : | |
| Hildegarde Bratts | Jill Powell |
| Sigfriede Holzhiem | Suzanne Henderson |
| Wolffe Bratts | Meg Tolin |
| Jimmys | David Jackson, Danny Strayhorn +3 |
| Chauffeur | Ben George |
| nowitz, the Lawyer | Merwin Goldsmith |
| dor, The Impresario | Mitchell Jason |
| tor Witt, Company Manager | Michel Moinot |
| lame Peepee | Kathi Moss +4 |
| eral Director Preysing | Timothy Jerome +5 |
| mmchen, the Typist | Lynette Perry +6 |
| o Kringelein, the Bookeeper | Chip Zien +7 |
| x Von Gaigern, the Baron | John Schneider +8 |
| aela, the Confidante | Caitlin Brown +9 |
| aveta Grushinskaya, the Ballerina | Zina Bethune +10 |
| llery Workers : | |
| Gunther Gustafsson | Walter Willison +11 |
| Werner Holst | David Elledge +12 |
| Franz Kohl | Jerry Ball +13 |
| Ernst Schmidt | Henry Grossman |
| el Courtesan | Suzanne Henderson |
| tsie | Meg Tolin |
| ective | David Elledge +14 |
| de, the Maid | Jill Powell |

**DERSTUDIES/STANDBYS:** Walter Willison (Baron), Jerry Ball
auffeur/Rhona/Zinnowitz), Gerrit de Beer (Sandor), David Elledge
auffeur/Rhona), Niki Harris (Countess/Grushinskaya/Peepee), Eivand Harum
auffeur/Zinnowitz), Rex D. Hays (Doctor), Ken Jennings (Kringelein/Witt), J.J.
son (Gigolo/Kringelein/Erik), Greg Zerkle (Preysing/Baron/Erik/
nowitz/Chauffeur), Merwin Goldsmith (Preysing), Lee Lobenhofer
eysing/Baron/Erik/Zinnowitz/ Chauffeur), Meg Tolin (Flaemmchen), Eric Bohus
k), Ben George (Baron) **SWINGS:** Rob Babbitt, Niki Harris, Eivand Harum, Greg
kle, Lee Lobenhofer, Glenn Turner, Eric Bohus, Ken Leigh Rogers

**USICAL NUMBERS:** The Grand Parade, Some Have Some Have Not, As It
uld Be, At the Grand Hotel, Table with a View, Maybe My Baby Loves Me, Fire
Ice, Twenty-two Years, Villa on a Hill, I Want to Go to Hollywood, Everybody's
ng It, The Crooked Path, Who Wouldn't Dance with You, The Boston Merger, No
ore, Love Can't Happen, What You Need, Bonjour Amour, Happy, We'll Take a
ss Together, I Waltz Alone, Roses at the Station, How Can I Tell Her?, Finale: The
nd Waltz

A musical in twenty scenes performed without intermission. The action takes place
Berlin's Grand Hotel in 1928.

osed April 19, 1992 after 1018 performances and 31 previews. Moved to the
shwin Theatre on Monday, February 3, 1992.

ucceeded by : 1.Edmund Lyndeck (during vacation) 2. Pascale Faye-Williams,
rick Taverna (during vacation) 3. Glenn Turner/ Ken Leigh Rogers (during illness),
chael Demby Cain 4. Brooks Almay 5. Merwin Goldsmith (During vacation)
ll Powell/ Meg Tolin (During vacation) 7.Austin Pendleton 8. Walter Willison
ring vacation), Greg Zerkle 9. Debbie de Coudreaux, Valerie Cutko 10. Penny
rth (during vacation), Cyd Charisse (Bdwy debut) 11. Abe Ribald (during
ation) 12. Michael Piehl 13. Abe Ribald (during illness) 14. Jerry Ball, Abe
ald

*Martha Swope Photos*

Tony Walton's set
**CENTER:** Zina Bethune, Walter Willison
**TOP:** John Schneider, Cyd Charisse

**57**

# LES MISERABLES

By Alain Boublil and Claude-Michel Schonberg; Based on the novel by Victor Hu
Music, Mr. Schonberg; Lyrics, Herbert Kretzmer; Original French Text, Mr. Bou
and Jean-Marc Natel; Additional Material, James Fenton; Direction/Adaptatio
Trevor Nunn and John Caird; Orchestral Score, John Cameron; Musical Supervis
Robert Billig; Musical Director, Jay Alger; Design, John Napier; Lighting, Dav
Hersey; Costumes, Andreane Neofitou; Casting, Johnson-Liff & Zerman; Origi
Cast Recording, Geffen; General Manager, Alan Wasser; Company Manager, Rob
Nolan; Stage Managers, Thom Schilling, Mary Fran Loftus, Gregg Kirsopp; Executi
Producer, Martin McCallum; Presented by Cameron Mackintosh; Press, Ma
Thibodeau/Merle Frimark; Previewed from Saturday, February 28; Opened in t
Broadway Theatre on Thursday, March 12, 1987* and moved to the Imperial Thea
on October 16, 1990.

## CAST

PROLOGUE: J. Mark McVey +1 (Jean Valjean), Robert Du Sold +2 (Javert), J.
Sheets, Joel Robertson, Alan Osburn Matt McClanahan, Drew Eshelman, Jose
Mahowald, Liam O'Brien, Dann Fink, Eric Kunze (Chain Gang), Frank Mastro
(Farmer), Mr. O'Brien (Labourer), Lucille DeCristofaro (Innkeeper's Wife), Ga
Lynch (Innkeeper), Kenny Morris (Bishop), Larry Alexander, Paul Avedisi
(Constables)

MONTREUIL-SUR-MER 1823: Christy Baron +3 (Fantine), Mr. Roberts
(Foreman), Mr. Mastrone, Mr. McClanahan (Workers), Jean Fitzgibbons, Diane De
Piazza, Cissy Lee Cates, Madeleine Doherty (Women Workers), Jessie Janet Richa
(Factory Girl), Mr. Fink, Mr. Sheets, Mr. McClanahan (Sailors), Ms. DeCristofa
Ms. Doherty, Ms. Cates, Lisa Ann Grant, Ms. Richards, Michele Maika, Melissa An
Davis, Sarah Litzsinger (Whores), Ms. Fitzgibbons (Old Woman), Ms. Della Piaz
(Crone), Mr. Morris (Pimp/Fauchelevent), Alan Osburn (Bamatabois)

MONTFERMEIL 1823: Lacey Chabert, Eliza Harris, Jessica Scholl (Young Cose
Young Eponine), Evalyn Baron (Mme. Thenardier), Drew Eshelman (Thenardier), M
Mastrone (Drinker), Mr. O'Brien, Ms. Litzsinger (Young Couple), Mr. Lynch (Drun
Paul Avedisian, Ms. Doherty (Diners), Mr. Morris, Mr. Osburn, Mr. Sheets, M
Fitzgibbons, Ms. Richards, Ms. DeCristofaro (Drinkers), Mr. Fink (Young Man), M
Cates, Ms. Grant (Young Girls), Ms. Piazza, Mr. McClanahan (Old Couple), M
Robertson, Mr. Alexander (Travelers)

PARIS 1832: Gregory Grant, Brian Press (Gavroche), Ms. DeCristofaro (Begg
Woman), Ms. Richards (Young Prostitute), Mr. Lynch (Pimp), Natalie Toro
(Eponine), Mr. O'Brien (Montparnasse), Mr. Alexander (Babet), Mr. Sheets (Brujo
Mr. Morris (Claquesous), Joseph Kolinski +5 (Enjolras), Matthew Porretta
(Marius), Jacquelyn Piro +7 (Cosette), Mr. Robertson (Combeferre), Mr. Fi
(Feuilly), Mr. Mastrone (Courfeyrac), Mr. McClanahan (Joly), Mr. Osburn (Grantair
Mr. Avedisian (Lesgles), Mr. Lynch (Jean Prouvaire)

**UNDERSTUDIES:** J.C. Sheets, Frank Mastrone, Joel Robertson (Valjean), Ga
Lynch, Alan Osburn (Javert), Paul Avedisian, Gary Moss (Bishop), Jessie Ja
Richards, Jean Fitzgibbons (Fantine), Kenny Morris, Liam O'Brien (Thenardier), M
Fitzgibbons, Diane Della Piazza (Mme. Thenardier), Lisa Ann Grant, Sara Litzsing
(Eponine), Larry Alexander, Matt McClanahan (Marius), Ms. Litzsinger, Cissy L
Cates (Cosette), Mr. Avedisian Dann Fink (Enjolras), Lacey Chabert (Gavroc
SWINGS: T. Ryan Barkman, Nina Hennessy, Christa Justus, Garry Moss

**MUSICAL NUMBERS:** Prologue, Soliloquy, At the End of the Day, I Dreame
Dream, Lovely Ladies, Who Am I?, Come to Me, Castle on a Cloud, Master of t
House, Thenardier Waltz, Look Down, Stars, Red and Black, Do You Hear the Peo
Sing?, In My Life, A Heart Full of Love, One Day More, On My Own, A Little Fall
Rain, Drink with Me to Days Gone By, Bring Him Home, Dog Eats Dog, Soliloq
Turning, Empty Chairs at Empty Tables, Wedding Chorale, Beggars at the Fea
Finale

A dramatic musical in two acts with four scenes and prologue.

*Still playing May 31, 1992. Winner of 1987 "Tonys" for Best Musical, Best Sco
Best Book, Best Featured Actor and Actress in a Musical (Michael Maguire, Fran
Ruffelle), Direction of a Musical, Scenic Design and Lighting.

+ Succeeded by: 1. Mark McKerracher 2. Richard Kinsey 3. Susan Dawn Cars
Rachel York 4. Debbie Gibson, Michele Maika 5. Joseph Mahowald 6. John Leo
Eric Kunze 7. Melissa Anne Davis

*Joan Marcus Photos*

**TOP LEFT: Joe Mahowald**
**TOP RIGHT: Melissa Anne Davis, John Leone**
**BOTTOM LEFT: Mark McKerracher, Richard Kinsey**
**BOTTOM RIGHT: Lacey Charbert**

# LOST IN YONKERS

By Neil Simon; Director, Gene Saks; Sets/Costumes, Santo Loquasto; Lighting, Tharon Musser; Sound, Tom Morse; Prod. Supervisor, Peter Larence; Casting, Jay Binder; Company Manager, Brian Dunbar; Stage Managers, Peter B. Mumford, Jim Woolley; Presented by Emanuel Azenberg; Press, Bill Evans/Jim Randolph; Previewed from Tuesday, February 12; Opened in the Richard Rodgers Theatre on Thursday, February 21, 1991*

## CAST

Jay ..................................................................................................Jamie Marsh
Arty ...........................................................................................Danny Gerard +1
Eddie ............................................................................................Mark Blum +2
Bella .....................................................................................Mercedes Ruehl +3
Grandma Kurnitz ........................................................................Irene Worth +4
Louie .........................................................................................Kevin Spacey +5
Gert ..........................................................................................Lauren Klein

**STANDBYS:** Pauline Flanagan, Irene Dailey (Grandma), Didi Conn, Leslie Ayvazian (Bella/Gert), David Chandler (Louie/Eddie), Justin Strock (Arty), David Neipris (Jay), Justin Scott Walker

A play in two acts with eight scenes. The action takes place in a two-bedroom apartment over Kurnitz's Kandy Store in Yonkers, NY, 1942.

*Closed January 3, 1993 after 780 performances and 11 previews. Winner of 1991 Pulitzer Prize and "Tonys" for Best Play, Leading Actress (Mercedes Ruehl), Featured Actress (Irene Worth), Featured Actor (Kevin Spacey)

+ Succeeded by: 1. Benny Grant  2. David Chandler, Steve Vinovich, Timothy Jerome 3. Didi Conn, Jane Kaczmarek, Lucie Arnaz  4. Mercedes McCambridge, Rosemary Harris, Anne Jackson, Isa Thomas  5. Bruno Kirby, Alan Rosenberg, Brian Markinson

*Martha Swope Photos*

**Benny Grant, Jane Kaczmarek, Jamie Marsh**
**CENTER: Bruno Kirby, Mercedes McCambridge**
**TOP: Bruno Grant, David Chandler, Jamie Marsh, Rosemary Harris**

# MISS SAIGON

Music, Claude-Michel Schonberg; Lyrics, Richard Maltby ,Jr., Alain Boublil; Adapted from Boublil's French lyrics; Book, Mr. Boublil, Mr. Schonberg; Additional Material, Mr. Maltby, Jr.; Director, Nicholas Hytner; Musical Staging, Bob Avian; Orchestrations, William D. Brohn; Musical Supervisors, David Caddick, Robert Billig; Associate Director, Mitchell Lemsky; Design, John Napier; Lighting, David Hersey; Costumes, Andreane Neofitou, Suzy Benzinger; Sound, Andrew Bruce; Conductor, Dale Rieling; Stage Managers, Fred Hanson, Sherry Cohen, Tom Capps; Cast Recording (London), Geffen; Presented by Cameron Mackintosh; Press, Fred Nathan/Marc Thibodeau, Merle Frimark; Previewed from Saturday, March 23; Opened in the Broadway Theatre on Thursday, April 11, 1991*

## CAST

SAIGON - 1975
The Engineer ........................................................Jonathan Pryce +1
Kim ..........................................................Lea Salonga +2, Kam Cheng +3
Gigi ...................................................................Marina Chapa
Mimi ...................................................................Sala Iwamatsu
Yvette ..............................................................Imelda De Los Reyes
Yvonne ...........................................................Joann M. Hunter +4
Bar Girls .......................Raquel C. Brown, Annette Calud, Mirla Criste, Jade Stice,
　　　　　　　　　　　　Melanie Mariko Tojio, Cheri Nakamura
Chris .....................................................................Willy Falk +5
John ...................................................................Hinton Battle +6
Marines.............................................Paul Dobie, Michael Gruber, Leonard Joseph,
　　　Paul Matsumoto, Sean McDermott, Thomas James O'Leary, Gordon Owens,
　　　　Christopher Pecaro, Matthew Pederson, Kris Phillips, W. Ellis Porter,
　　　　Alton F. White, Bruce Winant, Jarrod Emick, Sean Grant, General
　　　　　　　McArthur Hambrick, Kingsley Leggs, Herman Sebek
Barmen.................................................Zar Acayan, Alan Ariano, Jason Ma
Vietnamese Customers ........................Tony C. Avanti, Eric Chan, Francis J. Cruz,
　　　　　　　Darren Lee, Ray Santos, Nephi Jay Wimmer, Tito Abeleda
Thuy ...................................................................Barry K. Bernal
Embassy Workers, Vendors, etc.............................................Company

HO CHI MINH CITY (Formerly Saigon)-April 1978
Ellen .....................................................................Liz Callaway +7
Tam ...................................Phillip Lee Carabuena, Brandon Paragas Ngai
Guards......................................................Tony C. Avanti, Francis J. Cruz
Dragon Acrobats ........................Darren Lee, Michael Gruber, Nephi Jay Wimmer
Asst. Commissar..........................................................Jason Ma
Soldiers ..............................................Zar Acayan, Alan Ariano, Jason Ma,
　　　　　　　　Paul Matsumoto, Ray Santos, Nephi Jay Wimmer
Citizens, Refugees.......................................................Company

USA - September 1978
Conference Delegates ...................................................Company

BANGKOK - October 1978
Hustlers ......................................Mr. Acayan, Mr. Ma, Mr. Matsumoto,
　　　　　　　　　　　　　　　　Mr. Santos, Mr. Wimmer
Moulin Rouge Owner .....................................................Francis J. Cruz
Inhabitants, Bar Girls, Vendors, Tourists ....................................Company

SAIGON - April 1975
Shultz................................................................Thomas James O'Leary
Doc ...................................................................Kingsley Leggs
Reeves ..................................................................Bruce Winant
Gibbons ..................................................................Paul Dobie
Troy ...................................................................Leonard Joseph
Nolen .................................................General McArthur Hambrick
Huston ...............................................................Matthew Pederson
Frye ...................................................................Jarrod Emick
Marines, Vietnamese....................................................Company

BANGKOK - October 1978
Inhabitants, Moulin Rouge Customers.......................................Company

**UNDERSTUDIES:** Paul Matsumoto, Ray Santos, Herman Sebek (Engineer), Annette Calud, Imelda de los reyes, Melanie Mariko Tojio (Kim), Jarrod Emick, Christopher Pecaro (Chris), Leonard Joseph, Kingsley Leggs (John), Jane Bodle, Jade Stice (Ellen), Zar Acayan, Jason Ma, Marc Oka (Thuy) SWINGS: Sylvia Dohi, Henry Menendez, Marc Oka, Todd Zamarripa

**Sean McDermott, Leila Florentino**
**Top: Francis Ruivivar**

**MUSICAL NUMBERS:** The Heat Is on in Saigon, Movie in My Mind, T[ ] Transaction, Why God Why?, Sun and Moon, The Telephone, The Ceremony, L[a] Night of the World, Morning of the Dragon, I Still Believe, Back in Town, You W[ ] Not Touch Him, If You Want to Die in Bed, I'd Give My Life for You, Bui-Doi, Wh[ ] a Waste, Please, Guilt Inside Your Head, Room 317, Now That I've Seen H[ ] Confrontation, The American Dream, Little God of My Heart

A musical in two acts. The action takes place in Saigon, Bangkok, and the US[ ] between 1975-79.

*Still playing May 31, 1992. Winner of 1991 "Tonys" for Leading Actor in [ ] Musical (Jonathan Pryce), Leading Actress in a Musical (Lea Salonga) and Featur[ ] Actor in a Musical (Hinton Battle).

+ Succeeded by: 1. Francis Ruivivar 2. Leila Florentino 3. Annette Calud 4. Lyd-L[ ] Gaston 5. Sean McDermott 6. Alton F. White 7. Jane Bodle

*Joan Marcus, Michael LePoer Trench Photos*

# THE PHANTOM OF THE OPERA

sic, Andrew Lloyd Webber; Lyrics, Charles Hart; Additional Lyrics, Richard
goe; Book, Mr. Stilgoe, Mr. Lloyd Webber; Director, Harold Prince; Musical
ging/Choreography, Gillian Lynne; Orchestrations, David Cullen, Mr. Lloyd
bber; Based on the novel by Gaston Leroux; Design, Maria Bjornson; Lighting,
rew Bridge; Sound, Martin Levan; Musical Direction/Supervision, David Caddick;
ting, Johnson-Liff & Zerman; General Manager, Alan Wasser; Company Manager,
hael Gill; Stage Managers, Steve McCorkle, Bethe Ward, Frank Marino; Presented
Cameron Mackintosh and The Really Useful Theatre Co.; Press, Merle Frimark,
rc Thibodeau; Previewed from Saturday, January 9; Opened in the Majestic
atre on Tuesday, January 26, 1988*

## CAST

| | |
|---|---|
| Phantom of the Opera | Mark Jacoby |
| ristine Daae | Karen Culliver/Katherine Buffaloe |
| ul, Vicomte de Chagny | Hugh Panaro |
| lotta Giudicelli | Marilyn Caskey |
| nsieur Andre | Jeff Keller |
| nsieur Firmin | George Lee Andrews |
| dame Giry | Leila Martin |
| aldo Piangi | Gary Rideout |
| g Giry | Catherine Ulissey |
| Rever | Gary Barker |
| ctioneer | Richard Warren Pugh |
| ter/Marksman | Gary Lindemann |
| Lefevre | Kenneth Waller |
| eph Buquet | Philip Steele |
| n Attilio/Passarino | Thomas Sandri |
| ve Master | Wesley Robinson |
| nky/Stagehand | Jeff Siebert |
| iceman | Charles Rule |
| ge | Elena Jeanne Batman |
| rdrobe Mistress/Confidante | Mary Leigh Stahl |
| ncess | Raissa Katona |
| dame Firmin | Dawn Leigh Stone |
| keeper's Wife | Rebecca Eichenberger |
| let Chorus of the Opera Populaire | Tener Brown, Alina Hernandez, Cherylyn Jones, Lori MacPherson, Tania Philip, Kate Solmssen, Christine Spizzo |

**DERSTUDIES:** Gary Barker (Phantom/Andre), Jeff Keller (Phantom), Raissa
tona (Christine), Gary Lindemann, James Romick (Raoul), Paul Laureano (Firmin),
chard Warren Pugh (Firmin/Piangi), George Lee Andrews, James Romick
ndre),Elena Jeanne Batman, Rebecca Eichenberger, Dawn Leigh Stone (Carlotta),
zanne Ishee (Carlotta/Giry), Patrice Pickering, Mary Leigh Stahl (Giry), Maurizio
rbino (Piangi), Tener Brown, Cherylyn Jones, Kate Solmssen, Lori MacPherson
eg), Jeff Siebert (Master/Dancer) SWINGS: Denny Berry, Ms. Ishee, Paul
ireano, Mr. Romick

**USICAL NUMBERS:** Think of Me, Angel of Music, Little Lotte/The Mirror,
antom of the Opera, Music of the Night, I Remember/Stranger Than You Dreamt It,
gical Lasso, Notes/Prima Donna, Poor Fool He Makes Me Laugh, Why Have You
ought Me Here?/ Raoul I've Been There, All I Ask of You, Masquerade/Why So
ent?, Twisted Every Way, Wishing You Were Somehow Here Again, Wandering
ild/Bravo Bravo, Point of No Return, Down Once More/Track Down This
irderer, Finale

A musical in two acts with nineteen scenes and a prologue. The action takes place
and around the Paris Opera house, 1881-1911.
till playing May 31, 1992. Winner of 1988 "Tonys" for Best Musical, Leading Actor
a Musical (Michael Crawford), Featured Actress in a Musical (Judy Kaye),
rection of a Musical, Scenic Design and Lighting.

*Joan Marcus Photos*
**Top: Karen Culliver, Mark Jacoby**
**CENTER: The Company**
**RIGHT: Hugh Panaro, Culliver**

# THE SECRET GARDEN

Music, Lucy Simon; Lyrics/Book, Marsha Norman; Based on the novel by Fra
Hodgson Burnett; Director, Susan H. Schulman; Orchestrations, William D. Br
Musical Director/Vocal Arrangements, Michael Kosarin; Choreography, Mic
Lichtefeld; Sets, Heidi Landesman; Costumes, Theoni V. Aldredge; Lighting, Th
Musser; Original Cast Recording, Columbia; Dance Arrangements, Jeanine Leven
Sound, Otts Munderloh; Music Coordinator, John Miller; Hair/Makeup, Ro
DiNiro; Prod. Manager, Peter Fulbright; General Manager, David Strong War
Casting, Wendy Ettinger; Stage Managers, Perry Cline, Frances Lombardi, Max
Torres, Elizabeth Farwell; Producers, Greg C. Mosher, Rhoda Mayerson, Den
Dorothy and Wendell Cherry, Margo Lion, 126 Second Ave. Corp., Playhouse Sq
Center; Presented by Heidi Landesman, Rick Steiner, Frederic H. Mayerson, Eliza
Williams, Jujamcyn Theatres/TV Asahi and Dodger Productions; Press, Adrian Br
Brown, John Barlow, Cabrini Lepis; Previewed from Friday, April 5; Opened in the
James Theatre on Thursday, April 25, 1991*

## CAST

Lily ................................................................................Rebecca Luker
Mary ................................................................................Daisy Eagan +1
................................................................................Kimberly Mahon +2
Fakir ................................................................................Peter Marinos
Ayah ................................................................................Patricia Phillips +3
Ros ................................................................................Kay Walbye
Capt. Albert Lennox................................................................Michael DeVries +4
Lt. Peter Wright................................................................Drew Taylor
Lt. Ian Shaw................................................................Paul Jackel
Major Holmes................................................................Peter Samuel
Claire................................................................Rebecca Judd
Alice................................................................Nancy Johnston
Archibald................................................................Mandy Patinkin +5
Dr. Neville Craven................................................Robert Westenberg
Mrs. Medlock................................................................Barbara Rosenblat
Martha................................................................Alison Fraser
Dickon ................................................John Cameron Mitchell +6
Ben................................................................Tom Toner
Colin................................................................John Babcock + 7
Jane................................................................Teresa De Zarn +8
William................................................................Frank DiPasquale
Betsy................................................................Betsy Friday
Timothy................................................................Alec Timerman +9
Mrs. Winthrop................................................................Nancy Johnston

**UNDERSTUDIES:** Nancy Johnston, Laurie Gayle Stephenson (Lily), Cam
MacCardell-Fossel, Lee Alison Marino (Mary), Michael DeVries (Archibald/Nevi
Peter Samuel (Archibald), Rebecca Judd (Medlock/Ayah/Winthrop), Priscilla Qui
(Medlock/Claire/Alice), Betsy Friday (Martha/Rose/Claire/Alice), Jennifer Sm
(Martha/Ayah/Alice Winthrop), Kevin Ligon (Dickon/Fakir/Shaw), Brian Qu
(Dickon/Shaw), Bill Nolte (Ben/Wright/Holmes), Drew Taylor (Ben), Parker Con
Lance Robinson (Colin), Frank DiPasquale (Lennox/Fakir/Wright/Holmes), F
Jackel, Michael Brien Watson (Lennox) **SWINGS:** Mr. Ligon, Mr. Nolte,
Quinby, Ms. Smith, Mr. Watson

**MUSICAL NUMBERS:** Opening Dream, There's a Girl, House Upon the Hi
Heard Someone Crying, A Fine White Horse, A Girl in the Valley, It's a Ma
Winter's on the Wing, Show Me the Key, A Bit of Earth, Storm, Lily's Eyes, Rou
Shouldered Man, Final Storm, The Girl I Mean to Be, Quartet, Race You to the To
the Morning, Wick, Come to My Garden, Come Spirit Come Charm, Disappear, H
On, Letter Song, Where in the World, How Could I Ever Know, Finale

A musical in two acts with 18 scenes and prologue. The action takes place
Colonial India and at Misselthwaite Manor, North Yorkshire, England in 1906.

*Closed January 3, 1993 after 706 performances and 22 previews. Winner of 1
"Tonys" for Featured Actress in a Musical (Daisy Eagan), Best Book, and Best Sc
Design.

+ Succeeded by:1. Lydia Ooghe 2. Lee Alison Marino 3. Elizabeth Acosta 4. Da
Elledge 5. Howard McGillin 6. Jedidiah Cohen 7. Diedrich Stelljes 8. Laurie Ga
Stephenson 9. Brian Quinn

*Bob Marshak Photos*

**Top: Lydia Ooghe, Rebecca Luker, Howard McGillin
CENTER: Lydia Ooghe, Alison Fraser
LEFT: John Cameron Mitchell, Daisy Eagan**

# THE WILL ROGERS FOLLIES

Music/Arrangements, Cy Coleman; Lyrics, Betty Comden and Adolph Green; Book, Peter Stone; Director/Choreographer, Tommy Tune; Orchestrations, Billy Byers; Musical Director, Eric Stern; Musical Contractor, John Miller; Sets, Tony Walton; Costumes, Willa Kim; Lighting, Jules Fisher; Original Cast Recording, Columbia; Sound, Peter Fitzgerald; Projections, Wendall K. Harrington; Wigs, Howard Leonard; General Manager, Marvin A. Krauss; Casting, Julie Hughes, Barry Moss; Stage Managers, Peter von Mayrhauser, Patrick Ballard; Presented by Pierre Cossette, Martin Richards, Sam Crothers, James M. Nederlander, Stewart F. Lane, Max Weitzenhoffer in association with Japan Satellite Broadcasting; Press, Richard Kornberg; Previewed from Monday, April 1; Opened in the Palace Theatre on Wednesday, May 1, 1991*

## CAST

| | |
|---|---|
| Ziegfeld's Favorite | Cady Huffman +1 |
| Will Rogers | Keith Carradine +2 |
| Unicyclist/Roper | Vince Bruce |
| Wiley Post | Paul Ukena, Jr +3 |
| Clem Rogers | Dick Latessa |
| Will's Sisters/Betty's Sisters | Roxanne Barlow, Maria Calabrese, Colleen Dunn, Dana Moore, Wendy Waring, Leigh Zimmerman, Amy Heggins, Kimberly Hester, Lynne Michele, Betty Blake, Dee Hoty +4 |
| Wild West Show/Trainers/Madcap Mutts | Tom & Bonnie Brackney with B.A., Cocoa, Gigi, Rusty, Trixie, Zee |
| Will Rogers, Jr. | Rick Faugno +5 |
| Mary Rogers | Tammy Minoff +6 |
| James Rogers | Lance Robinson +7 |
| Freddy Rogers | Gregory Scott Carter +8 |
| Will Rogers Wranglers | John Ganun, Troy Britton Johnson Jerry Mitchell, Jason Opsahl |
| New Ziegfeld Girls | Ms. Barlow, Ms. Calabrese, Ganine Derleth, Rebecca Downing, Ms. Dunn, Sally Mae Dunn, Toni Georgiana, Eileen Grace, Luba Gregus, Tonia Lynn, Ms. Moore, Aimee Turner, Jillana Urbina, Ms. Waring, Christina Youngman, Ms. Zimmerman, Heather Douglas, Ganine Giorgione, Ms. Heggins, Ms. Hester, Ms. Michele, Carol Denise Smith, Susan Trainor |
| Indian Sun Goddess | Jillana Urbina |
| Indian of the Dawn | Jerry Mitchell |
| Mr. Ziegfeld's Stage Manager | Tom Flagg |
| Vaudeville Announcer | Jason Opsahl |
| Roper | Tomas Garcilazo |
| Radio Engineer | John Ganun |
| Voice of Mr. Ziegfeld | Gregory Peck |

**UNDERSTUDIES/STANDBYS:** David M. Lutken (Will), Luba Gregus (Betty/Ziegfeld's Favorite), Leigh Zimmerman (Ziegfeld's Favorite), Buddy Smith (Will Jr.), Tom Flagg (Clem), Eden Riegel (Mary/James/Freddy) SWINGS: Mary Lee DeWitt, Jack Doyle, Angie L. Schworer, Allyson Tucker

**MUSICAL NUMBERS:** Let's Go Flying, Will-a-Mania, Give a Man Enough Rope, It's a Boy, So Long Pa, My Unknown Someone, We're Heading for a Wedding, Big Time, My Big Mistake, Powder Puff Ballet, Marry Me Now/I Got You, Wedding Finale, Look Around, Favorite Son, No Man Left for Me, Presents for Mrs. Rogers, Without You, Never Met a Man I Didn't Like

A musical inspired by the words of Will and Betty Rogers, in two acts with twelve scenes and prelude. The action takes place in Broadway's Palace Theatre at present.

*Closed September 5, 1993 after 983 performances and 34 previews. Winner of 1991 "Tonys" for Best Musical, Best Score, Best Direction of a Musical, Best Costumes, Best Lighting, Best Choreography. Selected by the NY Drama Critics Circle as Best Musical of 1990-91.

+Succeeded by:1. Susan Anton, Cady Huffman, Marla Maples 2. Mac Davis 3.David Lutken 4. Nancy Ringham 5.James Zimmermann 6. Candace N. Walters 7. Buddy Smith 8. Jeffrey Stern

*Martha Swope, Edward Patino Photos*

**TOP: Mac Davis**
**LEFT: Mac Davis and New Ziegfeld Girls**

## THE AWARD AND OTHER PLAYS

Written/Directed by Warren Manzi; Sets, Jay Stone; Lighting, Patrick Eagelton; Costumes, Nancy Bush; Presented by The Actors Collective; Press, Michelle Vincents; Previewed from March 26, 1991; Opened in Theatre Four on Tuesday, April 2, 1991*
**PROGRAM: ONE FOR THE MONEY;** with Brian Dowd
**THE QUEEN OF THE PARTING SHOT;** with Catherine Russell, Dean Gardner
**THE AUDITION;** with James Farrell
**THE AWARD;** with Marcus Powell

  *Closed April 28, 1992 after playing Tuesday nights only, for the previous year.

**Warren Manzi**

## BREAKING LEGS

By Tom Dulak; Director, John Tillinger; Sets, James Noone; Costumes, David Woolard; Lighting, Ken Billington; Casting, Marjorie Martin; General Manager, Ra Roseman; Stage Manager, Elliott Woodruff; Presented by Elliott Martin, Bud Yor James & Maureen O'Sullivan Cushing; Press, Jeffrey Richards/David Le Sh Previewed from Saturday, April 27, 1991; Opened in the Promenade Theatre Sunday, May 19, 1991*

### CAST

| | |
|---|---|
| Lou Graziano | Vincent Gardenia |
| Angie | Sue Giosa +1 |
| Terence O'Keefe | Nicolas Surovy +2 |
| Mike Fransisco | Philip Bosco +3 |
| Tino De Felice | Victor Argo |
| Frankie Salvucci | Larry Storch |

**STANDBYS/UNDERSTUDIES:** Vince Viverito (Lou/Mike), Virgil Rober (Terence), Kelleigh McKenzie (Angie), Brian Dykstra (Tino/Frankie).

  A comedy in two acts. The action takes place at a present day restaurant in a N England university town.

*Closed May 3, 1992 after 401 performances.

+Succeeded by: 1. Karen Valentine  2. Nick Wyman  3. Joseph Mascolo

*Janet Van Ham Photo*

  **Joseph Mascolo, Vincent Gardenia**

# THE FANTASTICKS

Music, Harvey Schmidt; Lyrics/Book, Tom Jones; Director, Word Baker; Original
Musical Direction/Arrangements, Julian Stein; Design, Ed Wittstein; Musical Director,
Dorothy Martin; Stage Managers, Kim Moore, James Cook, Steven Michael Daly,
Matthew Eaton Bennett, Christopher Scott; Presented by Lore Noto; Associate
Producers, Sheldon Baron, Dorothy Olim, Jules Field; Cast Recording, MGM/Polydor;
Press, Ginnie Weidmann; Opened in the Sullivan Street Playhouse on Tuesday, May 3,
1960*

### CAST

The Boy ....................................................Kevin R. Wright/Matthew Eaton Bennett
The Girl ........................................................................Marilyn Whitehead
The Girl's Father .................................................................William Tost
The Boy's Father.................................................................George Riddle
Narrator/El Gallo ............................................Kenneth Kantor/Scott Willis
Mute...............................................Matthew Eaton Bennett/Christopher Scott
Old Actor ..........................................................................Bryan Hull
Man Who Dies ..........................................................Earl Aaron Levine

MUSICAL NUMBERS: Overture, Try to Remember, Much More, Metaphor, Never
Say No, It Depends on What You Pay, Soon It's Gonna Rain, Abduction Ballet, Happy
Ending, This Plumb is Too Ripe, I Can See It, Plant a Radish, Round and Round, They
Were You, Finale

A musical in two acts.

*Still Playing May 31, 1992. The world's longest running musical.

*Steve Young Photos*

**Top: William Tost, George Riddle
Below: Marilyn Whitehead, Kevin R. Wright**

**TOP LEFT:** Jeff Lyons, Mary Denise Bentley, Herndon Lackey, Susanne Blakeslee, Brad Ellis
**TOP RIGHT:** Jeff Lyons, Herndon Lackey
**RIGHT:** Susanne Blakeslee, Jeff Lyons
**BOTTOM:** Susanne Blakeslee, Mary Denise Bentley, Jeff Lyons, Herndon Lackey

# FORBIDDEN BROADWAY
## 1991-92 Season Editions

Created/Written/Directed by Gerard Alessandrini; Musical Director, Brad Ellis; Asst. Director, Phillip George; Costumes, Erika Dyson; Wigs, Teresa Vuoso; Consultant, Pete Blue; Stage Manager, Jerry James; Cast Recordings, DRG; Press, Shirley Herz/Glenna Freedman; Presented by Jonathan Scharer; Originally opened at Palssons (now Steve McGraw's) on January 15, 1982 and moved to Theatre East on September 15, 1988*

### THIS SEASON'S CASTS

| | | |
|---|---|---|
| Mary Denise Bently | Toni DiBuono | Susanne Blakeslee |
| Brad Ellis | Leah Hocking | Alix Korey |
| Herndon Lackey | Roxie Lucas | Jeff Lyons |
| Michael McGrath | Patrick Quinn | |

**PROGRAMS:** Forbidden Broadway 1991 1/2, Forbidden Christmas (Nov.19, 1991-Jan.12, 1992), Best of Forbidden Broadway-10th Anniversary Edition (Apr.6, 1992- )

**SELECTIONS INCLUDED:** 10th Anniversay Edition: Forbidden Bdwy 1992, Well Did You Evah? (Schuberts vs. Nederlanders), Evita, Annie, If I Sing It Slower (Topol), Richard Harris' Camelot, Hello Carol, Chita and Rita, I Ham What I Ham (George Hearn), Anything Goes, Hey Bob Fosse, Madonna's Brain, M. Butterfly, Into the Words, Julie Andrews, More Miserables, Abbodanza, I'm an Asian Too, Crazy for You, Raul of LaMancha, A Show for Me (Streisand), Grim Hotel, Somewhat Overindulgent (Patinkin), I'm One of the Girls (Lauren Bacall), Do I Shave? (Yul Brynner), Liza One Note, Cats, An Actor in NY, Finale

*Still playing May 31, 1992 (with lay-off between Jan.-Apr. 1992).

*Carol Rosegg/Martha Swope Photos*

# FOREVER PLAID

Written/Directed/Choreographed by Stuart Ross; Music/Lyrics, Various; Musical Arrangements/Continuity/Supervision, James Raitt; Sets, Neil Peter Jampolis; Lighting, Jane Reisman; Costumes, Debra Stein; Musical Director, David Chase; Sound, Marc Salzberg; Original Cast Recording, RCA; Stage Manager, Connie Drew; Presented by Gene Wolsk in association with Allen M. Shore and Steven Suskin; Press, Shirley Herz/Miller Wright, Glenna Freedman, Sam Rudy; Opened in Steve McGraw's on Friday, May 4, 1990*

## CAST

Jinx..............................................................................Stan Chandler +1
Smudge.......................................................................David Engel +2
Sparky.........................................................................Larry Raben +3
Francis......................................................................Guy Stroman +4

**UNDERSTUDIES:** Drew Geraci, Bruce Blanchard, Steven Michael Daley

**MUSICAL NUMBERS:** Anniversary Song, Catch a Falling Star, Chain Gang, Crazy 'bout ya Baby, Cry, Day-O, Dream Along with Me, Gotta Be This or That, Heart and Soul, Jamaica Farewell, Kingston Market, Lady of Spain (Ed Sullivan Show spoof), Love is a Many Splendored Thing, Magic Moments, Matilda, Moments to Remember, No Not Much, Papa Loves Mambo, Perfidia, Rags to Riches, Round and Round, Shangri-La, She Loves You, Sing to Me Mr. C, Sixteen Tons, Temptation, Theme from The Good The Bad The Ugly, Three Coins in the Fountain, Undecided

A musical for the "good guys" performed without intermission. The action takes place in 1964 and now.

Still playing May 31, 1992.

Succeeded by: 1. Paul Binotto 2. Gregory Jbara 3. Michael Winther 4. Neil Nash

*Carol Rosegg/Martha Swope Photos*

**RIGHT:** (clockwise from bottom) **Stan Chandler, Larry Raben, Guy Stroman, David Engel**
**BELOW:** **David Engel, Guy Stroman, Stan Chandler, Larry Raben**

# LIPS TOGETHER TEETH APART

By Terrence McNally; Director, John Tillinger; Set, John Lee Beatty; Costumes, Jane Greenwood; Lighting, Ken Billington; Sound, Stewart Werner, Chuck London; Fights, Jerry Mitchell; Stage Manager, Pamela Singer; Presented by Manhattan Theatre Club by special arrangement with Lucille Lortel; Press, Helene Davis, Deborah Warren; Opened at Manhattan Theatre Club's Stage 1 on Tuesday, May 28, 1991 and transferred to the Lucille Lortel Theatre on January 9, 1992*

## CAST

Chloe Haddock.....................................................................Hillary Bailey Smith +1
Sam Truman ......................................................................Jonathan Hadary +2
John Haddock ...................................................................Anthony Heald +3
Sally Truman.......................................................................Roxanne Hart +4

**UNDERSTUDIES:** Lou Williford (Chloe), Tom Bloom (Sam/John), Ken Kliban (Sam), Lee Brock (Sally)

A comic drama in three acts. The action takes place on Fire Island over a Fourth of July weekend.

*Closed June 27, 1992 after 169 performances at the Lortel and 250 performances previously at Manhattan Theatre Club.

+Succeeded by: 1. Christine Baranski (original), Lou Williford 2. Ken Kliban, Ethan Phillips 3. Brian Kerwin, Tom Bloom, Michael Countryman 4.Carolyn McCormick, Joanne Camp, Frances Conroy

*Gerry Goodstein Photos*

BELOW: (top) Roxanne Hart, Jonathan Hadary, (front) Anthony Heald, Hillary Bailey Smith
TOP: Christine Baranski, Brian Kerwin
CENTER: Jonathan Hadary, Roxanne Hart
BOTTOM RIGHT: Jonathan Hadary, Joanne Camp, Christine Baranski, Brian Kerwin

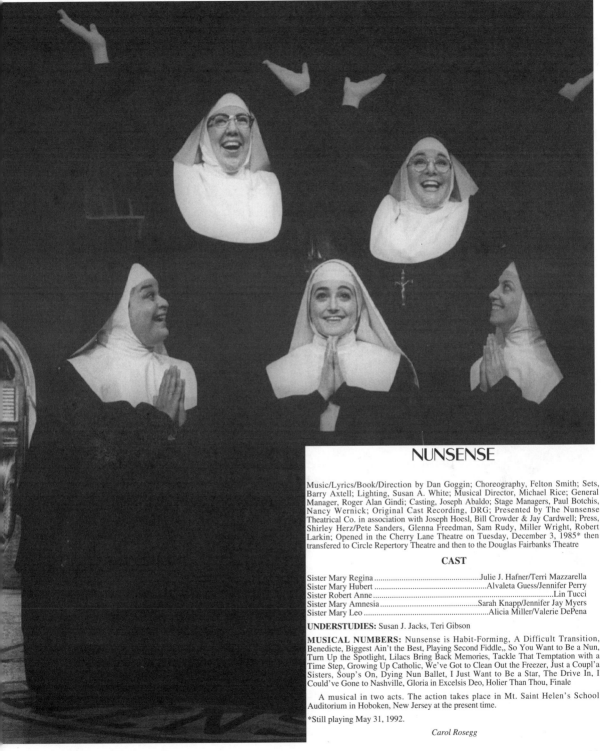

# NUNSENSE

Music/Lyrics/Book/Direction by Dan Goggin; Choreography, Felton Smith; Sets, Barry Axtell; Lighting, Susan A. White; Musical Director, Michael Rice; General Manager, Roger Alan Gindi; Casting, Joseph Abaldo; Stage Managers, Paul Botchis, Nancy Wernick; Original Cast Recording, DRG; Presented by The Nunsense Theatrical Co. in association with Joseph Hoesl, Bill Crowder & Jay Cardwell; Press, Shirley Herz/Pete Sanders, Glenna Freedman, Sam Rudy, Miller Wright, Robert Larkin; Opened in the Cherry Lane Theatre on Tuesday, December 3, 1985* then transfered to Circle Repertory Theatre and then to the Douglas Fairbanks Theatre

## CAST

Sister Mary Regina ..................................................Julie J. Hafner/Terri Mazzarella
Sister Mary Hubert ......................................................Alvaleta Guess/Jennifer Perry
Sister Robert Anne .........................................................................................Lin Tucci
Sister Mary Amnesia .............................................Sarah Knapp/Jennifer Jay Myers
Sister Mary Leo .........................................................Alicia Miller/Valerie DePena

**UNDERSTUDIES:** Susan J. Jacks, Teri Gibson

**MUSICAL NUMBERS:** Nunsense is Habit-Forming, A Difficult Transition, Benedicte, Biggest Ain't the Best, Playing Second Fiddle,, So You Want to Be a Nun, Turn Up the Spotlight, Lilacs Bring Back Memories, Tackle That Temptation with a Time Step, Growing Up Catholic, We've Got to Clean Out the Freezer, Just a Coupl'a Sisters, Soup's On, Dying Nun Ballet, I Just Want to Be a Star, The Drive In, I Could've Gone to Nashville, Gloria in Excelsis Deo, Holier Than Thou, Finale

A musical in two acts. The action takes place in Mt. Saint Helen's School Auditorium in Hoboken, New Jersey at the present time.

*Still playing May 31, 1992.

*Carol Rosegg*

# PAGEANT

Music, Albert Evans; Lyrics/Book, Bill Russell and Frank Kelly; Conception /Direction/ Choreography, Robert Longbottom; Co-Choreographer, Tony Parise; Musical Director/ Orchestrations/Arrangements/ Supervision, James Raitt; Set, Daniel Ettinger; Costumes, Gregg Barnes; Lighting, Timothy Hunter; Hairstylist, Lazaro Arencibia; Casting, Joseph Abaldo; General Management, Kevin Dowling/Gwen Cassel; Assoc. Producer, Chip Quigley; Presented by Jonathan Scharer; Press, Shirley Herz/Glenna Freedman; Previewed from Tuesday, April 23, 1991; Opened in the Blue Angel on Thursday, May 2, 1991*

## CAST

Miss Bible Belt ..............................................................................Randall Ash +1
Miss Deep South ..............................................................................David Drake +2
Miss Texas ...........................................................................................Russell Garrett
Miss Industrial Northeast ................................................................Joe Joyce +3
Miss West Coast .............................................................................Joe Salvatore +4
Miss Great Plains ...............................................................................Dick Scalan
Frankie Cavalier ...............................................................................J.T. Cromwell

**STANDBYS:** Tony Parise, Paul Ard, Jack Plotnick (Contestants-Miss U.S. Territories and Possessions), Larry Hansen (Frankie)

**MUSICAL NUMBERS:** Natural Born Females, Something Extra, Talent Competitions (Banking on Jesus, Camptown Races, Interpretative Dance etc...), It's Gotta Be Venus, Girl Power, Good Bye, Miss Glamouresse

A musical comedy beauty pageant performed without intermission. The audience picks the winner each night.

*Closed June 7, 1992 after 462 performances and 10 previews.

+Succeeded by: 1. Keith Allen 2. Dale Sandish 3. Jack Plotnick 4.Barry Finkel

*Scott Humbert Photos*

(clockwise from center) J.T. Cromwell, Dick Scanlan, Joe Joyce, Davi¢ Drake

# PERFECT CRIME

By Warren Manzi; Director, Jeffrey Hyatt; Set, Chris Pickart; Costumes, Barbar Blackwood; Lighting, Patrick Eagleton; Sound, David Lawson; Stage Manage¡ George E.M. Kelly; Press, Michelle Vinvents, Paul Lewis, Jeffrey Clarke; Opened i the Courtyard Playhouse on April 18, 1987* and later transferred to the Second Stage 47th St. Playhouse, Intar, Harold Clurman Theatre, and since January 3, 1991 ª Theatre Four*

## CAST

Margaret Thorne Brent....................................................................Catherine Russell
James Ascher ..............................................................................James Farrell/Warren Manzi
Lionel McAuley ........................................Brian Dowd/Trip Hamilton/J.A. Nelson
W. Harrison Brent.......................Marcus Powell/Graeme Malcolm/Mark Johannes
David Breuer ...........................................................................................Dean Gardner

A mystery.

*Still playing May 31, 1992.

**Catherine Russell**

# SONG OF SINGAPORE

Music/Lyrics by Erik Frandsen, Robert Hipkens, Michael Garin and Paula Lockheart; Book, Allan Katz, Mr. Frandsen, Mr. Hipkens, Mr. Garin, Ms. Lockheart; Director, A.J. Antoon; Orchestrations, John Carlini; Musical Supervision, Art Baron; Sets, John Lee Beatty; Costumes, Frank Krenz; Lighting, Peter Kaczorowski; Sound, Stuart J. Allyn; Vocal Arrangements, Yaron Gershovsky; Cast Recording, DRG; Stage Manager, Ron Nash; Presented by Steven Baruch, Richard Frankel, Thomas Viertel in association with Allen Spivak and Larry Magid; Press, Chris Boneau/Jackie Green; Opened at the Song of Singapore Nightclub (17 Irving Place) on Tuesday, May 7, 1991*

## CAST

| | |
|---|---|
| Spike Spauldeen | Erik Frandsen |
| Freddy S. Lyme | Michael Garin |
| Hans van der Last | Robert Hipkens |
| Rose | Donna Murphy +1 |
| Chah Li | Cathy Foy |
| Inspectors/Pilot/Hindu Messengers | Francis Kane |
| Kenya Ratamacue | Oliver Jackson, Jr. |
| Cigarette Girl | Stephanie Park |

**UNDERSTUDIES:** Michael Sansonia (Spike/Freddy/Kenya), Lon Hoyt (Freddy/Inspector), William Daniel Grey (Hans/Inspector), Stephanie Park (Chah Li), Erik Frandsen (Kenya), Allison Briner, Connie Kunkel (Rose)

**MUSICAL NUMBERS:** Song of Singapore, Inexpensive Tango, I Miss My Home in Harlem, You Gotta Do What You Gotta Do, Rose of Rangoon, Necrology, Sunrise, Never Pay Musicians What They're Worth, Harbour of Love, I Can't Remember, I Want to Get Off This Island, Foolish Geese, Serve It Up, Fly Away Rose, I Remember, Shake Shake Shake, We're Rich, Finale

A musical mystery in two acts. The action takes place on the Singapore waterfront, 1941.

*Closed June 30, 1992 after 459 performances and 18 previews.

+Succeeded by: 1.Jacquey Maltby, Andrea Green

*Martha Swope Photos*

**Michael Garin, Donna Murphy, Erik Frandsen**
**TOP: Cathy Foy**

# TONY N' TINA'S WEDDING

By Artificial Intelligence (Nancy Cassaro, Artistic Director); Conception, Ms. Cassaro; Director, Larry Pellegrini; Supervisory Director, Julie Cesari; Musical Director, Debra Barsha; Choreography, Hal Simons; design & Decor, Randall Thropp; Costumes/Hairstyles/Makeup, Juan DeArmas; General Manager, Leonard A. Mulhern; Company Manager, James Hannah; Stage Managers, K.A. Smith, Bernadette McGay; Presented by Joseph Corcoran & Daniel Corcoran; Press, David Rothenberg/Terence Wombie. Opened in the Washington Square Church & Carmelita's on Saturday, February 6, 1988.*

## CAST

Valentia Lynne Nunzio, the bribe ...................................................Kelly Cinnante+1
Anthony Angelo Nunzio, the groom ...................................................Robert Cea+2
Connie Mocogni, the maid of honor ..................................................Dina Losito+3
Barry Wheeler, the best man ...................................................Bruce Kronenberg+4
Donna Marsala, bridesmaid ...............................................................Lisa Casillo+5
Dominick Fabrizzi, usher...............................................................George Schifini+6
Marina Gulino, bridesmaid ............................................................Aida Turturro+7
Johnny Nunzio, usher and brother of groom ............................James Georgiades+8
Josephine Vitale, mother of the bride............................................Nancy TimPanaro
Joseph Vitale, brother of the bride...........................................................Paul Spencer
Luigi Domenico, great uncle of the bride................................Allen Lewis Rickman
Rose Domenico, aunt of the bride .......................................................Wendy Caplan
Sister Albert Maria, cousin of the bride .........................................Fran Gennuso
Anthony Angelo Nunzio, Sr., father of the groom .............................Dan Grimaldi
Madeline Monroe, Mr. Nunzio's girlfriend .................................Georgienne Millen
Grandma Nunzio, grandmother fo the groom .........................Bonnie Rose Marcus
Michael Just, Tina's ex-boyfriend ...................................................Anthony T. Lauria
Father Mark, parish priest.......................................................................Gary Schneider
Vinnie Black, caterer ...........................................................................Tom Karlya
Loretta Black, wife of the caterer .....................................................Victoria Constan
Mick Black, brother of the caterer ...........................................................Joe Bacino+9
Nikki Black, daughter of the caterer....................................................Jodi Grant+10
Mikie Black, son of the caterer ....................................................Anthony Luongo
Pat Black, sister of the caterer .............................................................Jody Oliver
Rick Demarco, the video man ..............................................................Marc Romeo
Sal Antonucci, the photographer ........................................................Glenn Taranto

An environmental theatre production. The action takes place at the wedding and reception, at the present time

*Still playing May 31, 1991 after moving to St. John's Church and Vinnie Black's Coliseum.

+Succeeded by: 1.Sharon Angela 2.Rick Pasqualone 3.Doma Villella, Susan Laurenzi 4.Keith Primi, Timothy Monagan 5.Susan Campanero 6. Lou Martini, Jr. 7.Celeste Russi 8.Michael Creo, Ken Garito 9.Tony Palellis 10.Maria Gentile

*Linda Alaniz Photos*

**RIGHT: Rick Pasqualone, Sharon Angela**

| PRODUCTIONS FROM PAST SEASONS THAT CLOSED DURING THIS SEASON | | | |
|---|---|---|---|
| **Production** | **Opened** | **Closed** | **Performances** |
| And The World Goes Round | 3/5/91 | 3/8/92 | 408 + 15 previews |
| Breaking Legs | 4/27/91 | 5/10/92 | 401 |
| City of Angels | 12/11/89 | 1/19/92 | 878 + 24 previews |
| Fiddler on the Roof (Revival) | 11/11/90 | 6/16/91 | 241 + 18 previews |
| Grand Hotel | 11/12/89 | 4/25/92 | 1018 + 31 previews |
| Gypsy (Return of Revival) | 4/28/91 | 7/28/91 | 105 + 12 previews |
| I Hate Hamlet | 4/8/91 | 6/22/91 | 88 + 24 previews |
| Jackie Mason: Brand New | 10/17/90 | 6/29/91 | 216 + 6 previews |
| Lips Together Teeth Apart | 5/28/91 | 6/27/92 | 250(MTC)+169(Lortel) |
| Once On This Island | 10/18/90 | 12/1/91 | 469 + 19 previews |
| Other People's Money | 2/7/89 | 6/30/91 | 990 |
| Our Country's Good | 4/27/91 | 6/8/91 | 48 + 12 previews |
| Pageant | 4/28/91 | 6/7/92 | 462 + 10 previews |
| Penn & Teller (Bdwy run) | 4/3/91 | 6/29/91 | 103 + 9 previews |
| Six Degrees of Separation | 5/16/90 | 1/5/92 | 681(496 Bdwy, 185OB) |
| Smoke On The Mountain | 5/10/90 | 6/30/91 | 452 + 11 previews |
| Song Of Singapore | 5/7/91 | 6/30/92 | 459 + 18 previews |

# OFF-BROADWAY PRODUCTIONS

### (June 1,1991 through May 31, 1992)

(Actors' Playhouse) Saturday, June 1-14, 1991 Lawrence Lane presents:
**THE HAUNTED HOST** by Robert Patrick and **SAFE SEX** by Harvey Fierstein; Director, Eric Concklin; Design, David Adams (*Host*), Michael R. Smith (*Sex*); Lighting, Tracy Dedrickson; Associate Producers, Steven J. Korwatch, Wayne Hamilton; Stage Manager, Kate Riddle; Press, Shirley Herz/Sam Rudy CAST: Harvey Fierstein (Jay Astor-*Host*/Ghee-*Sex*), Jason Workman (Frank-*Host*/Mead-*Sex*)
A revised version of *Safe Sex*, the middle play in Mr. Fierstein's *Safe Sex* trilogy, joined the continuing *Haunted Host,* which began its Actors' Playhouse run April 19, 1991.

(John Houseman Theatre) Tuesday, June 4-23, 1991 (24 performances) Takka Productions presents:
**SELLING OFF** by Harris W. Freedman; Director, Gene Feist; Sets, James Youmans; Costumes, David C. Woolard; Lighting, Donald Holder; Sound, Scott Lehrer; Stage Managers, David Hyslop, Deborah Cresswell; General Manager, Ralph Roseman; Press, Jeffrey Richards/David LeShay, Irene Gandy. CAST: Andrew Bloch (Leon Berkowitz), Deborah Cresswell (Sydney O'Leary), John Braden (Maurice Hughes), Dody Goodman (Ethel Berkowitz), Janet Zarish (Sally Lowell), Robert Stattel (Harvey Schnorr), John C. Vennema (Arnold Handler), Sofia Landon (Muriel Berkowitz), Larry Block (Bernie Weiner)
A comedy in two acts. The action takes place in New York City, at present.

(Orpheum Theatre) Tuesday, June 4-Aug. 25, 1991 (80 performances) Island Visual Arts, Mark Groubert & Ellen M. Krass present:
**MAMBO MOUTH;** Written & Performed by John Leguizamo; Director, Peter Askin; Sets, Philip Jung; Lighting, Natasha Katz; Sound, Bruce Ellman; Musical Supervisor, Jellybean Benitez; Stage Manager, Joseph A. Onorato; Executive Producer, Elizabeth Keller; Press, Peter Cromarty/David Lotz, David B. Katz. PROGRAM: Agamemnon, Angel Garcia, Loco Louie, Pepe, Manny the Fanny, Inca God, Crossover King
A comic voyage through the aspirations and frustrations of Hispanic America performed without intermission. The show played 107 performances during the 1990-91 season at the American Place Theatre.

(Theatre for The New City) Thursday, June 6-23, 1991 (12 performances) Theatre for the New City (George Bartenieff, Executive Director; Crystal Field, Artistic Director) presents:
**SKY WOMAN FALLING** by Toby Armour; Director, Muriel Miguel; Sets, Tom Moore; Lighting, Zdenek Kriz; Costumes, Barbara Little Bear; Stage Manager, Deborah Ratelle; Press, Jonathan Slaff. CAST: Muriel Borst (Young Mary), Hortensia Colorado (Middle Aged Mary), Lisa Mayo (Old Mary)
A drama performed without intermission about Mary Jemison, a white woman captured by Indians during the French & Indian Wars.

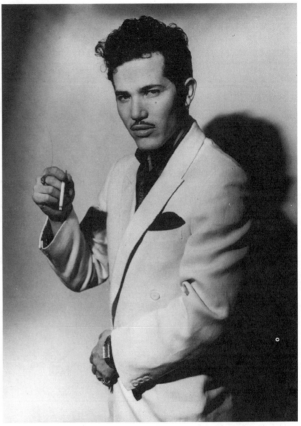

**John Leguizamo in "Mambo Mouth" (*David Hughes*)**

(Nuyonean Poets) Thursday, June 6-29, 1991 (12 performances)
**JULIUS CAESAR SET IN AFRICA;** Adaptation/Direction , Rome Neal; From William Shakespeare's play; Costumes, Charles Thomas; Sets, Chris Cumberbatch; Musical Director, Oba Tai-Ye; Choreography, Robert Turner; Lighting, Sandra Ross; Sound, David Wright; Stage Manager, Michael Thomas Newton. CAST: Christopher Adams, Vincent D'Arbouze, Akwesi Asante, Malika Batche, Kwame Isaac Boampong, Angela D. Brown, Queen Ye Boa, Robert Clements, Rochelle Cunningham, Clarence Cutherson, Randy Davis, Claire Floyd, James R. Garrett, Lloyd Goodman, Malika Iman, Ahmat Jallo, Keith Johnson, Robin McClamb, Rome Neal, Mac Powell, Rick Reid, Brandon Rosser, Gloria Sauve, Ed Sewer III, Jonathan D. Spooner, Robert Turner, Renauld White

(Third Step Studio) Thursday, June 6-30, 1991 (16 performances) Third Step Theatre Company presents:
**CRIME ON GOAT ISLAND** by Ugo Betti; Translation, Henry Reed; Director, Moshe Yassur; Sets, Jack Chandler; Lighting, Eric Cornwell; Stage Manager, Mindy Myers. CAST: Alison Brunell (Pia), Al D'Andrea (Angelo), Tamara Daniel (Agata), Margit Ahlin (Silvia)
A drama in two acts. The action takes place in an isolated house, surrounded by wasteland.

**Janet Zarish, Dody Goodman, Sofia Landon, (front) Andrew Bloch in "Selling Off" (*Martha Swope*)**

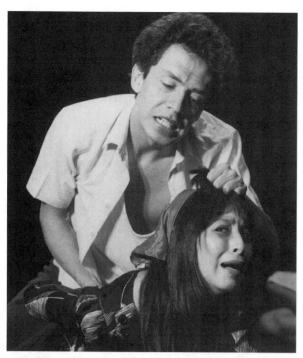

**Manuel Arenas, Ana Maria Estrada in "Night of the Murderers"** (*M. Arenas*)

(top) James Heatherly, Connie Ogden, Natasha Baron, David Phillips, (front) Dana Ertischek, Mark Traxler in "Prom Queens Unchained" (*Carol Rosegg*)

(Theatre Row Theatre) Friday , June 7-30, 1991 (25 performances) The Working Theatre presents:
**WORKING ONE ACTS '91;** Sets, Deborah Jasien; Lighting, Don Holder; Costumes, Lauren Press; Sound, Serge Ossorguine; Press, Bruce Cohen. CAST: Me Duane Gionson, Lyn Greene, Joseph Palmasm Dean Ryan Nichols, Roger Serbagi, Pamala Tyson, Kevin Davis, Allan Tung, Akira Takyama, Kiya Anne Joyce, Ian We Kevin Davis, Linda Marie Larson
**NEW HOPE FOR THE DEAD** by John Sayles; Director, Earl Hagan;with Joseph Palmas (Pharaoh), Linda Marie Larson (Candace)
**ABANDONED IN QUEENS** by Laura Maria Censabella; Director, Bill Mitchelson with Roger Serbagi (Father), Dean Nichols (Son)
**BETTING ON THE DUST COMMANDER** by Suzan-Lori Parks; Director, Liz Diamond; with Kevin Davis, Pamala Tyson

(Saval Theatre) Friday, June 7-30, 1991 (12 performances) American Ensemble Co. presents:
**RED SKY** by Robert Dominguez; Director, Antonio Valente; Film directed by Robe Dominguez. CAST: Steve Aronson (Cop), Michael Artura (Sonny), Sal Condoluci (Frankie the Nose), Ariel Cruz (Guillermo), Anthony Cucci (Toro), Steven Fucile (Billy), Harvey Kaufman (Pepe), Angie Kristic (Marisol/Mama), Manny Melendez (Young Sonny), Benny Nieves (Tex), Vinny Pastore (Fat Louie), Robert Petito (Vinny), John Vincent Vargas (El Ciego)
A multi-media drama in two acts. The action takes place in Texas, Brooklyn, and Mexico.

(Duality Playhouse) Friday, June 7-30, 1991 (16 peformances) Jeffrey Rosen & Rasgos Group Theatre present:
**THE NIGHT OF THE MURDERERS** by Jose Triana; Translation, Bill Blechingberg, Gabriela Kohen; Director, Manuel Arenas; Sets, Alejandro Sarmiento; Sound, Lizette Amado; Lighting, Mr. Blechingberg; Stage Manager, Ute Hansen; Press, Chris Boneau/Bob Fennell. CAST: Bill Blechingberg, Manuel Arenas (Lalo), Ana Maria Estrada (Cuca), Gabriela Kohen (Beba)
A drama taking place in any Latin American community at any given time.

(Village Gate/Downstairs) Friday, June 7-Aug. 18, 1991 (57 performances and 27 previews) PQU Productions presents:
**PROM QUEENS UNCHAINED** with Music by Keith Herrmann; Lyrics, Larry Goodsight; Book, Stephen Witkin; Conception, Mr. Goodsight, Mr. Herrmann; Director/Choreographer, Karen Azenberg; Music Director, Stuart Malina; Vocal/Dance Arrangements, Mr. Malina, Mr. Herrmann; Sets, Bob Phillips; Costumes, Robert Strong Miller; Lighting, Nancy Collings; Sound, Richard Dunning General Managers, Richard Berg, Patricia Berry; Stage Managers, Susan Whelan, Denise Laffer; Press, Peter Cromarty/David Lotz. CAST: Don Crosby (Mr. Kelty/Ro Mackelroy), Ron Kurowski (Mr. Sloan/Mr. McIssac/Mr. Cornelius/Miss Carlson/Mr Turk), James Heatherly (Grant Cassidy), Dana Ertischek (Cindy Mackelroy), Sandra Purpuro (Louise Blaine), Susan Levine (Carla Zlotz), David Phillips (Frank "Switch" Dorsey), Mark Edgar Stephens (Eddy "Wheels" Stevenson/Minka Lasky), Ilene Bergelson (Brenda Carbello), Mark Traxler (Richie Pomerantz), Becky Adams (Viol O'Grady), Gary Mendelson (Myron "Hicky" Greenberg), Connie Ogden (Sherry Va Heusen), David Brummel (Mr. Pike/Mario Lanza), Natasha Baron (Venulia), Kathy Morath (Mrs. Glick/Bunny Mackelroy)

(Gramercy Arts Theatre) Saturday, June 8-23, 1991 (14 performances) Repertorio Espanol in association with The New York International Festival of the Arts presents
**NEW OLD STORY (NOVA VELHA ESTORIA) ;** Conceived & Directed by Antunes Filho; Sets/Costumes, J.C. Serroni; Lighting, David De Brito; Sound, Raul Teixeira; Press, Ellen Jacobs. CAST: Samantha Monteiro (Little Red Riding Hood), Luis Melo (Wolf), Helio Cicero (Mother/Grandmother), Ondina Castilho (First Friend), Yara Nico (Second Friend), Geraldo Mario (Gnome/Hunter)
An adult adaptation of the Red Riding Hood fairy tale performed by Brazil's Grupo de Teatro Macunaima.

(Playhouse 125) Wednesday, June 12-23, 1991 (12 performances) The Royston Company presents:
**TWELFTH NIGHT** or **WHAT YOU WILL** by William Shakespeare; Director, Peter Royston; Musical Director/Composer, Peter Nissen; Costumes, Elizabeth Royston; Lighting, David Kramer; Choreography, Kathleen Dempsey. CAST: John Steber (Orsino), David Kinsey (Curio), Jack Smith (Valentine), Joanne Comerford (Viola), Mort Mortenson (Sea Captain), Jessica Givelber (Sailor), Lisa Langford (Maria), Charles Hall (Toby), James Corbett (Andrew), Paul Barry (Feste), Michele Remsen (Olivia), Ted Rooney (Malvolio), Christopher Batyr (Fabian), Soraya Butler (Handmaiden), James Bianchi (Sebastian), Kevin Alfred Brown (Antonio), Isiah Bard (Priest)
A Dixieland-flavored version of Shakespeare's comedy.

**Martin Outzen, Randall Denman in "Body and Soul"** (*Tony Savino*)

**Adam Long, Reed Martin, Jess Borgeson of "Reduced Shakespeare"**

**Marla Sucharetza, James Horan** (*Phillip Wong*)

(Courtyard Playhouse) Wednesday, June 12-Nov.4, 1991 (109 performances and 17 previews) The Glines presents:
**BODY AND SOUL**; Written and Directed by John Glines; Sets, David Jensen; Lighting, Tracy Dedrickson; Costumes, Ina Raye; Press, Chris Boneau/Bob Fennell
CAST: David Boldt succeeded by Tom Delling (Sky), Martin Outzen (Lou), Eddie Cobb succeeded by Robert Tierney, Casey Wayne, Michael McLernon (Max), Randall Denman succeeded by David Mitchell, John Jason (Denny), Douglas Gibson (Todd)
A romantic comedy in two acts. The action takes place in a country house during summer.

(Marymount Manhattan Theatre) Thursday, June 13-23, 1991 (8 performances) Maly Productions and Ken Marsolais present:
**THE REDUCED SHAKESPEARE COMPANY IN THE COMPLETE WORKS OF WILLIAM SHAKESPEARE (ABRIDGED)** by Jess Borgeson, Adam Long and Daniel Singer; Additional Material, Reed Martin; Costumes, Sa Thomson; Sets, Kent Elofson; Company Manager, Scott Ewing; Press, Terry M. Lilly and David J. Gersten
CAST: Reed Martin, Jess Borgeson, Adam Long
A high speed comic condensation of all of Shakespeare's plays. A presentation of The NY International Festival of the Arts.

(Federal Hall Steps) Thursday, June 13-28, 1991 (5 performances and 1 preview) Marquis Studios presents:
**BOLINAS...WHERE THE COWS KISS EACH OTHER GOODNITE**; Written and Performed by David Marquis; Director, Jaye Austin Williams; Lighting, Kristabelle Munson; Press, Ted Killmer/Tray Batres
A monologue exploring California hippie life circa 1968.

(29th St. Theatre) Thursday, June 13-30, 1991 (15 performances) Annette Moskowitz & Alexander E. Racolin present:
**DUSE, DUNCAN AND CRAIG** by Lemuel Borden; Director, Cara Caldwell-Watson; Sets, Mitchell J. Christenson; Lighting, Bruce Goldberg; Costumes, Liz Elkins; Dance Consultant, Julia Levien; Music, Lewis B. Flinn II; Stage Manager, David Lyons; Press, Chris Boneau/Bob Fennell CAST: James Horan (Gordan Craig), Marla Sucharetza (Isadora Duncan), Rita Crosby (Eleanora Duse), Judith Landon (Dancing Isadora)
A drama involving the actress, the dancer and a theatrical inventor. The action takes place in Paris, Florence, Berlin and Moscow.

(One Dream Theatre) Thursday, June 13-30, 1991 (14 performances) THECO in association with Annette Moskowitz & Alexander Racolin presents:
**PORTRAIT OF DORA** by Helene Cixous; Translation, Anita Barrows; Director, David M. Kronick; Sets, Alexander Brebner; Lighting, Laura Glover; Costumes, Veronica Worts; Music, Doug Cuomo; Stage Manager, Dwight R.B. Cook; Press, Chris Boneau/Bob Fennell. CAST: Giselle Liberatore (Dora), Emily Tetzlaff (Mrs. K), Brad Campbell (Freud), Tom Dale Keever (Mr. B), Peter Kisiluk (Mr. K)
A drama about Freud's first published case study.

(Joyce Theatre) Thursday, June 13-July 7, 1991 (28 performances) The Joyce Theatre Foundation and Lincoln Center Theatre in association with The New York International Festival of the Arts presents:
**THE STATE THEATRE OF LITHUANIA** ; Director, Eimuntas Nekrosius; Translations, Arunas Ciuberkis; Lighting, Michael Blanco, Gintautas Urba, Romualdas Treinys; Artistic Director, Ruta Wiman; Press, Merle Debuskey/Susan Chicoine
**UNCLE VANYA** by Anton Chekhov; Sets/Costumes, Nadiezda Gultiajeva; Music, Fautas Latenas; Stage Manager, Birute-Ona Jaruseviciene. CAST: Vladas Bagdonas (Alexandr Serebryakov), Dalia Storyk (Yelena), Dalia Overaite (Sofya), Elvyra Zebertaviciute (Marya), Vidas Petkevicius (Ivan), Kostas Smoriginas (Mihail), Juozas Pocius (Ilya Telyegin), Irena Tamosiunaite (Marina), Rimgaudas Karvelis, Jurate Aniulyte, Vytaukinaitis (Servants)
A drama performed in two acts. The action takes place on Serebryakov's estate.
**THE SQUARE** by Eimuntas Nekrosius; Sets/Costumes, Adomas Jacovskis. CAST: Kostas Smoriginas (He), Dalia Overaite, Janina Matekonyte (She), Remigijus Vilkaitis (Doctor/Announcer/Guard), Gerardas Zalenas (Prisoner)
A drama performed without intermission.

(St. Bartholomew's) Friday, June 14-23, 1991 (13 performances) Cindy Kaplan, Voza Rivers, The Hayworth Shakespeare Festival & The New York International Festival of the Arts present:
**THE TRAGEDY OF MACBETH** by William Shakespeare; Director, Stephen Rayne; Sets, Gerry Lidstone; Costumes, Emma Ryott; Lighting, Christopher Gorzelnik; Consultant, Diane Ward; Stage Manager, Melanie Adam; Press, Jeffrey Richards/Irene Gandy. CAST: Alex Tetteh-Lartey (Duncan/Old Man), Patrick Miller (Malcolm/Murderer), John Matshikiza (Macbeth), Trevor Gordan (Banquo), Burt Caesar (Macduff), Bhasker (Ross), Solomon (Fleance), Desmond McNamara (Seyton/Porter), Mona Hammond (Doctor/Sister), Caroline Lee-Johnson (Lady Macbeth), Clara Onyemere (Lady Macduff/Sister), Indra Ove (Gentlewoman/Sister)
   An adaptation set in modern day South Africa and featuring actors from The Royal Shakespeare Co. & The Royal National Theatre.

(Fifth Floor Theatre) Sunday, June 16-21, 1991 (7 performances) Studio Tisch (NYU/TSOA Graduate Acting & Directing Alumni) presents:
**TWO ONE ACT COMEDIES**; Sets, Cynthia Dorrel; Lighting, Jason Livingston; Sound, David Ratzlow; Stage Manager, Lisa Iacucci
PULLING TEETH by Jay Derrah; Director, Larry Pine. CAST: Marsha McKay (Joy), Jack Doulin (Will)
   The action involves two former lovers in a dentist's office.
21A by Kevin Kling; Directors, Fred Siegel, Paul Walker. CAST: Bob Kirsh (Ron Huber/Gladys/Chairman Francis/Student/Not Dave/Capt. Twelvepack/Steve/Jim Shipley)
   The action involves a bus driver and his off-center passengers.

(Carnegie Hall) Monday, June 17, 1991 (1 night only) The Museum of the City of New York presents:
**GIVE MY REGARDS TO BROADWAY**: A Salute To 125 Years of Musical Theatre; Writer/Director, David H. Bell; Musical Director, Paul Schwartz; Sets, Michael Anania; Lighting, Ken Billington; Sound, Robert Etter; Executive Producer, Robert Franz; Producer, Bonnie Nelson Schwartz; Press, Keith Sherman,/Chris Day, Jim Byk CAST: Diahann Carroll, Richard Kiley (Co-hosts), George Abbott, Michael Allison, Gene Barry, Laurie Beechman, Theodore Bikel, Jerry Bock, Betty Buckley,

**Emily Tetzlaff, Giselle Liberatore in "Portrait of Dora"** (*Carol Rosegg*)

Gregg Burge, David Carroll, Marge Champion, Carol Channing, Martin Charnin, Betty Comden, John Cullum, Carmen DeLavallade, Helen Gallagher, Adolph Green, Sheldon Harnick, Jerry Herman, Geoffrey Holder, Sally Ann Howes, Judy Kaye, Flo Lacey, Burton Lane, Carol Lawrence, Dorothy Loudon, Rebecca Luker, Patti LuPone, Manhattan Rhythm Kings, Andrea McArdle, Phyllis Newman, Jerry Orbach, Harold Prince, Lee Roy Reams, Ron Richardson, Chita Rivera, Donald Saddler, Paul Schwartz, Elaine Stritch, Charles Strouse, Jule Styne, Ben Vereen
   A benefit for the museum's theatre collection.

(New Stages) Thursday, June 20-24, 1991 (6 performances) New Stages Musical Arts (Joe Miloscia, Artistic Director) presents:
**THE NEW AMERICAN MUSICAL WRITERS COMPETITION 1991**; Producer Joe Miloscia; Design Russ Bralley; Manager, Kevin Young
AN ELEPHANT NEVER FORGETS with Music by John Kroner and Jerry Sternbach Lyrics, Faye Greenberg; Director, Jeff Martin; Musical Director, Vincent Trovato CAST: Bertilla Baker, Carolyn Berman, Carolyn Drascoski, Howard Katz Fireheart, David Jennings, Valerie Scott, John Sloman
THE AWAKENING OF SPRING with Music by Jane L. Komarow; Libretto, Judith C. Lane; Director, James A. Lopata; Music Director, Maria Delgado CAST: Liz Amberly (Knuppeldick), Michele Azar (Marta), Andrew Berman (Otto), Brigid Brady (Wendla), Bill Brooks (Stiefel/Eselohren), Terri Cannicott (Frau Gabor), Lauren Cohn (Sonnenstitch), Tim Connell (Hanschen), Nanette DeWester (Thea), Robert Ford (Ernst), Milica Govich (Frau Bergmann), David Gurland (Melchior), Billy Arthur Martel (Moritz), Marguerite MacIntyre (Ilse), Mark Peters (Pastor Kahlbauch), Tom Souhrada (Gabor/Fliegentod)
OEDIPUS, TEX. with Music/Lyrics/Book by Neal Herr and Brent Sanders; Director, Mary Elizabeth Carlin; Music Director, Catherine Reid CAST: Paul Malamphy (Judge), Tracey Moore (Egan), Andy Taylor (Billy), Barbara Tirrell (Miss Kitty), Bill Brooks, Adam Dyer, Anita Hollander, Susanne Lucia, Tom Souhrada, Annette Verdolino
   A festival of staged readings of the winning entries from a musical theatre competition.

**Marquerite MacIntyre, Billy Arthur Martel in "New American Musicals"**

(Trinity Theatre) Thursday, June 20-29, 1991 (7 performances) Calico Arts presents:
MORNINGSONG with Music/Lyrics/Book by Cordelia Jones-Post; Director, Rasa
Allan Kazlas; Musical Director, Mara Barth Waldman; Choreography, Maurice
Brandon Curry, Tina Bush; Costumes, Natalie Walker; Sets, Vicki Davis; Lighting,
Jeanne Koenig; Stage Manager, Thomas Morrissey; Press, Teressa Lynne Hoover
CAST: Lynn Alexander, Leslee Anne, Craig Batchker, Sandra Benton, Phillip Brown,
Tina Bush, Cedric D. Cannon, Shonnese C.L. Coleman, Toni Condos, Kathryn
Fowhey, Rochelle Cunningham, Maria-Patricia Donaldson, Ron Draeves, David
Preston Duret, Stanley Earl Harrison, John Humphreys, Fred John, Youssif Kamal,
Robert Laur, Denise Lock, Marvin Lowe, Gabrielle Mason, Andrea Mead, Darren
Perkins, Eric Sanders, Angela Simpson, Renard Steele, Lyn Tierney, Rachel White,
John Borras, Laura Lane, Dave McCracken, Kevin Weiler
An American opera. The action takes place on a plantation on the eve of the Civil War.

(Impact Theatre) Friday, June 21-30, 1991 (8 performances) Yaffa Prod.II, PM Prods.
presents:
MITOTE (WOMAN TALK) by Maisha Baton; Director, Patricia Floyd CAST: Linda
H. Humes, Jane Galvin-Lewis, Lorenzo, Yvonne Warden
A play about Afro-American women in Santa Fe at the turn of the century.

(Lucille Lortel Theatre) Friday, June 21-Sept.15, 1991 Theatre-In-Limbo, Manny
Kladitis, Drew Dennett, Shaun Huttar, & The WPA present:
RED SCARE ON SUNSET by Charles Busch; Director, Kenneth Elliott; Sets, B.T.
Whitehill; Costumes, Debra Tennenbaum; Lighting, Vivien Leone; Sound, Aural
Fixation; Wigs, Elizabeth Katherine Carr; Stage Manager, T.L. Boston; Press, Shirley
Herz/Sam Rudy CAST: Mark Hamilton (Ralph Barnes/Sales Girl/R.G.
Benson/Granny Lou), Roy Cockrum (Jerry/Bertram Barker), Julie Halston (Pat
Pilford), Arnie Kolodner (Frank Taggart), Charles Busch (Mary Dale), Andy Halliday
(Malcolm/Old Lady), Judith Hansen (Marta Towers), Ralph Buckley (Mitchell Drake)
A comic melodrama in two acts. The action takes place in Hollywood, 1951.

(Nat Horne Theatre) June 1991 Love Creek Productions and Isy Productions present:
CURRENTS TURNED AWRY by D.L. Coburn; Director, Philip Galbraith;
Lighting, Richard Kent Green MEET DOYLE MACINTYRE with Michael Cannis,
Larry Collis, Robert Lindley Sutton DINING OUT ALONE with Nick Stannard
Two one-acts involving suicide.

(Double Image Theatre) Saturday, July 6-Oct., 1991 Double Image Theatre presents:
DAMON RUNYON'S TALES OF BROADWAY; Adapted and Performed by John
Martello; Sets, Lutz Gock; Costumes, Thom Heyer; Stage Manager, Joe Caruso; Press,
David Rothenberg
Performed without intermission.

(Henry St. Settlement) Wednesday, July 10-20, 1991 (9 performances) Henry St.
Settlement presents:
THE EAGLE IN THE BUBBLE by Byron Ayanoglu and Jiri Schubert; Director, Mr.
Schubert; Music, Christopher Cherney; Lyrics, Jimmy Camicia; Press, Rhonda
Schaller CAST: Merek Vasut, Ron Jones, The Transformers
Three liars attempt to come to terms with New York City life.

(John Houseman Studio) Wednesday, July 10-Aug.4, 1991 Transferred to Judith
Anderson Theatre Tuesday, Aug.6, 1991 Eric Krebs presents:
A RENDEVOUS WITH GOD by Miriam Hoffman; Translation, Ms. Hoffman, Rena
Berkowicz Borow; Director, Sue Lawless; Musical Director, Ben Schaechter; Design,

**Michael Oberlander, Meghan Duffy in "Georgy"** (*Carol Rosegg*)

**Avi Hoffman in "Rendezvous with God"**

Don Coleman; Stage Manager, Karen Federing; Press, David Rothenberg CAST: Avi
Hoffman
A play of songs, poems and stories on the life of Yiddish poet Itzik Manger.
Performed without intermission.

(Wings Theatre) Tuesday, July 16-Aug.9, 1991 (16 performances) Wings Theatre Co.
& CityStock present:
GEORGY with Music by George Fischoff; Lyrics, Carol Bayer Sager; Book, Tom
Mankiewicz; Director, Morgan LaVere; Musical Director, Darren R. Cohen;
Choreography, Schellie Archbold; Sets, Vicki R. Davis; Lighting, Jeanne Koenig;
Costumes, Jane Epperson; Sound, Gerard Drazba; Press, Chris Boneau/Bob Fennell
CAST: Meghan Duffy (Georgy), Jon Lutz (James), Tracy Darin (George/Others), Joel
Goodness (Peter/Others), Michael Oberlander (Josh), Molly Scott (Meredith), Fredi
Walker (Peg/Others), Bill Wheeler (Ted) MUSICAL NUMBERS: Make It Happen
Now, Pease Puddin', Just for the Ride, So What?, Georgy, A Baby=Mrs. Jones, That's
How It Is, There's a Comin' Together, Half of Me, Gettin' Back to Me, Sweet
Memory, Toy Balloon (new), Finale
A revised version of the 1970 musical in two acts. The action takes place in
Greenwich Village.

(Irish Arts Center) Tuesday, July 16-Aug.17, 1991 (14 performances and 17 previews)
Gerald White presents:
MY SON THE DOCTOR by Marc J. Bielski; Director, Jeffrey B. Marx; Costumes,
Blair Hammond; Lighting, Thomas Simitzes; Sets, Bill M. Effrey; Production
Coordinator, Harold Bell; Stage Manager, Dennis Higgins; Press, Francine L.
Trevens/Robert J. Weston CAST: Matthew Boston (David), Colin Gray succeeded by
Gregory MacLaine (Doctor/Steve), Dan Gershwin (Leonard), Joyce Renee Korbin
(Dorothy), Bunny Levine (Phyllis/Nurse), Sheila Sawney (Sondra)
A comedy in two acts. The action takes place in the Maxwell family kitchen.

(West End Gate) Wednesday, July 17-Aug.2, 1991 (8 performances) Liberty Stage Co.
presents:
MARIE AND BRUCE by Wallace Shawn; Director, Ronald Bly; Lighting/Stage
Manager, Michael David Winter; Sound, Larry Luban CAST: Robin Poley (Marie),
Scott Klavan (Bruce), Kenneth Elchert (Herb/Fred), Wendy Forem (Enid/Jean), Deidre
Manganaro (Bettina/Ilsa/Roxanne), Laurence Gewirtz (Henry/Tim/Ed), Hal Cohen
(Antoine/Bert), Michael David Winter (Waiter)
Performed without intermission.

**Scott Klavan, Robin Poley in "Marie and Bruce" (*Ronald Bly*)**

**Chandra Wilson, Angela Goethals in
"The Good Times are Killing Me" (*Susan Cook*)**

(Tada Theatre) Friday, July 19-Aug.12, 1991 (35 performances) TADA! (Janine Nina Trevens, James Learned; Artistic Directors) presents:
**RABBIT SENSE** with Music by John Kroner; Lyrics, Gary Gardner; Book, Davidson Lloyd; Director, James Learned; Musical/Vocal Director, Wendell Smith; Choreography, Jan Johnson; Sets, Wendy Ponte; Costumes, Ann R. Emo; Lighting, Ellen R. Horaitis; Press, Chris Boneau CAST: Danielle Beauchamp, Latisha Capo, Joran Corneal, Javier Diaz, Patrick Dominguez, Katherine Dong, Colin Fisher, Ann Garcia, William Hernandez, Equiano Holman, Russell Jines, Richard Kydd, Aurora Nonas-Barnes, Mizuo Peck, Jordan Peele, Xiomara Reyes, Frances Rivera, Aaron Tollerson, Cui Wang
MUSICAL NUMBERS: Grab Some Magic, What's a Kid to Do?, Ballad of Brer Rabbit, Boss Bear, Skedeaddle, Race/We're a Family, Brer Fox Trot, The Magic's in You (Music/Lyrics, Joel Gelpe)
 A musical adaptation of the *Uncle Remus* tales performed without intermission.

(Rainbow & Stars) Tuesday, July 23-Aug.31, 1991 (60 performances) Rainbow & Stars presents:
**WHAT A SWELL PARTY!** : *The Cole Porter Revue*; Music/Lyrics, Cole Porter; Director, Fred Greene; Musical Director, Bruce Coyle; Conceived/Produced by Greg Dawson & Steve Paul; Press, Jessica Miller, David Lotz CAST: Mary Cleere Haran, Terri Klausner, Helen Schneider, Bruce Coyle, Ronny Whyte

(Minetta Lane Theatre) Tuesday, July 30-Nov.24, 1991 (136 performances) David Mirvish and Second Stage Theatre in association with Concert Productions Int'l, US present:
**THE GOOD TIMES ARE KILLING ME** by Lynda Barry; Director, Mark Brokaw; Sets, Rusty Smith; Lighting, Don Holder; Costumes, Ellen McCartney; Sound, Janet Kalas; Hairstylist, Antonio Soddu; Music Coordinator/Vocal Arrangements, Steve Sandberg; Script Consultant, Erin Sanders; Executive Producer, Brian Sewell; General Manager, Maria Di Dia; Stage Manager, James Fitzsimmons; Press, Richard Kornberg CAST: Angela Goethals (Edna Arkins), Lauren Gaffney (Lucy Arkins), Holly Felton

(Mom/Mrs. Doucette), Ellia English (Aunt Martha/Bonita), Wendell Pierce (Mr. Willis), Nora Cole (Mrs. Willis), Ruth Williamson (Aunt Margaret), John Lathan (Earl Stelly/Preacher/Marcus), Jennie Moreau (Cousin Ellen/Mrs. Hosey/Mrs. Mercer), Kathleen Dennehy (Sharon/Theresa Douchette), Harry Murphy (Uncle Jim), Peter Appel (Dad/Cousin Steve), Chandra Wilson (Donna Willis), Brandon Mayo (Elvin Willis)
 A comedy in two acts. The action takes place in a working class neighborhood, 1965-68.

(John Houseman Theatre) Tuesday, July 30, 1991-Jan.19, 1992 Richard Frankel, Thomas Viertel, Steven Baruch, Tim Jenison, and Paul Montgomery present:
**PENN & TELLER ROT IN HELL**; Sets, John Lee Beatty; Lighting, Dennis Parichy; Sound, T. Richard Fitzgerald; Costumes, Peter Fitzgerald; Director of Covert Activities, Robert P. Libbon; Director of Internal Affairs, Ken "Krasher" Lewis; Stage Manager, Cathy B. Blaser; Press, Chris Boneau/Jackie Green CAST: Penn Jillette, Teller, Carol Perkins
 Direct from last season's "Broadway tryout", a revised version of the magic act.

(NADA Theatre) Thursday, Aug.1-4, 1991 Reopened at Kaufman Theatre Thursday, Aug.22-24, 1991 (9 performances total) Audacious Productions present:
**THE 15TH WARD**; Written and Directed by James Dougherty; Producer, Ernest Ramirez; Choreography, Roberta Bender; Technical, Bill Swartz, Peter Conlin; Press, Barbara Atlee CAST: Barry Phillips (Harry Moncreif), Stephen Roylance (Fred), Bill Weeden (Judge/Gabe Wedmeyer/John Bentnor/Manning), Janet Geist (Dr. Susan Chafting), Lawrence Hubbell (Gervin Snitzer), Perry Zanett (Irving Snitzer), Joan Gainsley Mollison (Catherine O'Dwyer), Bob Manus (Frank Bancroft), Spencer Ross (Lionel Johnson), Howard Atlee (Sam), Manuel Brown (Burt Fluffner), David Watkins (Arnold Caesar), Bill Swartz (Gabe's Techie)
 A political farce. The action takes place in a Democratic neighborhood in Philadelphia.

**Helen Schneider, Bruce Coyle, Mary Clere Haran, Ronny White, Terri Klausner in "What a Swell Party!" (*Carol Rosegg*)**

**Anglea Goethals, Lauren Gaffney in
"The Good Times are Killing Me" (*Susan Cook*)**

**Adriano Gonzalez, Bersaida Vega in
"Los Jibaros Progresistas" (*Peter Krupenye*)**

**Isabelle Townsend, Claudia Beck-Mann in "Philosopher's Stone"**

(Puerto Rican Traveling Theatre) Aug.18-Sept.22, 1991 (33 performances) Puerto Rican Traveling Theatre presents:
**LOS JIBAROS PROGRESISTAS** with Music/Lyrics/Book by Ramon Mendez Quinones; Director/Music Director, David Crommett; Sets, Daniel Ettinger; Costumes, Amparo Fuertes; Sound, Gary Harris; Stage Manager, Hector Marin; Press, Max Eisen CAST: Bersaida Vega (Juaniya), Miriam Cruz (Chepa), George Bass (Cleto), Adriano Gonzalez (Anton), Anibal Lleras (Bruno), Rafael Picorelli (Don Pico)
A verse musical. The action takes place in the mountains of Northwest Puerto Rico in 1882. This production toured city parks before appearing at the 47th St. Theatre.

(Ballroom) Tuesday, Aug.20-Sept.8, 1991 (24 performances)
**THE FABULOUS LYPSINKA SHOW** with John Epperson; Press, Shirley Herz/Sam Rudy
A comedy variety show.

(John Houseman Theatre) Tuesday, Aug.27,1991-Jan.5, 1992 Transfered to Westside Theatre Downsairs Thursday, Jan.30-Mar. 8, 1992 Eric Krebs presents:
**FINKEL'S FOLLIES**; Conception, Fyvush Finkel; Music, Elliot Finkel; Lyrics, Philip Namanworth; Direction/Adaptation, Robert H. Livingston; Orchestrations, Ian Finkel; Sets/Costumes, Mimi Maxmen; Lighting, Robert Bessoir; Musical Director, Mike Huffman; Musical Staging, James J. Mellon; Stage Manager, Michael J. Chudinski; Press, David Rothenberg/Meg Gordean, Manuel Igrejas, Terence Womble CAST: Fyvush Finkel, Mary Ellen Ashley, Laura Turnbull, Avi Ber Hoffman
MUSICAL NUMBERS: Yiddish Vaudeville Tonight, Mom I Want to Be in Yiddish Vaudeville, You Were Meant For Me, A Kliene Soft Shoe, Ringa Zinga, Tankhum, Mi-Komash Melon, Rozinkes mit Mandelen, Di Greene Kuzeene, Yossel Yossel, Ich Hob Dich Tzufil Lieb, Belz, Not on the Top, That Something Special, Vee Zenen Meine Ziben Gute Yor, Oy Mama, The Fiddle, Tzi Vus Darf Ich Du?, These are the Jokes, Odenemya, Abi Tsu Zein mit Dir, Finale
A musical revue in two acts.

(Gas Station) Tuesday, Sept. 3-11, 1991 ( 8 performances)
**THE PHILOSOPHER'S STONE** by Par Lagerkvist; Director, Mihaly Kerenyi;

Set/Costumes, Melissa Lustgarten; Stage Manager, Gus Michaels CAST: Michael Skinner (Albertus), Claudia Beck-Mann (Maria), Isabelle Townsend (Catherine), Ira Rubin (Simonides), Jeff Dobbins (Jacob), Dave Knapp (Nightcock), Nolan Carley (Clemens/Blind Man), Joanne Singer (Tilda), Debra Vogel (Malena/Sister Teresia), Mihaly Kerenyi (Lucas Whorerake), Brian Catton (Prince)

(The Towers) Tuesday, Sept.3-29, 1991 (19 performances and 5 previews) En Garde Arts presents:
**ANOTHER PERSON IS A FOREIGN COUNTRY** by Charles L. Mee, Jr.; Director, Anne Bogart; Music, Daniel Schreier; Producers, Anne Hamburger, Portia Kamons; Sets, Kyle Chepulis; Props, Deborah Scott; Costumes, Claudia Brown; Lighting, Carol Mullins; Sound, Eric Liljestrand; Production Manager, Michael Casselli; Stage Managers, Paul J. Smith, Mary Elizabeth Carlin; Music Director, John M. Buchanan; Press, Ted Killmer CAST: Robert Beatty, Jr. ( Jimmy), Victoria Boomsma (Opera Singer-Linus), Rashid Brown (Manuel), Christine Campbell (Twin 1-Milicent), Maria Clarke (Isabella), Bruce Hlibok (Ajax), Marie Kalish (Fergie), Terence Mintern (Ethyl), Tom Nelis (Poet), Jennifer Rohn (Jennifer), David Steinberg (Mike), Kelly Taffe (Twin 2-Melody), Adam Auslander, Paul Carter, Irene Fitzpatrick, Erika Greene, Emily Knowles, Monica Koskey, David McIntyre, Mary McBride, Barry Rowell, Roy Scott, Richard Sheinmel, Natalie Trapnehis, Halina Ujda, Lora Zuckerman
A site-specific play with music, performed in the remains of the first American cancer hospital.

(45th St Theatre) Tuesday, Sept.3, 1991- Sage Theatre Co. presents:
**SPARKY'S LAST DANCE** by Richard Lay; Director, John Wall; Lighting, David Jensen; Stage Manager, Rick Foster CAST: Dennis Dooley (Hurricane Pox), Eric J. Wiggins III (Maximillian Bilge), Bob McGrath (Gov. Jinks), Tom Grasso (Attorney Theo), Bonnie Haagenbuch (Lily Pox), Helene Beth Abrams (Nancy Toot), John Tsakonas (Rainbow Gout/Executioner), Richard Lay (Teller), Larry McCue (Smile/Priest)
A black comedy about white trash.

**Laura Turnbull, Abi Ber Hoffman, Fyvush Finkel, Mary Ellen Ashley
in "Finkel's Follies"**

**Jennifer Rohn, David Steinberg, Tom Nelis in
"Another Person is a Foreign Country" (*William Rivelli*)**

(Living Theatre) Wednesday, Sept.4-29, 1991 (20 performances) The Living Theatre New Directors series presents:
**BEIRUT** by Alan Bowne; Director, Christina Kirk; Sets/Lighting, Tim Cunningham; Costumes, Romy Phillips; Sound, Judi Rymer CAST: David Zurav (Torch), Alene Dawson (Blue), Dora Litinaki (Guard)
   The 1987 drama performed without intermission.

(Orpheum Theatre) Wednesday, Sept.4-Dec.1, 1991 (87 performances and 16 previews) Michael Frazier, Richard Norton, and Ted Snowdon present:
**UNIDENTIFIED HUMAN REMAINS AND THE TRUE NATURE OF LOVE** by Brad Fraser; Director, Derek Goldby; Sets/Costumes, Peter Hartwell; Lighting, Kevin Rigdon; Music/Sound, Richard Woodbury; Prod. Supervisor, Frank Scardino; Stage Manager, George Boyd; Press, Edward Callaghan/Andrea Goldstein, Owen Levy CAST: Kimberley Pistone (Benita), Scott Renderer succeeded by Lou Liberatore (David), Lenore Zann (Candy), Clark Gregg succeeded by Mark Wilson (Bernie), Michael Connor (Kane), Michelle Kronin (Jerri), Sam Rockwell succeeded by Mark Kevin Lewis (Robert)
   An adult thriller in two acts. the action takes place in Edmonton, Alberta at present.

(Intar Stage II) Thursday, Sept. 5-Oct. 13, 1991 (30 performances) Vere Johns presents:
**THE BOXING DAY PARADE** by Clifford Mason; Director, Jennifer Vermont-Davis; Set/Lighting, Donald L. Brooks; Costumes, Myra Coola-Le, Ali Turns; Choreography, Jeffrey Dobbs CAST: Arthur French, Pam Hyatt, Carol London, Clifford Mason, Norman Matlock, Morgan, Monica Parks, John Steber
   A play about Jamaica's independence from Britain.

(Theatre Row Theatre) Thursday, Sept. 5, 1991- Merry Enterprises Theatre presents:
**SUBLIME LIVES** by Paul Firestone; Director, William E. Hunt; Sets, Don Jensen; Lighting, David Neville; Costumes, Traci di Gesu; Stage Manager, Otis White; Press, David Rothenberg CAST: William Verderber (Richard Mansfield), Jordan Charney (William Winter), Ron Keith (Fred), Lenny Singer (Henry Salomon), Pamela Cecil (Beatrice Cameron), Hans Freidrichs (Clyde Fitch), Susan Farwell (Constance Neville)
   A play in two acts, the action takes place in the Continental Hotel, Phialdelphia and the Madison Sq. Theatre, 1889-91.

(Soho Rep Theatre) Friday, Sept.13-Oct.5, 1991 (15 performances) Annette Moskowitz, Alexander E. Racolin & Salamander Repertory present:
**FRANKENSTEIN** by Joel Leffert and Nancy Nichols; Based on the novel by Mary Shelly; Director, Ted Davis; Sets, Bob Barnett; Lighting, Richard Schaefer; Costumes, Neville Bean; Creature Design, G. Duncan Eagleson; Makeup, Diana Mullen; Stage Manager, Scott Shook; Press, Chris Boneau/Bob Fennell CAST: Barry Craig Friedman (Henry), Larry Swansen (Prof. Waldman), Jean Tafler (Elizabeth), Jenn Thompson (Justine), James L. Walker (Victor Frankenstein), Timothy Wheeler (Creature)
   A new adaptation of the gothic tale.

**Michelle Kronin, Lenore Zann in "Unidentified Human Remains…"** (*Carol Rosegg*)

**Scott Renderer, Michael Connor in "Unidentified Human Remains…"** (*Carol Rosegg*)

(Harold Clurman and John Houseman Theatres) Sunday, Sept.15-16, 1991 (2 performances)
**HURRAY!HURRAY!HOLLYWOOD** with Music by Sam Harris; Lyrics/Book, Bruce J. Newberg, Mr. Harris; Press, Wallace Ross/Susan Dubow CAST: Kaye Ballard, Jodi Benson, Wallace Kurth
   Showcase of a new musical.

(William Redfield Theatre) Wednesday, Sept.18-22, 1991 (5 performances) Qwirk Productions present:
**RUMOR OF GLORY** by James Bosley; Director, Peter Dalto; Stage Manager, Christine Califra CAST: William Preston, Richard Psarros, Molly McKenna, Jennifer Jay Stewart, David Blackman, Simon Brooking, Daniel J. Leventritt, Diane Shore, Laurence Addeo, William Hill, Mark Hymen

**80**

**James L. Walker, Timothy Wheeler in "Frankenstein"** (*Carol Rosegg*)

apiro Theatre) Thursday, Sept.19-Oct.5, 1991 (16 performances) Playwrights'
iew Productions (Frances Hill, Artistic Director; Deborah Goodwin, Producer)
ents:
**O COLLECTS THE PAIN** by Sean O'Connor; Director, William Electric Black;
, E.F. Morrill; Lighting, Jeffrey S. Koger; Costumes, Robin Orloff; Sound, John H.
wn; Consultant, David Sheppard; Stage Manager, Yael Schuster CAST: Kelvin
vanne (Howard), Robert Colt (Ryan), Khalil Kain (Jeff), Gordon MacDonald
ckey), Angel Jemmott (Lorraine), Lloyd Goodman (Danny), Frank Guy (Mercy),
Rodriquez (Rafael)
drama in two acts. The action takes place at Columbia University in NYC during
ng of 1993.

t Horne Theatre) Thursday, Sept. 19, 1991- B&G Assoc. and William E. Lathan
sent:
**LKS REMEMBERS A MISSSING PAGE**; Written and Performed by James E.
nny Jim" Gaines; Director, Andre Mtumi; Set, Terry Chandler; Lighting, Sandra
s; Music, Bob La Pierre; Design, Eve Burris; Sound, Bill Milbrodt; Press, Barbara
e
e rise and fall of Harlem in a monologue.

sh Arts Center) Tuesday, Sept.24-Oct.13, 1991 (13 performances and 7 previews)
able W Prods. in association with Irish Arts Center presents:
**MIEN** by Aldyth Morris; Dialect Coach, Joann Dolan; Sets, David Raphel;
hting/Prod.Management, Kurt Wagemann; Sound, Larry Horne; Press, Francine L.
vens/Robert J. Weston CAST: William Walsh (Fr. Damien)
drama about a young Belgian priest who served lepers and contracted the disease.

arold Clurman Theatre) Thursday, Sept.26-Oct.6, 1991 (13 performances) Punch
d Judy Productions in association with Gail Bell presents:
**RIBBEAN COUPLES** by Carolyn Moses; Director, Deborah Roberts; Sets, Caty
xey; Costumes, David Toser; Lighting, John Wooding; Stage Manager, Warren
edman CAST: Diane Findlay, Larry Nicks

e Dream Theatre) Thursday, Sept.26-Oct.11, 1991 (11 performances) Under One
f Theatre Co. presents:
**LESTIAL ALPHABET EVENT** with Music by Carter Burwell; Book/Direction,
rienne Weiss; Lighting, Chris Akerlind; Costumes, Claudia Brown; Sets, Kristin
es, Andrew Ginzel; Press, David Rothenberg/Terence E. Womble CAST: Joan
sak, Shishir Kurup, Johnnie Morello, Helen Shumaker

llage Gate Downstairs) Thursday, Sept.26, 1991-June 14, 1992 (269 performances)
n Delsener, Soloway Sisters/Eric W. Waddell and Metraform's Annoyance Theatre
sent:
**AL LIVE TV NIGHT** featuring THE REAL LIVE BRADY BUNCH; Directors,
and Faith Soloway; Music, Faith Soloway, Frank De Vol; Costumes/Stage
nager, Thia Rogan; Sets, Dan Kipp, Jim Jatho, Terry Ayers; Press, PMK, David
thenberg CAST: Andy Richter (Mike), Jane Lynch (Carol), Pat Towne (Greg),
cky Thyre (Marcia), Benjamin Zook (Peter), Melanie Hutsell succeeded by Kathryn
ly (Jan), Tom Booker (Bobby), Susan Messing succeeded by Madeline Long
ndy), Mari Weiss (Alice), Guest stars included Davy Jones. Episodes of the tv
ies.and THE REAL LIVE GAME SHOW Cast: Wayne Waddell (Host), Dana
nningham, John Copeland (Models)

(top) Shaun P. Murphy, Brett Paesel, Bradford Draezen, (middle)
**Karen Grealti, Florence Sturgeon, James Grace, (bottom) Rachel**
**Dratch, David Koechner, Aaron Rhodes as "Real Live Brady Bunch"**

**Stephanie Zimbalist, Linda Purl in "Baby Dance"** (*T. Charles Erickson*)

(St. Bart's Playhouse) Friday, Sept.27-Oct.6, 1991 (9 performances) St. Bart's
Playhouse (Christopher Catt, Artistic Director) presents:
**STEEL MAGNOLIAS** by Robert Harling; Director, Jean Prinz Korf; Set, Josh
Rothenberg; Lighting, Karen Spahn; Costumes, Estella Marie; Sound, Kevin Mochel;
Stage Manager, Keith Garsson; Press, Peter Cromarty/Lynne McCreary CAST:
Tracey Cassidy (Truvy), Nancy Young (Annelle), Catherine Winters (Clairee), Kathy
Kirkpatrick (Shelby), Barbara Blomberg (M'Lynn), Maren Swenson (Ouiser)
  The 1987 comedy in two acts. the action takes place in Louisiana.

(Lucille Lortel Theatre) Friday, Sept.27-Dec.8, 1991 (61 performances and 23
previews) John A. McQuiggan, Lucille Lortel, Daryl Roth in association with Susan
Dietz present:
**THE BABY DANCE** by Jane Anderson; Director, Jenny Sullivan; Sets, Hugh
Landwehr; Costumes, David Murin; Lighting, Kirk Bookman; Sound, Brent Evans;
Co-General Manager, Patricia Berry; Stage Manager, Tammy Taylor; Press, Chris
Boneau/Adrian Bryan-Brown, Susanne Tighe, John Barlow, Bob Fennell, Jackie
Green, Cabrini Lepis CAST: Linda Purl (Wanda), Richard Lineback (Al), Stephanie
Zimalist (Rachel), Joel Polis (Richard), John Bennett Perry (Ron)
  A drama in two acts. The action takes place in Louisiana during a hot spring and
summer.

**Kathy Kirkpatrick, Tracy Cassidy, Catherine Winters, Nancy Young**
**in "Steel Magnolias" (*Carol Rosegg*)**

(Variety Arts Theatre) Friday, Sept.27, 1991-Apr.26, 1992  Andre Ptaszynski and Don Taffner present:

**RETURN TO THE FORBIDDEN PLANET**; Written and Directed by Bob Carlton; Musical Director, Kate Edgar; Sets, Rodney Ford; Costumes, Sally J. Lesser; Lighting, Richard Nelson; Sound, Bobby Aitkin, Autograph; Effects, Gerry Anderson; *Ariel* Costume Design, Adrian Rees; General Manager, Steven Warnick; Company Manager, Mark Johnson; Stage Manager, Bonnie Panson; Press, Chris Boneau/Adrian Bryan-Brown  CAST: Robert McCormick (Capt. Tempest), Steve Steiner (Dr. Prospero), Gabriel Barre (Ariel), Louis Tucci (Cookie), Julee Cruise (Science Officer), James H. Wiggins, Jr. (Bosun Arras), Mary Ehlinger (Navigation Officer), Erin Hill (Miranda), James Doohan (Chorus), Rebecca Ptaszynski (Infant Miranda), DAMAGE CONTROL CREW: Allison Briner (Ensign Betty Will), Chuck Tempo (Petty Officer Axel Rhodes), David LaDuca (Ensign Harry Saul Spray), Michael Rotondi (Ensign Dane G. Russ)

MUSICAL NUMBERS: Born To Be Wild, Don't Let Me Be Misunderstood, Gloria, Go Now, Good Golly Miss Molly, Good Vibrations, Great Balls of Fire, I Can't Turn You Loose, I Heard It Through the Grapevine, I'm Gonna Change the World, It's a Man's World, Mr. Spaceman, Monster Mash, Oh Pretty Woman, Only the Lonely, Robot Man, Shake Rattle and Roll, Shakin' All Over, She's Not There, Tell her, It's in His Kiss (Shoop Shoop Song), Telstar, Who's Sorry Now, Why Must I Be a Teenager in Love, Wipeout, Young Girl

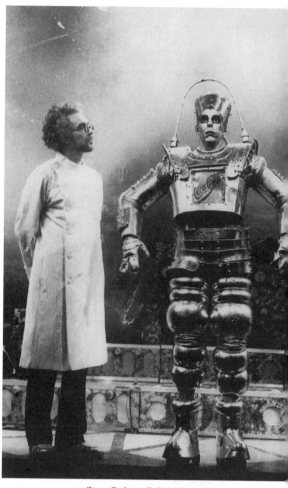

Louis Tucci, Julee Cruise in
**"Return to the Forbidden Planet"** (*Carol Rosegg*)

Steve Steiner, Gabriel Barre in
**"Return to the Forbidden Planet"** (*Carol Rosegg*)

A musical in two acts with a score comprised of 1950s-60s pop songs. Inspired by Shakespeare's *Tempest* and the 1956 MGM film *Forbidden Planet*. Guest rock stars included Lou Christie, The Crystals, the Shirelles, Martha Reeves, The Chiffons, Ga U.S. Bonds, The Coasters, the Platters, The Marvelettes, etc...

(Lambs Theatre) Wednesday, Oct.2, 1991-still playing May 31, 1992  Arthur Cantor Carol Ostrow and Libby Adler Mages present:
**BEAU JEST** by James Sherman; Director, Dennis Zacek; Production Design, Bruce Goodrich; Costumes, Dorothy Jones; Lighting, Edward R.F. Matthews; Stage Manager, Jana Llynn; Press, Mr. Cantor  CAST: Laura Patinkin (Sarah Goldman), John Michael Higgins (Chris), Tom Hewitt (Bob), Larry Fleischman (Joel), Rosalyn Alexander (Miriam), Bernie Landis (Abe)
  A romantic comedy in three acts.

Laura Patinkin, Tom Hewitt in "Beau Jest"

lement's Theatre) Thursday, Oct.3-19, 1991 (13 performances and 3 previews)
olis Brown Adaptors presents:

**ODANZ**: *The Dilema Of Desmondus & Diphylla* and **KOPPELVISION AND
ER DIGITAL DEITIES**; Written, Directed and Choreographed by Tony Brown
Kari Margolis; Lighting, Brian Aldous, Kyle Chepulis; Scenic Design, Rick Paul;
Mr. Chepulis; Costumes, Ms. Margolis, Carter Timmins, Donna Larsen, Debra
Press, Ted Killmer CASTS: *Decodanz* Tony Brown, Kari Margolis, Ed Alletto,
nanie Bienskie, Beth Brooks, Stephan Geras, Stephan Kohrherr, Deborah Marcus,
Merwyn, Kristi Schumacher, Carter Timmins, Robbie Walker *Koppelvision* Mr.
to, Mr. Bienskie, Ms. Brooks, Natalie Ferrier, Mr. Geras, Louise Heit, Mr.
err, Elizabeth Korabek, Ms. Marcus, Ms. Timmins, Ms. Walker, Kristin Stuart
movement theatre troup in a double bill. *Decodanz* involves a vampiric couple in
ywood. *Koppelvision* is a surreal twist of the tv dial.

**Robbie Walker, Stephen Kohrherr, Stephan Geras, Carter Timmins in
"Koppelvision..."** (*Ruby Levesque*)

th Anderson Theatre) Thursday, Oct.3-22, 1991 (16 performances and 4
ews) SeaCrest Associates and The Quaigh Theatre present:

**R LADY OF PERPETUAL DANGER** by Adam Kraar; Director, Joel Bishoff;
Steve Carter; Lighting, Matthew Frey; Costumes, Amy Lenzcewski; Producer,
Gabay; Stage Manager, Roger Lee; Press, Peter Cromarty/David B. Katz CAST:
n Cristaldi (Will), Nancy Kawalek (Concetta), Arija Bareikis (Sally), Mary
nin (Constanza), Robert Arcaro (Valducci)
omedy in two acts. The action takes place in South Brooklyn at present.

**Mary Tahmin, Kevin Cristaldi, Alexandra Reichler, Robert Arcaro in
"Our Lady of Perpetual Danger"** (*Carol Rosegg*)

angle Theatre) Thursday, Oct.3-27, 1991 (20 performances) Triangle presents:

**DGERS AND HART: A CELEBRATION** with Music by Richard Rodgers;
cs, Lorenz Hart; Concept, Richard Lewine, John Fearnly; Director, Michael
ach; Musical Director, Stuart Rosenthal; Costumes, Amanda J. Klein; Lighting,
cy Collings; Sets, Karl Carrigan, Peter R. Feuche; Stage Manager, Cathy Diane
mlin; Press, Jim Baldassare CAST: Gary Anderson, Suzanne Briar, Mark Doerr,
e Harris, Andy Taylor, Tracy Venner
SICAL NUMBERS: Overture, Jupiter Forbid, Falling in Love With love, Thou
ll, The Girl Friend, Where Or When, To Keep My Love Alive, With a Song in My
rt, Everthing I've Got, This Can't Be Love, Wait Till You See Her, My Heart
d Still, Isn't It Romantic, Here in My Arms, My Romance, Glad To Be Unhappy,
ish I Were In Love Again, It Never Entered My Mind, Happy Hunting Horn, How
ut It, Love Me Tonight, Mountain Greenery, It's a Lovely Day for a Murder, Little
Blue, Mimi, Prayer, Bad in Every Man, Manhattan Melodrama, Blue Moon,
ny One-Note, Way Out West, Give It Back to the Indians, I Gotta Get Back to
York, Manhattan, Any Old Place with You, On a Desert Island, Most Beautiful
in the World, Great Big Town, Song of Paree, Dear Old Syracuse, Ten Cents a
ce, Sing For Your Supper, I've Got Five Dollars, She Could Shake the Maracas, I
n't Know What Time It Was, You Took Advantage Of Me, You Mustn't Kick It
und, Cause We Got Cake, Dancing on the Ceiling, It's Got to Be Love, He & She,
e Room, I Could Write a Book, Ship Without a Sail, Nobody's Heart, Spring is
e, You're Nearer, There's a Small Hotel, This is My Night to Howl, Bewitched, I
ried An Angel, Lady is a Tramp, Have You Met Miss Jones?, Lover, Finale
musical revue in two acts.

**Suzanne Briar, Mark Doerr, Andy Taylor in
"Rodgers and Hart: A Celebration"** (*Carol Rosegg*)

u Theatre) Tuesday, Oct.8-27, 1991 (17 performances) Ubu Repertory (Francoise
urilsky, Artistic Director) presents:

**TEMPEST** by Aime Cesaire; Translation, Richard Miller; Director, Robbie
Cauley; Set, Jane Sablow; Lighting, Zebedee Collins; Costumes, Carol Ann
etier; Musical Director, Tiye Giraud; Movement, Marlies Yearby; Press, Peter
marty/Lynne McCreary CAST: Rafael Baez (Ariel), Robert G. Siveris
atswain/Friar), Allen Gilmore (Trinculo/Captain), Leo V. Finnie III (Stephano),
bert Ford (Gonzalo), Arthur French (Prospero), Bryan Hicks (Ferdinand),
wrence James (Alonso), Jasper McGruder (Eshu/MC), Sharon McGruder (Miranda),
rick Rameau (Sebastian), Leon Addison Brown (Caliban), Kim Sullivan (Antonio),
rlies Yearby (Goddess)

ichael's Pub) Tuesday, Oct.8-Nov.2, 1991 (27 performances and 1 preview)
wrence Kasha & Ronald A. Lachman in association with Warner/Chappell Music
oup present:

' **WIT'S END**; Written by Joel Kimmel; Based on the works of Oscar Levant;
ector, Barbara Karp; Set, Alan Kimmel; Lighting, Andrew Taines; Stage Manager,
b Thurber; Presented in cooperation with June Levant; Press, Terry Lilly/David
rsten CAST: Stan Freeman (Oscar Levant)
n irreverent musical evening in two acts.

**Sharon McGruder, Arthur French in
"A Tempest"** (*Carol Rosegg*)

**83**

(Ensemble Studio Theatre) Wednesday, Oct.9-31, 1991 Ensemble Studio Theatre (Curt Dempster, Artistic Director; Dominick Balletta, Managing Director) presents: **OCTOBERFEST '91;** Producer, Kevin Confoy; Featuring *Sam I Am* by Keith Reddin; Director, Billy Hopkins; with Macaulay Culkin, Lois Smith, John Christopher Jones, Leslie Lyles, Victor Slezak;*Two Bears Blinking* by Michael Brady; *The United Way* by Robert Shaffron; *You've Changed* by Bruce Ellman; *Heaven* by Barry Kaplan; *What Are Friends For?* and *Same Difference* by Michael Wells; *A Walk On Water* by Paul Minx; *Beginner's Mind* by Don Ponturo; *The Velocity of Gary* by James Still; *The End Of Our Rope* by Joe Gilford; *No More Flat World* by Jack Agueros; *Getting To Know You* by Billy Aronson; *Mama And Jack Carew* by Hal Corley; *Buster Breaker's Insomnia* by Rita Nachtman; *Mama Drama* by the Company; *Three Plays* by Will Scheffer; *Dream Of A Common Language* by Heather MacDonald; *Salvation* by Paul Weitz; *Nanna* by David Simpatico; *Dig & Arch* by Julie McKee; *Minna & The Space People* by Wendy Hammond; *Fran And Jane* by Billy Aronson; *Autumn Sonata* by Ingmar Bergman; *Dream Of Wealth* by Arthur Giron; *I Used To Know Buddy Rich!* and *Fax You!* by Yvonne Adrian; *Time* by Susann Brinkley; *Caught* by Michael John LaChiusa; *The Rose Quilt* by Debra Kaplan; *Blue Stars* by Stuart Spencer;*Senaca Links* by Peter Maloney; *Coyote Hangin' On A Barbed Wire Fence* by Percy Granger; *Blessed Events* by Charles Leaphart; *Busted* by Nicole Burdette; *Angel Of Mercy* by Jose Rivera; *Fasting* by Bill Bozzone; *Becoming Memories* by Arthur Giron; *Time's Up* by Clayton Brooks; *Sparrow* by Peter Manos; *Harry In The Night* by Julie Bovasso; *Heart's Location* by D.S. Moynihan with Music by Andrew Howard; *Four Play* by Gina Barnet; *Mentals* by Stephen Policoff; *Wild Mushrooms* by Robert Siegel; *Inciting Laughter* by David Margulies, Music and Comedy by Rusty Magee; *Deposing The White House* by Dan Isaac; *Doll* by Laura Maria Censabella; *The Confinement* by Charlene Redick; *Bedtime Story* by Leonard Melfi; *The Wild Goose* by John Patrick Shanley; *Patsys Brothers* by Edward Allan Baker; *Untitled* by Susan Cameron; *Survival Of The Species* by Robert Shaffron; *Against The Tide* by Bruce Ellman; *Open Window* by Brad Korbesmeyer; *Two Past Nam* by Alan Stoler; *Mother Earth* by Martin Duberman

(Theatre Row Theatre) Wednesday, Oct.9-Nov.3, 1991 (30 performances) J.B. Matthews in association with The Ensemble Studio Theatre (Kate Baggott, Producer) present:

**Stan Freeman in "At Wit's End"** (*Thomas A. Werner*)

**Will Lyman, Gretchen Walther in "The Novelist"** (*Carol Rosegg*)

**THE NOVELIST** by Howard Fast; Director, Sam Schacht; Sets, Jane Clark; Costumes, Kitty Leech; Lighting, Victor En Yu Tan; Music Arrangement, Joseph Bloch; Graphic Design, Denny Tillman; Stage Manager, Sara Gormley Plass; Press, Peter Cromarty/David B. Katz CAST: Gretchen Walther (Jane Austin), Will Lyman (Thomas Crighton)
A drama in two acts. the action takes place in Chawton, Hampshire, England in Apr 1817.

(Intar) Wednesday, Oct.9-Nov.10, 1991 (33 performances) Intar Hispanic American Arts Center (Max Ferra, Artistic Director) presents:
**OUR LADY OF THE TORTILLA** by Luis Santeiro; Director, Max Ferra; Sets, Charles E. McCarry; Lighting, Michael Chybowski; Costumes, Claudia Stephens; Sound, Gary Harris; Press, Peter Cromarty/David Lotz CAST: Carmen Rosario (Delores Cantu), Oscar de la Fe Colon (Nelson Cruz), Ilka Tanya Payan (Dahlia Cruz, Catherine Cobb Ryan (Beverly Barnes), Gary Perez (Eddy Cruz), Genevieve Daniels (Voice of Valerie Spinetti)
A comedy in two acts. The action takes place in a Latin New Jersey neighborhood a present.

**Catherine Cobb Ryan, Oscar de la Fe Colon in "Our Lady of the Tortilla"** (*Carol Rosegg*)

(Lamb's Little Theatre) Thursday, Oct.10, 1991- Lambs Theatre Co. presents:
**PROMISED LAND** with Music/Lyrics/Book by George Fischoff; Director, Peter Bennett; Choreography, Mercedes Ellington; Sets, Peter Harrison; Costumes, Kathry Wagner; Lighting, Robert Jared; Prod. Manager, Clark Cameron; General Manager, Nancy Nagel Gibbs; Stage Manager, Rachel S. Levine; Press, Chris Boneau/John Barlow, Adrian Bryan-Brown CAST: Dana Cote (Joshua), Jahneen (Pharoh's Daughter), Michael Oberlander (Pharaoh), Wendy Oliver (Zipporah), Francis Ruiviv (Moses)
A musical based on biblical tale of Moses and the Exodus from Egypt.

(Ohio Theatre) Thursday, Oct.10-20, 1991 (10 performances) Arden Party presents:
**UBU ROI** by Alfred Jarry; Director, Karin Coonrod; Lighting, Darrel Maloney CAST: Leslie Bogerhoff, Mary Christopher, Thom Garvey, James Urbaniak
The 1896 tragicomedy about war and power.

**84**    **James Urbaniak, Mary Christopher in "Ubu Roi"** (*Ken Van Sickle*)

po Cultral Center) Thursday, Oct.10-27, 1991 (16 performances) Signature
re Co. presents:
**SORROWS OF FREDERICK**; Written/Directed by Romulus Linney; Set, E.
Cosier; Lighting, Jeffrey S. Koger; Costumes, Teresa Snider-Stein; Stage
ager, James Marr; Press/Artistic Director, James Houghton CAST: Fred Burrell
erick William I), Claude D. File (Chancelor), Austin Pendleton (Frederick the
), Garrison Philips (Voltaire), Kernan Bell, Bryant Bradshaw, James Coyle,
a Commings, Elliot Fox, Mitchell Riggs, T. Ryder Smith, Richard Thomsen,
Woodson
vised version of the 1967 drama.

napalus) Friday, Oct.11-27, 1991 (13 performances) Quinapalus Theatre Co.
nts:
**ROVER** by Aphra Behn; Director, Joseph Garren; Costumes, Jeanne Bosse;
Anthony Ferrer; Fights, Michael G. Chin; Stage Manager, Ali Sherwin CAST:
e Balthrop, Bill Christ, David Conaway, Mark Edward Lang, Susan McBrien,
Parker, Daniel Platten, Kay Rothman, Janet Rust, Tony Rust, Donald Sadler,
Schmidt, Virginia Thomas, Ovidio Vargas, Tim Zay
estoration swashbuckler.

ed Angels) Friday, Oct.11-28, 1991 (14 performances) Naked Angels presents:
ARKER PURPOSE by Wendy Riss; Director, Charlie Schulman; Sets, George
s; Lighting, Jeffrey Whitsett; Costumes, Rosi Zingales; Sound, Charlie Bugbee
Music, Jonathan Larson; Advisor, Pippin Parker; Producers, Beth Emelson, Dana
; Stage Managers, Katherine Lumb, Ralph Fleischer CAST: Lisa Beth Miller
d Singer), Julianne Hoffenberg, Deborah Karpel (Backup Singers), Bruce
Vittie (Philip), Timothy Britten Parker (Frankie), Michael Mastrototaro (Paulie),
Jones (Joey), Jodie Markell (Louise), Bradley White (Mickey), Jim Broaddus
gman), Merrill Holtzman (Jack), Fisher Stevens (Wolf), Andrew Geotz (Man with
ken Arm)

antic Theatre) Friday, Oct.11-Dec.1, 1991 (39 performances and 4 previews)
ntic Theatre Co. by special arrangement with Evangeline Morphos Brinkley and
cy Richards presents:
TANT FIRES by Kevin Heelan; Director, Clark Gregg; Sets, Kevin Rigdon;
ting, Howard Werner; Costumes, Sarah Edwards; Stage Manager, Matthew Silver;
s, Jim Baldassare CAST: David Wolos-Fonteno (Raymond), Todd Weeks

**Garrison Phillips, Austin Pendleton in
"Sorrows of Frederick" (*Susan Johann*)**

**Ray Anthony Thomas, Giancarlo Esposito, Jordan Lage in
"Distant Fires" (*Carol Rosegg*)**

(Angel), Giancarlo Esposito succeeded by Isiah Washington (Foos), Ray Anthony
Thomas (Thomas), Jordan Lage (Beauty), Jack Wallace (General)
A drama in two acts. The action takes place in Ocean City, MD at present.

(Wings) Saturday, Oct.12-Nov.3, 1992 (24 performances) Wings Theatre Co. presents:
**DREAM MAN** by James Carroll Pickett and **INTIMACIES** by Michael Kearns;
Artistic Director/Press, Jeffery Corrick CAST: Michael Kearns
Two one-man pieces dealing with sex and AIDS.

(Provincetown Playhouse) Saturday, Oct.12-Nov.24, 1991 (60 performances) Al
Corley, Bart Rosenfeld & Marcy Drogin present:
**SERVY-N-BERNICE 4EVER** by Seth Zvi Rosenfeld; Director, Terry Kinney; Sets,
Edward T. Gianfrancesco; Costumes, Judy Dearing; Lighting, Kenneth Posner; Sound,
Jeffrey Taylor; Stage Manager, M.A. Howard; Press, Peter Cromarty/ David B. Katz,
David Lotz CAST: Lisa Gay Hamilton (Bernice), Cynthia Nixon (Carla), Ron Eldard
(Servy), Erik King (Scotty)
A drama in two acts. The action takes place in Boston and New York City at present.

(Open Eye Theatre) Saturday, Oct.12-Dec.29, 1991 (12 performances) Open Eye New
Stagings presents:
**EAGLE OR SUN** by Sabina Berman; Translation, Isabel Saez; Director/Editor, Amie
Brockway; Press, Shirley Herz/Sam Rudy CAST: Doug Jewell, Joey Chavez, Maria
A. Merullo, Ricky Genaro, Tara Mallen, John DiLeo
A drama on the destruction of the Aztec empire.

**Cynthia Nixon, Lisa Gay Hamilton, Erik King, Ron Eldard in
"Servy-n-Bernice 4Ever" (*Carol Rosegg*)**

**Donna English, Susan Mansur, Joel Vig, Joanne Baum in "Ruthless"**
*(Carol Rosegg)*

(Musical Theatre Works) Wednesday, Oct.16-Nov.2, 1991 (12 performances)
Reopened at Players Theatre Friday Mar.13, 1992-Jan.24, 1993 (302 performances and
40 previews) Musical Theatre Works (Anthony J. Stimac, Artistic Director), Kim Lang
Lenny, Wolfgang Bocksch and Jim Lenny present:
**RUTHLESS!** with Music by Marvin Laird; Lyrics/Book/Direction, Joel Paley;
Musical Directors, Mr. Laird, Dennis Buck; Sets, James Noone, Jeffrey Rathaus;
Costumes, Gail Cooper-Hecht, Mr. Rathaus; Lighting, Kenneth Posner; Sound, Tom
Sorce; Stage Manager, Pamela Edington; Press, Jeffrey Richards/David LeShay- Keith
Sherman CAST: Joel Vig succeeded by Sylvia Miles (Sylvia St. Croix), Donna
English (Judy Denmark), Laura Bundy (Tina Denmark), Susan Mansur succeeded by
Adinah Alexander (Myra Thorn/Reporter), Rae C. Wright (Myra-*Musical Theatre
Works)*, Joanne Baum (Louise Lerman/Eave), Rose Addesso (Louise-*MTW)* , Denise
Lor (Lita Encore)
MUSICAL NUMBERS: Tina's Mother, Born to Entertain, Talent, To Play This Part,
Third Grade, Where Tina Gets It From, Pippi Song, Kisses and Hugs, I Hate Musicals,
Angel Mom, A Penthouse Apartment, It Will Never Be That Way Again, Parents and
Children, Ruthless , In *MTW* prod: Tap Shoes, My Poodle Puddles, Sleep Now My
Child
  A musical comedy in two acts (one-act in *MTW* version). The action takes place in
Small Town, USA and New York City over a four year span.

(Synchronicity Space) Thursday, Oct.17-Nov.3, 1991 (16 performances) Art & Work
Ensemble presents:
**120 SECONDS** by Andrew Young; Director, Anthony DiPietro CAST: Nancy Castle
(Phyllis Babbs), David Frank (Dr. Harold Brogan), Curtis Anderson (Dr. Albert
Sweet), Tricia Kiley (Dr. Rebecca Sanford), Martha Gilpin (Elena Martinez)

(Theatre 22) Thursday, Oct.17-Nov.3, 1991 (12 performances) Oberon Theatre
Ensemble presents:
**ROSMERSHOLM** by Henrik Ibsen; Director, Richard Albert CAST: Mary Ann
Conk, Jim Connors, Michele Cuomo, Philip Cuomo, Tom Trenkle, Thomas F. Walsh
  The 1886 drama.

**86**

**Donna English, Laura Bundy in "Ruthless"** *(Carol Rosegg)*

...eatre at St. Paul & St. Andrew) Thursday, Oct.17-Nov.10, 1991 (16 performances) ...terfold/CAF present:

...E MALE ANIMAL by James Thurber and Elliott Nugent; Director, Robert ...ain; Producer, Mary Grace; Sets/Lighting, Kevin Ash; Stage Manager, Kim Wells ...ST: Becket Royce (Ellen Turner), John Eisner (Tommy Turner), Allegra Growdon ...ricia Stanley), Joshua Simon (Wally Myers), David Vogel (Dean Damon), James ...dsky (Michael Barnes), Jay Hammer (Joe Ferguson), Yvette Edelhart (Blanche ...non), Jim Siatowski (Ed Keller), Ann Yocum (Myrtle Keller), Ilene Lisak (Nutsy ...er), Kim Wells (Reporter)
...comedy in three acts. the action takes place in a mid-western university town, ...0.

...medy Cellar) Thursday, Oct.17-Dec.1, 1991 Comedy Cellar presents:
...SOLUTELY RUDE with Music/Lyrics by Rick Crom; Direction/Vocal ...angements, John McMahon; Lighting, Sean Haines; Press, Pete Sanders/Matt Lenz ...ST: Mark-Alan, Rick Crom, Frankie Mayo, Virginia McMath, Amy Ryder, Heidi ...llenhauer
...SICAL NUMBERS: The Tacky Opening Number, Party Line, Guardian Angels, ...Fine!, Reunion, Pee Wee's Warning, If I Only Were the Pope, Urge Durge, First ...ies First, You Don't Need Me Anymore, Kitty's Turn, Straight Man, Cole Porter's ...· Trek, Close That Show!, One Last Prince, Sondheim's Oklahoma, Tacky Closing ...mber

...thedral of St. John the Divine), Saturday Oct.19, 1991 (1 performance)
...ACE FOR GRACE by Robert Wilson; Press, Bruce Cohen CAST: Jessye ...rman, Philip Glass, Richard Landry, The Silver Belles, Christopher Knowles ...n experimental work for sound, light and air.

...lksbiene Playhouse) Saturday, Oct.19, 1991-Jan.12, 1992 (39 performances)
...E MARRIAGE CONTRACT by Edhraim Kishon; Yiddish Translation, Isreal ...ker; Director, Howard Rossen; Set, Harry Lines; Costumes, Susan Sigrist; Lighting, ...an Baron; Music, Ed Linderman; Arrangements, Barry Levitt; Stage Manager, ...ith Scher; Press, Max Eisen/Madelon Rosen CAST: David Rogow (Elimelech ...rozovsky), Zypora Spaisman (Shifra), Shira Flam (Ayala), Richard Carlow (Robert ...all), Diana Cypkin (Yaffa Birnbaum), Sandy Levitt (Buki)
...comedy with music in two acts. The action takes place in Tel-Aviv, early 1950s.

...anhattan Church of Christ) Wednesday, Oct.23-Nov.9, 1991 (12 performances)
...IE LOVING KNIFE by Albert Asermely; Director, Ross Meyerson; Set, Jannike ...ss; Lighting, Steve Greenberg; Costumes, Robert R. Bulla; Sound, Mark A. ...rlson; Press, Barbara Atlee CAST: Mihran Guian (Samir), George Michael Fenney ...ild), John Budzyna, Kari Luther, Christopher Brady, Adriana Inchaustegui, Brian ...ott, Walter Krochmal
...twenty-five year old drama predicting the Iraqi turmoil. The action takes place in ...ghdad, 1958.

...heatre Off Park) Thursday, Oct.24-Nov.8, 1991 (12 performances and 4 previews) ...el Wing Rep. Co. presents:
...FTH OF JULY by Lanford Wilson; Director, Richard Lollo; Sets, Eric Harriz; ...stumes, Cynthia Dumont; Lighting, David Lander; Producer, Elizabeth Bancroft; ...ge Manager, Lisa Gavaletz; Press, Chris Boneau/Bob Fennell CAST: Scott Mackin ...en), Jeff Gregory (Jed), Jill Perin (Gwen), John McNamara (John), Stephanie ...aylor (Shirley), Elizabeth Bancroft (June), Terese Hayden (Sally), Lee Scotten ...eston)
..., play in two acts. The action takes place near Lebanon, Missouri in the summer of ...77.

...ne Dream Theatre) Thursday, Oct.24-Nov.17, 1991 transferred to Intar Tuesday, ...c.3-15, 1991 Miranda d'Ancona, Doris Kaufman & Zaluma and Prima Artists ...esent:
...IE DROPPER; Written/Directed by Ron McLarty; Sets, Stephen Olson; Lighting, ...chael Stiller; Costumes, Traci de Gesu; Music, Wayne Joness; Stage Manager, Scott ...gg; Press, David Rothenberg CAST: Wendy Scharfman (Mo Polleni), Nick ...angiulio (Jack Polleni), Bob Horen (Old Shoe Horn), John Dawson Beard (Bobby ...rn), Richard Long (Young Shoe Horn)
...drama in two acts. The action takes place in Warrington, England and Bridgeton, ...aine between 1910-84.

**Heidi Mollenhauer, Frankie Maio, Rick Crom, Amy Ryder, (front) Mark-Alan in "Absolutely Rude"**

**Dian Cypkin, Shira Flam, Zypora Spaisman in "Marriage Contract"** (*Rebecca Lesher*)

LEFT: **Wendy Scharfman, Bob Horen**
RIGHT: **Richard Long, John Beard in "The Dropper"** (*Alex Rupert*)

**Elaine Stritch, Margaret Whiting in
"Rodgers and Hart Revue"** (*Carol Rosegg*)

**Carol A. Honda, Shizuko Hoshi, Mary Lee, (front) Constance
Boardman in "Dressing Room"** (*Carol Rosegg*)

(Ohio Theatre) Friday, Oct.25-Nov.3, 1991 (10 performances) T.W.E.E.D. in
association with Neo Labos Dancetheatre presents:
**ATOMIC OPERA**; Created by Kevin Malony, Michele Elliman & John O'Malley;
Concept/Text/Direction, Mr. Maloney; Choreography, Mr. O'Malley, Ms. Elliman;
Costumes, Anne Patterson; Lighting, Richard Schaefer; Score/Sound, Douglas J.
Cuomo; Production Design, Alexander Brebner; Press, Chris Boneau/Bob Fennell
CAST: Torrin Cummings, Michele Elliman, Audrey Fort, Lisa Gillette, Peggy Gould,
Renate Graziadei, Mia Kim, David McGrath, John O'Malley, Colleen O'Neill, Craig
Victor VOICES: Marleen Menard, Ernie Shaheen, Wade Oates, Stephen Pell, Kevin
Scullin, Diane Tyler, Lisa Carballo, Alex Guthrie
   A music theatre piece tracing the evolution of the Atomic Age.

(Atlantic Theatre) Friday, Oct.25-Nov.10, 1991 (12 performances) Atlantic Theatre
Co. presents:
**REUNION** by David Mamet; Director, Jordan Lage; Lighting, Howard Werner; Stage
Manager, Pamela Jean Schaffer; Press, Jim Baldassare CAST: Jack Wallace (Bernie),
Mary McCann (Carol)
   The action takes place in Bernie's apartment one March afternoon.

(Rainbow & Stars) Tuesday, Oct.29-Nov.23, 1991 (40 performances) Rainbow & Stars
presents:
**THE RODGERS AND HART REVUE**; Conceived/Produced by Steve Paul and
Greg Dawson; Musical Director, Fred Wells; Press, Jessica Miller/David Lotz CAST:
Elaine Stritch, Margaret Whiting, Judy Kuhn, Jason Graae, Jay Leonhart, Joe Cocuzzo,
Fred Wells
   A musical songbook.

(Judith Anderson Theatre) Tuesday, Oct.29-Nov.24, 1991 (28 performances) The
Women's Project & Productions (Julia Miles, Artistic Director) presents:
**APPROXIMATING MOTHER** by Kathleen Tolan; Director, Gloria Muzio; Sets,
David Jenkins; Costumes, Elsa Ward; Lighting, Jackie Manassee; Sound, Mark

Bennett; Stage Manager, Robert L. Young; Press, Fred Nathan/Merle Frimark CA
Mia Dillon (Molly), Shawana Kemp (Brena), Deidre O'Connell (Fran), Tonya Pin
(Ellie/Sylvia/Grace), Richard Poe (Jack/Eugene), Steven Ryan (Mac), Ali Thomas
(Jen)
   A drama performed without intermission. The action takes place in New York Ci
and Indiana at present.

(Playhouse 46) Tuesday, Oct.29-Nov.30, 1991 (25 performances and 5 previews) P
Asian Rep. (Tisa Chang, Artistic Director) presents:
**THE DRESSING ROOM** by Kunio Shimizu; Translation, John K. Gillespie;
Adaptor/Dramaturg, Chiori Miyagawa; Director, Kati Kuroda; Lighting, Tina
Charney; Composer, Bert Moon; Sets, Atsushi Moriyasu; Costumes, Eiko Yamagu
Sound, Ty Sanders; Stage Manager, Sue Jane Stoker; Press, Ted Killmer CAST:
Shizuko Hoshi (Actress A), Carol A. Honda (Actress B), Constance Boardman
(Actress C), Mary Lee (Actress D)
   A surreal drama performed without intermission. the action takes place in a theatr
dressing room.

(Circle in the Square Downtown) Tuesday, Oct.29-May 17, 1992 (218 performance
Susan Quint Gallin, Calvin Skaggs, Susan Wexler, Judith Resnick and Oprah Winf
present:
**FROM THE MISSISSIPPI DELTA** by Dr. Endesha Mae Holland; Director,
Jonathan Wilson; Sets/Costumes, Eduardo Sicangco; Lighting, Allen Lee Hughes;
Sound, Rob Milburn, David Budries; Traditional Music Arranged and Performed by
Michael Bodeen, Mr. Milburn; General Manager, Dana Sherman; Stage Managers,
Anthony Berg, Lydia J. Fox; Press, Jeffrey Richards/David LeShay CAST: Sybil
Walker (Woman One), Jacqueline Williams (Woman Two), Cheryl Lynn Bruce
(Woman Three), SUCCEEDING ACTORS: Tempestt Bledsoe, Shona Tucker
   A drama in two acts. The action takes place in the South and Midwest from the ea
1940s to the mid-1980s.

**Tonya Pinkins, Mia Dillon, Diedre O'Connell in
"Approximating Mother"** (*Martha Holmes*)

**Cheryl Lynn Bruce, Sybil Walker, Jacqueline Williams in
"From the Mississippi Delta"** (*T. Charles Erickson*)

**Ernestine Jackson, Carmen De Lavallade in "Island Memories"** (*Carol Rosegg*)

**Julie Ziegler, Adrian Davey, Bill Sorvillo in "Paradise Lost"** (*Gerry Goodstein*)

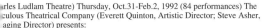

arles Ludlam Theatre) Thursday, Oct.31-Feb.2, 1992 (84 performances) The culous Theatrical Company (Everett Quinton, Artistic Director; Steve Asher, aging Director) presents:
**EBEARD** by Charles Ludlam; Director, Everett Quinton; Sets, T. Greenfield; umes, Toni Nanette Thompson; Lighting, Richard Currie; Music/Sound, Jim rak; Props, Tom Moore; Stage Manager, Karen Ott; Press, Judy Jacksina/Robin chek CAST: Kevin Scullin (Sheemish), Stephen Pell (Mrs. Maggot), Brian Neil vitch (Lamia, the Leopard Woman), Everett Quinton (Khanazar von Bluebeard), vn Nacol (Good Angel/Bad Angel), Lisa Herbold (Sybil), Bill Graber (Rodney er), Eureka (Miss Cubbidge), H.M. Koutoukas (Hecate)
elodrama in three acts. The action takes place off the Maine coast.

Rep. Theatre) Friday, Nov.1-5, 1991 (5 performances) Ubu Repertory presents:
**AND MEMORIES** by Ina Césaire; Translation, Christiane Makward, Judith er; Director, Dianne Kirksey-Floyd; Set, Jane Sablow; Lighting, Zebedee Collins; umes, Carol Ann Pelletier; Dance/Music Consultant, Marie Brooks; Sound, hael Sargeant; Press, Peter Cromarty/Lynne McCreary CAST: Carmen De allade (Aure), Ernestine Jackson (Hermance)

cadero) Friday, Nov.1-16, 1991 (9 performances) Crooked Foot Prods. presents:
**DOWN!!! CONVERSATIONS WITH THE MOB**; Written/Directed by Sam ry Kass; Set, Kimberly Stroup; Scenic Artist, Jim Myers; Lighting/Sound, George eron; Press, David Rothenberg CAST: Ray Mancini, Holt McCallany, Nicholas arro
ee short plays about men on the wrong side of the law.

fman Theatre) Friday, Nov.1, 1991-Jan.1992 Martin R. Kaufman presents:
**LE PORTER AT THE KAUFMAN: COLE & COWARD**; Set, Phillip win; Lighting, Douglas O'Flaherty; Press, John and Gary Springer CAST: Julie son, William Roy

rold Clurman Theatre) Tuesday, Nov.5-17, 1991 (14 performances) Opening Doors uctions (Jay B. Lesiger, Gen. Manager; Tom Klebba, Artistic Director) presents:
**MPANY** with Music/Lyrics by Stephen Sondheim; Book, George Furth; Director, Klebba; Musical Director, Milton Granger; Choreography, Don Johanson; Sets,

Bryan Johnson; Costumes, Norman Sweet; Lighting, Tracy Lee Wilson; Stage Manager, Irma Csermak; Press, Jay B. Lesiger CAST: Alan Osburn (Robert), Bette Glenn (Sarah), David Edwards (Harry), Kate Newlon (Susan), Steven Hauck (Peter), Cynthia Marty (Jenny), Steven Tracy Ross (David), Connie Baker (Amy), Tom Dusenbury (Paul), Jane Wasser (Joanne), Joseph Culliton (Larry), Joanne Lessner (Marta), Eileen Kaden (Kathy), Susan Hackett (April)
MUSICAL NUMBERS: Company, Little Things You Do Together, Sorry-Grateful, You Could Drive a Person Crazy, Have I Got a Girl for You, Someone is Waiting, Another Hundred People, Getting Married Today, Side by Side, What Would We Do Without You, Poor Baby, Tick Tock, Barcelona, Ladies Who Lunch, Being Alive
The 1970 musical in two acts. The action takes place in New York City. An Equity Fights Aids Production.

(Mazur Theatre) Wednesday, Nov.6-23, 1991 (14 performances) Playwright Preview Productions present:
**LAMB ON FIRE** by Phillip DePoy; Director, Andrew Burgreen; Music, Klimchak; Design, Anne Cox; Costumes, Robin Orloff; Lighting, Jeff Koger; Press, Laurel Spielman CAST: Jennifer Johnson, Scott Weir
The relationship of Charles and Mary Lamb during the 1800s

(Acting Studio) Wednesday, Nov.6-23, 1991 (14 performances) James Price, The Acting Studio, and Chelsea Repertory Co. Ensemble present:
**PARADISE LOST** by Clifford Odets; Director, John Grabowski; Set, Jay Durrwachter; Costumes, Robin Goldwasser; Lighting, Warren Karp CAST: Scott Ambrozy (Pike), Adrian Davey (Ben), Eddie Diaz (Paul), Robert Edwards (Williams), Gregory Fensterman (Gordon), Thom Hansen (Foley), Christian Jones (Felix), Joan Kindel (Bertha), Barbara Lynch (Clara), Janeene Maze (Libby), Peter Nevargic (May), Bart O'Brien (Post/Detective), Elizabeth Parish (Lucy), Michael Ricca, Bob Rueda, Benjamin Schiff (Cameraman/Detective), Bill Sorvillo (Julie), Christopher Torres (Kewpie), Edward Veneziano (Katz), John Austin Wiggins (Michaels), Zoran Zdravkovitch (Schnabel), Julie Ziegler (Pearl)
The 1936 drama in three acts. The action takes place in a middle class city neighborhood, 1934.

**Julie Wilson**

**Edwina Moore, Hugh Dane in "Willie & Esther"** (*James Russell*)

(Astor Place Theatre) Thursday, Nov.7, 1991-still playing May 31, 1992  Mark Dunn
and Makoto Deguchi present:
TUBES; Created and Written by Matt Goldman, Phil Stanton, Chris Wink,; Director,
Marlene Swartz; Artistic Coordinator; Caryl Glaab; Sets, Kevin Joseph Roach; Lighting,
Brian Aldous; Costumes, Lydia Tanji, Patricia Murphy; Sound, Raymond Schilke;
Computer Graphics, Kurisu-Chan; Stage Manager, Kevin Cunningham; Press, David
Rothenberg  CAST: Blue Man Group (Matt Goldman, Phil Stanton, Chris Wink)
 An evening with the performance group, performed without intermission.

illage Theatre) Wednesday, Nov.6-Dec.1, 1991 (19 performances) Village Theatre
. presents:
**IE RIVERS AND RAVINES** by Heather MacDonald; Director, Henry Fonte;
stumes, Marjorie Feenan; Set, Allen D. Hahn; Lighting, Douglas O'Flaherty;
und, Rick Sirois  CAST: Michelle Berke, Matthew Caldwell, Michael Curran,
san Farwell, Marjorie Feenan, Christie Harrington, Randy Kelly, Terrence Martin,
vid McConnell, Julia McLaughlin, Howard Thoresen, Zeke Zaccaro

'th St. Theatre) Thursday, Nov.7, 1991- Fontana Entertainment presents:
**ILLIE & ESTHER** by James Graham Bronson; Director, Diann McCannon; Stage
anager, Trell; Producers, Bern Nadette Stanis, Debbie Lytle; Press, Francine L.
evens/Robert J. Weston, Daphne Dennis  CAST: Hugh Dane, Emitt Thrower
illie), Bern Nadette Stanis (Esther)
. comedy in two acts. The action takes place outside of a Los Angeles bank.

valon Rep. Theatre) Thursday, Nov.7-24, 1991 (16 performances) Spectrum Stage
sents:
**' FOOTE: Two One-Acts By Horton Foote**; Sets, Lee Gundersheimer, Tanya
rduik; Costumes, Alyson Hui; Lighting, Michael Lincoln, Jennifer Primosch; Sound,
chael Grumer; Stage Managers, Georgia Buchanan, Michelle Cote
**IE MIDNIGHT CALLER**; Director, Emma Walton  CAST: Frances Robertson
ma Jean Jordan), Sheri Matteo (Cutie Spencer), Margaret Ritchie (Miss Rowena
uglas), Alice McLane (Mrs. Crawford), Charles Derbyshire (Mr. Ralph Johnston),
ti Specht (Helen Crews), Stephen Hamilton (Harvey Weems)
**IE OIL WELL**; Director, Stephanie Cassel Scott  CAST: Joan Matthiessen (Mrs.
ula Thornton), Nancy Jo Carpenter (Thelma Doris Thornton), Ian Cohen (Man),
lan Green (George Weems), Jack Poggi (Will Thornton), Kirk Tatnall (2nd Man),
cholas Eastman (Roy Thornton), Jacqueline DeCosmo (Mamie Bledsoe)

arles Ludlam Theatre) Friday, Nov.8-Dec.19, 1991 resumed full time Feb.14-June
1992 (74 performances) The Ridiculous Theatrical Co. presents:
**IE BELLS** by Leopold Lewis; Adapted from *The Polish Jew* by MM. Erckmann
Chatrian; Adapted again by Everett Quinton; Score, Mark Bennett; Press, Judy
ksina  CAST: Everett Quinton
late night attraction performed without intermission.

Barts Playhouse) Friday, Nov.8-24, 1991 (14 performances) St. Bart's Playhouse
sents:
**MN YANKEES** with Music/Lyrics by Richard Adler and Jerry Ross; Book,
rge Abbott and Douglas Wallop based on Wallop's novel *The Year The Yankees*
*t The Pennant ;* Director, Christopher Catt; Musical Director, Craig Kienle;
oreography, Kathi Jo Hubner; Sets, Nephelie Andonyadis; Costumes, Estella Marie;
hting, Karen Spahn; Sound, Kevin Mochel; Producer, Brett A. Crawford; Stage
nager, Tracey Cassidy; Press, Peter Cromarty/Lynne McCreary  CAST: Eric B.
telheim (Joe), Elizabeth Yawitz (Meg), Michael Waxenberg (Applegate), Jerilyn
kler (Doris), Catherine Yerly (Sister), Lucas Torres (Joe Hardy), John J. Bennett
nry), Richard Van Slyke (Sohovik), Steve Sabowitz (Smokey), Keith Garsson (Van
en), Bruce Lloyd (Rocky), Joann Baney (Gloria), Ken Altman (Welch), Lesley
menthal (Lola), Katherine Beitner (Miss Weston), Ferris Mack (Commisioner),

**Everett Quinton in "The Bells"**

**Ferris Mack, Bruce Lloyd, Jeff Peters, Lucas Torres in
"Damn Yankees" (Blanche Mackey)**

Mark A. Modano (Linville), Jeffery Peters (Postmaster), Ann Vawter, Nancy Young
MUSICAL NUMBERS: Six Months Out of Every Year, Goodbye Old Girl, Heart,
Shoeless Joe From Hannibal MO., A Man Doesn't Know, A Little Brains A Little
Talent, Whatever Lola Wants, Who's Got the Pain, The Game, Near To You, Those
Were the Good Old Days, Two Lost Souls, Finale
  The 1955 musical in two acts. The action takes place in Washington, D.C.

(Symphony Space) Sunday, Nov.10, 1991 (1 performance) New York Gilbert &
Sullivan Players present:
**PRINCESS IDA** with Music by Arthur Sullivan; Lyrics/Book, W.S. Gilbert; Musical
Director, Al Bergeret; Press, Francine L. Trevens/Robert J. Weston  CAST: John
Rubinstein (King Gama), Linda Milani (Princess Ida), Joy Hermalyn (Lady Blance),
Kae Egan (Lady Psyche), Jan Holland (Melissa), Philip Reilly, Paul Tomasko, Richard
Slade, Richard Holmes, Del-Bourree Bach (Arac), Michael Collins (Guron), Samuel
Shaw (Scynthius)
  The 1894 operetta.

(Ubu Rep Theatre) Tuesday, Nov.12-16, 1991 (5 performances) Ubu Repertory
presents:
**THE HILLS OF MASSABIELLE** by Maryse Conde; Translation, Richard Philcox;
Director, Cynthia Belgrave; Set, Jane Sablow; Lighting, Zebedee Collins; Costumes,
Carol Ann Pelletier; Press, Peter Cromarty/Lynn McCreary  CAST: April Armstrong
(Luana), Oliver Barrero (Sylvain), Arthur French (Reynalda), Clebert Ford (Theonce),
Yvette Hawkins (Titine), Robert Jimenez (Jean-Marie), Jack Landron (Leandre),
Cynthia Martells (Judith), Roger Chazz Robinson (Asst.)

**Liz Daniels, Mark Malone in "Night Dance" (*Carol Rosegg*)**

(Soho Rep Theatre) Thursday, Nov.14-24, 1991 (11 performances) The Basic Theatre presents:
**OFF THE BEAT & PATH**; Sets/Lighting, Marc D. Malamud; Costumes, Patty Burke, Jared Hammond; Stage Manager, Susan "Q" Gutmann ; *Mr. Big Stuff* by Ben Sahl; Director, Katherine Mayfield CAST: Nicolas Glaeser, Spruce Henry; *Five Burgers* by Jay Amari and Ben Sahl; Director, Jared Hammond CAST: Spruce Henry, Tom Spivey; *Words, Words, Words* by David Ives; Director, Robert Lee Martini CAST: Sarah Ford, Nicolas Glaeser, Jared Hammond; *a.k.a. Marleen* by Carol K. Mack; Director, Gary C. Walter CAST: Sheri Delaine, Loretta Toscano, Katherine Mayfield, Spruce Henry; *Sunstroke* by Ronald Ribman; Director, W.D. Charlton CAST: Craig Alan Edwards, David Goldman, Tom Spivey, Elizabeth Ann Townsend; *The Conquest of Everest* by Arthur Kopit; Director, Chuck Ferrero CAST: Eric Brandenburg, Margaret Burnham, Michael G. Chin; *Sure Thing* by David Ives; Director, Lester Shane CAST: Mindi L. Lyons, John Edmond Morgan
  Seven zany one-acts.

(Theatre at 224 Waverly Place) Thursday, Nov.14-30,1991 (15 performances) Cameron Merrick and the Scandalous Minds Theatre Co. present:
**I CAN'T STOP SCREAMING** by Andy Halliday; Director, Jeff Mousseau; Sets, Sherri Adler; Costumes, Bryant Hoven; Lighting, Eric Cornwall; Wigs, Elizabeth Katherine Carr, Sal Salandra; Stage Manager, Margaret Bodriguian; Press, Shirley Herz/Sam Rudy CAST: Thomas Bolster (Frankie Dane), Alan Pratt (Biff Conklin), Bill Tripician (Mr. Pettijohn), Michael Latshaw (Steven Dewear), Linda Evanson (Lulu Wells), Charles Kelly (Mr. Monique), Louis Silvers (Ted Willis), Matt Lenz (Tuck Stevens), Andy Halliday (Winky Terwilliger), Sal Mistretta (Everson Vail), Elaine Rinehart (Dr. Noria Lattimore), Ralph Buckley (Voice of Terror)
  A psychological-screwball-comedy-murder-mystery-thriller in two acts. The action takes place at Miraculous Pictures in Hollywood in 1929.

(One Dream Theatre) Thursday, Nov.14-Dec.1, 1991 (13 performances) Curious Theatre presents:
**NIGHT DANCE** by Reynolds Price; Director, Neel Keller; Sets, Jeff McDonald; Lighting, Betsy Finston; Costumes, Gay Howard; Sound, Donna Riley; Stage Manager, Damond Gallagher; Press, Chris Boneau/Adrian Bryan Brown, Wayne Wolfe CAST: Tom McBride (Neal Avery), Alexandra Styron (Taw Avery), Elizabeth Ann Daniels (Genevieve Watkins), Kathy Gerber (Roma Avery), Robert Kerbeck (Porter Farwell), Paul Barry (Dob Watkins), Mark Malone (Wayne Watkins)
  A drama in two acts. The action takes place in a small town in eastern No. Carolina, 1945.

(Duality Playhouse) Thursday, Nov.14-Dec.8, 1991 (20 performances) P.I.A. Productions presents:
**SEVEN PILLARS OF WICA-DICK : A TRIUMPH**; Written and Performed by Mark Ameen; Director, Rich Rubin; Lighting, Susan Hamburger; Sets, Angelo Underhill; Press, David Rothenberg
  Impressions, in two acts, of a gay man's sexual and emotional journey through mind, matter, and politics.

(Triplex) Saturday, Nov.16-23, 1991 (6 performances and 1 preview) Triplex Performing Arts presents:
**THE GUISE** by David Mowat; Director, Brian Astbury; Sets/Costumes, Katrina Bryceland; Music, William Hetherington; Stage Manager, Tony Kerr; Press, Ted Killmer CAST: Tania-Jane Bowers (Jane/Janine), Karen Bowlas (Bridget), Timothy Chipping (Andrew Decayne), Karl Collins (Milenko), Michael Hodgson (Dab/Prynne), Carnine Sinclair (Beryl), Andrew Weale (Richard Daborne)
  A satirical drama performed by London's Arts Threshold ensemble.

**Andy Halliday (center) in "I Can't Stop Screaming"** (*David Morga*

**Tim Halligan, Maureen Silliman in "Voice of the Prairie"** (*Carol Rosegg*)

(Holy Trinity) Thursday, Nov.21-Dec.15, 1991 (15 performances) Triangle Theatr Co.(Michael Ramach, Producing Director) presents:
**VOICE OF THE PRAIRIE** by John Olive; Director, Richard Harden; Music, Pe Ostroushko; Costumes, Amanda J. Klein; Lighting, Nancy Collings; Sets, Evelyn Sakash; Sound, David Hunter Koch; Stage Manager, Cathy Diane Tomlin; Press, Baldassare CAST: Fred Burrell (Poppy/David/Watermelon Man/Frankie's Father) Tim Halligan (Davy/Leon/James), Maureen Silliman (Frankie/Francis/Susie)
  A play in two acts. The action takes place in various locales in the US, jumping b and forth between 1895 and 1923.

(Open Eye Theatre) Saturday, Nov.23-Dec.15,1991 (16 performances) Open Eye N Stagings (Amie Brockway, Artistic Director) presents:
**THE DEATH AND LIFE OF SHERLOCK HOLMES** by Suzan L. Zeder; base Sir Arthur Conan Doyle's stories; Director, Russell Treyz; Costumes, Marianne Powell-Parker; Sets, Adrienne J. Brockway; Lighting, Spencer Mass; Stage Manag James Marr; Press, Shirley Herz/Sam Rudy CAST: George Cavey (Watson), Arle Richards (Mrs. Hudson/Madame Bergolia), Jim Helsinger (Office Hopkins/Swiss Messenger), Kermit Brown (Arthur Conan Doyle), Mitchell Greenberg (Sherlock Holmes), Elton Beckett (Lestrade/Zoltan/Clay), Tara Mallen (Wiggins), Amanda Gronich (Mary Doyle)
  A mystery in two acts. The action takes place in and around London and Europe March, 1893.

**Michelle Fairley, Ian Fitzgibbon in "Shadow of a Gunman"** (*Tom Lawlor*)

...ary Stage) Sunday, Nov.24-Dec.22,1991 (24 performances) Primary Stages Co.
...nts:

**...SOLUTION** by Stuart Duckworth; Director, Seth Gordon; Set, Bob Phillips;
...ing, Allen D. Hahn; Costumes, Martha Bromelmeier; Sound, Gayle Jeffery; Stage
...ger, Joe Maguire  CAST: Daniel Ahearn (Richard), Justin Cozier (Steve), Leigh
...n (Esther), Shareen Powlett (Valerie), Anne Newhall (Judith)
...omedy set in Detroit, 1970.

...phony Space) Monday, Nov.25-Dec.8, 1991 (15 performances) The O'Casey
...tre Co. presents:

**...SHADOW OF A GUNMAN** by Sean O'Casey; Director, Shivaun O'Casey;
...Brien Vahey, Josie MacAvin; Costumes, Jan Bee Brown; Lighting, Rory
...pster; Sound, Paul Bull; Music, Tommy Sands; Producer, Sally deSousa; Stage
...ager, Bryan Young; Press, Patt Dale  CAST: Niall Buggy (Seumas Shields),
...ard Cooper (Tommy Owens), Michelle Fairley (Minnie Powell), Ian Fitzgibbon
...al Davoren), Pauline Flanagan (Mrs. Grigson), Stephen Gabis (Auxiliary),
...ard Holmes (Maguire), Doreen Keogh (Mrs. Henderson), Shauna Rooney
...ement Resident), Sean McCarthy (Mr. Grigson), George Vogel (Mr.
...gher/Landlord)
...923 drama in two acts. The action takes place in a Dublin tenement, 1920s.

...atre of Riverside Church) Wednesday, Nov.27-Dec.22, 1991 (23 performances)
... Federal Theatre and Woodie King, Jr. present:

**...N!** by Beverly Trader; Director, Thomas W. Jones II; Sets/Lighting, Richard
...on; Costumes, Gregory Glenn; Sound, Carmen Griffin; Musical Director/
...ger, Uzee Brown; Music Consultant, Oral Moses; Stage Manager, Lisa L.
...on; Press, Max Eisen/Madelon Rosen  CAST: David Edwards (Posey Maddox),
... Fitzgibbon (David Dobbs), Lee James Ganzer (Thorton Burk), Roberta Illg
...tha Knight Massey), Maurice Langley (Profit Glover), Kathleen Masterson
...abeth Dobbs), Ronald Richardson (Ephraim B. Rucker), Phyllis Stickney (Hetty
...eod), Neal Tate (Phillip Dobbs), Michele Denise Woods (Dicy Dobbs)
... action takes place in Georgia, 1836-66.

...atre for the New city) Friday, Nov.29-Dec.15, 1991 (15 performances)
**...LO MRS. PRESIDENT** with Music/Lyrics/Book/Direction/Set/Musical
...ction by Phoebe Legére; Press, Tony Origlio  CAST: LaVern Baker (Mary Lou
...nington)

...rry Lane Theatre) Wednesday, Dec.4-12, 1991 (1 performance and 9 previews)
...an Tyree presents:

**...NOISE OF '92:** *Diversions From The New Depression;*  Sets, Ann Davis;
...umes, Gregg Barnes; Lighting, Douglas O'Flaherty; Sound, Serge Ossorguine;
...eography, Tony Musco; Musical Arrangements, Mario Sprouse; Press, David
...enberg  CAST: Neilan Tyree, Mink Stole, Timi Michael (Marie-France), Tom
...s( Hector), Kit McClure and Her All-Girl Orchestra.
...nusical revue in two acts.

...r Stage II) Wednesday, Dec.4-15, 1991 (12 performances) Performers At Work
...tre Co. presents:

**...W LEOPARDS** by Martin Jones; Director, Todd Stuart Phillips; Set, Chris
...er; Costumes, Constance Hoffman; Lighting/Stage Manager, David Alan
...stock  CAST: Patrice Grullion, Joy Passey

...npo Cultral Center) Wednesday, Dec.4-22, 1991 (12 performances) Signature
...tre Co. presents:

**...THEN VALLEY** by Romulus Linney; Directors, Mr. Linney, James Houghton;
... E. David Cosier; Costumes, Teresa Snider-Stein; Lighting, Jeffrey S. Koger
...T: Scott Sowers (Starns), Richard Bowden, Celia Howard, Jim Ligon, Peter G.
...se, Ann Sheehy
...Appalachian drama.

**Ron Richardson, Phyllis Stickney in "Zion!"** (*Bert Andrews*)

**Kit McClure, Neilan Tyree, Mink Stole in
"The Big Noise of '92"** (*Marc Karzen*)

**Vince O' Brien, Natalie Ross, Tom Riis Farrell, Marcia DeBonis,
(front) Aaron Goodwin in "Greetings"** (*Anthony Abercrombie*)

(St. Peter's) Wednesday, Dec.4, 1991-Feb.9, 1992 (70 performances and 9 previews)
American Cabaret Theatre (Peter Ligeti, Producing Director) presents:

**I WON'T DANCE:** *Steve Ross Sings Fred Astaire*; Production Supervisor, Michael
Sommers; Text, Steve Ross, Mr. Sommers; Musical Arrangements, Wally Harper, Mr.
Ross, Bruno David Casolari; Set, Jean Valente; Lighting, Matt Berman; Sound,
Cynthia Daniels; Press, Chris Boneau/Adrian Bryan-Brown, Susanne Tighe, John
Barlow, Bob Fennell  CAST: Steve Ross
PROGRAM: Top Hat, The Way You Look Tonight/Funny Face, Fascinating
Rhythm/Lady Be Good, Dancing in the Dark, Please Don't Monkey with Broadway,
Easter Parade, Kalmer & Ruby Sequence, Say Young Man of Manhattan, City of the
Angels, A Lot in Common with You, Shall We Dance, It Only Happens When I Dance
with You, Let's Face the Music and Dance, Let Yourself Go, Nevertheless, Entr'acte,
They All Laughed, Leading Lady Sequence, I Guess I'll Have to Change My Plan,
Mittel-Europa Sequence, Night and Day, Puttin' on the Ritz/Steppin' Out with My
Baby, They Can't Take That Away, By Myself, Cheek to Cheek, Finale

**Steve Ross in "I Won't Dance"** (*Peter Ligeti*)

**93**

**(clockwise from center) Joseph Adams, Monica Carr, Vicki Lewis, Polly Pen, Karen Mason in "Don Juan..." (*Carol Rosegg*)**

(Morningside Gardens) Thursday, Dec.5-15, 1991 (8 performances) The Morning Players present:

**THE HELLS OF DANTE** by Harry Granick; Director, Blair Park; Costumes, Va Stewart; Stage Manager, Francine Berman; Music, Lewis Papier CAST: Theo Pol (Tony Ramese), Paul DuBois (Jim Hunter), Terry Ann Bennett (Abby Knowles), Karen Elaine Wells (Mae Saunders), Howard Atlee (Will Kerringer), Chance Kell (Blake Gattling)

A drama in three acts with one intermission. The play is a fictional parallel to the story of President Warren Harding.

(One Dream Theatre) Thursday, Dec.5-22, 1991 (15 performances) The Barrow G presents:

**GREETINGS** by Tom Dudzick; Eileen H. Dougherty; Sound, David Schnirman; Stage Manager, Marjorie S. Goodsell; Press, Robert Shampain CAST: Natalie Ro (Emily) , Aaron Goodwin (Mickey), Tom Riis Farrell (Andy), Marcia DeBonis (Randi), Vince O'Brien (Phil)

A comedy in two acts.

(Vineyard-26th St.) Thursday, Dec.5-29, 1991 Vineyard Theatre (Douglas Aibel, Artistic Director; Barbara Zinn Krieger, Executive Director; Jon Nakagawa, Mana Director) presents:

**THE DON JUAN AND THE NON DON JUAN** with Music by Neil Radisch; Ly James Milton,David Goldstein; Book, Mr. Milton ; Based on writings of Marvin Cohen; Director, Evan Yionoulis; Musical Director, Dale Rieling; Sets, William Barclay; Lighting, A.C. Hickox; Costumes, Teresa Snider-Stein; Musical Supervis Jan Rosenberg; Stage Manager, Renee Lutz; Press, Shirley Herz/Sam Rudy CAST Joseph Adams (Al Lehman/Tom Gervasi), Karen Mason (Marge/Others), Polly Pe (Danielle/June/Brigit/Executive/Others), Vicki Lewis (Bernice/May/Gregory/Othe Monica Carr (Phyllis/April/Harriet/Others)

MUSICAL NUMBERS: Intangible Tom, Hello My Name is Al, Tonight Tom, Obituary, I'll Be Gone, Al's Letter/Tom's Reply, Love and Making Love, Married, Sister Brigit's Curse, Al's Dream, You're Fired, Tom's Disguise, Divorce, Tom in Hell, Love is the Way That We Live

A musical performed without intermission. The setting is New York City at prese

(Naked Angels) Friday, Dec.6-21, 1991 Naked Angels and Amnesty International present:

**NAKED RIGHTS**; Producer, Jenifer Estess; Co-Directors, Jace Alexander, Paul S Eckstein; Coordinator, Julianne Hoffenberg;Sets, George Xenos; Lighting, Brian MacDevitt; Sound, Aural Fixation/Guy Sherman; Costumes, Rosi Zingales; Music/Music Director, Bruce Mack; Choreography, Aziza; Stage Manager, Jenny PROGRAM: Ariel Dorfman Poems
LUCKY by Jan Jalenak; Director, Novella Nelson CAST: Kevin Thigpen (Russell Jacinto Taras Riddick (J.C.), Jeff Williams (Harpo)
MY WOLVERINE by Nathaniel Kahn; Director, Christie Wagner CAST: Billy Strong (Man)
COQ AU VIN by Jon Robin Baitz; Director, Joe Mantello CAST: Patrick Breen (Michael), Bradley White (Terry), Gareth Williams (Man)
EMPATHY by Ned Eisenberg; Director, Veronica Brady CAST: Mary Alice (Flo Seller)
PAY-PER-KILL by Warren Leight; Director, Jace Alexander CAST: Bradley Whi (Host), Gareth Williams (Dennis Tom Hokamp), Kevin Thigpen (Shamus Hoving), Billy Strong (Darryl Gates), Piper Ross (Deborah Allen), David Marshall Grant (Fr John), Julianne Hoffenberg, Tim Ransom (Reporters), Leon Addison Brown (Elder Bishop), Suzanne Dottino (Sarah Anne), Richard Poe (Gov. Thompson), Paul S. Eckstein (Joseph Hoving), Jimmy Antoine, Lisa Beth Miller (Guards)
LIMBO by Pippin Parker; Director, Seret Scott CAST: Leon Addison Brown (Josa Richard Poe (Peter), Frederica Meister (Mrs. Wickham), Julianne Hoffenberg (Waitress)
THE SUFFERING COLONEL by Kenneth Lonergan; Director, Matthew Broderic CAST: Timothy Britten Parker (Col. Vasti), Gareth Williams (Tsolvek), Nicole Burdette (Mrs. Vasti), Tim Ransom, Andy Yerkes (Voices)
THROWING YOUR VOICE by Craig Lucas; Director, Jace Alexander; CAST: Da Marshall Grant (Doug), Jenifer Estess (Lucy), Tim Ransom (Richard), Lisa Beth Miller (Sarah)
SONS OF THE SAME LION by Charles Fuller; Director, Paul S. Eckstein CAST: Michael Wright (Soldier #1), O.L. Duke (Soldier #2), Jeff Williams, Jimmy Antoin (Voices)

**Klea Scott, Jacqueline Wolff in "Sins & Virtues Pt. 1"**

Reggie Montgomery, Bruce McCarty in
"Raft of the Medusa" (*Tom McGovern*)

Melanie Demitri, James Barbosa, in
"Mr. Shakespeare and Mr. Porter"

Robin Spielberg, (on couch) Kristen Johnston, Steven Goldstein,
amian Young, (top) Mary McCann, Neil Pepe in "Five Very Live"
(*Carol Rosegg*)

(Musical Theatre Works) Friday, Dec.6-23, 1991 (12 performances) Actors' Alliance Inc. presents:

**SINS & VIRTUES: PART 1**; Conceived/Directed by Melanie Sutherland CAST: Mary Birdsong, Ronna Jeffries, Nancy Learmonth, Christal Lockwood, Jo Ann Peritz, Carl Ritchie, Klea Scott, Jacqueline Wolff

PROGRAM: *Backyard Bob* by Alred Tessier, *But If It Rage* by Arnold Johnston and Deborah Ann Percy, *Which Marriage?* by Nancy Dean

New one-acts on lust, envy and justice.

(Minetta Lane Theatre) Tuesday, Dec.10, 1991-Jan.12, 1992 (30 performances and 9 previews) Peggy Hill Rosenkranz presents:

**RAFT OF THE MEDUSA** by Joe Pintauro; Director, Sal Trapani; Sets, Phillip Baldwin; Costumes, Laura Crow; Lighting, Dennis Parichy, Mal Sturchio; Sound, Chuck London; Fights, Rick Sordelet; Stage Manager, Marjorie Horne; Press, Keith Sherman/Chris Day, Jim Byk, Frank Goodman CAST: Robert Alexander (Tommy), Annie Corley (Cora), Brenda Denmark (Nairobi), William Fichtner (Alec), Dan Futterman (Donald), Robert Jimenéz (Jimmy), Steven Keats (Jerry), David F. Louden (Bob), Bruce McCarty (Larry), Reggie Montgomery (Doug), Patrick Quinn (Michael), Abigael Sanders (Felicia), Cliff Weissman (Alan)

A drama performed without intermission. The action takes place at a group therapy session for people with AIDS or HIV infection.

(Colony Theatre) Tuesday, Dec.17, 1991-Jan.18, 1992 (16 performances) Colony Theatre presents:

**FOOLS** by Neil Simon; Director, Timothy Kelleher; Sets/Lighting, Nathanial Hussey; Press, Monika Mitchell CAST: Barry Levy (Leon), Stephen Christopher (Snetsky), Patrick McCullough (Magistrate), John Morrison (Slovitch), Darrell Wilks (Mishkin), Lisa Hughes (Yenchna), Jonathan T. Cook (Zubritsky), Rose Marie Norton (Lenya), Arija Bareikis (Sophia), Matt Kowalski (Gregor)

The 1981 comedy in two acts.

(Medicine Show) Wednesday, Jan.1-Mar.21, 1992 Medicine Show presents:

**MR. SHAKESPEARE AND MR. PORTER** with Music/Lyrics, Cole Porter; Text, William Shakespeare; Concept/Book, Barbara Vann, James Barbosa; Music Director, Randy Redd; Directors, Ms. Vann, Deloss Brown, Harvey Cort; Choreography, Sandra Stratton, Mark Haim; Sets, Timothy Cramer; Lighting, Paul Murphy, Michael Hunold, Tony de Rose CAST:Lisa Haim, Linda Witzel, Katherine Burger, James Barbosa, Michael Galante, Melanie Demitri, Carl J. Frano, Victor Venning, Richard Domenico, Barbara Vann, Mark J. Dempsey, Morton Banks, Maureen May, Becque Olson, Paul Murphy, Liana McCulloch, Bonnie Goodman, JoJo Gonzales

An absurdist musical comedy incorporating Cole Porter songs into *Macbeth*, *King Lear*, *As You Like It*, *Measure for Measure*, *Hamlet*, *Midsummer Night's Dream*

(Atlantic Theatre) Friday, Jan.3-18, 1992 (14 performances) Atlantic Theatre Co. presents:

**FIVE VERY LIVE**; Sets, James Wolk; Lighting, Howard Werner; Stage Manager, Matthew Silver; Press, Jim Baldassare

SURE THING by David Ives; Director, Scott Zigler CAST: Robert Bella (Bill), Mary McCann (Betty)

An examination of the art of the pick-up.

CALL OF THE WILD by Patrick Breen; Director, Neil Pepe CAST: David Pittu (Coyote)

A behind the scenes look at a coyote's true passions.

WONDERFUL PARTY by Howard Korder; Director, Todd Weeks CAST: Kristen Johnston (Tina), Mary McCann (Mandy), Steven Goldstein (Ed), Robin Spielberg (Laraine), Damian Young (Bruce), Neil Pepe (Ben), Robert Bella (Rudolph), David Pittu (Irving), Craig Addams, Julia Bradnan, David Branscombe, Christopher Burns, Fran Costello, Catherine Cushman, Sarah Eckhardt, Nancy Gartlan, Ken Glickfeld, Hilary Hinckle, Robin Lichtig, Barry Liebman, Connie Rafferty, Christopher Roberts, Kimberly Anne Ryan, Celia Schaefer, Eric Sherr, Matthew Silver, Liz Tucillo, Elizabeth Wells (Guests), Ron Butler (Kali)

A foray in the act of party giving.

FIVE VERY LIVE by David Van Matre; Director, Neil Pepe CAST: Robert Bella (Steve Basswood), Ron Butler (Tom Lather/Reporter), Kristen Johnston (Mom/Sylvia/Reporter), Mary McCann (Brook Hightower), Steven Goldstein (Dad/Chip/Reporter), Robin Spielberg (Yancy Yarlow/Daughter), Damian Young (Announcer)

A parody of a local news show.

THE AGE OF PIE; Written/Directed by Peter Hedges CAST: David Pittu (Clark), Steven Goldstein (Stan), Robin Spielberg (Betty O), Sarah Eckhardt (Joy), Robert Bella (Styart), Kristen Johnston (Ruth), Mary McCann (Connie), Damian Young (Skip)

A comedy about the desire to seek help from others through extraordinary means.

**95**

(Under One Roof Theatre) Thursday, Jan.9-Feb.2, 1992 (19 performances) Under One Roof presents:
**JOB: A CIRCUS** with Music/Conception/Direction by Elizabeth Swados; Clown Routines, Gabriel Barre, Mary Dino, Michael Gunst, Jeff Hess, Alan Mintz, Stephen Ringold; Sets/Costumes, Nephelie Andonyadis; Lighting, Kristabelle Munson; Vocal Arrangements, Ann Marie Milazzo, Cathy Porter, Michael Sottile; Stage Manager, Tori Evans; Press, David Rothenberg CAST: Mary Dino, Tori Evans, Michael Gunst, Jeff Hess, Ann Marie Milazzo, Alan Mintz, Daniel Neiden, Paul O'Keefe, Stephen Ringold, Michael Sottile
  A musical resetting the biblical Job story under the big top.

(St. Mark's Theatre) Thursday, Jan.9-Mar.1, 1992 (32 performances) The Ontological-Hysteric Theatre presents:
**THE MIND KING**; Written/Directed/Designed by Richard Foreman; Asst. Director, David Herskovits; Technical, Colin Hodgson; Sound, John Collins; Press, Sue Latham CAST: David Patrick Kelly, Henry Stram, Colleen Werthmann
  A series of hallucinatory stories performed without intermission.

(Haft Theatre) Saturday, Jan.11-17, 1992 (7 performances) New York State Theatre Institute presents:
**BEAUTY AND THE BEAST**; Adaptation by Ray Bono; Director, Ed Lange; Costumes, Karen Kammer; Sets, Victor A. Becker; Lighting, Betsy Adams; Sound, Dan Toma; Press, Chris Boneau/Wayne Wolfe CAST: Marlene Goudreau, David Bunce, Joel Aroeste, John Thomas McGuire III, Erika Johnson Newell, Etta Caren Fink, Skye McKenzie, Joseph Larrabee-Quandt, Betsy Riley, John Romeo, Mariye Inouye
  Set in Fourteenth Century England.

(St. Clements) Tuesday, Jan.14-Mar.14, 1992 Theatre For a New Audience (Jeffrey Horowitz, Producing Director) presents:
**THE COMEDY OF ERRORS** by William Shakespeare; Director, William Gaskill; Music, Deniz Ulben; Sets, Power Boothe; Costumes, Gabriel Berry; Lighting, Frances Aronson; Masks, Karin Weston, Mr. Berry; Fights, J. Allen Suddeth; Stage Manager, Carol Dawes; Press, Shirley Herz/Miller Wright CAST: Al Carmines (Duke/Balthazar), Donovan Dietz (Merchant/Officer/Emilia), Wally Dunn (Angelo), Karen Foster (Luciana), Jeffrey Guyton (Dromio of Ephesus), Robert Hock (Egeon), Polly Humphreys (Luce/Pinch's Asst.), Benjamin Lloyd (Jailer), Linda Maurel (Courtesan), Scott Rabinowitz (Jailer/Merchant/Asst.), Ramón Ramos (Antipholus of Ephesus), Michael Rogers (Antipholus of Syracuse), Elizabeth Meadows Rouse (Adriana), Peter Schmitz (Dromio of Syracuse), Richard Spore (Pinch)
  A comedy performed without intermission. The action takes place in Ephesus.

**Jeff Hess, Stephen Ringold on "Job: A Circus"** (*Everett Scott*)

(Actors' Playhouse) Wednesday, Jan.15-June 7, 1992 (125 performances and 20 previews) Drew Dennett presents:
**JULIE HALSTON'S LIFETIME OF COMEDY**; Written and Performed by Julie Halston; Director, Kenneth Elliott; Set, B.T. Whitehill; Lighting, Vivien Leone; Stage Manager, Allison Sommers; Press, Shirley Herz/Sam Rudy
  Performed without intermission.

(Avalon Theatre) Thursday, Jan.16-Feb.1, 1992 (15 performances) 5Men/5 Women presents:
**YEAR OF PILGRIMAGE** by Doug Grisson; Directors, Peter B. Weller, Todd Cash CAST: Tom Ellis, Bill C. Tate, Mr. Cash, Jim Doharty, Adenrele Ojo, Robin Sconyers, Jon Strange, Rebecca Weitman
  Three one-acts set in the deep South during the civil rights movement.

(Theatre 22) Thursday, Jan.16-Feb.2, 1992 (12 performances) Hawk and Handsaw presents:
**OTHELLO** by William Shakespeare; Director, Elfin Frederick Vogel CAST: Paul DuBois, Angela Foster, Caleb Hart, Alain Lozach, Judy Ramakers, Steven Viola, Mr. Vogel
  A modern dress production.

(Open Eye Theatre) Sunday, Jan.19-Feb.29, 1992 Open Eye Theatre presents:
**A WOMAN CALLED TRUTH** by Sandra Fenichel Asher; Director, Ernest Johns; Press, Shirley Herz/Sam Rudy CAST: Patricia R. Floyd (Sojourner Truth), Ricky Genaro, Jen Wolfe, Joe Clancy, James Duane Polk, Alicia Rene Washington
  The story of an early black and women's rights crusade.

**Julie Halston** (*Len Prince*)

...illiam Redfield Theatre) Wednesday, Jan.22-26, 1992 (5 performances) Alchemy ...eatre Co. presents:

...TY OF BROKEN DREAMS; Three John Cheever stories adapted by the ...mpany; Director, Debbie Saivetz; A Courthouse Repertory Co. Production; ...oducer, Gitta Donovan; *O City Of Broken Dreams* with Louise Freistadt (Narrator), ...el Van Liew (Evarts Mallory), Ellen Reilly (Alice Malloy), Kate Kearney-Patch ...ildred-Rose Malloy) *The Five-Forty-Eight* with Stephen O'Rourke (Narrator), ...ck Weber (Blake), Louise Freistadt (Miss Dent) *Christmas Is a Sad Season for the* ...or with Jase Draper (Charlie), Joel Van Liew (Narrator) ...erformed without intermission.

...op of the Village Gate) Thursday, Jan.23-Mar.7, 1992 Turner Monarch Productions ...esent:

...ST A NIGHT OUT ! *A Musical Love Story* with Music/Lyrics/Book by Richard ...d Susan Turner; Director/Choreography, Leslie Dockery; Sets, Lisa Watson; ...ostumes, Gregory Glenn; Lighting, Sandra Ross; Sound, Monarch Studios; Press, ...ter Cromarty/David Lotz, David B. Katz CAST: Zenzele Scott (Sylvia), Charlene ...zpatrick (BJ), Bruce Butler, Rufus James (Curtis), Tonya Alexander, Juju Harty ...enee), Deborah Keeling, Diane Weaver (Marlena Davis) ...USICAL NUMBERS(including standards): Just a Night Out, Just in Time/Lady is a ...amp, Misty, All of You, Everything Costs Money in New York, 6'2 & Ooh!, Here ...e Go Again, Don't Go to Strangers, What is She Doing Here, I'll Be There When ...ou Need Me, I've Got You Under My Skin, Renee's Lament, Let's Get One Thing ...raight, Showtime Is Mine, That Woman Is Me, Lovely Ladies, Finale ...musical in two acts. The action takes place in a midwestern, blue-collar town ...en people could earn a living singing and dancing.

...el's Down Under) Tuesday, Jan.28, 1992- Patricia Kearney presents: ...OVE SPIRIT; Written/Composed by Ernest McCarty; Musical Director, Levi ...rcourt; Sets/Costumes, Leon Munier; Press, Francine L. Trevens CAST: Natalie ...rter, Elana Cooper, Irene Dee, Keith Johnston, Christopher Richard

...heatre Row Theatre) Tuesday, Jan.28-30, 1992 (3 performances) The Class Acting ...pertory presents: ...URN OF EVENTS; Works by Joe Pintauro, David Ives, Frederick Stoppel, David ...arren, Katha Feffer; Press, Kevin P. McAnarney CAST: Tom Young, Nicholas ...stman, Katha Feffer, Holliston Hill, Susan Jacobson, Bruce Levy, Christa Roberts, ...aron Rowe, Kent Rulon, Deb Turcotte, Robert Veligdan

...illage Theatre) Wednesday, Jan.29-Feb.23, 1992 (20 performances) Village Theatre ...o. presents: ...MIMA MUNDI by Don Nigro; Director, Henry Fonte; Lighting, Craig Little; ...ostumes, Marj Feenan; Stage Manager, Lisa Jean Lewis CAST: Michelle Berke, ...ichael Curran, Susan Farwell, Marjorie Feenan, Christie Harrington, Randy Kelly, ...rrence Martin, David McConnell, Julia McLaughlin, Howard Thoresen, Patrick ...rner, Patrick White, Zeke Zaccaro ...A drama set in England, France and America.

...laster Theatre) Wednesday, Jan.29-Apr.12, 1992 (83 performances and 4 previews) ...e Artists' Perspective in association with Chess Players Ltd. present: ...HESS with Music by Benny Andersson and Bjorn Ulvaeus; Lyrics/Book, Tim Rice; ...rector, David Taylor; Musical Director/New Orchestrations, Phil Reno; Sets, Tony ...astrigno; Lighting, John Hastings; Costumes, Deborah Rooney; Sound, Creative ...udio Design; Stage Manager, Doug Fogel; Press, Judy Rabitcheff CAST: Kathleen ...owe McAllen (Florence Vassy), J. Mark McVey (Anatoly Sergievsky), Ray Walker ...rederick Trumper), Patrick Jude (Arbiter), Jan Horvath (Svetlana), Bob Frisch ...lexander Molokov), Mark Ankeny, Michael Gerhart, Mary Illes, David Koch, Nita ...oore, Ric Ryder, Carol Schuberg, Rebecca Timms ...USICAL NUMBERS: Merano, Where I Want to Be, How Many Women, US vs. ...SSR, Arbiter's Song, Chess Game #1, A Model of Decorum and Tranquility, Chess ...ymn, Someone Else's Story, Nobody's on Nobody's Side, Merchandiser's Song, ...ountain Top Duet, Who'd Ever Guess It?, Chess Game #2, Florence Quits, Pity the ...hild, Anthem, One Night in Bangkok, Heaven Help My Heart, Argument, ...onfrontation, No Contest, I Know Him So Well,The Deal, Endgame, You and ...Epilogue ...A revision of the 1986 London and 1988 Broadway musical in two acts. The action ...kes place in Merano, Italy and Bangkok, Thailand in 1972-73.

**Deborah Keeling, Bruce Butler, Messeret Stroman in "Just a Night Out"** (*Hugh Bell*)

**Irene Dee, Keith Johnston, Ilana Cooper, Christopher Richard, (front) Natalie Carter in "Love Spirit"** (*William Gibson*)

**Kathleen Rowe McAllen, Ray Walker in "Chess"** (*Beth Kelly*)

**Elvira and Hortensia Colorado in "Huipil"** (*Shirley Curtin*)

**Patrick Fitzgerald, Chris O' Neill in**
**"Grandchild of Kings"** (*Carol Rosegg*)

(Synchronicity Space) Thursday, Jan.30-Feb.15, 1992 (16 performances) Art & Work Ensemble presents:
**VINEGAR TOM** by Caryl Churchill; Director, Derek Todd; Set, Miguel Lopez-Castillo; Lighting, John Collins; Costumes, Alejandra Lopez CAST: Mary F. Unser (Alice), Norma Rockwood (Joan), Michael Gilpin (Jack), Martha Gilpin (Margery), Joseph Ricci, Susanna Page, Dawn Hunter, Curtis Anderson, Kathleen L. Warner, Nancy Castle, Karen Morgan, Kelly Cleary, Chris Taylor, Steven Rahav Rome, Cheryl Swift
A 1976 drama with music.

(Theatre for the New City) Thursday, Jan.30-Feb.16, 1992 (12 performances) Theatre for the New City and Coatlicue/Las Colorado Theatre Co. present:
**HUIPIL**; Written and Performed by Elvira Colorado and Hortensia Colorado; Sets, Tom Moore; Lighting, Zdenek Kriz; Costumes, Soni Moreno-Primeau; Music, Franc Menusan; Press, Jonathan Slaff/Shirley Curtin
A non-linear drama weaving dreams and myths with contemporary Native American Indian life.

(Kampo Cultral Center) Thursday, Jan.30-Feb.16, 1992 (16 performances) Signature Theatre Co. presents:
**A WOMAN WITHOUT A NAME** by Romulus Linney; Director, Thomas Allan Bullard; Set, E. David Cosier; Costumes, Teresa Snider-Stein; Lighting, Jeffrey S. Koger; Stage Manager, Dean Gray CAST: Barbara Andres (The Woman), Fred Burrell (William Craig), Elisabeth Lewis Corley (Fanny Knapp), Susan Ericksen (Calistra), Marin Hinkle (Susie Balis), Jim Ligon (Arthur Moore), Bernie McInerney (David), Peter G. Morse (Ed), Mark Niebuhr (Charlie)
A drama adapted from the novel *Slowly by Thy Hand Unfurled* by Mr. Linney.

(Alice's Fourth Floor) Thursday, Jan.30-Mar.1, 1992 (24 performances) Alice's Fourth Floor (Susan Brinkley, Artistic Director) presents:
**APPOINTMENT WITH A HIGH WIRE LADY** by Russell Davis; Director, Michael Mantell; Sets/Lighting, Michael Francis Moody; Costumes, David Sawaryn; Music, Jane Ira Bloom, Jayne Atkinson; Producers, Kate Baggott, Patricia Cornell; Stage Manager, Sally Plass; Press, Chris Boneau/Adrian Bryan-Brown, Bob Fennell

CAST: Victor Slezak (Richard Skelley), Jayne Atkinson (Louise Wick), Suzanne Shepard (Carla Ukmar)
A drama in two acts. The action takes place in a state psychiatric institution some years ago.

(St. Bart's Playhouse) Friday, Jan.31-Feb.9, 1992 (9 performances) St. Bart's Playhouse presents:
**BILOXI BLUES** by Neil Simon; Director, Christopher Catt; Sets, Fred Christoffel; Costumes, Estella Marie; Lighting, Karen Spahn; Sound, Kevin Mochell; Press, Pete Cromarty/Lynne McCreary CAST: Ken Altman, Dan Grinko, Jane Larkworthy, Jam Lurie, Brian Meyers, Mary Rodgers, Steve Ross, Richard Van Slyke, Randy Wilhelm
The 1985 comedy set in WWII boot camp.

(Theatre For The New City) Friday, Jan.31-May 10, 1992 (97 performances and 20 previews) The Irish Rep. Theatre Co. (Ciaran O'Reilly and Charlotte Moore, Artistic Directors) and One World Arts Foundation present:
**GRANDCHILD OF KINGS**; From the autobiographies of Sean O'Casey; Adaptation/Direction, Harold Prince; Sets, Eugene Lee; Lighting, Peter Kaczorowski; Costumes, Judith Anne Dolan; Sound, James M. Bay; Musical Director, Martha Hitc Conductor, Rusty Magee; Choreography, Barry McNabb; Stage Manager, Kathe Mu Press, Chris Boneau/Adrian Bryan-Brown, Susanne Tighe CAST: Chris O'Neill (Ol Sean), Pauline Flanagan (Sue), Terry Donnelly (Ella), Ciaran O' Reilly (Archie), Ciaran Sheehan (Tom), Michael Judd (Michael), Nesbitt Blaisdell (Conductor), Padd Croft (Mrs. Saunders), Chris Carrick (Headmaster), Denis O'Neill (Woods), Georgia Southcotte (Drunken Woman), Dermot McNamara (Rev.), Brian F. O'Byrne (Tomm Talton), Louise Favier (Daisy Battles), Rosemary Fine (Alice), Chris A. Kelly (Drummer Benson), Maeve Cawley (Jenny Cliteroe)
A drama in two acts. The action takes place in Dublin, 1880-1910.

(Westbeth Theatre Center) Monday, Feb.3-16, 1992 Westbeth presents:
**GERTRUDE, QUEEN OF DENMARK** by Pat Kaufman; Director, Vasek C. Sime CAST: Marilyn Sokol (Gertrude), Marissa Copeland (Ophelia), Mary Lou Rosato (Lady Jane), Jerry Matz (Polonius), John Daggen (Hamlet)
A spoof of *Hamlet*.

**Victor Slezak, Jayne Atkinson in**
**"Appointment with a High Wire Lady"** (*T. Charles Erickson*)

**"Grandchild of Kings" company** (*Carol Rosegg*)

Claudia Fielding, Catherine Curtin, Percy Granger in
"Making Book" (*Marvin Einhorn*)

Marjorie Austrian, Joyce Sozen in "Homesick"

mary Stages) Tuesday, Feb.4-Mar.1, 1992 (24 performances) Primary Stages
sey Childs, Artistic Director) presents:
KING BOOK by Janet Reed; Director, Susan Einhorn; Sets/Costumes, Bruce
odrich; Lighting, Spencer Mosse; Sound, One Dream; Stage Manager, Amy
pa CAST: Catherine Curtin (Kelly Clark), Daniel Ahearn (Joel Braun), Claudia
ding (Ellen Winston), Allison Janney (Megan Calember), Percy Granger (Dr.
ichton)
satire in two acts. The action takes place in New York classrooms and publishing
ces.

neyard Theatre) Wednesday, Feb.5-Mar.1, 1992 Vineyard 15th St. presents:
DY BRACKNELL'S CONFINEMENT by Paul Doust; and THE PARTY
pted by Ellen McLaughlin from three Virginia Woolf stories; Director, David
jornson; Sets, G.W. Mercier; Lighting, Phil Monat; Costumes, Muriel Stockdale;
ge Manager, Crystal Huntington; Press, Shirley Herz/Sam Rudy CAST: Edward
bert (Lady Augusta Bracknell), Kathleen Chalfant (*Party* women)
pair of one-character plays.

son Guild Theatre) Wednesday, Feb.5-Mar.8, 1992 (35 performances and 4
views) The Working Theatre (Bill Mitchelson, Artistic Director) presents:
CENSION DAY by Michael Henry Brown; Director, L. Kenneth Richardson;
s, Tavia Ito; Costumes, Lance Kenton; Lighting, R. Stephen Hoyes; Sound, Rob
rton; Fights, David Leong; Choreography, Donald Byrd; Music, Olu Dara; Stage
nager, Lisa L. Watson; Press, Bruce Cohen CAST: Andre De Shields
iot/Sam), Michael Beach (Nat Turner), Novella Nelson (Nancy), Betty K. Bynum
erry), Ving Rhames (Hark/Executioner), Arthur French (Henry), Rozwill Young
ill/Executioner), Jeremy Stuart (Travis/Overseer), Jesse Bernstein (Putnam
ore), Matthew C. Cowles (Master Turner/Brantley/John Brown), Colleen Quinn
argaret Whitehead), Earl Whitted (Randy/Executioner), Jack Gwaltney
yles/Executioner)
drama in two acts. The action takes place in Southampton County, Virginia
nning 1800-31.

(Billy Redfield Theatre) Thursday, Feb.6-22, 1992 (16 performances)
THE BOX/HOMESICK by John Monteleone; Director, Keith Fadelici; Press,
Barbara Atlee CAST: *Box* Jonathan Friedman, Philip Levy, Lane Luchert, Jeff
Streger, Elizabeth Klobe; *Homesick* Steve Abruscato, Marjorie Austrian, Cam
Sanders, Joyce Sozen
A pair of one-act comedies.

(Triangle Theatre) Thursday, Feb.6-Mar.1, 1992 (13 performances and 3 previews)
Triangle Theatre Co. (Michael Ramach, Producing Director) presents:
SALT-WATER MOON by David French; Director, Charles R. Johnson; Costumes,
Amanda J. Klein; Lighting, Nancy Collings; Set, Evelyn Sakash; Stage Manager,
Cathy Diane Tomlin; Press, Jim Baldassare CAST: Steve Dane (Jacob Mercer),
Mary Snow (Kimberly Topper)
The action takes place in a Newfoundland, Canada summmer home, 1926.

(Ensemble Studio Theatre) Friday, Feb.7- Ensemble Studio Theatre(Curt Dempster,
Artistic Director; Dominick Balletta, Managing Director) presents:
GEORGE WASHINGTON DANCES by David Margulies; Director, Jack Gelber;
Lighting, Greg MacPherson; Set, Sarah Lambert; Sound, Michael Sargent;
Costumes, David Sawaryn; Prod. Manager, Andrew Kaplan CAST: David
Margulies (Howell), Jahn Margulies (Harry)
Presented in EST's *In Pursuit of America* series.

(Studio Theatre 603) Friday, Feb.7-23, 1992 (16 performances) The Sputen Duyvil
Theatre Co. presents:
LA RONDE by Arthur Schnitler; Translation, Beatte Bennett; Director, Frederick
Wessler; Lighting, Chris Gorzelnik; Costumes, Noel Noblitt; Stage Manager, Lisa
Gavaletz; Press, Janelle Sperow CAST: Bill Costa, Jeff Hearn, Susan Jon, Casey
McDonald, Maureen MacDougall, Monika Mitchell, Rusty Owen, Garrison Phillips,
Janelle Sperow, Mary Kaye Swedish
A comedy in two acts set in turn-of-the-century Vienna.

Rozwill Young, Kevin N. Davis, Arthur French, Ving Rhames in
"Ascension Day" (*Carol Rosegg*)

Kimberly Topper, Steve Dane in
"Salt-Water Moon" (*Carol Rosegg*)

99

(Nat Horne Theatre) Tuesday, Feb.11-Mar.28, 1992 (20 performances and 4 previews) Love Creek Productions presents:
**THE MASK** by Bill Elverman; Director/Set, Les Wilhelm; Lighting, R.K. Green; Costumes, Tarayn Quinn; Stage Manager, Tracy Newirth; Press, Francine L. Trevens/Robert Weston, Daphne Dennis CAST: Dustye Winniford (Daniel Gregory), Carol Halstead (Anna-Marie Jensen), Peter Bock (Erik Jensen), Scott Sparks (Brian Tallman), Stephen Beach (Buddy Jackson/Reporter/Richard/Clerk), Jeff Paul (Dominic Rowlands/Detective/Paul), Jed Dickson (Dennis Chase, P.I./Coroner/Geoffrey Wickes), Katherine Parks (Alice Duggan/Reporter/Judge Nolan), Jeffrey J. Albright (D.A. Baldwin/Lawrence)
   A drama in two acts. The action takes place in New York City. Based on a notorious true sadomasochistic murder case.

(224 Waverly Place) Wednesday, Feb.12-Mar.6, 1992 Royston Theatre Co. presents:
**SAINT JOAN** by George Bernard Shaw; Director, Peter Royston; Music, William Catanzaro; Sets, Rhys Williams; Lighting, Jeffrey Whitsett; Costumes, Elizabeth Royston, Rebecca Schroyer CAST: Jerry Koenig (de Baudricourt/Soldier), Isiah Bard (Steward), Joanne Comerford (Joan), Philip Cuomo (de Poulengey/ D'Estivet), Gregory St. John (Archbishop), Ira Rubin (La Tremouille/1920 Gentleman), John Haggerty (Bluebeard/de Courcelles), Con Roche (La Hire/Executioner), Charles Hall (Dauphin-Charles VII), Kevin Brown (Dunois), Ted Hewlet (Page/Scribe), James R. Bianchi (de Beauchamp), James Corbett (Chaplain), John Steber (Bishop/Cauchon), Donald Grody (Inquisitor), William D. Michie (Ladvenu)
   A drama in two acts. The action takes place in France between 1429-56.

(29th St. Playhouse) Thursday, Feb.13-Mar.1, 1992 Annette Moskowitz and Alexander E. Racolin on behalf of Play Producers presents:
**RUTHERFORD AND SON** by Gita Sowerby; Director, Michael Hillyer; Set, Vicki R. Davis; Costumes, Natalie Bartha Walker; Lighting, Kristabelle Munson CAST: Saylor Creswell, John Hillyer, Holly Hawkins, Annette Hunt, Mark Edward Lang, Gwendolyn Lewis, Miller Lide, Joan Matthiessen

(Ensemble Studio Theatre) Thursday, Feb.13-Mar.4, 1992 (In Repertory) Ensemble Studio Theatre (Curt Dempster, Artistic Director; Dominick Balletta, Managing Director) presents:
**KOREA** by Bill Bozzone; Director, Kate Baggott; Sets, Sarah Lambert; Costumes, David Sawaryn; Lighting, Greg MacPherson; Sound, Mike Sargent CAST: Josh Hamilton (Bobby Costello), Pete Benson (Walter Dybek), Kevin O'Keefe (Stokes), Bai Ling (Chae), Bill Cwikowski (Wolff), Kevin Thigpen (Henley)
   A drama presented in EST's *In Pursuit of America* series.

(Diplomat Hotel) Thursday, Feb.13-Mar.14, 1992 (15 performances) Dar A. Lutz presents:
**THE LAW OF REMAINS**; Created/Directed by Reza Abdoh; Producer, Diane White; Asst. Director, Jennifer Loeb; Manager/Administrator, Rupert Skinner; Sets, Sonya Balassanian; Sound, Raul Vincent Enriques; Videos, Adam Soch; Costumes, Chip White; Lighting, Rand Ryan; Dances, M'Bewe Escobar, Stormy; Press, Jonathan

**Scott Sparks, Peter Bock, Carol Halstead in "The Mask"** (*Michael Bartley*)

**Josh Hamilton, Pete Benson, Bai Ling, Kevin O'Keefe in "Korea"**

Slaff CAST: Sabrina Artel, Brenden Doyle, Anita Durst, Stephan Francis, Giuliana Francis, Ariel Herrera, Priscilla Holbrook, Peter Jacobs, Sardar Singh Kahlsa, Tom Pearl, Tony Torn, Kathryn Walsh, Kwasi Boateng, Veronica Pawlowska, Raphael Pimental

(Musical Theatre Works) Friday, Feb.14-24, 1992 Theatre Outrageous presents:
**BOO ! 7 CHARACTERS/NO GUARANTEES** by Stephen Patterson; Director, Kenneth Mitchell; Sets, Agatha LaPlante; Costumes, Susan Monteagoudo; Lighting, Jodi Cooper; Music, Ellen Mandel CAST: Stephen Patterson
   A one-man, seven character monologue.

(Intar Theatre) Friday, Feb.14-Mar.1, 1992 (15 performances) Willow Cabin Theatre Co. presents:
**COWBOY IN HIS UNDERWEAR (A DARK JOURNEY)**; Written/Directed by Adam Oliensis; Sets, Miguel Lopez-Castillo; Lighting, Laura Manteuffel; Stage Manager, Linda Powell; Press, Jim Baldassare CAST: Darcy Brown (Woman/ Valerie/Voice), Edward Kassar (Shadowman), Jake Daehler (Ted), Tasha Lawrence (Stacey/Kathryn), Michael Rispoli (Mike), John Manfrellotti (Dom), Bob Taubman (Phil), Angela Nevard (Rita/Hooker #1), Alice Haining (Rebecca/Hooker #2), Olivia Birkelund (Mona/Shelia)
   A play in two acts. The action takes place in various Manhattan locales over a years time.

**Alice Haining, Jake Daehler in "Cowboy in His Underwear"** (*Andrea Bernstein*)

(Kaufman Theatre) Tuesday, Feb.18-Mar.22, 1992 Martin R. Kaufman presents:
**THE OTHER SIDE OF PARADISE** by John Kane; Director, Susie Fuller; Music/Producer, Fred Hellerman; Costumes, Mary Peterson; Lighting, Michael Nybowski; Sound, Raymond D. Schilke; Vocals, Michael Duffy; Sets, Pearl Broms; Stage Manager, Deborah Cressler; Press, Howard J. Rubinstein CAST: Keir Dullea (F. Scott Fitzgerald)
A monodrama in two acts. The action takes place in Hollywood in 1927 and 1940.

(Quality Playhouse) Thursday, Feb.20-Mar.8, 1992 (12 performances) First Step Productions presents:
**THE BLAMELESS**; Written/Directed by Eric Schaeffer; Press, Benita Gold CAST: Adam Shaw, Charles Ley, Emily Perret, Rini Stahl
A comedy on dating in the 1990s.

(Theatre for the New City) Thursday, Feb.20-Mar.8, 1992 (12 performances) Theatre for the New City presents:
**FELICIA** by Patricia Cobey; Director, Robert Bresnick; Music, Brian Johnson; Design, Maureen Schell, Karen Tsakos, Leslie Weinberg CAST: Adam Auslander, Teresa Della Valle, Philip Hackett, Scott Leonard, Cristina Sanjuan, Zoe Zimmerman
A farce inspired by the Roman comedy *Phormio* set in L.A. at present.

(Cornelia St. Cafe) Thursday, Feb.20-Mar.9, 1992 (16 performances) Cornelia St. Cafe presents:
**TALE OF TWO TOMS**; Written/Directed by Fred Kolo; Sets, Dario Nuñez; Costumes, Heidi Hollman; Lighting, Richard Schaefer CAST: Jeff Hasler, Dorie Herndon, Walter Lockwood, Brian Russell, Bob Sealy, Mimi Turque

(Ladines/Atlantic Theatre) Sunday, Feb.23-Mar.9, 1992 (6 performances) and *Rosemary* reopened at (Atlantic Theatre) Friday, Apr.3-25, 1992 (8 performances) Atlantic Theatre Co. presents:
**COCKTAILS AND CAMP** with *The Men in Her Life* and *Rosemary for Remembrance*; Written/Directed by David Pittu; *Rosemary* adapted from *Remembered Death* by Agatha Christie; Lighting, Laura Manteuffel, Howard Werner; Press, Jim Baldassare CAST: *Rosemary* Kristen Johnson (Rosemary Barton), David Pittu (George Barton), Mary McCann (Iris Marle), Hilary Hinckle (Ruth Lessing), Neil Pepe (Victor Drake), Paul Urciolo (Anthony Browne), Drew McVety (Stephen Farraday), Ana Hellman (Cassandra Farraday), Patrick Boll (Col. Race), Brian Quirk (Lucilla Drake), Sarah Eckhardt *Men* included Robin Spielberg

(Ohio Theatre) Thursday, Feb.27-Mar.8, 1992 (8 performances) T.W.E.E.D. presents:
**NERVOUS SPLENDOR : THE WORLD OF LUDWIG WITTGENSTEIN** by Larry Souchuk; Director, Rebecca Holderness; Set, David Landis; Costumes, Loren Bevins; Lighting, Richard Schaefer; Music, Jessica Murrow; Press, Chris Boneau/Adrian Bryan Brown, Bob Fennell CAST: Craig Victor, Randy Miles, David McGrath, Roberta Levine, Jason Bauer, Catherine Lloyd Burns, Jon Kinnaly, Rin Utley, Daniel Crozier, Erin Tavin, Bob Airhart, Jonathan Miller
The turbulent life of philosopher Wittgenstein set in 1930s-40s England.

**Keir Dullea in "The Other Side of Paradise"**

**David McGrath, Bob Airhart in "Nervous Splendor"** (*James White*)

(T. Schreiber Studio) Thursday, Feb.27-Mar.8, 1992 (6 performances) T. Schreiber Studio presents:
**I AM A CAMERA** by John Van Druten; Director, David S. Macy; Set, Richard Harrison; Lighting, Alexandra J. Pontone; Costumes, Kevin Kuney; Stage Manager, John Harmon CAST: Stephen Waldrup, Elizabeth Harpur, David Klionsky, Elaine Bradbury, Toby Poser, Sarah Ford, Nelson Avidon
The 1951 drama set in Berlin.

(All Souls Theatre) Thursday, Feb.27-Mar.15, 1992 (15 performances) All Souls Players, Marlene Greene and Wendell Kindberg presents:
**DEAR WORLD** with Music/Lyrics by Jerry Herman; Book, Jerome Lawrence and Robert E. Lee; Based on *The Madwoman of Chaillot* by Jean Giraudoux as adapted by Maurice Valency; Director, Jeffery K. Neill; Musical Directors, Joyce Hitchcock, David Jutt; Sets/Lighting, Tim Callery; Costumes, Chas W. Roeder; Stage Manager, Ralph Ortiz CAST: Tran Wm. Rhodes (Prospector), Marie Santell (Countess Aurelia), Winston (Corbett), Susan Hale (Nina), Joe Aronica (Deaf Mute), Branch Woodman (Alain), Lisa Dyson (Lili), Jean and Alex Turney (Fifi & Maurice), Pamela J. Nigro (Claudine), Beau Allen (President), William Zarriello (Julian), Gary Henderson (Lawyer), Robert W. Laur (Board Member), Scott Will (Policeman), Joan Jaffe (Madame Constance), Ariel Joseph (Mademoiselle Gabrielle), Stephen Brice (Sewerman), Marlene Greene (Monique), Ralph Ortiz (Alphonse)
MUSICAL NUMBERS: Through the Bottom of the Glass, Spring of Next Year, Each Tomorrow Morning, I Don't Want to Know, I've Never Said I Love You, Pretty Garbage/Ugly Garbage, One Person, Memory, Pearls, Dickie, Voices, Thoughts, Tea Part Trio, And I Was Beautiful, Dear World, Kiss Her Now, Finale
A revision of the 1969 musical in two acts. The action takes place in Paris.

**Ariel Joseph, Marie Santell, Joan Jaffe in
"Dear World"** (*Victor Plessner*)

**Kim Yancey, Claire Dorsey in "Late Bus to Mecca"** (*Bert Andrews*)

S. Hubbard (Michael Payne), Harold W. Smith (Eagle Barnes), Robert Michael Ka~ (Roy Gravinger), Donna Marie Johnson (Dianne Bell), Brian Egnew (Terrence Gravinger), Jonathan Spooner (Sean Davis), Randall Porter (Arthur/Waiter/Officer Gregg), Alphonso Johnson (Tony/Officer Collin), Joan Green (Mrs. Simpson), Tom McCullough (Sen. Bill Rubinstein), Sam Tallerico (Melvin Hobbs, FBI), Sean Coo~ (Comm. Tate), Leigh Smith (Cynthia Wilson)

A suspense mystery. The action takes place in Atlanta, 1982.

(John Houseman Studio) Friday, Feb.28-Mar.15, 1992 (18 performances) Eric Kreb: presents:
**NAPALM THE MAGNIFICENT**; Conceived/Performed by David Craig; Press, David Rothenberg

Monologue satarizing political correctness.

(Judith Anderson Theatre) Friday, Feb.28-Mar.22, 1992 (26 performances) The Women's Project & Productions (Julia Miles, Artistic Director) and New Federal Theatre (Woodie King Jr., Producer) present:
**CHAIN/LATE BUS TO MECCA** by Pearl Cleage; Director, Imani; Sets, George Xenos; Lighting, Melody Beal; Costumes, Ornyece; Sound, Bill Toles; Stage Mana Jacqui Casto; Press, Jeffrey Richards/Denise Robert  CASTS:*Chain* Karen Malina White (Rosa)  *Late Bus* Claire Dorsey (Black Woman), Kim Yancey (Ava)

Two one-acts. *Chain* is set in present day Harlem. *Late Bus* takes place in the Detr bus station, Oct. 1970.

**Laura Esterman, Lisa Emery in "Marvin's Room"** (*Marc Bryan-Brown*)

(Minetta Lane Theatre) Friday, Feb.28-Sept.6, 1992 (214 performances and 7 previews) Frederick Zollo, Howard Erskine, Richard Frankel, Steven Baruch, Thomas Viertel, Mitchell Maxwell, Alan Schuster, Peggy Hill Rosenkranz in association with The Goodman Theatre, Hartford Stage Co. and Playwrights Horizons present:
**MARVIN'S ROOM** by Scott McPherson; Director, David Petrarca; Sets, Linda Buchanan; Costumes, Claudia Boddy; Lighting, Robert Christen; Music/Sound, Rob Milburn; Stage Manager, Brian A. Kaufman; Press, Philip Rinaldi  CAST: Laura Esterman succeeded by Susan Pellegrino (Bessie), Tim Monsion (Dr. Wally), Alice Drummond succeeded by Mary Diveny (Ruth), Tom Aulino (Bob), Lisa Emery succeeded by Nance Williamson (Lee), Mark Rosenthal (Hank), Karl Maschek succeeded by Oren J. Mayo, Marty Zentz (Charlie), Adam Chapnick succeeded by Brad Newman (Marvin)

A drama in two acts. The action takes place in various Florida locations and an Ohio mental hospital, at present. This production played 92 performances and 24 previews earlier this season at Playwrights Horizons.

(Riant Theatre) Thursday, Feb.27-Mar.29, 1992 (25 performances) The Riant Theatre presents:
**THE ATLANTA AFFAIR**; Written/Directed by Van Dirk Fisher; Set, Tina Washington; Lighting, Pamela Fisher; Stage Manager, Doris Stewart; Press, Irene Gandy  CAST: Jane Dewey (Jane Teig), Keith Allen (Dan Buetell/John), Gabriela Kohen (Myra), Perry J. Zanett (Charles Widmire), Alexandra Calder (Melissa Widmire), Charles Ley (Alan Edwards), Suzanne Bayne, Doris Stewart (Sharon Cumbersome), Dee Dixon (Mrs. Edwards/Mrs. Barnes/Protestor/Miss Donovan), Dana

**Laura Esterman in "Marvin's Room"** (*Marc Bryan-Brown*)

il Bellows, Fiona Gallagher in "The Best of Schools" (*Carol Rosegg*)

Earl Fields Jr., Jessica Smith in "Lotto" (*Jessica Katz*)

nder One Roof) Saturday, Feb.29-Mar.22, 1992 (17 performances) Under One Roof
d Ridge Theatre present:
NGLE MOVIE by Hugh Esten; Director, Bob McGrath; Set, Laurie Olinder;
ghting, Joel Giguere; Sound, Jim Farmer; Slides, Dorey Eckhardt; Films, Susie
en, Bill Morrison, Karl Nussbaum, Don Campbell; Press, David Rothenberg
.ST: Damian DaCosta (Capt. Dan), Jay Derrah (Drummer), John Dossett (Dr.
usseau), Santo Fazio (Witch Doctor), Kimberly Flynn (Rima), James Godwin
eastman/Old Salt), Katherine Griffith (Mrs. Hampton), Jon Hayden (Native Chief),
vid Leslie (Tarzan), Rebecca Moore (Lita), Bill Reese (Native), M.W. Reid (Dr.
o), Julia Stiles (Felicity), Neal Sugarman (Musician), Fred Tietz (Pierre)
lulti-media theatre piece drawn from B-movies.

hio Theatre) Tuesday, Mar.3-7, 1992 (5 performances) T.W.E.E.D. presents:
LTA : OR THIS BROOCH FOR HIRE by Farran Smith; Director, Michael
:Quary; Sets, Virginia Farley; Gowns, Ossi; Choreography, Michael Kraus;
ghting, Richard Schaefer; Press, Chris Boneau/Adrian Bryan-Brown, Bob Fennell
.ST: Michael McQuary, William Rioux, Lisa Ebeyer, Jon M. Johnson, Rick
rwick, James Sexton, Bennett Mitten, Shane Haffey, Marcos Prado, Linda Ianella,
lly Dacus, Ching Gonzales, Claudine Kielson
. 1940s-style film noir.

(Intar Theatre) Tuesday, Mar.3-8, 1992 (8 performances) The Common Ground
Theatre Group presents:
**LOOSE ENDS** by Michael Weller; Director, Cheryl Rogers; Set, Daniel Ettinger;
Lighting, David Weiner; Stage Manager, Tiffany Marshall CAST: Cynthia Besteman,
Darcy Brown, Christopher Cabot, Cheryl Huggins, Justin Kirk, Tasha Lawrence, Ken
Schatz, Dustin Schell, Erich Schmidt, Steven Smith, Joel Van Liew
  The 1979 drama in two acts.

(Ubu Rep.) Tuesday, Mar.3-15, 1992 (12 performances) UBU Repertory (Francoise
Kourilsky, Artistic Director) presents:
**THE BEST OF SCHOOLS** by Jean-Marie Besset; Translation, Mark O'Donnell;
Director, Evan Yionoulis; Set, Karen TenEyck; Lighting, Greg MacPherson;
Costumes, Anky Frilles; Stage Manager, David Waggett; Press, Peter Cromarty/Lynne
McCreary CAST: Gil Bellows (Louis), Jonathan Friedman (Paul), Fiona Gallagher
(Agnes), Mira Sorvino (Emeline), Justin Scott Walker (Mecir), Danny Zorn (Bernard)
  A drama set on a campus outside Paris at present.

(24 Karat Club) Tuesday, Mar.3-May 11, 1992 (80 performances) Howard Perloff
presents:
**BERNIE'S BAR MITZVAH**; Written/Directed by Howard Perloff; Costumes, Dot
Liadakis; Stage Manager, Terry J. Moore; Press, Shirley Herz/Sam Rudy, Miller
Wright CAST: *Bernsteins* Ian Bonds (Bernie), Howard Segal (Mark), Carolyn
Beauchamp (Judy), Tiffany Garfinkle (Jodi), Barney Cohen (Sam), S. Rachel Herts
(Sara), Bob Garman (Neil), Laura Covello (Carol), David E. Rosenberg (Great Aunt
Bella), *Silverbergs* Benjamin Blum (Irving), Marjorie F. Orman (Mildred), *Gattons*
John DiDomenico (Robert), Anita Horwath (Debra), *Friends* Linda Jones (Leila
Jones), Brooke Johnson (Marsha Rosenthal), Louis Levy (Rabbi Schulberg), Fred
Daubert (Max), *Catering Staff* Thomas F. Barton (Scotti), Carl Glorioso (Bruno),
Charmaine Chester (Enya), Brian Jacobs (Jake), Suzanne Innes (LuAnne), Tony M.
Bishop (Morgan), Larry Malkus (Ralph), Rodney Bonds (Randy), Dolores McBride
(Ruby), Heidi Williams (Wednesday), *Band* Tony DeFabritus (Tony Richards), Diane
De Noble (Louise LaRue), Steve Strawitz (Guitar), Kenn Stranieri (Drums), David
Witkowski (Winds), Scott McLeod (Bass), *Children* Suzanna Duchon (Cyndee),
David Jackson (Reggie), Frank Paglisi (Aaron), Brian Pakulla (Kevin), Brandon Smith
(BJ), Jennifer Youssef (Ariel) UNDERSTUDIES: Brian Jacobs (Neil), Alan Palmer
(Jake), Matthew Karas (Mark)
  A theatrical spoof of an extravagant Bar Mitzvah.

(Heckscher Theatre) Wednesday, Mar.4 moved to Union Sq. Theatre Friday, June 19 -
still playing May 31, 1992 Lafayette Ltd., Barbara Lerman, C. Frazier Enlow in
association with Dick Scott and Executive Producer Aston Springer present:
**LOTTO :** *Experience The Dream*; Written/Directed by Cliff Roquemore;
Sets/Costumes, Felix E. Cochren; Lighting, Shirley Prendergast; Stage Manager,
Avan; Music, Joe Zamberlin, Melvin Brannon; Press, Peter Cromarty/David Katz
CAST: Earl Fields, Jr. (Horace Benson), Karl Calhoun (Spike), Peace Roberts
(Pearline Benson), Jessica Smith (Mildred Banks), Bryan Roquemore (Junebug),
Maurice Fontane (Lester Franklin), Ottis Young Smith (Blaze Jaxon), Elise Chinyere
Chance (Nett), John L. Bennett (Seth Goldberg), Steve Baumer (Nathan Stokes),
Bridget Kelso (Rochelle Moten)
  A comedy in two acts. The action takes place in Los Angeles at present.

John Dossett, Rebecca Moore in "Jungle Movie" (*Everett Scott*)   **103**

(Manhattan Class Company) Wednesday, Mar.4-21, 1992 (18 performances)
Manhattan Class Co.(Robert LuPone, Bernard Telsey, Executive Directors; W.D.
Cantler, Associate Director) presents:
CLASS 1 ACTS : '91-'92; Sets, Rob Odorisio; Lights, Howard Werner, Amy
Appleyard; Costumes, Dianne Rosetti-Finn; Sound, Raymond Schilke; Prod.
Supervisor, Laura Kravets Gautier; Prod. Manager, Ira Mont; Press, Peter
Cromarty/David Lotz
GROUP : A THERAPEUTIC MOMENT; Written/Directed by Ethan Silverman; Stage
Manager, Kristin Abernathy-West CAST: Sonja Lanzener (Norma Ballhouse), Karen
Evans-Kandel (Ola Stew Art), Michael Louden (David Johnston), Genie Francis
(Linda Wilson), Matthew Lewis (Charles Rosenthal), Jacquelyn Reingold (Sharon
Epstein)
MIXED BABIES by Oni Faidi Lampley; Director, Jennifer Nelson; Stage Manager,
Kathryn Brannach CAST: Kathryn Hunter (Reva Mae Dix), Elise Neal (Andee), Sonja
Martin (Dena), Gwen McGee (Shalanda), Lisa C. Arrindell (Thomasina), Afia Thomas
(Goddess)
A.M.L. by Jacquelyn Reingold; Director, Brian Mertes; Stage Manager, Wendy
Ouellette CAST: Calista Flockhart, Erin Cressida Wilson, Robin Morse, Michelle
Hurd, Ashley Crow
ST. STANISLAUS OUTSIDE THE HOUSE by Patrick Breen; Director, Ethan
Silverman; Stage Manager, Michelle Malloy McIntyre CAST: Curtis McClarin
(Manhole), Jamie Harrold (Zap), Danielle DuClos (Spit), Seth Gilliam (Curb), Portia
Johnson (Breeze)

(Lambs Theatre) Wednesday, Mar.4-May 3, 1992 (63 performances) Lamb's Theatre
Co. (Carolyn Rossi Copeland, Producing Director) presents:
OPAL with Music/Lyrics/Book, by Robert Nassif Lindsey; Director, Scott Harris;
Musical Staging, Janet Watson; Sets, Peter Harrison; Costumes, Michael Bottari;
Lighting, Don Ehman; Musical Director, Joshua Rosenblum; Sound, Jim Van Bergen;
General Manager, Nancy Nagel Gibbs; Prod. Manager, Clark Cameron; Stage
Manager, Sandra M. Franck; Press, Adrian Bryan-Brown, Chris Boneau/Wayne Wolfe
CAST: Reed Armstrong (Narrator), Mimi Bessette (Girl That Has No Seeing), Eliza
Clark, Tracy Spindler (Opal), Louisa Flannigam, Regina O'Malley (The Mama), Mark
Goetzinger (Man That Wears Gray Neckties/Angel Father), Sarah Knapp, Alfred
Lakeman , Judy Malloy (Narrators), Marni Nixon (Sadie McKibben), Pippa Winslow
(Thought-Girl with the Far-away Look in Her Eyes/Angel Mother)
   A musical performed without intermission. The action takes place in a lumber camp
in Oregon, 1904.

"Opal"

(Courtyard Playhouse) Wednesday, Mar.4-May 31, 1992 (78 performances) The
Glines presents:
GET USED TO IT with Music/Lyrics/Direction by Tom Wilson Weinberg;
Choreography, Jack Matter; Set, Edmond Ramage; Lighting, Tracy Dedrickson;
Costumes, Cantanese/Lauze; Press, Chris Boneau/Bob Fennell CAST: Sebastian
Herald, John O'Brien, Todd Whitley, Wayne Barker (piano)
   Musical revue on gay life.

(Westbeth Theatre Center) Thursday, Mar.5-15, 1992 (14 performances) Wild Virtue
Rep. presents:
ON THE VERGE by Eric Overmyer; Director, Daniel Tamm CAST: Carol
Chenoweth, Joanna Daniels, John Quinn, Ann Schulman

(Singers Forum) Thursday, Mar.5-23, 1992 (16 performances) The Singers Forum
presents:
PERPETRATOR by Tedd Smith; Director, Producer, Tom Ferriter; Lighting,
Michael Prosceo; Sound, Aural Fixation; Sets, Jared Saltzman; Costumes, Eva
Schegulla; Press, Peter Cromarty/David B. Katz CAST: Thomas Barbour (Penningto
Matthews), Stephen Bradbury (Sydney Chapin), Robert Mason Ham (Lloyd
Aberdeen), Frank Medrano (Clark/Guard 1), Brian Victor Johnson (Cyril Joe Carlin)
Dennis Jordan (Eddie), Oscar Koch (Paul), Anne Marie Campbell (Taffy), Jerry
McGee (Bank Guard/Guard 2), Mark Doerr (Philip), Sara Lea Taylor (Young Woma
   A drama in two acts. The action takes place in New York City and a prison in
Oregon. Inspired by Norman Mailer's association with Jack Henry Abbott.

(45th St. Theatre) Thursday, Mar.5-Apr.12, 1992 (46 performances) Sito Production
and Dave Feldman in association with Gentlemen Prods. present:
BERT SEES THE LIGHT; Conception/Direction/Sets, R.A. White; Lighting, Dave
Feldman; Costumes, Virginia M. Johnson; General Manager, Stephen W. Nebgen;
Stage Manager, Jill Cordle; Press, David Rothenberg CAST: Jack Black, Molly
Bryant, Michael Rivkin
   A comic play chronicling Bertolt Brecht's journey from Germany to Hollywood in
the 1940s.

Robert Mason Ham, Anne Marie Campbell, Mark Doerr in
"Perpetrator" (*Paula Court*)

Robin Morse, Erin Cressida Wilson, Calista Flockhart, Ashley Crow i
"Manhattan Class 1-Acts" (*Carol Rosegg*)

Michael Rivkin, Jack Black in
"Bert Sees the Light" (*Jason Keene*)

…eatre at 224 Waverly Place) Friday, Mar.6-22, 1992 (16 performances) Liberty
…ge Co. presents:
…RELAWNY OF THE 'WELLS' (NOW & THEN) by Sir Arthur Wing Pinero;
…aptation, Ronald Bly and Laurence Gewirtz; Director, Mr. Bly; Sets, R.J. Bila;
…ghting, Barbara Raguso; Costumes, Kathleen Beckett; Music Director, Sean Hartley;
…ss, Rachel Luxemburg CAST: Jody Barrett (Jody/Rose Trelawny), Jessica Beltz
…ssica/Avonia Bunn), David Cheaney (David/Arthur Gower), Hal Cohen (Hal), Craig
…dley (Craig/Ferdinand Gadd), Bob Horen (Bob/Ablett/ William Gower), Susannah
…cAdams (Susannah/Mrs. Mossop/Trafalgar Gower), Vicki Meisner (Vicki/Mrs.
…fer), Adam Michenner (Adam/Mr. Telfer/ Charles), Michael Morin
…ichael/Augustus Colpoys/O'Dwyer), Robin Poley (Robin/Imogene Parrott), Scott
…nters (Scott/Tom Wrench)
…comedy in two acts. The action takes place in present-day New York City and
…ctorian London.

…ty Center) Tuesday, Mar.10-14, 1992 (7 performances) Mito Kikaku Corp. and
…er Grilli present:
…NRAKU : THE NATIONAL PUPPET THEATRE OF JAPAN in *The Love*
…icides at Sonezaki* by Chikamatsu Monzaemon; Music, Mochizuki Tamekichi; Sets,
…nai Scene Shop; Lighting, Mark Stanley; Press, Zeisler Group/Kevin P. McAnarney
…AST: Toyotake Rodayu V, Tsuruzawa Seiji, Yoshida Minosuke III, Kiritake Itcho
…d the company

…estbeth Theatre Center) Tuesday, Mar.10-22, 1992 (10 performances) Theatre
…brador/New Georges presents:
…NEGAR TOM by Caryl Churchill; Director, Marjorie Ballentine; Set, William F.
…oser; Lighting, Betsy Finston; Stage Manager, Ruth Hackett CAST: Erik Tieze
…an/Dr./Bell Ringer/Sprenger), Susan Bernfield (Alice), James Rutigliano (Jack),
…eer Goodman (Margery), Carolyn Baemler (Betty), Charlotte Colavin (Joan),
…olleen McQuade (Susan), Deborah Kampmeier (Ellen), Patrick McCarthy
…acker/Kramer), Sally Ramirez (Goody)
…a 1976 drama.

**Jessica Beltz, Craig Dudley, Scott Winters in
"Trelawny of the Wells-Now and Then"**

**Kevin Thigpen, Robert Bella in "The Virgin Molly" (*Carol Rosegg*)**

(Atlantic Theatre) Saturday, Mar.14-Apr.12, 1992 (14 performances and 9 previews)
Atlantic Theatre Co. presents:
**THE VIRGIN MOLLY** by Quincy Long; Director, Sarah Eckhardt; Sets, George
Xenos; Lighting, Howard Werner; Sound, David Lawson; Movement, Rick Sordelet;
Stage Manager, Matthew Silver; Press, Jim Baldassare CAST: Robert Bella (Pvt.
Molly Peterson), William Mesnik (Corporal), Todd Weeks succeeded by Ronnie
Butler (Civilian), Kevin Thigpen (Jones), Neil Pepe (Capt.), Don Reilly (Harmon)
   A "modern miracle comedy" performed without intermission. The action takes place
in the "queerhouse" at a Marine Corps unit at present.

(Theatre at 224 Waverly Pl.) Tuesday, Mar.17, 1992 (1 night only) Liberty Stage Co.
presents:
**CROWN OF KINGS**; Based on Shakespeare's histories; Adapted and Directed by
Craig Dudley; Lighting, Barbara Raguso; Sound, Larry Luban; Stage Manager, Hal
Cohen CAST: Craig Dudley, David Cheaney

(Alice's Fourth Floor) Wednesday, Mar.18-Apr. 5, 1992 (15 performances) The
Miranda Theatre Co. in association with The Italian Gov't Institution for Dramatists
present:
**LOVERS** by Mario Fratti; Director, Raymond Haigler; Sets, Edmund A. Lefevre, Jr.;
Lighting, Scott Griffin; Costumes, Rodney Munoz; Stage Manager, Janie Schwartz;
Press, Chris Boneau/Adrian Bryan-Brown CAST: Alexandra Napier (Tess), Gwen
Torry-Owens (Marisa), Brian Poteat (Eugene), Susan Egbert (Ursula)
   A suspense drama in two acts. The action takes place in a movie theatre and
apartment, over a two year period.

(Intar Theatre) Wednesday, Mar.18-May 3, 1992 (42 performances) Intar (Max Ferra,
Artistic Director; Eva Brune, Managing Director) presents:
**THE LADY FROM HAVANA** by Luis Santeiro; Director, Max Ferrá; Set/Costumes,
Campbell Baird; Lighting, Debra Dumas; Sound, Fox & Perla; Music, Fernando Rivas;
Stage Manager, Sergio Cruz; Press, Peter Cromarty/David Lotz CAST: Georgia
Galvez (Marita/Gloria), Lillian Hurst (Mama/Rosa), Feiga M. Martinez (Zoila/Isabel)
   A comedy in two acts. The action takes place in Miami Beach, 20 years after the
Cuban revolution.

**Craig Dudley in "Crown of Kings"**

**Alexandra Napier, Gwen Torry-Owens, Susan Egbert in
"Lovers" (*William Gibson*)**

Peter Bretz, Nicolette Vajtay in "White Bear" (*Carol Rosegg*)

Steve Mellor, John Seitz in "7 Blowjobs" (*Shirley Curtin*)

Kitty Crooks, Gordon MacDonald, Crystal Field in
"Rivalry of Dolls" (*Jonathan Slaff*)

Daniel Marcus, Marion Adler, Scott Wentworth in
"Gunmetal Blues" (*Carol Rosegg*)

(Ubu Rep.) Tuesday, Mar.24-Apr.5, 1992 (12 performances) UBU Repertory presents
**THE WHITE BEAR** by Daniel Besnehard; Translation, Stephen J. Vogel; Director,
Peter Muste; Set, John Brown; Lighting, Greg MacPherson; Costumes, Carol Ann
Pelletier; Sound, Phil Lee, David Lawson; Stage Manager, David Waggett; Press,
Peter Cromarty/Lynne McCreary CAST: Peter Bretz, Kathryn Rossetter, Nicolette
Vajtay
A drama set on an oceanliner bound for Ellis Island at the turn of the century.

(Harold Clurman Theatre) Tuesday, Mar.24-Apr.12, 1992 (18 performances) Northern
Lights Theatre presents:
**HOUR OF THE LYNX** by Per Olov Enquist; Translation, Kjersti Board; Director,
Oeyvind Froeyland; Set, Campbell Baird; Lighting, Paul Bartlett; Costumes, Debora
Rooney; Music, Genji Ito; Stage Manager, Lillian Ann Slugocki; Press, Karen Rome
CAST: Rob Campbell, Heather Ehlers, Helen Harrelson, John Jacobs
A drama from Sweden.

(One Dream Theatre) Wednesday, Mar.25-29, 1992 (5 performances)
**SOVIETIQUETTE (MY DAYS IN RUSSIA)**; Written and Performed by David
Marquis; Director, Jaye Austin-Williams; Lighting, Kristabelle Munson
A one man show of stories, anecdotes and unpleasantries.

(Puerto Rican Traveling Theatre) Wednesday, Mar.25-Apr.28, 1992 Puerto Rican
Traveling Theatre presents:
**THE OXCART (LA CARRETA)** by Rene Marques; Translation, Dr. Charles
Pilditch; Director, Alba Oms; Set, H.G. Arrott; Lighting, Brian Haynsworth;
Costumes, Mary Marsicano; Stage Manager, Elizabeth Valsing; Press, Max Eisen/
Madelon Rosen CAST: Eddie Andino, Miriam Cruz, Chris De Oni, Ebony Diaz,
Jackeline Duprey, Norberto Kerner, Esther Mari, Iraida Polanco, Fernando Quinones,
Victor Sierra, Jeanette Toro, Walter Valentin
A drama based on a 1951 novel.

(Soho Rep.) Thursday, Mar.26-Apr.19, 1992 (16 performances) Soho Rep. (Marlene
Swartz, Julian Webber, Artistic Directors) presents:
**7 BLOWJOBS** by Mac Wellman; Director, Jim Simpson; Sets/Lighting, Kyle
Chepulis; Costumes, Caryn Neman; Sound, Mike Nolan; Stage Manager, Catherine A.
Heusel; Press, Jonathan Slaff CAST: Valerie Charles (Dot), Kristen Harris (Delivery
Person), Melissa Smith (Eileen), Reed Birney (Bruce), Steve Mellor (Tom), John Seitz
(Bob), John Augustine (Bob Jr.), Jon Tytler (BobBob Jr.)
A political primer that takes place in the Old Senate Office.

(Theatre for the New City) Thursday, Mar.26-Apr.19, 1992 (16 performances) Theatre
for the New City (Bartenieff/Field) presents:
**THE RIVALRY OF DOLLS** by James Purdy; Director, John Uecker; Sets, Myra
Duarte; Lighting, Zdenek Kriz; Costumes, Delia Doherty; Stage Manager, Judith
Sostek; Press, Jonathan Slaff CAST: William Alderson (Dr. Clyde Radwell), Kitty
Crooks (Amelia Radwell), Christine Langer (Sadie Radwell), Gordon McDonald
(Lester Fladgate), Crystal Field (Pauline Radwell), Paul Anthony Stewart (Cy Dunlap)
A drama in two acts. The action takes place in Midwestern farm country during the
1920s.

(Theatre Off Park) Friday, Mar.27-May 10, 1992 (46 performances) AMAS presents:
**GUNMETAL BLUES** with Music/Lyrics by Craig Bohmler and Marion Adler; Book,
Scott Wentworth; Director, Davis Hall; Co-Musical Staging, Patricia L. Paige; Music
Director/Arrangements/Orchestrations, Mr. Bohmler; Sets/Costumes, Eduardo
Sicangco; Lighting, Scott Zielinski; Stage Manager, Lisa Ledwich; Press, Peter
Cromarty/David B. Katz CAST: Daniel Marcus (Piano Player), Michael Knowles
(Barkeep), Marion Adler (Blondes), Scott Wentworth (Private Eye)
MUSICAL NUMBERS: Welcome to This, Don't Know What I Expected, Facts, Well-
to-Do Waltz, Spare Some Change, Mansion Hill, Shadowplay, Skeletons, Blonde
Song, Childhood Days, Take a Break, Not Available in Stores!, Gunmetal Blues, I'm
the One That Got Away, Jenny, Put it on My Tab, The Virtuoso, Finale
A musical in two acts. The action takes place in the Red Eye Lounge, tonight.

**Gil Bellows in "A Snake in the Vein"** (*Carol Rosegg*)

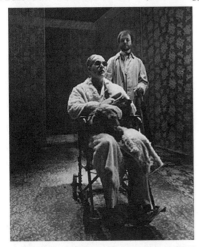

**Mark Waterman, Harris Berlinsky in "Endgame"** (*Shirley Curtin*)

**Larry Block, Richard B. Shull, Jack Hallet, (rear) Kim Chan, Lou Liberatore, Francine Beers, Renee Taylor, Helen Greenberg in "One of the All-Time Greats"** (*Carol Rosegg*)

(Manhattan Class Company) Friday, Mar.27-May 17, 1992 (40 performances) Manhattan Class Co. presents:
**A SNAKE IN THE VEIN** by Alan Bowne; Director, Jimmy Bohr; Sets, Rob Odorisio; Lighting, Howard Werner; Costumes, Dianne Rosetti-Finn; Sound, Lia Vollack; Stage Manager, James Marr; Press, Peter Cromarty/ David Lotz CAST: Gil Bellows (J.J.), Charles Cragin (The Man)
The 1985 drama performed without intermission. The action takes place at present, late at night.

(Bouwerie Lane Theatre) Friday, Mar.27-May 31, 1992 (22 performances) Jean Cocteau Repertory presents:
**ENDGAME** by Samuel Beckett; Director, Eve Adamson; Set, John Brown; Costumes, Jonathan Bixby; Press, Jonathan Slaff CAST: Harris Berlinsky (Clov), Mark Waterman (Hamm), Joseph Menino (Nagg), Angela Vitale (Nell)

(Westbeth Theatre Center) Monday, Mar.30-Apr.5, 1992 (8 performances) Metawhateverphor Theatre Co. presents:
**WHAT A ROYAL PAIN IN THE FARCE** by Leonard Jacobs; Director, David C. Wright; Sets/Lighting, Christopher O'Leary; Stage Manager, S.C. Corrington; Press, Howard and Barbara Atlee
A farce in three acts.

(Wings Theatre) Tuesday, Mar.31-May 15, 1992 (28 performances) Wings Theatre Co. presents:
**THE RUBY SLIPPERS** by Bill Solly and Neil Kennedy; Director, Duane Mazey; Sets/Lighting, Edmond Ramage; Costumes, Jeffrey Wallach; Sound, Gerard Drazba; Stage Manager, Steven Shelton CAST: John Clayton (Chris), Michael Lang (Sid/Sandy), Peter Coster (Alun/Miles), Carys Wayne (Waitress/TJ/Doreen), Blair Zoe Tuckman (Fay), Leona Toussaint (Mrs. Burley), David Toussaint (Mr. Salmon/John), Jeffrey Wallach (David/Lana), Edmond Ramage (Miss Death)
A drama about a young man's obsession with Judy Garland. The action takes place in London, 1971.

(New Dramatists) Wednesday, Apr.1, 1992 (1 performance) Arthur Shafman Int'l presents:
**A WALK IN THE WOODS** by Lee Blessing; Director, Ernie Barbarash CAST: Gregg Thomas (Honeyman), Jerry Rockwood (Botvinnik)
A play in two acts. The action takes place in a pleasant woods on the outskirts of Geneva.

(Village Theatre) Wednesday, Apr.1-25, 1992 (17 performances) Village Theatre Co. presents:
**THIS ONE THING I DO** by Claire Braz-Valentine in collaboration with Michael Griggs; Director, GiGi Rivkin; Lighting, Jason Livingston; Set, Henry Fonte; Costumes, Christie Harrington; Sound, Jim Harrington; Stage Manager, Lisa Jean Lewis CAST: Julia Flood (Susan B. Anthony), Marjorie Feenan (Elizabeth Cady Stanton), Ellen Barry, Allyn Burrows, James Fleming, Belynda Hardin, Randy Kelly, David McConnell, Edward Tully, Tim Zay

(Vineyard Theatre) Wednesday, Apr.1-May 24, 1992 Vineyard Theatre (Barbara Zinn Krieger, Executive Director; Douglas Aibel, Artistic Director; Jon Nakagawa, Managing Director) presents:
**ONE OF THE ALL-TIME GREATS** by Charles Grodin; Director, Tony Roberts; Sets, Allen Moyer; Lighting, Phil Monat; Costumes, Muriel Stockdale; Sound, Bruce Ellman; Stage Manager, Maura J. Murphy; Press, Shirley Herz/Sam Rudy CAST: Kim Chan (Waiter), Larry Block (Alvin), Renée Taylor (Lenore), Richard B. Schull (Ric), Lou Liberatore (Norman), Helen Greenberg (Darlene), Jack Hallett (Marty/Manny), Francine Beers (Claudia), Tom McGowan (Joe), Kimberleigh Aarn (Melanie Noelle)
A comedy in two acts. The action takes place in New York City.

(John Jay Theatre) Monday, Apr.6-15, 1992 (9 performances) The Acting Company (Zelda Fichandler, Artistic Director; Margot Harley, Executive Producer) presents:
**A MIDSUMMER NIGHT'S DREAM** by William Shakespeare; Director, Joe Dowling; Sets, Douglas Stein; Costumes, Catherine Zuber; Lighting, Allen Lee Hughes; Music, George Fulginiti Shakar; Stage Manager, Elizabeth Stephens; Press, Richard Kornberg CAST: Jonathan Earl Peck (Theseus), Trish Jenkins (Hippolyta), Major West (Egeus/Philostrate), Terra Vandergaw (Hermia), Mark Stewart Guin (Lysander), Rainn Wilson (Demetrius), Angie Phillips (Helena), Patrick Kerr (Peter Quince), Andrew Weems (Bottom), Duane Boutte (Flute), Derek Meader (Snout/Peaseblossom), Dan Berkey (Snug), Jed Diamond (Starveling/Mustardseed), Jeffrey Wright (Puck), Lisa Benavides (Cobweb), Kati Kuroda (Moth) and

Mark Stewart Guin, Terra Vandergaw in
"Midsummer Night's Dream" (*Diane Gorodnitzki*)

Sue Kenny, Alexander Webb, Kimberly Topper in
"More Fun Than Bowling" (*Carol Rosegg*)

**BLOOD KNOT** by Athol Fugard; Director, Tazewell Thompson; Sets, Douglas Stein; Costumes, Paul Tazewell; Lighting, Allen Lee Hughes; Sound, Susan R. White CAST: Jed Diamond (Morris), Jonathan Earl Peck (Zachariah)

(Theatre Row Theatre) Tuesday, Apr.7-25, 1992 (15 performances) Gryphon Co. presents:
**ON THE VERGE (OR THE GEOGRAPHY OF YEARNING)** by Eric Overmyer; Director, Peter Basch; Sets/Lighting, Joel Giguere; Costumes, Maud Kresnowski; Press, Shirley Herz/Sam Rudy CAST: Barbara Bragg, Adriana Maxwell, Teresa Wolf, Brian Howe
  Three Victorian women safari into the future.

(Provincetown Playhouse) Thursday, Apr.9-12, 1992 (5 performances) Curtis Entertainment 6 presents:
**A TERRIBLE BEAUTY**; Written/Directed by Kevin Breslin; Sets, Tony Dunne; Lighting, Gary Marder; Costumes, Barbara Schulman Breslin; Sound, Doug Kleeger; Producers, Ronald Curtis, Deren Getz, Hugh Bach, Peter Thomas Roth, Stage Manager, Paul D'Amato; Press, John and Gary Springer CAST: William Hickey (Pat McCann), Tatum O'Neal (Donna Murphy), Holt McCallany (John Murphy), Fiona Hutchison (Deirdre McCann), Michael A. Healy (Damon O'Leary)
  A drama in two acts. The action takes place in McCann's bar on St. Patrick's Day.

(Triangle Theatre) Thursday, Apr.9-May 3, 1992 (20 performances) Triangle Theatre Co. (Michael Ramach, Producing Director) presents:
**MORE FUN THAN BOWLING** by Steve Dietz; Director, John Seibert; Sets, Bob Phillips; Lighting, Nancy Collings; Costumes, Amanda J. Klein; Stage Manager, Cathy Diane Tomlin; Press, Jim Baldassare CAST: Fred Burrell (Jake), T. Cat Ford (Lois), Sue Kenny (Loretta), Kimberly Topper (Molly), Alexander Webb (Mr. Dyson)
  A comedy set in the small midwestern town of Turtle Rapids.

(Ubu Rep.) Tuesday, Apr.14-26, 1992 (12 performances) UBU Repertory (Francoise Kourilsky, Artistic Director) presents:
**FAMILY PORTRAIT** by Denise Bonal; Translation, Timothy Johns; Director, Shirley Kaplan; Set, John Brown; Lighting, Greg MacPherson; Costumes, Carol Ann Pelletier; Stage Manager, David Waggett; Press, Peter Cromarty/Lynne McCreary CAST: Joanna Merlin (Louise), Gareth Williams (Raymond), Paul Austin (Pinchard),

Alice Alvarado (Assia), Matthew Mutrie (Patrick), Alison Bartlett (Armelle), Robert Kerbeck (Albert)
  The action takes place in a French border town at present.

(Third Step Studio) Thursday, Apr.16-May 3, 1992 (12 performances) Third Step Theatre Co. presents:
**MORAL AND POLITICAL LESSONS ON WYOMING** by Vincent Sessa; Director, Elfin Frederick Vogel; Set, Alex Biagioli; Costumes, Jennifer Anderson; Stage Manager, Malik CAST: Kirk Duncan, William Ellis, R.K. Greene, Gordon Jorgensen, John Kozeluh, Barbara Sinclair, Michele Wagner
  A serious comedy on the power of theatre.

(Judith Anderson Theatre) Friday, Apr.17-May 3, 1992 (15 performances) Echo Rep. presents:
**FARTHER WEST** by John Murrell; Director, Victoria Liberatori; Sets, Sarah Edkins; Costumes, Barbara Beccio; Lighting, Warren Karp; Sound, Jessica Morrow; Sound, Tom Gould; Dance, Leslie Farlow; Fights, Jason Kushner; Press, Francine L. Trevens CAST: Richard Bierman, Milton Carney, Catherine Dudley, Jeff Dypwick, J.C. Islander, Michael O'Hare, Janice Orlandi, Jerry Silverstein, Sandra Waugh
  A drama set in Calgary, 1880.

(Union Square Theatre) Tuesday, Apr.21-May 24, 1992 (14 performances and 24 previews) Max Weitzenhoffer, Stewart F. Lane, Joan Cullman and Richard Norton present:
**EATING RAOUL** with Music by Jed Feuer; Lyrics, Boyd Graham; Book, Paul Bartel based on his screenplay with Richard Blackburn; Director, Toni Kotite; Orchestrations, Joseph Gianono; Musical Director, Albert Ahronheim; Sets, Loren Sherman; Costumes, Franne Lee; Lighting, Peggy Eisenhauer; Sound, Peter Fitzgerald; Cast Recording, Bay Cities; Vocal Arrangements, Mr. Feuer, Mr. Ahronheim; Choreography, Lynne Taylor-Corbett; Press, Keith Sherman/Chris Day, Joel W. Dein, Jim Byk; Stage Manager, Alan Hall CAST: Courtenay Collins (Mary Bland), Eddie Korbich (Paul Bland), M.W. Reid (Dr. Doberman/Ginger), Jonathan Brody (Mr. Kray/James/Junior), David Masenheimer (Mr. Leech/ Howard/Bobby), Lovette George (Cop/Inez-Raoulette), Cindy Benson (Donna the Dominatrix/Tyrone/Yolanda), Adrian Zmed (Raoul), Susan Wood (Gladys-Raoulette), Allen Hidalgo (Tourist/Swinger/Etc.)

William Hickey, Tatum O'Neal, Holt McCallany, Michael A. Healy, Fiona Hutchison in "A Terrible Beauty" (*Stephen Sands*)

Matthew Mutrie, Alice Alvarado in "Family Portrait" (*Carol Rosegg*)

**Eddie Korbich, Courtney Collins in**
**"Eating Raoul"** (*Anita & Steve Shevett*)

**Meg Wynn Owen, Maria Radman, Laurence Gleason in**
**"Like to Live"** (*Carol Rosegg*)

MUSICAL NUMBERS; Meet the Blands, A Small Restaurant, La La Land, Swing Swing Swing, Happy Birthday Harry, You Gotta Take Pains, A Thought Occurs, Experts, Empty Bed, Basketball, Tool for You, Think About Tomorrow, Opening, Hot Monkey Love, Momma Said, Lovers in Love, Mary, Eating Raoul, Mucho Macho Trio, One Last Bop, Finale
A musical comedy in two acts with fifteen scenes. The action takes place in Los Angeles, mid-1960s.

(Soho Rep Theatre) Wednesday, Apr.22-26, 1992 ( 7 performances) Bestboy Productions presents:
**ALL ABOUT JANICE**; Created/Composed by Tammy Andries, Greg Berry and Lisa Welti; Director, Ms. Andries; Lighting, Roma Flowers; Music, Kristian Roebling CAST: Daniel Andries, Greg Berry, Holli Harms, Brian Jucha, Richard Pait, Joe Rinaldi, Ted Schulz, Vincent Tangredi, Lisa Welti
Multi-media piece on Hollywood's view of actors.

(Primary Stages) Wednesday, Apr.22-May 17, 1992 (23 performances) Primary Stages presents:
**MURDER OF CROWS** by Mac Wellman; Director, Jim Simpson; Set, Kyle Chepulis; Costumes, Bruce Goodrich; Lighting, Brian Aldous; Composer/Sound, David Van Tieghem; Choreography, Tina Dudek; Stage Manager, Melanie White CAST: Anne O'Sullivan (Nella), Jan Leslie Harding (Susannah), William Mesnik Howard), Lauren Hamilton (Georgia), Steve Mellor (Raymond), Reed Birney (Andy), Tina Dudek (Crow #1), Ray Xifo (Crow #2), David Van Tieghem (Crow #3)
A black comedy performed without intermission.

(One Dream Theatre) Thursday, Apr.23-May 10, 1992 (15 performances) Willow Cabin Theatre Co. and Alexander E. Racolin present:
**LIKE TO LIVE/TISSUE** by Louise Page; Director, Edward Berkeley; Sets/Costumes, Miguel Lopez-Castillo; Lighting, Jane Reisman; Stage Manager, Julie Lancaster; Press, Jim Baldassare CASTS: *Tissue* Maria Radman (Sally Bacon), Meg Wynn Owen (Woman), Laurence Gleason (Man) *Live* Meg Wynn Owen (Hermoine), Maria Radman (Paulina)

(Triplex) Friday, Apr.24-May 3, 1992 (7 performances and 1 preview) The Asian American Performance Initiative, New York Chinese Cultral Center and Chinatown History Museum present:
**HAVOC IN GOLD MOUNTAIN**; Created/Performed by Ming Fay, Fred Wei-han Ho, Jia Lu Hu, Corky Lee, Siu Fai Pun, Liang Xing Tang, Liang Tee Tue; Press, Ted Killmer
Performance art creating a new mythology for Asian America.

(Kampo Cultral Center) Friday, Apr.24-May 17, 1992 (16 performances) Signature Theatre Co. presents:
**AMBROSIO** by Romulus Linney; Directors, Mr. Linney, James Houghton; Set, E. David Cosier; Costumes, Teresa Snider-Stein, Jonathan Green; Lighting, Jeffrey S. Koger; Stage Manager, Deborah Natoli CAST: Jacqueline Bertrand (Elvira), Craig Duncan (Rosario), Mark Alan Gordon (Lucero), Marin Hinkle (Antonia), Garrison Phillips (Inquisitor), T. Ryder Smith (Don Pedro), Peter Ashton Wise (Ambrosio)
A drama performed without intermission. The action takes place in Cordoba, Spain in 1500.

(Queens Theatre in the Park) Friday, Apr.24-May 24, 1992 (15 performances)
**VAGABOND STARS** by Nahma Sandrow; Lyrics, Alan Poul; Director, Christopher Catt; Choreography, Tom Polum; Sets, Sarah L. Lambert; Costumes, Jose M. Rivera; Press, Peter Cromarty/David Stepfanou CAST: Guylaine Laperrière, Fred Goldberg, Eugene Flam
Songs and routines of the Yiddish theatre.

(Our Lady of Vilnius) Friday, Apr.24-May 24, 1992 (16 performances) Arts Club Theatre presents:
**PROPHET JONAH** by Kazys Saja; Direction/Translation, Rasa Allan Kazlas; Music, Bruce Sales CAST: Petrus Antonius, Ron Botting, Dimitri Christy, Thomas Crouch, Marianne DeAngleis, Donald Broady, Gayle Hudson, Eric Sanders, John Steber, Kelly Taffe, Stephen Wyler

**Steve Mellor, Lauren Hamilton, Jan Leslie Harding, Annie O'Sullivan,**
**William Mesnick in "Murder of Crows"** (*Marvin Einhorn*)

**Marin Hinkle, Peter Ashton Wise in**
**"Ambrosio"** (*Susan Johann*)

(St. Paul's) Saturday, Apr.25-May 26, 1992 (7 performances) Grassroots Theatre Co. presents:

**EASTERN STANDARD** by Richard Greenberg; Director, Victoria McElwaine; Stage Manager, Larry Yalkowsky; Prod. Coordinator, Eric Schussel CAST: Stephen Delaney (Drew), Michael Perreca (Stephen), Carol Van Keuren (Ellen), Gretchen Claggett (May), Anthony M. Brown (Peter), Eileen Connolly (Phoebe)

The 1988 comedy-drama in two acts. The action takes place in Manhattan and the Hamptons at present.

(Playhouse 46) Tuesday, Apr.28-May 23, 1992 (21 performances) Pan Asian Repertory (Tisa Chang, Artistic/Producing Director) presents:

**FAIRY BONES** by Laurence Yep; Director/Music, Tina Chen; Set, Atsushi Moriyasu; Lighting, Deborah Canstantine; Costumes, Juliet Ouyoung; Sound, Jim Van Bergen; Stage Manager, Sue Jane Stoker; Press, Ted Killmer CAST: Raul Aranas (Con Man/Peter), Keenan Shimizu (Young Man), Lucy Liu (Young Woman), Christen Villamor (Spirit Woman)

Two one-act dramas. The action takes place in the Sacremont Delta, 1893.

(Theatre 22) Thursday, Apr.30-May 17, 1992 (15 performances) Terese Hayden presents:

**TEN BLOCKS ON THE CAMINO REAL** by Tennessee Williams; Director, Terese Hayden; Design, Fred Kolo; Press, Max Eisen/Madelon Rosen CAST: Jacqueline Brookes (Gypsy), Charles Cissel (Kilroy), Gregory Jones (Guard/ Instructor), Roger Kovary (Baron Charlus/Byron/Don Quixote), Tasha Lawrence (Esmeralda), Robert Maniscaico (Player), James Stevenson (Gutman), Charles Tuthill (Casanova), Elaine Valby (Margueritte Gautier)

The original version of William's later Broadway play *Camino Real*.

(St. Bart's) Friday, May 1-17, 1992 (14 performances) St. Bart's presents:

**HOW TO SUCCEED IN BUSINESS WITHOUT REALLY TRYING** with Music/Lyrics, by Frank Loesser; Book, Abe Burrows, Jack Weinstock, Willie Gilbert; Director, Steven Earl-Edwards; Musical Director, Steve Silverstein; Choreography, Jeffery Peters; Sets, Fred Christoffel; Costumes, Estella Marie; Lighting, Karen Spahn; Press, Peter Cromarty/Lynne McCreary CAST: Peter Yawitz (Finch), Jonathan Bennett, Tracy Cassidy, Jim Mullins, Ann Vawter, LuAnn Vispoli, Ken Altman,

Lucy Liu, Christen Villamor in "Fairy Bones" (*Carol Rosegg*)

Peter Yawitz, Tracey Cassidy, Ann Vawter in "How to Succeed..." (*Carol Rosegg*)

Katherine Beitner, Sean Dosil, Jonathan Foits, Dan Grinko, Denver Hart, Dan Josseph Jane Larkworthy, Matt Levine, Marcie Lopez, Paul Seymour, Jean Streit, Maren Swenson, Richard Van Slyke, Michael Waxenberg, Lizzie Yawitz

The 1961 musical in two acts. The action takes place on Park Ave.

(Henry St. Settlement) Friday, May 1-17, 1992 New Federal Theatre and Shoestring Prods. present:

**TESTIMONY** by Safiya Henderson-Holmes; Director, Raina von Waldenburg; Set, Nathan Jones; Lighting, Marty Liquori; Press, Max Eisen/Madelon Rosen CAST: Marty Liquori (Maceo), Julie Bray-Morris (Laura), Mantee M. Murphy (Taylor), Sonita Surratt (Jacintha)

A drama set in the Tombs, May 1989.

(Ballroom) Monday, May 4-30, 1992 (31 performances) Tim Jonson presents:

**DANCING ON THE WHITE HOUSE LAWN**; Written/Performed by Donna Blue Lachman; Director, David Petrarca; Press, David Rothenberg

An autobiographical monologue.

(Ubu Rep.) Tuesday, May 5-17, 1992 (12 performances) UBU Repertory (Françoise Kourilsky, Artistic Director) presents:

**JOCK** by Jean-Louis Bourdon; Translation, Timothy Johns; Director, André Ernotte; Set, John Brown; Lighting, Greg MacPherson; Costumes, Carol Ann Pelletier; Sound, Phil Lee, David Lawson; Stage Manager, David Waggett; Press, Peter Cromarty/Lynne McCreary CAST: Craig Wasson (Jock), Jim Abele (Jim), Margaret Klenck (Sonia)

American premiere of a French drama.

(Hudson Guild Theatre) Tuesday, May 5-24, 1992 (24 performances) The Actor's Company Theatre:

**TWELFTH NIGHT** by William Shakespeare; Director, David Perry; Set, Ray Recht; Costumes, Mimi Maxmen; Lighting, Robert Rosenthal; Sound, Tom Sorce; Press, Peter Cromarty/Lynne McCreary CAST: Maia Danziger, Francesca di Mauro, Gregory Salata, Mark Lewis, Robert Mason Ham, Mary Alice McGuire, Tony Hoty

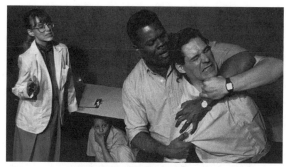

Juli Bray-Morris, Sonita Surratt, Mantee Murphy, Marty Liquori in "Testimony" (*Bert Andrews*)

Margaret Klenk, Jim Abelee in "Jock" (*Carol Rosegg*)

(Mazur Theatre) Wednesday, May 6-23, 1992 (15 performances) Playwrights' Preview Productions presents:
**ON SUMMER DAYS** by Roma Greth; Director, Frances Hill; Set, Ann Davis; Lighting, Judy Daitsman; Costumes, Robin Orloff; Musical Director, Virginia Becraft; Stage Manager, Yael Schuester CAST: Bill Bennett, Joan Bruemmer, Joanna Daniels, Barbara Raven, Mary Jane Wells
A drama set in Indiana, 1940.

(Mobile Home) Wednesday, May 6- moved to Atlantic Theatre Wednesday, June 3-Aug.5, 1992 Michael Cohen, Ron Kastner and Lyle Saunders present the Home for Contemporary Theatre & Art production:
**ONE NECK** by Todd Alcott; Director, Randy Rollison; Design, H.G. Arrott; Lighting, Mary Louise Geiger; Costumes, Carol Brys; Music/Sound, David Jackson; Action Sequence, Rick Sordelet; Press, Shirley Herz/Wayne Wolfe and David Rothenberg CAST: Frank Deal (Wes), Todd Alcott (Lucian), David Thornton (Guy), Melissa Hurst (Patina), Allison Janney (Nyla), Damian Young (Hack)
A thriller in two acts. The action takes place on Long Island, late summer.

(Amas Theatre) Thursday, May 7-31, 1992 (24 performances) Amas Musical Theatre presents:
**JUNKYARD** with Music by Michael Sahl; Lyrics, Manuel Mandel; Book, Mr. Mandel, Mr. Sahl; Director, Avi Ber Hoffman; Co-Musical Staging, Barry Finkel; Musical Director, Mr. Sahl; Set, John Farrell; Costumes, Jessica Doyle; Lighting, William Kradlak; Stage Manager, Joka Kops CAST: Nicholas Augustus, Richert Easley, Julie Jirousek, Peter-Michael Kalin, Rick Leon, Susan Levine, Chris N. Norris, Obie Story, Natalie Toro, Darlene B. Young

(Performing Garage) Thursday, May 7-June 7, 1992
**ROY COHN/JACK SMITH**; Conceived/Performed by Ron Vawter; *Roy Cohn* by Gary Indiana; *Jack Smith* by Jack Smith; Creation, Gregory Mehrten, Clay Shirky, Mr. Vawter, Marianne Weems; Director, Mr. Mehrten; Lighting, Jennifer Tipton
Two monologues.

(Chernuchin Theatre) Thursday, May 7-June 21, 1992 (35 performances) American Theatre of Actors presents:
**BROTHERLY LOVE** by John Fedele; Director, Frank Criscione; Set, Robert Bryson; Lighting, Bob Sesselberg; Costumes, Linda Luppino; Press, David Rothenberg CAST: John Fedele, Robert Arcaro, Jim Hance, Lynne Knight, Noemi Soulet
A drama about Italian-American brothers.

(clockwise) Frank Deal, Todd Alcott, Allison Janney, Damian Young, Melissa Hurst, David Thornton in "One Neck" (*William Gibson*)

Lynne Knight, Robert Arcaro, John Fedele in "Brotherly Love" (*William Gibson*)

(29th St. Playhouse) Monday, May 11-30, 1992 (17 performances) 29th St. Repertory presents:
**THE DUCK BLIND** by Peter Maeck; Director, David Dorwart; Set, Roger Mooney; Costumes, David Burke; Lighting, David Weiner; Sound, Vera Beren; Press, David Rothenberg CAST: Alison Lani Bronda, Tim Cocoran, Leo Farley, David Mogentale, Richard Sachar
A drama about war as experienced from the homefront.

(Judith Anderson Theatre) Wednesday, May 13-June 7, 1992 (27 performances) The Women's Project & Productions (Julia Miles, Artistic Director) presents:
**DREAM OF A COMMON LANGUAGE** by Heather McDonald; Director, Liz Diamond; Set, Anita Stewart; Costumes, Sally J. Lesser; Lighting, Michael Chybowski; Composer/Sound, Daniel Moses Schreier; Stage Manager, Jill Cordle; Press, Jeffrey Richards/Denise Robert CAST: Caris Corfman (Pola), Mia Katigbak (Dolores), Mary Mara (Clovis), J.R. Nutt (Mylo), Joseph Siravo (Victor), Rocco Sisto (Marc)
A drama in two acts. The action takes place outside Paris, 1874.

(Westbeth Theatre Center) Thursday, May 14-31, 1992 (16 performances) Watt Productions presents:
**STRIP TEASE** by Robin Moran Miller; Director, Donal Egan; Set, Mark Solan; Lighting, Chele Ware; Costumes, Jonathan Green; Stage Manager, Paul A. Kochman; Press, Ruta Vaisnys CAST: Elizabeth Schofield, Lynne McCollough, Richard Petrocelli, Didi Sinclair, Cynthia Babak, Jane Montgomery, Elissa Groh, Katrini Lantz
The lives of six strip dancers.

(Soho Rep) Thursday, May 14-June 7, 1992 (20 performances) Soho Rep (Marlene Swartz, Julian Webber, Artistic Directors) presents:
**TONE CLUSTERS** by Joyce Carol Oates; Director, Julian Webber; Sets, Kyle Chepulis; Costumes, Mary Myers; Sound, David Schnirman; Lighting, Don Holder; Video/Stage Manager, Mark Frankel; Press, Jonathan Slaff CAST: John Nacco (Frank Gulick), Black-Eyed Susan (Emily Gulick), Richard Adamson (Voice)
A one-act drama.

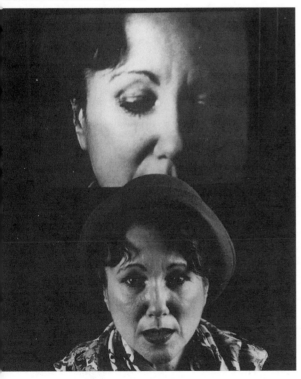
Black-Eyed Susan in "Tone Clusters" (*Jonathan Slaff*)

(Theatre for the New City) Thursday, May 14-31, 1992 (12 performances) Theatre for the New City presents:
**ANGELINA'S PIZZERIA** with Music/Lyrics/Book by Eddie DiDonna, Crystal Field, T. Scott Lilly, Mark Marcante, Michael Vazquez; Director, Mark Marcante; Set, Michael McGarty; Lighting, Tom Barker; Masks, Tony Angel; Costumes, Lolly Alejandro CAST: Arlana Blue, Stephen DeLorenzo, Mary Cunningham Eck, Henry Fandel, Crystal Field, Vicky Linchon, T. Scott Lilly, Mark Marcante, Craig Meade, Sheridan Roberts, Michael Vasquez, Barbara Wise
A musical in two acts.

(One Dream Theatre) Friday, May 15-June 7, 1992 (19 performances and 3 previews) Willow Cabin Theatre Co. presents:
**MACBETH** by William Shakespeare; Director, Edward Berkeley; Sets/Costumes, Miguel Lopez-Castillo; Lighting, Steven Rust; Fights, Bjorn Johnson; Press, Jim Baldassare CAST: John Bolger (Macbeth), Cecil Hoffmann (Lady Macbeth), John Billeci (Rosse), Maria Bolger (Fleance/Macduff's Son), Christopher Cabot (Angus), Angela Nevard, Dede Pochos, Linda Powell (Witches), Adam Oliensis (Macduff), Christine Radman (Gentlewoman), Maria Radman (Lady Macduff), Michael Rispoli (Banquo/Old Siward), Jonathan Sea (Malcolm), Alex Spencer (Lenox), Joel Van Liew (Donalbain/Murderer/Monteth), Ken Favre (Soldier/Murderer/Cathness), Laurence Gleason (Duncan/Porter/Old Man/Doctor).

(Beckmann Theatre) Monday, May 18-24, 1992 (7 performances) The Quaigh Theatre presents:
**BROADWAY AFTER DARK** by Ward Morehouse III; Director, Will Lieberson; Lighting, Joseph A. Goshert; Makeup, James Chai; Sound, George Jacobs; Stage Manager, Winifred Powers CAST: Steve Shoup (Ward Morehouse II)
A drama on the critic and columnist.

(Beacon Theatre) Tuesday, May 19, 1992- Barry Hankerson, Dimensions Unlimited, and New Regal Theatre present:
**THE FIRST LADY** with Music by Vickie Winans; Writer/Director, Chip Fields; Press, Irene Gandy CAST: Vickie Winans (Paula), Louis Price (Rev. Cooper), Donald Albert, Ernie Banks, Tina Brooks, Don Rico Brent, Cassandra Davis, Kellie Evans, Sandra Feva, Katrina Harper, Keneth Hickson, Bryan Jones, Hezekiah Williams, Glynis Martin, Marshall Titus

(Cherry Lane Theatre) Tuesday, May 19-June 14, 1992 Dowling Ent., John Walker and Pamela Gay, Hal "Corky" Kessler and Gintare Sileika Everett, in association with Charles J. Scibetti and Victory Gardens Theatre present:
**HAUPTMAN** by John Logan; Director, Terry McCabe; Set, James Dardenne; Costumes, Claudia Boddy; Lighting, Todd Hensley; Sound, Galen G. Ramsey; Choreography, Ann Hartdegen; Stage Manager, Kristin Laresen; Press, Chris Boneau/Adrian Bryan Brown, Cabrini Lepis, Craig Karpel CAST: Denis O'Hare (Richard Hauptman), Gunnar Branson (Charles Lindbergh), Donna Powers (Anne Morrow Lindbergh), Wendy Lueker (Anna Hauptman), Craig Spidle (Prosecuting Attorney Wilentz), Dev Kennedy (Dr. Condon), Rod McLachlan (Judge Trenchard)
The action takes place on Death Row, April 3, 1936.

(Ubu Rep.) Tuesday, May 26-June 7, 1992 (12 performances) UBU Repertory presents:
**NOWHERE** by Reine Bartève; Translation, Bruno Kernz, Lorraine Alexander; Director, Francoise Kourilsky; Set, John Brown; Lighting, Greg MacPherson; Costumes, Carol Ann Pelletier; Music, Genji Ito; Stage Manager, Teresa Conway; Press, Peter Cromarty/Lynne McCreary CAST: Julie Boyd (Marie), William Carden, Du-Yee Chang, Stephen Mendillo
A drama set at a deserted train station in France.

(Playhouse 125) Wednesday, May 27-June 21, 1992 (20 performances) Randy Norton in association with Eclipse Enterprise Prods. presents:
**A FRESH OF BREATH AIR**; Written/Performed by Dale Stein; Music, Charles Goldbeck; Lyrics, Ms. Stein; Director, Christopher Ashley; Set, Russell Metheny; Lighting, Daniel MacLean Wagner; Costumes, Sharon Lynch; Press, David Rothenberg
One-woman show with music.

(Theatre Row Theatre) Wednesday, May 27-June 28, 1992 (25 performances) New York Repertory Theatre Co. presents:
**NEBRASKA** by Keith Reddin; Director, Graf Mouen; Set, Christopher Barreca; Lighting, Mimi Jordan Sherin; Costumes, Connie Singer; Sound, Jeffrey Taylor; Stage Manager, Randy Lawson; Press, Peter Cromarty/David Bar Katz CAST: Michael Hayden (Dean Swift), Robert North (Jack Gurney), Cathy Reinheimer (Julie Swift),

**Cathy Reinheimer, Michael Hayden in "Nebraska"** (*Carol Rosegg*)

Michael Griffiths (Henry Fielding), Jon Patrick Walker (Ted Barnes), Paula Mann (Carol Gurney), Anne Torsiglieri (Kim Newman)
A drama in two acts. The action takes place in and around a Strategic Air Command base outside of Omaha, Nebraska at present.

(Steve McGraw's) Friday, May 29, 1992 (off-hour schedule)- Michael Gill presents:
**WHITE LIES** with Songs by Keith Thompson and Douglas Carter Beane; Sketches, Mr. Beane; Director/Choreography, Greg Ganakas; Set, Jeff Modereger; Costumes, John Sullivan; Lighting, Ken Smith; Press, Peter Cromarty/Lynne McCreary CAST: Nancy Johnson, Bill Kocis, Hugh Panaro, Jennifer Smith, Cheryl Stern
Musical comedy revue inspired by weekly tabloid headlines.

(Intar Theatre) Wednesday, June 3-28, 1992 (24 performances) Intar (Max Ferra, Artistic Director) presents:
**ANY PLACE BUT HERE** by Caridad Svich; Set, Bill Stabile; Costumes, Sally Lesser; Lighting, Ernie Barbarash; Sound, Alina Avila; Stage Manager, Jesse Wooden; Press, Peter Cromarty/David Bar Katz CAST: Jessica Hecht (Lydia), Peter McCabe (Chucky), Mimi Cichanowicz Quillin (Veronica), Jim Abele (Tommy)
A dark comedy set in a faded New Jersey town.

(Judith Anderson Theatre) Wednesday, June 10-21, 1992 (20 performances) Manhattan Punch Line presents:
**8TH ANNUAL FESTIVAL OF ONE-ACT COMEDIES**; Artistic Director, Steve Kaplan PROGRAM A: *The Fall of the House of Shlimowitz* by Michael Panes; Director, Peter Basch; *Trudy & Paul Come to the Rescue* by Michael Aschner; Director, Mr. Kaplan; *The John Philip Sousa Workshop* by Stephen Gregg; Director, Tracy Brigden; *Candy Hearts* by Theresa Rebeck; Director, Tracy Brigden; *Get a Stupid Answer* by John Holleman; Director, Margie Salvante PROGRAM B: *Monkey Business* by David Bottrell; Director, Louis Scheeder; *The Solution*; Written/Directed by Michael Panes; *Bus Face* by Larry Blamire; Director, Cynthia Stokes; *Sally Sees the Light* by Barbara Lindsay; Director, Stephanie Klapper; *Unabridged* by Michael Dempsey; Director, Charles Karchmer
The final New York productions of this company.

# OFF BROADWAY COMPANY SERIES

## AMERICAN JEWISH THEATRE

Eighteenth Season

stic Director, Stanley Brechner; Associate Artistic Director, Lonny Price; Resident
ctor, Richard Sabellico; Counsel, Walter Gidaly, Howard I. Golden; Manager,
a Small; General Manager, George Elmer; Development, Norman Golden; Press,
rey Richards/Ben Gutkin

aturday, November 2 - December 29, 1991 (59 performances)
GS: *Children Of The Wind*; Music, Charles Strouse; Lyrics, Stephen Schwartz;
k, Joseph Stein; Director/Choreographer, Richard Sabellico; Musical Director,
cent Trovato; Sets, Jeff Modereger; Costumes, Gail Baldoni; Lighting, Tom
ge; Sound, Randy Hanson; Stage Manager, Kim Vernace CAST: Rachel Black
stomer/Aunt/Shopper/Rosa/14th St. Ballet Dancer/Rag Picker), Ann Crumb
becca), Jonathan Kaplan (David), Crista Moore (Bella), Philip Hoffman
ram/Hamlet/Big Tim), Jan Neuberger (Landlady/Rachel/Ophelia/14th St. Ballet
cer/Sophie/Mrs. Sullivan), David Pevsner (Doctor/Saul/14th St. Ballet
cer/Nathan), Robert Tate (Immigrant/Guard/Editor/Klezmer
sician/Bronstein/14th St. Ballet Dancer/Man/Striker), Alec Timerman (Ben/14th St.
et Dancer) MUSICAL NUMBERS: Children Of The Wind, If We Never Meet
in (new song), Yankee Boy, Greenhorns, Brand New World, Penny A Tune, Easy
You, Hamlet, Summer Night, For My Mary, Rags, Cherry St. Cafe, Uptown,
nd Of Love, Three Sunny Rooms, Wanting, What's Wrong With That, Dancing
h The Fools, Finale
a revised version of the 1986 musical in two acts. The action takes place en route
nd in New York City around 1910.

"First is Supper" cast with Shelley Berman
Top: David Pevsner, Ann Crumb, (front) Jonathan Kaplan in "Rags"

Saturday, January 4 - February 2, 1992 (31 performances)
**INVENTION FOR FATHERS AND SONS** by Alan Brody; Director, Jay E.
Raphael; Sets, Bill Clarke; Costumes, Elizabeth Covey; Lighting, Kirk Bookman;
Composer, Worth Gardner; Stage Manager, Gail Eve Malatesta CAST: William
Verderber (Joel), Len Stanger (Max), Gordon MacDonald (Abe/Marty), Glynis Bell
(Rachel), Monica Bell (Arlene/Danielle), Ben Hammer (Elihu), Elaine Grollman (Eva)

Saturday, February 29 - March 29, 1992 (31 performances)
**FIRST IS SUPPER** by Shelley Berman; Director, Andre Ernotte; Sets, James Wolk;
Costumes, Muriel Stockdale; Lighting, Howard Werner; Sound, Bruce Ellman; Stage
Manager, David Horton Black CAST: Nile Lanning (Ida), Patricia Mauceri (Frieda),
Louis Falk (Solly), Barbara Andres (Lotte), Mark Zimmerman (Getz), Blaza Autumn
Berdahl (Rosey), Marilyn Salinger (Rachel), Donald Christopher (Victor)
A drama in two acts. The action takes place in Chicago, 1919.

Saturday, April 25 - July 19, 1992
**BIG AL/ANGEL OF DEATH**; Sets, James Wolk; Costumes, Sarah Edwards;
Lighting, Howard Werner; Sound, Bruce Ellman; Stage Manager, Mark Cole BIG AL
by Brian Goluboff; Director, Peter Maloney CAST: Evan Handler (Leo), Gus
Rogerson (Ricky)
The action takes place in a downtown basement apartment in New York on a rainy
night.
ANGEL OF DEATH by Charlie Schulman; Director, Bill Hopkins CAST: Daniel
Von Bargen (Gunther Ludwig), Steven Goldstein (Rolf), Keith Reddin (Bill Century),
Leslie Lyles (Betty Century), Anna Thomson (Woman/Melanie Baxter)
The resurrection of Joseph Mengele as a pop movie star.

Keith Reddin, Leslie Lyles, Daniel von Bargen in
"Angel of Death" (*Carol Rosegg/Martha Swope Photos*)
Top: Gus Rogerson, Evan Handler in "Big Al"

**113**

# AMERICAN PLACE THEATRE

Twenty-eighth Season

Director/Co-Founder, Wynn Handman; General Manager, Dara Hershman; Development/Marketing Director, Donna Moreau-Cupp; Office Manager, Elizabeth Gue; Theatre Education (Interplay) Director, Lloyd Davis, Jr.; Literary Associate, Elise Thoren; Production Manager, Patrick Heydenburg; Mr. Handman's Asst., Jane Ray; Press, David Rothenberg/Meg Gordean, Manuel Igrejas, Terence Womble

Friday, September 27 - October 27, 1991 (33 performances)
**THE RADIANT CITY;** Written/Designed/Directed by Theodora Skipitares; Music, Christopher Thall; Lyrics, Andrea Balis; Lighting, F. Mitchell Dana; Sound, David Wonsey; Kinetics, Raymond Kurshals; Technical Design, Nir Lilach; Dramaturg, Cynthia Jenner; Stage Managers, Lloyd Davis Jr., Michael Robin  CAST: William Badgett, Charles W. Croft, Edward Greenberg, Cora Hook, John Jowett, Lisa Kirchner, Michael Preston, Jane Catherine Shaw, Christopher Thall
A multimedia music-theatre work in two acts that uses life-sized puppets, kinetic sculpture, film, slides, and live music to examine the history of New York City.

Friday, November 8 - December 1991
**REALITY RANCH;** Written and Performed by Jane Gennaro; Director, Peter Askin; Set, John Esposito; Lighting, Natasha Katz; Music/Sound, Daniel Schreier
Comedy monologue set in the world of infotainment.

Wednesday, November 13, 1991 - January 19, 1992
**FREE SPEECH IN AMERICA;** Written and Performed by Roger Rosenblatt; Director, Wynn Handman; Lighting, Todd Bearden; Stage Manager, Matthew Farrell
The essayist looks at free speech.

Friday, February 21 - March 29, 1992 (19 performances and 14 previews)
**AND** by Roger Rosenblatt; Director, Wynn Handman; Sets, Kert Lundell; Lighting, Brian MacDevitt; Production Manager, Patrick Heydenburg; Stage Manager, Lloyd Davis, Jr.  CAST: Ron Silver
A monodrama performed without intermission.

Wednesday, April 29 - May 30, 1992 (29 performances)
**ZORA NEALE HURSTON** by Laurence Holder; Director, Wynn Handman; Lighting, Shirley Prendergast  CAST: Elizabeth Van Dyke (Zora), Joseph Edwards
A return engagement of the 1990 production.

*Gerry Goodstein, Martha Holmes Photos*

**BELOW: Roger Rosenblatt**
**TOP RIGHT: Ron Silver in "And"**
**RIGHT: Jane Gennaro in "Reality Ranch"**

# BROOKLYN ACADEMY OF MUSIC

dent/Executive Producer, Harvey Lichenstein; Executive Vice-President, Karen
ks Hopkins; Marketing/Promotion, Douglas W. Allan; Finance/Administration,
ues Brunswick; General Manager, James D. Nomikos; Next Wave Director, Liz
npson; Young Peoples Programs, Leanne Tintori Wells; Development Director,
s Azaro; Press, Peter B. Carzasty, Robert Boyd, Lapacazo Sandoval, Ben Hartley,
rt Marlin.

lajestic Theatre) Monday, June 10-20, 1991 (9 performances)
 ROYAL DRAMATIC THEATRE OF SWEDEN; Director, Ingmar Bergman;
stic Director, Lars Löfgren; Sets/Costumes, Gunilla Palmstierna-Weiss;
reography, Donya Feuer; Music, Daniel Bell; Stage Managers, Thomas
nerberg, Stephano Mariano

S JULIE by August Strindberg  CAST: Lena Olin (Miss Julie), Peter Stormare
), Gerthi Kulle (Kristin), Marie Richardson, Kicki Bramberg, Ingrid Böstrom, Per
sson, Björn Granath, Jakob Eklund
 drama performed without intermission.

 G DAY'S JOURNEY INTO NIGHT by Eugene O'Neill; Translation, Sven
hel  CAST: Jarl Kulle (James Tyrone), Bibi Andersson (Mary Cavan Tyrone),
nmy Berggren (Jim Tyrone), Peter Storemare (Edmund Tyrone), Kicki Bramberg
hleen)
 drama in two acts.

 OLL'S HOUSE by Henrik Ibsen; Translation, Klas Östergren  CAST: Per
sson (Torvald Helmer), Pernilla Östergren (Nora), Erland Josephson (Dr. Rank),
e Richardson (Mrs. Linde), Björn Granath (Krogstad), Erika Harrysson (Hilde)
 drama performed in two acts.

epercq Space) Wednesday, January 22-26, 1992 (5 performances)
MLET by William Shakespeare; Translation, Avraham Shlonski;
ction/Adaptation, Rina Yerushalmi; Design, Moshe Sternfeld; Costumes, Ofra
k; Lighting, Judy Kupferman; Musical Director, Shosh Reisman  CAST: Noam
Azar (Guildenstern), Chanan Ben Shabat Rosencrantz, Dina Blei (Ophelia), Pnina
t (Gertrude), Amnon Douieb (Ghost/Player), Efron Etkin (Claudius), Orna Katz
yer), Moshe Malka (Horatio), Elisha Nurieli (Player), Amihai Pardo (Laertes),
si Pershitz (Osrick/Player), Shuli Rand (Hamlet), Shlomo Sadan
onius/Gravedigger)
erformed in Hebrew in two parts.

 Opera House/Lepercq Space/Carey Playhouse) Sunday, Jan. 19-Feb. 2, 1992
 AEL: THE NEXT GENERATION; A festival of Israeli arts featuring HAMLET
 formed by the Cameri Theatre of Tel Aviv, ROSENCRANTZ AND
 ILDENSTERN ARE DEAD performed by the Gesher Theatre Company, THE
 MMER OF AVIYA a solo performance by Gila Almagor, and JABAR'S HEAD
 ormed by Beit Hagefen Jewish-Arabic Theatre.
 Vednesday, January 29 - February 2, 1992 (5 performances)
 SENCRANTZ AND GUILDENSTERN ARE DEAD by Tom Stoppard;
 nslation, Joseph Brodsy; Director, Yevgeny Arye; Sets, D. Krimov; Costumes,
 na Lioly; Lighting, Alan Bochinsky, Michael Cherniavsky; Music, R. Berchenko,
 Nedsvetaky, N. Artamonov  CAST: Boris Achanov, Michael Asinovsky,
 xander Demidov, Yevgenya Dodina, Shaul Elias, Yevegeny Gamburg, Vladimir
 emsky, Rolland Heilovsky, Mark Ivanir, Yevgeny Terletsky, Igor Voytulevitch,
 alya Voytulevitch
 erformed by an Israeli Company of émigré Russian actors.

*Bengt Wanselius Photos*

TOP RIGHT: **Pernilla Ostergren, Per Mattsson in "A Doll's House"**
CENTER: **Shuli Rand in "Hamlet"**
RIGHT: **Gila Almagor in "Summer of Aviya"**

# CIRCLE REPERTORY COMPANY

Artistic Director, Tanya Berezin; Managing Director, Terrence Dwyer; Associate Artistic Director, Mark Ramont; Lab Director, Michael Warren Powell; Literary Manager, Lynn M. Thomson; Dramaturgical Advisor, Milan Stitt; Development Director, Virginia Finn Lenhardt; Business Manager, Michael A. Ruff; Marketing Director, Phillip Matthews; Press, Bill Evans/Jim Randolph, Erin Dunn

Wednesday, September 25 - November 3, 1991 (53 performances)
**BABYLON GARDENS** by Timothy Mason; Director, Joe Mantello; Sets, Loy Arcenas; Sound, Scott Lehrer; Production Manager, Jody Boese; Stage Manager, Denise Yaney   CAST: Timothy Hutton (Bill), Bobo Lewis (Molly), Mary-Louise Parker (Jean), Cynthia Martells (Opal), Steve Bassett (Andrew), Lea Floden (Jessica), Bruce McCarty (Larry), Cordelia Richards (Robin), Robert Jiménez (Philippe), Hector M. Estrada (Hector)
A drama in two acts. The action takes place in New York City at present.

Wednesday, November 20 - December 29, 1991 (36 performances)
**THE ROSE QUARTET** by Thomas Cumella; Director, Tee Scatuorchio; Sets, Loren Sherman; Costumes, Thomas L. Keller; Lighting, Dennis Parichy; Sound, Stewart Werner, Chuck London; Stage Manager, Lori M. Doyle   CAST: Joan Copeland (Rose Brill), Anne Pitoniak succeeded by Ruby Holbrook (Helen Brauer), Larry Keith (Jack Singer), Mason Adams (Lou Gold)
A drama in two acts. The action takes place on the Upper West Side of New York City near the present time.

Wednesday, January 29 - March 15, 1992 (55 performances)
**THE BALTIMORE WALTZ** by Paula Vogel; Director, Anne Bogart; Sets, Loy Arcenas; Costumes, Walker Hicklin; Lighting, Dennis Parichy; Sound/Score, John Gromada; Hair/Wigs, Bobby H. Grayson; Stage Manager, Denise Yancey   CAST: Cherry Jones (Anna), Richard Thompson (Carl), Joe Mantello (Third Man)
A drama performed without intermission. The action takes place in Baltimore at present.

Wednesday, April 22 - June 14, 1992 (63 performances)
**EMPTY HEARTS;** Written/Directed by John Bishop; Sets, John Lee Beatty; Costumes, Ann Roth, Bridget Kelly; Lighting, Dennis Parichy; Sound, Stewart Werner, Chuck London; Music, Robert Waldman; Concert Sequence Staging, Marcia Milgram Dodge; Stage Manager, Leslie Loeb   CAST: Cotter Smith (Michael Shartel), Mel Harris (Carol Shartel), Edward Seamon (Attorney Bob Hutchins/John Wahlen), John Dossett (Detective, Dave Ennis/Hank Sweetzer), Joel Anderson (Tom Kyle/Earl Tracy/Dr. Maxwell), Susan Bruce (Attorney Jan Horvath/Deidre McCullough), Charis Erickson (Mrs. Cambridge/Sara Kohler/Judge Ruth Denhardt/Minister/Mrs. Shartel)
A courtroom drama performed with intermission.

*Gerry Goodstein, David Morgan, Paula Court Photos*

**TOP: Timothy Hutton, Mary-Louise Parker in "Babylon Gardens"**
**RIGHT: Mason Adams, Ruby Holbrook, Larry Keith, Joan Copeland in "Rose Quartet"**

**Cotter Smith, Mel Harris in "Empty Hearts"**

**Joe Mantello, Richard Thompson, Cherry Jones in "Baltimore Waltz**

# CSC REPERTORY
## CLASSIC STAGE COMPANY

Twenty-fifth Season

...stic Director, Carey Perloff; Managing Director, Patricia Taylor; Development
...ector, Catherine Pagès; Company Manager, Kelley Voorhees; Production Manager,
...rey Berzon; Principal Designer, Donald Eastman; Conservatory Director, Rebecca
...; Press, Jeffrey Richards/David LeShay, Irene Gandy, Ben Gutkin, Denise Robert

...Monday, September 16 - December 15, 1991 (27 performances)
...N APPETIT!; Two Musical Monologues; Music, Lee Hoiby; Words, Ruth Draper
...lian Lesson), Julia Child (Bon Appetit); Director, Carey Perloff; Sets, Donald
...tman; Musical Director, Todd Sisley; Lighting, Mary Louise Geiger; Costumes,
...a Riggs, Jean Putch; Adaptations, Mark Shulgasser; Stage Manager, Crystal
...ntington   CAST:  Jean Stapleton (Mrs. Clancy/Julia Child)   PROGRAM:  The
...an Lesson, Bon Appètit!
...erformed in two acts.

...Thursday, October 17 - November 24, 1991
...BARET VERBOTEN; Created by Jeremy Lawrence; Directed/Staged by Carey
...loff and Charles Randolph-Wright; from the works of William Bendow, Bertolt
...cht, Hanns Eisler, Werner Finck, Fritz Grunbaüm, Friederick Hollaender, Walter
...hring, Edmund Meisel, Rudolf Nelson, Marcellus Schiffer, Mischa Spoliansky,
...nrad Tom, Kurt Tucholsky, Karl Valentin; Arrangements, Marjorie Poe;
...nslations, Kathleen L. Komar, Laurence Senelick, John Willett; Sets, Donald
...tman; Costumes, Gabriel Berry; Lighting, Mary Louise Geiger  CAST:  Betsy
...lyn, Mark Nelson, John Rubinstein, Carole Shelly

...nday, January 27 - March 8, 1992 (42 performances)
...EDITORS by August Strindberg; Translation, Paul Walsh; Director, Carey
...loff; Sets, Donald Eastman; Costumes, Candice Donnelly; Lighting, Frances
...onson; Stage Manager, Richard Hester  CAST:  Nestor Serrano (Adolf), Zach
...enier (Gustav), Caroline Lagerfelt (Tekla), Elizabeth Beirne, Elena McGhee
...omen), Denis Sweeney (Porter)
...A new translation of the 1889 drama. The action takes place in the Swedish seaside,
...9.

...Tuesday, April 7 - May 17 (37 performances)
...NDIDE by Len Jenkin; Adapted from Book by Francois Marie Arouet de Voltaire;
...ectors, David Esbjornson, Carey Perloff; Sets, Hugh Landwehr; Costumes, Teresa
...der-Stein; Lighting, Brian MacDevitt; Music, David Lang; Sound, John Kilgore III;
...vement, Lesley Farlow; Stage Manager, Crystal Huntington   CAST:  William
...eler (Gentleman/Jacques/Giroflee/Ragotsky), Kent Gash (Gentleman/Don
...rnando/Martin), Victor Mack (Candide), Dennis Reid (Baron Sr./Cacambo),
...chael Gaston (Baron Jr. Vanderdendur), Edward Hibbert (Pangloss/Pococurante),
...ia Gibson (Cunegonde/King of Eldorado), Rebecca (Baroness/Old Woman),
...nberley Pistone (Paquette/Clairon), Ani Apardian, D'Metrius Fitzgerald Conley,
...berta Kastelic, Elena McGhee, Katherine Puma, Denis Sweeney, Julina Tatlock,
...alther Traber, Rebecca West, Michael R. Wilson
...The action takes place there, the time is then.

*Gerry Goodstein, Glenn Matsumura Photos*

**Carole Shelly, John Rubinstein, Mark Nelson, Betsy Joslyn in**  **117**
**"Cabaret Verboten"**
**CENTER: Jean Stapleton in "Bon Appetit"**
**TOP: Cast on Hugh Landwehr's "Candide" set**

# JEWISH REPERTORY THEATRE

### Eighteenth Season

Artistic Director, Ran Avni; Associate Director, Edward M. Cohen; Manag
Director, Nina Heller; Casting, Stephanie Klapper; Advisory Board, Martin Balsa
Irving Brodsky, Dustin Hoffman, Anne Jackson, Lucille Lortel, Walter Matthau, Ar
Meara, Tony Randall, Jules Rose, Florence Stanley, Jerry Stiller, Eli Wallach; Pro
Pete Sanders/Matthew Lenz

Saturday, Oct. 26 - Nov. 24, 1991 transferred to Houseman Theatre Tuesday, Mar
10 - May 10, 1992
**SHMULNIK'S WALTZ** by Allan Knee; Director, Gordon Hunt; Music, David Sh
Sets, Ray Recht; Costumes, David Loveless; Lighting, Betsy Finston, Bri
MacDevitt; Musical Direction/Adaptation, William Schimmel; Stage Manager, D
Rosenberg  CAST:  Steve Routman (Shmulnik), Stephen Singer, Jerry Matz (Frie
etc.) Wendy Kaplan (Rachel), Ilana Levine (Feyla), Robert Katims (Father), Mari
Pasekoff, Anna Bess Lank (Minnie), Rob Gomes (Jonathan)
A comedy in two acts.  The action takes place in New York City, turn of the century.

Saturday, February 8 - March 8, 1992
**A LIFE IN THE THEATRE** by David Mamet; Director, Kevin Dowling; Sets, R
Odorisio; Costumes, Therese Bruck; Lighting, Brian Nason; Sound, Jim Van Berg
Stage Manager, Nina Heller  CAST: F. Murray Abraham (Robert), Anthony Fus
(John), Larry Klein (Stage Manager)
The 1977 backstage drama.

Saturday, April 25 - May 24, 1992
**THE SUNSET GANG;** with Music by L. Russell Brown; Lyrics/Book, Warr
Adler; Director, Edward M. Cohen; Musical Director/Arrangements/Additio
Material, Andrew Howard; Choreography, Ricarda O'Conner; Sets, Ray Rec
Costumes, Edi Giguere; Lighting, Spencer Mosse; Stage Manager, Geraldi
Teagarden  CAST:  Irving Burton (Naftule/Male Yenta), Shifra Lerer (Yetta/Fem
Yenta), Alfred Toigo (Bill), Sheila Smith (Mimi), Chevi Colton (Jenny), Gene Varro
(David)  MUSICAL NUMBERS:  Activities, What's Wrong Bill, Maybe It's N
Laundry Room, I Miss My Mama, You're the Cause of It All, Yetta, Hawaiian Nig
It's Too Late for Love, Don't Tell Me This Isn't Love, I Miss Bill/I Miss Jenny, R
Eye Express, Shoichet, I Wish I Could Explain, I Was a Good Wife, You Passed N
By, From September to December.
A musical in two acts.  The action takes place in a Florida retirement community.

Saturday, June 13 -
**THE LAST LAUGH** by Michael Hardstark; Director, Lou Jacob; Set, Rob Odoris
Costumes, Teresa Snider-Stein; Lighting, Brian Nason  CAST:  Larry Block, R
Faber, Adam Heller, Nick Plankias, Barbara Spiegel
Two one-acts, *In The Cemetery* and *The Cure* adapted from Chekhov.  This was
last show at the 14th St. location.

*Carol Rosegg/Martha Swope Photos*

**TOP LEFT: Gene Varrone, Sheila Smith, Alfred Toigo, Irving Burton**
**Chevi Colton, Shifra Lerer in "Sunset Gang"**
**LEFT: Irving Burton, Shifra Lerer in "Sunset Gang"**

Ilana Levine, Robert Katims, Steven Routman, Jerry Matz, Wendy Kaplan, Rob Gomes in "Shmulnik's Waltz"

# LA MAMA ETC.

Founder/Director, Ellen Stewart; Business Manager, James W. Moore; Associate Director, Meryl Vladimer; Development Director, Maurice McClelland; Archivist, Doris Pettijohn; Art Director, Susan Haskins; Technical Director, Brad Phillips; Resident Set Design, Jun Maeda; Resident Lighting, Howard Thies; Resident Costume Design, Gabriel Berry; Music Director, Steven Antonelli; Press, Jonathan Slaff

Wednesday, June 5-8, 1991 (4 performances)
COLLATERAL DAMAGE: The Private Life of the New World Order; Works by Amiri Baraka, Daniel Berrigan, William Cooner, Migdalia Cruz, Allen Ginsberg, Scarlet Letter, Tony Harrison, Christopher Logue, Charles L. Mee, Jr., Mac Wellman and David Wojnarowicz; Artistic Director, Leonard Shapiro; Music, Marilyn S. Falken; Design, Kyle Chepulis CAST: Vanessa Redgrave, George Bartenieff, Cathy Shiro, Steve Dominquez, Helen Gallagher, Guillermo Gomez-Peña, Phoebe Legére, Ruth Maleczech, Steven Mellor, Nicky Paraiso, Rachel Rosenthal
Meditations on the wars.

Thursday, June 6-16, 1991 (8 performances)
THE BAY OF NAPLES by Joël Dragutin; Director, Mr. Dragutin CAST: Jean-Claude Bonnifait, Bernard Charance, Françoise d'Inca, Joël Dragutin, Elisabethe Tual
Performed in French by Théâtre 95.

Wednesday, June 12 - 23, 1991 (13 performances)
POLAND'S CRICOT 2; Created by Tadeusz Kantor; Sound, Marek Adamczyk; Presented with The New York International Festival of the Arts
THE DEAD CLASS CAST: Zbigniew Bednarczyk, Tomasz Dobrowolski, Zbigniew Kostomski, Ewa Janicka, Leslaw Janicki, Waclaw Janicki, Maria Stangret Kantor, Marie Krasicaka, Jan Ksiazek, Bogdan Renczynski, Mira Rychlicka, Roman Siwulak, Lech Stangret, Teresa Welminska, Andrzej Welminski
TODAY IS MY BIRTHDAY CAST: Loriano della Rocca, Leslaw Janicki, Waclaw Janicki, Ludmila Ryba, Marie Vayssière, Andrzej Welminski
Experimentalist dramas form the Polish theatrical troupe.

Friday, October 18 - November 3, 1991 (13 performances)
FUTZ by Rochelle Owens; Direction/Music/Sets, Tom O'Horgan; Lighting, Howard Thies; Costumes, Ellen Stewart; Stage Manager, Marybeth Ward CAST: John Bakos (Futz), John Moran (Oscar Loup), Penny Arcade, Kimberly Flynn (Mother), Peter Craig, Marilyn Roberts, Sheila Dabney, Jonathan Slaff, Paul Beauvais, Doug Von Nessen, Thomas Keith
The 1967 play is revived for La MaMa's 30th anniversary.

Friday, January 3-19, 1992 (13 performances)
EXPLOSIONS; Created by Virlana Tkacz and Wanda Phipps; Music, Roman Hurko; Director, Ms. Tkacz; Sets/Lighting, Watoku Ueno; Costumes, Carol Ann Pelletier, Yuko Yamamura; Movement, June Anderson; Projections, Rebecca Baron CAST: Richarda Abrams (Mother), Candace Dian Leverett, Jessica Hecht (Wife), Ralph B. Peña (Government), Jeffrey Ricketts (Engineer), Sean Runnette (Billionaire's Son), Shawn Saito (Receptionist), Olga Shuhan (Sleeper), Jeff Sugarman (Brother)
Yara Arts Group examines the impact of technological disaster on individuals.

Thursday, January 23 - February 9, 1992 (14 performances)

"Futz" cast

KAFKA: FATHER AND SON by Mark Rozovsky; Adapted from Kafka's *Letter to His Father* and *The Judgement*; Translation, Elena Prischepenko, Direction/Design, Leonardo Shapiro; Lighting, Blu; Music, Marilyn Zalkan; Sound, Kyle Chepulis; Costumes, Liz Widulski; Sets, Michael Casselli, Stage Manager, Paul J. Smith CAST: George Bartenieff (Father), Michael Preston (Son)

Saturday, February 15 - March 8, 1992 (17 performances)
AKIN; Conception/Choreography/Direction, John Kelly; Music, Richard Peaslee; Lyrics, Mark Campbell; Music Director, Roberto Pace; Sets, Huck Snyder; Costumes, Donna Zakowska; Lighting, Howell Binkley; Film, Anthony Chase; Hair/Makeup, Bobby Miller; Sound, Tim Schellenbaum; Stage Manager, Lisa Buxbaum CAST: Peter Becker (Father), Vivian Timble (Virgin/Wife/Denizen), Larry Malvern (Child/Denizen), Marleen Menard (Child/Joan of Arc/Denizen), Kyle de Camp (Child/Eve/Denizen), John Kelly (Son)
A music-theatre-dance work. Based on medieval troubadours and their experiences, both imagined and real.

Wednesday, March 11-22, 1992 (11 performances)
THE GOLEM by Moni Ovadia; Original Music, Alessandro Nidi; Traditional Arrangements, Maurizio Deho, Gian Pietro Marazza; Book, Mr. Ovadia, Danielle Abbado CAST: Moni Ovadia
A drama sung in Yiddish, Italian, German and English.

Thursday, April 16 - May 3, 1992 (14 performances)
EGYPT; Adapted from *Antony and Cleopatra* by William Shakespeare; Director, David Herskovits; Music, Thomas Cabiniss; Sets, Marsha Ginsberg; Lighting, Lenore Doxsee; Costumes, David Zinn; Sound, John Collins; Stage Manager, Christine Lemme CAST: William Badgett (Enobarbus), Neil Bradley (Alexas), Bradley Glenn (Eros), Mairhinda Groff (Octavia), James Hannaham (Mardian/Menas), Karl-Peter Hermann (Agrippa/Thidias), Daniel Pardo (Chairmian), Gregor Paslawsky (Lepidus/Clown), Erik Passoja (Soothsayer/Dolabella), Scott Rabinowitz (Pompey/Proculeius), Randolph Curtis Rand (Antony), Steven Rattazzi (Caesar), Thomas Jay Ryan (Cleopatra), Greig Sargeant (Iras), Yuri Skujins (Decretas)
Performed without intermission.

Friday, March 27 - April 12, 1992 (11 performances)
FALLEN ANGEL; with Music/Lyrics/Book by William L. Boesky; Director, Rob Greenberg; Music Director, Steve Postel; Set, David Birn; Lighting, Chris Akerlind; Costumes, Wendy Rolf; Stage Manager, Anna Palmer CAST: Jonathan Goldstein (Will), Michael McCoy (Luke), Amy Correia (Gretta), Eliza Foss (Dr. Newberger/Alex), Michael J. Twain (Father/Don)
A musical performed without intermission.

Thursday, May 28 - June 21, 1992 (16 performances)
GOD'S COUNTRY by Steven Dietz; Director, Leonard Foglia; Set, Michael McGarty; Costumes, Nina Canter; Lighting, Russell Champa, Sound, One Dream; Fights, Rick Sordelet; Supervisor, Nancy Kramer; Stage Manager, Christine Lemme; Press, Lee Brock CAST: Seth Barrish, Lee Brock, Marcia DeBonis, Tom Riis Farrell, Aaron Goodwin, Larry Green, Reade Kelly, Keigh Patellis, Wendee Pratt, Michael Elting Rogers, Stephen Singer, Colleen Gallagher
A drama in two acts. The action takes place in a Seattle courtroom, a Denver radio station and numerous other U.S. locations between 1983 and the present.

*Jonathan Slaff, Glenn Jussen, Shirley Curtin Photos*

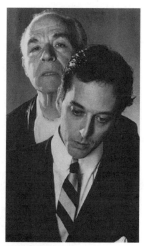

**LEFT:** Leigh Patellis in "God's Country"
**RIGHT:** George Bartenieff, Michael Preston in "Kafka: Father and Son"

# LINCOLN CENTER THEATER

Artistic Director, André Bishop; Executive Producer, Bernard Gersten; Resident Director, Gregory Mosher; General Manager, Steven C. Callahan; Production Manager, Jeff Hamlin; Development Director, Hattie K. Jutagir; Finance Director, David S. Brown; Marketing Director, Thomas Cott; Company Manager, Edward J. Nelson; Dramaturg, Anne Cattaneo; Musical Theatre Director, Ira Weitzman; Casting, Daniel Swee; Press, Merle Debuskey

(Cort Theatre) Tuesday, December 17, 1991 - February 9, 1992 (29 performances and 33 previews)
**TWO SHAKESPEAREAN ACTORS;** See Broadway Calendar

(Newhouse Theatre) Friday, January 31 - July 26, 1992 (205 performances)
**THE SUBSTANCE OF FIRE** by Jon Robin Baitz; Director, Daniel Sullivan; Sets, John Lee Beatty; Costumes, Jess Goldstein; Lighting, Arden Fingerhut; Sound, Scott Lehrer; Stage Manager, Roy Harris  CAST: Sarah Jessica Parker succeeded by Cordelia Richards (Sarah Geldhart), Patrick Breen (Martin Geldhart), Ron Rifkin (Issac Geldhart), Jon Tenney (Aaron Geldhart), Maria Tucci (Marge Tucci)
   A drama in two acts. The action takes place in a publishing office and Gramercy Park apartment in New York City Between 1987 - 1990. This production previously played 140 performances at Playwrights Horizons March - June, 1991.

(Booth Theatre) Friday, January 24 - August 30, 1992 (229 performances and 23 previews)
**THE MOST HAPPY FELLA;** See Broadway Calendar

(Beaumont Theatre) Saturday, February 22 - April 19, 1992 (38 performances and 26 previews)
**FOUR BABOONS ADORING THE SUN;** See Broadway Calendar

*Martha Swope Photos*

**120**

Jon Tenney, Patrick Breen, Sarah Jessica Parker, Ron Rifkin in "Substance of Fire"

# NEW YORK THEATRE WORKSHOP

istic Director, James C. Nicola; Managing Director, Nancy Kassak Diekmann;
istic Associate, Christopher Grabowski; Artistic Administrator, Martha Banta,
neral Manager, Esther Cohen; Development Director, Glen Knapp; Marketing
ector, Carla Forbes-Kelly; Production Manager, George Xenos; Technical Director,
m Loftis; Press, Richard Kornberg, Carol Fineman, James L.L. Morrison

All Productions at Perry St. Theatre) Friday, Nov. 22, 1991 - Feb. 2, 1992
**AD FOREST** by Caryl Churchill; Director, Mark Wing-Davey; Sets/Costumes,
rina Draghici; Lighting, Christopher Akerlind; Sound, Mark Bennett; Fights, David
ong; Stage Manager, Thom Widmann    CAST: Lanny Flaherty
gdan/Soldier/Translator), Randy Danson (Irina/Grandmother/Flowerseller), Calista
ckhart (Lucia/Student Doctor), Mary Mara (Florina/Student), Tom Nelson
abriel/Student), Mary Shultz (Flavia/Painter/Grandmother/Rodica), Christopher
Cann (Mihai/Dog/Bulldozer Driver), Joseph Siravo (Doctor/Priest/Vampire/
meone With Sore Throat/Officer/Old Aunt), Jake Weber (Radu/Soldier), Garret
lahunt (Ianos/Painter), Rob Campbell (Securitate Man/Angel/Patient/Toma/Ghost
iter/Student)
A drama in three acts, performed in two parts.  The action centers around the
manian Revolution.

Wednesday, February 19 - March 8, 1992 (21 performances)
**ME FLIES WHEN YOU'RE ALIVE;** Written and Performed by Paul Linke; Flag
sign, Anders Holmquist; Music, Francesca Draper Linke; Director, Mark W. Travis;
hting, Pat Dignan; Sound, Mark Bennett; Stage Manager, Liz Dreyer
A monologue performed without intermission.

Friday, March 20 - April 19, 1992 (35 performances)
**PSINKA!  A DAY IN THE LIFE;** Created and Performed by John Epperson;
rector/Choreography, Michael Leeds; Set, James Schuette; Costumes, Anthony
ong; Lighting, Mark L. McCullough; Sound, Mark Bennett, Jim Van Bergen; Puppet
ker, Randy Carfagno; Stage Manager, Kate Broderick    CAST: Mr. Epperson,
rico Kaklafraninalli, Puppets
Performance art performed without intermission.

Wednesday, May 27 - June 27, 1992 (33 performances)
**NCH ME IN THE STOMACH** by Deb Filler and Alison Summers; Director, Ms.
mmers; Set, George Xenos; Lighting, Pat Dignan; Sound, Mark Bennett; Stage
anager, Thom Widmann   CAST: Deb Filler
An autobiographical monologue performed without intermission.

*Martha Swope Photos*

**Top:** Garret Dillahunt, Tim Nelson, Jake Weber in "Mad Forest"
**Center:** Paul Linke in "Time Flies When You're Alive"
**Right:** John Epperson as Lypsinka

# MANHATTAN THEATRE CLUB

Twentieth Season

Artistic Director, Lynne Meadow; Managing Director, Barry Grove, General Manager, Victoria Bailey; Associate Artistic Director, Michael Bush; Casting, Donna Isaacson; Script Development, Kate Loewald; Writers-in-Performance Director, Alice Gordon; Development Director, Janet Harris; Business Manager, Michael P. Naumann; Company Manager, Harold Wolpert; Education Director, David Shookhoff; Marketing Director/Press, Helene Davis, Deborah Warren

(Stage II) Thursday, October 3 - December 8, 1991 (78 performances)
**BEGGARS IN THE HOUSE OF PLENTY** by John Patrick Shanley; Director, Mr. Shanley; Sets, Santo Loquasto; Costumes, Lindsay W. Davis; Lighting, Natasha Katz; Sound, Bruce Ellman; Stage Manager, Renee Lutz   CAST: Loren Dean (Johnny), Dana Ivey (Ma-Noreen), Daniel Von Bargen (Pop), Laura Linney (Sheila), Jon Tenney (Joey), Jayne Haynes (Sister Mary Kate)
A dark comedy performed without intermission.

(Stage I) Tuesday, May 28, 1991 - January 5, 1992 (250 performances)
**LIPS TOGETHER TEETH APART** by Terrence McNally; Director, John Tillinger; Sets, John Lee Beatty; Costumes, Jane Greenwood; Lighting, Ken Billington; Sound, Stewart Werner; Fights, Jerry Mitchell; Stage Manager, Pamela Singer   CAST: Christine Baranski succeeded by Deborah Rush, Hillary Bailey Smith (Chloe Haddock), Nathan Lane succeeded by Jonathan Hadary (Sam Truman), Anthony Heald (John Haddock), Swoosie Kurtz succeeded by Roxanne Hart (Sally Truman)
A comic drama in three acts.  The action takes place on Fire Island over a Fourth of July weekend.  The production transferred to the Lucille Lortel theatre on January 9, 1992.

(Union Square Theatre) Tuesday, October 15 - November 24, 1991 (48 performances & previews)
**A PIECE OF MY HEART** by Shirley Lauro; Suggested by the book by Keith Walker; Director, Allen R. Belknap; Sets, James Fenhagen; Costumes, Mimi Maxmen; Lighting, Richard Winkler; Sound, John Kilgore; Guitar/Vocal Arrangements, Cynthia Carle; Stage Manager, Richard Hester   CAST: Annette Helde (Martha), Cynthia Carle (Maryjo), Corliss Preston (Sissy), Sharon Schlarth (Whitney), Kim Miyori (Leeann), Novella Nelson (Steele), Tom Stechschulte (Men)
A drama in two acts.  The stories derive from the oral histories of women who served in Vietnam during the war.

(Stage II) Tuesday, January 7 - March 22, 1992 (88 performances and 15 previews) transfered to Orpheum Theatre Thursday, March 26 - September 6, 1992 (190 performances)

**TOP: Hillary Bailey Smith, Anthony Heald in "Lips Together Teeth Apart"**
**CENTER: (top) Kim Miyori, Tom Stechschulte, Cynthia Carle (front) Novella Nelson, Sharon Schlarth, Corliss Preston, Annette Helde in "A Piece of My Heart"**

Jon Tenney, Loren Dean in "Beggars in the House of Plenty"     Dana Ivey, Laura Linney in "Beggars in the House of Plenty"

Jon De Vries, Dennis Boutsikaris, Deborah Hedwall in
"Sight Unseen"
Top Right: Lynne Thigpen, Tsepo Mokone, Keith David in
"Boesman and Lena"
Right: David Schechter, Bill Buell, Anne Bobby in "Groundhog"

**SIGHT UNSEEN** by Donald Margulies; Director, Michael Bloom; Sets, James
Youmans; Costumes, Jess Goldstein; Lighting, Donald Holder; Music/Sound, Michael
Roth; Stage Manager, Harold Goldfaden CAST: Dennis Boutsikaris succeeded by
Lou Liberatore during vacation (Jonathan Waxman), Jon De Vries (Nick), Deborah
Hedwall succeeded by Margaret Colin (Patricia), Laura Linney (Grete)
A drama in two acts. The action takes place in the English countryside, London,
and New York over a period of seventeen years.

(Stage I) Tuesday, January 14 - March 22, 1992 (80 performances)
**BOESMAN AND LENA;** Written and Directed by Athol Fugard; Sets/Costumes,
Susan Hilferty; Lighting, Dennis Parichy; Stage Manager, Sandra Lea Williams
CAST: Keith David (Boesman), Lynne Thigpen (Lena), Tsepo Mokone (Outa)
A 1969 drama performed without intermission. The action takes place on the tidal
mudflats on the outskirts of Port Elizabeth, South Africa.

(Stage II) Tuesday, April 14 - May 17, 1992 (40 performances)
**GROUNDHOG;** Composed/Written/Directed by Elizabeth Swados; Sets/Costumes,
G.W. Mercier; Lighting, Natasha Katz; Sound, Ed Fitzgerald; Musical
Direction/Arrangements, Ann Marie Milazzo, Michael Sottile; Stage Manager,
Richard Hester CAST: Stephen Lee Anderson (Dr. R.T. Ebney/Etc.), Anne Bobby
(Gila), Bill Buell (Judge Alex T. Waldman/Etc.), Gilles Chiasson (Zoe/Etc.), Nora
Cole (Georgette Bergen), Ula Hedwig (D.A. Randall), Ann Marie Milazzo
(Weatherperson/Etc.), Lauren Mufson (Sandy/Etc.), Daniel Neiden (Mayor/Etc.),
Susan Postel (Lauree/Etc.), David Schechter (Groundhog), Tony Scheitinger
(Gomez/Etc.), Michael Sottile (Daniel Chelnik)
MUSICAL NUMBERS; Weather Report #1, Bathing Suits Stock Markets & Blimps,
Project Heal, One More Day, Willard Scott, Abduction, Weather Report #2, Street
People, Groundhog is Going to Trial, My Movie of the Week, Who Will I Be?, Flight
For Health, Bellevue and the Judge, Testimony, Experts, This Isn't How I Imagined a
Trial to Be, Just Trust Me, Yes/No, Doctor's Canon, Bill and Willa, Danilo's Rap,
Sweet Bitter Candy, Hey Groundhog, Why Did I Forget?, Ten Year Blues, Harmonica
Man, Weather Report #3, If I Am Released, Closing Arguments, Judge's Decision,
Little Hymn of Groundhog, Groundhog Has Won, Lawyer's Lament, Open the Door,
Groundhog is Becoming Important, Hearing Voices, Pay Phone, ACLU, Rewrite Your
Own Story, Hymn to Spring, Weather Report #4, What Could I Have Done?, Someone
Is Discovering Something
The action takes place in New York City, mid-1980s.

(Stage I) Tuesday, April 28 - June 21, 1992 (64 performances)
**THE EXTRA MAN** by Richard Greenberg; Director, Michael Engler; Set, Loy
Arcenas; Costumes, Jess Goldstein; Lighting, Donald Holder; Sound, Scott Lehrer;
Stage Manager, Robin Rumpf CAST: Laila Robins (Laura), Boyd Gaines (Keith),
Adam Arkin (Jess), John Slattery (Daniel)
A drama in two acts. The action takes place in New York City from fall to spring.

*Gerry Goodstein, Martha Swope Photos*

**Laila Robins, Adam Arkin, Boyd Gaines in "The Extra Man"** 123

# NEW YORK SHAKESPEARE FESTIVAL

Founder, Joseph Papp; Artistic Director, JoAnne Akalaitis; Producing Director, Jason Steven Cohen; Associate Artistic Director, Rosemarie Tichler; General Managers, Elizabeth Gardella, Sally Cambell Morse; Literary Consultant, Gail Merrifield; Literary Manager, Jason Fogelson; Casting, Nancy Piccione, Jordan Thaler; Development Director, Christine S. Peck; Press, Richard Kornberg, Bruce Campbell/Barbara Carroll, James L.L. Morrison

(Delacorte Theater/Central Park) Friday, June 21 - July 14, 1991 (21 performances) **OTHELLO** by William Shakespeare; Director, Joe Dowling; Sets, Frank Conway; Costumes, Jane Greenwood; Lighting, Richard Nelson; Music, Peter Golub; Fights, David Leong; Stage Managers, Karen Armstrong, Buzz Cohen CAST: Jake Weber (Roderigo), Christopher Walken (Iago), George Morfogen (Brabantio), Raul Julia (Othello), Michel R. Gill (Cassio), Frank Raiter (Duke of Venice), Daniel Oreskes (Gratiano), Bruce Katzman (Senator of Venice), Michael Gaston (Messenger/Herald), Kathryn Meisle (Desdemona), Christopher McHale (Montano), Jed Diamond, Robert Jimenez, Jeffrey Wright (Gentlemen), Mary Beth Hurt (Emilia), Miriam Healy-Louie (Bianca), Tom Hewitt (Lodovico), David Borror, Eddie Bowz, Torben Brooks, Josh Fardon, Eric LaRay Harvey, Richard Holmes, Nancy Hower, Nina Humphrey, Royal Miller, Adam Trese
Performed in two acts. This was production #18 in the Shakespeare Marathon.

(Delacorte/Central Park) Tuesday, July 30 - August 11, 1991 (12 performances) **A MIDSUMMER NIGHT'S DREAM** by William Shakespeare; Direction/Translation/Adaptation, Cacá Rosset; Sets/Costumes, José DeAnchieta Costa; Lighting, Peter Kaczorowski; Asst. Director, Maria Alice Vergueiro; Choreography, Val Folly; Musical Direction, Duca Franca; Circus Coach, José Wilson Leite; Gymnastic Coach, Regina Oliveira; Fencing Coaches, Peter Gidali, Erwin Leibl; Skating Coach, Luciano Marcelo Coutinho; Stage Managers, Antônio Marciano, Márcio Marciano, Clóvis Cardoso CAST: José Rubens Chachá (Theseus/Oberon), Christiane Tricerri (Hippolyta/Titania), Mario César Camargo (Egeus/Tom Snout), Elaine Garcia (Hermia), Rubens Caribé (Lysander), Richard Homuth (Demetrius), Carolina N. Ribeiro (Helena), Anton Chaves (Philostrate/Robin Starveling/Moon), Tácito Rochya (Peter Quince), Cacá Rosset (Bottom/Pyramus), Ary França (Flute/Thisby), Gerson Steves (Snug), Augusto Pompeo (Puck), Daniela De Carli (Lady/Falena/Valet/Singer), Débora Pacioni Zambon (Lady/Fairy/Valet), Meire Florio (Lady/Fairy/Belly Dancer), Mônica Monteiro (Peachblossom/Amazon/ Valet), Norma Gabriel (Mustardseed/Lady/Valet) André Caldas, Felipe Matsumoto, Gusto Vasconcelos, Kiko Belucci, Kiko Caldas, José Wilson Leite (Gentlemen/Elves/Acrobats)
Performed in two acts by Brazil's Teatro do Ornitorrinco.

**Christopher Walken, Kathryn Meisle, Raul Julia, Mary Beth Hurt i "Othello"**

**Sharon Washington, James McDaniel, Keith Randolph Smith in "Before it Hits Home"**

(Delacorte/Central Park) Tuesday, August 27 - September 8, 1991 (12 performance **THE TEMPEST** by William Shakespeare; Director, Carlos Gimenez; Adaptati Ugo Ulive; Sets, Marcelo Pont-Verges, Augusto Gonzalez; Lighting, Trevor Brov Mr. Gimenez; Costumes, Hugo Marquez, Mr. Pont-Verges, Mr. Gonzelez; Music, Ju Carlos Nunez; Sound, Eduardo Bolivar; Artistic Production, Jorge Borges, And Vazquez, Gabriel Flores; Technical Director, Freddy Belisario; Stage Managers, N Flores, George Hewit CAST: Erich Wildpret (Ariel), Jose Tejera (Propero), Natha Martinez (Miranda), Daniel Lopez (Caliban), Jesus Araujo (Fernando), Rodo Villafranca (Capt./Old Spirit), Norman Santana (Bosun/Spirit), German Mendi (Alonso), Francisco Alfaro (Antonio), Hugo Marquez (Gonzalo), Aitor Gavi (Sebastian), Ramon Goliz (Adrian), William Cuao (Black Spirit), Cosme Corta (Trinculo), Anibal Grunn (Estefano), Ricardo Martinez, Hector Becerra, Ism Monagas, Gregorio Milano (Spirits/Sailors), Ivezku Celis (Godesses/Nymph Alejandro Faillace (Sailor)
A spanish language version performed without intermission by Rajatabla, Natio Youth Theatre of Venezuela, and Venezuela's National Theatre Workshop.

(Public/Martinson) Tuesday, October 29 - November 24, 1991 (32 performances) **IN THE JUNGLE OF CITIES** by Bertolt Brecht; Director, Anne Bogart; Se Donald Eastman; Costumes, Gabriel Berry; Lighting, Heather Carson; Sound, Jac Burckhardt, L.B. Dallas; Composer, Judson Wright; Co-Produced with Mabou Min Stage Manager, Buzz Cohn CAST: Ruth Maleczech (Mae), Brian Juc (Skinny/Employee/Barman), Mario Arrambide (George Garga), Frederick Neuma (Shlink), Terry O'Reilly (C. Maynes/Sinner/Pat Mankey/Reporter), Greg Mehr (Worm), René Rivera (Baboon/Man), Karen Evans-Kandel (Jane Larry/Sinner), Fa Green (Mary Garga), Raul Aranas (Preacher/John Garga), David McIntyre, Royst Scott (Dock Workers)
A drama performed without intermission. The action takes place in Chicago 1912.

(Public/Newman Theatre) Tuesday, November 5 - December 22, 1991 (56 performanc **PERICLES** by William Shakespeare; Director, Michael Greif; Sets, John Arnor Costumes, Gabriel Berry; Lighting, Frances Aronson; Music/Music Direction, J Jaffe; Sound, Mark Bennett; Choreography, Kenneth Tosti; Hairstylist/Makeup, Bob Miller CAST: Robert Beatty, Jr. (Fisherman/Gentleman of Ephesus and Tyre), La Block (Lord/Fisherman/Cerimon/Pandar), Paul Butler (Helicanus), MacIntyre Dix (Escanes/Fisherman/Gentleman/Lord), Cordelia Gonzales (Thaisa), Joseph F (Thaliard/Sailor/Gentleman of Tyre), Byron Jennin (Antiochus/Simonides/Lysimachus), Bobo Lewis (Lychorida/Bawd), Saundra McCla (Dionyza), Don R. McManus (John Gower/Philemon/Diana, Arnold Moli

**Campbell Scott, Martha Plimpton in "Pericles"**
**Top Left: "Midsummer Night's Dream"**

ssenger/Boult), Steve Mellor (Cleon), Dan Moran (Lord/Knights/Leonine/Sailor), rtha Plimpton (Daughter of Antiochus/Marina), Campbell Scott (Pericles)
, drama in two acts. This marks the 19th production of the NYSF Shakespeare rathon.

Public/Anspacher) Sunday, December 1-15, 1991 (15 performances)
)VING BEYOND THE MADNESS: A FESTIVAL OF NEW VOICES; ator, George C. Wolfe; Technical Coordinator, Bill Barnes; Lighting, Dan lowitz PROGRAM: *Spic-O-Rama* with John Leguizamo; *An American Griot* by Bullins and Idris Ackamoor with Ackamoor; *Big Butt Girls, Hard-Hearted Women*, tten/Performed by Rhodessa Jones; *Tokyo Bound*, Written/Performed by Amy Hill; elle! *The Absolute Outrageous Truth 'Bout Us*, Written/Performed by Hazelle dman; *Remembrances and Dedications: A Haphazard Cabaret, Part I*, Conceived Vernon Reid; *Identities, Mirrors, and Distortions*, Written/Performed by Anna vere Smith; *Symposium in Manila* by Hans Ong; *Science and Ritual* with Derin ang; *Pomo Afro Homos* in Fierce Love and a new work; *Danitra Vance and the* -O Boys Revisited; *Relationships: Intimate and Not So Intimate* by Blondell mmings
heatre, music and dance by people of color.

Public/Anspacher) Wednesday, December 18, 1991 - January 5, 1992 (17 performances)
NO ONCE REMOVED; Conceived, Written and Performed by Reno; ector/Developed with Evan Yionoulis; Music, Mike Yionoulis; Lighting, Dan lowitz
Ionologue performed without intermission.

Public/Martinson) Tuesday, Jan. 14 - Feb. 16, 1992 (24 performances and 13 previews)
E HOME SHOW PIECES; Written and Directed by David Greenspan; Sets, liam Kennon; Costumes, Elsa Ward; Lighting, David Bergstein; Stage Manager, k McMahon CAST: David Greenspan, Ron Bagden, Tracey Ellis
our short plays covering seven years in the life of one principal character: *Doing Beast, Too Much in the Sun*, *Portrait of the Artist, The Big Tent*.

Public/Shiva) Saturday, February 15 - March 7, 1992 (4 performances)
SHAME; Presented with HOME For Contemporary Theatre and Art; HOST: t Mitler CAST: Linda Hill, The Poster Boys, Todd Alcott, and weekly rotating Playwrights, actors and poets perform short pieces.

Public/LuEsther) Tuesday, February 18 - March 22, 1992 (40 performances)
FORE IT HITS HOME by Cheryl L. West; Director, Tazewell Thompson; Sets, Arcenas; Lighting, Nancy Schertler; Costumes, Paul Tazewell; Sound, Susan te; Hairstylist, Antonio Soddu; Stage Manager, James Fitzsimmons CAST: James Daniel (Wendal), Sharon Washington (Simone/Miss Peterson), Keith Randolph th (Douglas), Yvette Hawkins (Reba), Marcella Lowery (Maybelle), Frankie R, on (Bailey), James Jason Liley (Dwayne), Carol Honda (Nurse), Beth Dixon (Dr. nberg), Monti Sharp (Junior)
, drama in two acts. The action takes place in the Midwest at present.

Public/Shiva) Tuesday, March 3-29, 1992 (24 performances)
MO SAPIEN SHUFFLE; Written and Directed by Richard Caliban; Music, John e; Sets, Kyle Chepulis; Costumes/Marionettes, Yvette Helin; Lighting, Brian ous; Sound, John Huntington; Stage Manager, Paul J. Smith CAST: Vivian Lanko eeler), Erica Gimpel (Moon), Diana Ridoutt (Stage Manager), Mark Dillahunt nge Hand), Martin Donovan (Craven), Sharon Brady (Willa), Lauren Hamilton madette), Glen M. Santiago (Rocky), Mollie O'Mara (Cleo)
, high-tech fantasy performed without intermission by the Cucaracha Theatre.

Public/Newman) Tuesday March 17 - April 19, 1992 (40 performances)
PITY SHE'S A WHORE by John Ford; Director, JoAnne Akalaitis; Sets, John klin; Costumes, Gabriel Berry; Lighting, Mimi Jordan Sherin; Music, Jan A.P. zmarek; Sound, John Gromada; Fights, David Leong; Choreography, Timothy

**Anna Deavere Smith in "Fires in the Mirror"**

**Elizabeth Peña, Al Rodrigo, Gloria Foster in "Blood Wedding"**
**TOP: Val Kilmer, Wendell Pierce in " 'Tis Pity She's a Whore"**

O'Slynne; Hair/Makeup, Bobby Miller; Stage Manager, Pat Sosnow **CAST: Val Kilmer** (Giovanni), Jeanne Tripplehorn (Annabella), April **Armstrong** (Singer/Townsperson), Erick Avair (Vasques), J. David Brimmer (Banditto/Party Guest), Soraya Burler, (Girl Scout/Townsperson), Helmar Augustus Cooper **(Donado)**, Adrian Danzig, (Juggler/Servant), Angel David (Banditto/Party Guest), Joan Elizabeth (Girl Scout/Townsperson), Jared Harris (Soranzo), Ross Lehman (Bergetto), **Larry** Grant Malvern (Banditto/Party Guest), Marlo Marron (Philotis), Ellen McEldudd (Hippolita), Tom Nelis (Cardinal), Deidre O'Connell (Putana), Daniel Oreskes (Lt. Grimaldi), Wendell Pierce (Friar Bonaventure), Frank Raiter (Florio), Giovanna Sardelli (Girl Scout/Townsperson), Rocco Sisto (Richardetto), Mark Kenneth Smaltz (Poggio), Doug Von Nessen (Juggler/Servant)
The 1624 drama, here set in Parma, Italy in the early 1930s.

(Public/Shiva) Friday, May 1 - June 28 moved to (Public/Anspacher) Tuesday, July 7 -August 16, 1992 (91 performances and 11 previews)
FIRES IN THE MIRROR: CROWN HEIGHTS, BROOKLYN AND OTHER IDENTITIES; Conceived, Written and Performed by Anna Deavere Smith; Director, Christopher Ashley; Set, James Youmans; Costumes, Candice Donnelly; Lighting, Debra J. Kletter; Projections, Wendall K. Harrington, Emmanuelle Krebs; Music, Joseph Jarman; Stage Manager, Karen Moore
A portrayal of 26 people involved in an urban riot.

(Public/Martinson) Tuesday, April 28 - May 31, 1992 (21 performances and 18 previews)
BLOOD WEDDING by Frederico Garcia Lorca; Translation, Langston Hughes; Director, Melia Bensussen; Sets, Derek McLane; Costumes, Franne Lee; Lighting, Peter Kaczorowski; Composer/Music Director, Michele Navazio; Choreography, Donald Byrd CAST: Phyllis Bash (Mother-in-Law), Omar Carter (Moon/Youth/Woodcutter), Ivonne Coll (Neighbor/Servant), Joaquim de Almeida (Leonardo), Sara Erde (Bridesmaid/Girl), Gloria Foster (Mother), Cordelia Gonzalez (Wife), Fanni Green (Beggar/Woman), Mike Hodge (Father), Michael Mandell (Youth/Woodcutter), Marchand Odette (Child/Bridesmaid/Girl), Elizabeth Peña (Bride), Tim Perez (Youth/Woodcutter), Al Rodrigo (Groom), Gina Torres (Bridesmaid/Girl)
A drama performed without intermission. This production uses the 1938 translation of the 1932 original.

*Martha Swope, William Gibson, Susan Cook Photos*

# PEARL THEATRE

Artistic Director, Shepard Sobel; General Manager, Mary L. Harpster; Developme
Director, Ivan Polley; Artistic Associate, Joanne Camp; Dramaturge, Dale Ramse
Resident Costume Designer, Barbara A. Bell; Resident Set Designer, Robert Jo
Schwartz; Voice/Text Coach, Robert Neff Williams; Press, Chris Boneau/Bob Fenne

Wednesday, July 7 - August 10, 1991 (16 performances)
**MOLIERE** Written & Performed by Richard Morse; Director, Alex Szogyi; Desig
Donald L. Brooks; Music, James Dowcett
  A one man celebration of the playwright.

Friday, September 9 - October 19, 1991 (45 performances)
**TARTUFFE** by Moliere; Translation, Donald M. Frame; Director, Shepard Sob
Sets, Robert Joel Schwartz; Costumes, Barbara A. Bell; Lighting, Richard
Kendrick; Sound, Donna Riley; Stage Manager, Lynn Bogarde  CAST: Anna Mir
(Madame Pernelle), Janine Lindsay (Flipote), Hank Wagner (Damis), Kathryn L
(Mariane), Julia Glander (Dorine), Dugg Smith (Cleante), Joanne Camp (Elmir
Frank Geraci (Orgon), Arnie Burton (Valere), Martin LaPlatney (Tartuffe), Ea
Edgerton (M. Loyal), Alex Leydenfrost (Gentleman)
  A comedy performed in two acts. The action takes place in Orgon's house in Paris.

Friday, October 25 - December 7, 1991 (45 performances)
**THE TROJAN WOMEN** by Euripides; Translation, Richmond Lattimore; Direct
Shepard Sobel; Set, Robert Joel Schwartz; Costumes, Barbara A. Bell; Lighting, Pa
Armstrong; Sound, Donna Riley; Stage Manager, Mary-Susan Gregson  CAST: Be
Jarrett (Hecuba), Donnah Welby (Andromache), Robin Leslie Brown (Helen), Lau
Rathgeb (Cassandra), Stuart Lerch (Menelaus), Carlo Alban (Astyanax), Arnie Burt
Joanne Camp, Belynda Hardin, Alex Leydenfrost, Diane Paulus, Hank Wanger

Friday, December 13, 1991 - January 25, 1992 (45 performances)
**AS YOU LIKE IT** by William Shakespeare; Director, Anthony Cornish; Sets, Rob
Joel Schwartz; Lighting, Paul Armstong; Costumes, Barbara A. Bell; Songs, G
Wilfenden; Fights, Rick Sordelet; Stage Manager, Liz Dreyer  CAST: Arnie Burt
(Orlando), Frank Lowe (Adam Martext), David Gottlieb (Oliver), David Edward Jor
(Dennis/Corin), Alex Leydenfrost (Charles/Forester/Williams/De Boys), Joanne Car
(Rosalind), Robin Leslie Brown (Celia), Craig Bockhorn (Touchstone), Hank Wagr
(Le Beau/Amiens/Hymen), Dan Daily (Frederick/Senior), Wynn Harmon (Silviu
Stuart Lerch (Jaques), Laura Rathgeb (Audrey), Donnah Welby (Phebe)
  The action takes place at the Royal Court and the forest of Arden.

Friday, January 31 - March 14, 1992 (45 performances)
**GHOSTS** by Henrik Ibsen; Director, Robert Brink; Set, Robert Joel Schwar
Costumes, Barbara A. Bell; Lighting, Vick Neal; Sound, Donna Riley; Stage Manag
Sue Jane Stoker  CAST: Edward Seamon (Engstrand), April Shawhan (Hele
Michael Levin (Manders), Arnie Burton (Oswald), Robin Leslie Brown (Regina)
  The 1882 drama.

Friday, March 20 - May 2, 1992 (45 performances)
**CHEKHOV VERY FUNNY**; Four one-acts by Anton Chekhov; Director, Shepa
Sobel; Sets, Robert Joel Schwartz; Costumes, Barbara A. Bell; Lighting, A.C. Hickc
Stage Manager, Mary-Susan Gregson
CONCERNING THE INJURIOUSNESS OF TOBACCO with Dan Daily THE BEA
with Frank Geraci, Robin Leslie Brown, Dan Daily THE MARRIAGE PROPOSA
with Frank Geraci, Dan Daily, Robin Leslie Brown SWAN SONG with Frank Gera
Dan Daily

Sunday, April 26 - May 9, 1992 (5 performances)
**PEACE IN A TRAVELING HEART** with Frank Geraci; Musical Director, K
Mallor
  A musical travelogue through the men of generations of a family.

*Carol Rosegg/Martha Swope Photos*

**TOP: Joanne Camp, Frank Geraci in "Taruffe"**
**SECOND PHOTO: Bella Jarrett in "Trojan Women"**
**THIRD PHOTO: Joanne Camp, Donnah Welby in "As You Like It"**
**LEFT: Robin Leslie Brown, Dan Daily in "Chekhov Very Funny"**

# RIVERSIDE SHAKESPEARE COMPANY

Fifthteenth Season

Artistic Director, Gus Kaikkonen; Managing Director, Stephen Vertano; Operations Director, Wyatt Obeid; Development Director, Jeannie Dobie; Academy Director, Laura Fine; Assistant Artistic Director, Tim Gable; Co-Founders, W. Stuart McDowell, Gloria Skurski; Artistic Associate, Timothy W. Oman; Press, Douglas Tuchman

(Playhouse 91) Friday, September 13 - October 27, 1991
**MACBETH** by William Shakespeare; Director, Gus Kaikkonen; Sets, Bob Barnett; Costumes, Pamela Scofield; Lighting, Stephen J. Backo; Music, Ellen Mandel; Fights, Ian Rose; Stage Managers, Matthew G. Marholin, Rona Bern CAST: Victor Raider-Wexler (Duncan/Porter), Don Reilly (Malcolm), Alex Spencer (Sgt./Caithness), Aaron Goodwin (Donalbain), Dan Daily (Ross), Olivia Charles (1st Witch/Gentlewoman), Jeannie Dobie (2nd Witch/Young English Woman), Kathleen Christal (Lady Macduff/3rd Witch), Stephen McHattie (Macbeth), Gilbert Cruz (Banquo), Jennifer Harmon (Lady Macbeth), Brian Mulligan (Seyton), Joseph Acosta (Fleance), Richard McWilliams (Macduff), Diane Ciesla (Lennox), Martin Hynes (Young Ross), Robert Ruffin, Steve Satta (Murderers), Richard Bereck, Edwin Hansen-Nelson (Boy Macduff), Abe Novick (Doctor)
Performed in two acts.

Wednesday, November 6 - December 1, 1991 (26 performances)
**IRON BARS** by Arpád Göncz; Translation, Katharina M. & Christopher C. Wilson; Directors, Andre De Szekely, László Vámos; Sets, Bob Barnett; Costumes, Pamela Scofield; Lighting, Stephen J. Backo; Music, Tommy Vig; Stage Managers, Matthew G. Marholin, Rona Bern CAST: Garry Goodrow (Emmanuel), Alice White (Dolores), Lisbeth Bartlett (Beata), Maureen Clarke (Woman Doctor), Richard Thomsen (President), David Lipman (Major/Upholsterer/Plainclothesman), Mark Young (Sgt./Delivery Man/Male Nurse), Christopher Mixon (Prosecutor/Telephone Man/Doctor), Dan Daily (Prosecutor/Gas Man/Plainclothesman), Bruce Edward Barton (Prisoner/Window Dresser/Police Minister), Briane Keane (Prisoner/Handyman/Male Nurse), James Matthew Ryan (Prisoner/Errand Boy/Lackey), Mikel Borden (Prisoner/Delivery Man/Policeman), Peter Brown (Prisoner/Handyman/Policeman)
A dark comedy in two acts.

Wednesday, December 11, 1991 - March 8, 1992 (93 performances)
**CINDERELLA** with Music/Arrangements by Dan Levy; Lyrics, Amy Powers, Mr. Levy; Book, Norman Robbins; Director, Laura Fine; Sets, Harry Feiner; Costumes, Gail Baldoni; Lighting, Stephen Petrilli; Stage Manager, Paula Gray CAST: Mark Honan (Buttons), Fredi Walker (Dandini), Melanie Wingert (Cinders), Pat Flick (Baron Hardupp), Diane Ciesla (Baroness Hardupp), Robert Mooney (Asphyxia), John Keene Bolton (Euthanasia), Jim Fitzpatrick (Ammer), Jay Brian Winnick (Tongs), Anthony Stanton (Prince Charming), Lora Lee Cliff (Old Lady/Fairy Godmother) MUSICAL NUMBERS: Bright Spring Morn, It's What You Do That Makes Your Wishes Come True, His Highness, I Am a Prince, Your Sticks Your Hat Your Hand, Getting Ready for the Ball, Dance at the Ball Tonight, Waitin' on the Women, Keep the Castle Warm, La Petite Oiseau, Delighted You Invited Me, Happy Ending
A musical in two acts in the English Panto tradition.

*Carol Rosegg/Martha Swope Photos*

**TOP LEFT: Stephen McHattie, Jennifer Harmon in "Macbeth"**
**LEFT: Garry Goodrow, Richard Thomsen in "Iron Bars"**

**LEFT: Robert Mooney**
**RIGHT: Lora Lee Cliff in "Cinderella"**

# PLAYWRIGHTS HORIZONS

Twentieth Season

Artistic Directors, Andre Bishop (outgoing), Don Scardino; Executive Director, Paul S. Daniels; Associate Artistic Director, Nicholas Martin; Literary Manager, Tim Sanford, Musical Theatre Program, Ira Weitzman; Casting, Susan Shaw; Production Manager, David A. Milligan; Development, Dale Daley; Press, Philip Rinaldi, Elisa Shevitz

Tuesday, September 24 - October 20, 1991 (30 performances)
**THE 1991 YOUNG PLAYWRIGHTS FESTIVAL;** Producing Director, Nancy Quinn; Managing Director, Sheri M. Goldhirsch; Selection Committee, Andre Bishop, Ruth Goetz, Carol Hall, David Henry Hwang, Ms. Quinn, Mary Rodgers, Stephen Sondheim, Alfred Uhry, Wendy Wasserstein, John Weidman; Sets, Allen Moyer; Costumes, Elsa Ward; Lighting, Pat Dignan; Sound, Janet Kalas; Production Manager, David A. Milligan; Stage Managers, Roy Harris, Liz Small
SECRETS TO SQUARE DANCING by Denise Maher; Director, Gloria Muzio CAST: Louis Falk (Karl), Anne Lange (Veronica), Ethan Phillips (Mr. Pondence), Peter Francis James (Mr. Lewis), Mary Testa (Gladys), Steve Hofvendahl (Bruce), Olga Merediz (Rhoda), S. Epatha Merkerson (Janet), Paul Bates (Brad)
I'M NOT STUPID by David E. Rodriguez; Director, Seret Scott   CAST: Curtis McClarin (Roger), Peter Francis James (Dr. Green), S. Epatha Merkerson (Margaret Fletcher)
DONUT WORLD by Matthew Peterson; Director, Michael Mayer CAST: Paul Bates (Bud), Ethan Phillips (Sparky), Steve Hofvendahl (Lester), Olga Merediz (Mavis)
MAN AT HIS BEST by Carlota Zimmerman; Director, Mar Brokaw   CAST: Seth Gilliam (Dean), James G. Macdonald (Skyler)
   The tenth annual festival featuring writers under the age of 19.

Friday, November 15, 1991 - February 23, 1991 (92 performances and 24 previews) then transferred to Minetta Lane Theatre Friday, February 28, 1992
**MARVIN'S ROOM** by Scott McPherson; Director, David Petrarca; Sets, Linda Buchanan; Costumes, Claudia Boddy; Lighting, Robert Christen; Music/Sound, Rob Milburn; Production Manager, David A. Milligan; Stage Manager, Roy Harris CAST: Laura Esterman (Bessie), Tim Monsion (Dr. Wally), Alice Drummond (Ruth), Tom Aulino (Bob), Lisa Emery (Lee), Shona Tucker (Dr. Charlotte/Retirement Director), Mark Rosenthal (Hank), Karl Maschek (Charlie), Adam Chapnick (Marvin)
   A drama in two acts.  The action takes place at various Florida locations and a mental institution in Ohio at present.

Wednesday, December 11-22, 1991 (14 performances)
**FOUR SHORT OPERAS** by Michael John LaChiusa; Director, Kirsten Sanderson; Musical Director, Joshua Rosenblum; Sets, Derek McLane; Costumes, David Sawaryn; Lighting, Debra J. Kletter; Stage Manager, Liz Small
BREAK with Chuck Cooper (Man 1), Joe Grifasi (Man 2), Mary Beth Peil (Mary)
   The action takes place at a construction site.
AGNES with Mary Beth Peil (Woman), Alice Playten (Agnes), Mr. Cooper (Man)
   The action takes place at a park.
EULOGY FOR MISTER HAMM with Mr. Grifasi (Man), Ms. Peil (Woman), Ms. Playten (Girl), Mr. Cooper (Man in Dirty Dungarees)
   The action takes place in a hallway in a SRO hotel.

**Laura Esterman, Alice Drummond in "Marvin's Room"**
**TOP: Laura Esterman, Mark Rosenthal in "Marvin's Room"**

LUCKY NURSE with Ms. Peil (Madge), Mr. Grifasi (Jerry), Ms. Playten (Sherri), Mr. Cooper (Cabbie)
The action takes place in a hospital nurses' lounge.

Tuesday, January 29 - February 9, 1992
MAN, WOMAN, DINOSAUR by Regina M. Porter; Director, Melia Bensussen; Sets, Allen Moyer; Costumes, Karen Perry, Brian MacDevitt; Sound, Bruce Ellman; Stage Manager, Liz Small   CAST: Clarice Taylor (Verve Willows), Jihmi Kennedy (Coochie Willows), Oni Faida Lampley (Bernadette Marsh), Robinson Frank Adu (Alan Marsh), Sharif Rashed (Li'l Samuel)
The action takes place in Savannah, Georgia

Friday, March 20 - May 24, 1992 (55 performances and 21 previews)
THE END OF THE DAY by Jon Robin Baitz; Director, Mark Lamos; Sets, John Arnone; Costumes, Jess Goldstein; Lighting, Pat Collins; Sound David Budries; Production Manager, David A. Milligan; Stage Manager, M.A. Howard   CAST: Roger Rees (Graydon Massey), John Benjamin Hickey (Jonathon Toffler/Young Graydon), Paul Sparer (Hilly Lasker/Swifty/Lord Kitterson), Philip Kerr (Jeremiah Barton/Tellman the Butler), Nancy Marchand (Rosemund Brackett/Jocelyn Massey), Jean Smart (Helen Lasker-Massey/Lady Hammersmith Urbaine Supton Stoat).
A dark comedy in two acts.  The action takes place in California and London, 1991.

Wednesday, April 29 - May 10, 1992 (14 performances)
LITTLE EGYPT by Lynn Siefert; Director, Roberta Levitow; Set, James Noone; Costumes, Mary Myers; Lighting, Robert Wierzel; Music/Sound, John Gomada; Fights, Rick Sordelet; Stage Manager, William H. Lang   CAST: John Griesemer (Victor Mulkey Hood), Mary Shultz (Celeste Waltz), Phyllis Somerville (Faye Waltz), J. Smith-Cameron (Bernadette Waltz), Richard Gilliland (Watson Mason), J.R. Horne (Hugh Door)
A comedy taking place in Cairo, Illinois during the 1980s.

*Marc Bryan-Brown, T. Charles Erickson Photos*

**RIGHT: Nancy Marchand, Roger Rees in "End of the Day"**
**BELOW: Jean Smart, Roger Rees in "End of the Day"**

129

# ROUNDABOUT THEATRE

## Twenty-sixth Season

Producing Director, Todd Haimes; Founding Director, Gene Feist; General Manager, Ellen Richard; Technical Director, Julia C. Levy; Technical Director, Mitch Christenson; Press, Joshua Ellis

(17th St) Tuesday, July 30 - September 22, 1991 (63 performances)
**THE MATCHMAKER** by Thornton Wilder; Director, Lonny Price; Sets, Russell Metheny; Costumes, Gail Brassard; Lighting, Stuart Duke; Sound, Philip Campanella; Music, Claibe Richardson; Stage Manager, Roy W. Backes   CAST: Joseph Bova (Horace Vandergelder), Jim Fyfe (Cornelius Hackl), Rob Kramer (Barnaby Tucker), Jarlath Conroy (Malachi Stack), Michael Hayden (Ambrose/August), Theodore Sorel (Joe Scanlon), Jack Cirillo (Rudolph), Dorothy Loudon (Dolly Levi), Eileen Letchworth (Flora Van Huysen), Lisa Emery (Irene Molloy), Lisa Dove (Minnie Fay), Wendy Lawless (Ermengarde), Mary Diveny (Gertrude/Cook)
   The 1955 comedy performed in three acts.  The action takes place in Yonkers, NY and NYC, just after the turn of the century.

For other Roundabout productions (*The Homecoming, The Visit, Hamlet, The Price*), see BROADWAY CALENDAR.

Dorothy Loudon in "The Matchmaker" (*Martha Swope*)

# SECOND STAGE THEATRE

## Thirteenth Season

Artistic Directors, Robyn Goodman & Carole Rothman; Literary Manager, Sanders; Production Manager, Carol Fishman; Managing Director, Dorothy J. Ma Marketing Director, Savannah Whaley; Development Director, Craig Raia; Busi Manager, Jerry Polner; Casting, Simon & Kumin; Press, Richard Kornberg

Monday, July 8 - August 10, 1991 (42 performances)
**HOME AND AWAY;** Written & Performed by Kevin Kling; Director/Sets, D Esbjornson; Lighting, Frances Aronson; Sound, Mark Bennett; Hairstylist, Ant Soddu; Stage Manager, Crystal Huntington
   A monologue performed in two parts.  The comic stories involve a Minne childhood and world travels.

Tuesday, December 3, 1991 - January 12, 1992 (45 performances)
**DEARLY DEPARTED** by David Bottrell and Jessie Jones; Director, Gloria Mu Sets, Allen Moyer; Lighting, Don Holder; Costumes, Ellen McCartney; Sound, N Bennett; Hairstylist, Antonio Soddu; Stage Manager, Stacey Fleischer  CAST: D Baker (Junior), Leo Burmester (Bud Turpin/Ray-Bud), Mary Fogarty (Rayne Sloane Shelton (Marguerite), Greg Germann (Royce), Jessie Jones (Lucille), L Cook (Suzanne), J.R. Horne (Rev. Hooker/Clyde/Norval), Wendy Law (Delightful/Nadine), Jill Larson (Juanita/Veda)
   A comedy in two acts.  The action takes place somewhere below the Mason-D line at present.

Tuesday, March 17 - April 26, 1992 (42 performances)
**RED DIAPER BABY;** Written and Performed by Josh Kornbluth; Director, Jo Mostel; Set, Randy Benjamin; Lighting, Pat Dignan; Costumes, Susan Lyall; So Aural Fixation; Hairstylist, Antonio Soddu; Stage Manager, Buzz Cohen
   Monologue about coming of age in a family of Jewish communists.

Tuesday, May 12 - July 4, 1992 (56 performances)
**SPIKE HEELS** by Theresa Rebeck; Director, Michael Greif; Sets, James Youn Lighting, Kenneth Posner; Costumes, Candice Donnelly; Sound, Mark Ben Hairstylist, Antonio Soddu; Stage Manager, Jess Lynn  CAST: Kevin Ba (Edward), Tony Goldwyn (Andrew), Saundra Santiago (Georgie), Julie White (Ly
   A comedy in two acts.  The action takes place in Boston at present.

*Susan Cook Photos*

**TOP LEFT: Greg Germann, Dylan Baker in "Dearly Departed"**
**CENTER: Saundra Santiago, Kevin Bacon in "Spike Heels"**
**BOTTOM LEFT: Tony Goldwyn, Santiago**

n Futterman, Danny Zorn, Lenny Venito, Aaron Harnick in "Club Soda"

Roger Howarth, Billy Morrissette, Michael Loudon, J.D. Cullum in
"White Rose"

Stephen Mailer, Ken Garito in "Peacetime"

Marguerite MacIntire, Ellen Greene, Jonathan Hadary, Valarie
Pettiford, Jessica Molaskey in "Weird Romance"

# WPA THEATRE
## (WORKSHOP OF THE PLAYERS ART)

Fourteenth Season

Artistic Director, Kyle Renick; Managing Director, Donna Lieberman; General Manager, Lori Sherman; Resident Designer, Edward T. Gianfrancesco; Resident Lighting Designer, Craig Evans; Production Manager, Augustus Perkins; Press, Jeffrey Richards Associates/David LeShay, Gary Brammick, Robert Marlin

Thursday, June 6 - July 14, 1991 (39 performances)
**CLUB SODA** by Leah Kornfeld Friedman; Director, Pamela Berlin; Sets, Edward T. Gianfrancesco; Lighting, Craig Evans; Costumes, Deborah Shaw; Sound, Aural Fixation; Choreography, John Carrafa; Musical Director, Edward Strauss; Stage Manager, Karen Moore   CAST: Alanna Ubach (Lillie), Patricia Mauceri (Lillie's Mother/Lady in Window/Blanche), Dan Futterman (Binnie), Danny Zorn (Louie/Dr. Toona), Lenny Venito (Vic/Soda Jerk), Aaron Harnick (Toss/Bert), Katherine Hiler (Gloria/Miss O'Brien/Dr. Levine)
A comedy set in Brooklyn, NY, 1947.

Thursday, October 15 - November 17, 1991 (35 performances)
**THE WHITE ROSE** by Lillian Garrett-Groag; Director, Christopher Ashley; Sets, Edward T. Gianfrancesco; Lighting, Debra Dumas; Costumes, Michael Krass; Sound, Aural Fixation; Stage Manager, Greta Minsky   CAST: Roger Howarth (Schmidt/Probst), J.D. Cullum (Hans Scholl), Melissa Leo (Sophie Scholl), Victor Slezak (Mahler), Larry Bryggman (Robert Mohr), Brad Greenquist (Bauer), Michael Louden (Alexander Schmorell), Billy Morrissette (Willi Graf)
The action takes place in Munich, Germany, 1942 - 1943.

Friday, January 3 - February 9, 1992 (39 performances)
**BELLA, BELLE OF BYELORUSSIA** by Jeffrey Essmann; Director, Christopher Ashley; Music, Michael John La Chiusa; Sets, James Youmans; Lighting, Debra Dumas; Costumes, Anne C. Patterson; Sound, Aural Fixation; Musical Staging, John Carrafa; Stage Manager, Karen Moore   CAST: Claire Beckman (Bella), Harriet Harris (Ludmilla/Waitress), Becca Lish (Sally), Joe Grifasi (Oglokov), Willis Sparks (Giorgi), Ann Mantel (Mamushka), Jefferson Mays (Sergei/Vladivostok Jimmy)
A Comedy with songs in two acts. The action takes place in Minsk, Byelorussia, 1989.

Saturday, February 22 - March 15, 1992 (25 performances)
**PEACETIME** by Elaine Berman; Director, Pamela Berlin; Sets, Edward T. Gianfrancesco; Lighting, Craig Evans; Costumes, Mimi Maxmen; Sound, David Wiggall; Choreography, Constance Valis Hill; Stage Manager, Karen Moore   CAST: Stephen Mailer (Morris Singer), Ken Garito (Jake Singer), Barry Snider (Hyman Singer), Jessica Queller (Frannie Singer), Suzanne Costallos (Adela Singer), Gordon Greenberg (Ben Singer), Kelly Wolf (Miriam Greenblatt), Sandra Laub (Blossom Goldman)
A drama in two acts. The action takes place in New York City during the winter of 1920 - 1921.

Tuesday, May 12 - July 2, 1992 (50 performances)
**WEIRD ROMANCE** with Music by Alan Menken; Lyrics, David Spencer; Book Alan Brennert; Director, Barry Harman; Orchestrations/Dance Arrangements, Douglas Besterman; Cast Recording, Columbia; Musical Director/Vocal Arrangements, Kathy Sommer; Choreography, John Carrafa; Sets, Edward T. Gianfrancesco; Lighting, Craig Evans; Costumes, Michael Krass; Sound, Aural Fixation; Stage Manager, Joseph A. Onorato
ACT I: *The Girl Who Was Plugged In*; Based on story by James Tiptree, Jr.   CAST: Valarie Pettiford (Shannara/Technician/Make-up Specialist/GTX Lady/Script Supervisor), Eric Riley (Zanth/Paramedic/Technician/Movement Coach), Ellen Greene (P. Burke), William Youmans (Vendor/Joe Hopkins), Sal Viviano (Paul), Marguerite MacIntyre (First Fan/Delphi), Jessica Molaskey (2nd Fan/Mugger/Technician/Voice Coach/Gtx Lady/2nd Director), Danny Burstein (3rd Fan/Paramedic/Technician/Reporter/Film Director), Jonathan Hadary (Isham)
MUSICAL NUMBERS: Weird Romance, Great Unknown, Stop and See Me, That's Where We Come In, Feeling No Pain, Pop! Flash!, Amazing Penetration, Eyes That Never Lie, No One Can Do, Worth It, Finale
This action takes place in a large metropolitan city, 2061

ACT II: *Her Pilgrim Soul*; based on Alan Brennert story   CAST: Danny Burstein (Daniel), Jonathan Hadary (Kevin), Sal Viviano (Johnny Beaumont), William Youmans (Clown/Chuck/Ruskin), Eric Riley (Boxer/George Lester), Marguerite MacIntyre (Bride/Susan), Jessica Molaskey (Carol), Valarie Pettiford (Rebecca), Ellen Greene (Nola)   MUSICAL NUMBERS: My Orderly World, Need to Know, Remember, Another Woman, Pressing Onward, I Can Show You a Thing or Two, A Man, Someone Else is Waiting
The action takes place in Cambridge, Massachusetts on the day after tomorrow.

*Martha Swope, Joe Schuyler, Blanche Mackey Photos*

# YORK THEATRE

Twenty-third Season

Founder/Producing Director, Janet Hayes Walker; Managing Director, Molly Pickering Grose; Artistic Advisors, John Newton, James Morgan; Technical Director, Sally Smith; Development, Brendi Drosnes; Business Manager, Charles Dodsley Walker; Press, Keith Sherman/Chris Day, Jim Byk

Friday, September 27 - October 20, 1991 (21 performances)
**THE MISANTHROPE** by Molière; Translation, Richard Wilbur; Director, Alex Dmitriev; Sets, James Mogan; Costumes, Barbara Beccio; Lighting, Jerold R. Forsyth; Stage Manager, Mary Ellen Allison   CAST: Patrick Stretch (Alceste), Gordana Rashovich (Arsinoé), Shari Simpson (Célimène), Andrew Borba, Lee Chew, Oliver Clark, Michael Hammond, Gillian Hemstead, Ian Trigger

Friday, December 6, 1991 - January 19, 1992
**WHAT ABOUT LUV?** with Music by Howard Marren; Lyrics, Susan Birkenhead; Book, Jeffrey Sweet; Director, Patricia Birch; Musical Director, Tom Helm; Sets, James Morgan; Costumes, Barbara Beccio; Lighting, Mary Jo Dondlinger; Stage Manager, William J. Buckley   CAST: Austin Pendleton (Harry Berlin), David Green (Milt Manville), Judy Kaye (Ellen Manville)   MUSICAL NUMBERS: Harry's Letter, Polyarts U., Why Bother?, Paradise, It's Love!, The Chart, Ellen's Credo, Somebody, The Test, How Beautiful the Night Is, What a Life!, Lady, If Harry Weren't Here, My Brown Paper Hat, Do I Love Him?
A revision of the 1984 musical *Love* in two acts. The action takes place in New York City during the recent past.

**Gordana Rashovich, Shari Simpson in "The Misanthrope"**
BELOW: **John Kozeluh, Michelle O'Steen in "After the Dancing in Jerich**

Friday, February 2 - 23, 1992
**AFTER THE DANCING IN JERICHO;** Written and Directed by P.J. Barry; Se Daniel Ettinger; Costumes, Barbara Beccio; Lighting, Mary Jo Dondlinger; Stage Manage Alan Fox; Choreography, Dennis Dennehy   CAST: Michelle O'Steen (Katie Driscol John Kozeluh (Jimmy Conroy), Ginger Prince (Kate Driscoll Thorp), Jack Davidson (Ji Conroy), James Congdon (Howard Thorp), Pamela Burrell (Gloria French Conroy)
A comedy set in New York City, New Jersey, and Rhode Island spanning 1947-1984.

Friday, March 20 - April 26, 1992
**LITTLE ME** with Music by Cy Coleman; Lyrics, Carolyn Leigh; Book, Neil Simo Based on the novel by Patrick Dennis; Director, Jeffrey B. Moss; Choreograph Barbara Siman; Musical Director, Leo P. Carusone; Sets, James E. Morgan; Costume Michael Bottari, Ronald Case; Lighting, Stuart Duke; Stage Manager, Alan F CAST: Jo Ann Cunningham (Older Belle), Stephen Joseph (Eggleston/Nurs Newsboy/Cop/Preacher/German Soldier/Patient/Passenger/Asst. Director/Victo Peasant), Denise Le Donne (Momma/Romona/Miss K/Cop/Colette/Girl Party/Nurse/Passenger/Newsboy/Secretary/Prop Boy/Peasant), Amelia Prenti (Young Belle/Baby), Jonathan Beck Reed (Noble/Pinchley/Val/Fre Otto/Prince/Noble Jr.), Russ Thacker (George/Kleeg/Bennie/Headwaiter/Soldie Steward/Sailor/Royal Doctor/Judge), Ray Wills (Brucey/Bentley/Pinchle Jr./Bernie/Lawyer/Waiter/Soldier/Sargent/General/Capt./King/Yulnick/Judg MUSICAL NUMBER: Overture, Don't Ask a Lady, Other Side of the Tracks, Ric Kids Rag, I Love You, Deep Down Inside, Be a Performer, Oh! Dem Doggor Dimples, Boom Boom, I've Got Your Number, Real Live Girl, Poor Little Hollywoo Star, Little Me, Goodbye, Here's To Us, Finale
The 1962 musical in two acts. The action takes place everywhere from Twin Jug Illinois in the past, to Hackensack, NJ at present.

*Carol Rosegg Photos*

**132**       **Jo Ann Cunningham in "Little Me"**
TOP LEFT: **David Green, Austin Pendleton, Judy Kaye in "What About! Luv?"**

## ANNIE WARBUCKS

sic, Charles Strouse; Lyrics, Martin Charnin; Book, Thomas Meehan; Director, Mr. rnin; Choreography, Peter Gennaro; Orchestrations, David Siegel; Musical ector, Michael Duff; Sets, Thomas M. Ryan; Costumes, Nancy Missimi; Lighting, ne Ferry Williams; Sound, Randy Allen Johns; Produced in workshop by dspeed Opera House; Press, Terry James; World Premiere on January 29, 1992 at riott's Licolnshire Theatre and toured after Chicago engagement.

### CAST

| | |
|---|---|
| ie Warbucks | Lauren Gaffney |
| dy | Chelsea |
| ke | Don Forston |
| . Pugh/Whittleby | Joan Krause |
| ver Warbucks | Harve Presnell |
| ce Farrell | Jennifer Nees |
| on Whitehead | Joel Hatch |
| Price/Ray Billy/David Lillianthal/Bert Healy | Fred Zimmerman |
| Waterhouse/Fletcher/Mr. Stanley/Marine | Rob Rahn |
| nmis. Harriet Stark | Alene Robertson |

Orphans:

| | |
|---|---|
| sie | Bebbie Wittenberg |
| lly | Andrea Costa |
| y | Raegen Kotz |
| per | Betsy Morgan |
| ches | Ali Pesche |
| fy | Natalie Berg |
| s Sherman | Jeanne Croft |
| anda Wagstaff | Jennifer Neuland |
| s Felicia Dabney | Karen Olson |
| . Florence Kelly | Mary Ernster |
| s Phillips/Gladys | Catherine Lord |
| y Ray/Steve McCall/Judge Brandeis | Dale Morgan |
| in T. Patterson | Kingsley Leggs |
| a Patterson | Seraiah Carol |
| . Patterson | Thomasina Gross |
| nklin Delano Roosevelt | Raymond Thorne |
| rine | William Berloni |

**DERSTUDIES:** Raegan Kotz (Annie), Fred Zimmerman (Warbucks), Catherine d (Grace), Jennifer Neuland (Mrs. Kelly), Rob Rahn (Drake), Joan Krause (Mrs. k)

**USICAL NUMBERS:** When You Smile, Above the Law, Changes, The Other man, That's the Kind of Woman, A Younger Man, 'Cause of You, But You Go On, rything is Nothing Without You, Love, Somebody's Gotta Do Somethin', You Owe Tootsie, All Dolled up, Tenement Lullaby, It Would Have Been Wonderful, I ss Things Happen for the Best, The Day They Say I Do, Finale

A musical in two acts with 13 scenes. Earlier versions of this sequel to *Annie* were sented under the title *Annie 2* in January 1990 at the Kennedy Center and May 1991 Goodspeed Opera House.

*Tom Maday Photos*

**Alene Robertson, Mary Ernster**
LEFT: **Harve Presnell, Lauren Gaffney**
ABOVE: **Lauren Gaffney**

133

# BYE BYE BIRDIE

Music, Charles Strouse; Lyrics, Lee Adams; Book, Michael Stewart; Director, Gene Saks; Choreography, Edmund Kresley; Musical Director, Michael Biagi; Sets, Peter Larkin; Costumes, Robert Mackintosh; Lighting, Peggy Eisenhauer; Sound, Peter Fitzgerald; Hairstylist, Robert DiNiro; Casting, Stuart Howard, Amy Schecter; General Manager, Barbara Darwall, Alecia Parker; Production Supervisor, Craig Jacobs; Technical Supervisor, Arthur Siccardi; Company Manager, Jim Brandeberry; Stage Managers, David Wolfe, Thomas Bartlett; Presented by Barry and Fran Weissler and Pace Theatrical Group; Press Judy Jacksina/Anita Dianak, Penny M. Landau. Opened May 9, 1991 in Long Beach, California after previous St. Louis engagement, and still touring May 31, 1992.

## CAST

| | |
|---|---|
| Rose Alvarez | Ann Reinking+1 |
| Albert Peterson | Tommy Tune |
| Ursula Merkle | Jessica Stone |
| Kim MacAfee | Susan Egan |
| Doris MacAfee | Belle Calaway |
| Harry MacAfee | Dale O'Brien |
| Randolph MacAfee | Joey Hannon |
| Mae Peterson | Marilyn Cooper |
| Conrad Birdie | Marc Kudisch |
| Hugo Peabody | Steve Zahn |
| Deborah Sue | Robyn Peterman |
| Suzie | Jane Labanz |
| Mayor | J. Lee Flynn |
| Mayor's Wife | Kristine Nevins |
| Mrs. Merkle | Mary Kilpatrick |
| Gloria Rasputin | Belle Calaway |
| TV Stage Manager | Martin Coles |
| Charles F. Maude | J. Lee Flynn |
| Harvey Johnson | Paul Castree |

**ENSEMBLE:** Paul Castree, Martin Coles, Vincent D'Elia, Michael Duran, Kim Frankenfield, Simone Gee, Elizabeth Green, Peter Gregus, Vanessa Handrick, Jorinda Junius, Brian Loeffler, Brian-Paul Mendoza, Elizabeth O'Neill, Robyn Peterman, Tracy Rosten, H. Hyland Scott II, Tara Sobeck, Wendy Springer, Shaver Tillitt

**UNDERSTUDIES/STANDBYS:** Belle Calaway (Rose), Dennis Daniels (Albert/Birdie), Tracy Rosten (Mae), Vincent D'Elia (Birdie), J. Lee Flynn (Harry), Mary Kilpatrick (Doris/Gloria), Jane Labanz (Kim), Wendy Springer (Randolph), Paul Castree (Hugo), Elizabeth Green (Ursula), Brian-Paul Mendoza (Harvey)

**MUSICAL NUMBERS:** An English Teacher, Telephone Hour, How Lovely to Be a Woman, Put on a Happy Face, Normal American Boy, One Boy, Honestly Sincere, Hymn for a Sunday Evening, One Last Kiss, What Did I Ever See in Him?  A Lot of Livin' to Do, Kids, Baby Talk to Me, Shriner's Ballet, A Giant Step (new song), He's Mine (new song), Rosie

A musical in two acts. The action takes place in New York and Ohio, 1959.

+: Succeeded by: I. Lenora Nemetz

**Ann Reinking, Tommy Tune in "Bye Bye Birdie"**

# A CHORUS LINE

Originally Conceived, Choreographed, and Directed by Michael Bennett; Mu[sic,] Marvin Hamlisch; Lyrics, Edward Kleban; Book, James Kirkwood, Nicholas Da[nte;] Restaged by Baayork Lee; Musical Director, Joseph Klein; Lighting, Richard Wink[;] Sound, Abe Jacob; Assistant Director, Jim Litten; General Manager, Robert V. Stra[;] Stage Manager, Joseph Sheridan; Presented by Robert L. Young, Richard Martini, Albert Nocciolino; Press, Molly Smith

## CAST

| | |
|---|---|
| Frank | Jim Athens |
| Al | Frank Kosik |
| Richie | Philip Michael Bakerville |
| Shelia | Gail Benedict |
| Connie | Melinda Cartwright |
| Judy | Janie Casserly |
| Butch | Kevin Chinn |
| Zach | Randy Clements |
| Don | Michael Danek |
| Roy | Morris Freed |
| Cassie | Wanda Richert-Preston |
| Diana | Deborah Geneviere |
| Bobby | Michael Gorman |
| Val | Kelli Fish |
| Tricia | Julia Gregory |
| Tom | Darrell Hankey |
| Kristine | Melissa Johnson |
| Greg | Doug Friedman |
| Vicki | Diana Kavilis |
| Maggie | Julie Pappas |
| Paul | Porfirio |
| Larry | Michael Biondi |
| Mike | Mark Santillano |
| Mark | Randy Slovacek |
| Lois | Anna Simonelli |
| Bebe | Beth Swearingen |

**UNDERSTUDIES:** Jim Litten (Mike/Larry/Al), Julia Greg[ory] (Maggie/Bebe/Kristine/Diana), Kevin Chinn (Richie/Paul), Anna Simone[lli] (Connie/Diana/Bebe), Jim Athens (Bobby/Greg/Paul), Morris Freed (Larry/Mar[k]) Darrell Hankey (Don/Al/Greg), Diana Kavilis (Val/Judy/Kristine/Cassie), Mich[ael] Danek (Zach), Janie Casserly (Shelia), Buddy Balou (Zach/Bobby), Danny Rou[] (Mark/Mike/Don), Beth Swearingen (Cassie), Karls Christensen (Don/Zach/[A]) Mindy Hull (Judy/Shelia)

A musical performed without intermission. The action takes place during [an] audition, circa 1975.

**"A Chorus Line"**

# CITY OF ANGELS

Music, Cy Coleman; Lyrics, David Zippel; Book, Larry Gelbart; Director, Michael Blakemore; Sets, Robin Wagner; Costumes, Florence Klotz; Lighting, Paul Gallo; Musical Staging, Walter Painter; Presented by Barry and Fran Weissler; Press, Anita Dloniak; Opened in Los Angeles' Shubert Theatre

## MOVIE CAST

| | |
|---|---|
| Stone | James Naughton succeeded by Jeff McCarthy |
| Orderlies | Jordan Leeds, Jeffrey Rockwell |
| Oolie | Randy Graff succeeded by Catherine Cox |
| Alaura Kingsley | Lauren Mitchell |
| Big Six | Darwyn Swalve |
| Sonny | Nick DeGruccio |
| Jimmy Powers | Bob Walton |
| Angel City 4 | Richard Kasper, Tampa Lann, Monica Mancini, Royce Reynolds |
| Munoz | Joe Lala |
| Pasco | Jeffrey Rockwell |
| Bobbi | Leslie Denniston |
| Irwin S. Irving | Charles Levin |
| Peter Kingsley | Andrew Husmann |
| Margaret | Sara Tattersall |
| Luther Kingsley | Jack Manning |
| Dr. Mandrill | Doug Carfrae |
| Mallory Kingsley | Anastasia Barzee |
| Mahoney | Jordan Leeds |
| Coroner | Alvin Ing |
| Gaines | Robert Rod Barry |
| Madame | Kathy Garrick |
| Tootsie | Christiane Noll |

## HOLLYWOOD CAST

| | |
|---|---|
| Stine | Stephen Bogardus |
| Buddy Fidler | Charles Levin |
| Gabby | Leslie Denniston |
| Barber | Doug Carfrae |
| Donna | Randy Graff succeeded by Catherine Cox |
| Masseuse | Kathy Garrick |
| Jimmy Powers | Bob Walton |
| Engineer | Robert Rod Barry |
| Carla Haywood | Lauren Mitchell |
| Del Dacosta | Doug Carfrae |
| Pancho Vargas | Joe Lala |
| Werner Kriegler | Jack Manning |
| Gerald Pierce | Andrew Husmann |
| Avril Raines | Anastasia Barzee |
| Gene | Jeffrey Rockwell |
| Cinematographer | Alvin Ing |
| Stand-In | Sara Tattersall |
| Buddy's Nephew | Jordan Leeds |
| Hairdresser | Kathy Garrick |
| Make-Up | Christiane Noll |
| Studio Cops | Nick DeGruccio, Darwyn Swalve |

A musical in two acts. The action takes place in Los Angeles in the 1940s. For original 1989 Broadway production see *Theatre World* Vol. 46.

*Craig Schwarz Photos*

**TOP: Lauren Mitchell**
**RIGHT: Catherine Cox, Jeff McCarthy**

# A FEW GOOD MEN

By Aaron Sorkin; Director, Don Scardino; Set, Ben Edwards; Costumes, David C. Woolard; Lighting, Thomas R. Skelton; Sound, John Gromada; Casting, Pat McCorkle; Stage Manager, David Hyslop; Tour presented by David Brown, Lewis Allen, Robert Whitehead, Roger L. Stevens, Kathy Levin, Suntory Int'l, The Shubert Organization and The Kennedy Center for the Performing Arts; Press, Bill Evans/William Schelble, Rick Miramontez (West Coast); Opened at the Bushnell Theatre in Hartford, Ct. on Tuesday, January 7, 1992, playing Baltimore, Memphis, Grand Rapids, Chicago, San Francisco and Los Angeles before closing May 10, 1992 in St. Paul.

## CAST

| | |
|---|---|
| Lance Cpl. Harold W. Dawson | Keith Diamond |
| Pfc. Louden Downey | David Van Pelt |
| Lt. J.G. Sam Weinberg | Michael Countryman |
| Lt. J.G. Daniel A. Kaffee | Michael O'Keefe |
| Lt. Cmdr. Joanne Galloway | Alyson Reed |
| Capt. Isaac Whitaker | Edmond Genest |
| Capt. Matthew A. Markinson | Ross Bickell |
| Pfc. William T. Santiago | John Ortiz |
| Col. Nathan Jessep | Scott Sowers |
| Lt. Jonathan James Kendrick | Conan McCarty |
| Lt. Jack Ross | Jordan Lage |
| Cpl. Jeffrey Owen Howard | Joshua Malina |
| Capt. Julius Alexander Randolph | Paul Winfield succeeded by Paul Butler in L.A. |
| Cmdr. Walter Stone | William Parry |
| Marines, Sailors, M.P.s, Lawyers | Jonathan Bustle, William J. Duffy, Noah Emmerich, Ken Marino, Monté Russell |

**UNDERSTUDIES:** William J. Duffy (Kaffee/Ross), Noah Emmerich (Kendrick), Jonathan Bustle (Whitaker/Markinson/Randolph), Monté Russell (Dawson/Santiago), Ken Marino (Downey/Howard), Ron Ostrow (Marines, etc.), Deirdre Madigan (Galloway)

A drama in two acts. The action takes place in various locations in Washington, D.C. and Guantanamo Bay, Cuba in 1986. For original 1989 Broadway production see *Theatre World* Vol. 46 (page 19).

*Joan Marcus Photos*

Michael O'Keefe, Alyson Reed

Michael O'Keefe, David Van Pelt, Michael Countryman, Alyson Reed, Scott Sowers, Monte Russell, William J. Duffy

Ross Bickell, Scott Sowers, Conan McCarty, Michael O'Keefe, Alyson Reed, Michael Countryman

David Van Pelt, Michael O'Keefe, Keith Diamond

Keith Diamond, Michael O'Keefe, Michael Countryman, Alyson Reed, Scott Sowers, (top) Paul Winfield, Jordan Lage

## FOREVER PLAID

r complete original creative credits see Off Broadway section;
ector/Choreography, Stuart Ross; Musical Director, Ron Roy; Company Manager,
en Szorady; Stage Manager, Mark Healy; Press, David Balsom; Opened in the
ston Park Plaza Hotel on Wednesday, October 9, 1991 and still playing May 31,
*2.

### CAST

ncis ..................................................Dale Sandish succeeded by Robert Lambert
rky......................................................David Benoit succeeded by Bruce Moore
x..............................................................Leo Daignault succeeded by Roy Chicas
udge .....................................................Jeff Bannon succeeded by Jeffrey Korn

**DERSTUDIES:** Gregory Bouchard, Jeffrey Korn
A musical performed without intermission. For original New York production see
*atre World* Vol. 46.

*Marc Teatum Photos*

**TOP: Jeff Bannon, Robert Lambert, Roy Chicas, Bruce Moore**
**RIGHT: Bruce Moore, Roy Chicas, Jeff Bannon, Robert Lambert**

(right) Julie Harris

Julie Harris, Roberta Maxwell

Marylouise Burke, Julie Harris, Roberta Maxwell

John Horton, Julie Harris

# LETTICE & LOVAGE

By Peter Shaffer; Director, Michael Blakemore; Design, Alan Tagg; Costum
Anthony Powell (Julie Harris), Frank Krenz; Lighting, Ken Billington; Stage Mana
Susie Cordon; Presented by The Shubert Organization, Roger Berlind and Ca
Cities/ABC; Tour opened in New Haven in April 1992 followed by Bos
Washington, etc ... and still touring May 31, 1992.

## CAST

Lettice Douffet ................................................................................Julie Harris
Surly Man ...........................................................................................Dane Knell
Lotte Schoen ...........................................................................Roberta Maxwell
Miss Framer ......................................................................Marylouise Burke
Mr. Bardolph ...............................................................................John Horton
Visitors ..............................................Miss Burke, Timm Fujiii, Bonnie Hess-Rose,
Mr. Knell, Barbara Lester, Sybil Lines, Hugh A. Rose,
Jill Tanner, Laurine Towler, Tyrone Wilson

**STANDBYS:** Jill Tanner (Lettice), Sybil Lines (Lotte/Framer), Hugh A. R
(Bardolph/Man)

A comedy in two acts. For original 1990 Broadway production with Maggie Sr
see *Theatre World* Vol. 46.

*Martha Swope Photos*

**138**

**Julie Harris**

# ONCE ON THIS ISLAND

Music, Stephen Flaherty; Lyrics/Book, Lynn Ahrens; Based on novel *My Love My Love* by Rosa Guy; Director/Choreography, Graciela Daniele; Orchestrations, Michael Starobin; Musical Director, Mark Lipman; Musical Supervisor, Steve Marzullo; Casting, Alan Filderman; Associate Choreographer, Willie Rosario; Sets, Loy Arcenas; Costumes, Judy Dearing; Lighting, Allen Lee Hughes; Sound, Scott Lehrer; Executive Producer, George MacPherson; Presented by The Nederlander Organization, Auditorium Theatre Council, Tom Mallow, ATP/Dodger, Pace Theatrical, Kennedy Center, Shubert Organization, Capital Cities/ABC, Suntory Int'l, James Walsh and Playwrights Horizons; Press, Patt Dale; Opened in the Subert Theatre, Chicago on Thursday, April 2, 1992 and still touring May 31, 1992.

## CAST

| | |
|---|---|
| Erzulie | Natalie Venetia Belcon |
| Andrea | Monique Cintron |
| Daniel | Darius de Haas |
| Asaka | Carol Dennis |
| Little Ti Moune | Nilyne Fields |
| Mama Euralie | Sheila Gibbs |
| Ti Moune | Vanita Harbour |
| Papa Ge | Gerry McIntyre |
| Agwe | James Stovall |
| Armand | Keith Tyrone |
| Tonton Julian | Miles Watson |

**STANDBYS:** Alvateta Guess (Mama/Asaka), Tonya L. Dixon (Ti Moune/Andrea/Erzulie), LaShonda Hunt (Little Ti Moune), Keith Tyrone (Daniel), James Stovall (Tonton), Steven Cates (Papa/Agwe/Armand)

**MUSICAL NUMBERS:** We Dance, One Small Girl, Waiting for Life, And the Gods Heard Her Prayer, Rain, Pray, Forever Yours, Sad Tale of the Beauxhommes, Ti Moune, Mama Will Provide, Some Say, Human Heart, Some Girls, The Ball, A Part of Us, Why We Tell the Story

A musical performed without intermission. The action takes place in the French Antilles during a night storm. For original 1990 Broadway production see *Theatre World* Vol. 47.

*Martha Swope Photos*

**TOP: Vanita Harbour, Carol Dennis and cast**
**CENTER: Monique Cintron, Darius de Haas**
**BOTTOM LEFT: The Company**

**Vanita Harbour, Darius de Haas**

# THE SECRET GARDEN

For complete original creative credits and Musical Numbers see Broadway Section; Director, Susan H. Schulman; Musical Director, Constantine Kitsopoulos; Stage Manager, Dan W. Langhofer; Executive Tour Producer, George MacPherson; Company Manager, John Pasinato; Press, Adrian Bryan-Brown, Jeff Finn; Opened in Cleveland on Tuesday, April 28, 1992 and still touring May 31, 1992.

## CAST

| | |
|---|---|
| Lily | Anne Runolfsson |
| Mary Lennox | Melody Kay, Kay Mahon |
| Fakir | Andy Gale |
| Ayah | Audra Ann McDonald |
| Rose | Jacquelyn Piro |
| Capt. Albert Lennox | Kevin Dearinger |
| Lt. Peter Wright | Ken Land |
| Lt. Ian Shaw | Mark Agnes |
| Major Holmes | Marc Mouchet |
| Claire | Roxann Parker |
| Alice | Mary Illes |
| Archibald Craven | Kevin McGuire |
| Dr. Neville Craven | Douglas Sills |
| Ms. Medlock | Mary Fogarty |
| Martha | Tracy Ann Moore |
| Dickon | Roger Bart |
| Ben | Jay Garner |
| Colin | Sean Considine, Luke Hogan |
| William | James Barbour |
| Betsy | Jill Patton |
| Timothy | Ty Hreben |
| Mrs. Winthrop | Roxann Parker |

**UNDERSTUDIES:** Jacquelyn Piro, Mary Illes (Lily), Douglas Sills, Marc Mouchet (Archibald), James Barbour, Ken Land (Neville), Roxann Parker (Medlock), Susie McMonagle, Jill Patton (Martha), Ty Hreben, Oliver Woodall (Dickon), Mr. Mouchet (Ben), Ms. Illes, Ms. Patton (Rose), Mark Agnes, Mr. Barbour (Albert), Mark Agnes, Mr. Woodall (Fakir), Ms. Patton, Ms. McMonagle (Ayah), Mr. Barbour, Todd Murray, Mr. Woodall (Wright/Shaw), Mr. Murray, Mr. Barbour (Holmes), Ms. Patton, Ms. McMonagle (Claire/Winthrop/Alice), Mr. Murray, Mr. Woodall (William), Ms. McMonagle (Betsy), Mr. Woodall, Mr. Murray (Swings)

A musical in two acts. The action takes place in India and an English mansion. For original 1991 Broadway production see *Theatre World* Vol. 47.

*Carol Rosegg/Martha Swope Photos*

**BELOW: Roger Bart, Melody Kay**
**TOP: Anne Runolfsson, Luke Hogan, Kevin McGuire, Melody Kay**
**RIGHT: Kevin McGuire, Douglas Sills**
**BOTTOM RIGHT: Kevin McGuire, Anne Runolfsson**

# PROFESSIONAL REGIONAL COMPANIES

## ACT/A CONTEMPORARY THEATRE

Seattle, Washington
Twenty-eighth Season

Founding Director, Gregory A. Falls; Artistic Director, Jeff Steitzer; Producing Director, Phil Scherner; Managing Director, Susan Trapnell Moritz; Production Manager, James Verdery; Marketing, Teri Mumme; Press, Michael Sande; Development, Mary K. Stevens; Directors, Steven Dietz, Gary Gisselman, David Ira Goldstein, Jeff Steitzer; Set Designers, Bill Forrester, Greg Lucas, Michael Olich, Shelley Henze Schermer, Vicki Smith, Scott Weldin, Lori Sullivan Worthman; Costume Designers, Gene Davis Buck, Laura Crow, Nanrose Buchman, Sam Fleming, Carolyn Keim, Rose Pederson; Lighting Designers, Richard Hogle, Peter Maradudin, Rick Paulsen, Phil Schermer; Sound Designers, Steven M. Klein, David Hunter Koch, Jim Ragland; Stage Managers, Jeff Hanson, Joan Toggenburger, Gretchen Van Horne, Craig Weinelling; Dramaturg, Steven E. Alter.

### PRODUCTIONS & CASTS

**MY CHILDREN! MY AFRICA!** by Athol Fugard with Jonathan Adams, Warren Bowles and Stephanie Kallos
**THE ILLUSION** by Tony Kushner with Laurence Ballard, Ted D'Arms, Robert Nadir, David Pichette, Faye M. Price, G. Valmont Thomas and Christopher Welch
**TEARS OF RAGE** by Doris Baizley with John Aylward, Linda Emond, Torrey Hanson, Stephanie Kallos, Christine McMurdo-Wallis, Karen Meyer and David P. Whitehead
**OUR COUNTRY'S GOOD** by Timberlake Wertinbaker with Jonathan Adams, Laurence Ballard, Linda Emond, Matthew Shawn Miller, Marianne Owen, Jeanne Paulsen, Larry Paulsen, Faye M. Price, Peter Silbert, Michael Winters and R. Hamilton Wright
**WILLI, AN EVENING OF WILDERNESS AND SPIRIT** written and performed by John Pielmeier
**HALCYON DAYS** by Steven Dietz with Laurence Ballard, Mark Chamberlin, Andrew DeRycke, Linda Emond, Peter Silbert, Stephanie Shine, Novel Sholars and Michael Winters
**A CHRISTMAS CAROL** by Charles Dickens, adapted by Gregory Falls with Mark Drusch, Brittany Duncan, Linda Emond, Tamu Gray, Eddie Levi Lee, Brian J. Martin, Lori McCracken, Rex McDowell, Robert Nadir, Ryan O'Connor, David Pichette, Peter Silbert, Harris D. Smith, Danny Swanson, Brian Thompson, Michael Seamus Tomkins, Claudine Isles Wallace and Grace Zandarski

*Chris Bennion Photos*

TOP: Linda Emond, David P. Whitehead in "Tears of Rage"
RIGHT: John Pielmeier in "Willi"

Warren Bowles, Stephanie Kallos in "My Children My Africa"

Peter Silbert, Stephanie Shine, Novel Sholars in "Halcyon Days"

# ACTORS THEATRE OF LOUISVILLE

Louisville, Kentucky
Twenty-eighth Season

Producing Director, Jon Jory; Executive Director, Alexander Speer; Associate Director, Marilee Hebert-Slater; Development, J. Christopher Wineman; Press, James Seacat; Sets, Paul Owen; Lighting, Karl E. Haas; Sound, Darron West; Props, Ron Riall; Production Manager, Frazier W. Marsh; Stage Manager, Debra Acquavella, Carey Upton; Technical Director, Steve Goodin.
RESIDENT COMPANY: Bob Burrus, Ray Fry, V. Craig Heidenreich, Fred Major, William McNulty, Adale O'Brien, Mark Sawyer-Dailey

## PRODUCTIONS & CASTS

**TALES FROM THE VIENNA WOODS** by Odon Von Horvath, adapted by Christopher Hampton; Director, Mladen Kiselov. CAST: V. Craig Heidenreich, Adale O'Brien, Georgine Hall, Mark Sawyer-Dailey, Mary Beth Peil, William McNulty, Liz Burmester, Fred Major, Ray Fry, Lisa McNulty, Claire Beckman, Bob Burrus, Mary Anne Rickert, Keith Grumet, Cheryl Jones, Elizabeth Daily, Tracy Effinger, Stacey Ivey, Christopher Franciosa, Kathryn Velvel.
**QUARTERMAINE'S TERMS** by Simon Gray; Director, Steven D. Albrezzi. CAST: William McNulty, June Ballinger, Fred Major, Ray Fry, V. Craig Heidenreich, Bob Burrus, Adale O'Brien.
**THE MYSTERY OF IRMA VEP** by Charles Ludlam; Director, Jon Jory. CAST: Peter Zapp, Bill Owikowski.
**A CHRISTMAS CAROL** by Jon Jory and Marcia Dixey; Director, Frazier W. Marsh. CAST: Vaughn McBride, William McNulty, Ann Hodapp, Raphael Nash, June Ballinger, Adale O'Brien, Bob Burrus, Mark Sawyer-Dailey, V. Craig Heidenreich, Fred Major, Jason Bumba, Ameer Rasool, Eleni Kotsonis, Deanna Wilkins, Don Spalding, John Bland, Susan Riley Stevens, Roxanne Chang, Kathryn Velvel, Joe Bashour, Daryl Swanson, Stacey Leigh Ivey, Steven C. Howard Jr., Justin McLeod, Shaun Powell, Todd Morgan.
**LETTICE AND LOVAGE** by Peter Shaffer; Director, Nagle Jackson. CAST: Peggy Cowles, Mark Sawyer-Dailey, Adale O'Brien, Ann Hodapp, Bob Burrus, Carmie Dailey, Johanna Fears, Steve Willis.
**PRELUDE TO A KISS** by Craig Lucas; Director, Bob Krakower. CAST: Gus Rogerson, V. Craig Heidenreich, Lauren Lane, Sonja Lanzener, Fred Major, William McNulty, Mara Swanson, Ray Fry, Percy Metcalf, Leslie Beatty, Alison Michel, S. Scott Shina, Daryl Swanson.
**THE HEIDI CHRONICLES** by Wendy Wasserstein; Director, Frazier W. Marsh. CAST: Colleen Gallagher, Tessie Hogan, Christopher Marobella, Brian Keeler, V. Craig Heidenreich, Veanne Cox, Kim Sykes, Diane Kinerk, Eric Ostrow.
**HYAENA** by Ross MacLean; Director, Mladen Kiselov. CAST: William McNulty, Michael Hartman, Sandra Sydney, Kathryn Layng, Mark Shannon, Christopher Franciosa, S. Scott Shina, Darly Swanson.
**BONDAGE** by David Henry Hwang; Director, Oskar Eustis. CAST: Kathryn Layng, B.D. Wong.
**DEVOTEES IN THE GARDEN OF LOVE** by Suzan-Lori Parks; Director, Oskar Eustis. CAST: Margarette Robinson, Esther Scott, Sandra Sydney.
**THE OLD LADY'S GUIDE TO SURVIVAL** by Mayo Simon; Director, Alan Mandell. CAST: Lynn Cohen, Shirl Bernheim.
**MARISOL** by Jose Rivera; Director, Marcus Stern. CAST: Karina Arroyave, V. Craig Heidenreich, Esther Scott, Susan Knight, Carlos Ramos.
**D. BOONE** by Marsha Norman; Director, Gloria Muzio. CAST: Gladden Schorck, Rod McLachlan, Catherine Christianson, Dave Florek, Chekotah Miskensack, Steve Willis, Mark Shannon, Skipp Sudduth, Kathryn Velvel, Eddie Levi Lee.
**THE CARVING OF MOUNT RUSHMORE,** written and directed by John Conklin. CAST: Eddie Levi Lee, Dave Florek, Skipp Sudduth, Catherine Christianson, Rod McLachlan, Scott Kasbaum.
**EVELYN AND THE POLKA KING** by John Olive; Music, Carl Finch, Bob Lucas; Lyrics, Bob Lucas; Director, Jeff Hooper. CAST: Tom Ligon, Seana Kofoed, Margo Skinner, Guy Klucevsek, Bob Lucas, Paul Culligan, Hunt Butler, Miles Davis.
**DRIVING MISS DAISY** by Alfred Uhry; Director, Ray Fry. CAST: Gloria Cromwell, Mark Sawyer-Dailey, Donnie L. Betts.
**ANTONY AND CLEOPATRA** by William Shakespeare; Director, Jon Jory. CAST: Clancy Brown, William McNulty, Bob Burrus, V. Craig Heidenreich, Mark Sawyer-Dailey, Christopher Franciosa, Mercedes Ruehl, Mary Beth Peil, Leslie Beatty, Mark Shannon, Eric Ostrow, Adale O'Brien, Joseph Fuqua, Fred Major, Vaughn McBride, Edward Hyland, Christopher Marobella, Ray Fry, Annette Helde.

*Richard Trigg Photos*

TOP: Mary Beth Piel, Mercedes Ruehl, Clancy Brown in "Antony and Cleopatra"
BELOW: Kathryn Layng, B.D. Wong in "Bondage"
THIRD PHOTO: Mark Shannon, Catherine Christianson in "D. Boone"
BOTTOM: Karina Arroyave, V. Craig Heidenreich in "Marisol"

# ALLENBURY PLAYHOUSE

Boiling Springs, Pennsylvania

Producer, John J. Heinze; Managing Director, Michael Rothhaar; Production Stage Manager/Lighting/Director, Richard J. Frost; Coordinator, Cate Van Wickler; Sets, Robert Klingelhoefer; Costumes, Rose Parent; Technical Director, Rob Murtoff; Advertising/Marketing, Deborah Giroux

## PRODUCTIONS & CASTS

**MY FAIR LADY** by Lerner & Loewe; Director, Michael Rothhaar CAST: Eddie Buffum, Holly Cruz, Tina Guice (Buskers), Michael McKenzie (Freddy), Debbie Lee Jones (Mrs. Eynsford-Hill), Bob Tron, Rexanne Wright, Lisa Lehr (Patrons), James Hayney (Doorman), Selena Nelson, Nina Noelle Genzel, Len Pfluger, James Jaeger, Patt Giblin, James Allen (Cockneys), Ellen Zachos (Eliza), Richert Easley (Pickering), Michael Haney (Higgins), J. Robert Garrity, Dan Sarnelli (Men), Bob Tron(George), James Jaeger (Harry), Len Pfluher (Jamie), Nick Cosco (Alfred Doolittle), Holly Cruz, Tina Guice (Cockneys), J. Robert Garrity (Drunk), Catherine Blaine (Mrs. Pearce), Debbie Lee Jones (Mrs. Hopkins), Mr. Hayney, Mr. Buffum, Ms. Jones, Mr. Jaeger, Ms. Nelson, Ms. Genzel, Ms. Wright (Servants), Amy Warner (Mrs. Higgins), Bob Tron (Charles), Mr. Buffum, Ms. Cruz (The Boxingtons), James Allen (Policeman), Mr. Sarnelli (Sir Reginald), Ms. Lehr (Lady Tarrington), Mr. Hayney (Ambassador), Ms. Jones (Queen of Transylvania)

**DAMN YANKEES** by Richard Adler, Jerry Ross and George Abbott; Director, Michael Rothhaar CAST: Richert Easley (Joe Boyd), Debbie Lee Jones (Meg Boyd), Len Pfluger, Eddie Buffum, James Jaeger, Patt Giblin, James Allen, J. Robert Garrity, Daniel Sarnelli (Fans), Holly Cruz, Tina Guice, Nina Noelle Genzel, Selena Nelson, Lisa Lehr, Rexanne Wright (Wives), Michael Nostrand (Applegate), Ms. Wright (Sister), Ms. Nelson (Doris), Michael McKenzie (Joe Hardy), Mr. Sarnelli (Henry), Mr. Giblin (Sohovik), Mr. Jaeger (Smokey), Mr. Buffum (Vernon), James Allen (McMillan), J. Robert Garrity (Franklin), Nick Cosco (Van Buren), Mr. Pfluger (Rocky), Ellen Zachos (Gloria), James Hayney (Lynch), Bob Tron (Welch), Rebecca Timms (Lola), Ms. Guice (Miss Weston)

**MAN OF LA MANCHA;** Music, Mitch Leigh; Lyrics, Joe Darion; Book, Dale Wasserman; Director, Michael Rothhaar CAST: Bob Tron (Capt.), Michael McKenzie (Cervantes/Quijana/Quixote), Michael Harrington (Gov./Innkeeper), Richard Adams (Duke/Carrasco/Knight of Mirrors), Michael Nostrand (Sancho), Selena Nelson (Maria), Len Pfluger, Eddie Buffum, James Jaeger, Daniel Sarnelli, Julian Garza, James Allen, J. Robert Garrity (Muleteers/Prisoners), Kate Kongisor Aldona/Dulcinea), Tina Guice (Fermina), Rebecca Timms (Antonia), Nick Cosco (Padre), Debbie Lee Jones (Housekeeper), Mr. Sarnelli (Barber), Nina Noelle Genzel (Moorish Dancer), James Hayney (Attendant)

**CAT ON A HOT TIN ROOF** by Tennessee Williams; Director, Michael Rothhaar CAST: James Jaeger (Lacy), Leah Burnette (Sookey), Amy Warner (Margaret), Paul Carlin (Brick), London Shover (Sonny), Will Rothhaar (Buster), Rachel Elizabeth Werner (Dixie), Debbie Lee Jones (Mae), Michael Harrington (Rev. Tooker), Jame Hayney (Baugh), Richard Adamson (Gooper), Nannette Rickert (Big Mama), Nick Cosco (Big Daddy), Rachel Felstein (Trixie), J. Robert Garrity (Small)

**LEND ME A TENOR** by Ken Ludwig; Director, Michael Rothhaar CAST: Rose Parent (Maggie), Richard Adamson (Max), Nick Cosco (Saunders), Catherine Blaine (Maria), Michael Harrington (Tito), James Jaeger (Bellhop), Amy Warner (Diana), Leanne Tron (Julia)

**SLEUTH** by Anthony Shaffer; Director, Richard J. Frost CAST: Michael Rothhaar (Andrew Wyke), Paul Carlin (Milo Tindle), Phillip Farrar (Doppler), Liam McNulty (Sgt. Tarrant), Bernard Jenkyns (Higgs)

**THE FOREIGNER** by Larry Shue; Director, Michael Rothhaar CAST: Bob Crawford (Froggy), James Michael Reilly (Charlie), Nanette Rickert (Betty), Paul Carlin (Rev. Lee), Rebecca Timms (Catherine), Steven Smyser (Owen), Ed Hammond (Ellard), Deighna De Riu, Bobo Rafkin (Townfolk)

**CHAPTER TWO** by Neil Simon; Director, Michael Rothhaar CAST: James Michael Reilly (George), Paul Carlin (Leo), Amy Warner (Jennie), Rebecca Tiims (Faye)

TOP: **Ellen Zachos, Michael Haney in "My Fair Lady"**
BELOW: **Ed Hammond, James Michael Reilly in "Foreigner"**

# ALLEY THEATRE

Houston, Texas
Forty-fourth Season

Artistic Director, Gregory Boyd; Executive Director, Stephen J. Albert; Assistant Director, Michael Wilson; Directors, Edward Albee, Christopher Baker, Anne Bogart, Gregory Boyd, Ron Link, Claude Purdy, Stuart Ross, Michael Wilson; Designers, Dwight Andrews, Howell Binkley, Anthony Bish, Ainslie Bruneau, Steffani Compton, Kevin Dunayer, Christina Gianelli, Lynda Kwallek, Donna M. Kress, Jay Michael Jagim, Susan Kijamichez, Derek McLane, Yael Pardess, Joe Pino, James D. Sandefur, Douglas Stein, Marty Vreeland, David Woolard; Christopher Baker, Literary Director/Director of Education; Francesca Madden, Marketing Director; Naomi Grabel, Communications Director; Rachel Edmonson, Public Relations Director.
**ACTORS:** Tyress Allen, Jonathon Allore, Akin Babatunde, Malinda Bailey, Jeffrey Bean, James Black, John Feltch, Bettye Fitzpatrick, Gerald Hiken, Annalee Jefferies, Constance Jones, Kimberly King, Shirley Knight, Tom Klunis, Andy Einhorn, Charles Krohyn, Robyn Lively, Jason London, Sharon Madden, Lisa McEwen, Lee Merrill, Alex Allen Morris, Robin Moreley, Jim Ponds, Charles Sanders, Peter Webster, Barney O'Hanlon, Robert Aberdeen, Tom Cayler, Adam Heller, Vernel Begneris, Gabby Turner, Sheryl Sutton, Arnie Burton, Willie Sparks, Diane Fratantoni, Patti Allison, Tina Sheperd, Alma Cuervo
**GUEST ARTISTS:** Edward Albee, Sidney Berger, Jose Quintero, Frank Wildhorn, Robert Wilson

**PRODUCTIONS THIS SEASON:** *Le Cirque, A Flea in Her Ear, Calliope Jam* (World Premiere), *A Christmas Carol, Marriage Play, The Kiddie Pool* (World Premiere), *The Baltimore Waltz, Forever Plaid, One Flew Over the Cuckoo's Nest*

*Jim Caldwell Photos*

# AMERICAN CONSERVATORY THEATRE

San Francisco, California
Twenty-sixth Season

Artistic Director, Edward Hastings; Managing Director, John Sullivan

## PRODUCTIONS & CASTS

**CAT ON A HOT TIN ROOF** by Tennessee Williams; Directed by Warner Shook. CAST: Andrea Marcovicci (Maggie), Daniel Reichert (Brick), Ken Ruta (Big Daddy), Joy Carlin (Big Mama), Lawrence Hecht (Gooper), Deborah Sussel (Mae), William Paterson (Doctor Baugh), Ed Hodson (Reverend Tooker), Nancy Carlin (Maggie - alternate).

**THE PIANO LESSON** by August Wilson; Directed by Lloyd Richards. CAST: Ed Bernard (Doaker), Isiah Whitlock, Jr. (Boy Willie), Michael Jayce (Lymon), L. Scott Caldwell (Bernice), Danyele Gossett (Maretha), Abdul Salaam El Razzac (Avery), Danny Robinson Clark (Wining Boy, Rosalyn Coleman (Grace).

**TAKING STEPS** by Alan Ayckbourn; Directed by Richard E.T. White. CAST: Ray Reinhardt (Roland Crabbe), Lorri Holt (Elizabeth Crabbe), Nancy Carlin (Kitty), Charles Lanyer (Mark), Howard Swain (Tristram Watson), Harold Surratt and Mark Silence (Leslie Bainbridge).

**A CHRISTMAS CAROL,** adapted by Laird Williamson and Dennis Powers; Directed by David Maier. CAST: William Paterson and Ken Ruta (Ebenezer Scrooge), Michael Scott Ryan (Ghost of Christmas Present/Charles Dickens), Richard Butterfield (Bob Cratchit), Judith Moreland (Mrs. Cratchit), Carl Quann (Tiny Tim), Rick Hamilton, Fredi Olster (The Fezziwigs), Josiah Polhemus (Young Scrooge), Laurie McDermott (Belle Cousins), Mark Silence (Fred), Adam Paul (Dick Wilkins), Kelvin Han Yee (Marley's Ghost), Frank Ottiwell (Ghost of Christmas Past), Adrian Roberts (Ghost of Christmas Future), Luis Oropeza (Old Joe), Susan Pilar (Mrs. Filcher), Alicia Sedwick (Mrs. Dilber).

**SOME ENCHANTED EVENING: THE SONGS OF RODGERS AND HAMMERSTEIN;** Direction Musical Staging by Paul Blake. CAST: Reveka Mavrovitis, Karen Morrow, Frances Epsen, Lara Teeter, Robert Yacko.

**CYRANO DE BERGERAC** by Edmond Rostand; Directed by Sabin Epstein. CAST: Peter Donat and Charles Layner (Cyrano), John DeMita (Christian), Michael Learned (Roxane), Michael Scott Ryan (Comte de Guiche), Kelvin Han Yee (Le Bret), Hector Correa (Rogueneau), Richard Butterfield (Vicomte de Valvert), Andrew Dolan (Marquis Chavigny), Eric Zivot (Marquis Cuigy), Bruce Williams (Montfleury), Adrian Roberts (Brissaille), Anne Lawder and Lynne Soffer (Duenna), Vilma Silva (Lise), Frank Ottiwell (Meddler/Capuchin Monk/Nobleman), Brian Lohmann (Ligniere/Reporter/First Poet), Ed Hodson (Jodelet/Musketeer), Adam Paul (Cut Purse/Second Poet/Page/Sentry), Alex Fernandez (Porter/Cadet), Alicia Sedwick (Sister Marthe/Orange Girl).

**CHARLEY'S AUNT** by Brandon Thomas; Directed by Edward Hastings. CAST: Drew Letchworth (Lord Fancourt Babberly), Josiah Polhemus (Jack Chesney), Mark Silence (Charles Wykeham), Laurie McDermott (Kitty Verdun), Susan Pilar (Amy Spettigue), Ray Reinhardt (Stephen Spettigue), Lawrence Hecht (Sir Francis Chesney), Luis Oropeza (Brassett), Kathryn Crosby (Donna Lucia d'Alvadorez), Julie Oda (Ela Delahay).

**THE COCKTAIL HOUR** by A.R. Gurney; Directed by Albert Takazauckas. CAST: William Paterson (Bradley), Anne Lawder (Ann), Mark Bramhall (John), Frances Lee McCain (Nina).

**GOOD** by C.P. Taylor; Directed by John C. Fletcher. CAST: William Hurt (John Halder), Philip Brotherton (Bok), Joy Carlin (Halder's Mother), Casey Daly (Crooner), Julia Fletcher (Helen Halder), Lawrence Hecht (Maurice), Stephen Paul Johnson (Hitler/Eichmann), David Maier (Freddie), Josiah Polhemus (Doctor), Vilma Silva (Elizabeth), Lynne Soffer (Nurse), Philip Stockton (Bouller/Hoss), Grace Zandarski (Anne), Mark Manske, Laurie McDermott, Julie Oda, Robert Parsons, Charlos Papierski, Shawn Michael Patrick, Adam Paul, Susan Pilar, Adrian Roberts, Alicia Sedwick, Mark Silence, Alison Kalison Strahan, Brenda Yungeberg.

*Ken Friedman, Larry Menkle Photos*

TOP: **Andrea Marcovicci, Daniel Reichert in**
**"Cat on a Hot Tin Roof"**
BELOW: **Michael Learned, Peter Donat in "Cyrano"**
THIRD PHOTO: **Laurie McDermott, Drew Letchworth, Susan Pilar in**
**"Charley's Aunt"**
BOTTOM: **William Hurt in "Good"**

**144**

# AMERICAN REPERTORY THEATRE

Cambridge, Massachusetts
Thirteenth Season

...stic Director, Robert Brustein; Managing Director, Robert J. Orchard; Associate ...stic Director, Ron Daniels; Press, Katalin Mitchell.

...SIDENT COMPANY: Candy Buckley, Lewis Black, Charles "Honi" Coles, ...oieta Czyzewska, Thomas Derrah, Alvin Epstein, Christine Estabrook, Jeremy ...dt, Joel Grey, Gustave Johnson, Cherry Jones, Mark Metcalf, Royal E. Miller, ...uel Perez, Anne Pitoniak, Martin Rayner, Stephanie Roth, Tisha Roth, Michael ...ko, Mark Rylance, John Seitz, Steven Skybell, Derek Smith, Sheryl Sutton, Bronia ...an Wheeler, Jon David Weigand.

...ODUCTIONS: *HAMLET* by William Shakespeare, Directed by Ron Daniels; ...SALLIANCE* by George Bernard Shaw, Directed by David Wheeler; *THE SEA ...LL* by Anton Chekhov, Directed by Ron Daniels; *HEDDA GABLER* by Henrik ...en, Directed by Adrian Hall; *THE SERVANT OF TWO MASTERS* by Carlo ...ldoni, Directed by Andrei Belgrader; *MEDIA AMOK* (World Premiere) by ...ristopher Durang, Directed by Les Waters; *OLEANNA* (World Premiere) written ...directed by David Mamet.

*Richard Feldman Photos*

Thomas Derrah, Mark Rylance, Michael Rudko in "Hamlet"

Candy Buckley, Steven Skybell in "Hedda Gabler"

Alvin Epstein, Anne Pitoniak in "Media Amok"

Christine Estabrook, Mark Metcalf in "Seagull"

Alvin Epstein, Stephanie Roth, Derek Smith, Jeremy Geidt in
"Misalliance"

145

# AMERICAN HEARTLAND THEATRE

Kansas City, Missouri

Executive Artistic Director, James Assod; Assistant Executive Director, Lilli Zarda; Assistant Artistic Director, Paul Hough.

**PRODUCTIONS:** Ain't Misbehavin', Lend Me a Tenor, Beehive, The Lion in

**RIGHT:** (top) Melissa Koonce, Kimberly Harris, Heidi Gutknecht, (center) Vikki Barret, (front) Becky Barta in "Beehive"

# ARENA STAGE

Washington, D.C.
Forty-first Season

Artistic Director, Douglas C. Wagner; Executive Director, Stephen Richard; Gene Manager, Guy Berguist; Founding Director, Zelda Fichandler; Resident Direct Tazewell Thompson; Associate Director/Dramaturg, Laurence Maslon; Costum Marjorie Slaiman; Designers, Loy Arcenas, Allen Lee Hughes, Tom Lynch, Na Schertler, Paul Tazewell; Production Manager, Martha Knight; Stage Managers, Renee Alexander, Maxine Krasowski Bertone, Jessica Evans, Tara M. Galvin, Wer Streeter, Robert Witherow.
**RESIDENT COMPANY:** Richard Bauer, Casey Biggs, Teagle F. Bougere, Ra Cosham, Terrence Currier, Franchelle Stewart Dorn, Gail Grate, M.E. Hart, Ta Hicken, Michael W. Howell, Jurian Hughes, David Marks, Pamela Nyberg, Saun Quarterman, Henry Strozier, Jeffrey V. Thompson, John Leonard Thompson, H Wines, Wendell Wright.

**PRODUCTIONS:** The Time of Your Life, Yerma, A Wonderful Life, Jar the Flo Trinidad Sisters (Premiere), The Father, The School for Wives, Mrs. Klein, The Visi

**A WONDERFUL LIFE** with Music by Joe Raposo; Lyrics/Book, Sheldon Harni based on film It's a Wonderful Life; Director, Douglas C. Wager; Choreography, Jo McKneely; Musical Direction/Arrangements, Jeffrey Saver; Orchestrations, Mich Starobin; Sets, Thomas Lynch; Costumes, Jess Goldstein; Lighting, Allen Hugh Stage Manager, Martha Knight   CAST: Casey Biggs (George), Scott Wise (Har Richard Bauer (Potter), James Hindman (Wainwright), Jeffrey V. Thomps (Clarence), Ralph Cosham (Joseph), Wendell Wright (Hepner/Morgan/Carte Terrence Currier (Martini/Tom), Tana Hicken (Mrs. Martini/Mrs. Hatch), Michael Howell (Ernie), Halo Wines (Molly), Henry Strozier (Uncle Billy), Harriet D. F (M.C./Teller), Deanna Wells (Violet), Brigid Brady (Mary), David Marks (Ma Pamela Nyberg (Lillian/Doroth), David Truskinoff (Stuart), Benjamin H. Sali (Walt), Kiki Moritsugu (Ruth), M.E. Hart (Minister), Michael L. Forrest (Accountan Tracy Flink (Harriet), Gabrielle Dunmyer, John MacInnis, Tyler John Chasez, J Eskovitz, Hannahlee Casler, Kari Ginsburg, Heather Casler, Embrey Min MUSICAL NUMBERS: George's Prayer, This Year Europe!, One of the Luc Ones/Can you Find Me a House, In a State, A Wonderful Life, If I Had a Wi Ruth/On to Pittsburgh, Good Night, Not What I Expected, Panic at the Building a Loan, Linguini, First Class All the Way, I Couldn't Be with Anyone But Y Welcome a Hero, Christmas Gifts, Precious Little, Unborn Sequence, Finale

A musical in two acts. The action takes place in Bedford Falls, NY from 192 1945 and Heaven.

*Joan Marcus Photos*

**TOP LEFT:** Pamela Nyberg, Casey Biggs in "Time of Your Life"
**BOTTOM:** Jeffrey V. Thompson, Casey Biggs in "A Wonderful Life"

# ARIZONA THEATRE COMPANY

Tucson, Arizona

stic Director, David Ira Goldstein; Managing Director, Robert Alpaugh; Artistic
ociate, Matthew Wiener; Production Manager, Kent Conrad; Company Manager,
en Bagnall; General Manager, James E. Cook; Press, Prindle Gorman-Oomens.
EST ARTISTS: Wendy Robie, Bruce Graham.

### PRODUCTIONS AND CASTS

E STOOPS TO CONQUER by Oliver Goldsmith; Director, Edward Payson Call;
s, Greg Lucas; Costumes, Peggy Kellner; Lighting, Don Darnutzer. CAST:
jamin Stewart (Mr. Hardcastle), Grace Keagy (Mrs. Hardcastle), Brenda Varda
e Hardcastle), Gerald Burgess (Tony Lumpkin), James Michael Connor (Young
low), Pascal Marcotte (George Hastings), Rebecca Marcotte (Constance Neville),
lie O'Carroll (Bouncer/Pimple), Rebecca Perrin (Audrey), Rick Long
alton/Servant), James Monitor (Sir Charles Marlow/Servant), Richard Trujillo, Bo
erts, Bill Parker (Servants)

N'T MISBEHAVIN' based on an original idea by Murray Horitz & Richard
tby, Jr.; Director/Musical Staging, Arthur Faria; Set/Lighting, Kent Dorsey;
tumes, Randy Barcelo. CAST: Eugene Barry-Hill, Evan Bell, Capathia Jenkins,
a Lema, Sharon Wilkins.

O'S AFRAID OF VIRGINIA WOOLF? by Edward Albee; Director, Austin
dleton; Set, Greg Lucas; Lighting, Tracy Odishaw; Costumes, Sigrid Insull.
ST: Rondi Reed (Martha), George Morfogen (George), Bryant Bradshaw (Nick),
ienne Thompson (Honey).

E HEIDI CHRONICLES by Wendy Wasserstein; Director, David Ira Goldstein;
s, Jeff Thomson; Lighting, Don Darnutzer; Costumes, Rose Pederson. CAST:
in Groves (Heidi Holland), Wendy Robie (Susan Johnston), Richard Hochberg
er Patrone), Mark Chamberlin (Scoop Rosenbaum), David V. Scully (Chris
er/Hippie/Mark/Steve/Attendant/Waiter/Ray), Carolyn Hennesy (Jill/Debbie/Lisa),
anne Bouchard (Fran/Molly/Betsy/April), Kimberly Davis (Becky/Clara/Denise).

NOR DEMONS by Bruce Graham; Director, Andrew Traister; Sets, Greg Lucas;
hting, Rick Paulsen; Costumes, Francis Kenny. CAST: Jack Wetherall (Deke
nters), Kathy Fitzgerald (Diane Kikorski), John Dennis Johnston (Vince DelGatto),
angelia Costa (Carmella DelGatto), Dean Thompson (Mr. O'Brien), Diane
bayashi (Mrs. Simmonds), Apollo Dukakis (Mr. Simmonds), Aron Eisenberg
nny Simmonds).

A MARKS by Gardner McKay; Director, Matthew Wiener; Music, Larry
inger; Sets, Greg Lucas; Lighting, Tracy Odishaw; Costumes, Kathy Kish. CAST:
th Scales (Colm Primose), Michele Marsh (Timothea Stiles).

*Tim Fuller Photos*

**TOP: "Ain't Misbehavin" cast
RIGHT: Bryant Bradshaw, Rondi Reed, George Morfogen in "Who's
Afraid of Virginia Wolf"**

# BARTER THEATRE

Abingdon, Virginia
Fifty-eighth Season

Artistic Director & Producer, Rex Partingon; Resident Directors: Ken Costigan,
Dorothy Marie Robinson; Youth Stage Director: John Hardy; Production Manager:
Tony Partingon; Assistant to the Production Manager: Majorie Terry; Stage
Managers: Tony Partingon, Majorie Terry, Myrle Curry; Scenic Designers: Kevin
Joseph Roach, Daniel Ettinger; Scene Shop Foreman/Master Carpenter: Gray Daniel;
Technical Consultant/Master Carpenter: Greg Owens; Master Carpenter: William D.
Gore; Master Electrician: William J. Sauerbrey III; Resident Costume Designer/Shop
Manager: Pamela Hale; Costumer: Kathryn K. Conrad; Assistant Costumer: Jennifer
Bengston; Wardrobe Mistresses: Claudia Hill, Stacey B. Riley; Properties Managers:
Barbara Carrier, David Montgomery; Director of Marketing and Promotions: Lori
Ward.

**PRODUCTIONS:** *Scapin, Greater Tuna, Arsenic and Old Lace, Oil City Symphony,
Steel Magnolias, Stage Struck, Driving Miss Daisy,* Spring Tour: *Greater Tuna,*
Harter Youth Stage: *Charlotte's Web, American Tall Tales.*

**LEFT: Scott Nagel, Nicholas Piper, John Fitzgibbon in
"Arsenic and Old Lace"** 147

# CALDWELL THEATRE COMPANY

Boca Raton, Florida

Artistic and Managing Director, Michael Hall; Director of Design, Frank Bennett; Company Manager, Patricia Burdett; Marketing Director, Kathy Walton; Press Representative/Photographer, Paul Perone; Accountant, Helen Mavromatis; Technical Director, Chip Latimer; Associate Technical Director and Master Electrician, Ken Melvin; Prop Master, George Sproul; Graphic Designer and Associate Scenic Designer, James Morgan; Lighting Designer, Mary Jo Dondlinger; Costumer, Bridget Bartlett; Scenic Artist, R.L. Markham; Asst. House Manager, Hank Allen; Asst. Company Manager, Nick Skoulaxenos; Administrative Asst., Noreen Petruff; Box Office Manager, Mike Cozzolino; Stage Managers, Bob Carter and Chip Latimer.
**GUEST ARTISTS:** Cliff Robertson, Beth Fowler

## PRODUCTIONS & CASTS

**THE MOUSETRAP** by Agatha Christie. Director, Michael Hall; Scenic Designer, Frank Bennett.   CAST:  John Felix, John Gardiner, Mark Irish, Elizabeth Moore, John G. Preston, Susan Russell, Thia Stephan, Kraig Swartz.
**LETTICE AND LOVAGE** by Peter Shaffer.  Director, Michael Hall; Scenic Designer, James Morgan. CAST: Margaret Hall, John Felix, Denise Du Maurier, Elizabeth Moore, John Gardiner, Vicki Boyle, Elizabeth A. Nemeth, Paul Everett, Justin Kane, Richard Marlow, Mikal Nilsen.
**NIGHT MUST FALL** by Emlyn Williams.  Director, Michael Hall; Scenic Designer, Frank Bennett. CAST: Peter Bradbury, Joy Johnson, Elizabeth A. Nemeth, Pat Nesbit, K. Lype O'Dell, Carmella Ross, Thia Stephan, Joe Warik.
**REEL MUSIC (Revue).**  Director, James Morgan; Musical Director, Kevin Wallace. CAST: Kim Cozort, Joe Gillie, Susan Russell, William Selby, Jean Tait
**FALSETTOLAND** by William Finn and James Lapine.  Director and Scenic Designer, James Morgan; Musical Staging, Tina Paul; Musical Director, Kevin Wallace.   CAST:  Jeffrey Blair Cornell, Kim Cozort, Sara-Page Hall, Michael Iannucci, Lenny Marine, Stuart Marland, Jean Tait
**THE TAFFETAS** by Rick Lewis.  Director, Michael Hall; Musical Staging, Tina Paul; Musical Director Kevin Wallace; Scenic Designer, James Morgan. CAST: Kim Cozort, Susan Hatfield, Elizabeth A. Nemeth, Jean Tait, Kevin Wallace
**OH COWARD!** devised by Roderick Cook.  Director, Michael Hall; Musical Staging, Tina Paul; Musical Director, Kevin Wallace.  CAST: Beth Fowler, Kip Niven, James Weatherstone
**REEL MUSIC 2 (Cabaret)**  Musical staging, Tina Paul; Musical Director, Kevin Wallace.  CAST: Kim Cozort, Michael Iannucci, Ted Keegan, Perry Ojeda, Jean Tait, Jody Walker

*Paul Perone Photos*

**Top: Carmella Ross, Peter Bradbury, Elizabeth A. Nemeth in "Night Must Fall"**
**Right: James Weatherstone, Beth Fowler, Kip Niven in "Oh Coward"**

# CAPITAL REPERTORY COMPANY

Albany, New York

Artistic Director, Bruce Bouchard; Director of Development, Deborah J. Lee; Busin[...] Manager, Deborah Brownell; Production Manager Julie A. Fife; Director [...] Marketing, Mark Rossier Equity; Stage Manager, Julie A. Hileman, Michele San[...] Technical Director, Marc Goursage; Artistic Associate, Mark Dalton.

## PRODUCTIONS & CASTS

**THE HOUSE OF BLUE LEAVES** by John Guare; Director, Michael J. Hume; [...] Donald Eastman; Costumes, Lynda L. Salsbury; Lighting, Kenneth Posner; Sou[...] David Wiggall.  CAST: William Carden, David Dodge, Susan Pellegrino, Kate Ke[...] Forbesy Russell, Elaine Grollman, Julia Walter, Alison Cowell, Mark Dalton, [...] Moseley, Darren Kelly.
**REMEMBRANCE** by Graham Reid; Director, Bruce Bouchard; Sets, Rick Den[...] Costumes, Martha Hally; Lighting, Brian MacDevitt.  CAST: Jack Aranson, Dar[...] Kelly, Anita Gillette, Kate Kelly, Tracy Swallows, Tara Hugo.
**PEACETIME** by Elaine Berman (World Premiere; in association with WPA Thea[...] NY); Director, Pamela Berlin; Set, Edward Gianfrancesco; Lighting, Craig Eva[...] Costumes, Mimi Maxman.  CAST: Ken Garito, Stephen Mailer, Kelly Wolf, Sar[...] Laub, Barry Snider, Gordon Greenberg, Jessica Queller, Suzanne Costallos.
**HOW I GOT THAT STORY** by Amlin Gray; Director, Mark Dalton; Set, T[...] Usher; Costumes, James Scott; Lighting, David Wiggall.  CAST:  Michael J. Hur[...] Phil Kaufman.
**THE SUM OF US** by David Stevens; Director, Jamie Brown; Set, James Noo[...] Costumes, Randall E. Klein; Lighting, Phil Monat.  CAST: Mitchell Riggs, Jan[...] Doerr, Jeffrey Plunkett, Marion McCorry.
**BROADWAY BOUND** by Neil Simon; Director, John Pynchon Holms; Set, Da[...] Gallo; Costumes, Lynda L. Salsbury; Lighting, David Wiggall.  CAST:  Max[...] Taylor-Morris, Michael Marcus, Rick Lawless, Todd Merrill, Leigh Dillon, [...] Robinson.

*Joseph Schuyler Photos*

**Left: Tracy Sallow, Anita Gillette in "Remembrance"**

# CENTER STAGE

Baltimore, Maryland

Artistic Director, Irene Lewis; Managing Director, Peter W. Culman; Associate Managing Director, Patricia Egan.

## PRODUCTIONS & CASTS

**THE QUEEN AND THE REBELS** by Ugo Betti; Director, Irene Lewis; Set, Christopher Barreca; Costumes, Catherine Zuber; Lighting, Stephen Strawbridge. CAST: Thomas Ikeda, Robertson Dean, Jan Triska, Gregory Wallace, Elizabeth Van Dyke, Caitlin Clarke, Dominic Chianese, Gordon Joseph Weiss, James Brown, Linda Powell, Liam Hughes, George Matthew, Elizabeth Vaughn.

**MY CHILDREN! MY AFRICA!** by Athol Fugard; Director, Lisa Peterson; Set, Derek McLane; Costumes, Catherine Zuber; Lighting, Peter Kaczorowski. CAST: Moses Gunn, Victor Mack, Kathleen McKenny.

**A DOLL HOUSE** by Henrik Ibsen; Director, Jackson Phippin; Set, Tony Straiges; Costumes, Catherine Zuber; Lighting, Stephen Strawbridge. CAST: Caitlin O'Connell, Richard Bekins, Keith Langsdale, Cara Duff-MacCormick, Stephen Marle, Trinity Thompson, Jake Martin, David J. Offenheimer, Sanford C. Keith, Adam Bennett, Laini Nemett, Katie Offenheiser.

**PERICLES PRINCE OF TYRE** by William Shakespeare; Director, Irene Lewis; Set, John M. Conklin; Costumes, Susan Hilferty; Lighting, Pat Collins. CAST: Robert Cornthwaite, Charles Shaw Robinson, Gina Torres, Kate Forbes, Robertson Dean, June Gable, Kenneth Gray, Thomas Ikeda, Carlos Juan Gonzalez, David J. Steinberg, Clayton LeBouef.

**POLICE BOYS** (World Premiere) by Marion Isaac McClinton; Director, Marion Isaac McClinton; Set, Donald Eastman; Costumes, Paul Tazewell; Lighting, James F. Ingalls. CAST: David Alan Anderson, Bobby Bermea, Ron Richardson, Faye M. Price, Jacinto Taras Riddick, Eric A. Payne, Liann Pattison, Terry E. Bellamy, Paul Emanuel Morgan.

**THE BALTIMORE WALTZ** by Paula Vogel; Director, Michael Greif; Set, Donald Eastman; Costumes, Paul Tazewell; Lighting, James F. Ingalls. CAST: Kristine Nielsen, Jonathan Fried, Robert Dorfman.

**THE MISANTHROPE** by Moliere; Director, Irene Lewis; Set, Kate Edmunds; Costumes, Catherine Zuber; Lighting, Pat Collins. CAST: Stephen Markle, Keith Langdale, Tony Amendola, Lynnda Ferguson, Oni Faida Lampley, Judith Marx, Michael Early, John Lathan, David J. Steinberg.

*Richard Anderson Photos*

**Caitlin Clarke in "The Queen and the Rebels"**

**Kristine Nielsen, Jonathan Fried, Robert Dorfman in "Baltimore Waltz"**
**Top Left: Bobby Bermea in "Police Boys"**

**Robertson Dean, David J. Steinberg, Gina Torres, Robert Cornthwaite, Kenneth Gray in "Pericles"**
**Center: Moses Gunn, Kathleen McKenny in "My Children My Africa"**

149

# CINCINNATI PLAYHOUSE IN THE PARK

Cincinnati, Ohio

Artistic Director (acting), Michael Murray; Managing Director, Kathleen Norris; Production Manager, Phil Rundle; Technical Director, Shawn Nolan; Business Manager, Gail Lawrence; Development Director, Cynthia Colebrook; Director of Marketing, Kimberly Cooper; Public Relations Director, Peter Robinson; Production Stage Manager, Tom Lawson; Stage Managers, Bruce E. Coyle, Candace LoFrumento; Sound Designer, David Smith; Literary Manager, Susan Banks.

## PRODUCTIONS & CAST

**THE MYSTERY OF IRMA VEP** by Charles Ludlam. Director, David Holdgrive; Stage Manager, Bruce E. Coyle; Set Designer, Jay Depenbrock; Costume Designer, Martha Hally; Lighting Designer, James Fulton. CAST: Simon Brooking (Nicodemus Underwood/Lady Enid Hillcrest/Alcazar), Russell Goldberg (Jane Twisden/Lord Edgar Hillcrest/Intruder).
**OUR TOWN** by Thornton Wilder. Director, Jay E. Raphael; Stage Manager, Tom Lawson; Set Designer, Joseph P. Tilford; Costumes, Elizabeth Covey; Lighting Designer, Kirk Bookman. CAST: T. Thomas Brown (Stage Player/Townsperson/Assistant Stage Manager), Robertson Carricart (Editor Webb), Clyde Cash (Sam Craig), Tim DeKay (George Gibbs), Mara DeMay (Townsperson/Audience Member), Kevin Donovan (Howie Newsome), Larry Golden (Simon Stimson), Michael Hartman (Dr. Gibbs), J. Thomas Hodges (Joe Crowell/Si Crowell), Mike Ingram (Wally Webb), Susan J. Jacks (Mrs. Soames), Dane Knell (Joe Stoddard), Raye Lankford (Emily Webb), Darrie Lawrence (Mrs. Manager), Pirie MacDonald (Stage Manager), Sioux Madden (Townsperson/Audience Member), Mark Mocahbee (Baseball Player/Townsperson/Audience Member), Herman Petras (Professor Willard), Carol Schultz (Mrs. Gibbs), Robert Stocker (Constable Warren), Christina Trefzger (Rebecca Gibbs), Maria Whitley (Townsperson/Dead Woman).
**SPEED-THE-PLOW** by David Mamet. Director, Jay E. Raphael; Stage Manager, Candace LoFrumento; Set Designer, G.W. Mercier; Costume Designer, Jan Finnell; Lighting Designer, Jackie Manassee. CAST: Mark Arnold (Charlie Fox), Sheridan Crist (Bobby Gould), Tracy Thorne (Karen).
**A CHRISTMAS CAROL** by Charles Dickens, adapted by Howard Dallin (World Premiere). Director, Howard Dallin; Stage Manager, Bruce E. Coyle; Set Designer, James Leonard Joy; Costume Designer, David Murin; Lighting Designer, Kirk Bookman. CAST: Bonnie Black (Patience/Scrubwoman/Mrs. Dilber), Michael Brian (Fred/Tailor), T. Thomas Brown (Peter Cratchit/Poulterer), Yusef Bulos (Ebenezer Scrooge), Darryl Croxton (Jacob Marley/Young Jacob/Old Joe), Andy Cullison (Matthew/Rich Boy/Urchin), Shelly Delaney (Ghost of Christmas Past/Martha Cratchit), Mara DeMay (Fan/Boy Baker/Rose), Tom Dunlop (Young and Mature Scrooge/Ghost of Christmas Yet to Come), Patrick Farrelly (Fezziwig/Ghost of Christmas Present), Rebecca Finnegan (Caroler/Laundress), Russell Goldberg (Topper/Accountant), Derek Hake (Boy Scrooge/Simon), Michael Haney (Bob Cratchit), James Harris (Mr. Cupp/Fezziwig's Lawyer), Katie Harris (Child at Fezziwig's), Matthew Harris (Tiny Tim), Rosie Harris (Little Girl), Sara Harris (Belle/Catherine Margaret), Steven Hendrickson (Mr. Sosser/Schoolmaster/Percy), Dale Hodges (Mrs. Peake/Mrs. Fezziwig), Daniel Hood (Gregory/Apprentice), Kyle Legg (Caroler/Constable), Maya Elaine Lilly (Girl at Fezziwig's), Betsy Lippitt (Fiddler), Sioux Madden (Maid), Michael Ogley (Charles/Boy Guest/Urchin), Gregory

Ebony Jo-Ann, LaChanze, Kim Brockington in "From the Mississippi Delta"

Procaccino (Undertaker's Assistant/Dick Wilkins), Hannah Reck (Belin[..] Cratchit/Girl at Fezziwig's), Ron Lee Savin (Undertaker), George B. Smart [..] (Caroler/Rich Father), Greta Storace (Rich Girl), Kathryn Gay Wilson (Mrs. Cratchi[..] Maria Whitley (Caroler/Rich Wife).
**JAPANGO** by Richard Epp (World Premiere). Director, Kent Stephens; Sta[..] Manager, Candace LoFrumento; Set Designer, Victor A. Becker; Costume Design[..] Susan E. Mickey; Lighting Designer, Kirk Bookman. CAST: Kent Broadhurst (Ki[..] Ferdinand), Josh Brockhaus (The Boy), Celeste Ciulla (Beatrice), Monique Fowl[..] (Queen Isabella), Curt Karibalis (Christopher Columbus), Russell Leib (Francis[..] Bobadilla/Knight Commander/Luis Santangel/Receiver General), Tim Perez (T[..] Indian), Herman Petras (Fra Juan Perez).
**FROM THE MISSISSIPPI DELTA** by Dr. Endesha Ida Mae Holland. Director, C[..] Scott; Stage Manager, Tom Lawson; Set and Costume Designer, G.W. Merce[..] Lighting Designer, Kirk Bookman. CAST: Kim Brockington (Woman Two), Ebon[..] Jo-Ann (Woman Three), LaChanze (Woman One).
**BILLY BISHOP GOES TO WAR** by John Gray in collaboration with Eric Peterso[..] Director, Howard Dallin; Stage Manager, Bruce E. Coyle; Set Designer, Lori Sulliva[..] Worthman; Costume Designer, Delmar L. Rinehart, Jr.; Lighting Designer, Ki[..] Bookman. CAST: David Anthony Brinkley(Billy Bishop/Upperclassman/Adjuta[..] Perrault/Officer/Sir Hugh Cecil/Lady St. Helier/Cedric/Doctor/ Instructor/Gener[..] John Higgins/Tommy/Lovely Helene/Albert Ball/Walter Bourne/Germa[..] Soldier/General Hugh Trenchard/Servant/King George V), Richard Oberack[..] (Narrator/Pianist).
**THE COCKTAIL HOUR** by A.R. Gurney. Director, Christopher Ashley; Stag[..] Manager, Candace LoFrumento; Set Designer, James Leonard Joy; Costume Design[..] Lisa Molyneux; Lighting Designer, Kirk Bookman. CAST: Frank Hankey (John[..] Katherine Leask (Nina), Dolores Sutton (Ann), William Swan (Bradley).
**ACCORDING TO COYOTE** by John Kaufman. Stage Manager, Christi-An[..] Sokolewicz; Set Designer, Don Yanik; Sound Designer, Michael Holten. Producti[..] of Berkeley Repertory Theatre. CAST: Victor Toman (Storyteller).
**PICKLE FAMILY CIRCUS** Conceived by Larry Pisoni. Director, Lu Yi and Lar[..] Pisoni; Stage Manager: Allis Antler; Set Designer, Barbara Mesney; Costum[..] Designer, Beaver Bauer; Lighting Designer, Kurk Landisman; Choreographer, Emil[..] Keeler; Music Director, Jeffrey Gaeto. CAST: Charlotte Backman, Jay Laverdur[..] Cindy Marvel, Montana Miller, Laura Pape, Jeff Raz, Diane Wasnak, Zhuo Yue.
**PERFECT FOR YOU, DOLL** By Steven Sater (World Premiere). Director, Be[..] Schachter; Stage Manager, Bruce E. Coyle; Set and Costume Designer, Craig Clippe[..] Lighting Designer, Victor En Yu Tan. CAST: Rita Gardner (Barone), David [..] Howard (Arnold), Jane LeGrand (Beth), Erica Mitchell (Betty), Ted Neusta[..] (Bradley), Constance Shulman (Candi), Nadja Stokes (Barbara), William Verderb[..] (Barry).
**HOT'N COLE** with Music and Lyrics by Cole Porter. Devised by David Holdgriv[..] Mark Waldrop, and George Kramer (World Premiere). Director and Choreographe[..] David Holdgrive; Musical Director, George Kramer; Set Designer, James Leonard Jo[..] Costume Designer, Mariann Verheyen; Lighting Designer, Kirk Bookman. CAS[..] Deb G. Girdler, Mark Martino, Pamela Myers, Amelia Prentice, Jonathan Smedle[..] Mark Waldrop. Accompanists: George Kramer, Scot Woolley.
**LADY DAY AT EMERSON'S BAR AND GRILL** by Lanie Robertson. Directo[..] Jonathan Wilson; Stage Manager, Candace LoFrumento; Set Designer, Joseph [..] Tilford; Lighting Designer, Kirk Bookman. CAST: Robert Galbreath, Jr. (Jimm[..] Powers), Ernestine Jackson (Billie Holiday).

*Sandy Underwood Photos*

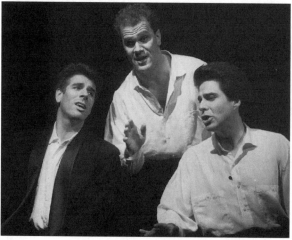
**150**   Mark Martino, Jonathan Smedley, Mark Waldrop in "Hot 'n Cole"

# CENTER THEATRE GROUP/AHMANSON THEATRE UCLA
## JAMES A. DOOLITTLE THEATRE

Los Angeles, California
Twenty-fifth Season

ducing Director, Gordon Davidson; Managing Director, Charles Dillingham; neral Manager, Douglas C. Baker; Press, Tony Sherwood, Joyce Friedmann, Julie ser; Staff Liaison to Mr. Davidson, Susan Obrow; Audience Development Director, bert Schlosser; Casting Director, Stanley Soble, C.S.A.; Development Director, ristine Fiedler; Technical Director, Robert Routolo; Central Services Director, Faith guel.

### PRODUCTIONS & CASTS

IE MOST HAPPY FELLA based on Sidney Howard's *They Knew What They nted,* Book, Music and Lyrics by Frank Loesser; Director, Gerald Gutierrez; oreography, Liza Gennaro; Musical Direction, Tim Stella; Scenery Design, John e Beatty; Costume Design, Jess Goldstein; Lighting Design, Craig Miller; Duo- no Arrangements, Robert Page, under the supervision of Frank Loesser; Sound sign, Jon Gottlieb; Associate Producer, Sue Frost; Casting, Warren Pincus; Artistic sociate, Jo Sullivan; Production Stage Manager, Michael Brunner; Stage Manager, chael McEowen; Conductor/Pianist, Tim Stella; Assistant Conductor/Pianist, David ans. Center Theatre Group/Ahmanson Theatre presents the Goodspeed Opera use production. Originally produced for the Goodspeed Opera House by Michael P. ce. CAST: Claudia Catania (Marie), Buddy Crutchfield (Ciccio), Tad Ingram octor/Cashier/Postman), Liz Larsen (Cleo), Mark Lotito (Pasquale), Spiro Malas ony Esposito), Mary Gordon Murray (Rosabella), Bill Nabel (Giuseppe), Charles stone (Joe), Scott Waara (Herman), John Aller, Anne Allgood, Robert Ashford, Bill dolato, Molly Brown, Kyle Craig, Mary Helen Fisher, Bob Freschi, Ramon lindo, Keri Lee, T. Doyle Leverett, Ken Nagy, Gail Pennington, Ed Romanoff, Jane ulyan, John Soroka, Laura Streets, Thomas Titone, Melanie Vaughan.

VO TRAINS RUNNING by August Wilson; Directed by Lloyd Richards; Scenic sign, Tony Fanning; Costume Design, Christi Karvonides; Lighting Design, Geoff orf; Casting, Meg Simon; Executive Producer, Benjamin Mordecai; General anager, Laurel Ann Wilson; Company Manager, Noel Gilmore; Production Stage anager, Karen L. Carpenter; Stage Manager, Fred Seagraves. Center Theatre oup/Ahmanson Theatre and Yale Repertory Theatre production. Presented in sociation with Huntington Theatre Company, Seattle Repertory Theatre and The Old obe Theatre. CAST: Roscoe Lee Browne (Holloway), Anthony Chisholm (Wolf), rry Fishburne (Sterling), Cynthia Martells (Risa), Chuck Patterson (West), Sullivan alker (Hambone), Al White (Memphis), Willie Carpenter, Sarah Davis, Lee mpton, Nick LaTour.

'S ONLY A PLAY by Terrence McNally; Directed by John Tillinger; Scenic esign, John Lee Beatty; Costume Design, Tom Rand; Lighting Design, Paulie nkins; Sound Design, Jon Gottlieb; Casting, Stanley Soble, C.S.A.; Production Stage anager, Mark Wright; Stage Manager, James T. McDermott; Fight Direction, Randy ovitz. Originally produced by the Manhattan Theatre Club. CAST: Paul Benedict a Drew); Eileen Brennan (Virginia Noyes); Zeljko Ivanek (Peter Austin), Dana Ivey ulia Budder); Sean O'Bryan (Gus); David Pierce (Frank Finger); Charles Nelson eilly (James Wicker); Doris Roberts (Emma), Valorie Armstrong, Richard Ballin, dy McCutcheon, Michael Spound.

OST IN YONKERS by Neil Simon; Directed by Gene Saks; Scenery and Costumes, nto Loquasto; Lighting, Tharon Musser; Sound, Tom Morse; Production Supervisor, m Barlett; Casting, Jay Binder; General Manager, Leonard Soloway; Company anager, Laura Green; Stage Manager, Terry Witter. Center Theatre oup/Ahmanson Theatre presents the American Express Gold Card and Emanuel zenberg production. CAST: Mercedes McCambridge (Grandma Kurnitz), Brooke dams (Bella), Ned Eisenberg (Louie), Alex Dezen (Arty); Jeff Maynard (Jay), Martin nakar (Eddie), Polly Adams (Gert), Taro Alexander, Ross F. Goldberg, Rhonda ayter, Murray Rubinstein, Isa Thomas.

*Jay Thompson Photos*

TOP: Željko Ivanek, David Pierce in "It's Only a Play"
CENTER: Larry Fishburne, Cynthia Martells in "Two Trains Running"
BOTTOM: Spiro Malas, Charles Pistone in "Most Happy Fella"

# CENTER THEATRE GROUP/MARK TAPER FORUM

Los Angeles, California
Twenty-fifth Season

Artistic Director/Producer, Gordon Davidson; Managing Directors, Stephen J. Albert, Charles Dillingham; Associate Artistic Director, Robert Egan; Resident Director, Oskar Eustis; Managers, Karen S. Wood, Michael Solomon; Staff Director for ITP, Peter C. Brosius; Staff Producer, Corey Beth Madden; Literary Manager, Frank Dwyer; Development Director, Christine Fiedler; Technical Director/CTG, Robert Routolo; Production Supervisor, Frank Bayer; Production Administrator, Jonathan Barlow Lee; Casting Director, Stanley Soble, CSA; Press, Nancy Hereford, Phyllis Moberly, Evelyn Kiyomi Emi, Ken Werther; Audience Development, Robert J. Schlosser.

## PRODUCTIONS & CASTS

**SPUNK; Three tales by Zora Neale Hurston,** Adapted by George C. Wolfe (West Coast Premiere): Director, George C. Wolfe; Choreography, Hope Clarke; Original Music, Chic Street Man; Sets, Loy Arcenas; Costumes, Toni-Leslie James; Lighting, Donald Holder; Mask and Puppets, Barbara Pollitt; Vocal Improvisations, Ann Duquesnay; Associate Producer, Corey Beth Madden; Production Stage Manager, Mary K. Klinger; Stage Manager, James T. McDermott; presented in association with the New York Shakespeare Festival, Joseph Papp, Producer; Associate Producer for NYSF, Jason Steven Cohen; CAST: Bruce Beatty (Man Two, Jelly, Voice Three, Clerk), Ann Duquesnay (Blues Speak Woman, Voice Two, Voice for Joe Clark, Joe's Mother), Kevin Jackson (Joe, Slang Talk Man, Man One), Chic Street Man (Guitar Man), Stanley Wayne Mathis (Man Two, Jelly, Voice Three, Clerk), Reggie Montgomery (Sykes, Sweek Back, Voice One), Danitra Vance (Delia, Girl Missie May).

**HENCEFORWARD** by Alan Ayckbourn (West Coast Premiere); Director, Tom Moore; Sets, Ralph Funicello; Costumes, Robert Blackman, Lighting, Peter Maradudin; Sound, Jon Gottlieb; Original Music, Larry Delinger with Craig Sibley; Video Design, Evan Mower, Jon Gottlieb; Casting, Stanley Soble, Lisa Zarowin; Production Stage Manager, Mary Michele Miner; Stage Manager, Tami Toon; CAST: Brandi Chrisman (Geain, age 9), Nike Doukas (Rita), John Glover (Jerome), Ellen Idelson (Geain, Age 13), Jane Krakowski (Zoe), Dakin Matthews (Mervyn), Alan Shearman (Lupus), Paula Wilcox (Corinna).

**THE KENTUCKY CYCLE** by Robert Schenkkan: Director, Warner Shook; Sets, Michael Olich; Costumes, Frances Kenny; Lighting, Peter Maradudin; Original Music/Sound Design, Jim Ragland; Dramaturg, Tom Bryant; Fight Director, Randy Kovitz; Casting, Stanley Soble, Lisa Zarowin; Production Stage Manager, Joan Toggenburger; Stage Manager, Cari Norton; produced in association with Intiman Theatre Company, Seattle, Washington; CAST: Lillian Garrett-Groag, Martha Hackett, Charles Hallahan, Katherine Hiler, Ronald Hippe, Gregory Itzin, Sheila Renee Johns, Roger Kern, Erik Kilpatrick, Matthew Kimbrough, Ronald William Lawrence, Scott MacDonald, Vince Melocchi, Tuck Milligan, Randy Oglesby, Jeanne Paulsen, Jim Ragland, Novel Sholars, Laurie Souza, Michael Winters.

**RICHARD II** by William Shakespeare: Director, Robert Egan; Sets, Yael Pardess; Costumes, Robert Blackman; Lighting, R. Stephen Hoyes; Music and Sound, Nathan Birnbaum; Text Editor and Collator, Diana Maddox, Fight Director, Randy Kovitz; Production Stage Manager, Mary Michele Miner; CAST: Carlos Carrasco (Northumberland), Michael Cerveris (Duke of Aumerle), Ryan Cutrona (Greene, Earl of Salisbury), Tom Fitzpatrick (1st Murderer, Bushy, Sir Stephen Scroope), Kelsey Grammer (Richard II), Melora Hardin (Queen), Barry Shabaka Henley (John of Gaunt, Sir Pierce of Exton), Robert Jason (Bolingbroke), Eugene Lee (Duke of Gloucester, Lord Ross, Groom of the Stable), Philip Moon (Lord Willoughby, Exton's Man), Natsuko Ohama (Duchess of Gloucester, Servant, Duchess of York), Albert Owens (Abbot), Luis Antonio Ramos (Henry Percy), Winston José Rocha-Castillo (2nd

Michael Cerveris, Ryan Cutrona, Kelsey Grammer, Tom Fitzpatrick, Norman Snow in "Richard II"

Tuck Milligan, Charles Hallahan, Ronald Hippe in "Kentucky Cycle"
CENTER: John Glover, Jane Krakowski in "Henceforward"
TOP: Danitra Vance, Kevin Jackson in "Spunk"

urderer, Lord Fitzwater), Jeanne Sakata (Servant, Gardener), Armin Shimerman ·uke of York), Norman Snow (Lapoole, Bagot, Welsh Captain, Keeper), John ckery (Mowbray, Bishop of Carlisle).

NFINISHED STORIES by Sybille Pearson (World Premiere): Director, Gordon vidson; Sets, Peter Wexler; Costumes, Csilla Marki; Lighting, Martin Aronstein; und, Jon Gottlieb; Production Stage Manager, Mary K. Klinger; Stage Manager, sbeth M. Collins; CAST: Christopher Collet (Daniel), Fionnula Flanagan (Gaby), l Linden (Yves), Joseph Wiseman (Walter).

RE IN THE RAIN ... SINGER IN THE STORM, Conceived and Developed by nothy Near and Holly Near, produced in association with the San Jose Repertory eatre: Director, Timothy Near; Musical Director/Arrangements, John Bucchino; Set, te Edmunds; Costumes, Marianna Elliott; Lighting, Peter Maradudin CAST: Holly ar

## TAPER, TOO

SNOWBALL'S CHANCE IN HELL, Written and Performed by John Fleck; Set l Lighting, Kevin Adams; Sound, Nathan Birnbaum.

## IMPROVISATIONAL THEATRE PROJECT

CCORDING TO COYOTE by John Kauffman; Director, Peter C. Brosius; oreography, Gary Mascaro; Set, Victoria Petrovich; Costumes, Csilla Marki; hting, Michael Gilliam; Sound and Music Composition, Trinidad Krystall, Marty ystall and John Fitzgerald; Producer, Josephine Ramirez; CAST: Katrina Alexy, olfe Boward, Peter Kors, Michele Mais.

## SUNDAYS AT THE ITCHEY FOOT

LUN CANAN - The Nine Guardians by Rosario Castellanos, Translated by ne Nicholson, Adapted by Josephine Ramirez: Directed by Jose Luis Valenzuela; hting, Jose Lopez; Musical Direction and Arrangements, Mark Sanchez: CAST: ique Castillo, Sal Lopez, Vanessa Marquez, William Marquez, Lupe Ontiveros; rk Sanchez, Percussion.

MES AGEE: A HEART'S EYE, Adapted for the stage with additional dialogue Emmett Jacobs and Tony Plana from the book "Let Us Now Praise Famous Men" James Agee and Walker Evans: Director, Tony Plana; Set, Edward E. Haynes Jr.; hting, Philip D. Widmer; CAST: John Bellucci.

TTING AWAY WITH MURDER, Two stories by James M. Cain - "Dead Man" "The Baby in the Icebox:" Adapted and Directed by Ellen Sandler; Set and hting, D. Martyn Bookwalter; Original Music and Sound Design, Mitchell enhill; CAST: Dwier Brown, Anne Heche, Paul Perri, Steve Rankin.

Holly Near in "Fire in the Rain"
Top: Christopher Collet, Joseph Wiseman in
"Unfinished Stories"

**153**

# THE COCONUT GROVE PLAYHOUSE

Miami, Florida

Producing Artistic Director, Arnold Mittelman; Associate Producer, Lynne Peyse
Production Manager, Jay Young; Technical Director, David L. Radunsky; Reside
Costume Designer/Costumier, Ellis Tillman; Property Master, Stephen M. Lamber
Master Electrician, Todd Wren; Head Audio Engineer, Steve Shapiro; Productic
Stage Manager, Rafael V. Blanco; Assistant Stage Managers, Karen E. Eichne
Heather Dale Mackenzie, Jancie C. Lane and Connie M. Silver; Director of Educatic
Judith Delgado; Director of Finance and Operations, Vicki Grayson; Developme
Director, Lisa A. Pearson; Director of Marketing and Sales, Mark D. Sylveste
Communications Manager, Savannah Whaley; Company Manager, Terri Scherme
Casting by Stuart Howard and Amy Schecter.

## PRODUCTIONS & CASTS

**BLUES IN THE NIGHT:** Conceived, Staged and Directed by Sheldon Epps; Set an
Lighting Design by Douglas D. Smith; Costume Design by Ellis Tillman; Sour
Design by Philip G. Allen; Musical Direction by Rahn Coleman; Assistant Direct
and Choreographer, Patricia Wilcox. CAST: Roz Ryan, Vivian Reed, Leilani Jon
and Alan Weeks.
**TALES OF TINSELTOWN:** Book and Lyrics and Michael Colby; Music by Pa
Katz; Directed and Choreographed by Tony Stevens; Set Design by James Tiltc
Costume Design by Lindsay W. Davis; Lighting Design by John Hasting; Sou
Design by Philip G. Allen; Orchestrations by Larry Moore, Larry Hochman and Dav
Krane; Musical Direction by David Krane; Produced in association with Sond
Gilman Productions, Inc. CAST: Keith Devaney, Peter Ermides, Melinda Gilb, Ell
Harvey, Marcia Lewis, Karyn Quackenbush, John Scherer and Michael Tucci.
**FOREVER PLAID:** Written, Directed and Choreographed by Stuart Ross; S
Design by Neil Peter Jampolis; Costume Design by Debra Stein; Lighting Design I
Jane Reisman; Sound Design by Philip G. Allen; Musical Direction, Continui
Arrangements and Musical Supervision by James Raitt. CAST: Paul Binotto, Greg
Jbara, Neil Nash and Michael Winther.
**I HATE HAMLET:** Written by Paul Rudnick; Directed by Robert Kalfin; Set Desi
by Tony Straiges; Costume Design by Ellis Tillman, Lighting Design and Scer
Consultation by James Tilton; Sound Design by Steve Shapiro; Fight Direction by
Allen Suddeth. CAST: Scott Hylands; Adinah Alexander, Peter Bradbury, Jul
DePaul, Howard Samuelsohn and Jane White.
**THE SUBSTANCE OF FIRE:** Written by Jon Robin Baitz; Directed by To
Giordano; Set and Lighting Design by James Tilton; Costume Design by Ellis Tillma
Sound Design by Steve Shapiro. CAST: Mark Margolis, Mark Gaylord, Micha
Mastrototaro, Nancy McDoniel, Crista Moore.
**TOO SHORT TO BE A ROCKETTE!** (World Premiere) Written by Buz Kohan a
Bruce Vilanch; Original Music by Larry Grossman; Original Lyrics by Buz Koha
Conceived and Directed by Gary Smith; Musical Staging & Choreography by Wal
Painter; Set Design by Roy Christopher; Lighting Design by Ken Billington; Costu
Design by Ret Turner; Sound Design by Philip G. Allen; Musical Direction by Vince
Falcone; Arrangements by Bill Byers; Don Costa, Vincent Falcone, Robert Farne
Peter Matz and Sam Nestico; Production Consultant, Tino Barzie; Produced
association with Smith-Hemion Productions, Inc. CAST: Pia Zadora, Curt Anthe
Julie A. Delgado, Bernard Dotson, Judette Warren and Kady Zadora.
**THE LADY FROM HAVANA/LA SENORA DE LA HABANA** (World Premie
of Spanish Language **LA SENORA DE LA HABANA**) Written by Luis Santei
Directed by Max Ferra; Set Design by Stephen Lambert; Costume Design by E
Tillman; Lighting Design by Todd Wren; Sound Design by Steve Shapiro. CAS
Xonia Benguria, Alina Troyano, Marta Velasco.
**FAMILY SECRETS:** Written by Sherry Glaser and Greg Howells; Directed by Ir
Pinn; Original Direction by Art Wolff; Set Design by Stephen Lambert; Lighti
Design by Todd Wren; Costumes Coordinated by Ellis Tillman; Sound Design
Steve Shapiro; Presented in association with Harriet Newman Leve. CAST: She
Glaser.
**AGAPE'** (World Premiere) In-School Touring Production: Written and Directed
Patricia Dolan Gross from an original concept by Judith Delgado and Patricia Do
Gross; Musical Direction and Original Music by Fred Desena, Original Lyrics
Patricia Dolan Gross; Set Design by Stephen Lambert; Costume Design by E
Tillman; Sound Design by Steve Shapiro; Stage Manager, Karen Delaney; Sou
Technician, John Beers. CAST: Isadore Geller, Kathy Kay Kurtz, Luis Marce
Janet Raskin and Reggie Wilson.

*Luis Castaneda and Jo Winstead Photos*

**TOP:** Vivian Reed, Alan Weeks, Roz Ryan, Leilani Jones in
"Blues in the Night"
**BELOW:** Peter Ermides, Keith Devany, John Scherer, Marcia Lewis
Ellen Harvey, Michael Tucci, Karyn Quackenbush, Melinda Gilb i
"Tales of Tinseltown"
**THIRD PHOTO:** (clockwise) Crista Moore, Mark Gaylord, Nancy
McDoniel, Michael Mastrototaro, (seated) Mark Margolis in
"Substance of Fire"
**BOTTOM:** Sherry Glaser in "Family Secrets"

# CROSSROADS THEATRE COMPANY

New Brunswick, New Jersey
Fourteenth Season

Producer/Artistic Director, Ricardo Kahn; Associate Producer, Kenneth Johnson; Director of Play Development, Sydne Mahone; Interim Managing Director, Paul R. Tertreault; Director of Development, Mercia Weyand; Marketing, Sheila Phillips-Murph; Business Manager, Louise Smythe; Director of Operations/Production, Gary Kechely; Company Manager, Cheri B. Kechely; Production Stage Manager, Patreshettarlini Adams.

## PRODUCTIONS & CASTS

**BILL COSBY - LIVE**
**BLACK ORPHEUS;** CAST: A'lain Adams, Julia Aponte, Akwesi Asante, Cameron Boyd, Coleman Butler, Helmar Augustus Cooper, Sandra Daley, Marshall R. Facotra, Jack Landron, Carol-Jean Lewis, James Lockhart, Larry Marshall, Siobhan McCarty, Jesse Moore, Kim Weston-Moran, Kimi Ann Stephenson, Theara Ward, Ming-Na Wen.
**OAK AND IVY;** CAST: Melissa Fontes, Michelle Hurd, Robert Jason, Peter McCabe, Lizan Mitchell, Joy Moss, Carla Maria Sorey, Scott Whitehurst.
**THE LOVE SPACE DEMANDS;** CAST: Demitri Corbin, Ezra Knight, William "Spaceman" Patterson, Jackie Mari Roberts, Ntozake Shange, Theara Ward.
**GENESIS 1992; A CELEBRATION OF NEW VOICES AT CROSSROADS**
**THE TALENTED TENTH;** CAST: Avery Brooks, Graham Brown, Mathew Idason, Phyllis Yvonnne Stickney, Pamala Tyson, David Wolos-Fonteno.

*Rich Pipeling Photos*

TOP: (front) Robert Jason, Melissa Fontes,
(rear) Peter McCabe, Lizann Mitchell, Michelle Hurd,
Carla-Maria Sorey, Scott Whitehurst in "Oak and Ivy"
CENTER: Kim Weston-Moran, Jesse Moore, Carol Jean-Lewis in
"Black Orpheus"
BOTTOM: (clockwise) Ezra Knight, Demitri Corbin, Jackie Mari
Roberts, William "Spaceman" Patterson, Ntozake Shange,
Theara J. Ward in "Love Space Demands"

**155**

# DELAWARE THEATRE COMPANY

Wilmington, Delaware
Thirteenth Season

Cleveland Morris, Artistic Director; David Edelman, Managing Director; Danny Peak, Assistant to the Artistic Director; Patricia Christian, Production Stage Manager; Eric Schaeffer, Resident Scene Designer/Production Manager; Marla Jurglanis, Costume Designer; Bruce K. Morriss, Resident Lighting Designer; James Darkey, Assistant to the Stage Manager; Paul Taylor and Tim Baumgartner, Props Master; Charles O'Lone, Master Carpenter; Laura Miller and Melissa R. Hagman, Lighting Assistants; Melody Holton and Wendy Parker Fariss, Costume Assistants; Jason Sean Hettel, Scenic Artist; Shoshana Bobkoff, Artistic Associate; Ann Schenck, Director of Development; Sheri M. Johnson, Development Associate; Donna-Marie King, Director of Marketing; Lori A. Cartwright, Box Office Manager; Marcia B. Spivack, Group Sales; Donna Pody, Business Manager; Charles J. Conway, Student Outreach Coordinator; Joan Beatson, Administrative Assistant; Sets, Eric Schaeffer, Rebecca G. Frederick, Karen TenEyck, William Werner; Lights, Bruce K. Morriss; Costumes, Marla Jurglanis.

## PRODUCTION AND CASTS

**AMADEUS** by Peter Shaffer; Directed by Cleveland Morris; Sound Designer, Joseph K. Dombrowski; Cast: Peter Bretz (Antonio Salieri), Jeffrey Guyton and Nick Santoro (The Venticelli), Christopher Roberts (Salieri's Valet), Mario Scalora (Salieri's Cook), Steve Cowie (Joseph II), Richard Henrich (Johann Kilian von Strack), Joe Palmieri (Count Orsini-Rosenberg), Joe Muzikar (Baron van Swieten), Fred Royal (Giuseppe Bonno), Susan Huey (Teresa Salieri), Shawn Dorazio (Katherina Cavalieri), Diana LaMar (Constanze Weber), Ron Palillo (Wolfgang Amadeus Mozart), Kip Veasey (Major Domo), Robert Eppes and David Houser (Valets)
**COTTON PATCH GOSPEL** by Tom Key and Russell Treyz with Music and Lyrics by Harry Chapin; Directed by Danny Peak; Musical Director, Steve Steiner; CAST: Irwin Appel (Matthew), Andy Taylor (Jack), Kelleigh McKenzie (Andi), Kevin Edward Fox (Jim), Lachlan Macleay (Tom)
**T BONE N. WEASEL** by Jon Klien; Directed by Cleveland Morris; Musical accompaniment arranged and performed by Tom Eppes; Cast: Kim Sullivan (T. Bone), Andrew Prosky (Weasel), Ralph Buckley (3rd Actor)
**NOEL COWARD ... AT THE CAFE DE PARIS, The Words and Music of Sir Noel Coward** devised by Will Stutts; Directed by Adelle S. Rubin; Stage Manager, Joseph Domin; Musical Director and Pianist, Kevin Arruda; Cast: Will Stutts.
**THE PRICE** by Arthur Miller; Directed by Alex Dmitriev; Cast: David Bailey (Victor Franz), Susanne Marley (Esther Franz), Sam Gray (Gregory Solomon), Richard M. Davidson (Walter Franz).

*Richard C. Carter Photos*

BELOW: Richard Davidson, David Bailey in "The Price"
TOP: Peter Bretz, Ron Palillo in "Amadeus"
BOTTOM RIGHT: Kim Sullivan, Ralph Buckley, Andrew Prosky in
"T Bone N Weasel"

156

# DENVER CENTER THEATRE COMPANY

Denver, Colorado
Twelfth Season

novan Marley, Artistic Director; Kevin K. Maifeld, Executive Director; Barbara E.
lers, Producing Director; Tony Church, Associate Artistic Director, Artist Training;
hard L. Hay, Associate Artistic Director, Design; Randal Myler, Associate Artistic
rector, Casting; Anthony Powell, Assistant to the Artistic Director; Tom
ntgyorgyi, Associate Artistic Director, New Play Development; Laird Williamson,
sociate Artistic Director; Alan Bailey, Israel Hicks, Nagle Jackson, Donovan
rley, Randal Myler, Anthony Powell, Laird Williamson, Evan Yionoulis;
signers, (Costumes, Sets, and Lights), Robert Blackman, Barbara Bush, Bill Curley,
n Darnutzer, Pavel M. Dobrusky, Michael Ganio, Richard L. Hay, Charles R.
cLeod, Vicki Smith, Patricia Ann Whitelock, Andrew V. Yelusich; Playwrights,
zabeth Egloff, Garrison Esst, Nagle Jackson, Mark D. Kaufman, Dennis Powers,
bert Sprayberry, Laird Williamson.

TING COMPANY: Michael Keith Allen, Jacqueline Antaramian, Leigh Armor,
rod Sidney Arnold, Jim Baker, Jodi Baker, Lisa Barnes, Mimi Bessette, Harvy
nks, Paul Borrillo, Kathleen Brady-Garvin, William Brenner, Yuri Brusilovsky,
rc Bryman, Alice Cadogan, Gabriella Canino, Cynthia Carle, Gabriella Cavallero,
y Church, Bobby Clark, Ryan MacMillian Cole, Mark Colson, Jeffrey Combs,
es Michael Connor, Tracey J. Copeland, Susan d'Autremont, Darren Davis, Kay
bleday, Pi Douglass, Robert Eustace, Hugh Sadler Foley, Suzanne Fountain,
cent Garcia, Frank Georgianna, Sam Gregory, Ann Guilbert, Mark Hardy, Douglas
msen, Amy Harris, Michael Hartman, Katrina Hays, Ron Headlee, Katherine
sley, Leslie Hendrix, Jamie Horton, Tessie Hogan, James Hummert, John Hutton,
son Iovin, Johanna Jackson, Leticia Jaramillo, Eric J. Johann, Patricia Jones,
hael Kevin, Brad Kindall, James J. Lawless, Kipp Lockwood, Gary Logan, Julian
ez-Morillas, Gail P. Luna, William P. Lutz-Recht, Dee Maaske, Randolph
ntooth, Mary Martello, Jeff McCarthy, Paul Mockovak, Kathy Morath, Iona
rris, Jamin Morrison, G. Leslie Muchmore, Jordan Muraglia, Thomas Nahrwold,
n Onickel, Deborah Persoff, Andrew Philpot, Madeleine Pollak, Anthony Powell,
liss Preston, James Puig, Wendy Radford, Guy Raymond, Jamey Roberts, Devin
te Robinson, Vincent C. Robinson, Alice Rorvik, Blair Ross, Drew Rowley, Mark
bald, Ruthay, John E. Sauer, Jr., Carlotta Scarmack, Louis Schaefer, Callie
riener, Rachel Seay, Ean Seeb, Luke Simmons, Lise Simms, Archie Smith, Henry
m, Danny Swartz, Rosie Waters, Lisa Weaver, William M. Whitehead, Don
liams, Fredye Jo Williams, Olivia Williams, Alex Wyatt, Paul Wyatt, Briana
ker.

ODUCTIONS: THE ROSE TATTOO by Tennessee Williams; OTHER PEOPLE'S
NEY by Jerry Sterner; HOME by Samm-Art Williams; A CHRISTMAS CAROL by
rles Dickens, adapted for the stage by Laird Williamson; JULIUS CAESAR, by
liam Shakespeare; TO KILL A MOCKINGBIRD, based on the novel by Harper Lee,
matized by Christopher Sergel; TARTUFFE, by Moliere; ARSENIC AND OLD
CE, by Joseph Kesselring; WOLF-MAN, by Elizabeth Egloff; THEY SHOOT
RSES, DON'T THEY? (World Premiere) based on the novel by Horace McCoy,
k and lyrics by Nagle Jackson, music by Robert Sprayberry; UNCERTAINTY
rld Premiere) by Garrison Esst; EVIL LITTLE THOUGHTS (World Premiere) by
k D. Kaufman.

*Nicholas DeSciose and Terry Shapiro Photos*

Jeff McCarthy in "They Shoot Horses..."

**Patricia Jones, James Michael Connor in "Evil Little Thoughts"**

# DETROIT REPERTORY THEATRE

Detroit, Michigan
Thirty-fourth Season

Artistic Director: Bruce E. Millan; Group Sales/Marketing Director: Dino A. Valdez;
Outreach Director: Dee Andrus; Literary Manager: Barbara Busby; Costume
Designer: B.J. Essen; Set Designers: Bruce E. Millan, Robert Katkowsky and
Marylynn Kacir; Scenic Artist: John Knox; Lighting Designer: Kenneth R. Hewitt, Jr.;
Sound Designer: Burr Huntington; Stage Managers: William Boswell, Dee Andrus

## PRODUCTION & CASTS

**DETROIT STORIES** by Kim Carney, Stephen Mack Jones and Janet Pound.
Director, Barbara Busby. CAST: J. Center, Sabrina Childers, James Griffin, Tim
Holton, Roosevelt Johnson, Keegan-Michael Key, Ronald B. Mitchell, Mack Palmer,
Madelyn Porter, Demetris Dennis Taylor, Dianne Sievers.
**MISS EVERS' BOYS** by David Feldshuh; Director, Yolanda Fleischer. CAST:
Wayne Preston Chambers, Thomas Fiscella, Harold Hogan Sr., Michael Jay, Rod
Johnson, Charlotte J. Nelson, David Ramsey.
**OTHER PEOPLE'S MONEY** by Jerry Sterner; Director, Bruce E. Millan. CAST:
Sandra Aldridge, Barbara Busby, Council Cargle, Andrew Dunn, Harry Wetzel.
**SCULLY AND ROYCE** by Jeffrey Haddow; Director, Dee Andrus. CAST: Rod
Johnson, Mack Palmer.

*Bruce E. Millan Photos*

ockwise) Harold Hogan, Rod Johnson, David Ramsey, Michael Jay,
Charlotte Nelson in "Miss Evers' Boys"

# GEORGE STREET PLAYHOUSE

New Brunswick, New Jersey

Gregory S. Hurst: Producing Artistic Director; Diane Claussen: Managing Director; Wendy Liscow: Associate Artistic Director; Heidi W. Giovine: Director of Press & PR; Rick Engler: Director of Marketing & Sales; Karen S. Price: Business Manager; Sylvia R. Wolf: Director of Development; Susan Kerner: Director of Outreach/Resident Director; Deborah Jasien: Director of Design and Production; Barbara Forbes: Resident Costume Designer; Donald Holder: Resident Lighting Director; Rick Sordelet: Resident Fight Director; Thomas L. Clewell: Resident Stage Manager; Mark A. Collino: Technical Director.

**THE ENGAGEMENT** by Richard Vetere (World Premiere); Director, Matthew Penn; Set Designer, Deborah Jasien; Costume Designer, Barbara Forbes; Lighting Designer, Paul Armstrong; Stage Manager, Thomas L. Clewell. CAST: Joel Anderson (Tom), Richmond Hoxie (Jeffrey), Michael Countryman (Pat), Joseph Siravo (Tony), Melinda Mullins (Susan)

**ANNA CHRISTIE** by Eugene O'Neill; Director, Kevin Dowling; Set Designer, Jane Musky; Costume Designer, Barbara Forbes; Lighting Designer, Donald Holder; Music Composition and Sound, Randy Courts; Stage Manager, Anne C. Popper. CAST: Edwin J. McDonough (Johnny-The-Priest), Ralph Waite (Chris Christopherson), Diane Tarleton (Marthy Owen), Monique Fowler (Anna Christopherson), Neil Maffin (Mat Burke), Mark A. Collino (Longshoreman), Jay Duckworth (Longshoreman).

**I OUGHT TO BE IN PICTURES** by Neil Simon; Director, Gregory S. Hurst; Set Designer, Deborah Jasien; Costume Designer, Sue Ellen Rohrer; Lighting Designer, Donald Holder; Stage Manager, Thomas L. Clewell. CAST: Dorrie Joiner (Libby), Suzzanne Douglas (Steffy), John P. Connolly (Herb).

**SEPARATION** by Tom Kempinski (American Premiere); Director, Susan Kerner; Set Designer, Deborah Jasien; Costume Designer, Barbara Forbes; Lighting Designer, Michael Giannitti; Stage Manager, Anne C. Popper. CAST: Richard Poe (Joe Green), Jordan Baker (Sarah Wise).

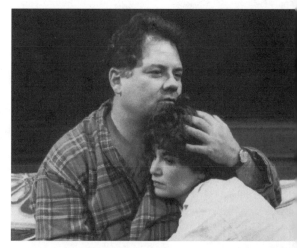

**SARAH AND ABRAHAM** by Marsha Norman (World Premiere); Director, Jack Hofsiss, Set Designer, David Jenkins; Costume Designers, Julie Weiss & Gary Lisz; Lighting Designer, Beverly Emmons; Music Composer, David Yazbek; Choreographer, Lynne Taylor-Corbett; Stage Manager, Thomas L. Clewell. CAST: William Katt (Abraham/Cliff), John Hickok (Tom), Steven Keats (Jack), Tovah Feldshuh (Sarah/Kitty), Christine Andreas (Hagar/Monica), Lee Chamberlin (Virginia), Carlo Alban (Issac), Bryan Gill, Ted Nolan (Stage Crew), Billy Duvall, Jr., Kristina Scalone.

**OTHER PEOPLE'S MONEY** by Jerry Sterner; Director, Wendy Liscow; Set Designer, Atkin Pace; Costume Designer, Barbara Forbes; Lighting Designer, Donald Holder; Stage Manager, Anne C. Popper. CAST: Terry Layman (William Coles), Gil Rogers (Andrew Jorgenson), Beth Fowler (Bea Sullivan), Tony Hoty (Lawrence Garfinkle), Valerie Leonard (Kate Sullivan).

**ZARA SPOOK AND OTHER LURES** by Joan Ackermann, Director, Pamela Berlin; Set Designer, Loren Sherman; Costume Designer, Barbara Forbes; Lighting Designer, Donald Holder; Stage Manager, Thomas L. Clewell. CAST: Matthew Bennett (Talmadge), Calista Flockhart (Evelyn), Shelley Rogers (Teale), Glynis Bell (Margery), Tom Tammi (Joe), Carolyn McCormick (Romona).

*Miguel Pagliere Photos*

**158**    **Ralph Waite, Monique Fowler in "Anna Christie"**

**Tovah Feldshuh, William Katt in "Sarah and Abraham"**
**CENTER: John P. Connolly, Dorrie Joiner in "I Ought to be in Picture**
**TOP: Calista Flockhart, Shelly Rogers in "Zara Spook..."**

# GOODMAN THEATRE

Chicago, Illinois

[Art]istic Director, Robert Falls; Producing Director, Roche Schulfer.

## PRODUCTIONS & CASTS

[BO]OK OF THE NIGHT (Premiere) by Louis Rosen and Thom Biship; Director, [Ro]bert Falls; Set, Michael Philippi; Costumes, Gabriel Berry; Lighting, James Ingalls; [Ch]oreographer, Marcia Milgram Dodge; Sound, Rob Milburn; Projections, John [Bo]esche; Stage Managers, Joseph Drummond, T. Paul Lynch. CAST: Hollis Resnik [Jill], David Studwell (Jill's Husband), Keith Byron-Kir (The Wishing Man), Vicki [Le]wis (The Wishing Woman), Jessica Molaskey (The Woman from Room 220), [B]rian Bailey (The Gypsy), Ora Jones (The Streetsinger/Juanita), John Herrera (The [Tram]p/The Desk Clerk), Paula Newsome (The Young Widow), Christian Dornseif (The [Wishing] Widow's Son), Jim Corti (The Dealer), David Bedelia (Carlos), Charlotte [Jav]ier (Jack's Wife).

[MI]SS EVERS' BOYS by David Feldshuh; Director, Kenny Leon; Set, Michael Olich; [Co]stumes, Susan E. Mickey; Lighting, Robert Peterson; Choreographer, Darlene [Bla]ckburn; Sound, Dwight Andrews; Stage Managers, Lois Griffing, Jill Larmett. [CA]ST: Celeste Williams (Eunice Evers), Donald Griffin (Hodman Bryan), Tab Baker [(W]illie Johnson), Danny Johnson (Caleb Humphries), Frederick Charles Canada (Ben [Wa]shington), Patrick Clear (Dr. John Douglas), Ernest Perry, Jr. (Dr. Eugene Brodus).

[A] CHRISTMAS CAROL by Charles Dickens; Adaptation by Tom Creamer; [Di]rector, Steve Scott; Set, Joseph Nieminski; Lighting, Robert Christen; Sound, Rob [Mil]burn; Choreographer, Beatrix Rashid; Music/Arrangement, Larry Schanker; Stage [Ma]nager/The Desk Clerk, Joseph Drummond, T. Paul Lynch. CAST: Tom Mula [(E]benezer Scrooge), Marilynn Bogetich (Mrs. Fezziwig/Charwoman), Henri Boyd [(W]ilmoena/Mrs. Dilber), Ray Chapman (Scrooge as a Young Man/Fred's Party [Gu]est), Patrick Clear (Bob Cratchit), Melissa Daye (Martha Cratchit), Adam Dylewski [(Ig]norance), Joan Elizabeth (Belle/Young Woman), Christopher Erwin (Tiny Tim), [Lau]rence Gallagher (Fred/Ghost of Christmas Yet to Come), Jeffrey Hutchinson [(Bu]sinessman), Mario Johnson (Peter Cratchit), Ora Jones (Mrs. Cratchit), Dennis [Ke]nnedy (Mr. Fezziwig/3rd Businessman), Bridgett Ane Lawrence (Fan/Belinda [Cr]atchit), Kingsley Leggs (Topper), Michael McAlister (Businessman), Johanna [Mc]Kay (Abby, Fred's Wife), Taryn Dai McKennie (Emily Cratchit/Want), Scott [Na]kita (Fiddler/Fred's Party Guest/Ghost of Christmas Yet to Come), Olumiji [Ol]awumi (Scrooge as a Boy/Turkey Boy), Ernest Perry, Jr. (Ghost of Christmas [Pr]esent), Darryl Alan Reed (Schoolmaster/Undertaker), Carmen Roman (Ghost of [Ch]ristmas Past/Fred's Party Guest), Robert Scogin (Marley's Ghost/Joe), James Sie [(Di]ck Wilkins/Young Man/Ghost of Christmas Yet to Come)

[T]WELFTH NIGHT by William Shakespeare; Director, Neil Bartlett; Set/Costumes, [Ri]chard Hudson; Lighting, Scott Zielinski; Sound, Rob Milburn; Stage Managers, Lois [Gr]iffing, Jill Larmett; Music, Nicholas Bloomfield. CAST: Josette DiCarlo (Orsino), [Jan]e E. Lew (Curio), Renee Albert (Valentine), Nikkieli Lewis (Viola), Paula Killen [(The] Captain), George Merritt (Feste), Lola Pashalinski (Sir Toby Belch), Jeannette [Sc]hwaba (Sir Andrew Aguecheek), Robin Baber (Maria), Shannon Cochran (Olivia), [Pe]ggy Roeder (Antonio), William Jones (Sebastian), Suzanne Petri (Malvolio), Lynn [Ba]ber (Fabian).

[O]N THE OPEN ROAD (Premiere) by Steve Tesich; Director, Robert Falls; Set, [Ge]orge Tsypin; Costumes, Gabriel Berry; Lighting, Michael Philippi; Sound, Rob [Mil]burn; Projections, John Boesche; Stage Managers, T. Paul Lynch, Joseph [Dr]ummond. CAST: Jordan Charney (Al), Steve Pickering (Angel), Denisha Powell [(The] Little Girl), Christopher Pieczynski (The Monk), Andy Taylor (Jesus).

[TH]E GOOD PERSON OF SETZUAN by Bertolt Brecht; English Translation by [She]ldon Patinkin; Director, Frank Galati; Set, Loy Arcenas; Costumes, Susan Hilferty; [Li]ghting, James F. Ingalls; Sound, Rob Milburn; Choreographer, Peter Amster; [Dra]maturg, Tom Creamer; Music, Claudia Schmidt; Stage Managers, Lois Griffing, [Jill] Larmett. CAST: Bruce Norris (Yang Sun), Claudia Schmidt (The Singer), Jim [Je]ue (Wang), William J. Norris (The First God), Mindy Bell (The Second God), Ajay [Na]idu (The Third God), Cherry Jones (Shen Teh), Kenny Ingram (Mrs. Shin), Larry [Ru]sso (Ma Fu), Ora Jones (His Wife), Charley Sherman (Her Nephew), Mark D. [Es]pinoza (An Unemployed Man), Christopher Donahue (Lin To), David Bonanno [(Y]ung), Doris DiFarnecio (His Wife), Olumiji Olawumi (Their Son/A Child), John [Mo]hrlein (The Grandfather), Teria Gartelos (Mrs. Ma Fu's Neice), Bellary Darden [(M]rs. Mitzu), Steve Pickering (Policeman), Aisha deHaas (Older Prostitute), Paul [K]ovall (Transvestite), John Reeger (Shu Fu), Linda Kimbrough (Mrs. Yang), Sarah [Un]derwood (A Saxophone Player), David Alan Novak (A Priest), Willy Schwarz [(Ac]cordianist), Miriam Sturm (Violinist), Anthony Diaz-Perez (Percussionist), Shana [Wi]nter (A Girl).

## STUDIO THEATRE PRODUCTIONS & CASTS

[D]OWN THE SHORE (Premiere) by Tom Donaghy; Director, David Petrarca; Set, [Li]nda Buchanan; Lighting, Robert Christen. CAST: Bruce MacVittie (MJ), Hynden [W]alch (Luke), Robert Mohler (Phippsey), Rick Snyder (Stan Man).

[H]OME AND AWAY written and performed by Kevin Kling; Director, Steven Dietz; [Li]ghting, Robert Christen.

[S]PUNK by Zora Neale Hurston; Adapted by George C. Wolfe; [Di]rector/Choreographer, Donald Douglass; Set, Amy Smith; Costumes, Birget [Rat]tenburg Wise; Lighting, Ken Bowen. CAST: Robert Barnett, Ellis Foster, Donald [Gri]ffin, Jonell Kennedy, Stevie Robinson, Shari A. Seals, Wanda Christine.

*Eric Y. Exit, Liz Lauren, Chris Bennion Photos*

**Paula Killen, Nikkiela Lewis, Renee Albert, Jane E. Lew in "Twelfth Night"**
**TOP: Cherry Jones, Bruce Norris in "Good Person of Setzuan"**

Sophie Hayden, Spiro Malas in "Most Happy Fella"

Carolle Carmello, Gregg Edelman, Jane Kean in "Arthur"

# GOODSPEED OPERA HOUSE

East Haddam, Connecticut
Twenty-ninth Season

Executive Director, Michael P. Price; Associate Producer, Sue Frost; Casting Director, Warren Pincus; Public Relations, Kay McGrath; Development Director, Heidi C. Freeman; Theatre Manager, Edward C. Blaschik, New York Press, Max Eisen/Madelon Rosen

## PRODUCTIONS & CASTS (1991)

**THE MOST HAPPY FELLA** with Music/Lyrics/Book by Frank Loesser; Director, Gerald Gutierrez; Musical Director, Tim Stella; Choreography, Liza Gennaro; Duo-Piano Arrangements, Robert Page; Sets, John Lee Beatty; Costumes, Jess Goldstein; Lighting, Craig Miller; CAST: Claudia Catania (Marie), Buddy Crutchfield (Ciccio), Sophie Hayden (Rosabella), Tad Ingram (Cashier/Postman/Doctor), Liz Larsen (Cleo), Mark Lotito (Pasquale), Spiro Malas (Tony), Bill Nabel (Giuseppe), Charles Pistone (Joe), Guy Stroman (Herman), Bill Badolato, Molly Brown, Kyle Craig, John Easterline, Mary Helen Fisher, Bob Freschi, Ramon Galindo, T. Doyle Leverett, Ken Nagy, Gail Pennington, Steven Petrillo, Roma Prindle, Ed Romanoff, Jane Smulyan, John Soroka, Laura Streets (Ensemble)

**ARTHUR: THE MUSICAL** with Music by Michael Skloff; Lyrics/Book, David Crane and Marta Kauffman; Based on screenplay by Steve Gordon; Director, Joseph Billone; Choreography, Tony Stevens; Musical Director, Tim Stella; Orchestrations, Bob Freedman; Sets, Linda Hacker; Costumes, Beba Shamash; Lighting, John Hasting; Stage Manager, Michael Brunner. CAST: Michael Allison (Hobson), Doug Andros (Ralph), Carolee Carmello (Linda), David Cryer (Johnson), Greg Edelman (Arthur Bach), Jane Kean (Martha), Jan Neuberger (Susan), Michael Shelle (Stanford), Deborah Carlson, Maureen Dodson, Leslie Feagan, Barry Finkel, Jack Hayes, K. Craig Innes, Anne Kulakowski, Jeanine Lamanna, Greta Martin, Sam Scalamoni (Ensemble) MUSICAL NUMBERS: A Child is Born, Hold That Thought, We'll Get Through This, Love in Bergdorf Goodman, Really Great Mood, Carried Away, Coney Island, Memory of Tonight, I Love a Romance, You Can't Have Everything, Magical Night, What I Never Knew, Champagne, Can I Live Without the Man, A Job I Highly Recommend, What Am I Doing Here, One More Day, We'll Get Through This, Try to Remember It All, Finale

**HERE'S LOVE** with Music/Lyrics/Book by Meredith Willson; Direction/Adaptation, Larry Carpenter; Choreography, Daniel Pelzig; Musical Director/Vocal Arrangements, Mark Mitchell; Conductor, Mark Mitchell; Sets, James Leonard Joy; Costumes, John Falabella; Lighting, Craig Miller; Stage Manager, Donna Cooper Hilton    CAST: Nesbitt Blaisdell (Drunken Santa/Judge), Erica Dutko (Susan), Denis Homes (Kris Kringle), Jerry Lanning (Macy), Jan Maxwell (Doris), Lowry Miller (Sawyer), Max Robinson (Shellhammer), Paul Schoeffler, David Ames, Peggy Bayer, Alan Gilbert, Bryan Harris, Marnee Hollis, Jennifer Kay Jones, Russ Jones, Guylaine Laperrière, Mark Manley, Jeanne-Marie Markwardt, Eric J. Paeper, Barbara Scanlon, Christopher Zelno, Robert Torres, Emily Rose Murphy (Hendricka), Adam Sanders (Tommy), Jason Williams (Harry) MUSICAL NUMBERS: Overture, It's Beginning to Look a Lot Like Christmas, Adeste Fideles March, Arm in Arm, Plastic Alligator, The Bugle, Here's Love, Pine Cones and Holly Berries, Look Little Girl, May the Good Lord Bless and Keep You, You Don't Know, Entracte, Expect Things to Happen/Ballet, My Wish, She Hadda Go back, That Man Over There, Fa La La, Marine March, Love Come Take Me Again, Finale

## NORMA TERRIS THEATRE

**WOODY GUTHRIE'S AMERICAN SONG** with Songs/Writings by Woody Guthrie; Direction/Conception/Adaptation, Peter Glazer; Musical Director, Malcolm Ruhl; Orchestration/Vocal Arrangements, Jeff Waxman; Choreography, Jennifer Martin; Sets, Philipp Jung; Costumes, Baker S. Smith; Lighting, David Noling; Stage Manager, Elizabeth Potter-Murray CAST: Brian Gunter, Ora Jones, Susan Moniz, John Reeger, Christopher Walz

*Diane Sobolewski, Mark Avery Photos*

Christopher Walz, John Reeger, Ora Jones in
"Woody Guthrie's American Song"
CENTER: Erica Dutko, Denis Holmes, Jan Maxwell in "Here's Love"

# GREAT LAKES THEATER FESTIVAL

Cleveland, Ohio

...istic Director, Gerald Freedman; Managing Director, Mary Bill; Associate Artistic
...rector, John Ezell; Associate Directors, Bill Rudman, Victoria Bussert; Assistant
...rector, Rob Ruggiero.

## PRODUCTIONS & CASTS

**...NCLE VANYA** by Anton Chekhov; Director, Gerald Freedman; Scenic Design,
...nn Ezell; Costume Design, Lawrence Casey; Lighting Design, Thomas Skelton;
...und Design, Stan Kozak; Stage Managers, Richard Costabile, Deidre Fudge.
...AST: Wendy Barrie-Wilson, Jacqueline Coslow, Robert Foxworth, Jim Hillgartner,
...l Holbrook, Annalee Jefferies, Betty Low, Kevin McCarty, Ron Miller, Neil
...pond
**...AUL ROBESON** by Phillip Hayes Dean; Directed by Harold Scott; Lighting by
...irley Prendergast; Special Arrangements and Orchestration by Eva C. Brooks;
...iginal Choreography by Dianne McIntyre; Company Manager, Paul Morer; Stage
...anagers: Doug Hosney, Richard Costabile; Musical Direction and Arrangements by
...nie Scott CAST: Avery Brooks, Ernie Scott
**...CHRISTMAS CAROL** by Charles Dickens; Original adaption and direction by
...erald Freedman; This production staged by Victoria Bussert; Scenic Design by John
...ell and Gene Emerson Friedman; Costume Design by James Scott; Lighting Design
...Mary Jo Dondlinger; Music adapted and arranged by Robert Waldman; Musical
...rector, Stuart Raleigh; Dance Staging by David Shimotakahara; Sound Design by
...m Mardikes and Stan Kozak; Stage Managers, Deidre Fudge, Richard Costabile
...AST: Elizabeth Boggio, Rick Boynton, J. Michael Brennan, John Buck, Jr., Phillip
...rroll, Amanda Chubb, Molly Daw, Donna English, Danny Flave-Novak, Michael
...awic, Tommy Krecic, William Leach, Lisa Leigh Lewis, Danielle Long, Kevin
...cCarty, Kenn McLaughlin, Robert Meksin, Adam Moeller, Colin Moeller, Maryann
...gel, Jim Ortlieb, Billy Radin, Candice Radin, Eric Radin, Gregory Violand
**...HIO STATE MURDERS** by Adrienne Kennedy (World Premiere); Directed by
...erald Freedman; Set Design conceived by Gerald Freedman and executed by John
...ell; Costumes Coordinated by Alfred Kohout; Projections by Kurt Sharp and Jesse
...ostein; Lighting Design by Cynthia Stillings; Sound Design by Stan Kozak; Stage
...anagers: Richard Costabile, Deidre Fudge CAST: Allan Byrne, Bellary Darden,
...by Dee, Michael Early, Irma P. Hall, Leslie Holland, Rick Williams
**...OTHER COURAGE** by Bertolt Brecht; Directed by Gerald Freedman; Scenic
...esign by Douglas Stein; Costume Design by Jeanne Button; Lighting design by Mary
...Dondlinger; Sound Design by Stan Kozak; Stage Managers, Richard Costabile,
...eidre Fudge CAST: Peter Aylward, John Buck, Jr., Joe Costa, Suzanne Costollos,
...D. Cover, Olympia Dukakis, Maurey Efrems, Ben Evett, William Duff Griffin,
...ichael Krawic, James Moore, Dan Putnam, David Ruckman, Darrell Starnik, Ray
...irta, Tina Walton-Virta, Ralph Williams, Christina Zorich

*Roger Mastroianni, Teresa Snider-Stein Photos*

**BELOW:** Ruby Dee in "Ohio State Murders"
**RIGHT:** Olympis Dukakis in "Mother Courage"
**BOTTOM RIGHT:** Hal Holbrook, Betty Low in "Uncle Vanya"

# GUTHRIE THEATER

Minneapolis, Minnesota

Artistic Director, Garland Wright; Executive Director, Edward A. Martenson; Producing Director, Madeline Puzo; Technical Director, Ray Forton; Costume Director, Maribeth Hite; Stage Managers: Jeffery A. Alspaugh, Tree O'Halloran; Education Coordinator, Sheila Livingston; Communications Director, Lendre Kearns.
**RESIDENT COMPANY:** Christopher Bayes, Bruce Bohne, John Bottoms, Jennifer Campbell, Bob Davis, Kristin Flanders, Nat Fuller, June Gibbons, Richard Grusin, Richard Iglewski, Charles Janasz, Shawn Judge, Jaqueline Kim, John Lewin, Sarah Long, John Lynch, Bill McGuire, Isabell Monk, Richard Ooms, Stephen Pelinski, Peter Thoemke, Brenda Wehle, James Williams, Sally Wingert, Stephen Yoakam

**SEASON PRODUCTIONS:** *IPHIGENIA AT AULIS* by Euripides; *AGAMEMNON and ELECTRA* by Aeschylus and Sophocles; *PRIVATE LIVES* by Noel Coward; *THE WINTER'S TALE* by William Shakespeare; *THE SEAGULL* by Anton Chekhov; *A CHRISTMAS CAROL* by Charles Dickens; *THE GOOD HOPE* by Herman Heijermans

*Michal Daniel Photos*

BELOW: "Marat/Sade" Company
RIGHT: Mel Winkler, Isabell Monk in "Death of a Salesman"
BOTTOM RIGHT: Nathaniel Fuller, Bruce Bohne in "Fantasio"

**Don Reilly, Lisa C. Arrindell in "All's Well That Ends Well"**

# HARTFORD STAGE COMPANY

Hartford, Connecticut
Twenty-ninth Season

[Ma]rk Lamos, Artistic Director; David Hawkanson, Managing Director; Greg Leaming, [As]sociate Artistic Director/Dramaturg; Howard Sherman, Public Relations Director; [Nan]cy Lindeman, Press Representative; Michael Ross, Business Manager; Candice [Ar]gotis, Production Manager; Jim Keller, Technical Director; Kathryn Foust, [Co]stume Shop Manager; Jerry Gardner, Properties Director; Bette Regan, Master [Ele]ctrician; Frank Pavlich, Audio Department Head; Casting, Ellen Novack, C.S.A.

## PRODUCTIONS & CASTS

**[M]ARCH OF THE FALSETTOS** Book, Lyrics and Music by William Finn; **[FA]LSETTOLAND** by William Finn & James Lapine; Music and Lyrics by William [Fin]n; Directed by Graciela Daniele; Orchestrations and Musical Supervision by [Mi]chael Starobin; Musical Direction, Henry Aronson; Set Design, Ed Wittstein; [Co]stume Design, Judy Dearing; Lighting Design, David F. Segal; Sound Design, [Da]vid Budries; Production Stage Manager, Barbara Reo; Stage Manager, Deborah [Va]ndergrift. CAST: Roger Bart (Whizzer), Joanne Baum (Cordelia), Ted Brunetti [M]arvin - alternate), Andrea Frierson (Dr. Charlotte), Adam Heller (Mendel), Etan [Cr]ane (Jason, Act II), Josh Ofrane (Jason, Act I), Evan Pappas (Marvin) and Barbara [Wa]lsh (Trina).

**Joanne Baum, Roger Bart, Andrea Frierson, Evan Pappas, Barbara Walsh, Adam Heller in "Falsettoland"**

**Heather Ehlers, Robert Foxworth, Burke Moses, Marlo Thomas in "...Virginia Wolf"**

**[AL]L'S WELL THAT ENDS WELL** by William Shakespeare; Directed by Mark [Lam]os; Set Design, Loy Arcenas; Costume Design, Catherine Zuber; Lighting Design, [Ch]ristopher Akerlind; Sound Design, David Budries; Dramaturg, Greg Leaming; [Pro]duction Stage Manager, Barbara Reo. CAST: Susan Appel (Helena), Lisa C. [Ar]rindell (Diana), Robin Chadwick (Parolles), Kevin Cristaldi, Trevor Davis, Steven [En]nis, Stephen DeRosa, Robert Dolan, Joshua Donoghue, Frank Geraci, Craig [He]rmes, John Hickok (2nd Lord Dumaine), Curt Hostetter (1st Lord Dumaine), Peggy [Joh]nson (Mariana), Delphi Lawrence (Widow), John McDonough (Clown), James [Mi]chael Nolan, Frank Raiter (Lafew), Kate Reid (Countess), Don Reilly (Bertram), [Joh]n Straub (King), Max Trace and Michael Wallace

**[W]HO'S AFRAID OF VIRGINIA WOOLF?** by Edward Albee; Directed by Paul [We]idner; Set Design, John Conklin; Costume Design, Jess Goldstein; Lighting Design, [Na]tasha Katz; Stage Manager, Deborah Vandergrift. CAST: Heather Ehlers (Honey), [Ro]bert Foxworth (George), Burke Moses (Nick) and Marlo Thomas (Martha).

**[HI]DDEN LAUGHTER** (American Premiere) by Simon Gray; Directed by Mark [Lam]os; Set Design, Christopher Barreca; Costume Design, Candice Donnelly; [Lig]hting Design, Stephen Strawbridge; Sound Design, David Budries; Dramaturg, [Gr]eg Leaming; Production Stage Manager, Barbara Reo. CAST: David Alford [(Nig]el Pertwee), Penny Balfour (Natalie Pertwee), Gloria Biegler (Naomi Hutchins), [Ju]dy Geeson (Louise Pertwee), Mark Hammer (Ben Pertwee), Jack Stehlin (Sam [Gr]aycott), Simon Templeman (Harry Pertwee) and James R. Winker (Ronnie [Ch]ambers).

**Mark Hammer, David Alford in "Hidden Laughter"**

**[HE]ARTBREAK HOUSE** by George Bernard Shaw; Directed by Michael Langham; [Se]t Design, Douglas Stein; Costume Design, Ann Hould-Ward; Lighting Design, Pat [Col]lins; Music, Stanley Silverman; Sound Design, David Budries; Dramaturg, Greg [Le]aming. CAST: Helen Carey (Hesione Hushabye), Randy Danson (Lady Ariadne [Ut]terword), Mary Diveny (Nurse Guinness), Lisa Dove (Ellie Dunn), Ron Faber (Billy [Du]nn), John Franklyn-Robbins (Captain Shotover), Jerry Lanning (Boss Mangan), [Al]an Dexter Lawson (An Indian Boy), Samuel Maupin (Randall Utterword), Larry [Pi]ne (Hector Hushabye) and Theodore Sorel (Mazzini Dunn).

**[RE]CKLESS** by Craig Lucas; Directed by Lisa Peterson; Set Design, Anita Stewart; [Co]stume Design, Melina Root; Lighting Design, Peter Kaczorowski; Sound Design, [Da]vid Budries; Production Stage Manager, Barbara Reo. CAST: David Bishins [(T]om), Patrick Garner (Tim Timko/Talk Show Host), Lisa Gay Hamilton (Pooty), [Su]san Knight (Rachel), Christopher McCann (Lloyd), Lola Pashalinski (Doctors One [th]rough Six) and Polly Pen (Trish Hammers).

*T. Charles Erickson Photos*

**Christopher McCann, Susan Knight, Lisa Gay Hamilton in "Reckless"**

**163**

# HUNTINGTON THEATRE COMPANY

Boston, Massachusetts
Tenth Season

Producing Director, Peter Altman; Managing Director, Michael Maso; Press, Robert Sweibel.

## PRODUCTIONS & CASTS

**THE SNOW BALL** (Premiere) by A. R. Gurney; Director, Jack O'Brien; Set, Douglas W. Schmidt; Choreographer, Graciela Daniele; Costumes, Steven Rubin; Lighting, David F. Segal; Sound, Jeff Ladman. CAST: George Deloy (Cooper Jones), Katherine McGrath (Liz), Deborah May (Lucy Dunbar), Christopher Wells (Jack Daley as a young man), Donald Wayne (Jack Daley as an older man), Susan J. Coon (Kitty Price as a young woman), Rita Gardner (Kitty Price as an older woman), Tom Lacy (Mr. Van Dam/Bladwin Hall), Robert Phalen (Saul Radner/Workman/Fritzi Klinger), Deborah Taylor (Joan Daley/Barbara Fiske/Rhoda Radner), Cynthia D. Hanson (Ginny Waters/TV interviewer), Terrence Caza (Billy Wickwire/TV Cameraman), Brian John Driscoll (Clavin Potter/Workman/Waiter), Pamela Blasetti (Heather Healy/Waitress), Gordon Clapp (Brewster Dunn/Mr. Smithers/Workman), Sandra Ellis-Troy (Mary Montesano/Others)

**TARTUFFE** by Moliere; English verse translation by Richard Wilbur; Director, Jacques Carter; Set, Hugh Landwehr; Costumes, John Falabella; Lighting, Roger Meeker. CAST: Louis Turenne (Orgon), Joan McMurtrey (Elmire), Etain O'Malley (Madame Pernelle), Linda Kates (Flipote), Tara Steinberg (Mariane), David Adkins (Damis), Munson Hicks (Cleante), Monti Sharp (Valere), Laurie Walters (Dorine), John Vickery (Tartuffe), Earle Edgerton (Monsieur Loyal), James Bodge (King's Officer), Steven F. Anderson, Liam Vincent (King's Soldiers/Servants).

**THE LITTLE FOXES** by Lillian Hellman; Director, Kyle Donnelly; Sets, Linda Buchanan; Costumes, Lindsay W. Davis; Lighting, Rita Pietraszek. CAST: Hazel J. Medina (Addie), Herbert Mark Parker (Cal), Laurie Kennedy (Birdie Hubbard), Jordan Charney (Oscar Hubbard), David Whalen (Leo Hubbard), Linda Gehringer (Regina Giddens), Munson Hicks (William Marshall), J. Kenneth Campbell (Benjamin Hubbard), Sue-Anne Morrow (Alexandra Giddens), Nicholas Hormann (Horace Giddens).

**CYMBELINE** by William Shakespeare; Director, Larry Carpenter; Set, John Falabella; Lighting, Marcia Madeira; Music, Scott Killian; Costumes, David Murin. CAST: John Innes (Cornelius), Richard J. McGoniagle (Lord/Brother of Posthumus), Sheila Allen (Queen), Bryant Weeks (Posthumus Leonatus), Lyn Wright (Imogen), Howard Witt (Cymbeline), Dan Mason (Pisanio), John Christopher Jones (Cloten), James Bodge (Lord), Roberta Willison (Helen/Mother of Posthumus), Jonathon Wood (Philario/Gaoler), Gary Sloan (Iachimo), Christopher Vasquez (Frenchman/Sicilius Leonatus), Raphael Nash (Caius Lucius), Jack Aranson (Belarius), Matthew Loney (Guiderius), Keith Hamilton Cobb (Arviragus), Kip Keith (Captain/Brother of Posthumus)

**THE WAY OF THE WORLD** by William Congreve; Director, Sharon Ott; Set, Kate Edmunds; Costumes, Erin Quigley; Lighting, Stephen Strawbridge; Music, Stephen LeGrand; Choreographer, Michael Oster. CAST: Francois Giroday (Mirabell), J. Michael Flynn (Fainall), James Bodge (Bentley), Robert Devaney (Mirabell's Servant/Lady Wishfort's Butler), Richard J. McGoniagle (Attendant), Hank Stratton (Witwoud), Wynn Harmon (Petulant), Monique Fowler (Mrs. Fainall), Mary Layne (Marwood), Ellen Karas (Millamant), Carol Hanpeter (Mincing), Dan Hiatt (Waitwell), Priscilla Shanks (Foible), Frances Cuka (Lady Wishfort), Kate Bennis (Peg), Charles Dean (Sir Willful Witwoud), Peter Connelly, Amy Shanik Langer (Ensemble)

**A CHRISTMAS CAROL** adapted from Charles Dickens by Larry Carpenter; Director, Larry Carpenter; Sets, James Leonard Joy; Costumes, Mariann Verheyen; Choreographer, Catherine Stornetta. CAST: Nicholas Pennell (Ebenezer Scrooge), Ron Holgate (Christmas Present), George Ede (Ghost of Marley), Roberta Maxwell (Mrs. Cratchit), Gary Rayppy (Bob Cratchit), Roxann Parker, Lisa Anne Barrett, Sara deLima, Paul Kirby, James Coelho, Katie Armour, Caroline de Lima, Andrew Goldstein, Matt Krouner, Amy Kumpel, Toby Moore, Peter Neudell, Katie Rourke, Eric Simundza, Joe Tremblay,

*Richard Feldman Photos*

TOP: Louis Turene, Joan McMurtrey, John Vickery in "Tartuffe"
BELOW: Jordan Charney, Hazel Medina, J. Kenneth Campbell, Linda
Gehringer, Munson Hicks in "Little Foxes"
THIRD PHOTO: "Cymbeline" cast
BOTTOM: J. Michael Flynn, Mary Layne in "Way of the World"

# ILLINOIS THEATRE CENTER

Park Forrest, Illinois
Sixteenth Season

...aging Director, Etel Billig; Directors, Steve S. Billig, Wayne Adams, Jonathan
...rk; Sets/Lighting, Archway Scenic, Wayne Adams, Jonathan Roark; Costumes Pat
...ker, Jewel-Ann, Elea Crowther

## PRODUCTIONS AND CASTS

...TER THE DANCING IN JERICHO by P.J. Barry  CAST: Cynthia Suarez, Bret
...einrich, Judy McLaughlin, Tom Cassidy, Shelley Crosby, Aaron H. Alpern
...NCES by August Wilson  CAST: Jim Jackson, Sam Sanders, Laura Collins,
...rles Glenn, J. Michael Jones, Gary De Witt Marshall, Alani Hicks-Batlett
...ernate Mescha Joy Grammer)
...NY by S.N. Behrman, Joshua Logan, Harold Rome  CAST: M. Nunzio Cancilla,
...id Six, Mary J. Adams, David Weiss-Lipschutz, Kamal J. Hans, Wayne Adams,
... McGrew, John B. Boss, Marijo Williamson, Shelley Crosby, Siobahn Sullivan,
..., Nykaza-Jones, David G. Peryam, Dean Scalzitti
...E CEMETERY CLUB by Ivan Menchell  CAST: Rebecca Borter, Etel Billig,
...la D'Angelo, Howard Hahn, Karen Lazarus
...E RABBIT FOOT by Leslie Lee  CAST: Bernadette L. Clarke, Laura Collins, J.
...hael Jones, Gary De Witt Marshall, Paulette McDaniels, Nathaniel Sanders
... NOT RAPPAPORT by Herb Gardner  CAST: Steve S. Billig, Sam Sanders,
... Cassidy, Diane Smith, David Ames, Judy McLaughlin, Sam Nykaza-Jones
...ENNY SERENADE by S. Billig  CAST: Karen Wheeler, David Six, Etel Billig,
... McGrew, Shelley Crosby, Miles Phillips, Sara Louise Dritz, Katie Kelly

**Bernadette Clarke, Nathaniel Sanders, Laura Collins, J. Michael Jones
in "Rabbit Foot"** (*Glenn Davidson*)

# INDIANA REPERTORY THEATRE

Indianapolis, Indiana
October 15, 1991 - May 17, 1992

Associate Artistic Director, Janet Allen; Managing Director, Victoria Nolan; Associate
Artist, Nicholas Hormann; Artistic Administrator, Jane Robison; Development
Director, Martha J. Bracher; Special Events, Juli A. Strattman; Production Stage
Manager, Joel Grynheim; Marketing Director, Michael O'Rand

## PRODUCTIONS & CASTS

**MAJOR BARBARA;** Director, John David Lutz; with Jennifer Sternberg (Lady
Undershaft), Andrew Barr (Stephen), Alexandra Reichler (Sarah), Cynthia Huse
(Barbara Undershaft), Philip Lehl (Adolphus), Bob Kirsh (Lomax), David Moffat
(Morrison), Howard Witt (Andrew), Jeanette Landis (Rummy), Michael McCauley
(Snobby Price), Kristin Lennox (Jenny), Michael Lipton (Peter), Richard Wharton
(Walker), Priscilla Lindsay (Mrs. Baines), Rockland Mers (Bilton), Ellery A. Bardos,
Marlene M. Dickinson (Maids/Streetpeople), Sets, Craig Clipper; Costumes, Catherine
F. Norgren; Lighting, Stuart Duke
**CHARLEY'S AUNT;** Director, Gavin Cameron-Webb; Sets, G.W. Mercier;
Costumes, Gail Brassard; Lighting, Rachel Budin  CAST: Martin Kildare (Jack),
Brad Bellamy (Brassett), Brian Howe (Wykeham), Marcus Olson (Babberley), Brenda
Foley (Kitty), Orlagh Cassidy (Amy), Evan Thompson (Chesney), Kensyn Crouch
(Spettigue), Julia Gibson (Ela), Donna Wandrey (Donna Lucia)
**THE ROAD TO MECCA;** Director, Amy Saltz; Sets/Costumes, G.W. Mercier;
Lighting, Robert Wierzel  CAST: Lenka Peterson (Miss Helen), Julie Boyd (Elsa),
John Leighton (Marius)
**SPUNK;** by George C. Wolfe; Director, Tom Jones; Sets, Russell Metheny;
Costumes, Goldie Dicks; Lighting, Michael Lincoln  CAST: Bo Diddley, Jr. (Guitar
Man), Bernardine Mitchell (Blues Speak Woman), Brian Chandler, Donald Griffin,
Monica Parks, Eric Ware (Folks)
**THE COCKTAIL HOUR** by A.R. Gurney; Director, Nicholas Hormann;
Sets/Costumes, Ann Sheffield; Lighting, Donald Holder
**TWELFTH NIGHT or WHAT YOU WILL** by Shakespeare; Director, Travis
Preston; Sets, Christopher Barreca; Costumes, Ann Sheffield; Lighting, Stephen
Strawbridge  CAST: Bob Field (Sax), Neil Larson (Orsino), David Barnes (Curio),
Brad Griffith (Valentine), Margaret Diaz-Padilla (Viola/Cesario), Clayton Nemrow
(Capt./Antonio), Marcell Rosenblatt (Maria), William Foeller (Toby), Tom Beckett
(Aguecheek), Donald Berman (Feste), Bob Kirsh (Malvolio), Rafeal Clements
(Fabian), Elina Löwensohn (Olivia), Reese Madigan (Sebastian), Jonathan Watkins
(Priest), Todd Brenneman, David Dreyfoos, Andy Mills, Michael Mills, Toni Smith,
Tom Stambaugh, Jonathan Watkins
**THE GIFTS OF THE MAGI** by Mark St. Germain; Director, Laurel E. Goetzinger;
Choreography, Michelle Jarvis; Musical Director, Terry Woods  CAST: Rick Walters
(Willy), Luther Creek (Jim), Emily Leatha Everson (Della), David Alan Anderson
(City Him), Kimberly Wurster (City Her), Andy White (Soapy)
**HUCK FINN'S STORY** by Aurand Harris; Director, Michael Lipton; Sets, Chib
Gratz; Lighting, Betsy Cooprider-Bernstein; Costumes, Deborah L. Shippee  CAST:
Luther Creek (Huck), Lynne Perkins (Widow/Miss Watson/River Woman/Aunt Sally),
Langstan Martin Smith (Jim), Rick Walters (Pap/Duke), Andy White (Slave
Hunter/King)
**THE SECRET HISTORY OF THE FUTURE** by James Still; Director, Janet Allen
CAST: Luther Creek (Diego/Student), Emily Leatha Everson (Lindsay/Mona Lisa),
Tif Luckenbill (Jason/Prince Juan), Lynne Perkins (Shelly), Langstan Martin Smith
(William), Rick Walters (Stevens/Da Vinci), Andy White (Buzz)

*Tod Martens Photos*

**Brian Chandler, Monica Parks, Don Griffin in "Spunk"**
TOP LEFT: Lenka Peterson in "Road to Mecca"

Nat Chandler, Beau Allen and men in "Carousel"
TOP RIGHT: Lannyl Stephens, Christopher Durham, Ben Hammer in
"Prelude to a Kiss"

# JUPITER THEATRE

Jupiter, Florida

Executive Producer, Richard C. Akins; Artistic Director, Avery Schreiber; Assoicate Producers, Brian M. Cronin, Norb Joerder; General Manager, Paulette Winn; Creative Director, Janina Akins; Public Relations Director, Pamela Smith

## PRODUCTIONS & CASTS

**AIN'T MISBEHAVIN'** by Fats Waller and others; Director, Norb Joerder  CAST: Ken Ard, Doug Eskew, Cleo King, Reva Rice, Cynthia Thomas
**OKLAHOMA** by Rodgers and Hammerstein; Director, Norb Joerder  CAST: Grant Norman, Gay Willis, Kevin Bernard, Lisa Merrill McCord, Michael Mulheren, Les Marsden, Harvey Philips, Elizabeth Dimon, Mary Jane Waddell, Lenny Daniel, Eileen Kaden
**A CHORUS LINE** by Marvin Hamlisch, Ed Kleban, James Kirkwood and Nicolas Dante  CAST: Michael Licata, Kerry Casserly, Robert Montano, Susan Santoro, Ernest Toussant, Others
**PRELUDE TO A KISS** by Craig Lucas; Director, Avery Schreiber  CAST: Christopher Durham (Peter), Lannyl Stephens (Rita), Ben Hammer (Old Man), Edward Dante (Dr. Boyle), Lourelene Snedeker (Mrs. Boyle), Andre Montgomery, Jimmy Ashmore, Brendan Broms, Theresa Cantone, Cynthia Collins, Marti Holmes, Beverly D. MacKeen, Cory P. Marin, Dana Schwartz, Ali Sharaf, Mark Jude Tarnacki, Suzie Vignon
**PUMP BOYS AND DINETTES;** Conceived/Written by John Foley, Mark Hardwick, Debra Monk, Cass Morgan, John Schimmel and Jim Wann; Director/Choreography, Norb Joerder  CAST: Bertilla Baker, Teri Furr, Kevin Hayes, Tim Howard, Raymond Leoni, James J. Stein, Jr.
**SHOW BOAT** by Jerome Kern and Oscar Hammerstein II; Director/Choreography, Norb Joerder; Lighting, Joanne D. Tooher; Sets, Stephen Placido, Jr.; Costumes, A. Jackson Pinkey; Stage Manager, Warren S. Geyer  CAST: Walter Willison (Gaylord Ravenal), Elizabeth Walsh (Magnolia), Alexander Barton (Joe), Avery Schreiber (Cap'n Andy), Beth McVey (Julie), Cleo King (Queenie), Lourelene Snedeker (Parthy), Gwen Arment (Ellie), Richard Smith (Steve), Wayne Steadman (Vallon), Harvey Phillips (Windy), Kenneth McMullen (Pete), Norb Joerder (Frank), Obie Story, Steve Asciolla, Kelli Lang, Quanda Dawnyell Johnson, Paul Everett, Andrea E. Rivette, Shelly Cohen, Jerry Zeigler
**DRIVING MISS DAISY** by Alfred Uhry; Director, Avery Schreiber  CAST: Ronnie Claire Edwards (Daisy), Ted Lange (Hoke), Michael Mulheren (Boolie)
**LEND ME A TENOR** by Ken Ludwig; Director, Avery Schreiber  CAST: Craig Wells, Ellen Zachos, Rose Alaio, Edwin C. Owens, Lourelene Snedeker, Jay Stuart, Marlene Elizabeth Vieira, Kitty Reidy
**CAROUSEL** by Rodgers and Hammerstein; Director, Andrew Gland-Linden  CAST: Nat Chandler (Billy), Michele Ragusa (Julie), Beau Allen (Jigger), Michele Pigliavento (Carrie), Richard Smith (Enoch), Mary Lou Reiner (Nettie), Connie Day (Mrs. Mullin), Harvey Phillips (Starkeeper/Sheldon), Jilanne Marie Klaus, Wayne Steadman, Eddie Buffum, Jonathan Ridgely Lewis

*Greg Allikas Photos*

Elizabeth Walsh, Walter Willison in "Show Boat"

# LONG WHARF THEATRE

New Haven, Connecticut
Twenty-seventh Season

stic Director, Arvin Brown; Executive Director, M. Edgar Rosenblum; Literary
sultant, John Tillinger; Artistic Administrator, Janice Muirhead; General Manager,
n K. Conte; Development, Pamela Tatge, Ana Silfer; Technical, Ben Baker; Props,
id Fletcher; Wardrobe, Jean Routt; Electrician, Jay Strevey; Press, Jeff Fickes

## PRODUCTIONS & CASTS

**OTH IS BACK** by Austin Pendleton; Director, Arvin Brown; Sets, John Lee
atty; Costumes, Jess Goldstein; Lighting, Dennis Parichy; Wigs by Cynthia
nand; Stage Manager, Anne Keefe. CAST: Maureen Anderman (Mary Ann), Beth
on (Adelaide), Joyce Ebert (Mrs. Hill), Alexander Enberg (Johnny Booth), Frank
gella (Junius Brutus Booth), Bob Morrisey (Baxter), Isabel Rose (Asia Booth),
hael Sbarge (Edwin Booth), Ralph Williams (Page).

**VENTURES IN THE SKIN TRADE** by Dylan Thomas; adapted by John
inger and James Hammerstein; Music by Tom Fay; Lyrics by James Hammerstein;
ector, John Tillinger; Sets, John Lee Beatty; Costumes, Jane Greenwood; Lighting,
ron Musser; Choreography, Danny Herman; Wigs, Paul Huntley; Stage Manager,
es Harker. CAST: Susan Antinozzi (Ensemble), Victoria Boothby (Mrs.
van/Mrs. Dacey), Victoria Clark (Winnie/Rose/Ensemble), Paddy Croft (Mrs.
nnet/Ensemble), John Curless (Tom/Ensemble), Thomas Hill (Mr.
nnet/Allingham), Daniel Jenkins (Sam Bennet), Lily Knight
ggy/Polly/Lola/Ensemble), Albert Macklin (Dave/George Ring), Scott Murphree
semble), Erin J. O'Brien (Lou/Lucy/Ensemble), William Parry (Harold/Ensemble),
Trigger (Mr. O'Brien/Ensemble), Michael Waldron (Reverend Bevan/Walter/Ron
hop/Ensemble)

**E PHILANTHROPIST** by Christopher Hampton; Director, Gordon Edelstein;
s, Hugh Landwehr; Costumes, Candice Donnelly; Lighting, Peter Kaczorowski;
ge Manager, Tammy Taylor. CAST: Gillian Anderson (Celia), Tim Choate
illip), Margaret Gibson (Araminta), Ronald Guttman (Braham), Lily Knight (Liz),
Reilly (John), Sam Tsoutsouvas (Don)

**ENEMY OF THE PEOPLE** by Henrik Ibsen; adapted by Arthur Miller;
ector, John Tillinger; Sets, Donald Eastman; Costumes, Robert Wojewodski;
hting, Arden Fingerhut; Wigs, Paul Huntley; Stage Manager, Diane DiVita.
ST: Paul Barry (Morten Kiil), John Peter Basinger (Ensemble), Lee Bergman
semble), Andrew Borba (The Drunk), Lewis Dube (Ensemble), Michael Gaston
ptain Horster), Nicholas Kepros (Peter Stockmann), Damien Leake (Hovstad),
rgery Murray (Catherine), Albie Powers (Ejlif), Ken Sawicki (Ensemble),
herine K. Slusar (Ensemble), Josh Soboslai (Morten), Sam Tsoutsouvas (Dr.
ckmann), Oliver Wadsworth (Billing), Margaret Welsh (Petra), Sewell Whitney
semble), Ralph Williams (Aslaksen)

**TOUCH OF THE POET** by Eugene O'Neill; Director, Arvin Brown; Sets,
hael Yeargan; Costumes, David Murin; Lighting, Christopher Akerlind; Music,
nton Evans; Wigs, Paul Huntley; Stage Manager, Tammy Taylor. CAST: Paul
ry (Patch Riley), Eddie Bowz (Mickey Malloy), Len Cariou (Cornelius Melody),
ath Conroy (Jamie Cregan), Joyce Ebert (Nora Melody), Melissa Leo (Sara
lody), Paul O'Brien (Dan Roche), Alexandra O'Karma (Deborah), Doug Stender
holas Gadsby), Sewell Whitney (Paddy O'Dowd).

**E INNOCENTS' CRUSADE** by Keith Reddin; Director, Joe Mantello; Sets,
gh Landwehr; Stage Manager, Ruth M. Feldman. CAST: Maggie Burke (Mame),
e Halston (Ms. Connel/Waitress/Ms. Cabot/Helen), Edmund Lewis (Eddy/Mr.
ncy/Evan/Stephen), Christopher Shaw (Bill), Welker White (Laura), William Wise
rl)

**POINTMENT WITH A HIGH WIRE LADY** by Russell Davis; Director,
hael Mantell; Music, Jane Ira Bloom; Sets, Hugh Landwehr; Stage Manager, Tom
rger. CAST: Jayne Atkinson (Louise Wick), Suzanne Shepherd (Carla Ukmar),
tor Slezak (Richard Skelley)

**AZY HORSE AND THREE STARS** by David Wiltse; Director, Mark Brokaw;
s, Hugh Landwehr; Stage Manager, Ruth M. Feldman. CAST: James Andreassi
Clark), Frank Converse (General Crook), Tracey Griswold (Guard), Machiste
itnake), Barry Mulholland (Crazy Horse)

**E DAY THE BRONX DIED** by Michael Henry Brown; Director, Gordon
elstein; Sets, Hugh Landwehr; Stage Manager, Tom Aberger. CAST: Michael Ian
ck (Billy), Craig Green (Daniel), Dwayne Gurley (Silk), Marjorie Johnson
other), Aaron Martin (Butter), Daryl "Chill" Mitchell (Alexander), Reggie
ntgomery (Big Mickey), Greg Mouning (Policeman), Kelly Neal (The Prince),
li Prince (Young Mickey), Herbert Rubens (Mr. Kornblum/Doctor), Troy Winbush
d Job)

**L BE SEEING YOU: THE MUSIC OF SAMMY FAIN** Staged by Dan Siretta;
sical Director, Rod Hausen; Stage Manager, Diane DiVita. CAST: Gregg Burge,
gi Grant, Jennifer Prescott, Ron Raines, KT Sullivan

*T. Charles Erickson Photos*

**TOP: Raphael Sbarge, Frank Langella in "Booth is Back"**
**BELOW: Daniel Jenkins, Lily Knight in**
**"Adventures in the Skin Trade"**
**THIRD PHOTO: Don Reilly, Tim Choate, Sam Tsoutsouvas in**
**"Philanthropist"**
**RIGHT: Melissa Leo, Len Cariou in "Touch of the Poet"**

167

Mel Duane Gionson, (top) Peter Jay Fernandez, Robert Joy in "Indians"

Mary Stuart Masterson, Linda Hunt, Frances McDormand in "Three Sisters"

# McCARTER THEATRE

Princeton, New Jersey

Artistic Director, Emily Mann; Managing Director, Jeffrey Woodward; Spe
Programming Director, W.W. Lockwood, Jr.; General Manager, Timothy J. Shie
Dramaturg, Janice Paran; Development Director, Susan F. Reeves; Assistant to Arti
Director, Loretta Greco; Stage Managers, Susie Cordon, Paul Mills Holmes, Elise-/
Konstantin, Cheryl Mintz, Fredric H. Orner, Jonathan D. Secor; Production Mana
Ruth E. Steinberg; Company Manager, Lori Robishaw; Casting Directors, F
Fouquet, Stuart Howard, Joanna Merlin, Elissa Myers, Amy Schecter; Costume Sk
Supervisor, Catherine Homa-Rocchio; Marketing/Press, David Mayhew, Daniel
Bauer

## PRODUCTIONS & CASTS

**INDIANS** by Arthur Kopit; Director, George Faison; Set, Eduardo Sicang
Costumes, Randy Barcelo; Lighting, Timothy Hunter; Properties, Sandy Stru
Composer/Music, David Bishop; Native American Music, Kenneth Little Ha
CAST: Robert Joy (Buffalo Bill), Jay Patterson (Stage Manager/Wild Bill Hicko
Rosa Evangelina Arredondo (Indian Maiden), Mel Duane Gionson (Sitting Bull), J
Tillotson (Senator Logan), Don Perkins (Senator Morgan/Ol' Time President), Gor
Stanley (Senator Dawes/Colonel Forsyth), Peter Jay Fernandez (John Grass), F
Lemos (Spotted Tail/Billy the Kid), Lewis Black (Ned Buntline/Lieutenant), R
Zieff (Grand Duke Alexis/Uncas/Poncho), Gregory Zaragoza (Geronimo/Jesse Jam
Shelley Wald (Teskanjavila), Julia Kiley (First Lady), Kenneth Little Hawk (Ch
Joseph), Victor Barbella, Sandra Coulboume, Bruce Harris, Roland Hayes, S
Inglese, Jr., Jorge V. Ledesma, Brian McMonagle, Jaclde Mauder

**A CHRISTMAS CAROL** by Charles Dickens; Adaptation, David Thomps
Director, Scott Ellis; Set, Michael Anania; Costumes, Lindsay Davis; Lighting, P
Kaczorowski; Properties, Sandy Struth; Sound, Abe Jacob; Original Song, Je
Kander and Fred Ebb; Music Composed and Adapted, Louis Rosen. CAST: Jar
Weatherstone (Bob Cratchit), Burt Edwards (Ebenezer Scrooge), Charles Cra
(Jacob Marley), Charles Antalosky, Raymond Anthony Arroyo, David Aaron Bak
Susan Batson, Ellen M. Bethea, Bill Camp, Lily Cheng, Tara Devlin, Rufus C. Gibs
Jared Green, Lyn Greene, Patricia Guinan, Thomas Guiry, Farley Gwazda, Dy
Haggerty, Ralf Hetzel, Mike Horgan, Andrea Hutnik, Michael John Ladolce
Meredith Landis, Mary Lee, Megan Livingston, Jennifer Lopez, Chris Laugh
Charlotte Maier, Kyle Petersen, Christina Prospero, Paola Renzi, Christopher Sco
Ching-Lee Shen, Michelle Towey, Daya Washington, James Wilby, Mira Wilcz
Greg Wu, Jenny Zhao, Kang Zhuang

**THREE SISTERS** by Anton Chekhov; Translation, Lanford Wilson; Director, Err
Mann; Set, Michael Yeargan; Costumes, Jennifer von Mayrhauser; Lighting, P
Collins; Properties, Sandy Struth; Original Music Composer, Mel Marvin; Movem
Consultant, Rob Marshall. CAST: Linda Hunt (Olga), Mary Stuart Masterson (Iri
Frances McDormand (Masha), Mark Nelson (Baron Tuzenbach), Josef Somr
(Chebutykin), Peter Francis James (Solyony), Myra Carter (Anfisa), Allen Sw
(Ferapont), Edward Herrmann (Vershinin), Paul McCrane (Andrei), John Christop
Jones (Kulygin), Laura San Giacomo (Natasha), Robert Baumgardner, Kurt W. Co
Sandra Coulboume, Alexander Draper, Mark Feuerstein, Jeff Glasse, Gregory Wag
Mira Wilczek

**MARRIAGE PLAY;** Written and Directed by Edward Albee (American Premier
Set and Costume, Derek McLane; Lighting, Howell Binkley; Movement Coordina
Chuck Hudson. CAST: Shirley Knight (Gillian), Tom Klunis (Jack).

**THE TRIUMPH OF LOVE** by Pierre Carlet de Marivaux (American Premier
Adaptation/Director, Stephen Wadsworth; Translation, Stephen Wadsworth w
Nadia Benabid; Set, Thomas Lynch; Costumes, Martin Pakledinaz; Lighti
Christopher Akerlind. CAST: Tom Brennan (Dimas), Katherine Borowitz (Leonic
Brooke Smith (Corine), John Michael Higgins (Harlequin), Mark Deakins (Ag
Mary Lou Rosato (Leontine), Robin Chadwick (Hermocrate)

*T. Charles Erickson Photos*

Tom Klunis , Shirley Knight in "Marriage Play"

John Michael Higgins, Katherine Borowitz, Tom Brennan in
"Triumph of Love"

**Michael James Laird, Eric Hissom, Stephen Daley, Daryl Edwards in "Cobb"**
TOP LEFT: **Geoffrey Beauchamp, Richard Schrot, Maureen McDevitt in "Ten Little Indians"**
CENTER: **Eric Tavares, Jeanne Arnold in "Gin Game"**
BOTTOM LEFT: **Julia Lema, Clent Bowers, Cynthia Thomas, Gene Barry-Hill, Terri White in "Ain't Misbehavin'"**

# MEADOW BROOK THEATRE

Rochester, Michigan
October 3, 1991 - May 17, 1992

Artistic/General Director, Terence Kilburn; Managing Director, James P. Spittle; Director of Cultral Affairs, Stuart C. Hyke; Sets, Peter W. Hicks, C. Lance Brockman; Costumes, Barbara Jenks, Randy Barcelo, Mr. Hicks; Lighting, Reid G. Johnson; Stage Managers: Robert Herrle, Terry W. Carpenter; Corporate Relations, Mary Bonnell

## PRODUCTIONS & CASTS

**INHERIT THE WIND** by Lawrence & Lee; Director, Charles Nolte  CAST: Arthur J. Beer, Mary Bremer, Booth Colman, Roy K. Dennison, Andrew Dunn, Paul Hopper, Sue Kenny, Julian Lindig, Phillip Locker, Thomas D. Mahard, John-Michael Manfredi, Wayne David Parker, Glen Allen Pruett, Joseph Reed, Carl Schurr, John Seibert

**TEN LITTLE INDIANS** by Agatha Christie; Director, Terence Kilburn  CAST: Paul Hopper (Rogers), Sue Kenny (Mrs. Rogers), Thomas D. Mahard (Narracott), Maureen McDevitt (Vera), Geoffrey Beauchamp (Lombard), Richard A. Schrot (Marston), Eric Tavares (Blore), Phillip Locker (Mackensip), Julian Lindig (Emily), Wil Love (Wargrave), Carl Schurr (Armstrong)

**A CHRISTMAS CAROL** by Charles Dickens, Adaptation/Direction, Charles Nolte  CAST: Booth Colman (Scrooge), Geoffrey Beauchamp, Paul Hopper, Sue Kenny, Julian Lindig, Phillip Locker, Thomas D. Mahard, Maureen McDevitt, Glen Allen Pruett, Joseph Reed, John Seibert

**THE GIN GAME** by D.L. Coburn; Director, Terence Kilburn  CAST: Jeanne Arnold (Fonsia), Eric Tavares (Weller)

**COBB** by Lee Blessing; Director, John Ulmer  CAST: Stephen Daley (Cobb over 70), Eric Hissom (Ty at 20), Michael James Laird (Ty at 40), Daryl Edwards (Charleston)

**PRIVATE LIVES** by Noel Coward; Director, Terence Kilburn  CAST: Leslie Lynn Meeker (Sibyl), Carl Schurr (Elyot), Wil Love (Victor), Sherry Skinker (Amanda), Karen Sheridan (Louise)

**AIN'T MISBEHAVIN'** with Music/Lyrics by Fats Waller; Director/Choreography, Arthur Faria; Musical Director, Ron Metcalf  CAST: Gene Barry-Hill, Clent Bowers, Julia Lema, Cynthia Thomas, Terri White

*Tim Fuller Photos*

# MILWAUKEE REPERTORY THEATER

Milwaukee, Wisconsin
Twenty-eighth Season

Artistic Director, John Dillon; Managing Director, Sara O'Connor; Associate Artistic Director, Kenneth Albers; Artistic Administrator/Resident Director, Norma Saldivar; Resident Composer, John Tanner; Resident Designers, Sam Fleming, John Story; Resident Playwright, John Leicht; Associate Artists: Amlin Gray, Sharon Ott; Technical Production Supervisor, Richard Rogers; Lighting Supervisor, Chester Loeffler-Bell; Production Stage Manager, Diane Carlin-Bartel; Stage Manager, Mark Baughman; Stage Manager, Joan Foster McCarty; Stage Manager, Mark A. Sahba; Assistant Stage Manager, Leslie Woodruff; Costume Shop Manager, Carol Kotsifakis; Properties Manager, Samuel A. Garst.
**RESIDENT COMPANY:** Kenneth Albers, Tom Blair, Catherine Lynn Davis, Richard Halverson, Johanna Melamed, Daniel Mooney, Ric Oquita, James Pickering, Rose Pickering, Linda Stephens, Gregory Steres, Adolphus Ward, Celeste Williams.

## PRODUCTIONS AND CASTS

**OUR TOWN** by Thornton Wilder; Director, John Dillon; Assistant Director, Marcia Tilchin; Set Design, Steve Rubin,; Costume Design, Michael Krass; Lighting Design, William H. Grant, III; Music Director, John Tanner; Scenic Artist, John Story. CAST: Chuck Baird, Mondy Carter, Pat Graybill, Richard Halverson, Monique Holt, Johanna Melamed, Daniel Mooney, Freda C. Norman, Maureen O'Dowd, Ric Oquita, Will Rhys, Kara T. Schuette, Steve Siegler, Linda Stephens, Gregory Steres, Andrew Vasnick, T. Patrick Walsh, Nancy Webber
**THE HOUSE OF BERNARDA ALBA** by Frederico Garcia Lorca, translated by Michael Dewell and Carmen Zapata; Director, Rene Buch; Set Design, Pavel Dobrusky; Costume Design, Sam Fleming; Lighting Design, Jason Sturm; Music by Rigoberto Obando and Pable Zinger of Repertorio Espanol; Casting Consultant, Ellen Novack, CSA. CAST: Liza Balestrieri, Miriam Colon, Catherine Lynn Davis, Ellyn Duncan, Feiga M. Martinez, Johanna Melamed, Caitlin O'Connell, Rose Pickering, Jill Steeg, Linda Stephens, Trinity Thompson
**THE GIN GAME** by D.L. Coburn; Director, Libby Appel; Set Design, Michael C. Smith; Costume Design, Constanza Romero; Lighting Design, Peter Maradudin CAST: Jon Farris, Rosemary Prinz
**A CHRISTMAS CAROL** by Charles Dickens, Adapted by Amlin Gray; Director, Kenneth Albers; Set Design, Stuart Wurtzel; Costume Design, Carol Oditz; Lighting Design, Dan Kotlowitz; Composer/Music Director, John Tanner; Choreographer, Cate Deicher; Vocal Coach, Robert Neff Williams; Stage Manager, Kimberley Barry; Assistant Stage Manager, Judy Berdan; Assistant Director for the Children, Shawn Gulyas. CAST: Jonathan Adams, Tom Blair, Catherine Lynn Davis, James DeVita, Richard Halverson, Anthony Lee, Johanna Melamed, Michael W. Nash, James Pickering, Walker Richards, Linda Stephens, Gregory Steres, Celeste Williams
**ALL THE TRICKS BUT ONE** (World Premiere) by Gilles Ségal, translated by Sara O'Connor; Director, Kenneth Albers; Set Design, Victor A. Becker; Costume Design, Sam Fleming; Lighting Design, Robert Jared. CAST: Tom Blair, Catherine Lynn Davis, Troy Dunn, Michael W. Nash, James Pickering, Rose Pickering, Will Rhys, Gregory Steres, Jeff Lee, Brady Moran.
**DEATH OF A SALESMAN** by Arthur Miller; Director, John Dillon; Set Design, Laura Maurer; Costume Design, Sam Fleming; Lighting Design, Robert Peterson; Incidental Music Composer, Alex North. CAST: Kenneth Albers, LeWan Alexander, Liza Balestrieri, Tom Blair, Richard Halverson, Ric Oquita, James Pickering, Rose Pickering, Kara T. Schuette, Jill Steeg, Linda Stephens, Gregory Steres, C. Michael Wright.
**MOOT** (World Premiere) by John Leicht; Director, John Dillon; Set Design, John Story; Costume Design, Charles Berliner; Lighting Design, Chester Loeffler-Bell, Speciality Wigs, Jim Ponder; Composer/Sound Design, John Tanner. CAST: Derek Craig, Saralynne Crittenden, James DeVita, Richard Halverson, Anthony Lee, Terry Merrill, Daniel Mooney, Rose Pickering, Stephan Roselin, Gregory Steres, Adolphus Ward, C. Michael Wright.

Gregory Steres, Anthony Lee, C. Michael Wright in "Moot"

Miriam Colon, Trinity Thompson in "House of Bernarda Alba"

## STIEMKE THEATRE

**OTHER PEOPLE'S MONEY** by Jerry Sterner; Director, Joseph Hanreddy; S Designer, Kenneth Kloth; Costume Designer, Dawna Gregory; Lighting Design Thomas C. Hase; Stage Manager, Joan Foster McCarty. CAST: Kenneth Albe Catherine Lynn Davis, James Pickering, Trinity Thompson, Adolphus Ward.
**MEETINGS** by Mustapha Matura; Director, Tim Bond; Set Designer, Ri Rasmussen; Costume Designer, Ellen Kozak; Lighting Designer, Kenneth Kloth; Sta Manager, Joan Foster McCarty. CAST: Anthony Lee, Amanda Ward, Cele: Williams
**AN EVENING OF MAMET, GRAY AND LINNEY** by David Mamet, Amlin Gra and Romulus Linney; Director, Norma Saldivar; Set Designer, Pat Doty; Costu Designer, Cecilia Mason; Lighting Designer, Linda Essig; Stage Manager, Joan Fos McCarty. CAST: James DeVita, Gwyn Fawcett, Richard Halverson, Johan Melamed.
**IMAGO: THEATRE MASK ENSEMBLE** Stage Manager, Conrad Burmeiste CAST: Conrad Burmeister, Jerry Mouawad, James J. Peck, Carol Uselman.

## STACKNER CABARET

**2X5X4** Conceived by Seth Glassman, Music by John Kander, Lyrics by Fred Eb Director, Pamela Hunt; Stage Manager, Mark Baughman. CAST: Susan Edward Melinda MacDonald, Mark Martino, Jack Forbes Wilson.
**GREATER TUNA** by Jaston Williams; Joe Sears and Ed Howard; Director, Kenne Albers; Stage Manager, Mark Baughman; Master Electrician, John W. Hanse CAST: Richard Halverson, James Pickering
**APPALACHIAN VOICES** (World Premiere) by Edward Morgan; Director, Edwa Morgan; Stage Manager, Mark Baughman; Master Electrician, John W. Hanse CAST: Steve Hickman, Edward James Morgan, John Newlin.
**LADY DAY** by Lanie Robertson; presented by Cricket Theatre; Director, Willia Partlan; Original Set Design, Jack Barkla; Set Adaptation, Steve Krahnke; Costu Coordinator, Dawna Gregory; Set Design, Steve Krahnke; Costu Manage Janice F. Campbell; Assistant Stage Manager, Leslie Woodruff; Master Electricia John W. Hansen; Tour Manager, Joel Olson; Production Manager, Mike Klaer CAST: Chuck Adams, Dan Chouinard, Shirley Witherspoon.
**MOTHER JONES** (World Premiere) Book by Ronnie Gilbert, Words and Music by Kahn; Director, Norma Saldivar; Set Design, Kate Henderson; Costume Design, Daw Gregory; Stage Manager, Mark Baughman; Stage Management Apprentice, Bec Owczarski; Assistant Director, Lee Wichman; Master Electrician, John W. Hanse CAST: Michael Dubay/Mark Lea Clark, Ronnie Gilbert, Jack Forbes Wilson.

*Mark Avery Photos*

Linda Stephens, Freda C. Norman in "Our Town"

# NEXT THEATRE COMPANY

Evanston, Illinois

...tistic Director, Harriet Spizziri; Managing Director, Jim Keister; Production ...nager, Tim Engle; Artistic Associates, Dexter Bullard, Matt DeCaro; Sets/Lighting, ...bert E. Smith; Sound, Larry Hart; Production Assistant, Katey Schwartz; Public ...lations, Cheryl J. Lewin Associates

**...RODUCTIONS:** *Two Rooms, Love & Anger, Bang the Drum Slowly, Turcaret the ...nancier, Irish Coffee, Blue Champagne, Scarecrows, The Enormous Room, ...usoria, Hunting of the Snark*

*Jennifer Girard Photos*

**RIGHT: Stephen Colbert, Michele Cole in "Infusoria"**

# ODYSSEY THEATRE ENSEMBLE

Los Angeles, California

Artistic Director, Ron Sossi; Literary Manager, Jan Lewis; Production Manager, Jody Roman; Technical Director, Duncan Mahoney; Business Manager, David Mills; Marketing Director, Lucy Pollak

### PRODUCTIONS & CASTS

**ONLY KIDDING** by Jim Geoghan; Director, Larry Arrick; Set, Karen Schulz; Lighting, Joe Damiano; Costumes, Jeffrey L. Ullman   CAST: Larry Keith, Andrew Hill Newman, Paul Provenza, Howard Spiegel, Sam Zap
**A MAP OF THE WORLD** by David Hare; Director, Allan Miller; Set, Paul Hawker; Lighting, Gary Floyd; Costumes, Pauline Cronin   CAST: James Caviezal, Philip Baker Hall, Christopher Paul Hart, Michael Holmes, Lani Hyatt, Randy Lowell, Andra Millian, Lynne Moody, Michael Nordstrom, Tucker Smallwood, Gilbert Stuart, Eric Underwood, Andrea Whitney

*Jan Deen Photos*

**LEFT: Christopher Paul Hart, Andra Millian, Philip Baker Hall in "Map of the World"**
**BOTTOM LEFT: Paul Provenza, Sam Zapp, Andrew Hill Newman in "Only Kidding"**
**BOTTOM RIGHT: Howard Spiegel, Larry Keith in "Only Kidding"**

# OLD GLOBE THEATRE

San Diego, California
Fifty-Seventh Season
June 28, 1991 - June 21, 1992

Executive Producer, Craig Noel; Artistic Director, Jack O'Brien; Managing Director, Thomas Hall; Play Development, Mark Hofflund; Business Director, Derek Harrison Hurd; Development Director, Demenick Ietto; Marketing Director, Joe Kobryner; Public Relations, Charlene Baldridge

## PRODUCTIONS & CASTS

**THE MERCHANT OF VENICE** by Shakespeare; Director, Jack O'Brien; Sets, Ralph Funicello; Costumes, Lewis Brown; Lighting, Peter Maradudin; Composer, Bob James   CAST: Richard Kneeland (Duke of Venice/Tubal), Aldo Billingslea (Prince of Morocco), Jonathan McMurtry (Prince Arragon), Richard Easton (Antonio), Geoffrey Lower (Bassanio), Kandis Chappell (Portia), Hal Holbrook (Shylock), James R. Winker (Gratiano), Henry J. Jordan (Salerio), Nicholas Martin (Solanio), Bo Foxworth (Lorenzo), June Gable (Nerissa), Andrea Fitzgerald (Jessica), Alex Perez (Leonardo), Eric Liddell (Stephano), Mary Elizabeth McGlynn (Bianca), Therese Walden (Maria), Triney Sandoval (Launcelot), Jim Morley (Old Gobbo), Will Crawford (Vittorio), Donald Sager (Angelo), Jesus Ontiveros (Clerk), Ted Deasy (Gaoler), David Huber, Marc Wong (Attendants), James Ingle, Richard Rennoll (Waiters), Amy Beth Cohen, Evangeline Fernandez, Sara Lindberg (Tourists)

**FOREVER PLAID;** Written/Directed/Choreographed by Stuart Ross; Arrangements, James Raitt; Set, Neil Peter Jampolis; Costumes, Debra Stein; Lighting, Jane Reisman; Stage Manager, Peter Van Dyke   CAST: Stan Chandler (Jinx), David Engel (Smudge), Larry Raben (Sparky), Guy Stroman (Francis)

**NECESSITIES** by Velina Hasu Houston; Director, Julianne Boyd; Sets, Cliff Faulkner; Costumes, Shigeru Yaji; Lighting, Ashley York Kennedy; Stage Manager, Robert Drake   CAST: Jennifer Savidge (Zelda Kelly), Jonathan Nichols (Kale Smith), William Anton (Daniel Kelly), Suzanna Hay (Christina), Bray Poor (Tommy), Freda Foh Shen (Elizabeth), Tara Marchant (Janine), Sue-Anne Morrow (Mary)
A world premiere. The action takes place in L.A. and Phoenix at present.

**THE TEMPEST** by Shakespeare; Director, Adrian Hall; Sets, Ralph Funicello; Costumes, Lewis Brown; Lighting, Peter Maradudin; Composer, Larry Delinger; Stage Manager, Douglas Pagliotti   CAST: Dierk Torsek (Alonso), Julian Gamble (Sebastian), Richard Easton (Prospero), Vaughn Armstrong (Antonio), Eric Liddell (Ferdinand), Jonathan McMurtry (Gonzalo), Marc Wong (Adrian), Donald Sager (Francisco), Stephen Markle (Caliban), Sean Murray (Ariel), Allen McCalla (Trinculo), Richard Kneeland (Stephano), Aldo Billingslea (Ship Master), Triney Sandoval (Boatswain), Mary Elizabeth McGlynn (Miranda), Ted Deasy, David Huber, James Ingle, Alex Perez, Bray Poor, Richard Rennoll, Ian Ross, Donald Sager, Triney Sandoval, Harry Zimmerman

**LA FIACA** by Ricardo Talesnik; Translation, Raúl Moncada; Director, Lillian Garrett-Groag; Sets, Robert Brill; Costumes, Robert Wojewodski; Lighting, Barth Ballard; Stage Manager, Maria Carrera   CAST: Luther Hanson (Boss), John Kassir (Nestor), Cristina Soria (Martha), Helena Carroll (Mrs. V), Jonathan Nichols (Peralta), Jesus Ontiveros (Jauregui)

**THE SHOW-OFF** by George Kelly; Director, Jack O'Brien; Sets, Cliff Faulkner; Costumes, Robert Wojewodski; Lighting, Peter Maradudin; Stage Manager, Robert Drake   CAST: Lynne Griffin (Clara), Sada Thompson (Mrs. Fisher), Jennifer Van Dyck (Amy), William Anton (Frank), Don Sparks (Aubrey), Mitchell Edmonds (Mr.

(seated) Richard Easton, Hal Holbrook in "Merchant of Venice"

(clockwise) Stan Chandler, Larry Raben, Guy Stroman, David Engel in "Forever Plaid"

**Richard Easton, Mary Elizabeth McGlynn in "The Tempest"**

Gordon Paddison, Susan Wands in "School for Husbands"

**172**

Rosemary Murphy, Christopher Collet, John Getz in "The Old Boy"

Fisher), Philip Charles Sneed (Joe), Will Crawford (Mr. Gill), Nicholas Martin (Mr. Rogers)

**THE OLD BOY** by A.R. Gurney; Director, Paul Benedict; Sets/Lighting, Kent Dorsey; Costumes, Christine Dougherty; Stage Manager, Peter Van Dyke  CAST: Christopher Collet (Perry), Franklin Cover (Dexter), Rob Neukirch (Bud), John Getz (Sam), Rosemary Murphy (Harriet), Harriet Hall (Alison)

**THE SCHOOL FOR HUSBANDS AND THE FLYING DOCTOR** by Molière; School Translation by Richard Wilbur; Doctor Translation/Adaptation, Albert Bermel; Director, Edward Payson Call; Sets, Robert Andrew Dahlstrom; Costumes, Michael Krass; Lighting, David F. Segal; Composer, Larry Delinger; Stage Manager, Douglas Pagliotti  CAST: Doctor Paul James Kruse (Gorgibus), Amy Beth Cohn (Lucile), Susan Wands (Sabine), Robert Petkoff (Valere), Tom Harrison (Arlecchino), Andrea D. Fitzgerald (Gros-Rene), Richard Easton (Lawyer), Evangeline Fernandez (Villbreuin), Alex Perez, Donald Sager (Zanies), School Richard Easton (Artiste), Tom Harrison (Ergaste), Gordon Paddison (Sganarelle), Robert Petkoff (Valere), Susan Wands (Isabelle), Andrea D. Fitzgerald (Lenor), Evangeline Fernandez (Lisette), Paul James Kruse (Magistrate), Alex Perez, Donald Sager (Zanies)

**SHIRLEY VALENTINE** by Willy Russell; Director, Craig Noel; Sets, Nick Reid; Costumes, Robert Wojewodski; Lighting, Barth Ballard; Stage Manager, Jerome J. Sheehan  CAST: Katherine McGrath (Shirley)

**BARGINS** (World Premiere) by Jack Heifner; Director, Jack O'Brien; Sets, Ralph Funicello; Costumes, Robert Wojewodski; Lighting, Ashley York Kennedy; Stage Manager, Douglas Pagliotti  CAST: Stephen Caffrey (Mr. Mead), Jeb Brown (Dennis), Linda Hart (Sally), Kellie Overby (Tish), Marcia Rodd (Mildred), Gregory Grove (Lothar)

**MR. RICKEY CALLS A MEETING** by Ed Schmidt; Director, Sheldon Epps; Sets, Ralph Funicello; Costumes, Christina Haatainen; Lighting, Barth Ballard; Stage Manager, Jerome J. Sheehan  CAST: Jeremiah Wayne Birkett (Clancy Hope), Arlen Dean Snyder (Branch Rickey), Sterling Macer Jr. (Jackie Robinson), Ron Canada (Joe Louis), Willie C. Carpenter (Paul Robeson), Nick LaTour (Bojangles Robinson)

**A ... MY NAME IS STILL ALICE;** Conception/Direction, Joan Micklin Silver and Julianne Boyd; Material by Dan Berkowitz, Douglas Bernstein, Randy Courts, David Friedman, John Gorka, Carol Hall, Georgia Holof, Ursaline Kairson, Doug Katsaros, Christine Lavin, Lisa Loomer, Denis Markell, Mel Marvin, Amanda McBloom, J.D. Mercier, David Mettee, Jimmy Roberts, Muriel Robinson, Glen Roven, Mark Saltzman, Luis Santeiro, Ellen Sebastian, Kate Shein, June Siegel, Mark St. Germain, Steve Tesich, David Zippel; Musical Director, Henry Aronson; Choreography, Liza Gennaro; Orchestrations, Robby Merkin; Sets, Cliff Faulkner; Costumes, David C. Woolard; Lighting, David F. Segal; Stage Manager, Douglas Pagliotti  CAST: Roo Brown, Randy Graff, Alaina Reed Hall, Mary Gordon Murray, Nancy Ticotin  World premiere of musical sequel.

*Ken Howard, Will Gullette Photos*

Sterling Macer Jr., Arlen Dean Snyder in "Mr. Rickey Calls a Meeting"

**Alaina Reed Hall, Mary Gordon Murray, Randy Graff in "A...My Name is Still Alice"**

173

Renee Stork, David Bedella, Rick Manning, Lauri Landry, Scott Carollo, Angelo Fraboni in "West Side Story"

James Brennan, Larry Grey, Joseph Mahowald, Mari Nelson, (floor) John Williams in "Camelot"

Darren Edward Higgins, Elizabeth Franz, Jennifer Holmes in "Great Expectations"

John DeLuca and ensemble in "Chess"

# PAPER MILL PLAYHOUSE

Millburn, New Jersey
Sixty-second Year
September 11, 1991 - June 28, 1992

Executive Producer, Angelo Del Rossi; Artistic Director, Robert Johanson; Gene Manager, Geoffrey Cohen; Company Manager, Steven Myers; Development Direct John McEwen; Public Relations, Albertina Reilly; Marketing Director, Debra Waxman

## PRODUCTIONS & CASTS

**WEST SIDE STORY** with Music by Leonard Bernstein; Lyrics, Stephen Sondhei Book Arthur Laurents; Set, Campbell Baird; Lighting, Ken Billington; Costumes, G Cooper-Hecht; Musical Director, Richard Parrinello; Direction/Choreography, Al Johnson; Stage Manager, Arturo E. Porazzi CAST: Angelo Fraboni (Riff), Sc Carollo (Tony), Michael Paternostro (Action), Bill Brassea (A-Rab), An Blankenbuehler (Baby John), Tim Schultheis (Snowboy), Michael Gerhart (Big Dea Michael Berresse (Diesel), Michael Arnold (Gee-Tar), Susie Foust (Graziella), Boni Lynn (Velma), Angela Garrison (Minnie), Kriss Dias (Clarice), Diana Laurens (Anybodys), Rick Manning (Bernardo), Lauri Landry (Maria), Renée Stork (Anit David Bedella (Chino), Julio Monge (Pepe), Eddie Otero (Indio), David Enriqu (Luis), Stephen Nunley (Anxious), Erik Chechak (Nibbles), Miguel Aviles (Juan Lyd-Lyd Gaston (Rosalia), Trish Reidy (Consuelo), Kelly Groniger (Teresita), Shar Moore (Francisca), Kriss Dias (Estella), Bob Jordan (Doc), David Brummel (Schran Bob Ari (Krupke), Frank O'Brien (Gladhand)

**CAMELOT** with Music by Frederick Loewe; Lyrics/Book, Alan Jay Lerne Director/Choreography, Robert Johanson; Musical Director, Jim Coleman; Se Michael Anania; Costumes, Gregg Barnes; Lighting, Mark Stanley; Stage Manag Jim Semmelman CAST: Larry Grey (Merlyn), James Brennan (Arthur), Mari Nels (Guenevere), Jeffrey Wilkins (Dinadan), John Williams (Lionel), George Ewas (Sagramore), Rod McCune, Jack Salley (Tumblers), Julietta Marcelli (Nimue Maureen McNamara (Nimue Voice), Joseph Mahowald (Lancelot), Raymond Sa (Squire Dap), Mr. Grey (Pellinore), Dudley (Horrid), Cheryl Allison (Lady Anne Robert Johanson (Mordred), Barbie Shallenberger (Morgan Le Fey), Noah Jarre (Tom), James Barbour, R.F. Dailey, Ron Dwenger, Thomas Foust, Rod McCune, J Montgomery, Todd Murray, Raymond Sage, Mr. Salley (Knights), Ms. Allison, Cari Andersson, Darlene Bel Grayson, Eva Grant, Ms. Marcelli, Ms. McNamara, Kar Rich, Ms. Shallenberger (Ladies), Greg Bernstein, Mr. Jarrett, Aaron Levy, Domin Scaglione, Melissa Stanley, Marc Skarecki (Pages)

**RUMORS** by Neil Simon; Director, John Brigleb; Sets, Tony Straiges; Costume Joseph G. Aulisi; Lighting, Timothy Hunter; Costumes, José M. Rivera; Sta Manager, Bonnie L. Becker CAST: Linda Cameron (Chris), Ken Kliban (Ker Suzanne Dawson (Claire), Stephen Berger (Lenny), Heather MacRae (Cookie), Rer Roop (Ernie), Michael Minor (Glenn), Catherine Campbell (Cassie), Wiley Moo (Welch), Carol Hanpeter (Pudney)

**GREAT EXPECTATIONS** by Charles Dickens; Adaptation/Direction, Robe Johanson; Sets, Michael Anania; Costumes, Gregg Barnes; Lighting, Timothy Hunte Music, Albert Evans; Stage Manager, Michael McEowen CAST: Michael Jam Reed (Pip), Daren Edward Higgins (Young Pip), Joe Ambrose, Carina Andersso Nancy Bell, Emily Blau, Kermit Brown, Dante Deiana, Elizabeth Franz, Ji Hillgartner, Larry Grey, Jennifer Holmes, Marceline Hugot, Michael Lewis, Joh MacKay, Robert Molnar, Michael O'Gorman, Linda Poser, Chris Rempfer, Ky Saunders, Jeff Seelbach, Suzanne Toren, Timothy Wheeler, Jeff Woodman, Richa Woods

**OKLAHOMA** with Music by Richard Rodgers; Lyrics/Book, Oscar Hammerstein Director, James Rocco; Musical Director, Tom Helm; Choreography, Sharon Halle Sets, John Lee Beatty; Costumes, Gregg Barnes; Lighting, Jeff Davis; Stage Manage Lora K. Powell CAST: Georgia Creighton (Aunt Eller), Richard White (Curley Susan Powell (Laurey), Michael Hayward-Jones (Skidemore), Mark Chmiel (Slim John Scherer (Will), Robert Cuccioli (Jud), Jennifer Allen (Ado Annie), Les Marsde (Ali Hakim), Mary Jo Limpert (Gertie), Ralston Hill (Carnes), Joan Mirabella (Drea Laurey), Marty McDonough (Dream Curley), Tim Schultheis (Dream Jud), Jeann Abolt, Linda Goodrich, Conny Lee Sasfai (Postcard Girls), Robert Jensen (Elam), Bc Wrenn (Fred), John Howell, Mark Hoebee (Dancing Boys), Diana Brownstone, Aldri Gonzalez, Eva Grant, Jim Gricar, Zoie Lam, Anna McNeely, William Paul Michal Joan Mirabella, Catherine Ruivivar, Barbie Shallenberger, Alex Sharp, Diana Steckle

**CHESS** with Music by Benny Andersson and Björn Ulvaeus; Lyrics, Tim Rice; Boc Richard Nelson; Director/Choreography, Rob Marshall; Musical Director, Jeff Rizz Sets, Michael Anania; Costumes, Gregg Barnes; Lighting, Tim Hunter; Stag Manager, Stephen J. Chaiken CAST: Al DeCristo (Gregor), Erin Ann Abrahamso (Young Florence), John DeLuca (Arbiter), Keith Rice (Anatoly), Steve Blachar (Freddie), David Cryer (Molokov), Judy McLane (Florence), P.J. Benjamin (Walter Michael Licata (Nikolai), Vivien Eng (Hostess), Timothy Warmen (KGB), J.C Montgomery (Harold), Barbara Haag (Reporter), Ron Dwenger (Joe), William Thoma Evans (Reporter), Troy Lambert (Christoff), Joseph Savant (Sergei), Susan Daw Carson (Svetlana), Donna Pompei (TV Interviewer), Timothy Albrecht, Tina Beli Jack Hayes, Sarah Miles, Elizabeth Mozer

*Gerry Goodstein, Jerry Dalia Photos*

# PENGUIN REPERTORY COMPANY

Stony Point, New York
Fifteenth Season
June 13, 1991 - May 31, 1992

Artistic Director, Joe Brancato; Executive Director/Producer, Andrew M. Horn; Production Stage Manager, Kathleen J. Dooner

## PRODUCTIONS & CASTS

**THE VALUE OF NAMES** by Jeffrey Sweet; Director, Joe Brancato; Sets, Mindy Feman; Lighting, William J. Plachy; CAST: Peter De Maio, Kurt Goldschmidt, Deborah Laufer
**WAY-OUT WEST** *Mae's Life in Musical Revue*; Conception/Direction, Joe Brancato; Music/Lyrics/Continuity, Ellen May Schwartz and Bonnie Lee Sanders; Musical Director, Alki Steriopoulos; Sets, Michael E. Downs; Costumes, David R. Zyla; Lighting, David Neville; Choreography, Cynthia Khoury CAST: Adinah Alexander, Jay Kiman, Charlie Marcus, Kevin McGlynn
**WE ARE NOT STRANGERS** *The Songs of Elizabeth Swados*; Director/Choreography, Bill Castellino; Musical Direction/Arrangements, Michael Sottile, Ann Marie Milazzo; Sets/Lighting, Don Coleman; Costumes, David R. Zyla CAST: Gilles Chiasson, Lothair Eaton, Ann Marie Milazzo, Lauren Mufson, Kate Ostrow, Ira Sakolsky, Michael Sottile
**GREATER TUNA** by Jaston Williams, Joe Sears and Ed Howard; Director, Craig W. Van Gundy; Sets, Jason Sturm; Lighting, David Neville; Costumes, Kevin Kuney CAST: David Ruckman, Robert Keith Watson
**ELEEMOSYNARY** by Lee Blessing; Director, Joe Brancato; Sets/Lighting, Jason Sturm; Music, Alex Clemente CAST: Ann Dowd, Denise Du Maurier, Heather Gottlieb

*Kerwin McCarthy Photos*

**RIGHT:** Ann Marie Milazzo, Gilles Chiasson, (rear) Lothair Eaton, Lauren Mufson, Kate Ostrow in "We are Not Strangers"
**TOP RIGHT:** Kevin McGlynn, Adinah Alexander, Charlie Marcus, Jay Kiman in "Way-Out West"

# PENNSYLVANIA STAGE COMPANY

Allentown, Pennsylvania
September 25, 1991 - June 21, 1992

Producing Artistic Director, Peter Wrenn-Meleck; Artistic Director, Scott Edmiston; Directors: Charles Richter, Mercedes Ellington, Howard Rossen, Peter Wrenn-Meleck, Scott Edmiston, Dennis Delaney; Sets: Paul Wonsek Sarah Baptist, Curtis Dretsch, Paul Wonsek, Bennet Averyt; Costumes: Patricia Adshead, George Bergerand, Jose Rivera, Charlotte M. Yetman, Audrey Stables, Barbara Kravitz, Margaret Shyne Benson; Lights: Paul Wonsek, Kenneth Posner, Tom Sturge, Curtis Dretsch, Joey Arnold, John Rankin, Bennet Averyt; Stage Managers: David Bennett, Christine M. Terchek; Technical Director/Production Manager: William Kreider; Press, Michael Traupman.

## PRODUCTIONS & CASTS

**THE IMMIGRANT** by Mark Harelik, Conceived by Mark Harelik and Randal Myler. CAST: Joel Fredericks, John Ramsey, Tanny McDonald and Stacie Chaiken.
**AIN'T MISBEHAVIN' The New Fats Waller Musical Show,** Based on an idea by Murray Horowitz and Richard Maltby, Jr. CAST: Cleo King, Michael Mandell, Keith Robert Bennett, Lovette George, and Amy Jo Phillips. Choreography by Mercedes Ellington, Muscial Direction by Carl Maultsby.
**SMILING THROUGH** (World Premiere Musical) by Ivan Menchell, Conceived by Ivan Menchell and Vicki E. Stuart. CAST: Vicki E. Stuart. Musical Director: Rod Hausen.
**THE COCKTAIL HOUR** by A.R. Gurney. CAST: Forrest Compton, Geoffrey Wade, Joanne Bayes and Mary Francina Golden.
**THEME AND VARIATIONS** by Samuil Aloyshin, Translated by Michael Glenny. CAST: Herman Petras, Kathleen McCall and Michael Elich.
**CANDIDA** by George Bernard Shaw. CAST: Joseph Culliton, Ellen Fiske, John Edmond Morgan, Jim Hillgartner, Warren Kelley and Sarah Standing.
**LEND ME A TENOR** by Ken Ludwig. CAST: Thomas Carson, Michael Crider, Carl Wallnau, Raye Lankford, Suzanne Grodner, Peg Small, Ione Saroyan, Claude Choukrane.

*Gregory Fota Photos*

**TOP LEFT:** Joel Fredericks, Stacie Chaiken in "The Immigrant" **175**
**BOTTOM:** Herman Petras, Kathleen McCall in "Theme and Variations"

# PIONEER THEATRE COMPANY

Salt Lake City, Utah

Charles Morey, Artistic Director; Christopher Lino, Managing Director; Colleen Lindstrom, Box Office Treasurer; D. Dale Dean, Company Manager; Helen Royle, Business Manager; Pat Wells, Executive Secretary; Susan Appleby Koles, Development Director; Cynthia Spoor, Marketing & Communications Director; Kimberly Leslie Garcia, Annual Giving Director; Lee Bellavance, Publicist; David Deike, Production Manager/Technical Director; John W. Caywood, Jr., Production Stage Manager; George Maxwell, Resident Designer/Set Decorator; Ariel Ballif, Resident Scenic Designer; James Prigmore, Musical Director; Carol Wells-Day, Costume Shop Manager/Resident Costume Designer; Linda Sarver, Resident Costume Designer; Kevin Phillips, Wig Master/Make-up Designer; Peter L. Willardson, Lighting Director; Casting, Michele Ortlip.
**RESIDENT COMPANY:** Margaret Crowell, Frank Gerrish, Rebecca Holt, David Jensen, Alfred Lakeman, Richard Mathews, Conan McCarty, K. Lype O'Dell, Robert Peterson, Sam Stewart, David Valenza, Craig Wroe.

## PRODUCTIONS & CASTS

**THE GRAPES OF WRATH;** Director, Charles Morey; Set Designer, George Maxwell; Costume Designer, Elizabeth Novak; Lighting Design, Karl E. Haas; Original Music Composed by Michael Smith; Production Stage Manager, John W. Caywood, Jr. CAST: Christopher Borg, Holly Claspill, Lurissa LaShay Gines, Ellen Graham, Charlotte Scott Guyette, Raymond Hoskins, David Jensen, Alfred Lakeman, Jayne Luke, Lois Markle, Conan McCarty, Clark Morgan, Aaron Nelson, K. Lype O'Dell, Trevor H. Olsen, Gene Pack, Robert Peterson, Jean Roberts, Michael Ruud, Josie Scothern, Richard Scott, L.J. Slavin, Michael Smith, David Valenza, Myk Watford, Jon Wilde, Craig Wroe.
**HENRY V;** Director, Charles Morey; Set Designer, Gary English; Costume Designer, Carol Wells-Day; Lighting Design, Peter L. Willardson; Original Music Composed by James Prigmore; Stage Manager, Barbara Rollins; Fight Director, David Boushey. CAST: Michael Behrens, Christopher A. Borg, Margaret Browell, Frank Gerrish, Lurissa La Shay Gines, Raymond Hoskins, Thomas E. Jacobsen, David Jensen, Curt Karibalis, Tom Markus, Richard Mathews, Conan McCarty, Steve Mehmert, Scott D. Nielson, K. Lype O'Dell, Trevor H. Olsen, Patrick Page, Robert Paterson, Britt Sady, Sam Stewart, David Valenza, Myk Watford, Craig Wroe.
**1940'S RADIO HOUR;** Director, Richard Russell Ramos; Musical Director, James Prigmore; Set Designer, Peter Harrison; Costume Designer, Linda Sarver; Lighting Design, Peter L. Willardson; Choreography, Jayne Luke; Production Stage Manager, John W. Caywood, Jr.; Stage Manager, D. Dale Dean CAST: Christopher Borg, Alan Brodine, John Guerrasio, Rebecca Holt, Stacy Todd Holt, Alfred Lakeman, Richard Mathews, Trevor H. Olsen, Jill Patton, Amelia Prentice, James Prigmore, Richard Scott, Mone Walton, Craig Wroe.
**IRMA VEP;** Director, John W. Caywood, Jr.; Set Designer, George Maxwell; Costume Designer, David C. Paulin; Lighting Design, Angelo O'Dierno; Stage Manager, Barbara Rollins. CAST: Davis Hall, Craig Wroe
**UNCLE VANYA;** Director, Charles Morey; Original Music Composed by James Prigmore, Set Designer, K.L. Alberts; Lighting Design, Peter L. Willardson; Production Stage Manager, John W. Caywood, Jr. CAST: Joyce Cohen, Bonnie Durrance-Doyle, Raye Lankford, Rica Martens, Richard Mathews, Robert Peterson, Max Robinson, Richard Scott, Craig Wroe.
**LETTICE & LOVAGE;** Director, Libby Appel; Original Music Composed by James Prigmore; Set Designer, Peter Harrison; Costume Designer, Carol Wells-Day; Lighting Design, Peter L. Willardson, Stage Manager, Barbara Rollins CAST: Mary Bishop, Richard Bowden, Rene Chadwick, Susan Dolan, Rai French, Libby George, Richard Scott, Maribeth Thueson, Jette Halladay, Darrie Lawrence, Richard Mathews, Trevor H. Olsen, Margo Prey, Randy Reys.
**MY FAIR LADY;** Director, Charles Morey; Musical Director, James Prigmore, Set Designer, George Maxwell; Costume Designer, David C. Paulin; Light Design, Richard Winkler; Choreography, Jayne Luke; Production Stage Manager, John W. Caywood, Jr.; Stage Manager, Barbara Rollins. CAST: Sarah Anderson, Dorothy Briggs Arnold, Daniel Baum, Lee Beckstead, Shawn Bender, Carol Call, Margaret Crowell, James Dale, Bonnie Durrance-Doyle, Frank Gerrish, Ann Hamilton, Rebecca Holt, Jim Jansen, Jen Jones, Ann Kittredge, Ann Stewart Mark, Mearle Marsh, Richard Mathews, Hannah Meadows, Patti M. Olsen, Robert Peterson, Richard Scott, Sam Stewart, Sam Smith, Andrew Williams, Debra Woods.

*Robert F. Clayton Photos*

**TOP RIGHT:** "Grapes of Wrath" company
**CENTER:** Mone Walton, Trevor H. Olsen, Amelia Prentice, Stacey Todd Holt in "1940's Radio Hour"
**RIGHT:** Craig Wroe, Davis Hall in "Irma Vep"

176

Paul Bates, Mary Alice in "A Sunbeam"

Alvin Epstein, Mark Rylance, Michael Rudko, Thomas Derrah in "Hamlet"

# PITTSBURGH PUBLIC THEATER

Pittsburgh, Pennsylvania
Seventeenth Season
October 10, 1991 - July 19, 1992

oducing Director, William T. Gardner; Managing Director, Dan Fallon; Technical
rector, A.D. Carson; Assistant to Producing Director, Les Kniskern; Costume
anager, Dolores Guertin; Public Relations, Elvira DiPaolo, Nancy Gleason;
arketing Director, Rosalind Ruch

## PRODUCTIONS & CASTS

SUNBEAM by John Henry Redwood; Director, Claude Purdy; Sets, James D.
ndefur; Costumes, Felix E. Cochren; Lighting, Phil Monat; Stage Manager, Julie
le CAST: Thomas Martell Brimm (Maceo Gilchrist), Mary Alice (Celia Gilchrist),
ble Lee Lester (Melvin McDaniels), Paul Bates (Sol Gilchrist), Dorothy Holland
r. Lefcourt), Rosalyn Coleman (Lynda Knox)
AMLET by Shakespeare; Director, Ron Daniels; Set/Costumes, Antony McDonald;
ghting, Frances Aronson; Music, Claire Van Kampen; Stage Manager, Julie Pyle
ST: Jon David Weigand (Bernardo/Player/Gentleman/Gravedigger), Royal Miller
rancisco/Reynaldo/Fortinbras), Steven Skybell (Horatio), Gustave Johnson
arcellus/Capt./Priest), Miguel Perez (Ghost of Hamlet's Father), Mark Metcalf
laudius), Jeremy Geidt (Voltemand/Gravedigger), Derek Smith (Laertes), Alvin
stein (Polonius), Mark Rylance (Hamlet), Christine Estabrook (Gertrude), Stephanie
th (Ophelia), Thomas Derrah (Rosencrantz/Osric), Michael Rudko (Guildenstern),
ndy Buckley (Player Queen), Ponny Conomos, James Cook, Thom Deventhal,
rol Ferguson, Christopher Hutchison, Donald Marshall, Americus Rocco, Charles
resinic
DO! I DO!; with Music by Harvey Schmidt; Lyrics/Book, Tom Jones; Director,
aureen Heffernen; Musical Director, Nathan Hurwitz; Choreography, David
anstreet; Sets, Ray Recht; Costumes, Michael J. Cesario; Lighting, Phil Monat;
age Manager, Jane Rothman CAST: Anthony Cummings, Ann Kittredge
IREE SISTERS by Chekhov; Adaptation, Corinne Jacker; Director, Bill Garner;
ts, Charles E. McCarry; Lighting, Brian MacDevitt; Costumes, Laura Crow; Stage
anager, Julie Pyle CAST: Caryn West (Olga), Susan J. Coon (Irina), Helena Ruoti
tasha), William Jay Marshall (Chebutykin), Lance Lewman (Baron), Kevin
novan (Afisa), Eugenia Rawls (Anfisa), William Thunhurst (Ferapont), Kenneth
eseroll (Vershinin), Rob Gomes (Andrei), Larry John Meyers (Kulygin), Catherine
tterfield (Natasha), Christopher Hutchison (Fedotik), Thom Delventhal (Rodé),
lleen Delaney (Maid)
IE COCKTAIL HOUR by A.R. Gurney; Director, Peter Bennett; Set, Gary
glish; Costumes, Laura Crow; Lighting, Andrew David Ostrowski, Stage Manager,
d Noel CAST: Burt Edwards (Bradley), Mark Hofmaier (John), Kim Hunter
nn), Margery Shaw (Nina)
MOON FOR THE MISBEGOTTEN by Eugene O'Neill; Director, Lee
nkowich; Sets, Anne Mundell; Lighting, Phil Monat; Costumes, Barbara Anderson;
age Manager, Julie Pyle CAST: Caryn West (Josie), Christopher R. Hutchison
like Hogan), Larry John Meyers (Phil), Tom Atkins (James Tyrone, Jr.), Michael
rns (Harder)
IE SUM OF US by David Stevens; Director, Marshall W. Mason; Sets, John Lee
atty; Costumes, Laura Crow; Lighting, Mal Sturchio; Stage Manager, Fred Noel
ST: Jordan Mott (Jeff), Russel Lunday (Harry), Anthony Meindl (Greg), Pamela
nlap (Joyce)

*Ric Evans, Gerry Goodstein Photos*

Helena Ruoti, Susan J. Coon, Caryn West in "Three Sisters"

Tom Atkins, Caryn West in "Moon for the Misbegotten"

# PLAYHOUSE THEATER COMPANY

Pittsburgh, Pennsylvania

**ME AND MY GIRL;** Book and Lyrics by L. Arthur Rose and Douglas Furber; Music by Noel Gay; Book revised by Stephen Fry (with Mike Ockrent); Directed by Steve Pudenz; Choreographed by Donna Drake; Scenery by Dick Block; Costumes by Don DiFonso; Lighting by Cindy Limauro; Musical Director, Nathan Hurwitz; Properties by Tracey Evans; Production Stage Manager, Eric Sprosty   CAST: Jonathan Beck Reed, Linda Gabler, Steve Pudenz, Pam Klinger, Barbara Porteus, Paul Depasquale, Mark Agnes, Ralston Hill, E. Bruce Hill, Etta Cox, Toni Schlemmer
**NOISES OFF** by Michael Frayn; Directed by Raymond Laine; Scenery by Anne Mundell; Costumes by Don DiFonso; Lighting by William O'Donnell; Assistant Director, Sheila McKenna; Properties by Tracey Evans; Production Stage Manager, Eric Sprosty   CAST: Hugh Alexander Rose, William Duncan, Linda Holeva, Susan McGregor-Laine, Tom J. Schaller, Robin Walsh, Paul Mochnick, Zachary Mott, Judy Ferguson Small
**BIG RIVER The Adventures of Huckleberry Finn;** Book by William Hauptman; Music and Lyrics by Roger Miller; Directed and Choreographed by Edie Cowan; Scenery by Anne Mundell; Costumes by Joan Markert; Lighting by Jennifer Ford; Musical Director, Nathan Hurwitz; Assistant Director, Teri McIntyre; Dialect Coach, Kathryn Aronson; Properties by Tracey Evans; Production Stage Manager, Eric Sprosty, Jon Bicsey, Jon Cannard, Renata Carreon, Kurt Cerny, Lanene Charters, Tome Cousin, Anthony Dixon, Sandra Dowe, Robert DuSold, Joe Dwyre, Melissa Eddy, Steve Geyer, Jeff Howell, James Judy, Seana Kate Livingston, Gavan Pamer, Lisa Panza, Angelo Reid, Stacey Robinson, Ron Lee Savin, Christopher Sciullo, Mark Thompson, Dixie Tymitz, Rema Webb

*John Fobes Photos*

**ABOVE: Gavan Pamer, Stacey Robinson in "Big River"**

# PLAYMAKERS REPERTORY COMPANY

Chapel Hill, North Carolina
September 14, 1991 - May 10, 1992

Executive Producer, Milly S. Barranger; Artistic Director, David Hammon; Administrative Director, Mary Robin Wells; Production Manager, Michael Roll; Sets and Costumes, Sharon K. Campbell, McKay Coble, Bobbi Owen; Sound, Pan Emerson; Stage Manager, Robert D. Russo; Assistant Stage Manager, Tanya Strickland; Voice Coach, Nancy Lane; Movement Coach, Craig Turner; Dramat; Adam Versenyi; Development, Gary Gambrell; Press and Marketing, Sharon Bro; Business Manager, Jack R. Bowen; Company Manager, Donna Bost Heins; Audie; Development Coordinator, Christopher Briggs, Box Office Manager, Stepha; Draper; Assistant Box Office Manager, Paul Goodson.
RESIDENT COMPANY: Gene Alper, Timothy Altmeyer, Elizabeth Anderson, D; Corvinus, Ray Dooley, Eve Eaton, Mark Ransom Eis, Barbara Ellingson, Step; Haggerty, Brett Halna du Fretay, Charles McIver, Connan Morrissey, Ronda Mus; Emily Newman, Donna Peters, Susanna Rinehart, Andrew Sellon, Alexander Yan; Stephano, Kristine Watt.
GUEST ARTISTS: Actors: Avril Gentles, Matthew Lewis, Anderson Matthews, M; O'Brady, Ron Parady, Judith Roberts, Ken Strong, Jeff Woodman. Director; William Woodman, Kathryn Long, Martin L. Platt. Designers: Bill Clarke, Mar; Dilliard, Mary Louise Geiger, Russell Parkman, Anita C. Stewart, Robert Wierzel.

**PRODUCTIONS:** Charles Dickens' *HARD TIMES*, adapted by Stephen Jeffre; Director, David Hammond. *A SHAYNA MAIDEL* by Barbara Lebow; Director, R; Dooley. *THE NUTCRACKER: A PLAY*, adapted from the stories of E.T.A. Hoffma; by David Hammond; Director, David Hammond. Edward Albee's *WHO'S AFR; OF VIRGINIA WOOLF?;* Director, William Woodman. *ELEEMOSYNARY* by L; Blessing; Director, Kathryn Long. *TWELFTH NIGHT* by William Shakespea; Director, Martin L. Platt.

*Kevin Keister Photos*

**TOP LEFT: Connan Morrissey, Mary O'Brady in "A Shayna Maidel";**
**BOTTOM: Connan Morrissey, Gene Alper, Ray Dooley in "Nutcracke;**

178

Bruce Norris in "The Actor Retires"

# REMAINS THEATRE

Chicago, Illinois

Artistic Director, Larry Sloan; Producing Director, R.P. Sekon; Ensemble Directors, Amy Morton, William Peterson; Operations Director, Christian Peterson; Development Director, Laura Samson; General Manager, Janis Post; Public Relations Director, Wendy Jacobson

## PRODUCTIONS & CASTS

**THE ACTOR RETIRES** (World Premiere) by Bruce Norris; Director, Mary Zimmerman; Sound, Eric Huffman; Stage Manager, Richard Lundy  CAST: Bruce Norris (The Actor), Martha Lavey (The Actor's Girlfriend/The Agent/The Casting Assist./The Script Girl/The Actor's Sister), Christopher Donahue (The Businessman/The Serious Actor/The Casting Agent), David Kersnar (The Actor's Friend/The Director)
 A comedy performed without intermission chronicling the actor's repeated failed attempts to retire from his life in theatre, film and tv.
**THE CHICAGO CONSPIRACY TRIAL** by Ron Sossi and Frank Condon; Director, Mr. Condon; Sets/Lighting, Kevin Snow; Costumes, Sraa Davidson; Sound/Musical Direction, Michael Bodeen; Stage Manager, Mary McAuliffe  CAST: Daniel Blinkoff (Tom Hayden), Magica Bottari (Spectator), Ted Gerald Brown (Seale's Custodian), Dale Calandra (Allen Ginsberg), Ruth Carter (Spectator), Deane Clark (Richard Grandholm/James B. Hatlin), Del Close (David Dellinger), Scott Cummins (Robert Connelly/Robert Peterson), David Geiselhart (Marshal), Kate Gleason (Kristi A. King/Spectator), Reginald C. Hayes (Black Panther), Chris Hogan (John Froines), Gary Houston (Thomas Aquinas Foran), Bruce Jarchow (William Kunstler), Scott Lowell (Rennie Davis), Geoffrey MacKinnon (Marshall Dobrowski), Brian Mendes (Jerry Rubin), George Murdock (Judge Julius Hoffman), Larry Newman, Jr. (Richard G. Shultz), Jill Nicholson (Reporter), David Alan Novak (Leonard Weinglass), Michael Novak (Lee Weiner), David Pasquesi (Abbie Hoffman), Lindsay Porter (Spectator), Joel Pownall (Sgt. Bailey/Mayor Daley), Bob Prado (Marshal), Kent Reed (David E. Stahl), Peter Reinemann (William Albright), Molly Reynolds (Barbara Braddock), Matt Robison (Marshal), Margie Rynearson (Ruth Peterson), Tony Sacre, Britton Walker (Spectators), Ed Wheeler (Bobby Seale), Gary Wilmes (Stewart Albert)
 A theatrical arrangement of the original trial transcripts.
**MISHUGANISMO;** Written and Performed by Susan Nussbaum; Director, Mike Nussbaum; Design, Sraa Davidson; Sound, Christian Petersen; Lighting/Stage Manager, Richard Lundy
**LAUGHTER IN THE DARK** by Vladimir Nabokov; Adaptation/Direction, Mary Zimmerman; Sets, John Musial; Costumes, Sarah J. Holden; Lighting, Kenneth Moore; Sound/Music, Michael Bodeen; Stage Manager, Mary McAuliffe  CAST: Gerry Becker (Albinus), Thomas Carroll (Dr. Lampert/Others), David Catlin (Otto), Marilyn Dodds Frank (Dorianna Karenina), Christopher Donahue (Axel Rex), Martha Lavey (Elisabeth), Oriana Mastro (Irma), Rebecca Melsky (Irma), David Alan Novak (Udo Conrad/Others), Craig Spidle (Paul), Heidi Stillman (Margot Peters), Jim True (Kaspar/Others)
**I WANT SOMEONE TO EAT CHEESE WITH;** Written and Performed by Jeff Garlin; Director, Mick Napier; Stage Manager, Janis Post
**ONCE IN DOUBT;** Written and Directed by Raymond J. Barry; Sets/Lighting, Kevin Snow; Costumes, Laura Cunningham; Sound, Christian Petersen; Stage Manager, Patty Lyons  CAST: William Petersen (Harry), Amy Morton (Flo), Gerry Becker (Mr. Wagner)

*Mary Zimmerman, Liz Lauren Photos*

**William Petersen, Amy Morton in "Once in Doubt"**
**CENTER: Christopher Donahue, Heidi Stillman in "Laughter in the Dark"**

179

# REPERTORY THEATRE OF ST. LOUIS

St. Louis, Missouri
September 4, 1991 - April 12, 1992

Artistic Director, Steven Woolf; Managing Director, Mark D. Bernstein

## PRODUCTIONS & CASTS

**CYRANO** by Edmond Rostand; Translation Brian W. Hooker; Director, Martin L. Platt; Sets, David Crank; Costumes, Alan Armstrong; Lighting, Peter E. Sargeant; Stage Manager, Glenn Dunn   CAST: Greg Thornton (Cyrano), Lisa Benedict (Roxanne), David Harum (de Neuvillette), John-Frederick Jones (de Guiche), A.D. Cover (Ragueneau), Geoffrey Beauchamp (le Bret), Bruce Longworth, Danny Robinson Clark, Shaun Hanson, Steven Lee Ramshur, Christopher, E. Sanders, David B. Heuvelman, Christopher Reilly, Sara Zahendra, Alan Clarey, Christian Malmin, John Milligan, Jodie Lynne McClintock, Whit Reichert, Donald Christopher, Kermit Brown, Michael Agnew, Kari Ely, Christine Hagel, Jean Lange, Ian Christopher, Randle Roper, Patti Lewis, Jim Dickerson, Jack Lippard, Jeff Stockberger, Tim Steiner, Roldan Lopez, Ian Novak, James R. Wehn, Bill Church, Christine Brooks, Rachel B. Newhouse, Coco Sansoni, Gregory Alan Iken, Amanda Sher

**OTHER PEOPLE'S MONEY** by Jerry Sterner; Director, Steve Woolf; Sets, Carolyn L. Ross; Costumes, Holly Poe Durbin; Lighting, Max De Volder; Stage Manager, T.R. Martin   CAST: William Keeler (Coles), Addison Powell (Jorgenson), Tony Hoty (Garfinkle), Mary Fogarty (Bea), Glynis Bell (Kate)

**THE 1940's RADIO HOUR** by Walton Jones; Director, John Going; Choreography, Rob Marshall; Musical Director, Byron Grant; Sets, John Roslevich Jr.; Costumes, Dorothy L. Marshall; Lighting, Peter E. Sargent; Stage Manager, Glenn Dunn   CAST: Irv Ziff (Pops), Paul Harmen (Johnny), Chad Kraus (Stanley), Tony Hoty (Lou), Rob Dorn (Wally), Peter Shawn (Clifton), Christa Germanson (Connie), Dorothy Stanley (Ginger), Kevin Chamberlin (Neal), Richard Gervais (B.J.), Judy McLane (Ann), Vanessa Shaw (Geneva), Bill Ullman (Biff)

**MISS EVERS' BOYS** by David Feldshuh; Director, Libby Appel; Music/Movement, Doris J. Bennett-Glasper; Sets, Joel Fontaine; Costumes, Arthur Ridley; Lighting, Robert Peterson; Stage Manager, T.R. Martin   CAST: Leah Maddrie (Eunice), Roy R. Wilson (Willie), Tyrone Wilson (Caleb), Francaswell Hyman (Hodman), William Hall Jr. (Ben), Jim Abele (Douglas), Ron Himes (Brodus)

**A VIEW FROM THE BRIDGE** by Arthur Miller; Director, Edward Stern; Sets, John Jensen; Costumes, Dorothy L. Marshall; Lighting, Rob Murphy; Music, Larry Bailey; Stage Manager, Glenn Dunn   CAST: Jerry Russo (Louis), Whit Reichert (Mike), Joneal Joplin (Alfieri), Robert Elliot (Eddie), Candace Dian Leverett (Catherine), Carol Schultz (Beatrice), Martino Pistone (Marco), Ian Christopher (Tony Immigration), Chris Hietikko (Rondolpho), Peter Hynds (Immigration), Steve Ramshur, Eddie Thompson (Submarines), Todd Luethans (Lipari), Jeanette Myers (Mrs. Lipari)

**ALMOST SEPTEMBER** with Music by Steven Lutvak; Lyrics/Book, David Schechter; Mr. Lutvak; Conception/Direction, Mr. Schechter; Musical Director, Wendy Bobbitt; Orchestrations, Joseph Church, Lawrence Yurman; Sets, John Ezell; Costumes, John Carver Sullivan; Lighting, Max De Volder; Stage Manager, T.R. Martin   CAST: Scott Schafer (Eustace), Nancy Opel (Theodora), Philip Lehl (Alexander), Skip Lackey (Herbert), Debbie Laumand (Hermione), Amanda Butterbaugh (Molly), Alastair Mole

**OKIBOJI** by Conrad Bishop and Elizabeth Fuller; Director, Susan Gregg; Sets/costumes, Arthur Ridley; Lighting, Mark P. Wilson; Stage Manager, Champe Leary   CAST: Dawn Didawick (Mag), Jodie Lynne McClintock (Rae)

**THE SWAN** by Elizabeth Egloff; Director, Susan Gregg; Sets/Lighting, Dale F. Jordan; Costumes, John Carver Sullivan; Music, Stephen Burnes Kessler; Stage Manager, Champe Leary   CAST: Sherry Skinker (Dora), Bruce Longworth (Kevin), Richard Victor Esvang (Bill)

**MARCH OF THE FALSETTOS and FALSETTOLAND** with Music/Lyrics by William Finn; Book, Mr. Finn, James Lapine; Director/Choreography, Pamela Hunt; Musical Director, Larry Pressgrove; Sets, Daniel Robinson; Costumes, J. Bruce Summers; Lighting, Peter Sargent; Stage Manager, Champe Leary   CAST: Tim Ewing (Marvin), Carol Dilley (Trina), Adam Harris (Jason), Ray Benson (Whizzer), Jack Cirillo (Mendel), Kathy Morath (Dr. Charlotte), Tia Speros (Cordelia)

*Judy Andrews Photos*

**Top:** Mary Fogarty, William Keller, Tony Hoty, Addison Powell in
"Other People's Money"
**Second Photo:** Fracaswell Hyman, Roy R. Wilson, William Hall Jr.,
Tyrone Wilson, Leah Maddrie in "Miss Ever's Boys"
**Third Photo:** Skip Lackey, Nancy Opel, Debbie Laumand in
"Almost September"
**Right:** Jack Cirillo, Ray Benson, Tim Ewing, Adam Harris in
"March of the Falsettos"

# SAN DIEGO REPERTORY THEATRE

San Diego, California

n Woodhouse, Producing Director; Adrian W. Stewart, Managing Director; glas Jacobs, Artistic Director; Richard Robertson, Marketing Director; Joan ter, Assoicate Producer; Kirsten Brandt, Communications and Development ector; John Redman, General Production Manager; Todd Salovey, Associate stic Director

## PRODUCTIONS & CASTS

**LL LIFE** by Emily Mann. CAST: Bill Maass, Darla Cash and Anasa Briggs ves.

**IN'T YO' UNCLE** by Robert Alexander. CAST: Sharon Lockwood, B.W. azalez, Michael Sullivan, Edris Cooper, Lonnie Ford, Paul K. Killam, Jim Griffiths, ot Kavee, Guy Totaro, Keiko Shimosato, Greta R. Bart, Dred Scott, and Dan Hart.

**ALE OF TWO CITIES** by Everett Quinton. CAST: Ron Campbell.

**NGDON SQUARE** by Maria Ines Fornes. CAST: Elizabeth Clemens, Julian ez-Morillas, Bray Poor, Richard Ortega, Giselle Rubino, Myriam Tubert, Andres real, and Anthony Wineski.

**BY'S BUCKET OF BLOOD** by Julie Hebert. CAST: Amanda White, Natalie man, Rick Sparks, Deborah Van Valkenburgh, Antonio (T.J.) Johnson, Ken ant, Tammy Casey, Cynthia Hammond, Definique Juniel, Damon Lamont, and ris White.

**RANDOLINA** by Carlo Goldoni, adapted by Melissa Cooper. CAST: Leon ger, Ollie Nash, Bray Poor, Kim McCallum, Tracey A. Leigh, and Peter J. Smith.

**E WOMEN** by Clare Booth Luce. CAST: Roxane Carrasco, Darla Cash, Linda tro, Barbara Chisholm, Sandie Church, Susan Gelman, Eleni Kelakos, Dochia ox, Sandra L'Italien, Linda Libby, Susy McWilliams, Amber Rae, Karen June chez, Joan Schirle, Regina Byrd Smith, Lorna Raver, and Marta Zekan.

**EST ARTISTS THIS SEASON:** San Francisco Mime Troupe, Maria Irene nes, and Anne Bogart.

Spiro Veloudos, Anne-Marie Cusson in
"Other People's Money"

# SEACOAST REPERTORY COMPANY

Portsmouth, New Hampshire

Directors, Roy M. Rogosin, Nancy Saklad, Eileen Rogosin, Scott Severence, Spiro Veloudos; Sets, Gary Newton, Tom St. Laurent, Susan Van Schaick; Costumes, Celinda English, Amanda Klein, Barbara Newton; Lighting, Nancy Collings, Ellen Gould, Scott Lozier; Stage Managers, Bobby Iyer, Bobby Fonacier; Executive Assistant, Jean Benda

**PRODUCTIONS:** *OTHER PEOPLE'S MONEY, OLIVER*

*Deb Cram Photos*

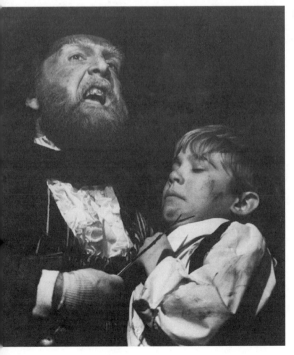

**LEFT: Bill Humphreys, Case Prince in "Oliver"**

**Top Left:** Kimiko Cazanov, David Morse in "Redwood Curtain"
**Top Right:** Kevin Tighe, Barbara Dirickson in "Hedda Gabler"
**Right:** William Biff McGuire in "Twelve Night"

# SEATTLE REPERTORY THEATRE

Seattle, Washington

Artistic Director, Daniel Sullivan; Managing Director, Benjamin Moore; Associate Artistic Director, Douglas Hughes; Artistic Associate/Dramaturg, Mary Bly; Artistic Administrator, Peggy Scales; Public Relations, M. Mark Bocek: Directors, Douglas Hughes, David Saint, Marshall Mason, Nagle Jackson, Mark Brokaw, Dan Sullivan, Robin Lynn Smith.

**PRODUCTIONS:** *TWELFTH NIGHT* by William Shakespeare; *M. BUTTERFLY* by David Henry Hwang; *REDWOOD CURTAIN* (World Premiere) by Lanford Wilson; *WHEN WE ARE MARRIED* by J.B. Priestley; *HEDDA GABLER* by Henrik Ibsen; *THE GOOD TIMES ARE KILLING ME* by Lynda Barry; *THE LISBON TRAVIATA* by Terrence McNally; *INSPECTING CAROL* (World Premiere) by Daniel Sullivan & The Resident Acting Company; *MARVIN'S ROOM* by Scott McPherson.

*Chris Bennion Photos*

# STUDIO ARENA THEATRE

Buffalo, New York
Twenty-seventh Season
September 22, 1991 - May 31, 1992

istic Director, David Frank/Gavin Cameron-Webb; Executive Director, Raymond
nnard; Associate Artistic Director/Dramaturg, Kathryn Long; Marketing Director,
urtney J. Walsh; Development Director, Anne E. Hayes; Press, Kelli G. Bocock,
sabeth Fleshler

## PRODUCTIONS & CASTS

**VEET 'N' HOT IN HARLEM: A Harold Arlen Revue**; Conception/Direction,
bert Elliot Cohen; Musical Director/Orchestrations, M. Michael Fauss;
oreography, Evelyn Thomas, Harold Nicholas; Sets, John Bonard Wilson;
stumes, Judy Dearing; Lighting, Peter Kaczorowski CAST: Keith Davis, Eugene
ming, Julia Lema, Monica Pège, Gwen Stewart

**HER PEOPLE'S MONEY** by Jerry Sterner; Director, Kathryn Long; Sets, Steven
rry; Costumes, Lauren K. Lambie; Lighting, Nancy Schertler; Music, Robert
lkman; Stage Manager, Sally Ann Wood CAST: Frank Hankey (Coles), Leon B.
vens (Jorgenson), John Camera (Garfinkle), Lydia Bruce (Bea), Katherine Leask
ate)

**CHRISTMAS CAROL** by Dickens; Adaptation, Amlin Gray; Director, David
nk; Sets/Lighting, Paul Wonsek; Costumes, Mary Ann Powell; Choreography,
nda H. Swiniuch; Stage Manager, Glenn Bruner CAST: Robert Spencer
rooge), Kevin Donovan, William Gonta, Saul Elkin, Robertson Carricart, Arn
einer, Jane Macfie, Chris Vasquez, Meghan Rose Krank, Roma Maffia, Patty
oper, Lacey Saunders, Amber Rae Sulick, Bobby Dela Plante, Ali Raza, Hope Olani
ve, Stacy Peters, Justin Jarosz, Jay Yeagle, Philip Jarosz, Sebastian Nicholas Pratt,
uren-Marie Pratt, Robin Teleford, Thane Schulz, Ron Veiders, Adrian Ingersoll,
n Kiouses

**ATCH ME IF YOU CAN** by Jack Weinstock and Willie Gilbert; Director,
ederick King Keller; Sets, Gary Eckhart; Costumes, Lauren K. Lambie; Lighting,
ul Wonsek; Stage Manager, Sally Ann Wood CAST: Terrell Anthony (Daniel),
chael Schacht (Levine), Vincent O'Neill (Kelleher), Pamela Gray (Elizabeth), Arn
einer (Sidney), Margret Kinney (The Woman), Brad Bellamy (Everett Parker, Jr.)

**NCES** by August Wilson; Director, Edward G. Smith; Sets, Felix E. Cochren;
stumes, Donna Massimo; Lighting, Dennis Parichy; Stage Manager, Glenn Bruner
ST: Stephen McKinley Henderson (Troy), Billy Ray Tyson (Bono), Elain Graham
ose), Stanley Earl Harrison (Lyons), Quinton Cockrell (Gabriel), French Napier
ory), Jessica Lynn Pratt/Lacey Saunders (Raynell)

**E IMMIGRANT: A Hamilton County Album**; Conceived by Mark Harelik and
ndal Myler; Director, Howard J. Millman; Sets, Kevin Rupnick; Costumes, Maria
rrero; Lighting, Phil Monat; Stage Manager, Sally Ann Wood CAST: David
eitbarth (Haskell), Jayne Houdyshell (Ima), John Sterling Arnold (Milton), Devora
lman (Leah)

**VE LETTERS** by A.R. Gurney; Director, Warren Enters; Set, Gerard P. Vogt;
hting, Dennis Parichy; Stage Manager, Glenn Bruner CASTS: William Daniels &
nnie Bartlett, John Schuck & Tandy Cronyn, Keir Dullea & Bonnie Franklin

*Rand Schuster Photos*

TOP: **Pamela Gray, Terrell Anthony, Michael Schacht in
"Catch Me if You Can"**
CENTER: **Brigid Cleary, Mary Tucker, Becky Woodley, Pamela Orem
in "The Women"**

# THE STUDIO THEATRE

Washington, D.C.
Fourteenth Season

Artistic/Managing Director, Joy Zinoman; Associate Managing Director, Keith Alan
Baker; Public Relations/Marketing Director, Marilyn Newton; Development Director,
Morey Epstein; Dramaturg, Maynard Marshall; Literary Manager, Serge Seiden;
Production Manager, Kathi Lee Redmond; Stage Manager, Serge Seiden

## PRODUCTIONS & CASTS

**WHEN I WAS A GIRL I USED TO SCREAM AND SHOUT** by Sharman
MacDonald; Director, Joy Zinoman; Sets, Russell Metheny; Lighting, Daniel MacLean
Wagner; Costumes, Ric Thomas Rice CAST: Sarah Marshall (Fiona), June Hansen
(Morag), Jennifer Mendenhall (Vari), James Ream (Ewan)
**THE WOMEN** by Clare Booth Luce; Director, John Going; Sets, Russell Methany;
Costumes, Don Newcomb; Lighting, Daniel MacLean Wagner CAST: Julie Bayer
(Jane), Mary A. Tucker (Sylvia), Laura Giannarelli (Nancy), Pamela Orem (Peggy),
Megan Morgan (Edith), Brigid Cleary (Mary), Nancy Paris (Countess), Prudence
Barry (Hairdresser/Saleswoman/Lucy/Dowager), Lois Kelso Hunt
(Hairdresser/Fitter/Maggie/Society Woman), Becky Woodley (Miriam/Model), Robin
Baxter (Olga/Salesgirl/Cutie), Dana Gillespie
(Pedicurist/Model/Timmerback/Cigarette Girl), Kaia Calhoun
(Euphie/Salesgirl/Nurse/Sadie), Dori Legg (Fordyce/Princess/Exercise/Cutie), Kristen
Minor (Little Mary), Joan Durr (Mrs. Morehead), Kimberly Schraf
(Saleswoman/Watts/Society Woman/Helene), Jennifer Mendenhall (Crystal), Beck
Woodley (Model), Meredith Patterson (Debutante)
**THE AMERICAN PLAN** by Richard Greenberg; Director, Rob Barron; Sets, James
Kronzer; Lighting, Daniel MacLean Wagner; Costumes, Helen Q. Huang CAST: Joy
Ehrlich (Lili), James Ream (Nick), Beverly Cosham (Olivia), Arlene Sterne (Eva),
Serge Seiden (Gil)
**THE WIZARD OF HIP or When in Double Slam Dunk**; Written and Performed by
Thomas W. Jones, II; Director, Kenny Leon; Stage Manager, Malik
**FALSETTOLAND** by William Finn
**NOBODY HERE BUT US CHICKENS** by Peter Barnes
**ALFRED AND VICTORIA: A Life** by Donald Freed
**SINCERITY FOREVER** by Mac Wellman

*Joan Marcus, John Long, Ken Cobb, Stan Barouh Photos*

**Joy Ehrlich, James Ream in "American Plan"**

# SYRACUSE STAGE

Syracuse, New York
Eighteenth Season

Producing Artistic Director, Arthur Storch; Managing Director, James A. Clark; Business Director, Diana Coles; Development, Shirley Lockwood; Marketing, Barbara Beckos; Press, Barbara Haas; Company Manager, Peter Sandwall; Literary Coordinator, Howard Kerner; Production Manager, Don Buschmann; Technical Director, William S. Tiesi; Lighting Coordinator, Sandra Schilling; Sound Designer, James Wildman; Properties Coordinator, Dana Baker; Costumer, Maria Marrero.

## PRODUCTIONS & CASTS

**THE COUNTRY WIFE** by William Wycherley; Director, Julianne Boyd; Set, Jim Youmans; Costumes, David C. Woolard; Lighting, Michael Newton Brown; Sound, James Wildman. CAST: Grant Albrecht (Mr. Horner), Kate Arecchi (Servant/Townsperson), Jeff Bell (Servant/Townsperson), Jason Cicci (Servant/Townsperson), Natascia Diaz (Mrs. Squeamish), Michael Elich (Mr. Harcourt), Edith Fischer (Old Lady Squeamish), Louis Fischer (Parson & Clasp), Libby George (Lady Fidget), Davis Hall (Mr. Sparkish), Jaquelyn Hodges (Servant/Townsperson), Ken Kliban (Mr. Pinchwife), Kathleen McCall (Mrs. Alithea), Diane McLaughlin (Servant/Townsperson), William Pitts (A Quack), David Ponting (Sir Jasper Fidget), Stephanie Seeley (Mrs. Dainty Fidget), Brian Stepanek (Head Servant), Maggie Topkis (Lucy, Alithea's Maid), Charles Tuthill (Mr. Dorilant), Susan Wands (Mrs. Margery Pinchwife).

**TEA** by Velina Hasu Houston; Director, Julianne Boyd; Set, Craig Lathrop; Costumes, C.L. Hunley; Lighting, Victor En Yu Tan; Sound, Bruce Ellman. CAST: Takayo Fischer (Setsuko Banks), Susan Haruye Ioka (Teruko MacKenzie), Dian Kobayashi (Atsuko Yamamoto), Jeanne Sakata (Himiko Hamilton), Diana Tanaka (Chizuye Juarez).

**ANDROCLES AND THE LION** By George Bernard Shaw; Director, Arthur Storch; Set, Victor A. Becker; Costumes, Pamela Scofield; Lighting, Phil Monat; Sound, James Wildman; Fight-Choreographer, Patrick Mulcahy. CAST: Andrew Butler (A Soldier), Jennifer Catney (Bag Lady/Courtesan), Michael Cherniak (Beggar Child), Gerardine Clark (Magaera), Brian Curley (A Christian), Peter DelGiornio (A Christian), Alaina Dyne (Beggar Child), Ben Elms (A Soldier), Kevin Grastorf (A Soldier), Bari Hochwald (Lavinia), Mark Hutchison (Secutor), John Innes (Caesar), Jane Keegan (A Christian), Victor Lazarow (Lentulus), Michael Jane Keegan (A Christian), Victor Lazarow (Lentulus), Michael Jane Keegan (A Christian), Victor Lazarow (Lentulus), Michael Montgomery (Soldiers), Gerard Moses (Spintho), Patrick Mulcahy (Retiarius), Patrick O'Connor (Menagerie Keeper), Michael James Reed (Captain), Mark Roth (Metellus), Ann M. Rott (A Christian), Anthony Salatino (The Lion), Andrew Sgroi (Christian/Lion Understudy), Brian Stepanek (Veteran), David Teschendorf (Ferrovius), James E. Tookle (A Christian), Tim Wheeler (Centurion), William Youmans (Androcles), Joe Zaloom (Editor).

**THE SUM OF US** by David Stevens; Director, Jamie Brown; Set, James Noone; Costumes, Randall E. Klein; Lighting, Sandra Schilling; Sound, James Wildman. CAST: James Doerr (Dad), Susanne Marley (Joyce), Jeffrey Plunkett (Greg), Mitchell Riggs (Jeff).

**THE IMMIGRANT** by Mark Harelik; Director, Howard Millman; Set, Kevin Rupnick; Costumes, Maria Marrero; Lighting, Phil Monat; Sound and Projection, Jeffrey Karoff. CAST: John Sterling Arnold (Milton Perry), David Brietbarth (Haskell Harelik), Jayne Houdyshell (Ima Perry),, Devora Millman (Leah Harelike).

**LOVE LETTERS** by A.R. Gurney; Director, Arthur Storch; Costumes, Maria Marrero; Lighting, Sandra Schilling; Sound James Wildman. CAST: Virginia Kiser (Melissa Gardner), Arthur Storch (Andrew Makepeace Ladd III).

*Lawrence Mason Jr. Photos*

RIGHT: (top) John Innes, Victor Lazarow, Mark Roth in "Androcles and the Lion"
CENTER: Jeanne Sakata, Takayo Fischer in "Tea"
TOP: James Doerr, Mitchell Riggs in "Sum of Us"

Adrian Latourelle, Brian Thompson, Louis Lotorto
in "Orphans"
TOP RIGHT: Tim McCuen Piggee in "Christmas Carol"
RIGHT: Lizanne Schader, Cynthis Jones in "A...My Name is Alice"
BOTTOM: Brad Curtis, Rachel Coloff, Peggy O'Connell, Wesley Rice in
"Guys and Dolls"

# TACOMA ACTORS GUILD

Tacoma, Washington

Artistic Director, Bruce K. Sevy; Managing Director, Kate Haas; Production Manager, Hal Meng; Company/Literary Manager, Nancy Hoadley; Public Relations/Marketing, Elizabeth Tudor-Scharnhorst; Development Director, Karen Dietz; Box Office Manager, Kelly Gardner; Stage Managers, Hal Meng, Liisa Talso; Lighting Designer, Robert A. Jones; Sound Designer, Tom Utterback; Technical Director, Will Rayburne; Stage Directors, Bruce K. Sevy, John Monteith, Christine Sumption, William Becvar, Beth Henley; Musical Directors, Teresa Metzger, Richard Gray; Choreographers, Jayne Muirhead, Stephen Terrell; Set Designers, Carey Wong, Jeff Konja, Peggy McDonald, Bill Forrester; Costume Designers, Ron Erickson, Jeanne Arnold, Josie Gardner; Lighting Designers, Patty Mathieu, Michael Wellborn.

### PRODUCTIONS & CASTS

**LEND ME A TENOR** by Ken Ludwig, CAST: Todd Jamieson, Jane Jones, Brian Thompson, Bill Ontiveros, Tina Marie Goff, Andrew Wilder, Kamella Tate, Zoaunne LeRoy.
**STRAIGHT ARROWS;** Written and performed by Colleen Dodson; Stage Manager, Frank Meiman
**CHRISTMAS CAROL;** Adaptation by Chad Henry, from the novel by Charles Dickens; CAST: C.R. Gardner, Laura Kenney, Justin Davis, Elwood Keith, Melinda Deane, Timothy McCuen Piggee, Andrew DeRycke, Charles Leggett, Diana Hedgepeth, Joshua Wingerter, Todd Jamieson, Jessica Wallenfels, Jane Jones.
**A... MY NAME IS ALICE;** Conceived by Joan Micklin Silver and Julianne Boyd; CAST: Cynthia Jones, Lizanne Schader, Melany Lynn Bell, Laura Kenney, Joanne Klein.
**ORPHANS** by Lyle Kessler; CAST: Adrian Latourelle, Louis Lotorto, Brian Thompson.
**RUMORS** by Neil Simon; CAST: Victoria Otto, Clayton Corzatte, Eric Ray Anderson, Susan Corzatte, Joanne Klein, Stephanie Shine, David Silverman, Elwood Keith, David Mong, Claire Sigman
**GUYS AND DOLLS;** Music and Lyrics by Frank Loesser; Book Jo Swerling & Abe Burrows; Based on a story and characters by Damon Runyon; CAST: Brad Curtis, Rachel Coloff, Wesley Rice, Peggy O'Connell, Floyd Van Buskirk, Dee Dee Van Zyl, David Silverman, Patricia Britton, Eric Ray Anderson, Jane Jones, Kevin Loomis, Tanya Perkins, John Lowrie, Chad Henry, Carroll Hovland, Thomas Arthur Grant, Stephen Terrell, Frank Joachimsthaler, Mark Padgett, Liz McCarthy, Michael Sharon, Kevin Hadley, Eric Jensen

*Fred Andrews, Gary Smith Photos*

# THEATRE THREE

Dallas, Texas
Thirtieth Season

Norma Young, Founding/Artistic Director; Jac Alder, Executive Producer-Director; Lora Hinson, Managing Director; Laurence O'Dwyer, Associate Director; Gary Yawn, Publicist; Tristan Wilson, Production Manager; Terry Dobson, Musical Director, Assistant to Mr. Alder; Linda Blase, Lighting Designer; Diana Figueroa Story, Costumer; J. Kyle Hannah, Journeyman; Nancy Losey, Intern.

## PRODUCTIONS & CASTS

**CAROLE COOK IN DRESS UP;** Directed by Tom Troupe; Musical Accompaniment by Terry Dobson; Scenic Design by Cheryl Denson; Lighting Design by Linda Blase; Sound Design & Technical Director, Tristan Wilson; Production Stage Manager, Terry Tittle Holman.

**STRINGBEAN** by Lanie Robertson; Directed by Glenn Casale; Musical Director and Arranger, Danny Holgate; CAST: Leslie Uggams; Akin Babatunde; Grover Coulson, Jr.; John S. Davies; Billy Jones; Connie Nelson; Dean Nolen; Jason Pratt; Michael Cal Stewart; Scenic Design, Harland Wright; Lighting Design, Linda Blase; Costume Design, Diana Figueroa Story; Sound Effects & Technical Director, Tristan Wilson; Production Stage Manager, Terry Tittle Holman (World Premiere)

**WAITING FOR GODOT** by Samuel Beckett; Directed by Norma Young; featuring Laurence O'Dwyer; Terry Vandivort; Hugh Feagin; John Rainone; Elliot Figg; Lighting Design by Linda Blase; Scenic Design by Jac Alder & Cheryl Denson; Costume Design by Cheryl Denson; Sound Design & Technical Director, Tristan Wilson; Production Stage Manager, Jac Alder; Production Assistant, J. Kyle Hannah.

**HEARTBEATS;** Book, Music and Lyrics by Amanda McBroom; created by Amanda McBroom and Bill Castellino; Directed by Jac Alder; Musical Direction by Terry Dobson; Musical Arrangements by Jerry Sternbach; Choreography by Fern Tresvan-Seibles; Lighting Design by Linda Blase; Scenic and Costume Design by Cheryl Denson; Wig & Hair Design by Russell Latham; Sound Design and Technical Director, Tristan Wilson; Production Stage Manager, Laurence O'Dwyer; Production Assistant, Nancy Losey; featuring Sally Soldo; John Taylor, Amy Mills, Michael Justis; Julie Lea Johnson; Paul Taylor.

**THE HEIDI CHRONICLES** by Wendy Wasserstein; Directed by Cheryl Denson; featuring Cheryl Norris; Mary Anna Austin; Scott Everhart; Linda Ford; Jim Jorgensen; Johna Sprizzo; Paul Tigue; Peggy Pharr Wilson; Scenic Design by Wade J. Giampa; Costume Design by Diana Figueroa Story; Lighting Design by Linda Blase; Wig & Hair Design by Russell Latham; Sound Design and Technical Director, Tristan Wilson; Production Stage Manager, Laurence O'Dwyer; Production Assistant, Nancy Losey; Assistant to the Director, Peggy Kruger.

**HOMEWARD BOUND** by Elliott Hayes; Directed by Norma Young; featuring Esther Benson; Jerry Haynes; Connie Nelson; Artie Olaisen; Jerry Crow; Bill Jenkins; Associate Director, Laurence O'Dwyer; Scenic and Sound Design by Tristan Wilson; Lighting Design by Linda Blase; Costume Design by Rick Tankersley; Production Stage Manager, Laurence O'Dwyer; Production Assistant, Nancy Losey.

**AMATEURS** by Tom Griffin; Directed by Jac Alder; Featuring Laurence O'Dwyer; Sharon Bunn; Terry Vandivort; Robert Andrews; Jerry Crow; R. Bruce Elliott; Kalen Hoyle; Elizabeth Mitchell; Jill Christine Peters; Production Stage Manager, Norma Young; Scenic Design by Jac Alder; Lighting Design by Linda Blase; Costume Design by Diana Figueroa Story; Sound Design by Tristan Wilson; Production Assistants, Nancy Losey; Vern McKinney.

*Linda Blase, Susan Kandell Photos*

**186**    **Sally Soldo, Julie Lea Johnson, Amy Mills in "Heartbeats"**

**Cheryl Norris in "Heidi Chronicles"**
**TOP: Leslie Uggams in "Stringbean"**

# TRINITY REPERTORY COMPANY

Providence, Rhode Island

[Arti]stic Director, Richard Jenkins; Resident Designer, Eugene Lee; Composer-in-[res]idence, Richard Cumming; Set Designer, Robert D. Soule; Costume Designer, [Wil]liam Lane; Lighting Designer, John F. Custer; Assistant to Richard Jenkins, Neal [---]on; Production Manager, Dennis Blackledge; Stage Managers: Thomas M. [H]uffman, Bonnie Baggesen, Richard Scott; Technical Director, David Rotondo; [Gra]nic Artist, Jennifer Didriksen; General Manager, Dennis E. Conway; Audience [De]velopment Director, Pamela Messore; Public Relations Director, Lynn Kelly; [Gra]phic Designer, Michael Guy; Director of Development, Kibbe Reilly.
[RE]SIDENT COMPANY: *IT'S ONLY A PLAY;* Allen Oliver, Peter Gerety, Margo [Ski]nner, Dan Welch, Cynthia Strickland, Timothy Crowe, Jonathan Fried, Janice [Dus]cos. *THE GLASS MENAGERIE;* Patricia Dunnock. *THE CHRISTMAS CAROL;* [Bri]an McEleney, Ed Shea, Ken Cheeseman, Fred Sullivan, Jr., Howard London, [Ann]ette Van Wright, Julia Langham, Dee Nelson, James Porter, Stephanie Clayman, [Geor]ge Rogers. *FENCES;* Gustave Johnson, Ricardo Pitts-Wiley, Barbara Meek, Jomo [K]ay, Rochel Coleman, Fyzah Cotman-El, Nicole-Nzinga Darden. *PRELUDE TO A [KIS]S;* Nance Williamson, Jay Blakemore, Barbara Blossom, Jack Willis, Paul Buxton, [Cat]herine Freedman, Richard Kneeland. *MACBETH;* Anne Scurria, Robert Colonna, [Wil]liam Damkoehler, David C. Jones, Phyllis Kay, Chip Lamb, George Saulnier, [Ch]ristopher Cooper, Gunnar Waldman, Robert Hofmann. *THE HEIDI [CH]RONICLES;* Brenda Corwin, Andrew Mutnick, Linda Amendola, James O'Brien, [Fre]d Sullivan, Jr.

[PR]ODUCTIONS THIS SEASON: *It's Only a Play, The Glass Menagerie, The [Chr]istmas Carol, Fences, Prelude to a Kiss, Macbeth, The Heidi Chronicles, Burn [Thi]s*

*Mark Morelli Photos*

**RIGHT: Gustave Johnson, Barbara Meek in "Fences"**
**TOP RIGHT: Dan Welch, Olympia Dukakis, Jonathan Fried in "Glass Menagerie"**

**Michael-Leon Wooley (L) in "Ain't Misbehavin'"**

# VIRGINIA STAGE COMPANY

Norfolk, Virginia
Twelfth Season

Kathleen P. Bateson, Executive Director; Julie Stafford, Director of Marketing, Barbara Peck, Director of Development; Tenna Matthews, Production Manager; Kathleen M. Cunneen, Production Stage Manager; Christopher Fretts, Technical Director; Lisa A. Vollrath, Resident Costume Designer; Laura Richin and Joe Abaldo of Joe Abaldo, Casting.
**RESIDENT COMPANY:** *WHO'S AFRAID OF VIRGINIA WOOLF?;* Barbara Andres, Ross Bickell, Kathy Danzer, Jack Koenig. *AIN'T MISBEHAVIN';* Allen Hidalgo, Kyme, Gwen Stewart, Cynthia Thomas, Michael-Leon Wooley. *ARMS AND THE MAN;* Julie Fishell, Marty McGaw, Erin J. O'Brien, Gary Sloan, John Tyson, Mark Vietor, Howard Witt. *BROADWAY BOUND;* David Bachman, David Burke, Tandy Cronyn, Bobby Ramsen, Barbara Spiegel, William Verderber.
**GUEST ARTISTS THIS SEASON:** *WHO'S AFRAID OF VIRGINIA WOLF?;* Charles Towers, Director, E. David Cosier, Set Designer; Nancy Schertler, Lighting Designer. *AIN'T MISBEHAVIN'* Marcia Milgram Dodge, Director and Choreographer; Reginald Royal, Musical Director; Anthony Dodge, Assistant Director; James Noone, Set Designer, Kenneth Posner, Lighting Designer; Laura Hassell, Guest Stage Manager. *ARMS AND THE MAN;* Christopher Hanna, Director; Bill Clarke, Set Designer; Candice Cain, Guest Costume Designer; Mary Louise Geiger, Lighting Designer; Steven Bryant, Wig Master. *BROADWAY BOUND;* Tom Gardner, Director; John Falabella, Set Designer; Terry Cermack, Lighting Designer.

*CJ Parker Photos*          **187**

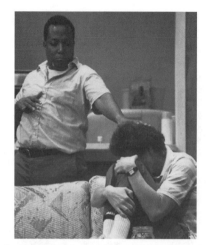

**Herbert Mark Parker, James Bunzli in "Boys Next Door"**

# WAYSIDE THEATRE

Winchester, Virginia
Thirtieth Season

Artistic Director, Christopher Owens; General Manager, Donna Johnson; Productic Stage Manager, Liz Reddick; Lighting, Chuck Arnaud.

## PRODUCTIONS & CASTS

**SUMMER AND SMOKE** by Tennessee Williams; Director/Set/Sound, Christoph Owens; Costumes, Kat Moon. CAST: T. Ryder Smith (John Buchanan, Jr.), Barba Bauer (Mrs. Winemiller), Jeffrey D. Eiche (Rev. Winemiller), Tamara Johnson (Aln Winemiller), Sema Osman (Rosa Gonzalez), Joanne Lessner (Nellie Ewell), Christia Kuser (Roger Doremus), John Cooke (Dr. John Buchanan, Sr.), Jennifer Yeo (Mr Bassett), Jeremy Priddy (Vernon/Dusty), Kim Franklin (Rosemary), Clif Mor (Gonzales), M. Scott Wood (Archie Kramer).

**THE BOYS NEXT DOOR** by Tom Griffin; Director, Traber Burns; Set, Christoph Owens; Costumes, Kat Moon. CAST: Clif Morts (Arnold Wiggins), Herbert Ma Parker (Lucien P. Smith), John Cooke (Jack), Frank Anderson (Norman Bulansky Richard C. Bennett (Mr. Hedges/Mr. Corbin/Senator Clarke), Jennifer Yeo (Mr Fremus/Mrs. Warren/Clara), Tamara Johnson (Sheila), Jeffrey D. Eiche (M Klemper).

**THE LION IN WINTER** by James Goldman; Director, Christopher Owens; Se Gregg Hillmar; Costumes, Bob Schramm. CAST: Frank Anderson (Henry), Joann Lessner (Alais), Jason Katz (John), Jeffrey D. Eiche (Geoffrey), J. Barrett Coop (Richard), Kathy Lichter (Eleanor), James Bunzli (Philip), Christian Kuser, Sen Osman (Servants).

**CORPSE!** by Gerald Moon; Director, John Cooke; Set/Costumes/Sound, Christoph Owens. CAST: Jeffrey D. Eiche (Evelyn Farrant/Rupert Farrant); Kathy Licht (Mrs. McGee), Frank Anderson (Maj. Ambrose Powell), Christian Kuser (Hawkins).

**THE PRICE** by Arthur Miller; Director/Set, Christopher Owens; Costumes, Chari Showalter. CAST: Dana Bate (Victor Franz), Kathy Lichter (Esther Franz), Jeffrey I Eiche (Gregory Soloman), Frank Anderson (Walter Franz).

**HOW THE OTHER HALF LOVES** by Alan Ayckbourn; Director/Set/Costume Christopher Owens. CAST: Barbara Anderson (Fiona Foster), Berkely Rhode (Theresa Phillips), Joseph Parra (Frank Foster), Stephen Gleason (Bob Phillips), Jaso Katz (William Featherstone), Dawn Tuttle (Mary Featherstone).

**A CHRISTMAS CAROL;** adapted from Charles Dickens by Christopher Owen Director, Christopher Owens; Musical Director, Donna Johnson; Costumes, Harri Engler. CAST: Jeffrey D. Eiche (Ebenezer Scrooge), Patrick Lawlor Bo Cratchit/Businessman), David Johnson (Fred/Dick Wilkins), Joseph Parra (1 Gentleman/Fezziwig/Old Joe), Joe McCullough (Jacob Marley/Party Guest/Spirit Christmas Present), Tod Williams (2nd Gentleman/Guest/Grocer/Neville Businessman), Eric Kinnie (Spirit of Christmas Past/Peter Cratchit), Jonathan Chezic (Tiny Tim), Jeremy Butterfield (Boy Scrooge/Turkey Boy), Ellen Nichols (Part Guest/Mrs. Cratchit/Mrs. Dilber), Barbara Bauer (Mrs. Fezziwig/Charwoman), Kev Connell (Topper/Young Scrooge), Sally Groth (Lucy/Fiddler/Martha Cratchit Jocelyn Beam (Jane Fezziwig/Lizzie Cratchit), Nancy Gunn (Belle/Denise), Eric Simon (Party Guest).

**GREATER TUNA** by Joe Sears, Jaston Williams & Ed Howard; Director/Se Christopher Owens; Costumes, Harriet Engler. CAST: Nick Stannard, Jeffrey I Eiche.

*Westervelt Photos*

**Jeffrey D. Eiche, Frank Anderson in "Corpse"**

**Jeffrey D. Eiche, Dana Bate in "The Price"**

**Nick Stannard in "Greater Tuna"**

**ABOVE: "A Chorus Line"**
**LEFT: "Me and My Girl"**
**BOTTOM: "Gypsy"**

# WESTCHESTER BROADWAY THEATRE

Elmsford, New York

President, Bill Stutler; Vice President/Treasurer, Bob Funking; Executive Assistant, Lisa Tiso; Public Relations, Bob Fitzsimmons; Artistic Consultants: Michael Bottari, Ronald Case

## PRODUCTIONS AND CASTS

**ME AND MY GIRL** with Music by Noel Gay; Lyrics/Book, Arthur Rose, Douglas Furber; Revisions, Mike Ockrent, Stephen Fry; Director, Charles Repole; Choreography, Michael Lichtefeld; Musical Director, John Mulcahy; Sets/Costumes, Michael Bottari, Ronald Case; Lighting, Andrew Gmoser; Stage Manager, Dawn A. Groenewegen CAST: James Young (Bill), Stephanie Douglas (Sally), William McCauley (Tremayne), Karen Curlee (Lady Jacqueline), Darcy Pulliam (Duchess), Michael Calkins (Gerald), Dick Decareau (Parchester), Haskell Gordon (Heathersett), Franz C. Alderfer, Brian Chenoweth, Becky Garrett, James Gerth, Elizabeth Green, Michael Kumor, Nancy Lyn Miller, Cyndi Neal, Michael J. Novin, Heather Spears, John M. Wiltberger, Gina Broetsky, Timothy Riches.

**A CHORUS LINE** with Music by Marvin Hamlisch; Lyrics, Edward Kleban; Book, James Kirkwood, Nicholas Dante; Conception, Michael Bennett; Director/Choreography, Rob Marshall, Kathleen Marshall; Musical Director, John Mulcahy; Sets/Costumes, Michael Bottari, Ron Case; Lighting, Andrew Gmoser; Stage Manager, Peter Barbieri, Jr. CAST: Karen Babcock (Lois), Keith Bernardo (Don), Andy Blankenbuehler (Mark), Stephen Bourneuf (Al), Bill Brassea (Mike), Beverly Britton (Val), Brian Chenoweth (Bobby), Randy Donaldson (Richie), Doug Friedman (Greg), Lauren Goler (Sheila), Christine Gradl (Maggie), Allen Hidalgo (Paul), Zoie Lam (Connie), LuAnn Leonard (Judy), Todd Lindamood (Frank), Susan Misner (Christine), Naomi Reddin (Tricia), Joseph Ricci (Roy), Susan Santoro (Diana), Pamela Sousa (Cassie), Brian Sutherland (Zach), Ernest Toussant (Larry), Valerie Wright (Bebe)

**GYPSY** with Music by Jule Styne; Lyrics, Stephen Sondheim; Book, Arthur Laurents; Director, Charles Repole; Choreography, Susan Stroman; Musical Director, John Mulcahy; Sets/Costumes, Michael Bottari, Ron Case; Lighting, Andrew Gmoser; Stage Manager, James Gerth CAST: Beth Fowler succeeded by Jana Robbins (Rose), Jamie Ross (Herbie), Jacquelyn Piro (Louise), Susan Gail Bernstein (June), Michael O'Steen (Tulsa), Isabelle Farrell (Tessie), Louisa Flaningam (Electra), Debbie Petrino (Mazeppa), Don Bradford (George/Weber/Cigar), Jerold Goldstein (Pop/Kringelein), Robin Boudreau (Agnes), Timothy Ford (L.A.), Stacia Goad (Blonde), Jennifer B. Skinner (Blonde/Maid), Jay Bodin (Jocko/Goldstone/Phil), Mark L. Greenley (Yonkers/Pastey), Bill Rolon (Kansas), Kimberly Abruzese, Lauren Auslander, Jason Robert Redford, Laura Donaldson, Anne Woodward Doss, Alexis Dale Fabricant, Thomas Montgomery, Jeffrey Selman, Laruen Thomas, Seth Neil Watsky.

# YALE REPERTORY THEATRE

New Haven, Connecticut
October 3, 1991 - May 23, 1992

Stan Wojewodski, Jr., Artistic Director; Benjamin Mordecai, Managing Director; Ming Cho Lee, Set Design Advisor; Jane Greenwood, Costume Design Advisor; Jennifer Tipton, Lighting Design Advisor; Barbara Somerville, Speech Advisor; Wesley Fata, Movement Advisor; Michael Yeargan, Resident Set Designer; Jess Goldstein, Resident Costume Designer; William B. Warfel; Lighting Director; Wendy Ettinger, Casting; Gitta Honegger, Resident Dramaturg; Joel Schechter, Dramaturg/Associate Director for Special Projects; Buzz Ward, General Manager; Robert Wildman, Director of Institutional Development; Thomas W. Clark, Audience Services Director; William J. Reynolds, Operations Manager; Bronislaw J. Sammler, Production Supervisor; Don Harvey, David L. Sword, Technical Directors; Tom McAlister, Costume Shop Manager; Brian Cookson, Properties Master; Anne Matteson, Resident Scenic Artist; Donald W. Titus, Resident Master Electrician; James Ward, Stage Carpenter; Wendy Beaton, Production Stage Manager; Margaret Adair Quinn, Resident Stage Manager; Mary-Susan Gregson, Stage Managers, Debra J. Justice, Renée Lutz, Renée Mesard, Susan Slagle, Stage Managers.

## PRODUCTIONS & CASTS

**ON THE VERGE OR THE GEOGRAPHY OF YEARNING** by Eric Overmyer; Directed by Stan Wojewodski, Jr.; Set, Matthew Moore; Costumes, Anna R. Oliver; Lighting, Robert Wierzel; Sound, Rob Gorton; Composer, Kim D. Sherman; Movement Consultant, Wesley Fata; Production Dramaturg, Stephen Haff. CAST: Jayne Atkinson, Tracey Ellis, Boyd Gaines, Harriet Harris; Musician, Kim D. Sherman.

**MY CHILDREN! MY AFRICA!** by Athol Fugard; Directed by Elizabeth Margid; Setting, Susan Branch; Costumes, Dennita Sewell; Lighting, Rick Martin; Sound, Mark D. Dingley; Composer, Jeffrey Hardy; Production Dramaturg, Dominica Borg. CAST: Ray Aranha, Kate Forbes, Eric LaRay Harvey.

**FEFU AND HER FRIENDS** by Maria Irene Fornes; Directed by Lisa Peterson; Set, Michael Vaughn Sims; Costumes, Maggie Morgan; Lighting, Trui Malten; Sound: Jon Newstrom; Production Dramaturg: Steven Oxman. CAST: Mary Magdalena Hernández, Sarah Long, Julianna Margulies, Joyce Lynn O'Connor, Pippa Pearthree, Tonia Rowe, Camilla Sanes, Kim Yancey.

**THE DEATH OF THE LAST BLACK MAN IN THE WHOLE ENTIRE WORLD** by Suzan-Lori Parks; Directed by Liz Diamond; Set, Riccardo Hernandez; Costumes, Caryn Neman; Lighting, Glen Fasman; Sound, Dan Moses Schreier; Production Dramaturg, Christina Sibul. CAST: Karen A. Bishop, Ron Brice, Leon Addison Brown, Reg E. Cathey, Leo V. Finnie III, Reginald Lee Flowers, Melody J. Garrett, Fanni Green, Michael Potts, Darryl Theirse, Pamala Tyson.

**DEMOCRACY IN AMERICA** by Colette Brooks; Directed by Travis Preston; Set, Christopher Barreca; Costumes, Tom Broecker; Lighting, Stephen Strawbridge; Sound, David Budries; Movement Consultant, Carl R. Hudson; Production Dramaturg, Karen E. Lordi. CAST: Christopher Bauer, Reg E. Cathey, Marissa Chibas, Brendan Corbalis, Reginald Lee Flowers, Melody J. Garrett, Carl R. Hudson, Elina Löwensohn, Adina Porter, Corliss Preston, John Gould Rubin, Elaine Tse, Francine Zerfas.

**EDWARD THE SECOND** by Christopher Marlowe; Directed by Stan Wojewodski, Jr.; Set, Michael Yeargan; Costumes, Tom Broecker; Lighting, Jennifer Tipton; Composer/Conductor, Kim D. Sherman; Sound, Darren Clark; Speech Consultant, Tim Monich; Production Dramaturgs, Karin McCully, Charles J. McNulty. CAST: Dallas Adams, Sarah Brown, Joseph Costa, Cara Duff-MacCormick, Reginald Lee Flowers, Peter Gantenbein, Malcolm Gets, Thomas Gibson, Michel R. Gill, Sam Groom, Sean Haberle, Byron Jennings, James Kall, Sarah Knowlton, Michael Manuel, Craig Mathers, Gregory McClure, Edwin J. McDonough, Dan Moran, Derek Murcot, Andrew Pang, Lance Reddick, Liev Schreiber, Bernie Sheredy, Anthony Ward. Musicians: Kim D. Sherman, Edwin Canning.

**THE BEAUTY PART** by S.J. Perelman; Directed by Walton Jones; Set, Nicholas Lundy; Costumes, Susan Branch; Lighting, Lynne Chase; Sound, Martin Desjardins; Production Dramaturgs, Jill Rachel Morris, Christina Sibul. CAST: Robert Beatty, Jr., Cynthia Darlow, MacIntyre Dixon, Richard Frank, Malcolm Gets, Jefferson Mays, Stephen Mendillo, Amy Povich, Judith Roberts, Reg Rogers, Scott Sherman, Richard Topol.

*Gerry Goodstein Photos*

TOP: Boyd Gaines, Harriet Harris in "On the Verge"
BELOW: Kate Forbes, Ray Aranha, Eric LaRay Harvey in
"My Children My Africa"
THIRD PHOTO: Byron Jennings, Cara Duff-MacCormick, (rear) Sam
Groom, Edwin J. McDonough, Michel R. Gill, Joseph Costa in
"Edward the Second"
RIGHT: Jefferson Mays, Amy Povich in "Beauty Part"

**190**

## ALABAMA SHAKESPEARE FESTIVAL

Montgomery, Alabama
Twentieth Season

stic Director, Kent Thompson; Managing Director, Tim Langan; Associate Artistic
ector, Charlie Caldwell; Production Manager, Terry Cermak; Costumes, Pam
liz; Casting, Bob Vardaman
**EST ARTISTS:** Directors: Vincent Murphy, Benn Sato Ammbush, Stephen
is, Charles Towers, Gavin Cameron-Webb; Designers: Paul Wonsek, William
odgood, David Crank, Jim Maronek; Costumes, Michael Krass, Alan Armstrong,
ne Button
**ODUCTIONS:** *THE MISANTHROPE* by Moliere; *PETER PAN* by James M.
rie, Mark Charlap, Carolyn Leigh, Jule Styne and Comden & Green; *MISS EVERS'*
*YS* by David Feldshuh; *THE LITTLE FOXES* by Lillian Hellman; *ARMS & THE*
*N* by Shaw; *KING LEAR* by Shakespeare; *SHADOWLANDS* by William
holson; *THE COMEDY OF ERRORS, LEND ME A TENOR* by Ken Ludwig;
*HARD II* by Shakespeare

*Scarsbrook/ASF Photos*

**BELOW:** John Milligan, Philip Pleasants in "Cherry Orchard"
**BOTTOM LEFT:** Frank Corrado in "Richard III"
**TOP RIGHT:** Michael Mandell, Kent Gash, Derrick Lee Weeden,
Charles Branklyn in "Miss Ever's Boys"
**RIGHT:** Joan Ulmer, Mark Capri in "The Rivals"
**BOTTOM RIGHT:** Candace Haas-Johnson, Candance Taylor in
"...Earnest"

## COLORADO SHAKESPEARE FESTIVAL

Boulder, Colorado
Thirty-fourth Season

Artistic Director, Richard Devin; Public Relations Director, Patricia McFerran;
Casting Director, Joel G. Fink; Directors, Peggy Shannon, James M. Symons, Robert
Robinson; Production Manager, Stephanie Young; Technical Director, Stancil
Campbell
**GUEST ARTISTS:** June Compton, Frank Corrado, Sean Hennigan, Dudley Knight
**PRODUCTIONS:** *Richard III, Julius Caesar, The Comedy of Errors, The*
*Importance of Being Earnest* by Oscar Wilde

*J. Martin Natvig Photos*

# NEW JERSEY SHAKESPEARE FESTIVAL

Drew University, Madison, New Jersey
June 4 - September 21, 1991

Artistic Director, Bonnie J. Monte; General Manager, Michael Stotts; Press, Carol S. Cornman

## PRODUCTIONS & CASTS

**THE TEMPEST** by Shakespeare; Director, Bonnie J. Monte; Sets, Michael Ganio; Costumes, Christine McDowell; Lighting, Bruce Auerbach; Sound, Andrew Bellware CAST: Gordon Stanley (Alonso), Tom Pasley (Sebastian), Miguel Perez (Prospero), Doug Krizner (Antonio), Barnaby Spring (Ferdinand), William Preston (Gonzalo), Sean Moynihan (Adrian), Francis Henry (Francisco), Conan McCarty (Caliban), James Michael Reilly (Trinculo), Fred Sullivan, Jr. (Stephano), Greg Steinbruner (Ship Master), Peter Husovsky (Boatswain), Joe Discher, Jason Smith (Mariners/Reapers), Julie Moses (Miranda), A. Bernard Cummings (Ariel), Kim Francis (Iris), Alice Saltzman (Ceres), Wendy Welch (Juno), Jennifer Potts, Lisa Berte, Stephanie Heller, Nicole Ricciardi (Nymphs/Creatures)

**THE SKIN OF OUR TEETH** by Thornton Wilder; Director, Kay Matschullat; Sets, Christine Jones; Costumes, David Burke; Lighting, Michael Giannitti; Sound, Andrew Bellware CAST: Faye Grant (Sabina), Craig Wasson (Mr. Antrobus), Christine Mourad (Mrs. Antrobus), Ephron Catlin (Henry), Alene Dawson (Gladys), Bill Kux (Mr. Fitzpatrick), James Michael Reilly (Telegraph Boy), Peter Husovsky (Dinosaur), Thomas Pasley (Homer), Christopher Grossett (Fred Bailey), Alice Saltzman (Ivy), Berley Rhodes (Miss E. Muse), Wendy Welch (Miss M. Muse), Julie Moses (Pageant Girl), Kim Francis (Madame Curie), Sean Moynihan (Usher/Sailor), Greg Steinbruner (Mammoth), Francis Henry (Broadcast Official), Edouard DeSoto (Moses), Holmes Morrison (Refugee/Chairpusher), Jimmy Bleyer/Gary Pinsky (Ushers/Wolves), Mary Louise (Fortune Teller), Jason Smith (Animal)

**A MIDSUMMER NIGHT'S DREAM** by Shakespeare; Director, Dylan Baker; Sets, James Sandefur; Costumes, Cynthia M. Dumont; Lighting, Phil Monat; Sound, Andrew Bellware; Composer, Jonathan Larson; Choreography, Jeni Breen CAST: Douglas Krizner (Theseus), Berkely Rhodes (Hippolyta), Sean Moynihan (Lysander), David Thornton (Demetrius), Alice Saltzman (Hermia), Becky Ann Baker (Helena), Fred Sanders (Egeus/Quince), Deborah Snyder (Philostrate), A. Benard Cumming (Oberon), Alene Dawson (Titania), Myra Taylor (Puck), Lisa Berte (Peaseblossom), Christopher Grossett (Cobweb), Jennifer Potts (Moth), Nicole A. Ricciardi (Mustardseed), Marcus Giamatti (Bottom), Paul Mullins (Flute), Peter Husovsky (Snout), Greg Steinbruner (Snug), Thomas Pasley (Starveling)

**DARK OF THE MOON** by Howard Richardson and William Berney; Director, Jimmy Bohr; Sets, Rob Odorisio; Costumes, Christine McDowell; Lighting, Bill Berner; Sound, Andrew Bellware; Stage Manager, Dan Bello CAST: Lou Milione (John), Charles Craigin (Conjur Man), Christopher Grossett (Dark Witch), Berkely Rhodes (Fair Witch), Wendy Welch (Conjur Woman), Sam Catlin (Hank), Alice Saltzman (Edna), Tom Pasley (Summey), Mary Lowry (Mrs. Summey), Kate Schlesinger (Miss Metcalf), Nick Plakias (Mr. Atkins), Gordon Stanley (Uncle Smelicue), Greg Steinbruner (Floyd), David Flynn (Berger), Kim Francis (Mrs. Bergen), Sean Moynihan (Dinwitty), Lynda Bookwalter (Greeny), Julie Moses (Hattie), Peter Husovsky (Hudges), Tracy Sallows (Barbara Allen), Fran Anthony (Mrs. Allen), Ed Mahler (Mr. Allen), Meg DeFoe (Ella Bergen), Tom Brennan (Preacher), Micah Walsh, Alice Francis (Children)

**TWELFTH NIGHT** by Shakespeare; Director, Bonnie J. Monte; Sets, Charles McCarry; Costumes, Hwa Park; Lighting, Steven Rosen; Sound, Andrew Bellware; Fights, Robert Walsh; Stage Manager, Renee Lutz CAST: Mark Wilson (Orsino), Graham Winton (Sebastian), Thomas Pasley (Antonio), Sean Moynihan (Curio/Capt.), Joe Discher (Valentine), Patrick Tull (Belch), James Michael Reilly (Aguecheek), Edward Herrmann (Malvolio), Peter Husovsky (Fabian), Paul Mullins (Feste), Laila Robins (Olivia), Elizabeth McGovern (Viola), Alice Saltzman (Maria), Frank Occhiogrosso (Priest), Charlotte Twine (Marion)

*Jane VanWert, Gerry Goodstein Photos*

TOP: David Thornton, A. Bernard Cummings in
"Midsummer Night's Dream"
CENTER: Edward Herrmann in "Twelfth Night"
RIGHT: Graham Winton, Laila Robins, Mark Wilson, Elizabeth
McGovern in "Twelfth Night"

**Robin Rodriguez, Cindy Basco, Jonathan Hogan in "Playboy of the Western World"**

**Remi Sandri, Adam Michael Hogan, Rick Hamilton, Robert Lisell-Frank, Michael Hume in "Conclusion of Henry VI"**

**Emilie Talbot, LeWan Alexander in "Othello"**

**Terri McMahon, Dominique Lozano, Remi Sandri in "As You Like It"**

# OREGON SHAKESPEARE FESTIVAL

Ashland & Portland, Oregon

istic Director, Henry Woronicz; Composer/Musical Director, Todd Barton; ident Set Designer, William Bloodgood; Associate Director/Production, Kirk yd; Scenic/Theatre Design, Richard L. Hay; Vocal Coach, Susan Murray Miller; ociate Artistic Director, Pat Patton; Director Emeritus, Jerry Turner; Development, nthia White

**EST DIRECTORS:** Barbara Damashek, Penny Metropulos, Fontaine Syer
**TING COMPANY:** Victoria Adams, Linda Alper, Kelly AuCoin, Cindy Basco, t Bernhardt, Aldo Billingslea, Mark Booher, Bruce Brownlee, Mimi Carr, Carol son, Jillian Crane, Philip Davidson, Tony DeBruno, Anthony DeFonte, Hugh non, James Edmondson, Richard Elmore, Kevin Fabian, Aileen Fitzpatrick, Debra khouser, Shawn Galloway, Bill Geisslinger, B.W. Gonzalez, Rick Hamilton, Luck i, Jonathan Hogan, Richard Howard, Philip Hubbard, David Kelly, Dan Kremer, vn Lisell-Frank, Robert Lisell-Frank, Douglas Markkanen, Molly Mayock, Sandy Callum, Terry McMahon, Michelle Morain, Mark Murphey, Maurya Murphey, es Newcomb, Paul Vincent O'Connor, Fredi Olster, J.P. Phillips, Ray Porter, John yl, Dennis Rees, Dennis Robertson, Robynn Rodriguez, Matthew Smith, Emilie bot, U. Jonathan Toppo, Eddie Wallace, Michael Weber, Derrick Lee Weeden
**ODUCTIONS:** *ALL'S WELL THAT ENDS WELL* by Shakespeare, *TOYS IN THE IC* by Lillian Hellman, *PLAYBOY OF THE WESTERN WORLD* by J.M. Synge, *BÊTE* by David Hirson, *LADIES OF THE CAMELLIAS* by Lillian Garrett, *STORATION* by Edward Bond, *THE FIREBUGS* by Max Frisch, *HEATHEN LLEY* by Romulus Linney, *OTHELLO* by Shakespeare, *CONCLUSION OF HENRY* by Shakespeare, *AS YOU LIKE IT* by Shakespeare

*Christopher Briscoe Photos*

**Mimi Carr, Fredi Olster in "Ladies of the Camellias"**      **193**

# STRATFORD FESTIVAL

Stratford, Ontario, Canada
Thirty-ninth Season

Artistic Director, David William; General Manager, Gary Thomas; Producer, Colleen Blake; Design Head, Debra Hanson; Music Director, Berthold Carrière; Communications Director, Ellen T. Cole; Development Director, Shawn St. Michael
**ACTING COMPANY:** Paul Aikins, Edward Atienza, Ann Baggley, Marsha Bagwell, Rodger Barton, Hume Baugh, Nancy Beatty, Brian Bedford, Wayne Best, James Binkley, Mervyn Blake, James Blendick, Mary Hitch Blendick, Stephen Bogaert, Sidonie Boll, Geoffrey Brumlik, Barbara Byrne, Anne-Marie Cadieux, Douglas Chamberlain, Patrick Chilvers, Juan Chioran, Antoni Cimolino, Patricia Collins, John Devorski, Sara Dickinson, Andrew Dolha, Peter Donaldson, Eric Donkin, William Dunlop, Michael Fawkes, Colm Feore, Michael Fisk, Richard Fitzpatrick, David Fox, John Franklyn-Robbins, Timothy French, Barbara Fulton, Pat Galloway, Peter Gaudreult, Lewis Gordon, Rose Graham, Allison Grant, Michael Halberstam, Ron Hastings, Kate Hennig, Larry Herbert, Roger Honeywell, Ellen Horst, Neil Ingram, Ellen Wilkes Irmisch, Melanie Janzen, Marcel Jeannin, Lorne Kennedy, Robert King, Tim Koetting, Jeffrey Kuhn, Adam Large, Shannon Lawson, Julia Lenardon, Monique Lund, Lori A. Martin, Roberta Maxwell, Geoff McBride, Tim McDonald, Mervon Mehta, Rod Menzies, Dale Mieske, Albert Millaire, Paul Miller, Kiri-Lyn Muir, William Needles, Louis Negin, Daniel T. Nelson, Ted Pearson, Nicholas Pennell, Miles Potter, Leon Pownall, Michael Querin, Douglas Rain, Claire Rankin, Kate Reid, Bradley C. Rudy, Todd Samdomirsky, Ronn Sarosiak, Natalie Sebastian, Goldie Semple, Michael Separd, Martin Spencer, Donna Starnes, Ordena Stephens, Brian Tree, Ian White, Jim White, Dathan B. Williams, N. Shawn Williams, Julia Winder, Karen Wood, Tom Wood, Anne Wright, Janet Wright, Susan Wright, Cavan Young
**PRODUCTIONS:** *HAMLET* by Shakespeare, *MUCH ADO ABOUT NOTHING* by Shakespeare, *CAROUSEL* by Rodgers & Hammerstein, *TREASURE ISLAND* by Elliott Hayes, *OUR TOWN* by Thornton Wilder, *TWELFTH NIGHT* by Shakespeare; *LES BELLES SOEURS* by Michel Trembly, *THE SCHOOL FOR WIVES* by Molière, *AN ENEMY OF THE PEOPLE* by Ibsen, *TIMON OF ATHENS* by Shakespeare, *HOMEWARD BOUND* by Elliott Hayes (World Premiere), *THE RULES OF THE GAME* by Luigi Pirandello, Translation, Robert Rietty, *THE KNIGHT OF THE BURNING PESTLE* by Francis Beaumont, *LOVE LETTERS* by A.R. Gurney Jr., *EIGHT SONGS FOR A MAD KING* and *MISS DONNITHORNE'S MAGGOT* by Peter Maxwell Davies

*Tom Skudra Photos*

# UTAH SHAKESPEAREAN FESTIVAL

Cedar City, Utah

Founder and Executive Producer, Fred C. Adams; Producing Artistic Director, Douglas N. Cook, Cameron Harvey; Managing Director, R. Scott Phillips; Finan Director, G. McClain McIntyre; Director of Marketing and Public Relations, Ro Bean; Publications Director, Bruce Lee; Art Director, Michelle Livermo Development Director, Jyl L. Shuler; Associate Finance Director, Suzanne Mor Assistant Marketing Director, Robert A. Reich; Operations Manager, Rick VanN Company Manager, James W. Loder; Production Manager, Tom Burke; Costume Sl Supervisor, Jeffrey Lieder; Master Electrician, John Sofranko; Choreograph Chrissie Scoville; Technical Directors, Gary P. Jung, Roger Sherman.

## PRODUCTIONS & CASTS

**DEATH OF A SALESMAN** by Arthur Miller; Director, Eli Simon; Set, Richard Isackes; Costumes, James Berton Harris; Lighting, Pat Simmons; Make-up and H Larry Pennington; Composer and Music Designer, Christine Frezza; Sound, James Capenos; Music Director, Brian Erle; Stage Manager, Anne Kearson. CAST: Jar Anzide, David Cheaney, T. Scott Cunningham, David Davalos, Deborah Har Carole Healey, David Janoviak, William Leach, Bets Malone, Ivars Mikels Elisabeth Ritson, Paul Sandberg, Susan Sweeney, Doug Zschiegner.
**HAMLET** by William Shakespeare; Director, Malcolm Morrison; Dramatu Michael Flachmann; Set, John Iacovelli; Costumes, Mark Pirollo; Lighting, Li Essig; Make-up and Hair, Larry Pennington; Music Composer, Christine Frez Sound, Pam Emerson; Music Director, Brian Erle; Fight Director, David Boush Vocal Coach, Jan Gist; Stage Manager, Karen Quisenberry. CAST: James Anz Thad S. Avery, Richard Bugg, Danny Campbell, Melissa Chalsma, T. Sc Cunningham, David Davalos, Kevin Durkin, Deborah Harris, Andrei Hartt, Joe Hils David Janoviak, George Judy, Harrison Long, Deven S. May, Michael McAlis Ivars Mikelson, Eric W. Porter, David Rogers, Dennis Ryan, Paul Sandberg, Chri Scoville, Patrick Ellison Shea, Gayle Staffanson, Jon A. Stewart, Price Waldn Doug Zschiegner.
**MISALLIANCE** by George Bernard Shaw; Director, John Neville-Andrews; : Richard M. Isackes; Costumes, James Berton Harris; Lighting, Pat Simmons; Make and Hair, Larry Pennington; Music, Christine Frezza; Sound, James M. Caper Speech and Dialect Coach, Jan Gist; Stage Manager, Tracy Burns. CAST: J Barrett, Michael Boudewyns, David Cheaney, Brad DePlanche, Marvin Gree Richard Kinter, William Leach, Elisabeth Ritson, Susan Sweeney.
**THE TAMING OF THE SHREW** by William Shakespeare; Director, Kathleen Conlin; Set, Richard M. Isackes; Costumes, James Berton Harris; Lighting, Simmons; Make-up and Hair, Larry Pennington; Music Composer, Christine Fre Sound, James M. Capenos; Music Director, Brian Erle; Fight Director, Da Boushey; Stage Manager, Jenny A. Batten. CAST: James Anzide, Mich Boudewyns, David Davalos, Brad DePlanche, Carole Healey, Joe Hilsee, Jef Ingman, Harrison Long, Michael McAlister, Eric W. Porter, Dennis Ryan, Chri Scoville, Patrick Ellison Shea, Jon A. Stewart, Melanie van Betten, Doug Zschiegne
**TWELFTH NIGHT** by William Shakespeare; Director, David Hammo Dramaturg, Michael Flachmann; Set, John Iacovelli; Costumes, McKay Col Lighting, Linda Essig; Make-up and Hair, Larry Pennington; Composer and M Designer, Christine Frezza; Sound, Pam Emerson; Music Director, Brian Erle; F Director, David Boushey; Vocal Coach, Jan Gist; Stage Manager, Evelyn Mat CAST: Thad S. Avery, Jody Barrett, Richard Bugg, Danny Campbell, Mel Chalsma, Kevin Durkin, Nancy C. Elliott, Marvin Greene, Andrei Hartt, Joe Hil George Judy, Harrison Long, Emily Nehus, Eric W. Porter, David Rogers, Der Ryan, Patrick Ellison Shea, Jon A. Stewart, Melanie van Betten, Price Waldman.
**VOLPONE** by Ben Jonson; Director, Richard Risso; Dramaturg, Michael Flachm Set, John Iacovelli; Costumes, Elizabeth A. Novak; Lighting, Linda Essig; Makc and Hair, Larry Pennington; Music Composer, Christine Frezza; Sound, Pam Emers Music Director, Brian Erle; Vocal Coach, Jan Gist; Stage Manager, Mandy Ba CAST: Thad S. Avery, Anthony Beckman, Brian Baker, Richard Bugg, Da Campbell, Melissa Chalsma, David Cheaney, Kevin Durkin, Marvin Greene, Deb Harris, Bruce Hassard, Andrei Hartt, Jeanne M. Homer, David Janoviak, George Ju Richard Kinter, Deven S. May, Robert Richardson, Elisabeth Ritson, Paul Sandb Brian Vaughn, Price Waldman, Buddy Waters.

*Jess Allen Photos*

**194** **Brian Bedford, Ann Baggley in "School for Wives"**
**TOP RIGHT: T. Scott Cunningham, Dennis Ryan in "Hamlet"**

# 1992 THEATRE WORLD AWARD RECIPIENTS

### (Outstanding New Talent)

**TALIA BALSAM**
of "Jake's Women"

**GRIFFIN DUNNE**
of "Search and Destroy"

**LARRY FISHBURNE**
of "Two Trains Running"

**LINDSAY CROUSE**
of "The Homecoming"

195

**JONATHAN KAPLAN**
of "Falsettos" and "Rags"

**MEL HARRIS**
of "Empty Hearts"

**JESSICA LANGE**
of "A Streetcar Named Desire"

**SPIRO MALAS**
of "Most Happy Fella"

**LAURA LINNEY**
of "Sight Unseen"

**MARK ROSENTHAL**
of "Marvin's Room"

**AL WHITE**
of "Two Trains Running"

**HELEN SHAVER**
of "Jake's Women"

197

THEATRE WORLD AWARDS presented Monday, June 1, 1992 in the Roundabout Theatre
Top: Presenters (all former recipients): Kevin Ramsey, Brenda Vaccaro, Ralph Carter, Bernadette Peters, Alec Baldwin, Dorothy Loudon; Patricia Elliot; Carol Channing, Peter Gallagher, Rosemary Harris, Gregory Hines, Crista Moore, Harry Groener  Below: Harry Groener, Helen Shaver, Jonathan Kaplan, Crista Moore, Gregory Hines, Lindsay Crouse, Rosemary Harris, Griffin Dunne  Bottom Row: Carol Channing, Mark Rosenthal Peter Gallagher, Mel Harris, Dorothy Loudon, Spiro Malas  Above: Bernadette Peters, Alec Baldwin, Dorothy Loudon, Laura Linney, Alec Baldwin, Bernadette Peters, Ralph Carter
*Photos by Michael Riordan, Michael Viadé, Peter L. Warrack, Van Williams*

Top: Ralph Carter, Laurence Fishburne, Jessica Lange, Patrick Mason, Rosaleen Linehan, Carol Channing, Peter Gallagher, Rosemary Harris, Kevin Ramsey, Brenda Vaccaro Below: Rosemary Harris, Spiro Malas, Crista Moore, Al White, Talia Balsam, LaChanze, Frances Ruivivar Bottom Row: Harry Groener, Jonathan Kaplan, Conchata Ferrell, SuEllen Estey, Jess Richards, John Martin, Rosemary Harris, Barnard Hughes Above Josh Ellis, Joyce Van Patten, Brenda Vaccaro, Talia Balsam, Alec Baldwin, Helen Shaver, Griffin Dunne, Alan Alda, Carol and Charles Lowe

*Photos by Michael Riordan, Michael Viadé, Peter L. Warrack, Van Williams*

**Karen Akers**

**Dylan Baker**

**Laurie Beechman**

# PREVIOUS THEATRE WORLD RECIPIENTS

**1944-45:** Betty Comden, Richard Davis, Richard Hart, Judy Holliday, Charles Lang, Bambi Linn, John Lund, Donald Murphy, Nancy Noland, Margaret Phillips, John Raitt
**1945-46:** Barbara Bel Geddes, Marlon Brando, Bill Callahan, Wendell Corey, Paul Douglas, Mary James, Burt Lancaster, Patricia Marshall, Beatrice Pearson
**1946-47:** Keith Andes, Marion Bell, Peter Cookson, Ann Crowley, Ellen Hanley, John Jordan, George Keane, Dorothea MacFarland, James Mitchell, Patricia Neal, David Wayne
**1947-48:** Valerie Bettis, Edward Bryce, Whitfield Connor, Mark Dawson, June Lockhart, Estelle Loring, Peggy Maley, Ralph Meeker, Meg Mundy, Douglass Watson, James Whitmore, Patrice Wymore
**1948-49:** Tod Andrews, Doe Avedon, Jean Carson, Carol Channing, Richard Derr, Julie Harris, Mary McCarty, Allyn Ann McLerie, Cameron Mitchell, Gene Nelson, Byron Palmer, Bob Scheerer
**1949-50:** Nancy Andrews, Phil Arthur, Barbara Brady, Lydia Clarke, Priscilla Gillette, Don Hanmer, Marcia Henderson, Charlton Heston, Rick Jason, Grace Kelly, Charles Nolte, Roger Price
**1950-51:** Barbara Ashley, Isabel Bigley, Martin Brooks, Richard Burton, Pat Crowley, James Daley, Cloris Leachman, Russell Nype, Jack Palance, William Smithers, Maureen Stapleton, Marcia Van Dyke, Eli Wallach
**1951-52:** Tony Bavaar, Patricia Benoit, Peter Conlow, Virginia de Luce, Ronny Graham, Audrey Hepburn, Diana Herbert, Conrad Janis, Dick Kallman, Charles Proctor, Eric Sinclair, Kim Stanley, Marian Winters, Helen Wood
**1952-53:** Edie Adams, Rosemary Harris, Eileen Heckart, Peter Kelley, John Kerr, Richard Kiley, Gloria Marlowe, Penelope Munday, Paul Newman, Sheree North, Geraldine Page, John Stewart, Ray Stricklyn, Gwen Verdon
**1953-54:** Orson Bean, Harry Belafonte, James Dean, Joan Diener, Ben Gazzara, Carol Haney, Jonathan Lucas, Kay Medford, Scott Merrill, Elizabeth Montgomery, Leo Penn, Eva Marie Saint
**1954-55:** Julie Andrews, Jacqueline Brookes, Shirl Conway, Barbara Cook, David Daniels, Mary Fickett, Page Johnson, Loretta Leversee, Jack Lord, Dennis Patrick, Anthony Perkins, Christopher Plummer
**1955-56:** Diane Cilento, Dick Davalos, Anthony Franciosa, Andy Griffith, Laurence

Harvey, David Hedison, Earle Hyman, Susan Johnson, John Michael King, Jayne Mansfield, Sara Marshall, Gaby Rodgers, Susan Strasberg, Fritz Weaver
**1956-57:** Peggy Cass, Sydney Chaplin, Sylvia Daneel, Bradford Dillman, Peter Donat, George Grizzard, Carol Lynley, Peter Palmer, Jason Robards, Cliff Robertson, Pippa Scott, Inga Swenson
**1957-58:** Anne Bancroft, Warren Berlinger, Colleen Dewhurst, Richard Easton, Tim Everett, Eddie Hodges, Joan Hovis, Carol Lawrence, Jacqueline McKeever, Wynne Miller, Robert Morse, George C. Scott
**1958-59:** Lou Antonio, Ina Balin, Richard Cross, Tammy Grimes, Larry Hagman, Dolores Hart, Roger Mollien, France Nuyen, Susan Oliver, Ben Piazza, Paul Roebling, William Shatner, Pat Suzuki, Rip Torn
**1959-60:** Warren Beatty, Eileen Brennan, Carol Burnett, Patty Duke, Jane Fonda, Anita Gillette, Elisa Loti, Donald Madden, George Maharis, John McMartin, Lauri Peters, Dick Van Dyke
**1960-61:** Joyce Bulifant, Dennis Cooney, Sandy Dennis, Nancy Dussault, Robert Goulet, Joan Hackett, June Harding, Ron Husmann, James MacArthur, Bruce Yarnell
**1961-62:** Elizabeth Ashley, Keith Baxter, Peter Fonda, Don Galloway, Sean Garrison, Barbara Harris, James Earl Jones, Janet Margolin, Karen Morrow, Robert Redford, John Stride, Brenda Vaccaro
**1962-63:** Alan Arkin, Stuart Damon, Melinda Dillon, Robert Drivas, Bob Gentry, Dorothy Loudon, Brandon Maggart, Julienne Marie, Liza Minnelli, Estelle Parsons, Diana Sands, Swen Swenson
**1963-64:** Alan Alda, Gloria Bleezarde, Imelda De Martin, Claude Giraud, Ketty Lester, Barbara Loden, Lawrence Pressman, Gilbert Price, Philip Proctor, John Tracy, Jennifer West
**1964-65:** Carolyn Coates, Joyce Jillson, Linda Lavin, Luba Lisa, Michael O'Sullivan, Joanna Pettet, Beah Richards, Jaime Sanchez, Victor Spinetti, Nicolas Surovy, Robert Walker, Clarence Williams III
**1965-66:** Zoe Caldwell, David Carradine, John Cullum, John Davidson, Faye Dunaway, Gloria Foster, Robert Hooks, Jerry Lanning, Richard Mulligan, April Shawhan, Sandra Smith, Leslie Ann Warren
**1966-67:** Bonnie Bedelia, Richard Benjamin, Dustin Hoffman, Terry Kiser, Reva Rose,

**Judy Kaye**

**Anthony Heald**

**Cynthia Nixon**

**Len Cariou**

**Laura Dean**

**Giancarlo Esposito**

Robert Salvio, Sheila Smith, Connie Stevens, Pamela Tiffin, Leslie Uggams, Jon Voight, Christopher Walken

**1967-68:** David Birney, Pamela Burrell, Jordan Christopher, Jack Crowder (Thalmus Rasulala), Sandy Duncan, Julie Gregg, Stephen Joyce, Bernadette Peters, Alice Playten, Michael Rupert, Brenda Smiley, Russ Thacker

**1968-69:** Jane Alexander, David Cryer, Blythe Danner, Ed Evanko, Ken Howard, Lauren Jones, Ron Leibman, Marian Mercer, Jill O'Hara, Ron O'Neal, Al Pacino, Marlene Warfield

**1969-70:** Susan Browning, Donny Burks, Catherine Burns, Len Cariou, Bonnie Franklin, David Holliday, Katharine Houghton, Melba Moore, David Rounds, Lewis J. Stadlen, Kristoffer Tabori, Fredricka Weber

**1970-71:** Clifton Davis, Michael Douglas, Julie Garfield, Martha Henry, James Naughton, Tricia O'Neil, Kipp Osborne, Roger Rathburn, Ayn Ruymen, Jennifer Salt, Joan Van Ark, Nell Carter, Mary Woronov, Sammy Cahn (Special Award)

**1971-72:** Jonelle Allen, Maureen Anderman, William Atherton, Richard Backus, Adrienne Barbeau, Cara Duff-MacCormick, Robert Foxworth, Elaine Joyce, Jess Richards, Ben Vereen, Beatrice Winde, James Woods

**1972-73:** D'Jamin Bartlett, Patricia Elliott, James Farentino, Brian Farrell, Victor Garber, Kelly Garrett, Mari Gorman, Laurence Guittard, Trish Hawkins, Monte Markham, John Rubinstein, Jennifer Warren, Alexander H. Cohen (Special Award)

**1973-74:** Mark Baker, Maureen Brennan, Ralph Carter, Thom Christopher, John Driver, Conchata Ferrell, Ernestine Jackson, Michael Moriarty, Joe Morton, Ann Reinking, Janie Sell, Mary Woronov, Sammy Cahn (Special Award)

**1974-75:** Peter Burnell, Zan Charisse, Lola Falana, Peter Firth, Dorian Harewood, Joel Higgins, Marcia McClain, Linda Miller, Marti Rolph, John Sheridan, Scott Stevensen, Donna Theodore, Equity Library Theatre (Special Award)

**1975-76:** Danny Aiello, Christine Andreas, Dixie Carter, Tovah Feldshuh, Chip Garnett, Richard Kelton, Vivian Reed, Charles Repole, Virginia Seidel, Daniel Seltzer, John V. Shea, Meryl Streep, A Chorus Line (Special Award)

**1976-77:** Trazana Beverley, Michael Cristofer, Joe Fields, Joanna Gleason, Cecilia Hart, John Heard, Gloria Hodes, Juliette Koka, Andrea McArdle, Ken Page, Jonathan Pryce, Chick Vennera, Eva LeGallienne (Special Award)

**1977-78:** Vasili Bogazianos, Nell Carter, Carlin Glynn, Christopher Goutman, William Hurt, Judy Kaye, Florence Lacy, Armelia McQueen, Gordana Rashovich, Bo Rucker, Richard Seer, Colin Stinton, Joseph Papp (Special Award)

**1978-79:** Philip Anglim, Lucie Arnaz, Gregory Hines, Ken Jennings, Michael Jeter, Laurie Kennedy, Susan Kingsley, Christine Lahti, Edward James Olmos, Kathleen Quinlan, Sarah Rice, Max Wright, Marshall W. Mason (Special Award)

**1979-80:** Maxwell Caulfield, Leslie Denniston, Boyd Gaines, Richard Gere, Harry Groener, Stephen James, Susan Kellermann, Dinah Manoff, Lonny Price, Marianne Tatum, Anne Twomey, Dianne Wiest, Mickey Rooney (Special Award)

**1980-81:** Brian Backer, Lisa Banes, Meg Bussert, Michael Allen Davis, Giancarlo Esposito, Daniel Gerroll, Phyllis Hyman, Cynthia Nixon, Amanda Plummer, Adam Redfield, Wanda Richert, Rex Smith, Elizabeth Taylor (Special Award)

**1981-82:** Karen Akers, Laurie Beechman, Danny Glover, David Alan Grier, Jennifer Holliday, Anthony Heald, Lizbeth Mackay, Peter MacNicol, Elizabeth McGovern, Ann Morrison, Michael O'Keefe, James Widdoes, Manhattan Theatre Club (Special Award)

**1982-83:** Karen Allen, Suzanne Bertish, Matthew Broderick, Kate Burton, Joanne Camp, Harvey Fierstein, Peter Gallagher, John Malkovich, Anne Pitoniak, James Russo, Brian Tarantina, Linda Thorson, Natalia Makarova (Special Award)

**1983-84:** Martine Allard, Joan Allen, Kathy Whitton Baker, Mark Capri, Laura Dean, Stephen Geoffreys, Tod Graff, Glenne Headly, J.J. Johnston, Bonnie Koloc, Calvin Levels, Robert Westenberg, Ron Moody (Special Award)

**1984-85:** Kevin Anderson, Richard Chaves, Patti Cohenour, Charles S. Dutton, Nancy Giles, Whoopi Goldberg, Leilani Jones, John Mahoney, Laurie Metcalf, Barry Miller, John Turturro, Amelia White, Lucille Lortel (Special Award)

**1985-86:** Suzy Amis, Alec Baldwin, Aled Davies, Faye Grant, Julie Hagerty, Ed Harris, Mark Jacoby, Donna Kane, Cleo Laine, Howard McGillin, Marisa Tomei, Joe Urla, Ensemble Studio Theatre (Special Award)

**1986-87:** Annette Bening, Timothy Daly, Lindsay Duncan, Frank Ferrante, Robert Lindsay, Amy Madigan, Michael Maguire, Demi Moore, Molly Ringwald, Frances Ruffelle, Courtney B. Vance, Colm Wilkinson, Robert DeNiro (Special Award)

**1987-88:** Yvonne Bryceland, Philip Casnoff, Danielle Ferland, Melissa Gilbert, Linda Hart, Linzi Hately, Brian Kerwin, Brian Mitchell, Mary Murfitt, Aidan Quinn, Eric Roberts, B.D. Wong

**1988-89:** Dylan Baker, Joan Cusack, Loren Dean, Peter Frechette, Sally Mayes, Sharon McNight, Jennie Moreau, Paul Provenza, Kyra Sedgwick, Howard Spiegel, Eric Stoltz, Joanne Whalley-Kilmer, Special Awards: Pauline Collins, Mikhail Baryshnikov

**1989-90:** Denise Burse-Mickelbury, Erma Campbell, Rocky Carroll, Megan Gallagher, Tommy Hollis, Robert Lambert, Kathleen Row McAllen, Michael McKean, Crista Moore, Mary-Louise Parker, Daniel von Bargen, Jason Workman, Special Awards: Stewart Granger, Kathleen Turner

**1990-91:** Jane Adams, Gillian Anderson, Adam Arkin, Brenda Blethyne, Marcus Chong, Paul Hipp, LaChanze, Kenny Neal, Kevin Ramsey, Francis Ruivivar, Lea Salonga, Chandra Wilson, Special Awards: Tracey Ullman, Ellen Stewart

**Mark Jacoby**

**Brenda Vaccaro**

**Robert Westenberg**

201

# Pulitzer Prize Productions

**1918**-Why Marry?, **1919**-No award, **1920**-Beyond the Horizon, **1921**-Miss Lulu Bett, **1922**-Anna Christie, **1923**-Icebound, **1924**-Hell-Bent fer Heaven, **1925**-They Knew What They Wanted, **1926**-Craig's Wife, **1927**-In Abraham's Bosom, **1928**-Strange Interlude, **1929**-Street Scene, **1930**-The Green Pastures, **1931**-Alison's House, **1932**-Of Thee I Sing, **1933**-Both Your Houses, **1934**-Men in White, **1935**-The Old Maid, **1936**-Idiot's Delight, **1937**-You Can't Take It with You, **1938**-Our Town, **1939**-Abe Lincoln in Illinois, **1940**-The Time of Your Life, **1941**-There Shall Be No Night, **1942**-No award, **1943**-The Skin of Our Teeth, **1944**-No award, **1945**-Harvey, **1946**-State of the Union, **1947**-No award, **1948**-A Streetcar Named Desire, **1949**-Death of a Salesman, **1950**-South Pacific, **1951**-No award, **1952**-The Shrike, **1953**-Picnic, **1954**-The Teahouse of the August Moon, **1955**-Cat on a Hot Tin Roof, **1956**-The Diary of Anne Frank, **1957**-Long Day's Journey into Night, **1958**-Look Homeward, Angel, **1959**-J.B., **1960**-Fiorello!, **1961**-All the Way Home, **1962**-How to Succeed in Business without Really Trying, **1963**-No award, **1964**-No award, **1965**-The Subject Was Roses, **1966**-No award, **1967**-A Delicate Balance, **1968**-No award, **1969**-The Great White Hope, **1970**-No Place to Be Somebody, **1971**-The Effect of Gamma Rays on Man-in-the-Moon Marigolds, **1972**-No award, **1973**-That Championship Season, **1974**-No award, **1975**-Seascape, **1976**-A Chorus Line, **1977**-The Shadow Box, **1978**-The Gin Game, **1979**-Buried Child, **1980**-Talley's Folly, **1981**-Crimes of the Heart, **1982**-A Soldier's Play, **1983**-'night, Mother, **1984**-Glengarry Glen Ross, **1985**-Sunday in the Park with George, **1986**-No award, **1987**-Fences, **1988**-Driving Miss Daisy, **1989**-The Heidi Chronicles, **1990**-The Piano Lesson, **1991**-Lost in Yonkers, **1992**-The Kentucky Cycle

# New York Drama Critics Circle Awards

**1936**-Winterset, **1937**-High Tor, **1938**-Of Mice and Men, Shadow and Substance, **1939**-The White Steed, **1940**-The Time of Your Life, **1941**-Watch on the Rhine, The Corn Is Green, **1942**-Blithe Spirit, **1943**-The Patriots, **1944**-Jacobowsky and the Colonel, **1945**-The Glass Menagerie, **1946**-Carousel, **1947**-All My Sons, No Exit, Brigadoon, **1948**-A Streetcar Named Desire, The Winslow Boy, **1949**-Death of a Salesman, The Madwoman of Chaillot, South Pacific, **1950**-The Member of the Wedding, The Cocktail Party, The Consul, **1951**-Darkness at Noon, The Lady's Not for Burning, Guys and Dolls, **1952**-I Am a Camera, Venus Observed, Pal Joey, **1953**-Picnic, The Love of Four Colonels, Wonderful Town, **1954**-Teahouse of the August Moon, Ondine, The Golden Apple, **1955**-Cat on a Hot Tin Roof, Witness for the Prosecution, The Saint of Bleecker Street, **1956**-The Diary of Anne Frank, Tiger at the Gates, My Fair Lady, **1957**-Long Day's Journey into Night, The Waltz of the Toreadors, The Most Happy Fella, **1958**-Look Homeward Angel, Look Back in Anger, The Music Man, **1959**-A Raisin in the Sun, The Visit, La Plume de Ma Tante, **1960**-Toys in the Attic, Five Finger Exercise, Fiorello!, **1961**-All the Way Home, A Taste of Honey, Carnival, **1962**-Night of the Iguana, A Man for All Seasons, How to Succeed in Business without Really Trying, **1963**-Who's Afraid of Virginia Woolf?, **1964**-Luther, Hello Dolly!, **1965**-The Subject Was Roses, Fiddler on the Roof, **1966**-The Persecution and Assassination of Marat as Performed by the Inmates of the Asylum of Charenton under the Direction of the Marquis de Sade, Man of La Mancha, **1967**-The Homecoming, Cabaret, **1968**-Rosencrantz and Guildenstern Are Dead, Your Own Thing, **1969**-The Great White Hope, 1776, **1970**-The Effect of Gamma Rays on Man-in-the-Moon Marigolds, Borstal Boy, Company, **1971**-Home, Follies, The House of Blue Leaves, **1972**-That Championship Season, Two Gentlemen of Verona, **1973**-The Hot l Baltimore, The Changing Room, A Little Night Music, **1974**-The Contractor, Short Eyes, Candide, **1975**-Equus, The Taking of Miss Janie, A Chorus Line, **1976**-Travesties, Streamers, Pacific Overtures, **1977**-Otherwise Engaged, American Buffalo, Annie, **1978**-Da, Ain't Misbehavin', **1979**-The Elephant Man, Sweeney Todd, **1980**-Talley's Folley, Evita, Betrayal, **1981**-Crimes of the Heart, A Lesson from Aloes, Special Citation to Lena Horne, The Pirates of Penzance, **1982**-The Life and Adventures of Nicholas Nickleby, A Soldier's Play, no musical honored, **1983**-Brighton Beach Memoirs, Plenty, Little Shop of Horrors, **1984**-The Real Thing, Glengarry Glen Ross, Sunday in the Park with George, **1985**-Ma Rainey's Black Bottom (no musical), **1986**-A Lie of the Mind, Benefactors, no musical, Special Citation to Lily Tomlin and Jane Wagner, **1987**-Fences, Les Liaisons Dangereuses, Les Misérables, **1988**-Joe Turner's Come and Gone, The Road to Mecca, Into the Woods, **1989**-The Heidi Chronicles, Aristocrats, Largely New York (Special), (no musical), **1990**-The Piano Lesson, City of Angels, Privates on Parade, **1991**-Six Degrees of Separation, The Will Rogers Follies, Our Country's Good, Special Citation to Eileen Atkins, **1992**-Two Trains Running, Dancing at Lughnasa

# American Theatre Wing Antoinette Perry (Tony) Award Productions

**1948**-Mister Roberts, **1949**-Death of a Salesman, Kiss Me, Kate, **1950**-The Cocktail Party, South Pacific, **1951**-The Rose Tattoo, Guys and Dolls, **1952**-The Fourposter, The King and I, **1953**-The Crucible, Wonderful Town, **1954**-The Teahouse of the August Moon, Kismet, **1955**-The Desperate Hours, The Pajama Game, **1956**-The Diary of Anne Frank, Damn Yankees, **1957**-Long Day's Journey into Night, My Fair Lady, **1958**-Sunrise at Campobello, The Music Man, **1959**-J.B., Redhead, **1960**-The Miracle Worker, Fiorello! tied with The Sound of Music, **1961**-Becket, Bye Bye Birdie, **1962**-A Man for All Seasons, How to Succeed in Business without Really Trying, **1963**-Who's Afraid of Virginia Woolf?, A Funny Thing Happened on the Way to the Forum, **1964**-Luther, Hello Dolly!, **1965**-The Subject Was Roses, Fiddler on the Roof, **1966**-The Persecution and Assassination of Marat as Performed by the Inmates of the Asylum of Charenton under the Direction of the Marquis de Sade, Man of La Mancha, **1967**-The Homecoming, Cabaret, **1968**- Rosencrantz and Guildenstern Are Dead, Hallelujah Baby!, **1969**-The Great White Hope, 1776, **1970**-Borstal Boy, Applause, **1971**-Sleuth, Company, **1972**-Sticks and Bones, Two Gentlemen of Verona, **1973**-That Championship Season, A Little Night Music, **1974**-The River Niger, Raisin, **1975**-Equus, The Wiz, **1976**-Travesties, A Chorus Line, **1977**-The Shadow Box, Annie, **1978**-Da, Ain't Misbehavin', Dracula, **1979**-The Elephant Man, Sweeney Todd, **1980**-Children of a Lesser God, Evita, Morning's at Seven, **1981**-Amadeus, 42nd Street, The Pirates of Penzance, **1982**-The Life and Adventures of Nicholas Nickleby, Nine, Othello, **1983**-Torch Song Trilogy, Cats, On Your Toes, **1984**-The Real Thing, La Cage aux Folles, **1985**-Biloxi Blues, Big River, Joe Egg, **1986**-I'm Not Rappaport, The Mystery of Edwin Drood, Sweet Charity, **1987**-Fences, Les Misérables, All My Sons, **1988**-M. Butterfly, The Phantom of the Opera, **1989**-The Heidi Chronicles, Jerome Robbins' Broadway, Our Town, Anything Goes, **1990**-The Grapes of Wrath, City of Angels, Gypsy, **1991**-Lost in Yonkers, The Will Rogers' Follies, Fiddler on the Roof, **1992**-Dancing at Lughnasa, Crazy For You, Guys & Dolls

Daniel Ahearn

Liz Amberly

Robert Alexander

Lisa C. Arrindell

Kevin Bacon

Kaye Ballard

# Biographical Data On This Season's Casts

## (June 1, 1991-May 31, 1992)

**BELE, JIM**. Born November 14, 1960 in Syracuse, NY. Graduate Ithaca Col. Debut 1984 OB in *Shepardsets*, followed by *The Cabbagehead, The Country Girl, Any Place but Here, Jock*.

**BRAHAM, F. MURRAY**. Born October 24, 1939 in Pittsburgh, Pa. Attended U. Tex. Debut 1967 OB in *The Fantasticks*, followed by *An Opening in the Trees, 14th Dictator, Young Abe Lincoln, Tonight in Living Color, Adaptation, Survival of St. Joan, The Dog Ran Away, Fables, Richard III, Little Murders, Scuba Duba, Where Has Tommy Flowers Gone? Miracle Play, Blessing, Sexual Perversity in Chicago, Landscape of the Body, The Master and Margarita, Biting the Apple, The Sea Gull, The Caretaker, Antigone, Uncle Vanya, The Golem, The Madwoman of Chaillot, Twelfth Night, Frankie and Johnny in the Clair de Lune, A Midsummer Night's Dream, Life in the Theatre*, Bdwy in *The Man in the Glass Booth (1968), 6 Rms Riv Vu, Bad Habits, The Ritz, Legend, Teibele and Her Demon, Macbeth, Waiting for Godot*.

**BUBA, ERNEST**. Born August 25, 1947 in Honolulu, HI. Attended Southwestern Col. Bdwy debut 1976 in *Pacific Overtures*, followed by *Loose Ends, Zoya's Apartment, Shimada*, OB in *Sunrise, Monkey Music, Station J. Yellow Fever, Pacific Overtures, Empress of China, The Man Who Turned into a Stick, Shogun Macbeth, Three Sisters, Song of Shim Chung*.

**ACKERMAN, LONI**. Born April 10, 1949 in NYC. Attended New School. Bdwy debut 1968 in *George M!*, followed by *No No Nanette, So Long 174th Street, The Magic Show, Evita, Cats*, OB in *Dames at Sea, Starting Here Starting Now, Roberta in Concert, Brownstone, Diamonds*.

**ADAMS, JANE**. Born April 1, 1965 in Washington, DC. Juilliard graduate. 1986 OB in *The Nice and the Nasty*, followed by *Young Playwrights Festival*, Bdwy in *I Hate Hamlet* for which she received a Theatre World Award, *The Crucible*.

**ADAMS, JOSEPH**. Born February 4, 1956 in Concord, Ca. Debut 1980 in ELT's *Romeo and Juliet*, followed by *Don Juan and the Non Don Juan*, Bdwy in *The Survivor* (1981).

**ADAMS, MASON**. Born February 26, 1919 in NYC. Graduate U. Wisc. Bdwy credits include *Get Away Old Man, Public Relations, Career Angel, Violet, Shadow of My Enemy, Tall Story, Inquest, Trial of the Catonsville 9, The Sign in Sidney Brustein's Window*, OB in *Meegan's Game, Shortchanged Review, Checking Out, The Soft Touch, Paradise Lost, The Time of Your Life, Danger: Memory, The Day Room, Rose Quartet*.

**ADLER, BRUCE**. Born November 27, 1944 in NYC. Attended NYU. Debut 1957 OB in *It's a Funny World*, followed by *Hard to Be a Jew, Big Winner, The Golden Land, The Stranger's Return, The Rise of David Levinsky, On Second Avenue*, Bdwy in *A Teaspoon Every Four Hours* (1971), *Oklahoma!* (1979), *Oh, Brother!, Sunday in the Park with George, Broadway, Those Were the Days, Crazy for You*.

**A'HEARN, PATRICK**. Born September 4, 1957 in Chappaqua,NY. Graduate Syracuse U. Debut 1985 OB in *Pirates of Penzance*, followed by *Forbidden Broadway*, Bdwy in *Les Misérables* (1987).

**AHEARN, DANIEL**. Born August 7, 1948 in Washington, DC. Attended Carnegie Mellon. Debut OB 1981 in *Woyzek*, followed by *Brontosaurus Rex, Billy Liar, Second Prize, Two Months in Leningrad, No Time Flat, Hollywood Scheherazade, Better Days, Joy Solution, Making Book*.

**AHLIN, MARGIT**. Born February 23, 1960 in Chappaqua, NY. Graduate NYU, AMDA. Debut 1982 OB in *Romeo and Juliet*, followed by *Social Event, Vanities, Standing on the Cheese Line, Company, Onlyman, In Available Light, The Elephant Piece, Crime on Goat Island*.

**AKERS, KAREN**. Born October 13, 1945 in NYC. Graduate Hunter Col. Bdwy debut 1982 in *Nine* for which she received a Theatre World Award, followed by *Jacques Brel Is Alive and Well and Living in New York, Grand Hotel*.

**ALDA, ALAN**. Born January 28, 1936 in NYC. Graduate Fordham U., Cleveland Playhouse. Bdwy credits include *Only in America, Purlie Victorious, Fair Game for Lovers* for which he received a Theatre World Award, *Cafe Crown, The Owl and the Pussycat, The Apple Tree, Jake's Women*, OB in *Darwin's Theories, A Whisper in God's Ear, Second City*.

**ALEXANDER, JACE**. Born April 7, 1964 in NYC. Attended NYU. Bdwy debut 1983 in *The Caine Mutiny Court Martial*, followed by *Six Degrees of Separation*. OB in *I'm Not Rappaport, Wasted, The Good Coach, Heart of a Dog, Price of Fame, Assassins*.

**ALEXANDER, JANE**. Born October 28, 1939 in Boston, MA. Attended Sarah Lawrence Col, U. Edinburgh. Bdwy debut 1968 in *The Great White Hope*, for which she received a Theatre World Award, followed by *6 Rms Riv Vu, Find Your Way Home, Hamlet (LC), The Heiress, First Monday in October, Goodbye Fidel, Monday after the Miracle, Shadowlands, The Visit*. OB in *Losing Time, Approaching Zanzibar*.

**ALEXANDER, ROBERT**. Born December 16, 1967 in Portsmouth, Va. Attended SUNY/Purchase. Debut 1991 OB in *Raft of the Medusa*.

**ALLEN, BEAU**. Born March 2, 1950 in Wilmington, De. Graduate Tufts U. Bdwy debut 1972 in *Jesus Christ Superstar*, followed by *Two Gentlemen of Verona, Best Little Whorehouse in Texas*, OB in *Dear World*.

**ALLEN, JOHN**. Born July 5, 1957 in Cuba. Graduate Hofstra U. Debut 1985 OB in *Pacific Overtures*, followed by *Encore, Maiami*, Bdwy in *Rags* (1986), *Chess, The Most Happy Fella* (1991).

**ALMY, BROOKS**. Born July 15 in Fort Belvoir, VA. Attended U. Hawaii. Bdwy debut 1981 in *The Little Prince and the Aviator*, followed by NYC Opera's *Music Man, Candide, Sweeney Todd and Pajama Game, A Change in the Heir*, OB in *Shylock, Nunsense*.

**ALDREDGE, TOM**. Born February 28, 1928 in Dayton, Oh. Attended Daton U. Goodman Theatre. Bdwy debut 1959 in *The Nervous Set*, followed by *UTBU, Slapstick Tragedy, Everything in the Garden, Indians, Engagement Baby, How the Other Half Loves, Sticks and Bones, Where's Charley?, Leaf People, Rex, Vieux Carre, St. Joan, Stages, On Golden Pond, The Little Foxes, Into the Woods, Two Shakespearean Actors*, OB in *The Tempest, Between Two Thieves, Henry V, The Premise, Love's Labour's Lost, Troilus and Cressida, The Butter and Egg Man, Ergo, Boys in the Band, Twelfth Night, Colette, Hamlet, The Orphan, King Lear, The Iceman Cometh, Black Angel, Getting Along Famously, Fool for Love, Neon Psalms, Richard II*.

**AMBERLY, LIZ**. Born October 2 in Poughkeepsie, NY. Attended Syracuse U. LAMDA. Debut 1989 OB in *Leave It to Jane*, followed by *The Awakening of Spring*.

**ANDERSON, CHRISTINE**. Born August 6 in Utica, NY. Graduate U. Wis. Bdwy debut in *I Love My Wife* (1980), OB in *I Can't Keep Running in Place, On the Swing Shift, Red, Hot and Blue, A Night at Texas Guinan's, Nunsense*.

**ANDERSON, FRED**. Born July 11, 1964 in Memphis, TN. Attended NC Sch. of Arts, Joffrey Ballet Sch. Debut 1988 OB in *Lost in the Stars*, followed by *Telltale Hearts*, Bdwy in *Crazy for You* (1992).

**ANDERSON, GILLIAN**. Born August 9, 1968 in Chicago, IL. Graduate Goodman Th. Sch. Debut 1991 OB in *Absent Friends* for which she received a Theatre World Award.

**ANDERSON, JOEL**. Born November 19, 1955 in San Diego, Ca. Graduate U. Utah. Debut 1980 OB in *A Funny Thing Happened on the Way to the Forum*, followed by *Joan of Lorraine, Last of the Knucklemen, The Widow Claire, The Heidi Chronicles, Fighting Light, Empty Hearts*.

**ANDERSON, KEVIN P**. Born January 5, 1960 in Peoria, IL. Attended U. WY. N. TX State. Debut 1990 in NYC Opera's *A Little Night Music*, followed by *Street Scene*.

**ANDERSON, LAWRENCE**. Born May 18, 1964 in Poughkeepsie, NY. Graduate U Col. Bdwy debut 1992 in *Phantom of the Opera* followed by *Les Misérables*.

**ANDRES, BARBARA.** Born February 11, 1939 in NYC. Graduate Catholic U. Bdwy debut 1969 in *Jimmy*, followed by *The Boy Friend, Rodgers and Hart, Rex, On Golden Pond, Doonesbury, OB in Threepenny Opera, Landscape of the Body, Harold Arlen's Cabaret, Suzanna Andler, One-Act Festival, Company, Marathon '87, Arms and the Man, A Woman without a Name, First is Supper.*

**ANDREWS, GEORGE LEE.** Born October 13, 1942 in Milwaukee, WI. Debut OB in *Jacques Brel Is Alive and Well ...*, followed by *Starting Here Starting Now, Vamps and Rideouts, The Fantasticks*, Bdwy in *A Little Night Music* (1973), *On the 20th Century, Merlin, The Phantom of the Opera, A Little Night Music* (NYCO).

**ANKENY, MARK.** Born October 9, 1958 in Austin, Mn. Debut 1985 OB in *She Loves Me* followed by *Murder Game, Hannah 1939, Chess.*

**ARANAS, RAUL.** Born October 1, 1947 in Manilla, P.I. Graduate Pace U. Debut 1976 OB in *Savages*, followed by *Yellow Is My Favorite Color, 49, Bullet Headed Birds, Tooth of the Crime,Teahouse, Shepard Sets, Cold Air, La Chunga, The Man Who Turned into a Stick, Twelfth Night, Shogun Macbeth, Boutique Living & Disposable Icons, Fairy Bones, In the Jungle of Cities*, Bdwy in *Loose Ends* (1978).

**ANTON, SUSAN.** Born October 12, 1950 in Yucaipa, CA. Attended Bernardino Col. Bdwy debut 1985 in *Hurlyburly*, followed by *The Will Rogers Follies*, OB's *Xmas a Go-Go.*

**ARCARO, ROBERT.** (a.k.a. Bob), Born August 9, 1952 in Brooklyn, NY. Graduate Wesleyan U. Debut 1977 OB in *New York City Street Show*, followed by *Working Theatre Festival, Man with a Raincoat, Working One-Acts, Henry Lumpur, Special Interests, Measure for Measure, Our Lady of Perpetual Danger, Brotherly Love.*

**ARKIN, ADAM.** Born August 19, 1956 in Brooklyn, NY. Bdwy debut 1991 in *I Hate Hamlet* for which he received a Theatre World Award followed by OB in *Sight Unseen.*

**ARNAZ, LUCIE.** Born July 17, 1951 in Los Angeles, Ca. Bdwy debut 1979 in *They're Playing Our Song* for which she received a Theatre World Award, followed by *Lost in Yonkers* (1992).

**ARNOTT, MARK.** Born June 15, 1950 in Chicago, Il. Graduate Dartmouth Col. Debut 1981 OB in *The Hunchback of Notre Dame* followed by *Buddies, Love's Labour's Lost, Two Gentlemen of Verona, The Dining Room, The Knack, Marmalade Skies, The Homecoming*, Bdwy debut 1992 in *A Small Family Business.*

**AROESTE, JOEL.** Born April 10, 1949 in NYC. Graduate SUNY. Bdwy debut 1986 in *Raggedy Ann*, OB in *Beauty and the Beast.*

**ARRAMBIDE, MARIO.** Born March 1, 1953 in San Antonio, Tx. Attended RADA. Debut 1985 OB in *Aunt Dan and Lemon*, followed by *The Death of Garcia Lorca, The Golem, Hamlet, Measure for Measure, In the Jungle of Cities.*

**ARRINDELL, LISA.** Born March 24, 1969 in Bronx, NY. Juilliard graduate. Debut 1990 in *Richard III*, followed by *Earth and Sky, Mixed Babies.*

**ASH, RANDL.** Born October 15, 1959 in Elmhurst, IL. Attended Central CT State Col. Debut 1977 OB in *The Comic Strip*, followed by *Elegies for Angels. Punks and Raging Queens, Pageant.*

**ASHFORD, ROBERT.** Born November 19, 1959 in Orlando, FL. Attended Washington & Lee U. Bdwy debut 1987 in *Anything Goes*, followed by *Radio City Music Hall Christmas Spectacular, The Most Happy Fella* (1992).

**ASHLEY, MARY ELLEN.** Born June 11, 1938 in Long Island City, NY. Graduate Queens Col. Bdwy debut 1943 in *Innocent Voyage*, followed by *By Appointment Only, Annie Get Your Gun, Yentl*, OB in *Carousel, Polly, Panama Hattie, Soft Touch, Suddenly the Music Starts, The Facts of Death, A Drifter, The Grifter and Heather McBride, Leave It To Me, Finkel's Follies.*

**ATKINSON, JAYNE.** Born February 18, 1959 in Bournemouth, Engl. Graduate Northwestern U., Yale. Debut 1986 OB in *Bloody Poetry*, followed by *Terminal Bar, Return of Pinocchio, The Art of Success, The Way of the World, Appointment with a High Wire Lady*, Bdwy in *All My Sons* (1987).

**ATLEE, HOWARD.** Born May 14, 1926 in Bucyrus, OH. Graduate Emerson Col. Debut 1990 OB in *Historical Prods,*followed by *The 15th Ward, The Hells of Dante, What a Royal Pain in the Farce.*

**AUBERJONOIS, RENE.** Born June 1, 1940 in NYC. Graduate Carnegie Inst. With LCRep in *A Cry of Players, King Lear*, and *Twelfth Night*, Bdwy in *Fire* (1969), *Coco, Tricks, The Good Doctor, Break a Leg, Every Good Boy Deserves Favor, Big River, Metamorphosis, City of Angels*, BAM Co. in *The New York Idea, Three Sisters, The Play's the Thing*, and *Julius Caesar.*

**AUGUSTINE, JOHN.** Born March 5, 1960 in Canton, OH. Attended Baldwin-White Col. Debut in 1988 OB in *Young Playwrights Festival '88*, followed by *Insatiable/Temporary People, A Walk on Lake Erie, Marathon '91, Seven Blowjobs.*

**AUGUSTUS, NICHOLAS.** Born July 22, 1959 in NYC. Attended Denison U. Debut 1989 OB in *Gigi*, followed by *Forbidden Broadway, Junkyard.*

**AUSTRIAN, MARJORIE.** Born February 3, 1934 in the Bronx, NY. Attended Syracuse U. Kansas. OB in *Henry V, All's Well That Ends Well, Sylvia Plath, Jonah, Ivanov, Loyalties, The House of Bernarda Alba, Lucky Rita, The Diary of Anne Frank, A Day in the Death of Elizabeth, Dodger Blue, Homesick.*

**AVARI, ERICK.** Born April 13, 1952 in Calcutta, In. Graduate Charleston (SC) Col. Debut 1983 OB in *Bhutan*, followed by *Comedy of Errors, Map of the World, A Midsummer Night's Dream, 'Tis a Pity She's a Whore.*

**AVIDON, NELSON.** Born February 23, 1957 in Brooklyn, NY. Debut in *Second Avenue* followed by *The Green Death, Cheapside, Chee-Chee, Three Sisters, Unnatural Acts, Progress, I Am A Camera.*

**AVNER, JON.** Born June 24, 1953 in NYC. Graduate Syracuse U. St. John's U. Debut 1986 OB in *Murder on Broadway*, followed by *Radio Roast, Crimes of Passion,*

*The World of Sholem Aleichem, Penguin Blues, Rasputin, Sarah, Currents Turn Awry.*

**BABBITT, ROB.** Born July 28, 1954 in Olean, NY. Attended N. Texas State Debut 1980 OB in *Blues in the Night*, Bdwy in *Stepping Out, Grand Hotel.*

**BACON, KEVIN.** Born July 8, 1958 in Philadelphia, Pa. Debut 1978 OB in *Gettin Out*, followed by *Glad Tidings, Album, Flux, Poor Little Lambs, Slab Boys, M without Dates, Loot, The Author's Voice, Road, Spike Heels.*

**BAEZ, RAFAEL.** Born August 3, 1963 in NYC. Attended CCNY. Debut 1987 C in *La Puta Vita*, followed by *Enough Is Enough, Ariano, Kate's Diary, A Tempest.*

**BAGDEN, RONALD.** Born December 26, 1953 in Philadelphia, PA. Gradua Temple U., RADA. Debut 1977 OB in *Oedipus Rex*, followed by *Oh! What a Love War, Jack, Gonza the Lancer, Dead Mother, The Home Show Pieces*, Bdwy *Amadeus* (1980).

**BAILEY, ADRIAN.** Born September 23, in Detroit, Mi. Graduate U. Detroit. Bdv debut 1976 in *Your Arms Too Short to Box with God*, followed by *Prince of Centr Park, Jelly's Last Jam*, OB in *A Thrill a Moment.*

**BAIN, CONRAD.** Born February 4, 1923 in Lethbridge, Can. Attended AAD. Bdwy in *Sixth Finger in a Five Finger Glove* (1956), *Candide, Hot Spot, Advise a Consent, The Cuban Thing, Twigs, Uncle Vanya, On Borrowed Time* (1991), *T MakropoulosSecret, The Queen and the Rebels, Hogan's Goat, The Kitchen, Scul Duba, Nobody Hears a Broken Drum, Steambath, Play Strindberg* (LC).

**BAKER, ANGELA.** Born February 3, 1973 in Cleveland, Oh. Attended NYT AADA. Debut 1989 OB in *Romeo and Juliet*, followed by Bdwy in *The Crucibl* (1991), *The Master Builder, A Little Hotel on the Side.*

**BAKER, CONNIE.** Born May 29, in Ft. Worth, Tx. Graduate TCU. Debut 1986 O in *The Pajama Game*, followed by *Company.*

**BAKER, DYLAN.** Born in Lackey, VA. Graduate Wm. & Mary, Yale. Debut 198 OB in *Not about Heroes*, followed by *Two Gentlemen of Verona, The Commo Pursuit, Much Ado about Nothing, Eastern Standard, Wolf-Man, Dearly Departe* Bdwy (1989) in *Eastern Standard* for which he received a Theatre World Award, *I Bete.*

**BAKER, ROBERT MICHAEL.** Born February 28, 1954 in Boston, Ma. Attende Boston U. AADA. Debut 1984 OB in *Jessie's Land* followed by *Enter Laughin, Happily Ever After, Company, The Education of Hyman Kaplan, Yiddle with a Fiddl* Bdwy in *Guys and Dolls* (1992).

**BALDWIN, ALEC.** Born April 3, 1958 in Massepequa, NY. Attended Georg Washington U. NYU. Bdwy debut 1986 in *Loot* for which he received a Theati World Award, followed by *Serious Money, A Streetcar Named Desire*, OB in *Prelu to a Kiss.*

**BALL, JERRY.** Born December 16, 1956 in New Lexington, OH. Graduate Capit U., NYU. Bdwy debut 1990 in *Grand Hotel.*

**BALLARD, KAYE.** Born November 20, 1926 in Cleveland, Oh. Debut 1954 OB *The Golden Apple*, followed by *Cole Porter Revisited, Hey Ma Kaye Ballard, Sh Stoops to Conquer, Working 42nd Street at Last!, Hurry! Hurry! Hollywood!*, Bdwy *The Beast in Me* (1963), *Royal Flush, Molly, Pirates of Penzance.*

**BALSAM, TALIA.** Born March 5, 1959 in NYC. Bdwy debut 1992 in *Jake Women* for which she received a Theatre World Award.

**BARANSKI, CHRISTINE.** Born May 2, 1952 in Buffalo, NY. Graduate Juilliar Debut OB 1978 in *One Crack Out*, followed by *Says I Says He, The Trouble wi Europe, Coming Attractions, Operation Midnight Climax, Sally and Marsha, Midsummer Night's Dream, It's Only a Play, Marathon '86, Elliot Loves, Lip Together Teeth Apart*, Bdwy in *Hide and Seek* (1980), *The Real Thing, Hurlyburl House of Blue Leaves, Rumors, Nick & Nora.*

**BARBOUR, THOMAS.** Born July 25, 1921 in New York City. Graduate Princeto Harvard. Bdwy debut 1968 in *Portrait of a Queen*, followed by *The Great White Hope Scratch, Lincoln Mask, Kingdoms*, OB in *Twelfth Night, Merchant of Venice Admirable Bashful, The Lady's Not for Burning, The Enchanted, Antony an Cleopatra, The Saintliness of Margery Kemp, Dr. Willy Nilly, Under the Sycamor Tree, Epitaph for George Dillon, Thracian Horses, Old Glory, Sgt. Musgrave's Danc Nestless Bird, The Seagull, Wayside Motor Inn, Arthur, The Grinding Machine, M Simian, Sorrows of Frederick, Terrorists, Dark Ages, Royal Bob, Relatively Speakin Aristocrats, The Taming of the Shrew, The Perpetrator.*

**BARCROFT, JUDITH.** Born July 6 in Washington, D.C. Attended Northwestern U Stephens Col. Bdwy debut 1965 in *The Mating Game* followed by *Dinner at 8, Plaz Suite, All God's Chillun Got Wings, Betrayal, Elephant Man, Shimada*, OB in *M Amilcar, Cloud 9, For Sale, Songs of Twilight, Solitaire/Double Solitaire, Breaking th Prairie Wolf Code.*

**BARON, EVALYN.** Born April 21, 1948 in Atlanta, GA. Graduate Northwestern U U. Min. Debut 1979 OB in *Scrambled Feet*, followed by *Hijinks, I Can't Kee, Running in Place, Jerry's Girls, Harvest of Strangers, Quilters*, Bdwy in *Fearles Frank* (1980), *Big River, Rages, Social Security, Les Miserables.*

**BARRE, GABRIEL.** Born August 26, 1957 in Brattleboro, Vt. Graduate AADA Debut 1977 OB in *Jabberwock* followed by *T.N.T., Bodo, The Baker's Wife, The Tim of Your Life, Children of the Sun, Wicked Philanthropy, Starmites, Mistress of the Inr Gifts of the Magi, The Tempest, Return to the Forbidden Planet*, Bdwy in *Rags* (1986)

**BARRIE-WILSON, WENDY.** Born June 9 in Loveland, OH. Graduate Denison UNC. Bdwy debut 1987 in *All My Sons*, OB in *The Voice of the Prairie.*

**BARSHA, DEBRA.** Born March 19, 1959 in Syracuse, NY. Attended Eastma School of Music, NY debut OB 1991 in *Tony 'n' Tina's Wedding.*

**BARTENIEFF, GEORGE.** Born January 24, 1933 in Berlin, Ger. Bdwy debut 1947 in *The Whole World Over*, followed by *Venus Is*, *All's Well That Ends Well*, *Quotations from Chairman Mao Tse-Tung*, *The Death of Bessie Smith*, *Cop-Out*, *Room Service*, *Unlikely Heroes*, OB in *Walking in Waldheim*, *Memorandum*, *The Increased Difficulty of Concentration*, *Trelawny of the Wells*, *Charley Chestnut Rides the IRT*, *Radio (Wisdom): Sophia Part I*, *Images of the Dead*, *Dead End Kids*, *The Blonde Leading the Blonde*, *The Dispossessed*, *Growing Up Gothic*, *Rosetti's Apologies*, *On the Lam*, *Samuel Beckett Trilogy*, *Quartet*, *Help Wanted*, *A Matter of Life and Death*, *The Heart That Eats Itself*, *Coney Island Kid*, *Cymbeline*, *Better People*.

**BARTLETT, ALISON.** Born in Massachusetts July 14, 1971. Debut 1984 OB in *Landscape of the Body*, followed by *Jersey City*, *Family Portrait*, *Approximating Mother*.

**BARTLETT, LISABETH.** Born February 28, 1956 in Denver, Co. Graduate Northwestern U. Bdwy debut 1981 in *The Dresser*, followed by *Execution of Justice*, OB in *The Lady's Not for Burning*, *The Rachel Plays*, *Iron Bars*.

**BARTON, STEVE.** Born in Arkansas. Graduate U. Texas. Bdwy debut 1988 in *Phantom of the Opera*.

**BASCH, PETER.** Born May 11, 1956 in New York City. Graduate Columbia Col. UC/Berkeley. Debut 1984 in *Hackers*, followed by *Festival of I-Act Comedies*, EST *Marathon '92*.

**BATEMAN, BILL.** Born December 10 in Rock Island, IL. Graduate Augustana Col Debut 1974 OB in *Anything Goes*, followed by Bdwy in *Hello Dolly* (1978), *Bring Back Birdie*, *Peter Pan* (1991).

**BATTLE, HINTON.** Born November 29, 1956 in Neubraecke, Ger. Joined Dance Theatre of Harlem before making Bdwy debut in *The Wiz* (1975), followed by *Dancin'*, *Sophisticated Ladies*, *Dreamgirls*, *The Tap Dance Kid*, *Miss Saigon*.

**BEAL, JOHN.** Born August 13, 1909 in Joplin, Mo. Graduate U. Pa. His many credits include *Wild Waves*, *Another Language*, *She Loves Me Not*, *Russet Mantle*, *Soliloquy*, *Miss Swan Expects*, *Liberty Jones*, *Voice of the Turtle*, *Lend an Ear*, *Teahouse of the August Moon*, *Calculated Risk*, *Billy*, *Our Town* (1970), *The Crucible*, *The Master Builder*, *A Little Hotel on the Side*, OB in *Wilder's Triple Bill*, *To Be Young, Gifted and Black*, *Candyapple*, *Long Day's Journey into the Night*, *Rivers Return*.

**BEDFORD, BRIAN.** Born February 16, 1935 in Morley, Eng. Attended RADA. Bdwy debut 1960 in *Five Finger Exercise* followed by *Lord Pengo*, *The Private Ear*, *The Astrakhan Coat*, *The Unknown Soldier and His Wife*, *The Seven Descents of Myrtle*, *Jumpers*, *The Cocktail Party*, *Hamlet*, *Private Lives*, *School for Wives*, *The Misanthrope*, *Two Shakespearean Actors*, OB in *The Knack*, *The Lunatic The Lover and the Poet*.

**BEDFORD, PATRICK.** Born May 30, 1932 in Dublin, Ire. Appeared with Dublin Gate Theatre before Bdwy bow 1966 in *Philadelphia, Here I Come!*, followed by *The Mundy Scheme*, *Equus*, OB in *Small Craft Warnings*, *Home*, *Grandchild of Kings*.

**BEECHMAN, LAURIE.** Born April 4, 1954 in Philadelphia, PA. Attended NYU. Bdwy debut 1977 in *Annie*, followed by *Pirates of Penzance*, *Joseph and the Amazing Technicolor Dreamcoat* for which she received a Theatre World Award, *Cats*, *Les Misérables*, OB in *Some Enchanted Evening*, *Pal Joey in Concert*.

**BEERS, FRANCINE.** Born November 26 in NYC. Attended Hunter Col., CCNY. Debut 1963 OB in *King of the Whole Damned World* followed by *Kiss Mama*, *Monopoly*, *Cakes with Wine*, *The Grandma Plays*, Bdwy in *Cafe Crown*, *6 Rms Riv Vu*, *The American Clock*, *Curse of an Aching Heart*, *One of the All-Time Greats*.

**BELMONTE, VICKI.** Born January 20, 1947 in U.S.A. Bdwy debut 1960 in *Bye Bye Birdie*, followed by *Subways Are for Sleeping*, *All American*, *Annie Get Your Gun* LC), OB in *Nunsense*.

**BELTZ, JESSICA.** Born in St. Louis, Mo. Graduate Ind. U. Brandeis U. Debut 1988 OB in *Gifts of the Magi*, followed by *Susan B.*, *Conversations in Black and White*, *Trelawney of the Wells*.

**BENSON, CINDY.** Born October 2, 1951 in Attleboro, MA. Graduate St. Leo Col, J. IL. Debut 1981 OB in *Some Like It Cole*, followed by *Eating Raoul*, Bdwy *Les Misérables* (1987).

**BENSON, JODI.** Born October 10, 1961 in Rockford, Il. Attended Millkin U. Debut 1983 in *Marilyn, An American Fable* followed by *Smile*, *Welcome to the Club*, *Crazy for You*, OB in *Hurry! Hurry! Hollywood!*

**BENTLEY, MARY DENISE.** Born December 28 in Indianapolis, IN. Graduate Ind. J. Bdwy debut 1983 in *Dreamgirls*, OB in *Little Shop of Horrors* (1987), followed by *Forbidden Broadway*.

**BERTISH, SUZANNE.** Born August 7, 1951 in London, Eng. Attended London Drama School. Bdwy debut 1981 in *Nicholas Nickleby*, followed by *Salome*, OB in *Skirmishes* for which she received a Theatre World Award, followed by *Rosmersholm*, *Art of Success*.

**BESSETTE, MIMI.** Born January 15, 1956 in Midland, Mi.Graduate TCU, RADA. Debut 1978 OB in *The Gifts of the Magi*, followed by *Bugles at Dawn*, *On the 20th Century*, *Opal*, Bdwy in *The Best Little Whorehouse in Texas*.

**BETHUNE, ZINA.** Born in NYC. Appeared with NYC Ballet before making Bdwy debut in *The Most Happy Fella* (1956), followed by *Grand Hotel*, OB in *Monday's Heroes* (1954).

**BEVERLEY, TRAZANA.** Born August 9, 1945 in Baltimore, MD. Graduate NYU. Debut 1969 OB in *Rules for Running*, followed by *Les Femmes Noires*, *Geronimo*, *Antigone*, *The Brothers*, *God's Trombones*, *Marathon '91*, Bdwy in *My Sister My Sister*, *For Colored Girls Who Have Considered Suicide* for which she received a Theatre World Award, *Death and the King's Horseman* (LC), *The Crucible*.

**BIANCHI, JAMES R.** Born June 21, 1949 in Cleveland, Oh. Attended Bowling Green State U. Debut 1991 OB in *Twelfth Night*, followed by *St. Joan*.

**BIRKELUND, OLIVIA.** Born April 26, 1963 in New York City. Graduate Brown U. Debut 1990 OB in *Othello*, followed by *Cowboy in His Underwear*.

**BIRNEY, REED.** Born September 11, 1954 in Alexandria, Va. Attended Boston U. Bdwy debut 1977 in *Gemini*, OB in *The Master and Margarita*, *Bella Figura*, *Winterplay*, *The Flight of the Earls*, *Filthy Rich*, *Lady Moonsong*, *Mr. Monsoon*, *The Common Pursuit*, *Zero Positive*, *Moving Targets*, *Spare Parts*, *A Murder of Crows*, *7 Blowjobs*.

**BISHOP, KELLY** (formerly Carole). Born February 28, 1944 in Colorado Springs, CO. Bdwy debut 1967 in *Golden Rainbow*, followed by *Promises, Promises*, *On the Town*, *Rachel Lily Rosenbloom*, *A Chorus Line*, *Six Degrees of Separation*, OB in *Piano Bar*, *Changes*, *The Blessing*, *Going to New England*, *Six Degrees of Separation*.

**BLACK, RACHEL.** Born September 15 in NYC. Attended U. Buffalo. Debut 1989 OB in *Land of Dreams*, followed by *The Fifth Romance Language*, *Yiddle with a Fiddle*, *Rags*.

**BLOCH, SCOTTY.** Born January 28 in New Rochelle, NY. Attended AADA. Debut 1945 OB in *Craig's Wife*, followed by *Lemon Sky*, *Battering Ram*, *Richard III*, *In Celebration*, *An Act of Kindness*, *The Price*, *Grace*, *Neon Psalms*, *Other People's Money*, *Walking the Dead*, EST *Marathon '92*, Bdwy in *Children of a Lesser God* (1980).

**BLOCK, LARRY.** Born October 30, 1942 in NYC. Graduate URI. Bdwy debut 1966 in *Hail Scrawdyke*, followed by *La Turista*, OB in *Eh?*, *Fingernails Blue as Flowers*, *Comedy of Errors*, *Coming Attractions*, *Henry IV Part 2*, *Feuhrer Bunker*, *Manhattan Love Songs*, *Souvenirs*, *The Golem*, *Responsible Parties*, *Hit Parade*, *Largo Desolato*, *The Square Root of 3*, *Young Playwrights Festival*, *Hunting Cockroaches*, *Two Gentlemen of Verona*, *Yello Dog Contract*, *Temptation*, *Festival of I Acts*, *The Faithful Brethern of Pitt Street*, *Loman Family Picnic*, *One of the All-Time Greats*, *Pericles*.

**BLOOM, TOM.** Born November 1, 1944 in Washington, D.C. Graduate Western MD Col., Emerson Col. Debut 1989 OB in *The Widow's Blind Date*, followed by *A Cup of Coffee*, *Major Barbara*, *A Perfect Diamond*, *Lips Together Teeth Apart*.

**BLUE, ARLANA.** Born November 15, 1948 in Passaic, NJ. Attended NY School of Ballet. Debut 1971 OB in *Fear of Love*, followed by *Paranoia Pretty*, *Sgt. Pepper's Lonely Hearts Club Band*, *Machinal*, *I Was Madelaine*, *Shewing Up of Blanco Posnet*, *Angelina's Pizzeria*.

**BLUM, JOEL.** Born May 19, 1952 in San Francisco, CA. Attended Marin Col., NYU. Bdwy debut 1976 in *Debbie Reynolds on Broadway*, followed by *42nd Street*, *Stardust*, *Radio City Easter Show*, OB in *And the World Goes Round*.

**BLUM, MARK.** Born May 14, 1950 in Newark, NJ. Graduate U. PA, U. MN. Debut 1976 OB in *The Cherry Orchard*, followed by *Green Julia*, *Say Goodnight Gracie*, *Table Settings*, *Key Exchange*, *Loving Reno*, *Messiah*, *It's Only a Play*, *Little Footsteps*, *Cave of Life*, *Gus & Al*, Bdwy in *Lost in Yonkers* (1991).

**BOBBIE, WALTER.** Born November 18, 1945 in Scranton, PA. Graduate U. Scranton, Catholic U. Bdwy debut 1971 in *Frank Merriwell*, followed by *The Grass Harp*, *Grease*, *Tricks*, *Going Up*, *History of the American Film*, *Anything Goes*, *Getting Married*, *Guys and Dolls*, OB in *Drat!*, *She Loves Me*, *Up from Paradise*, *Goodbye Freddy*, *Cafe Crown*, *Young Playwrights '90*.

**BOBBY, ANNE MARIE.** Born December 12, 1967 in Paterson, NJ. Attended Oxford U. Debut 1983 OB in *American Passion*, followed by *Class I Acts*, *Godspell*, *Progress*, *Groundhog*, Bdwy in *The Human Comedy*, *The Real Thing*, *Hurlyburly*, *Precious Sons*, *Smile*.

**BODLE, JANE.** Born November 12 in Lawrence, KS. Attended U. Utah. Bdwy debut 1983 in *Cats*, followed by *Les Miserables*, *Miss Saigon*.

**BOGARDUS, STEPHEN.** Born March 11, 1954 in Norfolk, VA. Princeton graduate. Bdwy debut 1980 in *West Side Story*, followed by *Les Miserables*, *Falsettos*, OB in *March of the Falsettos*, *Feathertop*, *No Way to Treat a Lady*, *Look on the Bright Side*, *Falsettoland*.

**BOGOSIAN, ERIC.** Born April 24, 1953 in Woburn, MA. Graduate Oberlin Col. Debut 1982 OB in *Men Inside/Voices of America*, followed by *Funhouse*, *Drinking in America*, *Talk Radio*, *Sex Drugs Rock & Roll*, *Notes from Underground*.

**BOHUS, ERIC.** Born June 1, 1959 in Trenton, NJ. Graduate High Point Col. Bdwy debut 1991 in *Grand Hotel*.

**BOLTON, JOHN KEENE.** Born December 29, 1963 in Rochester, NY. Graduate St. John Fisher Col. Debut 1991 OB in *Cinderella*.

**BOSCO, PHILIP.** Born September 26, 1930 in Jersey City, NJ. Graduate Catholic U. Credits: *Auntie Mame*, *Rape of the Belt*, *Ticket of Leave Man*, *Donnybrook*, *A Man for All Seasons*, *Mrs. Warren's Profession*, with LCRep in *A Great Career*, *In the Matter of J. Robert Oppenheimer*, *The Miser*, *The Time of Your Life*, *Camino Real*, *Operation Sidewinder*, *Amphitryon*, *Enemy of the People*, *Playboy of the Western World*, *Good Woman of Setzuan*, *Antigone*, *Mary Stuart*, *Narrow Road to the Deep North*, *The Crucible*, *Twelfth Night*, *Enemies*, *Plough and the Stars*, *Merchant of Venice*, *A Streetcar Named Desire*, *Henry V*, *Threepenny Opera*, *Streamers*, *Stages*, *St. Joan*, *The Biko Inquest*, *Man and Superman*, *Whose Life Is It Anyway?*, *Major Barbara*, *A Month in the Country*, *Bacchae*, *Hedda Gabler*, *Don Juan in Hell*, *Inadmissable Evidence*, *Eminent Domain*, *Misalliance*, *Learned Ladies*, *Some Men Need Help*, *Ah Wilderness!*, *The Caine Mutiny Court Martial*, *Heartbreak House*, *Come Back Little Sheba*, *Loves of Anatol*, *Be Happy for Me*, *Master Class*, *You Never Can Tell*, *Devil's Disciple*, *Lend Me a Tenor*, *Breaking Legs*.

205

**BOSTWICK, BARRY.** Born February 24, 1945 in San Mateo, Ca. Graduate Cal. Western, NYU. Bdwy debut with APA in *War and Peace*, followed by *Pantegleize, The Misanthrope, Cock-a-doodle Dandy, Hamlet, Grease, The Robber Bridegroom, She Loves Me, Nick and Nora*, OB in *Salvation, Colette, Soon, Screens, They Knew What They Wanted*.

**BOUTSIKARIS, DENNIS.** Born December 21, 1952 in Newark, NJ. Graduate Hampshire Col. Debut 1975 OB in *Another Language* followed by *Funeral March for a One-Man Band, All's Well That Ends Well, A Day in the Life of the Czar, Nest of the Wood Grouse, Cheapside, Rum and Coke, The Boys Next Door, Sight Unseen*, Bdwy in *Filumena* (1980), *Bent, Amadeus*.

**BOVA, JOSEPH.** Born May 25 in Cleveland, Oh. Graduate Northwestern U. Debut 1959 OB in *On the Town*, followed by *Once upon a Mattress, House of Blue Leaves, Comedy, The Beauty Part, Taming of the Shrew, Richard III, Comedy of Errors, Invitation to a Beheading, Merry Wives of Windsor, Henry V, Streamers, The Matchmaker*, Bdwy in *Rape of the Belt, Irma La Douce, Hot Spot, The Chinese, American Millionaire, St. Joan, 42nd Street*.

**BOWDEN, RICHARD.** Born May 21 in Savannah, Ga. Graduate U. Ga., U. Bristol/Eng. Bdwy debut 1964 in *Don Carlos* (Schiller Theatre) followed by *Captain Brassbound's Conversion*, OB in *Mlle. Colombe, Pocahontas, Freedom Train, As You Like It, The Tavern, Revenger's Tragedy, Heathen Valley*.

**BOWEN, ROBERT.** Born April 8, 1949 in New Haven, Ct. Graduate R.I. School of Design. Debut 1975 OB in *Boy Meets Boy*, followed by *A Theatre History, The Importance of Being Earnest*.

**BOYD, JULIE.** Born January 2 in Kansas City, Mo. Graduate U. Utah, Yale. Bdwy debut 1985 in *Noises Off*, followed by OB in *Only You, Working I Acts, Hyde in Hollywood, Nowhere*.

**BRASINGTON, ALAN.** Born in Monticello, NY. Attended RADA. Bdwy debut 1968 in *Pantegleize*, followed by *The Misanthrope, Cock-a-doodle Dandy, Hamlet, A Patriot for Me, Shakespeare's Cabaret, Merlin, Into the Light, Two Shakespearean Actors*, OB in *Sterling Silver, Charlotte Sweet*.

**BREEN, J. PATRICK.** Born October 26, 1960 in Brooklyn, NY. NYU Graduate. Debut 1982 OB in *Epiphanyu*, followed by *Little Murders, Blood Sports, Class 1 Acts, Baba Goya, Chelsea Walls, Naked Rights, The Substance of Fire*, Bdwy in *Brighton Beach Memoirs* (1983).

**BRENNAN, NORA.** Born December 1, 1953 in East Chicago, IN. Graduate Purdue U. Bdwy debut 1980 in *Camelot*, followed by *Cats*.

**BRIAR, SUZANNE.** Born February 8, 1946 in Washington, DC. Graduate U. Syracuse. Debut 1985 OB in *Tatterdemalion*, followed by *Princess Pat, The Red Mill, Oh, Boy!, No No Nanette, Can't Help Singing Kern, Rodgers and Hart: A Celebration*, Bdwy in *Chess* (1988), *Aspects of Love*.

**BRIGHTMAN, JULIAN.** Born March 5, 1954 in Philadelphia, Pa. Graduate U. PA. Debut 1987 OB in *1984*, followed by *Critic, Leaves of Grass*, Bdwy in *Peter Pan* (1990/1991).

**BRILL, FRAN.** Born September 30 in PA. Attended Boston U. Bdwy debut 1969 in *Red, White and Maddox*, OB in *What Every Woman Knows, Scribes, Naked, Look Back in Anger, Knuckle, Skirmishes, Baby with the Bathwater, Holding Patterns, Festival of One Acts, Taking Steps, Young Playwrights Festival, Claptrap, Hyde in Hollywood, Good Grief*.

**BRODERICK, MATTHEW.** Born March 21, 1963 in New York City. Debut 1981 OB in *Torch Song Trilogy*, followed by *The Widow Claire*, Bdwy 1983 in *Brighton Beach Memoirs* for which he received a Theatre World Award, followed by *Biloxi Blues, A Christmas Carol*.

**BRODY, JONATHAN.** Born June 16, 1963 in Englewood, NJ. Debut 1982 OB in *Shulamith*, followed by *The Desk Set, Eating Raoul*, Bdwy in *Me and My Girl* (1986).

**BROOKES, JACQUELINE.** Born July 24, 1930 in Montclair, NJ. Graduate U. Iowa, RADA. Bdwy debut 1955 in *Tiger at the Gates*, followed by *Watercolor, Abelard and Heloise, A Meeting by the River*, OB in *The Cretan Woman* (1954) for which she received a Theatre World Award, *The Clandestine Marriage, Measure for Measure, The Duchess of Malfi, Ivanov, 8 Characters in Search of an Author, An Evening's Frost, Come Slowly Eden, The Increased Difficulty of Concentration, The Persians, Sunday Dinner, House of Blue Leaves, Owners, Hallelujah, Dream of a Black-listed Actor, Knuckle, Mama Sang the Blues, Buried Child, On Mt. Chimorazo, Winter Dancers, Hamlet, Old Flames, The Diviners, Richard II, Vieux Carre, Tall Hookup, Home Sweet Home/Crack, Approaching Zanzibar, Ten Blocks on the Camino Real*.

**BROOKING, SIMON.** Born December 23, 1960 in Edinburgh, Scot. Graduate SUNY/Fredonia, U. Wash. Debut 1989 OB in *American Bagpipes*, followed by *The Mortality Project, Prelude & Liebestod, Rough Crossing, Rumor of Glory, King Lear*.

**BROOKS, JEFF.** Born April 7, 1950 in Vancouver, Can. Attended Portland State U. Debut 1976 OB in *Titanic*, followed by *Fat Chances, Nature and Purpose of the Universe, Actor's Nightmare, Sister Mary Ignatius Explains It All, Marathon 84, The Foreigner, Talk Radio, Washington Heights*, Bdwy in *A History of the American Film* (1978), *Lend Me A Tenor, Gypsy, Nick & Nora*.

**BROWN, BRANDY.** Born in 1976 in Mobile, AL. Bdwy debut 1987 in *Les Miserables*, returned in 1992.

**BROWN, CAITLIN.** Born January 27, 1961 in Marin, CA. Attended Sacramento State U. Bdwy debut 1990 in *Grand Hotel*.

**BROWN, DARCY.** Born April 7, 1968 in Poughkepsie, NY. Graduate Brown U. Debut 1992 OB in *Cowboy in His Underwear*, followed by *Loose Ends*.

**BROWN, KERMIT.** Born February 3, 1937 in Asheville, NC. Graduate Duke U. With APA in *War and Peace, Judith, Man and Superman, The Show-Off, Pantagle and The Cherry Orchard, Salome*, OB in *The Millionairess, Things, Lulu, Heartbre House, Glad Tidings, Anyone Can Whistle, Facade, The Arcata Promise, Midsummer Night's Dream, The Death and Life of Sherlock Holmes*.

**BROWN, KIMBERLY JEAN.** Born November 16, 1984 in Gaithersburg, M Bdwy debut 1992 in *Four Baboons Adoring the Sun*.

**BROWN, ROBIN LESLIE.** Born January 18, in Canandaigua, NY. Graduate L Debut 1980 OB in *The Mother of Us All*, followed by *Yours Truly, Two Gentlemen Verona, Taming of the Shrew, The Mollusc, The Contrast, Pericles, Androma Macbeth, Electra, She Stoops to Conquer, Berenice, Hedda Gabler, A Midsumm Night's Dream, Three Sisters, Major Barbara, The Fine Art of Finesse, 2 Schnitz One-Acts, As You Like It, Ghosts, Chekhov Very Funny*.

**BROWN, WILLIAM SCOTT.** Born March 27, 1959 in Seattle, WA. Attended WA. Bdwy debut 1986 OB in *Juba*, Bdwy in *Phantom of the Opera* (1988).

**BROWNE, ROSCOE LEE.** Born in 1925 in Woodbury, NJ. Attended Lincoln Columbia. Debut OB in *Julius Caesar*, followed by *Taming of the Shrew, Tit Andronicus, Romeo and Juliet, Othello, Aria da Capo, The Blacks, Brecht on Brec King Lear, Winter's Tale, The Empty Room, Hell Is Other People, Benito Cerer Troilus and Cressida, Danton's Death, Valpone, Dream on Monkey Mountain, Behi the Broken Words*, Bdwy in *General Seeger* (1992), *Tiger Tiger Burning Brig Ballad of the Sad Cafe, A Hand Is on the Gate, My One and Only, Two Tra Running*.

**BROWNING, SUSAN.** Born February 25, 1941 in Baldwin, NY. Graduate Per State. Bdwy debut 1963 in *Love and Kisses*, followed by *Company* for which s received a Theatre World Award, *Shelter, Goodtime Charley, Big River*, OB in Dime a Dozen, Seventeen, The Boys from Syracuse, Collision Course, Whiskey, As Y Like It, Removalists, Africanus Instructus, The March on Russia*.

**BRUMMEL, DAVID.** Born November 1, 1942 in Brooklyn, NY. Bdwy debut 19 in *The Pajama Game*, followed by *Music Is, Oklahoma!*, OB in *Cole Porter, T. Fantasticks, Prom Queens Unchained*.

**BRYANT, DAVID.** Born May 26, 1936 in Nashville, TN. Attended TN State Bdwy debut 1972 in *Don't Play Us Cheap*, followed by *Bubbling Brown Sug Amadeus, Les Miserables*, OB in *Up in Central Park, Elizabeth and Essex, Appear a Show Cause*.

**BRYGGMAN, LARRY.** Born December 21, 1938 in Concord, GA. Attend CCSF, Am. Th. Wing. Debut 1962 OB in *A Pair of Pairs*, followed by *Live Like Pi Stop, You're Killing Me, Mod Donna, Waiting for Godot, Ballymurphy, Marco Po Sings a Solo, Brownsville Raid, Two Small Bodies, Museum, Winter Dance Resurrection of Lady Lester, Royal Bob, Modern Ladies of Guanabacoa, Rum a Coke, Bodies Rest and Motion, Blood Sports, Class 1 Acts, Spoils of War, Coriolan Prelude to a Kiss, Macbeth, Henry IV Parts 1 and 2, The White Rose*, Bdwy in *Ulyss in Nighttown* (1974), *Checking Out, Basic Training of Pavlo Hummel, Richard I Prelude to a Kiss*.

**BUELL, BILL.** Born September 21, 1952 in Paipai, Taiwan. Attended Portland Sta U. Debut 1972 OB in *Crazy Now*, followed by *Declassee, Lorenzaccio, Promena The Common Pursuit, Coyote Ugly, Alias Jimmy Valentine, Kiss Me Quic BadHabits, Groundhog*, Bdwy in *Once a Catholic* (1979), *The First, Welcome to t Club, The Miser, Taking Steps*.

**BURK, TERENCE.** Born August 11, 1947 in Lebanon, IL. Graduate S. IL. U. Bdw debut 1976 in *Equus*, OB in *Religion, The Future, Sacred and Profane Love, Crin and Punishment*.

**BURKHARDT, GERRY.** Born June 14, 1946 in Houston, Tx. Attended Lon Mor Col. Bdwy debut 1968 in *Her First Roman*, followed by *The Best Little Whorehouse Texas, Crazy for You*, OB in *Girl Crazy, Leave It to Me*.

**BURNETT, ROBERT.** Born February 28, 1960 in Goshen, NY. Attended H Studio. Bdwy debut 1985 in *Cats*.

**BURRELL, FRED.** Born September 18, 1936. Graduate UNC, RADA. Bdwy deb 1964 in *Never Too Late*, followed by *Illya Darling*, OB in *The Memorandu Throckmorton, Texas, Voices in the Head, Chili Queen, The Queen's Knight, Pursuit of the Song of Hydrogen, Unchanging Love, More Fun Than Bowling, Woman without a Name, The Sorrows of Fredrick, The Voice of the Prairie*.

**BURRELL, PAMELA.** Born August 4, 1945 in Tacoma, WA. Bdwy debut 1966 Funny Girl*, followed by *Where's Charley?, Strider, Sunday in the Park with Georg OB in *Arms and the Man* for which she received a Theatre World Award, *Berkele Square, The Boss, Biography: A Game, Strider: Story of a Horse, A Little Madnes Spinoza, After the Dancing in Jericho*.

**BURRELL, TERESA** (formerly Terry) Born February 8, 1952 in Trinidad, W. Attended Pace U. Bdwy debut 1977 in *Eubie!*, followed by *Dreamgirls, Honky To Nights*, OB in *That Uptown Feeling They Say It's Wonderful, George White Scandals, Just So, And the World Goes 'Round*.

**BURSE-MICKLEBURY, DENISE.** Born January 13 in Atlanta, Ga. Gradua Spellman Col., Atlanta U. Debut 1990 OB in *Ground People* for which she received Theatre World Award.

**BURSTEIN, DANNY.** Born June 16, 1964 in NYC. Graduate UCal/San Dieg Moscow Art Theatre. Debut 1991 OB in *The Rothchilds, A Weird Romance*, Bdwy A Little Hotel on the Side* (1992).

**BURSTYN, ELLEN.** Born December 7, 1932 in Detroit, Mi. Attended Actor Studio. Bdwy debut 1957 (as Ellen MacRae) in *Fair Game*, followed by *Same Tim Next Year, 84 Charing Cross Road, Shirley Valentine, Shimada*, OB in *Three Sister Andromeda II, Park Your Car in Harvard Yard*.

**URTON, ARNIE.** Born September 22, 1958 in Emmett, ID. Graduate U. Ariz. dwy debut 1983 in *Amadeus*, OB in *Measure for Measure, Major Barbara, hnitzler One Acts, Tartuffe, As You Like It, Ghosts*.

**URTON, IRVING.** Born August 5, 1923 in NYC. Bdwy debut 1951 in *Peer Gynt*, llowed by *Chu Chem*, OB in *3 Unnatural Acts, Pal Joey, Keegan & Lloyd Again, ne Act Festival, The Sunset Gang*, and 25 Years with Paper Bag Players, *If Walls ould Talk, Why Can't We Talk?*

**URTON, KATE.** Born September 10, 1957 in Geneva, Switz. Graduate Brown U., ale. Bdwy debut 1982 in *Present Laughter*, followed by *Alice in Wonderland, oonesbury, Wild Honey, Some Americans Abroad, Jake's Women*, OB in *Winners* for hich she received a 1983 Theatre World Award, *Romeo and Juliet, TheAccrington als, Playboy of the Western World, Measure for Measure*.

**USCH, CHARLES.** Born August 23, 1954 in New York City. Graduate orthwestern U. Debut OB 1985 in *Vampire Lesbians of Sodom*, followed by *Times quare Angel, Psycho Beach Party, The Lady in Question, Red Scare on Sunset*, all of hich he wrote.

**UTLER, BRUCE.** Born March 11, 1954 in Clanton, NC. Graduate NC Central U. ebut 1983 OB in *Street Scene*, followed by *Freedom Days, Just a Night Out*.

**UTT, JENNIFER.** Born May 17, 1958 in Valparaiso, IN. Stephens Col. graduate. ebut 1983 OB in *The Robber Bridegroom*, followed by *Into the Closet*, Bdwy in *Les iserables* (1987).

**AHN, LARRY.** Born December 19, 1955 in Nassau, NY. Graduate Northwestern . Bdwy debut 1980 in *The Music Man*, followed by *Anything Goes, Guys and Dolls*, B in *Susan B!, Jim Thorpe, All American, Play to Win*.

**AIN, WILLIAM.** Born May 27, 1931 in Tuscaloosa, Al. Graduate U. Wash., atholic U. Debut 1962 OB in *Red Roses for Me*, followed by *Jericho Jim Crow, enry V, Antigone, Relatively Speaking, I Married an Angel in Concert, Buddha, opperhead, Forbidden City*, Bdwy in *Wilson in the Promise Land* (1970), *You Can't ke It with You, Wild Honey, The Boys in Autumn, Mastergate, A Streetcar Named esire*.

**ALABRESE, MARIA.** Born December 7, 1967 in Secone, PA. Bdwy debut 1991 The Will Rogers Follies.

**ALLAWAY, LIZ.** Born April 13, 1961 in Chicago, IL. Debut 1980 OB in odspell*, followed by *The Matinee Kids, Brownstone, No Way to Treat a Lady, Marry e a Little, 1-2-3-4-5*, Bdwy in *Merrily We Roll Along* (1981), *Baby, The Three usketeers, Miss Saigon*.

**AMBELL, AMELIA.** Born August 4, 1965 in Montreal, Can. Graduate Syracuse . Debut 1988 OB in *Fun*, followed by *A Member of the Wedding*, Bdwy in *Our ountry's Good* (1991).

**AMP, JOANNE.** Born April 4, 1951 in Atlanta, GA. Graduate Fl. Atlantic U., eo. Wash. U. Debut 1981 OB in *The Dry Martini*, followed by *Geniuses* for which e received a Theatre World Award, *June Moon, Painting Churches, Merchant of enice, Lady from the Sea, The Contrast, Coastal Disturbances, The Rivals, ndromache, Electra, Uncle Vanya, She Stoops to Conquer, Hedda Gabler, The Heidi hronicles, Importance of Being Earnest, Medea, Three Sisters, A Midsummer Night's ream, School for Wives, Measure for Measure, Dance of Death, Two Schnitzler One- cts, Tartuffe, Lips Together Teeth Apart, As You Like It*, Bdwy in *The Heidi hronicles* (1989).

**AMPANARO, SUSAN.** Born June 2, 1966 in The Bronx, NY. Graduate Fl. State . Debut 1991 OB in *Tony 'n' Tina's Wedding*.

**AMPBELL, AMELIA.** Born August 4, 1965 in Montreal, Can. Graduate Syracuse . Debut 1988 OB in *Fun*, followed by *Member of the Wedding*, Bdwy in *Our ountry's Good* (1991), *A Small Family Business*.

**ARABUENA, PHILIPP LEE.** Born October 18, 1986 in NYC. Bdwy debut 1991 Miss Saigon.

**ARDEN, WILLIAM.** Born February 2, 1947 in NYC. Attended Lawrence U., randeis U. Debut 1974 OB in *Short Eyes*, followed by *Leaving Home, Back in the ace, Thin Ice, Bloodletters, Dennis Nowhere*.

**ARHART, TIMOTHY.** Born December 24, 1953 in Washington, DC. Graduate U. . Debut 1984 OB in *The Harvesting*, followed by *The Ballad of Soapy Smith, Hitch- ikers, Highest Standard of Living, Festival of I-Acts*, Bdwy in *A Streetcar Named esire* (1992).

**ARLE, CYNTHIA.** Born March 4, 1951 in Hollywood, Ca. Graduate Carnegie- Iellon U. Bdwy debut 1978 in *The Crucifer of Blood*, followed by *Piaf, Is There Life fter High School?*, OB in *A Piece of My Heart*.

**ARRADINE, KEITH.** Born August 8, 1949 in San Mateo, CA. Attended Col. State . Bdwy debut 1969 in *Hair*, followed by *Foxfire, The Will Rogers Follies*, OB in ake Up It's Time to Go to Bed.

**ARROLL, ROCKY.** Born July 9, 1963 in Cincinnati, OH. Graduate Webster U. ebut 1986 OB in *Macbeth*, followed by *As You Like It, Romeo and Juliet, Henry IV, ichard II*, Bdwy in *The Piano Lesson* (1990) for which he received a Theatre World ward.

**ASNOFF, PHILIP.** Born August 3, 1953 in Philadelphia, PA. Graduate Wesleyan . Debut 1978 OB in *Gimme Shelter*, followed by *Chincilla, King of Schnorrers, Iary Stuart, Henry IV, Marathon '89, Up Against It*, Bdwy in *Grease* (1973), *Chess* or which he received a Theatre World Award, *Devil's Disciple, Shogun*.

**AVEY, GEORGE.** Born February 25, 1934 in Ridley Park Pa. Graduate U. Del., enn State. Debut 1967 OB in *Shoemaker's Holiday*, followed by *Dulcy, Romeo and uliet, The Death and Life of Sherlock Holmes*, Bdwy in *Three Men on a Horse* (1970).

**AVISE, JOE ANTONY.** Born January 7, 1958 in Syracuse, NY. Graduate Clark U. ebut 1981 OB in *Street Scene*, followed by Bdwy 1984 in *Cats*.

**CECIL, PAMELA.** Born December 20 in Newport, R.I. Attended Midland Lutheran Col., Iowa State U. Bdwy debut 1981 in *Can-Can*, followed by *42nd Street, La Cage aux Folles*, OB in *Sublime Lives*.

**CHALFANT, KATHLEEN.** Born January 14, 1945 in San Francisco, Ca. Graduate Stanford U. Bdwy debut 1975 in *Dance with Me*, followed by *M. Butterfly*, OB in *Jules Feiffer's Hold Me, Killings on the Last Line, The Boor, Blood Relations, Signs of Life, Sister Mary Ignatius Explains It All, Actor's Nightmare, Faith Healer, All the Nice People,, Hard Times, Investigation of the Murder in El Savador, 3 Poets, The Crucible, The Party*.

**CHAN, KIM.** Born December 28, 1917 in China. Debut 1969 OB in *Fame*, followed by *One of the All-Time Greats*.

**CHANDLER, DAVID.** Born February 3, 1950 in Danbury, Ct. Graduate Oberlin Col. Bdwy debut 1980 in *The American Clock*, followed by *Death of a Salesman, Lost in Yonkers*, OB in *Made in Heaven, Black Sea Follies*.

**CHANDLER, JEFFREY ALLAN.** Born September 9 in Durham, NC. Graduate Carnegie-Mellon U. Bdwy debut 1972 in *Elizabeth I*, followed by *The Dresser, Whodunnit, Two Shakespearean Actors*, OB in *The People vs. Ranchman, Your Own Thing, PenguinTouquet*.

**CHANNING, STOCKARD.** Born February 13, 1944 in NYC. Attended Radcliffe Col. Debut 1970 in *Adaptation/Next*, followed by *The Lady and the Clarinet, The Golden Age, Woman in Mind, Six Degrees of Separation*, Bdwy in *Two Gentlemen of Verona, They're Playing Our Song, The Rink, Joe Egg, House of Blue Leaves, Six Degrees of Separation, Four Baboons Adoring the Sun*.

**CHAPMAN, KAREN.** Born February 29, 1960 in Virginia Beach, Va. Attended U. Del., U. Bath/Eng. Debut 1989 OB in *Enrico IV*, Bdwy in *A Little Hotel on the Side* (1992).

**CHARNEY, JORDAN.** Born in NYC; graduate Brooklyn Col. OB in *Harry, Noon and Night, A Place for Chance, Hang Down Your Head and Die, The Pinter Plays, Telemachus Clay, Zoo Story, Viet Rock, MacBird, Red Cross, Glorious Ruler, Waiting for Godot, Slow Memories, One Flew over the Cuckoo's Nest, Boy Who Came to Leave, Cretan Bull, Naomi Court, Sublime Lives*, Bdwy in *Slapstick Tragedy* (1966), *The Birthday Party, Talley's Folly*.

**CHENG, KAM.** Born March 28, 1969 in Hong Kong. Attended Muhlenberg Col. Bdwy debut 1991 in *Miss Saigon*.

**CHEW, LEE.** Born February 8 in Roanoke, Va. Graduate Va. Com. U. Debut 1978 OB in *Can-Can*, followed by *Light Up the Sky, She Loves Me, The Misanthrope*.

**CHILSON, KATHRYN.** Born January 31, 1955 in Louisiana, Mo. Graduate Webster U. Debut 1982 OB in *The Cherry Orchard*, followed by *The Constant Wife, Full Circle*.

**CHONG, MARCUS.** Born July 8, 1967 in Seattle, Wa. Attended L.A. Valley Col., Santa Monica CC. Bdwy debut 1990 in *Stand-up Tragedy* for which he received a Theatre World Award.

**CHRISTOPHER, DONALD.** Born May 16, 1939 in Terre Haute, In. Graduate Ind. State U. Debut 1992 OB in *First the Supper*.

**CHRISTOPHER, THOM.** Born October 5, 1940 in Jackson Heights, NY. Attended Ithaca Col., Neighborhood Playhouse. Debut 1972 OB in *One Flew Over the Cuckoo's Nest*, followed by *Tamara, Investigation fo the Murder in El Salvador, Sublime Lives*, Bdwy in *Emperor Henry IV* (1973), *Noel Coward in two Keys* for which he received a Theatre World Award, *Caesar and Cleopatra*.

**CHRYST, GARY.** Born in 1959 in LaJolla, Ca. Joined Joffrey Ballet in 1968. Bdwy debut 1979 in *Dancin'*, followed by *A Chorus Line, Guys & Dolls*, OB in *One More Song One More Dance, Music Loves Me*.

**CIESLA, DIANE.** Born May 20, 1952 in Chicago, Il. Graduate Clark Col. Debut 1980 OB in *Uncle Money*, followed by *Afternoons in Vegas, The Taming of the Shrew, Much Ado about Nothing, Macbeth, Cinderella*.

**CIOFFI, CHARLES.** Born October 31, 1935 in New York City. Graduate U. Minn. OB in *A Cry of Players*, followed by *King Lear, In the Matter of J. Robert Oppenheimer, Antigone, A Whistle in the Dark, Hamlet, Self Defense, Real Estate*, Bdwy in *Stand-Up Tragedy* (1990), *Chinese Coffee*.

**CLARK, OLIVER.** Born January 4, 1939 in Buffalo, NY. Graduate Buffalo U. Bdwy debut 1963 in Arturo Ui, followed by*Ben Franklin in Paris, Caucasian Chalk Circle, Don't Drink the Water, In Spiro Who?, Two Times One, Passing Through from Exotic Places, Next, The Misanthrope*.

**CLARKE, RICHARD.** Born January 31, 1933 in England. Graduate U. Reading. With LCRep in *St. Joan* (1968), *Tiger at the Gates, Cyrano de Bergerac*, Bdwy in *Conduct Unbecoming, The Elephant Man, Breaking the Code, The Devils Disciple, M. Butterfly, Six Degrees of Separation, Two Shakespearean Actors*, OB in *Old Glory, Trials of Oz, Looking Glass, Trataurny of McWille*.

**CLAYTON, LAWRENCE.** Born October 10, 1956 in Mocksville, NC. Attended NC Central U. Debut 1980 in *Tambourines to Glory*, followed by *Skyline, Across the Universe, Two by Two, Romance in Hard Times, Juba*, Bdwy in *Dreamgirls* (1984), *High Rollers*.

**CLOSE, GLENN.** Born May 19, 1947 in Greenwich, CT. Graduate William & Mary Col. Bdwy debut 1974 with Phoenix Co. in *Love for Love, Member of the Wedding*, and *Rules of the Game*, followed by *Rex, Crucifer of Blood, Barnum, The Real Thing, Benefactors, Death and the Maiden*, OB in *The Crazy Locomotive, Uncommon Women and Others, Wine Untouched, The Winter Dancers, The Singular Life of Albert Nobbs*.

**COCHRAN, RAY.** Born September 4, 1964 in Lebanon, KY. Debut 1989 OB in *Young Playwrights Festival*, followed by *Down the Stream, Six Degrees of Separation* (also Bdwy).

**COCKRUM, ROY**. Born June 29, 1956 in Knoxville, TN. Graduate Northwestern U. Debut 1991 OB in *The Broken Pitcher*, followed by *Vampire Lesbians of Sodom, Red Scare on Sunset*.

**COHEN, JEDIDIAH**. Born October 30, 1976 in Ann Arbor, MI. Bdwy debut 1992 in *The Secret Garden*. OB in *Amahl and the Night Visitors, The Turn of the Screw*.

**COHENOUR, PATTI**. Born October 17, 1952 in Albuquerque, NM. Attended U. NM. Bdwy debut 1982 in *A Doll's Life*, followed by *Pirates of Penzance, Big River, The Mystery of Edwin Drood, Phantom of the Opera*, OB in *La Boheme* for which she received a Theatre World Award.

**COLE, NORA**. Born September 10, 1953 in Louisville, Ky. Attended Beloit Col., Goodman School. Debut 1977 OB in *Movie Buff*, followed by *Cartoons for a Lunch Hour, Boogie-Woogie Rumble, Ground Hog*, Bdwy in *Your Arms Too Short to Box with God* (1982), *Inacent Black, Runaways*.

**COLL, IVONNE**. Born November 4 in Fajardo, PR. Attended UPR, LACC. Debut 1980 OB in *Spain 1980* followed by *Animals, The Wonderful Ice Cream Suit, Cold Air, Fabiola, Concerto in Hi-Fi, A Burning Beach, The Promise, Blood Wedding*, Bdwy in *Goodbye, Fidel* (1980), *Shakespeare on Broadway*.

**COLLINS, JOAN**. Born May 21, 1933 in London. After many years on stage in England, on film and TV, she made her Bdwy debut in the 1992 revival of *Private Lives*.

**COLLIS, LARRY K.**. Born February 21, 1936 in Lohrville, Ia. Graduate State U. Ia. Bdwy debut 1988 in *Mail*, followed by OB in *Currents Turned Awry*.

**COLTON, CHEVI**. Born December 21, in NYC. Attended Hunter Col. OB in *Time of Storm, The Insect Comedy, The Adding Machine, O Marry Me, Penny Change, The Mad Show, Jacques Brel Is ..., Bits and Pieces, Spelling Bee, Uncle Money, Miami, Come Blow Your Horn, Almost Perfect, The Sunset Gang*, Bdwy in *Over Here, Carbaret, Grand Tour, Torch Song Trilogy, Roza*.

**CONAWAY, DAVID**. Born March 30, 1964 in Portland, Or. Graduate SUNY/Genesco. Debut 1989 OB in *Best Friends*, followed by *Scaramouche, Daddy's Gone, Slam, The Rover*.

**CONNELL, JANE**. Born October 27, 1925 in Berkeley, Ca. Attended U. Cal. Bdwy debut in *New Faces of 1956*, followed by *Drat! The Cat!, Mame* (1966/1983), *Dear World, Lysistrata, Me and My Girl, Lend Me a Tenor, Crazy for You*, OB in *Shoestring Revue, Threepenny Opera, Pieces of Eight, Demi-Dozen, She Stoops to Conquer, Drat!, The Real Inspector Hound, The Rivals, The Rise and Rise of Daniel Rocket, Laughing Stock, The Singular Dorothy Parker, No, No Nanette in Concert*.

**CONNOR, MICHAEL P.**. Born November 5, 1968 in Detroit, Mi. Graduate Boston U. Debut 1991 OB in *Romeo and Juliet* (1990) followed by *Unidentified Human Remains and the True Nature of Love*, Bdwy in *A Streetcar Named Desire* (1992).

**CONOLLY, PATRICIA**. Born August 29, 1933 in Tabora, E. Africa. Attended U. Sydney. With APA in *You Can't Take it With You, War and Peace, School for Scandal, The Wild Duck, Right You Are, We Comrades Three, Pantagleize, Exit the king, The Cherry Orchard, The Misanthrope, The Cocktail Party*, and *Cock-a-doodle Dandy*, followed by *A Streetcar Named Desire, The Importance of Being Earnest, The Circle, A Small Family Business*, OB in *Blithe Spirit, Woman in Mind*.

**CONROY, FRANCES**. Born in 1953 in Monroe, Ga. Attended Dickinson Col., Juilliard, Neighborhood Playhouse. Debut 1978 OB with the Acting Co. in *Mother Courage, King Lear*, and *The Other Half*, followed by *All's Well That Ends Well, Othello, Sorrows of Stephen, Girls Girls Girls, Painting Churches, Uncle Vanya, Romance Language, To Gillian on Her 37th Birthday, Man and Superman, Zero Positive, Secret Rapture, Some Americans Abroad, Bright Room Called Day, Lips Together Teeth Apart*, Bdwy in *The Lady from Dubuque* (1980), *Our Town* (1989), *The Secret Rapture, Some Americans Abroad, Two Shakespearean Actors*.

**CONROY, JARLATH**. Born September 30, 1944 in Galway, Ire. Attended RADA. Bdwy debut 1976 in *Comedians*, followed by *The Elephant Man, Macbeth, Ghetto, The Visit*, OB in *Translations, The Wind that Shook the Barley, Gardenia, Friends, Playboy of the Western World, One-Act Festival, Abel & Bela/Architect, The Matchmaker*.

**COOK, LINDA**. Born June 8 in Lubbock, Tx. Attended Auburn U. Debut 1974 OB in *The Wager*, followed by *Hole in the Wall, Shadow of a Gunman, Be My Father, Ghosts of the Loyal Oaks, Different People Different Rooms, Saigon Rose, Romantic Arrangements, No Time Flat, Dearly Departed*.

**COOPER, CHUCK**. Born November 8, 1954 in Cleveland, Oh. Graduate Ohio U. Debut 1982 OB in *Colored People's Time*, followed by *Riff Raff Revue, Primary English Class, Break/Agnes/Eulogy/Lucky*, Bdwy in *Amen Corner* (1983).

**COPELAND, JOAN**. Born June 1, 1922 in NYC. Attended Brooklyn Col, AADA. Debut 1945 OB in *Romeo and Juliet*, followed by *Othello, Conversation Piece, Delightful Season, End of Summer, American Clock, The Double Game, Isn't It Romantic? Hunting Cockroaches, Young Playwrights Festival, The American Plan, Rose Quartet*, Bdwy in *Sundown Beach, Detective Story, Not for Children, Hatful of Fire, Something More, The Price, Two by Two, Pal Joey, Checking Out, The American Clock*.

**CORFMAN, CARIS**. Born May 18, 1955 in Boston, MA. Graduate Fla. St. U., Yale. Debut 1978 OB in *Wings*, followed by *Fish Riding Bikes, Filthy Rich, Dry Land, All This and Moonlight, Cezanne Syndrome, Tea with Mommy and Jack, Equal Wrights, Mi Vida Loca, The Way of the World, Henry IV Parts 1 and 2, Dream of a Common Language*, Bdwy in *Amadeus* (1980).

**CORMIER, TONY**. Born November 2, 1951 in Camp Roberts, Ca. Attended Pierce Col., Wash. State U. Debut 1984 in *Kennedy at Colonus*, followed by *Pericles, Something Cloudy Something Clear, Three Sisters*.

**COSTALLOS, SUZANNE**. Born April 3, 1933 in New York City. Attended NYU, Boston Consv., Juilliard. Debut 1977 OB in *Play and Other Play by Beckett*, followed by *Elizabeth I, The White Devil, Hunting Scenes from Lower Bavaria, Selma, In Miami*

*As It Is in Heaven, Peacetime*, Bdwy in *Zorba* (1983).

**COUNCIL, RICHARD E.**. Born October 1, 1947 in Tampa, Fl. Graduate U. F Debut 1973 OB in *Merchant of Venice*, followed by *Ghost Dance, Look We've Co Through, Arms and the Man, Isadora Duncan Sleeps with the Russian Navy, Arth The Winter Dancer, The Prevalence of Mrs. Seal, Jane Avril, Young Playwrig Festival, Sleeping Dogs, The Good Coach, Subfertile*, Bdwy in *Royal Family* (197 *Philadelphia Story, I'm Not Rappaport, Conversations with My Father*.

**COUNTRYMAN, MICHAEL**. Born September 15, 1955 in St. Paul, MN. Graduate Trinity Col., AADA. Debut 1983 OB in *Changing Palettes*, followed by *June Moc Terra Nova, Out!, Claptrap, The Common Pursuit, Woman in Mind, Making Movie The Tempest, Tales of the Lost Formicans, Marathon '91, The Stick Wife, Li Together Teeth Apart*, Bdwy in *A Few Good Men* (1990).

**COYLE, JAMES**. Born August 15, 1954 in Culver City, Ca. Graduate Santa Clara Debut 1990 OB in *Smoke on the Mountain*, followed by *The Sorrows of Frederick*.

**CRAGIN, CHARLES**. Debut 1960 OB in *Borak*, followed by *Life in the Third R Burr, Caligula, Crambo, The Fantasticks, German Requiem, A Snake in the Ve* Bdwy in *Salome* (1992).

**CREMIN, SUSAN**. Born in NYC. Bdwy debut 1989 in *Gypsy*, followed by 19 revival.

**CRESSWELL, DEBORAH**. Born May 7 in Atlanta, Ga. Graduate Vanderbilt Debut 1973 OB in *Miss Collins the English Chairman*, followed by *A Litt Renaissance at Molly's O, Diary of a Scoundrel, Overruled, The Shewing Up Blanco Posnet, Box and Cox, Selling Off, The Bald Soprano, Ladies at the Alam Crimes of the Heart, Summer and Smoke, Macbeth, Death of a Salesman*.

**CRESWELL, SAYLOR**. Born November 18, 1939 in Pottstown, Pa. Gradua Brown U. Debut 1968 OB in *Carving a Statue*, followed by *Room Service, Savage Under Milk Wood, Rutherford & Son*, Bdwy in *Herzl* (1976).

**CRISTOFER, MICHAEL**. Born January 22, 1945 in Trenton, NY. Attend Catholic U. Debut 1977 OB in *The Cherry Orchard* for which he received a Thea World Award, followed by *Conjuring an Event, Chinchilla, No End of Blame, Bdv* in *Hamlet* (1992).

**CRIVELLO, ANTHONY**. Born Aug 2, 1955 in Milwaukee, WI. Bdwy debut 198 in *Evita*, followed by *The News, Les Miserables*, OB in *The Juniper Tree*.

**CROFT, PADDY**. Born in Worthing, Eng. Attended Avondale Col. Debut 1961 C in *The Hostage*, followed by *Billy Liar, Live Like Pigs, Hogan's Goat, Long Day Journey into Night, Shadow of a Gunman, Pygmalion, The Plough and the Stars (LC Kill, Starting Monday, Philadelphia Here I Come!, Grandchild of Kings*, Bdwy in *T Killing of Sister George, The Prime of Miss Jean Brodie, Crown Matrimonial, Maje Barbara*.

**CROMWELL, J.T.**. Born March 4, 1935 in Ann Arbor, MI. Graduate U. Cin Bdwy debut 1965 in *Half a Sixpence*, followed by *Jacques Brel is Alive..., 160 Pennsylvania Avenue*, OB in *Pageant*.

**CROMWELL, JAMES**. Born January 27, 1940 in Los Angeles, Ca. Attende Middlebury Col., Carnegie Tech. Debut 1960 OB in *Port Royal*, followed by *AC/D 3 Acts of Recognition, Hamlet*, Bdwy in *Othello* (1971), *Hamlet* (1992).

**CROOKS, KITTY**. Born February 23, 1958 in Doylestown, PA. Graduate Yale Bdwy debut 1986 in *Wild Honey*, OB in *One-Act Festival, Subfertile, The Rivalry Dolls*.

**CROUSE, LINDSAY**. Born May 12, 1948 in New York City. Graduate Radclif Col. Bdwy debut 1972 in *Much Ado About Nothing*, followed by *A Christmas Carol* OB in *The Foursome, Fishing, Long Day's Journey into Night, Total Recall, Father Day, Hamlet, Reunion, Twelfth Night, Childe Byron, Richard II, Serenading Loui Prairie/Shawl, The Stick Wife*, Bdwy 1991 in *The Homecoming* for which she receive a Theatre World Award.

**CROWNINGSHIELD, KEITH**. Born August 26, 1964 in Syracuse, NY. Gradua St. Lawrence U. Debut 1987 OB in *Starmites*, Bdwy in *Grand Hotel* (1989).

**CRUTCHFIELD, BUDDY**. Born June 4, 1957 in Dallas, Tx. Graduate SMU. Deb 1979 *Radio City Christmas Spectacular*, followed by OB *HMS Pinafore, Pirates Penzance, Tent Show, A Church Is Born, Senior Discretion, The Widow Clair*, Bdw in *The Most Happy Fella* (1992).

**CRUZ, FRANCIS J.**. Born October 4, 1954 in Long Beach, CA. Attended F.I.D.N Bdwy debut 1991 in *Miss Saigon*.

**CUCCIOLI, BOB**. Born May 3, 1958 in Hempstead, NY. Graduate St. John's Debut 1982 OB in *H.M.S. Pinafore*, followed by *Senor Discretion, Gigi, Th Rothschilds, And the World Goes Round*.

**CULKIN, MACAULAY**. Born August 26, 1981 in NYC. Debut 1985 OB in *Bac Babies*, followed by *After School Special, Buster B and Olivia, Sam I Am*.

**CULLITON, JOSEPH**. Born January 25, 1948 in Boston, Ma. Attended CalState L Debut 1982 OB in *Francis*, followed by *Flirtations, South Pacific (LC), Julius Caesa King John, Company*, Bdwy 1987 in *Broadway*.

**CULLUM, J.D.**. Born March 1, 1966 in NYC. Bdwy debut 1977 in *Kings* followe by *Shenandoah, You Never Can Tell, Getting Married*, OB in *Romance Language Losing It, Madwoman of Chaillot, Clarence, Abingdon Square, Woman in Mind, Wc Against Women;The White Rose*.

**CUNNINGHAM, JOHN**. Born June 22, 1932 in Auburn, NY. Graduate Yale Dartmouth U. OB in *Love Me a Little, Pimpernel, The Fantasticks, Love and L Love, The Bone Room, Dancing in the Dark, Father's Day, Snapshot, Head Ove Heels, Quartermaine's Terms, Wednesday, On Approval, Miami, Perfect Party, Bird of Paradise, Six Degrees of Separation*, Bdwy in *Hot Spot* (1963), *Zorba, Company 1776, Rose, The Devil's Disciple, Six Degrees of Separation*.

**RLESS, JOHN.** Born September 16 in Wigan, Eng. Attended Central Schl. of ...eech. NY debut 1982 OB in *The Entertainer*, followed by *Sus, Up 'n' Under, ...ogress, Prin, Nightingale, Absent Friends*, Bdwy in *A Small Family Business* ...92).

**RTIS, KEENE.** Born February 15, 1925 in Salt Lake City UT. Graduate U. Utah. ...wy debut 1949 in *Shop at Sly Corner*, with APA in School for *Scandal, The Tavern, ...atole, Scapin, Right You Are, Importance of Being Earnest, Twelfth Night, King ...ar, Seagull, Lower Depths, Man and Superman, Judith, War and Peace, You Can't ...ke It with You, Pantaglieze, Cherry Orchard, Misanthrope, Cocktail Party, Cock-a-...odle Dandy*, and *Hamlet, A Patriot for Me, The Rothschilds, Night Watch, Via ...lactica, Annie, Division Street, La Cage Aux Folles*, OB in *Colette, Ride Across ...nmark. ...ke Constance, The Cocktail Hour*.

**ELIA, CHET.** Born November 19, 1944 in Bridgeport, Ct. Attended Boston Cons. ...wy debut 1974 in *Mack and Mabel*, followed by *The Lieutenant, Man of La Mancha ...92).

**ABDOUB, JACK.** Born February 5 in New Orleans, La. Graduate Tulane U. OB in ...at's Up, Time for the Gentle People, The Peddler, The Dodo Bird, Annie Get Your ...n, Lola*, Bdwy in *Paint Your Wagon* (1951), *My Darlin' Aida, Happy Huntings, Hot ...ot, Camelot, Baker Street, Anya, Her First Roman, Coco, Man of LaMancha, ...igadoon, Moose Murders, One Touch of Venus, Sally in Concert, The Most Happy ...lla* (1992).

**AGGAN, JOHN.** Born April 18, 1954 in Camden, NJ. Graduate UNC. Debut 1980 ...B in *The Devil's Disciple*, followed by *Elmatha's Apology, Gertrude, Queen of ...nmark*.

**AILY, DANIEL.** Born July 25, 1955 in Chicago, IL. Graduate Notre Dame, U. ...ash. Debut 1988 OB in *Boy's Breath*, followed by *A Ronde, Iron Bars, Chekhov ...ry Funny, Macbeth, As You Like It*.

**ALEY, R.F.** Born April 16, 1955 in Denver, Co. Attended N. Co. U. Bdwy debut ...88 in *Chess, Sweeney Todd, Guys and Dolls*.

**ANNER, BRADEN.** Born in 1976 in Indianapolis, IN. Bdwy debut 1984 in *Nine*, ...llowed by *Oliver!, Starlight Express, Les Miserables*, OB in *Genesis*.

**ANSON, RANDY.** Born April 30, 1950 in Plainfield NJ. Graduate Carnegie-Mellon ... Debut 1978 OB in *Gimme Shelter*, followed by *Big and Little, The Winter Dancers, ...me Steps, Casualties, Red and Blue, The Resurrection of Lady Lester, Jazz Poets at ...e Grotto, Plenty, Macbeth, Blue Window, Cave Life, Romeo and Juliet, One-Act ...stival, Mad Forest*.

**AVID, KEITH.** Born May 8, 1954. Juilliard graduate. Debut1979 OB in *Othello*, ...llowed by *The Haggadah, Pirates of Penzance, Macbeth, Coriolanus, Titus ...dronicus*, Bdwy in *Jelly's Last Jam* (1992).

**AVIS, BRUCE ANTHONY.** Born March 4, 1959 in Dayton, Oh. Attended ...illiard. Bdwy debut 1979 in *Dancin'*, followed by *Big Deal, A Chorus Line, High ...ollers*.

**AVIS, HOPE.** Born March 23, 1964 in Englewood, NJ. Graduate Vassar Col. ...ebut 1991 OB in *Can-Can*, followed by Bdwy in *Two Shakespearean Actors* (1991).

**AVIS, MAC.** Born January 21, 1942 in Lubbock, Tx. Attended Emory U. Bdwy ...but 1992 in *The Will Rogers Follies*.

**AVIS, MARY BOND.** Born June 3, 1958 in Los Angeles, Ca. Graduate Cal. State ...Northridge, LACC. Debut 1985 OB in *Trousers*, Bdwy in *Mail* (1988), *Jelly's Last ...m*.

**AVIS, MELISSA ANNE.** Born November 14 in Nashville, Tn. Attended Belmont ... Bdwy debut 1990 in *Les Miserables*.

**AVISON, JACK.** Born July 17, 1936 in Worcester, Ma. Graduate Boston U. Debut ...68 in *Moon for the Misbegotten*, followed by *Big and Little, Battle of Angels, A ...idsummer Night's Dream, Hot 1 Baltimore, A Tribute to Lili Lamont, Ulysses in ...action, Lulu, Hey Rube!, In the Recovery Lounge, The Runner Stumbles, Winter ...gns, Hamlet, Mary Stuart, Ruby Ruby Sam Sam, The Diviners, Marching to Georgia, ...unting Scenes from Lower Bavaria, Richard II, The Great Grandson of Jedediah ...ohler, Buck, Time Framed, Love's Labour's Lost, Bing and Walker, After the ...ancing in Jericho*, Bdwy in *Capt. Brassbound's Conversion* (1972), *Anna Christie, ...imada*.

**AVYS, EDMUND C.** Born January 21, 1947 in Nashua, NH. Graduate Oberlin Col. ...ebut 1977 OB in *Othello*, Bdwy in *Crucifer of Blood* (1979), *Shadowlands, A Small ...mily Business*.

**EAL, FRANK.** Born October 7, 1958 in Birmingham, AL. Attended Duke U. ...ebut 1982 OB in *The American Princess*, followed by *Richard III, Ruffian on the ...air, A Midsummer Night's Dream, We Shall Not All Sleep, The Legend of Sleepy ...ollow, Three Sisters, The Triangle Project, One Neck*.

**EALMEIDA, JOQUIM.** Born March 15, 1957 in Portugal. Attended Lisbon Cons. ...B in *The Marriage Proposal, The Sign in Sidney Brustein's Window, A Chrismas ...arol, Talk to Me like Rain, What Would Jeanne Moreau Do?, Roosters, Blood ...edding*.

**EAN, LAURA.** Born May 27, 1963 in Smithtown, NY. Debut 1973 OB in *The ...ecret Life of Walter Mitty*, followed by *A Village Romeo and Juliet, Carousel, Hey ...ube, Landscape of the Body, American Passion, Feathertop, Personals, Godspell, ...estival of One-Acts, Catch Me If I Fall*, Bdwy in *Doonesbury* (1983), for which she ...ceived a Theatre World Award.

**EAN, LOREN.** Born July 31, 1969 in Los Vegas, Nv. Debut 1989 OB in *Amulets ...gainst the Dragon Forces*, for which he received a Theatre World Award, followed ... Beggars in the House of Plenty*.

**EBEER, GERRIT.** Born June 17, 1935 in Amsterdam, Neth. Bdwy debut 1965 in ...ickwick*, followed by *Illya Darling, Zorba, Pajama Game, All Over Town, Grand Hotel*.

**DeCOSMO, JACQUELINE.** Born January 1, 1943 in Canton, Oh. Graduate Kent State U. Debut 1973 OB in *Two Noble Kinsmen*,followed by *One Flew over the Cuckoo's Nest, In Circles, Joe Eggs, Deep to Center, 2 by Horton Foote*.

**deGANON, CAMILLE.** Born in Springfield, OH. Appeared with several dance companies before making her Bdwy debut in 1986 in *The Mystery of Edwin Drood*, followed by *Jerome Robbins' Broadway, Brigadoon* (NYCO/LC).

**DeGONGE, MARCY.** Born May 4, 1957 in Newark, NJ. Graduate Hart Col. Bdwy debut 1989 in *Cats*.

**DEL POZO, EMILIO.** Born August 6, 1948 in Havana, Cuba. Attended AMDA. Debut 1983 OB in *Union City Thanksgiving*, followed by *El Grande de Coca Cola, Senorita from Tacna, Twelfth Night, The Wonderful Ice Cream Suit, In Miami as It Is in Heaven*, Bdwy in *Salome* (1992).

**DeLAURENTIS, SEMINA.** Born January 21 in Waterbury, CT. Graduate Southern CT State Col. Debut 1985 OB in *Nunsense*, followed by *Have I Got a Girl for You*.

**deLAVALLADE, CARMEN.** Born March 6, 1931 in New Orleans, La. Bdwy debut 1954 in *House of Flowers*, followed by *Josephine Baker and company*, OB in *Othello, Departures, The Dreams of Clytemnestra, Island Memories*.

**DELLA PIAZZA, DIANE.** Born September 3, 1962 in Pittsburgh, PA. Graduate Cincinnati Consv. Bdwy debut 1987 in *Les Miserables*.

**DeSHIELDS, ANDRE.** Born January 12, 1946 in Baltimore, MD. Graduate U. Wis. Bdwy debut 1973 in *Warp*, followed by *Rachel Lily Rosenbloom, The Wiz, Ain't Misbehavin'* (1978/1988), *Haarlem Nocturne, Just So, Stardust, OB in 2008-1/2, Jazzbo Brown, The Soldier's Tale, The Little Prince, Haarlem Nocturne, Sovereign State of Boogedy Boogedy, Kiss Me When It's Over, Saint Tous, Ascension Day, Casino Paradise*.

**DeVRIES, JON.** Born March 26, 1947 in NYC./Graduate Bennington Col., Pasadena Playhouse. Debut 1977 OB in *The Cherry Orchard*, followed by *Agamemnon, The Ballad of Soapy Smith, Titus Andronicus, The Dreamer Examines his Pillow, Sight Unseen*, Bdwy in *The Inspector General, Devour the Snow, Major Barbara, Execution of Justice*.

**DeVRIES, MICHAEL.** Born January 15, 1951 in Grand Rapids, MI. Graduate U. Wash. Debut 1987 OB in *Ready or Not*, Bdwy in *Grand Hotel* (1989), *The Secret Garden*.

**deWOLF, CECILIA.** Born May 9, 1952 in Glen Cove, NY. Gradutate Denver U. PennState U., Columbia. OB in *Beautiful Dreamer* (1986), followed by *Family Life, Julie Johnson*.

**DIENER, JOAN.** Born February 24, 1934 in Cleveland, Oh. Attended Sarah Lawrence Col. Bdwy debut 1948 in *Small Wonder*, followed by *Season in the Sun, Kismet*, for which she received a Theatre World Award, *Cry for Us All, Man of LaMancha* (1965/1992), *Home Sweet Home*.

**DILLON, MIA.** Born July 9, 1955 in Colorado Springs, Co. Graduate Penn State U. Bdwy debut 1977 in *Equus*, followed by *Da, Once a Catholic, Crimes of the Heart, The Corn is Green, Hay Fever, The Miser*, OB in *The Crucible, Summer, Waiting for the Parade, Crimes of the Heart, Fables for Friends, Scenes from La Vie de Boheme, Three Sisters, Wednesday, Roberta in Concert, Come Back Little Sheba, Vienna Notes, George White's Scandals,Lady Moonsong, Mr. Monsoon, Almost Perfect, The Aunts, Approximating Mother*.

**DiPASQUALE, FRANK.** Born July 15, 1955 in Whitestone, NY. Graduate USC. Bdwy debut in *La Cage aux Folles* (1983), followed by *Radio City Christmas Spectacular 1990, The Secret Garden*.

**DIVENY, MARY.** Born in Elmira, NY. Attended Elmira Col., AADA. Bdwy debut 1946 in *The Playboy of the Western World*, followed by *Crime and Punishment, Life with Mother*, OB in *The Matchmaker, Marvin's Room*.

**DIXON, ED.** Born September 2, 1948 in Oklahoma. Attended U. Okla. Bdwy in *The Student Prince*, followed by *No No Nanette, Rosalie in Concert, The Three Musketeers, Les Miserables*, OB in *By Bernstein, King of the Schnorrers, Rabboni, Moby Dick, Shylock, Johnny Pye and the Foolkiller*.

**DIXON, MacINTYRE.** Born December 22, 1931 in Everett, Ma. Graduate Emerson Col. Bdwy debut 1965 in *Xmas in Las Vegas*, followed by *Cop-Out, Story Theatre, Metamorphosis, Twigs, Over Here, Once in a Lifetime, Alice in Wonderland, 3 Penny Opera*, OB in *Quare Fellow, Plays for Bleecker Street, Stewed Prunes, The Cat's Pajamas, Three Sisters, 3 X 3, Second City, Mad Show, Meow!, Lotta, Rubbers, Conjuring an Event, His Majesty the Devil, Tomfollery, A Christmas Carol, Times and Appetites of Toulouse-Lautrec, Room Service, Sills and Company, Little Murders, Much Ado about Nothing, A Winter's Tale, Arms and the Man, Hamlet, Pericles*.

**DOERR, MARK.** Born July 6, 1965 in Ann Arbor, Mi. Graduate U. Mich., Juilliard. Debut 1991 OB in *Unchanging Love*, followed by *Rodgers & Hart: A Celebration, The Perpetrator*, Bdwy in *The Visit* (1992).

**DOHI, SYLVIA.** Born February 2, 1965 in Hollywood, Ca. Attended UCLA, Portland CC. Bdwy debut 1991 in *Miss Saigon*.

**DONNELLY, DONAL.** Born July 6, 1931 in Bradford, Eng. Bdwy debut 1966 in *Philadelphia, Here I Come!*, followed by *A Day in the Death of Joe Egg, Sheuth, The Faith Healer, The Elephant Man, Execution of Justice, Sherlock's Last Case, Ghetto, Dancing at Lughnasa*, OB in *My Astonishing Self* (solo), *The Chalk Garden, Big Maggie*.

**DOTRICE, ROY.** Born May 26, 1925 in Guernsey, Channel Islands. Bdwy debut 1967 in *Brief Lives, A Return Engagement in 1974*, followed by *Mr. Lincoln, A Life, Hay Fever, The Homecoming*, OB in *An Enemy of the People*.

**DOVE, LISA.** Born December 23, 1964 in Moorhead, Mn. Graduate U. Evansville, Juilliard. Debut 1991 OB in *The Matchmaker*.

Gabriel Barre

Rachel Black

James R. Bianchi

Fran Brill

Mark Blum

Darcy Brown

Jonathan Brody

Kate Burton

Terence Burk

Kathleen Chalfant

William Cain

Nora Cole

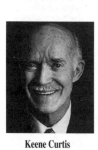

Marcus Chong

Joan Copeland

Michael Connor

Kitty Crooks

Tony Cormier

Hope Davis

Keene Curtis

Mary Diveny

Frank Deal

Donna English

Andre De Shields

Laura Esterman

Craig Dudley

Rosemary Fine

Richard Ferrone

Mary Fogarty

Henderson Forsythe

David Marshall Grant

**OWNING, REBECCA.** Born November 30, 1962 in Birmingham, AL. Graduate Oklahoma City U. Debut 1989 OB in *Wonderful Town*, Bdwy in *The Will Rogers Follies* (1991).

**OYLE, JACK.** Born June 7, 1954 in Brooklyn, NY. Graduate Adelphi U. Debut 3 in *New Faces of 1952*, followed by *Tomfoolery*, Bdwy in *The Will Rogers Follies* (1991).

**RAKE, DAVID.** Born June 27, 1963 in Baltimore, Md. Attended Essex Col., Peabody Consv. Debut 1984 in *Street Theatre*, followed by *Pretty Boy, Vampire Lesbians of Sodom, TheLife, The Night Larry Kramer Kissed Me, Pageant.*

**REYFUSS, RICHARD.** Born Oct. 29, 1947 in Brooklyn, NY. Bdwy debut 1969 in *Dut Seriously*, followed by *Total Abandon, Death and the Maiden,* OB in *Line, Julius Caesar, Othello.*

**RUMMOND, ALICE.** Born May 21, 1929 in Pawtucket, RI. Attended Pembroke ol. Bdwy debut 1963 in *Ballad of the Sad Cafe*, followed by *Malcolm, The Chinese, Thieves, Summer Boys, Some of My Best Friends, You Can't Take It with You,* OB in *Royal Gambit, Go Show Me a Dragon, Sweet of You to Say So, Gallows Humor, American Dream, Giants' Dance, Carpenters, Charles Abbot & Son, God Says There No Peter Ott, Enter a Free Man, A Memroy of Two Mondays, Secret Service, Boy Meets Girls, Savages, Killings on the Last Line, Knuckle, Wonderland, Endgame, Edecker, Marvin's Room.*

**CLOS, DANIELLE.** Born September 29, 1974 in Warwick, NY. Debut 1988 OB in *Rimers of Eldritch*, followed by *Asleep on the Wind, Working One Acts, St. Stanislaus Outside the House*, Bdwy in *Aspects of Love* (1990).

**UDLEY, CRAIG.** Born January 22, 1945 in Sheepshead Bay, NY. Graduate ADA, Am. Th. Wing. Debut 1970 OB in *Macbeth*, followed by *Zou, I Have Always Believed in Ghosts, Othello, War and Peace, Dial "M" for Murder, Misalliance, Crown of Kings, Trelawny of 'The Wells'.*

**UDLEY, GEORGE.** Born April 6, 1958 in Santa Monica, CA. Graduate Humboldt State U. Bdwy debut 1990 in *Grand Hotel.*

**ULAINE, PIERRE.** Born April 23 in Jaffa, Palestine. Bdwy debut 1989 in *Grand Hotel.*

**ULLEA, KEIR.** Born May 30, 1936 in Cleveland, NJ. Attended Neighborhood Playhouse. Debut 1959 OB in *Season of Choice*, followed by *Sweet Prince, Uncle Vanya, The Other Side of Paradise*, Bdwy in *Dr. Cook's Garden, Butterflies Are Free, P.S. Your Cat Is Dead.*

**MONT, JAMES.** Born August 12, 1965 in Chicago, IL. Attended Boston U. Debut 1988 OB in *Tony 'n' Tina's Wedding*, followed by *Waiting for Lefty, Not Me, American Buffalo, Special Interests, Down and Out, EST Marathon '92*, Bdwy in *Six Degrees of Separation* (1990).

**UNNE, GRIFFIN.** Born June 8, 1955 in NYC. Attended Neighborhood Playhouse. Debut 1974 OB in *White Album*, followed by *Coming Attractions, Hooters*, Bdwy in *Search and Destroy* for which he received a 1992 Theatre World Award.

**URAND, le CLANCHE.** Born in South Africa. Graduate Rhodes U. NYU, U. Cal/Berkeley. Debut 1977 OB in *Unfinished Women Cry in No-Man's Land*, followed by *Twelfth Night, What the Butler Saw, On Approval*, Bdwy in *Whose Life Is It Anyway* (1979), *Blithe Spirit, Einstein and the Polar Bear, Two Shakespearean Actors.*

**USOLD, ROBERT.** Born June 7, 1959 in Waukesha, WI. Attended U. Cinn. Consv. Bdwy debut in *Les Miserables* (1991).

**AGAN, DAISY.** Born November 4, 1979 in Brooklyn, NY. Attended Neighborhood Playhouse. Debut 1988 OB in *Tiny Tim's Christmas Carol*, Bdwy in *Les Miserables* (1989), followed by *The Secret Garden.*

**O, JONATHAN BECK.** Born July 9, 1959 in Oklahoma City, OK. Graduate Ok. U. Debut 1991 OB in *Little Me.*

**DELHART, YVETTE.** Born March 26, 1928 in Oak Park, IL. Attended Wright Col. Debut 1984 OB in *Office Mishegoss*, followed by *Home Movies, Night Must Fall, The Miser, Heart of a Dog, Peg' My Heart, The Dreams of Clytemnestra, The Male Animal.*

**DELMAN, GREGG.** Born September 12, 1958 in Chicago, IL. Graduate Northwestern U. Bdwy debut 1982 in *Evita*, followed by *Oliver!, Cats, Cabaret, City of Angels*, OB in *Weekend, Shop on Main Street, Forbidden Broadway, She Loves Me, Babes in Arms.*

**OMEAD, WENDY.** Born July 6, 1956 in New York City. Graduate NYCU. Bdwy debut 1974 in *The Wiz*, followed by *Stop the World..., America, Dancin', Encore, Cats.*

**DMONDS, MITCHELL.** Born January 24, 1940 in Knoxville, Th. Bdwy debut 1969 in *Red, White and Maddox*, followed by *Two Shakespearean Actors*, OB in *The Importance of Being Earnest, A Midsummer Night's Dream, A Maid's Tragedy.*

**DWARDS, DAVID.** Born December 13, 1957 in NYC. Graduate NYU. Bdwy debut 1972 in *The Rothschilds*, followed by *The Best Little Whorehouse in Texas, 42nd Street, A Chorus Line*, OB in *Wish You Were Here, Bittersuite, One More Time, Zion!, Company.*

**HLINGER, MARY.** Born August 17 in Green Bay, Wi. Graduate St. Norbert Col. SU. Debut 1989 OB in *Oil City Symphony*, followed by *Return of the Forbidden Planet.*

**IGENBERG, DAVID M.** Born May 17, 1964 in Manhasset, NY. Graduate AADA. Debut 1989 OB in *Young Playwright's Festival/Finnagan's Funeral Parlor & Ice Cream Shop*, followed by *Six Degrees of Separation, The My House Play, EST Marathon '92*, Bdwy in *Six Degrees of Separation* (1990).

**LDARD, RON.** Born in 1964 in New York City. Attended HS Performing Arts. Bdwy debut 1986 in *Biloxi Blues*, OB in *Tony 'n' Tina's Wedding*, followed by *Servy-Bernice 4 Ever.*

**LDER, DAVID.** Born July 7, 1966 in Houston, Tx. Attended U. Houston. Bdwy debut 1992 in *Guys and Dolls.*

**ELIZONDO, HECTOR.** Born December 12, 1936 in NYC. Attended CCNY. Bdwy debut 1968 in *The Great White Hope*, followed by *Prisoner of Second Avenue, Sly Fox, The Price*, OB in *Drums in the Night, Steambath, Dance of Death* (LC).

**ELLEDGE, DAVID.** Born July 27, 1957 in Omak, WA. Graduate U. Utah. Debut 1984 OB in *Clarence*, followed by *Cole Cuts*, Bdwy in *Grand Hotel* (1989), followed by *The Secret Garden.*

**ELLIS, BRAD.** Born October 5, 1960 in Lexington, MA. Attended Berklee Col. Debut 1990 OB in *Forbidden Broadway, Forbidden Broadway 10th Anniversary.*

**ELLIS, WILLIAM.** Born December 5, 1929 near Cincinnati, OH. Graduate Goodman School, Columbia, NYU. Debut 1953 OB in *One Foot to the Sea*, followed by *Murder in the Cathedral, Hill of Beans, Rags to Reubens, Hidden Away in Stores, Today's Children, The Marriage Proposal, Much Ado About Nothing, Writers, A Doll's House, Legend of Sleepy Hollow, Yesterday in Warsaw, Moral and Political Lessons on Wyoming.*

**EMERY, LISA.** Born January 29 in Pittsburgh, PA. Graduate Hollins Col. Debut 1981 OB in *In Connecticut*, followed by *Talley & Son, Dalton's Back, Grownups!, The Matchmaker, Marvin's Room*, Bdwy in *Passion* (1983), *Burn This, Rumors.*

**EMMET, ROBERT.** Born October 3, 1952 in Denver, CO. Graduate U. Wash. Debut 1976 OB in *The Mousetrap*, followed by *The Seagull, Blue Hotel, Miss Jairus, Hamlet, Deathwatch, Much Ado About Nothing, Songs and Ceremonies, Mass Appeal, Macbeth, Bell Book and Candle, Comes the Happy Hour, The Gift, The Merchant of Venice, Arms and the Man, The Lady from the Sea, Two Gentlemen from Verona, Andromache, Hamlet, The Diaries of Adam and Eve*, Bdwy in *The Devil's Disciple, Dancing at Lughnasa.*

**ENGEL, DAVID.** Born October 19, 1959 in Orange, CA. Attended U. Cal/Irvine. Bdwy debut 1983 in *La Cage aux Folles*, OB in *Forever Plaid.*

**ENGLISH, DONNA.** Born January 13, 1962 in Norman, Ok. Graduate Northwestern U. Bdwy debut 1987 in *Broadway*, OB in *Company, The Last Musical Comedy, Kiss Me Quick, Ruthless!*

**EPPERSON, JOHN.** Born 1956 in Hazelhurst, Ms. Debut 1988 OB in *I Could Go on Lypsynching*, followed by *The Fabulous Lypsinka Show, Lysinka! A Day in the Life!*

**ERDE, SARA.** Born March 18, 1970 in NYC. Debut 1987 OB in *Roosters*, followed by *Dancing Feet, A Midsummer Night's Dream, Don Juan of Seville, Occasional Grace, Blood Wedding.*

**ERICKSON, CLARIS.** Born December 13, 1940 in Aurora, Il. Graduate Northwestern U. Edinburgh U. Debut 1962 OB in *Little Eyolf*, followed by *A Tribute to Lili Lamont, As Is, Empty Hearts.* Bdwy in *As Is* (1985).

**ESHELMAN, DREW.** Born October 12, 1946 in Long Beach, Ca. Graduate Shimer Col., AmConsTh. Broadway debut 1992 in *Les Miserables.*

**ESPOSITO, GIANCARLO.** Born April 26, 1958 in Copenhagen, Den. Bdwy debut 1968 in *Maggie Flynn*, followed by *The Me Nobody Knows, Lost in the Stars, Seesaw, Merrily We Roll Along, Don't Get God Started, 3 Penny Opera*, OB in *Zooman and the Sign* for which he received a 1981 Theatre World Award, *Keyboard, Who Loves the Dancer, House of Ramon Iglesias, Do Lord Remember Me, Balm in Gilead, Anchorman, Distant Fires.*

**ESTERMAN, LAURA.** Born April 12 in NYC. Attended Radcliffe Col., LAMDA. Debut 1969 OB in *The Time of Your Life*, followed by *Pig Pen, Carpenters, Ghosts, Macbeth, The Sea Gull, Rubbers, Yankees 3, Detroit O., Golden Boy, Out of Our Father's House, The Master and Margarita, Chinchilla, Dusa, Fish, Stas and Vi, A Midsummer Night's Dream, The Recruiting Officer, Oedipus the King, Two Fish in the Sky, Mary Barnes, Tamar, Marvin's Room*, Bdwy in *Waltz of the Toreadors* (1973), *God's Favorite, Teibele and Her Demon, The Suicide, Metamorphosis.*

**ESTEY, SUELLEN.** Born November 21 in Mason City, IA. Graduate Stephens Col., Northwestern U. Debut 1970 OB in *Some Other Time*, followed by *June Moon, Buy Bonds Buster, Smile Smile Smile, Carousel, Lullaby of Broadway, I Can't Keep Running, The Guys in the Truck, Stop the World..., Bittersuite—One More Time, Passionate Extremes, Sweeney Todd, Love in Two Countries*, Bdwy in *The Selling of the President* (1972), *Barnum, Sweethearts in Concert, Sweeney Todd* (1989).

**ESTRADA, HECTOR M.** Born November 11, 1977 in Brooklyn, NY. Debut 1991 OB in *Babylon Gardens.*

**EVANS, HARVEY.** Born January 7, 1941 in Cincinnati, OH. Bdwy debut 1957 in *New Girl in Town*, followed by *West Side Story, Redhead, Gypsy, Anyone Can Whistle, Hello Dolly!, George M!, Our Town, The Boy Friend, Follies, Barnum, La Cage aux Folles*, OB in *Sextet.*

**EVANS-KANDEL, KAREN.** Born August 11 in NYC. Graduate Queens Col. Debut 1977 OB in *Nightclub Cantata*, followed by *1951 in The Making of Americans, Underfire, Alice in Concert, Dispatchers, Human Nature, Group*, Bdwy in *Runaways* (1978).

**EVERS, BRIAN.** Born February 14, 1942 in Miami, FL. Graduate Capital U., U. Miami. Debut 1979 OB in *How's the House?*, followed by *Details of the 16th Frame, Divine Fire, Silent Night Lonely Night, Uncommon Holidays, The Tamer Tamed, Death of a Buick, The Racket, Six Degrees of Separation*, Bdwy in *House of Blue Leaves, Six Degrees of Separation.*

**EWING, J. TIMOTHY** (a.k.a. Tim). Born April 3, 1954 in Evansville, IN. Graduate Okla. State U. Debut 1972 OB in *Colette Collage*, followed by *Promenade, Pacific Overtures, Good Times, Charley's Tale, Love in Two Countries, Rodgers and Hart: A Celebration.*

**FALK, WILLY.** Born July 21 in New York City. Harvard, LAMDA graduate. Debut 1982 OB in *The Robber Bridegroom*, followed by *Pacific Overtures, The House in the Woods, Elizabeth and Essex*, Bdwy in *Marilyn: An American Fable, Starlight Express, Les Miserables, Miss Saigon.*

**FARINA, MARILYN J.** Born April 9, 1947 in New York City. Graduate Sacred Heart Col. Debut 1985 OB in *Nunsense.*

**FAUGNO, RICHARD** (Rick). Born November 8, 1978 in New York City. Bdwy debut 1991 in *The Will Rogers Follies.*

**FAVIER, LOUISE.** Born March 25, 1964 in Auckland, NZ. Graduate U. College Cork. Debut 1992 OB in *All Must Be Admitted,* followed by *Grandchild of Kings.*

**FAYE, PASCALE.** Born January 6, 1964 in Paris, France. Bdwy debut 1991 in *Grand Hotel,* followed by *Guys and Dolls.*

**FEAGAN, LESLIE.** Born January 9, 1951 in Hinckley, Oh. Graduate Ohio U. Debut 1978 OB in *Can-Can,* followed by *Merton of the Movies, Promises Promises, Mowgli,* Bdwy in *Anything Goes* (1987), *Guys and Dolls.*

**FELDSHUH, TOVAH.** Born December 28, 1953 in New York City. Graduate Sarah Lawrence Col., U. Minn. Bdwy debut 1973 in *Cyrano,* followed by *Dreyfus in Rehearsal, Rodgers and Hart, Yentl* for which she received a Theatre World Award, *Sarava, Lend Me a Tenor,* OB in *Yentl the Yeshiva Boy, Straws in the Wind, Three Sisters, She Stoops to Conquer, Springtime for Henry, The Time of Your Life, Children of the Sun, The Last of the Red Hot Lovers, Mistress of the Inn, A Fierce Attachment, Custody.*

**FERLAND, DANIELLE.** Born January 31, 1971 in Derby, CT. Debut 1983 in *Sunday in the Park with George,* followed by *Paradise,* Bdwy in *Sunday in the Park with George* (1984), *Into the Woods* for which she received a Theatre World Award, *A Little Night Music* (NYCO/LC), *Crucible, A Little Hotel on the Side.*

**FERRARA, ANDY.** Born September 2, 1960 in Los Gatos, CA. Bdwy debut 1990 in *Peter Pan,* also 1991.

**FERRONE, RICHARD.** Born May 7, 1946 in Newton, MA. Graduate Holy Cross Col., Boston Law Col. Debut 1980 OB in *The Caine Mutiny Court-Martial,* followed by *Romeo and Juliet,* Bdwy in *The Crucible* (1991), *A Little Hotel on the Side.*

**FIEDLER, JOHN.** Born February 3, 1925 in Plateville, Wi. Attended Neighborhood Playhouse. OB in *The Sea Gull, Sing Me No Lullaby, The Terrible Swift Sword, The Raspberry Picker, The Frog Prince, Raisin in the Sun, Marathon '88, Human Nature,* Bdwy in *One Eye Closed* (1954), *Howie, Raisin in the Sun, Harold, The Odd Couple, Our Town, The Crucible, A Little Hotel on the Side.*

**FIELD, CRYSTAL.** Born December 10, 1942 in NYC. Attended Juilliard, Hunter Col. Debut 1960 OB in *A Country Scandal,* followed by *A Matter of Life and Death, The Heart That Eats Itself, Ruzzante Returns from the Wars, An Evening of British Music Hall, Ride That Never Was, House Arrest, Us, Beverly's Yard Sale, Bruno's Donuts, Coney Island Kid, Till The Eagle Hollars, The Rivalry of Dolls.*

**FIERSTEIN, HARVEY.** Born June 6, 1954 in Brooklyn, NY. Graduate Pratt Inst. Debut 1971 OB in *Pork,* followed by *International Stud, Figures in a Nursery, Haunted Host, Pouf Positive, Safe Sex,* Bdwy in *Torch Song Trilogy* for which he recieved a Theatre World Award, *Safe Sex.*

**FINE, ROSEMARY.** Born December 9, 1961 in Limerick, Ire. Graduate Trinity Col./Dublin. Bdwy debut 1988 in *Juno and the Paycock,* OB in *Grandchild of Kings* (1992).

**FINKEL, FYVUSH.** Born October 9, 1922 in Brooklyn, NY. Bdwy debut 1970 in *Fiddler on the Roof* (also 1981 revival), followed by *Cafe Crown* (1989), OB in *Gorky, Little Shop of Horrors, Cafe Crown, Dividends, Finkel's Follies.*

**FINN, JOHN.** Born September 30, 1952 in NYC. Debut 1985 OB in *The Last of the Knucklemen,* followed by Bdwy in *Biloxi Blues* (1987).

**FISHBURNE, LAURENCE "LARRY".** Born July 30, 1961 in Augusta, Ga. Attended NYC High Schoool of Performing Arts. Debut 1976 OB in *Eden,* followed by *In My Many Names and Days.* Bdwy 1992 in *Two Trains Running* for which he received a Theatre World Award.

**FISHER, MARY HELEN.** Born July 17 in Oklahoma City, Ok. Debut 1976 OB in *Spoon River Anthology,* followed by *Aladdin, Bar Mitzvah Boy.* Bdwy in *The Most Happy Fella* (1992).

**FITZGIBBON, JOHN.** Born September 13, 1946 in New York City. Graduate Fordham U. LAMDA. Debut 1967 in *Macbeth,* followed by *Macbird!, Screens, False Confessions, Julius Caesar, Gaugin in Tahiti, Moon Mysteries, Twelfth Night, Zion!,* Bdwy in *The Incomparable Max* (1981).

**FITZPATRICK, JIM.** Born November 26, 1950 in Omaha, Ne. Attended U. Neb. Debut 1977 OB in *Arsenic and Old Lace,* followed by *Merton of the Movies, Oh Boy!, Time and the Conways, Street Scene, The Duchess of Malfi, Comedy of Errors, Much Ado about Nothing, Cinderella.*

**FLANAGAN, PAULINE.** Born June 29, 1925 in Sligo, Ire. Debut 1958 OB in *Ulysses in Nighttown,* followed by *Pictures in the Hallway, Later, Antigone, The Crucible, The Plough and the Stars, Summer, Close of Play, In Celebration, Without Apologies, Yeats, A Celebration, Philadelphia Here I Come!, Grandchild of Kings, Shadow of a Gunman.* Bdwy in *God and Kate Murphy, The Living Room, The Innocents, The Father, Medea, Steaming, Corpse.*

**FLANINGAM, LOUISA.** Born May 5, 1945 in Chester SC.Graduate U. Md. Debut 1971 OB in *The Shrinking Bridge,* followed by *Pigeons on the Walk, Etiquette, The Knife, Say It with Music, Opal.* Bdwy in *Magic Show, Most Happy Fella* (1979), *Play Me a Country Song.*

**FLEISS, JANE.** Born January 28 in NYC. Graduate NYU. Debut 1979 OB in *Say Goodnight Gracie,* Followed by *Grace, The Beaver Coat, The Harvesting, D., Second Man, Of Mice and Men, Niedecker.* Bdwy in *5th of July* (1981), *Crimes of the Heart, I'm Not Rappaport, Search and Destroy.*

**FLEISS, NOAH.** Born April 16, 1984 in New Rochelle, NY. Bdwy debut 1992 in *Four Baboons Adoring the Sun.*

**FLODEN, LEA.** Born February 13, 1958 in Rockford, IL. Graduate Ind. U. Debut

**1980 OB** in *The Ladder,* followed by *Cherokee County, Short Change, Murder in Mummy's Tomb, Babylon Gardens.*

**FOGARTY, MARY.** Born in Manchester, NH. Debut 1959 OB in *The Well of Sc* followed by *Shadow and Substance, Nathan the Wise, Bonjour La Bonjour, Fa Comedy, Steel Magnolias, Dearly Departed.* Bdwy in *National Health* (1974), *W on the Rhine* (1980), *Of the Fields Lately.*

**FORD, CLEBERT.** Born January 29, 1932 in Brooklyn, NY. Graduate CC Boston U. Bdwy debut 1960 in *The Cool World,* followed by *Les Blancs, A Supposed to Die a Natural Death, Via Galactica, Bubbling Brown Sugar, The Minstrel Show, Mule Bone,* OB in *Romeo and Juliet, The Blacks, Antony Cleopatra, Ti-Jean and His Brothers, Ballad for Bimshire, Daddy, Gib Coriolanus, Before the Flood, The Lion and the Jewel, Branches from the Same T Dreams Deferred, Basin Street, 20 Year Friends, Celebration, Stories About the Days, A Tempest, The Hills of Massabielle.*

**FORSYTHE, HENDERSON.** Born September 11, 1917 in Macon, MO. Atter U. Iowa. Debut 1956 OB in *The Iceman Cometh,* followed by *The Collection, Room, A Slight Ache, Happiness Cage, Waiting for Godot, In Case of Accident, N An Evening with the Poet Senator, Museum, How Far Is It to Babylon?, Wild A Other Places, Clifthanger, Broadcast Baby, After the Fall, Some Americans Abr Fridays,* Bdwy in *The Cellar and the Well* (1950), *Miss Lonelyhearts, Who's Afrai Virginia Woolf?, Malcolm, Right Honourable Gentleman, Delicate Balance, Birth Party, Harvey, Engagement Baby, Freedom of the City, Texas Trilogy, Best L Whorehouse in Texas, Some Americans Abroad, 110 in the Shade* (NYCO/LC).

**FOSTER, DAN.** Born March 3, 1957 in Gary Ind. Graduate Providence Col. D OB 1989 in *Cymbeline,* followed by Bdwy in *City of Angels* (1991).

**FOSTER, GLORIA.** Born November 15, 1936 in Chicago, Il. Attended Ill. State Goodman Theatre. Debut 1963 OB in *In White America,* followed by *Medea* for wh she received a 1966 Theatre World Award, *Yerma, A Hand Is on the Gate, Bl Visions, The Cherry Orchard, Agamemnon, Coriolanus, Mother Courage, Long D Journey into Night, Trespassing, Forbidden City, Hamlet, Blood Wedding.*

**FOWLER, SCOTT.** Born March 22, 1967 in Medford, MA. Debut 1989 on Bdw *Jerome Robbins' Broadway,* followed by *Brigadoon* (NYCO/LC).

**FRANCIS-JAMES, PETER.** Born September 16, 1956 in Chicago, IL. Grad RADA. Debut 1979 OB in *Julius Caesar,* followed by *Long Day's Journey I Night, Antigone, Richard II, Romeo and Juliet, Enrico IV, Cymbeline, Hamlet, Lear Ladies, 10th Young Playwrights Festival.*

**FRANZ, ELIZABETH.** Born June 18, 1941 in Akron, OH. Attended AADA. De 1965 in *In White America,* followed by *One Night Stands of a Noisey Passenger, Real Inspector Hound, Augusta, Yesterday Is Over, Actor's Nightmare, Sister M Ignatius Explains It All, The Time of Your Life, Children of the Sun,* Bdwy *Rosencrantz and Guildenstern are Dead, The Cherry Orchard, Brighton Be Memoirs, The Octette Bridge Club, Broadway Bound, The Cemetery Club, Gett Married.*

**FRASER, ALISON.** Born July 8, 1955 in Natick, MA. Attended Carnegie-Mell Boston Consv. Debut 1979 OB in *In Trousers,* followed by *March of the Falset Beehive, Four One-Act Musicals, Tales of Tinseltown, Next Please!, Up Against* Bdwy in *The Mystery of Edwin Drood* (1986), *Romance Romance, The Secret Gard*

**FREEMAN, STAN.** Born April 3, 1920 in Waterbury, Ct. Graduate Hartt School Music. Bdwy debut 1967 in *An Evening with Marlene Dietrich* (also 1968), OB in *Wit's End* (1991).

**FRENCH, ARTHUR.** Born in New York City and attended Brooklyn Col. De 1962 OB in *Raisin' Hell in the Sun,* followed by *Ballad of Bimshire, Day of Absen Happy Ending, Brotherhood, Perry's Mission, Rosalee Pritchett, Moonlight Arm Dark Tower, Brownsville Raid, Nevis Mountain Dew, Julius Caesar, Friends, Cour Miracles, The Beautiful LaSalles, Blues for a Gospel Queen, Black Girl, Driving M Daisy, The Spring Thing, George Washington Slept Here, Ascension Day, Boxing L Parade, A Tempest, The Hills of Massabielle,* Bdwy in *Ain't Supposed to Di Natural Death, The Iceman Cometh, All God's Chillun Got Wings, The Resurrection Lady Lester, You Can't Take It with You, Design for Living, Ma Rainey's Blc Bottom, Mule Bone.*

**FRIDAY, BETSY.** Born April 30, 1958 in Chapel Hill, NC. Graduate NC Schl. Arts. Bdwy debut 1980 in *The Best Little Whorehouse in Texas,* followed by *Bra Back Birdie, The Secret Garden,* OB in *I Ought to Be in Pictures, Smile, Ace Diamonds.*

**FYFE, JIM.** Born September 27, 1958 in Camden, NJ. Graduate Allentown C Bdwy debut 1985 in *Biloxi Blues,* followed by *Legs Diamond, Artist Descending Staircase,* OB in *Remedial English, Moonchildren, Privates on Parade, T Matchmaker.*

**GAINES, BOYD.** Born May 11, 1953 in Atlanta, GA. Graduate Juilliard. Deb 1978 OB in *Spring Awakening,* followed by *A Month in the Country* for which received a Theatre World Award, BAM Theatre Co.'s *Winter's Tale, The Barbaria and Johnny on a Spot, Vikings, Double Bass, The Maderati, The Heidi Chronicles, T Extra Man, The Comedy of Errors,* Bdwy in *The Heidi Chronicles* (1989).

**GALANTICH, TOM.** Born in Brooklyn, NY. Debut 1985 OB in *On the 2G Century,* followed by *Mademoiselle Colombe,* Bdwy in *Into the Woods* (1989), *City Angels.*

**GALBRAITH, PHILIP.** Born December 12, 1950 in Toronto, Can. Graduate Windsor. Debut 1982 OB in *Nymph Errant,* followed by *The Mask.*

**GALINDO, RAMON.** Born June 3 in San Francisco, CA. Graduate U. of Cal Berkeley. Bdwy debut 1979 in *Carmelina,* followed by *Merlin, Cats, Song a Dance, Jerome Robbins' Broadway,* OB in *Funny Feet* (1987).

**LLAGHER, PETER.** Born August 19, 1955 in Armonk, NY. Bdwy debut 1977 *Hair*, followed by *Grease, A Doll's Life* for which he received a 1983 Theatre *rld* Award, *The Corn is Green, The Real Thing, Long Day's Journey into Night* '86), *Guys and Dolls* (1992).

**NUN, JOHN.** Born August 23, 1966 in Blissfeld, MI. Graduate U. Mich. Bdwy *ut* 1991 in *The Will Rogers Follies*.

**RBER, VICTOR.** Born March 15, 1949 in London, Can. Debut 1973 OB in *osts* for which he received a Theatre World Award, followed by *Joe's Opera, acks, Wenceslas Square, Love Letters, Assassins*, Bdwy in *Tartuffe, Deathtrap, eeney Todd, They're Playing Our Song, Little Me, Noises Off, You Never Can Tell, il's Disciple, Lend Me a Tenor, Two Shakespearean Actors*.

**RDENIA, VINCENT.** Born January 7, 1923 in Naples, It. Debut 1955 OB in *In il Once*, followed by *Man with the Golden Arm, Volpone, Brothers Karamazov, wer of Darkness, Machinal, Gallows Humor, Theatre of the Absurd, Lunatic View, le Murders, Passing Through from Exotic Places, Carpenters, Buried Inside Extra, aking Legs*, Bdwy in *The Visit* (1958), *Rashomon, The Cold Wind and the Warm, ly in America, The Wall, Daughter of Silence, Seidman & Son, Dr. Fish, The soner of Second Avenue, God's Favorite, California Suite, Ballroom, Glengarry n Ross*.

**RITO, KEN.** Born December 27, 1968 in Brooklyn, NY. Graduate Brooklyn Col. *but* 1991 OB in *Tony 'n' Tina's Wedding*, followed by *Peacetime, A Map of the y*.

**RRETT, RUSSELL** (formerly Giesenschlag). Born July 8, 1959 in San Diego, *.* Attended San Diego State U. Bdwy debut 1982 in *Seven Brides for Seven thers*, followed by *42nd Street*, OB in *Girl Crazy, Pageant*.

**RRICK, BARBARA.** Born February 3, 1962 in NYC. Debut 1986 OB in *Today I a Fountain Pen*, followed by *A Midsummer Night's Dream, Rosencrantz and ildenstern Are Dead, Eastern Standard*. Bdwy in *Eastern Standard* (1988), *A Small mily Business*.

**IZZARA, BEN.** Born August 28, 1930 in NYC. Attended CCNY. Bdwy debut *3* in *End as a Man* for which he received a Theatre World Award, followed by *Cat a Hot Tin Roof, Hatful of Rain, Night Circus, Strange Interlude, Traveller without ggage, Hughie, Duet, Who's Afraid of Virginia Woolf?, Shimada*.

**LFER, STEVEN.** Born February 21, 1949 in Brooklyn, NY. Graduate NYU, Ind. *.* Debut 1968 OB and Bdwy in *The Best Little Whorehouse in Texas*, followed by *s.*

**NNUSO, FRAN.** Born June 23, 1954 in Brooklyn, NY. Attended NY/Farmingdale. Debut 1990 OB in *Tony 'n' Tina's Wedding*.

**NTILE, MARIA.** Born May 21, 1962 in Boston, Ma. Debut 1991 OB in *Tony 'n' a's Wedding*.

**ORGE, BEN.** Born June 7, 1947 in Oxford, Eng. Attended Leeds Music Col. *but* 1984 OB in *Last of the Knucklemen*, Bdwy in *The Best Little Whorehouse in as* (1985), *Grand Hotel*.

**ORGIANA, TONI.** Born December 14, 1963 in Uniontown, PA. Attended lliard. Bdwy debut 1991 in *The Will Rogers Follies*.

**RACI, FRANK.** Born September 8, 1939 in Brooklyn, NY. Attended Yale. *but* 1961 OB in *Color of Darkness*, followed by *Mr. Grossman, Balm in Gilead, e Fantasticks, Tom Paine, End of All Things Natural, Union Street, Uncle Vanya, ccess Story, Hughie, Merchant of Venice, Three Zeks, Taming of the Shrew, The dy from the Sea, Rivals, Deep Swimmer, The Imaginary Invalid, Candida, Hedda bler, Serious Co., Berenice, The Philanderer, All's Well That Ends Well, Three ters, A Midsummer Night's Dream, Medea, The Importance of Being Earnest, jor Barbara, Measure for Measure, The Fine Art of Finesse, Two Schnitzler One ts, Peace in a Traveling Heart, Tartuffe*, Bdwy in *Love Suicide at Schofield racks* (1972).

**RARD, DANNY.** Born May 29, 1977 in New York City. Bdwy debut 1986 in *o the Light*, followed by *Les Miserables, Lost in Yonkers*, OB in *Today I Am a untain Pen, Second Hurricane, Falsettoland*.

**RBER, CHARLES E.** Born April 2, 1949 in Chicago, Il. Attended Wright Col., lliard. Bdwy debut 1981 in *Oh! Calcutta!*, followed by *Hamlet* (1992), OB in *A dsummer Night's Dream, One-Act Festival*.

**RBER, KATHY.** Born July 18, 1946 in Baltimore, Md. Attended U. Md., AADA. *but* 1975 OB in *The Zykovs*, followed by *Night Dance*.

**RETY, PETER.** Born May 17, 1940 in Providence, RI. Attended URI, Boston U. *but* 1964 OB in *In The Summer House*, followed by *Othello, Baal, Six Characters Search of an Author*. Bdwy in *The Hothouse* (1982), *Conversations with My Father*.

**RROLL, DANIEL.** Born October 16, 1951 in London, Eng. Attended Central *.* of Speech. Debut 1980 OB in *Slab Boys*, followed by *Knuckle and Translations* which he received a Theatre World Award, *The Caretaker, Scenes from La Vie de heme, The Knack, Terra Nova, Dr. Faustus, Second Man, Cheapside, Bloody etry, The Common Pursuit, Woman in Mind, Poets' Corner, The Film Society, erald City, Arms and the Man*, Bdwy in *Plenty* (1982), *The Homecoming* (1991).

**WIRTZ, LAURENCE.** Born January 19, 1953 in Brooklyn, NY. Graduate andeis U., Yale. Debut 1978 OB in *Decathlon*, followed by *A Day at Harmenz, hsemane Springs, Marie and Bruce*.

**ANGIULIO, NICHOLAS J.** Born February 25, 1953 in Bryn Mawr, Pa. Graduate Dayton. Debut 1991 OB in *The Dropper*.

**BBS, SHEILA.** Born February 16, 1947 in New York City. Graduate NYU. Debut 71 in *Two Gentlemen of Verona*, followed by *Runaways, Once on This Island*, OB *Last Days of British Honduras, Poets from the Inside, Once on This Island*.

**BSON, DEBBIE.** Born in 1971 in Merrick, NY. Bdwy debut 1992 in *Les Miserables*.

**GIBSON, JULIA.** Born June 8, 1962 in Norman, OK. Graduate U. Iowa, NYU. Debut 1987 OB in *A Midsummer Night's Dream*, followed by *Love's Labor Lost, Crucible, The Man Who Fell in Love with His Wife, Learned Ladies, Candide*.

**GILLAN, TONY.** Born August 15, 1963 in NYC. Attended Queens Col., California Inst. Debut 1990 OB in *Rosetta Street*, Bdwy 1992 in *Conversations with My Father*.

**GIONSON, MEL DUANE.** Born February 23, 1954 in Honolulu, HI. Graduate U. HI. Debut 1979 OB in *Richard II*, followed by *Sunrise, Monkey Music, Behind Enemy Lines, Station J, Teahouse, A Midsummer Night's Dream, Empress of China, Chip Shot, Manoa Valley, Ghashiram, Shogun, Macbeth, Life of the Land, Noiresque, Three Sisters, Lucky Come Hawaii, Henry IV Parts 1 & 2, Working 1-Acts '91.*

**GIOSA, SUE.** Born November 23, 1958 in Connecticut. Graduate Queens Col. RADA, LAMDA. Debut OB 1988 in *Tamara*, followed by *Breaking Legs*.

**GLANDER, JULIA.** Born December 22 in Detroit, Mi. Graduate Central Mi. U. U. Iowa. Debut 1987 OB in *The Misanthrope*, followed by *A Midsummer Night's Dream, Macbeth, The Lodger, Rain, Some Fish, No Elephants, Tartuffe*.

**GLEASON, JOANNA.** Born June 2, 1950 in Toronto, Can. Graduate UCLA. Bdwy debut 1977 in *I Love My Wife* for which she received a Theatre World Award, followed by *The Real Thing, Social Security, Into the Woods, Nick & Nora*, OB in *A Hell of a Town, Joe Egg, It's Only a Play, Eleemosynary*.

**GLEASON, LAURENCE.** Born November 14, 1956 in Utica, NY. Graduate Utica Col. Debut 1984 OB in *Romance Lanuage*, followed by *Agamemnon, A Country Doctor, The Misanthrope, The Sleepless City, Electra, Morning Song, Like to Live, Macbeth.*

**GLENN, BETTE.** Born December 13, 1946 in Atlantic City, NJ. Graduate Montpelier Col. Debut 1971 Ob in *Ruddigore*, followed by *Maggie Flynn, Company*, Bdwy in *Irene, She Loves Me.*

**GLOVER, SAVION.** Born November 19, 1973 in Newark, NJ. Bdwy debut 1984 in *The Tap Dance Kid*, followed by *Black and Blue, Jelly's Last Jam.*

**GLUSHAK, JOANNA.** Born May 27, 1958 in New York City. Attended NYU. Debut 1983 OB in *Lenny and the Heartbreakers*, followed by *Lies and Legends, Miami, Unfinished Song, A Little Night Music* (NYCO), Bdwy in *Sunday in the Park with George* (1984), *Rags, Les Miserables.*

**GOETHALS, ANGELA.** Born May 20, 1977 in NYC. Bdwy debut 1987 in *Coastal Disturbance, Four Baboons Adoring the Sun*, OB in *Positive Me, Approaching Zanzibar, The Good Times are Killing Me.*

**GOLDSTEIN, STEVEN.** Born October 22, 1963 in New York City. Graduate NYU. Debut 1987 OB in *Boy's Life*, followed by *Oh Hell, Three Sisters, Marathon '91, Angel of Death, Five Very Live, Casino Paradise*, Bdwy in *Our Town* (1988).

**GOLDWYN, TONY.** Born May 20, 1960 in Los Angeles, CA. Graduate Brandeis U., LAMDA. Debut 1985 OB in *Digby*, followed by *Messiah, The Sum of Us, Spike Heels.*

**GOLER, LAUREN.** Born November 10, 1961 in Washington,DC. Bdwy debut 1980 in *Happy New Year*, followed by *Onward Victoria!, Smile, Late Night Comic*, OB in *Joseph, Eating Raoul.*

**GONZALEZ, CORDELIA.** Born August 11, 1958 in San Juan, PR. Graduate UPR, Yale. Debut 1985 OB in *Impact*, followed by *The Love of Don Perlimplin, Sabina and Lucrecia, Blood Wedding, Pericles*, Bdwy in *Serious Money* (1988).

**GOODMAN, DODY.** Born October 28, 1915 in Columbus, Oh. Bdwy debut 1947 in *High Button Shoes*, followed by *Miss Liberty, Call Me Madam, Wonderful Town, Fiorello!, A Rainy Day in Newark, My Daughter, Your Son, Front Page, Lorelei*, OB in *Shoestring Revue, Shoestring 57, Parade, New Cole Porter Revue, Ah Wilderness!, Selling Off.*

**GOODNESS, JOEL.** Born January 22, 1962 in Wisconsin Rapids, WI. Graduate U. Wisc. Debut 1991 OB in *Custody*, followed by *Georgy*, Bdwy in *Crazy for You* (1992).

**GOODROW, GARRY.** Born Noveber 5, 1938 in Malone, NY. Debut 1960 OB in *Many Loves*, followed by *The Connection, Tonight We Improvise, In the Jungle of Cities, National Lampoon's Lemmings, Taming of the Shrew, Sills & Co., Iron Bars*, Bdwy in *The Connection, Story Theatre.*

**GORDON-CLARK, SUSAN.** Born December 31, 1947 in Jackson, MS. Graduate Purdue U. Debut 1984 OB in *The Nunsense Story*, followed by *Chip Shot, Nunsense.*

**GOTTLIEB, DAVID.** Born October 6, 1959 in Chicago, Il. Graduate Amherst Col., UNC. Debut 1991 OB in *As You Like It.*

**GRAAE, JASON.** Born May 15, 1958 in Chicago, IL. Graduate Cincinnati Consv. Debut 1981 OB in *Godspell*, followed by *Snoopy, Heaven on Earth, Promenade, Feathertop, Tales of Tinseltown, Living Color, Just So, Olympus on My Mind, Sitting Pretty in Concert, Babes in Arms, The Cat and the Fiddle, Forever Plaid, A Funny Thing Happened on the Way to the Forum, 50 Million Frenchmen, Rodgers and Hart Revue.*

**GRACE, EILEEN.** Born July 25 in Pittsburgh, PA. Graduate Point Park Col. Bdwy debut in *42nd Street*, followed by *My One and Only, The Will Rogers Follies.*

**GRAFF, RANDY.** Born May 23, 1955 in Brooklyn, NY. Graduate Wagner Col. Debut 1978 OB in *Pins and Needles*, followed by *Snoopy, A...My Name Is Alice, Once on a Summer's Day*, Bdwy in *Sarava, Grease, Les Miserables, City of Angels.*

**GRANT, DAVID MARSHALL.** Born June 21, 1955 in New Haven, Ct. Attended Conn. Col., Yale U. Debut 1978 OB in *Sganarelle*, followed by *Table Settings, The Tempest, Making Movies, Naked Rights*, Bdwy in *Bent* (1979), *The Survivor.*

**GRANT, JODI.** Born September 1, 1966 in Brooklyn, NY. Graduate Kingsborough Col., Brooklyn Col. Debut 1991 OB in *Tony 'n' Tina's Wedding*.

**GRAY, KEVIN.** Born February 25, 1958 in Westport, CT. Graduate Duke U. Debut 1982 OB in *Lola*, followed by *Pacific Overtures, Family Snapshots, The Baker's Wife, The Knife, Magdalena in Concert*, Bdwy in *The Phantom of the Opera* (1989).

**GREEN, ANDREA.** Born Octdebut 1980 in *They're Playing Our Song*, followed by *Little Me*, OB in *And the World Goes Round, Yiddle with a Fiddle, Song of Singapore*.

**GREEN, DAVID.** Born June 16, 1942 in Cleveland, Oh. Attended Kan. State U. Bdwy debut 1980 in *Evita, Teddy and Alice, The Pagama Game* (LC), OB in *Once on a Summer's Day, Miami, On the 20th Century, What About Luv?*

**GREENBERG, HELEN.** Born September 28, 1961 on Long Island, NY. Graduate NYU. Debut 1987 OB in *Words Words Words*, followed by *Double Blessing, Love Lemmings, Occasional Grace, One of the All-Time Greats*.

**GREENBERG, MITCHELL.** Born September 19, 1950 in Brooklyn, NY. Graduate Harpur Col., Neighborhood Playhouse. Debut 1979 OB in *Two Grown Men*, followed by *Scrambled Feet, A Christmas Carol, A Thurber Carnival, Isn't It Romantic?, Crazy Arnold, Yiddle with a Fiddle, The Death and Life of Sherlock Holmes*, Bdwy in *A Day in Hollywood/A Night in the Ukraine* (1980), *Can-Can, Marilyn, Into the Light, 3 Penny Opera*.

**GREENE, ELLEN.** Born February 22 in NYC. Attended Ryder Col. Debut 1973 on Bdwy in *Rachel Lily Rosenbloom*, followed by *The Little Prince and the Aviator*, OB in *In the Boom Boom Room, Threepenny Opera, Disrobing the Bride, The Little Shop of Horrors, Starting Monday, Weird Romance*.

**GRENIER, ZACH.** Born February 12, 1954 in Englewood, NJ. Graduate U. Mich., Boston U. Debut 1982 OB in *Baal*, followed by *Tomorrowland, Water Music, Morocco, The Cure, Birth of the Poet, Talk Radio, Marathon '90, Lilith, Arturo Ui, Creditors*, Bdwy (1989) in *Mastergate*.

**GRIESEMER, JOHN.** Born December 5, 1947 in Elizabeth, NJ. Graduate Dickinson Col, URI. Debut 1981 OB in *Turnbuckle*, followed by *Death of a Miner, Little Victories, Macbeth, A Lie of the Mind, Kate's Diary, Little Egypt*, Bdwy in *Our Town* (1989).

**GRIFFITH, KRISTIN.** Born September 7, 1953 in Odessa, Tx. Graduate Juilliard. Bdwy debut 1976 in *A Texas Trilogy*, OB in *Rib Cage, Character Lines, 3 Friends 2 Rooms, A Month in the Country, Fables for Friends, The Trading Post, Marching in Georgia, American Garage, A Midsummer Night's Dream, Marathon '87, Bunker Reveries, On the Bench, EST Marathon '92*.

**GROENER, HARRY.** Born September 10, 1951 in Augsburg, Ger. Graduate U. Wash. Bdwy debut 1979 in *Oklahoma!* for which he received a Theatre World Award, followed by *Oh, Brother!, Is There Life after High School, Cats, Harrigan 'n' Hart, Sunday in the Park with George, Sleight of Hand, Crazy for You*, OB in *Beside the Seaside*.

**GROSSMAN, HENRY.** Born October 11, 1938 in New York City. Attended Actors Studio. Debut 1961 OB in *The Magistrate*, followed by *Galileo*, Bdwy 1989 in *Grand Hotel*.

**GUITTARD, LAURENCE.** Born July 16, 1939 in San Francisco, Ca. Graduate Stanford U. Bdwy debut 1965 in *Baker Street*, followed by *Anya, Man of La Mancha* (1970/1992), *A Little Night Music* for which he received a Theatre World Award, *Rodgers and Hart, She Loves Me, Oklahoma!* (1979), *The Sound of Music* (LC), OB in *Umbrellas of Cherbourg*.

**GWILYM, ROBERT.** Born December 2, 1956 in Neath, Wales. Bdwy debut 1991 in *Dancing at Lughnasa*.

**HACK, STEVEN.** Born April 20, 1958 in St. Louis, MO. Attended Cal. Arts, AADA. Debut 1978 OB in *The Coolest Cat in Town*, followed by Bdwy in *Cats* (1982).

**HACKMAN, GENE.** Born Jan. 30, 1930 in San Bernardino, CA. Bdwy debut 1963 in *Children From Their Games*, followed by *Any Wednesday, Death and the Maiden*.

**HADARY, JONATHAN.** Born October 11, 1948 in Chicago, IL. Attended Tufts U. Debut 1974 OB in *White Nights*, followed by *El Grande de Coca Cola, Songs from Pins and Needles, God Bless You Mr. Rosewater, Pushing 30, Scrambled feet, Coming Attractions, Tom Foolery, Charley Bacon and Family, Road Show, 1-2-3-4-5, Wenceslas Square, Assassins, Lips Together Teeth Apart, Weird Romance*, Bdwy in *Gemini* (1977 also OB), *Torch Song Trilogy, As Is, Gypsy*.

**HAFNER, JULIE J.** Born June 4, 1952 in Dover, OH. Graduate Kent State U. Debut 1976 OB in *The Club*, followed by *Nunsense*, Bdwy in *Nine*.

**HAGAN, JOHN.** Born May 24, 1950 in New York City. Graduate NYU. Debut 1979 OB in *Disparate Acts*, followed by *Chang in a Void Moon, Two Nietzches in Love, Deep Sleep, Peter and Noel and Noel and Gertie, Dark Shadows, All That Fall, The River Runs Deep, In Time's Course, When Lithuania Ruled the World: Part III*.

**HALL, CHARLES EDWARD.** Born November 12, 1951 in Franfort, KY. Graduate Murray St. U. Debut 1977 OB in *Molly's Dream*, followed by *Sheridan Square, The Doctor in Spite of Himself, Loudspeaker, Action, The Tavern, Snow White, Radio City's Christmas Spectacular, As You Like It*.

**HALL, DAVIS.** Born April 10, 1946 in Atlanta, Ga. Graduate Northwestern U. Bdwy debut 1973 in *Butley*, followed by *Dogg's Hamlet and Cahoot's Macbeth*, OB in *The Promise, The Team, Dreamboats, The Taming of the Shrew, Donkey's Years, Love's Labour's Lost, Betrayal, The Travelling Squirrel, Gunmetal Blues*.

**HALLETT, JACK.** Born November 7, 1948 in Philadelphia, Pa. Attended AADA. Debut 1972 OB in *Servant of Two Masters*, followed by *Twelfth Night, The Education of Hyman Kaplan, One of the All-Time Greatest*, Bdwy in *The 1940's Radio Hour, The First*.

**HALLIDAY, ANDY.** Born March 31, 1953 in Orange, CT. Attended USIU/San Diego. Debut OB 1985 in *Vampire Lesbians of Sodom*, followed by *Times Square Angel, Psycho Beach Party, The Lady in Question, Red Scare on Sunset, I Can't Stop*

*Screaming.*

**HALLIGAN, TIM.** Born May 17, 1952 in Chicago, Il. Graduate U. Col. Debut 19 OB in *Responsible Parties*, followed by *Rain, Some Fish No Elephants, The Voic the Prairie.*

**HALSTEAD, CAROL.** Born September 12, 1959 in Hempstead, Ny. Graduate State U. Debut 1992 OB in *The Mask.*

**HALSTON, JULIE.** Born December 7, 1954 in New York. Graduate Hofstra Debut OB 1985 in *Times Square Angel*, followed by *Vampire Lesbians of Soa Sleeping Beauty or Coma, The Dubliners, The Lady in Question, Money Talks, Scare on Sunset, I'll Be the Judge of That, A Lifetime of Comedy.*

**HAMILTON, LAUREN.** Born November 10, 1959 in Boston, MA. Graduate I Col., Neighborhood Playhouse. Debut 1988 OB in *Famine Plays*, followed by *Dimes, Rodents and Radios, Hunger, Homo Sapien Shuffle, Famine Plays, A Mu of Crows, Homo Sapien Shuffle.*

**HAMMOND, MICHAEL.** Born April 30, 1951 in Clinton, Ia.Graduate U. I LAMDA. Debut 1974 OB in *Pericles*, followed by *The Merry Wives of Windso Winter's Tale, Barbarians, The Purging, Romeo and Juliet, The Merchant of Ver The Misanthrope*, Bdwy in *M. Butterfly* (1989), *Search and Destroy.*

**HANDLER, EVAN.** Born January 10, 1961 in New York City. Attended Juilli Debut 1979 OB in *Biography A Game*, followed by *Striker, Final Orders, Mara '84, Found a Peanut, What's Wrong with This Picture?, Bloodletters, Yo Playwrights Festival, Human Nature, Six Degrees of Separation, Marathon '91, Al*, Bdwy in *Solomon's Child* (1982), *Biloxi Blues, Brighton Beach Memo Broadway Bound, Six Degrees of Separation, I Hate Hamlet.*

**HARAN, MARY-CLEERE.** Born May 13, 1952 in San Francisco, Ca. Attended Francisco State U. Bdwy debut 1979 in *The 1940's Radio Hour*, followed by *OB Hollywood Opera, What a Swell Party!*

**HARDING, JAN LESLIE.** Born in 1956 in Cambridge, MA. Graduate Boston Debut 1980 in *Album*, followed by *Sunday Picnic, Buddies, The Lunch Gi Marathon '86, Traps, Father Was a Peculiar Man, A Murder of Crows.*

**HARDY, MARK.** Born October 25, 1961 in Reidsville, NC. Gradu UNC/Greensboro. Debut 1990 OB in *The Rothschilds*, followed by *Juba*, Bdwy in Miserables (1990).

**HARRIS, BAXTER.** Born November 18, 1940 in Columbus, KS. Attended U. K Debut 1967 OB in *America Hurrah*, followed by *The Serpent, Battle of Angels, De by the River..., Ferocious Kisses, The Three Sisters, The Dolphin Position, Bro Eggs, Paradise Lost, Ghosts, The Time of Your Life, The Madwoman of Chaillot, Reckoning, Wicked Women Revue, More Than You Deserve, Him, Pericles, Sel Gradual Clearing, Children of the Sun, Marathon '90, Go to Ground, EST Marat '92*, Bdwy in *A Texas Trilogy* (1976), *Dracula, The Lady from Dubuque.*

**HARMON, JENNIFER.** Born December 3, 1943 in Pasadena, Ca. Attended UI With APA in *Right You Are, You Can't Take It with You, War and Peace, The W Duck, School for Scandal*, OB in *The Effect of Gamma Rays on Man-in-the-Me Marigolds, The Hot 1 Baltimore, Learned Ladies, The Holly and the Ivy, In Perpet throughout the Universe, Macbeth.*

**HARNICK, AARON.** Born October 25, 1968 in NYC. Graduate Syracuse U. De 1991 OB in *Club Soda.*

**HARRELSON, HELEN.** Born in Missouri, graduate Goodman Theatre. Bdwy de 1950 in *The Cellar and the Well*, followed by *Death of a Salesman, Days in the Tre Romeo and Juliet, John in Our Town, His and Hers, House of Atreus, He and s Missing Persons, Laughing Stock, The Art of Self-Defense, The Hour of the Lynx.*

**HARRIS, JULIE.** Born December 2, 1925 in Grosse Pointe, MI. Yale gradua Bdwy debut 1945 in *It's a Gift*, followed by *Henry V. Oedipus, Playboy of the Weste World, Alice in Wonderland, Macbeth, Sundown Beach* for which she receive Theatre World Award, *The Young and the Fair, Magnolia Alley, Montserrat Member of the Wedding, I Am a Camera, Mlle. Colombe, The Lark, Country W Warm Peninsula, Little Moon of Alban, A Shot in the Dark, Marathon '33, Sca When You Are C. B., Hamlet (CP),Skyscraper, 40 Carats, And Miss Reardon Drink Little, Voices, The Last of Mrs. Lincoln, Au Pair Man, In Praise of Love, Belle Amherst, Mixed Couples, Break a Leg, Lucifer's Child, A Christmas Carol.*

**HARRIS, MEL.** Born July 12, 1958 in Bethlehem, Pa. NY debut 1992 OB in *Em Hearts* for which she received a Theatre World Award.

**HARRIS, NIKI.** Born July 20, 1948 in Pittsburgh, PA. Graduate Duquesne Bdwy debut 1980 in *A Day in Hollywood/A Night in the Ukraine*, followed by *My C and Only, Grand Hotel*, OB in *Leave It to Jane, No No Nanette, Berkeley Square.*

**HARRISON, STANLEY EARL.** Born September 17, 1955 in Cheverly, N Graduate Morgan State U. Debut 1978 OB in *The Phantom*, followed by *The Boo Woogie Rumble of a Dream Deferred, The Medium, Mud, The Mighty Gen Abyssinia, A Matter of Conscience, Morningsong*, Bdwy in The King and I (1985).

**HART, MELISSA (JOAN).** Born April 18, 1976 in Smithtown, Ny. Debut 1989 ( in *Beside Herself*, followed by *Imaging Brad*, Bdwy in *The Crucible* (1991).

**HART, ROXANNE.** Born in 1952 in Trenton, NJ. Attended Skidmore, Princeton Bdwy debut 1977 in *Equus*, followed by *Loose Ends, Passion, Devil's Disciple, Wa Winter's Tale, Johnny on a Spot, The Purging, Hedda Gabler, Waiting for the Para La Brea Tarpits, Marathon '84, Digby, Lips Together Teeth Apart.*

**HARUM, EIVIND.** Born May 24, 1944 in Stavanger, Norway. Attended Utah St U. Credits include *Sophie, Foxy, Baker Street, West Side Story* (1968), *A Chorus Li Woman of the Year, Grand Hotel.*

**HAUCK, STEVEN.** Born September 10, 1959 in Princeton, NJ. Graduate Trinity U. Wisc. Debut 1991 OB in *The Tempest*, followed by *Company.*

**WKINS, HOLLY**. Born August 22, 1959 in Shreveport, La. Attended Tulane U. MDA, NC School of Arts. Debut 1988 OB in Man and *Superman*, followed by *herford & Son*.

**YDEN, SOPHIE**. Born February 23 in Miami, Fl. Graduate Northwestern U. *wy* debut 1979 in *Whoopee!*, followed by *Barnum, Comedy of Errors, The Most *ppy Fella* (1992), OB in *She Loves Me, Jessie's Land, Passover, Lies My Father *d Me, Torpedo Bra, Fun*.

**YDEN, TERESE**. Born February 25 in Nashville, Tn. Attended Vanderbilt U. *DA, Actors Studio*. One of ELT founders and participated in its productions of *asure for Measure* (1944), *One Man Show, Live Life Again, Jason, Fanny, First *, The Millionairess*, and *Candida*, followed by *5th of July* (1991), Bdwy in *Joan of *raine* (1946), *Red Gloves, Wedding Breakfast*.

**YS, REX**. Born June 17, 1946 in Hollywood, CA. Graduate San Jose State U., *ndeis U*. Bdwy debut 1975 in *Dance with Me*, followed by *Angel, King of Hearts, *a, Onward Victoria!, Woman of the Year, La Cage aux Folles, Grand Hotel*, OB in *rley's Tale*.

**ALD, ANTHONY**. Born August 25 1944 in New Rochelle, NY. Graduate Mich. *e U*. Debut 1980 OB in *Glass Menagerie*, followed by *Misalliance* for which he *eved a Theatre World Award, The Caretaker, The Fox, Quartermaine's Terms, The *lanthropist, Henry V, Digby, Principia Scriptoriae, Lisbon Traviata, Elliot Loves, *malion, Lips Together Teeth Apart*, Bdwy in *Wake of Jamey Foster* (1982), *riage of Figaro, Anything Goes, A Small Family Business*.

**ATHERLY, JAMES**. Born August 10, 1965 in Jefferson City, Tn. Graduate West *as State U*. Debut 1991 OB in *Prom Queens Unchained*.

**DWALL, DEBORAH**. Born in 1952 in Washington State. OB credits include *nd Date, Intimacy, Amulets against the Dragon Forces, Savage in Limbo, *remities, Sight Unseen*, Bdwy in *Heidi Chronicles* (1989).

**INSOHN, ELISA**. Born October 11, 1962 in Butler, PA. Debut 1984 OB in *Oy *ma Am I in Love*, followed by *Scandal*, Bdwy in *42nd Street* (1985), *Smile, *antom of the Opera*.

**LDE, ANNETTE**. Born November 14 in Long Beach, Ca. Graduate U. Santa *bara, U. Wash*. Debut OB 1982 in *Antigone*,followed by *Hamlet, Ballad of Soapy *th, Virginia, Free Fall, A Piece of My Heart, Merchant of Venice, As You Like It, *wning in Loch Ness*, Bdwy in *Macbeth* (1988), *A Few Good Men*.

**LLER, ADAM**. Born June 8, 1960 in Englewood, NJ. Graduate NYU. Debut *4 OB in *Kuni-Leml*, followed by *The Special, Half a World Away, Encore!*, Bdwy *es Miserables* (1989).

**NDERSON, SUZANNE**. Born May 21, 1960 in New Jersey. Attended U. Del. *ut 1981 OB in *City Suite*, Bdwy in *Grand Hotel* (1989).

**NRITZE, BETTE**. Born May 23 in Betsy Layne, Ky. Graduate U. Tn. OB *n in Love, Abe Lincoln in Illinois, Othello, Baal, A Long Christmas Dinner, Queens *France, Rimers of Eldritch, Displaced Person, Acquisition, Crime of Passion, *ppiness Cage, Henry VI, Richard III, Older People, Lotta, Catsplay, A Month in *untry, The Golem, Daughters, Steel Magnolias*, Bdwy in *Jenny Kissed Me* (1948), *tures in the Hallway, Giants Sons of Giants, Ballad of the Sad Cafe, The White *use, Dr. Cook's Garden, Here's Where I Belong, Much Ado about Nothing, Over *re, Angel Street, Man and Superman, Macbeth* (1981), *Present Laughter, The *ette Bridge Club, Orpheus Descending, Lettice and Lovage, On Borrowed Time*.

**BBERT, EDWARD**. Born September 9, 1955 in NYC. Attended Hurstpierpont *, RADA*. Bdwy debut 1982 in *Alice in Wonderland*, followed by *Me and My Girl, *in *Candide in Concert, Dandy Dick, Privates on Parade, Lady Bracknell's *finement, Candide*.

**CKEY, WILLIAM**. Born 1928 in _____ Bdwy includes *Make a Million, On the *vn, Saint Joan, The Body Beautiful, Mourning Becomes Electra, Thieves, Tovarich, *enic and Old Lace*, OB in *Small Craft Warnings, Adaptation/Next, Happy Birthday *nda June, Cole Porter Revisited, A Terrible Beauty*.

**DALGO, ALLEN**. Born December 15, 1967 in NYC. Attended NY U. Debut *2 OB in *Eating Raoul*.

**GGINS, JOEL**. Born September 28, 1943 in Bloomington, Il. Graduate Mich. *te U*. Bdwy debut 1975 in *Shenandoah* for which he received a Theatre World *vard*, followed by *Music Is, Angel, Oklahoma!* (1980), *City of Angels*, OB in *Camp *eting*.

**GGINS, JOHN MICHAEL**. Born February 12, 1963 in Boston, MA. Graduate *aherst Col*. Debut 1986 in *National Lampoon's Class of '86*, followed by *Neddy, *f-torture and Strenuous Exercise, Trumps, Comic Safari, Maids of Honor, Beau *, Bdwy in *Mastergate* (1990), *La Bete*.

**LER, KATHERINE**. Born June 24, 1961 in Carson City, Nv. Graduate Mt. *lyoke Col*. Bdwy debut 1985 in *Hurlyburly*, OB in *Liebelei* (1987), *The Year of the *ck, A Shayna Maidel, Temptation, What A Man Weighs, Macbeth, Young *ywrights Festival, Club Soda*.

**LL, ERIN**. Born February 13, 1968 in Louisville, Ky. Graduate Syracuse U. Debut *1 OB in *Return to the Forbidden Planet*.

**LLINER, JOHN**. Born November 5, 1952 in Evanston, Il. Graduate Deniston U. *ut 1977 OB in *Essential Shepard*, followed by Bdwy in *They're Playing Our Song, *le Me, Woman of the Year, Crazy for You*.

**LLYER, JOSEPH**. Born March 6, 1962 in New London, Ct. Graduate St. *chael's Col, U. S. Dak*. Bdwy Debut 1990 OB in *Cornish Game*, followed by *Whose Child *t Anyway, Hamlet, The Boy Who Cried Elvis, Wiring Electra, Nutcracker in the *nd of Nuts, Winter Songs, Rutherford & Son*.

**NES, GREGORY**. Born February 14, 1946 in NYC. Bdwy debut 1954 in *The Girl *Pink Tights*, followed by *Eubie!* for which he received a Theatre World Award,

---

*Comin' Uptown, Black Broadway, Sophisticated Ladies, Jelly's Last Jam*, OB in *Twelfth Night*.

**HINES, MIMI**. Born July 17, 1933 in Vancouver, Can. Bdwy debut 1965 in *Funny Girl*, OB in *From Rodgers and Hart with Love, Little Me* (in previews).

**HIRSCH, JUDD**. Born March 15, 1935 in NYC. Attended AADA. Bdwy debut 1966 in *Barefoot in the Park*, followed by *Chapter Two, Talley's Folly, Conversations with My Father*, OB in *On the Necessity of Being Polygamous, Scuba Duba, Mystery Play, The Hot 1 Baltimore, Prodigal, Knock Knock, Life and/or Death, Talley's Folly, The Sea Gull, I'm Not Rappaport, Conversations with My Father*.

**HLIBOK, BRUCE**. Born July 31, 1960 in NYC. Debut OB and Bdwy 1978 in *Runaways*, followed by OB in *Wonderland in Concert, Another Person Is a Foreign Country, Passion, Rainfall, Lovelost*.

**HOCK, ROBERT**. Born May 20, 1931 in Phoenixville, Pa. Yale graduate. Debut 1982 OB in *Romeo and Juliet*, followed by *Edward II, Macbeth, The Adding Machine, Caucasian Chalk Circle, Kitty Hawk, Heathen Valley, Comedy of Errors*.

**HODGES, PATRICIA**. Born in Puyallup, Wa. Graduate U. Wa. Debut 1985 OB in *The Normal Heart*, followed by *No End of Blame, On the Verge, Hard Times, One-Act Festival*, Bdwy in *Six Degrees of Separation* (1991), *Dancing at Lughnasa*.

**HOEBEE, MARK S.** Born July 2, 1960 in NYC. Graduate Northwestern U. Bdwy debut 1989 in *Jerome Robbins Broadway*, followed by *Street Scene* (NYC Opera), *Nick and Nora*.

**HOFFMAN, AVI**. Born March 3, 1958 in The Bronx, NY. Graduate U. Miami. Debut 1983 OB in *The Rise of David Levinsky*, followed by *It's Hard to Be a Jew, A Rendezvous with God, The Golden Land, Songs of Paradise, Finkel's Follies*.

**HOFFMAN, JANE**. Born July 24 in Seattle, Wa. Graduate U. Cal. Bdwy debut 1940 in *Tis of Thee*, followed by *Crazy with the Heat, Something for the Boys, One Touch of Venus, Calico Wedding, Mermaids Singing, Temporary Island, Story for Strangers, Two Blind Mice, The Rose Tattoo, The Crucible, Witness for the Prosecution, Third Best Sport, Rhinoceros, Mother Courage and Her Children, Fair Game for Lovers, A Murderer among Us, Murder among Friends, Some Americans Abroad, Lost in Yonkers*, OB in *American Dream, Sandbox, Picnic on the Battlefield, Theatre of the Absurd, Child Buyer, A Corner of the Bed, Slow Memories, Last Analysis, Dear Oscar, Hocus Pocus, Lessons, The Art of Dining, Second Avenue Rag, One Tiger to a Hill, Isn't It Romantic, Alto Part, Frog Prince, Alterations, The Grandma Plays*.

**HOFFMAN, PHILIP**. Born May 12, 1954 in Chicago, IL. Graduate U. Ill. Bdwy debut 1981 in *The Moony Shapiro Songbook*, followed by *Is There Life after High School?, Baby, Into the Woods, Falsettos*, OB in *The Fabulous 50's, Isn't It Romantic, 1-2-3-4-5, Rags*.

**HOFVENDAHL, STEVE**. Born September 1, 1956 in San Jose, CA. Graduate U. Santa Clara, Brandeis U. Debut 1986 OB in *A Lie of the Mind*, followed by *Ragged Trousered Philanthropists, The Miser, A Midsummer Night's Dream, Light Shining in Buckinghamshire, 10th Young Playwrights Festival, Marvin's Room*, Bdwy 1989 in *Mastergate*.

**HOGAN, JONATHAN**. Born June 13, 1951 in Chicago, IL. Graduate Goodman Th. Debut 1972 OB in *The Hot 1 Baltimore*, followed by *The Mound Builders, Harry Outside, Cabin 12, 5th of July, Glorious Morning, Innocent Thoughts Harmless Intentions, Sunday Runners, Threads, Time Framed, Burn This!, The Balcony Scene*, Bdwy in *Comedians* (1976), *Otherwise Engaged, 5th of July, The Caine Mutiny Court-Martial, As Is, Burn This!, Taking Steps, The Homecoming*.

**HOLBROOK, RUBY**. Born August 28, 1930 in St. John's Nfd. Attended Denison U. Debut 1963 OB in *Abe Lincoln in Illinois*, followed by *Hamlet, James Joyce's Dubliners, Measure for Measure, The Farm, Do You Still Believe the Rumor?, The Killing of Sister George, An Enemy of the People, Amulets against the Dragon Forces, The Rose Quartet*, Bdwy in *Da* (1979), *5th of July, Musical Comedy Murders of 1940*.

**HOLLIDAY, DAVID**. Born August 4, 1937 in Illinois. Attended Carthage Col. Bdwy debut 1968 in *Man of La Mancha*, followed by *Coco* for which he received a Theatre World Award, *Music Is, Perfectly Frank, Man of La Mancha* (1991), OB in *Nevertheless They Laugh*.

**HOLLIS, TOMMY**. Born March 27, 1954 in Jacksonville, TX. Attended Lon Morris Col., U. Houston. Debut 1985 OB in *Diamonds*, followed by *Secrets of the Lava Lamp, Paradise, Africanus Instructus, The Colored Museum*, Bdwy 1990 in *The Piano Lesson* for which he received a Theatre World Award.

**HOLTZMAN, MERRILL**. Born September 1, 1959. Bdwy debut 1989 in *Mastergate*, OB in *Chelsea Walls, Nebraska, A Darker Purpose*.

**HONDA, CAROL A.** Born November 20 in Kealakekua, HI. Graduate U. HI. Debut 1983 OB in *Yellow Fever*, followed by *Empress of China, Manoa Valley, Once Is Never Enough, Life of the Land, Rosie's Cafe, And the Soul Shall Dance, The Wash, Before It Hits Home, The Dressing Room*.

**HOOVER, PAUL**. Born June 20, 1945 in Rockford, Il. Graduate Pikeville Col., Pittsburgh Sem. Debut 1980 OB in *Kind Lady*, followed by *Prizes, As You Like It*.

**HOREN, BOB**. Born October 12, 1925 in Aberdeen, SD. Graduate U. Min., U. Mo. OB in *Hogan's Goat, The 13th Chair, The Dropper*, Bdwy in *An Enemy of the People, A Minor Miracle, The Great White Hope*.

**HORVATH, JAN**. Born January 31, 1958 in Lake Forest, Il. Graduate Cinn. Conservatory. Bdwy debut 1983 in *Oliver!*, followed by *Sweet Charity, Phantom of the Opera, 3 Penny Opera*, OB in *Sing Me Sunshine, Jacques Brel Is Alive and Well ..., Chess*.

**HOTY, DEE**. Born August 16, 1952 in Lakewood, OH. Graduate Otterbein Col. Debit 1979 in *The Golden Apple*, followed by *Ta-Dah!, Personals*, Bdwy in *The 5 O'Clock Girl* (1981), *Shakespeare Cabaret, City of Angels, The Will Rogers Follies*.

**HOWARD, CELIA.** Born August 23, 1937 in Oakland, CA. Graduate Stanford U. Debut OB in *Cat and the Canary* (1965), followed by *Whitsuntide, Last Summer at Blue Fish Cove, After the Rain, Midsummer, Heathen Valley.*

**HOWES, SALLY ANN.** Born July 20, 1934 in London, England. Has appeared in *My Fair Lady, Kwamina, Brigadoon, What Makes Sammy Run?, A Little Night Music* (NYCO).

**HOYT, J.C.** Born March 6, 1944 in Mankato, MN. Graduate U. Minn. Debut 1975 OB in *Heathen Piper*, followed by *La Ronde, Two Gentlemen of Verona, The Comedy of Errors, Rivers and Ravines.*

**HUDSON, TRAVIS.** Born February 2 in Amarillo, TX. U. TX graduate. Bdwy debut in *New Faces of 1962*, followed by *Pousse Cafe, Very Good Eddie, The Grand Tour,* OB in *Triad, Tattooed Countess, Young Abe Lincoln, Get Thee to Canterbury, The Golden Apple, Annie Get Your Gun, Nunsense.*

**HUFFMAN, CADY.** Born February 2, 1965 in Santa Barbara, CA. Debut 1983 OB in *They're Playing Our Song*, followed by *Festival of 1 Acts, Oh Hell!,* Bdwy 1985 in *La Cage aux Folles*, followed by *Big Deal, The Will Rogers Follies.*

**HUNT, ANNETTE.** Born January 31, 1938 in Hampton, Va. Graduate Va. Intermont Col. Debut 1957 OB in *Nine by Six*, followed by *Taming of the Shrew, Medea, Anatomist, The Misanthrope, The Cherry Orchard, Electra, Last Resort, The Seducers, A Sound of Silence, Charades, Dona Rosita, Rhimestones, Where's Charley?, The White Rose of Memphis, M. Amilcar, The Sea Gull, Rutherford & Son,* Bdwy in *All the Girls Came Out to Play* (1972).

**HURT, MARY BETH.** Born September 26, 1948 in Marshalltown, Ia. Attended U. Iowa, NYU. Debut 1972 OB in *More Than You Deserve*, followed by *As You Like It, Trelawny of the Wells, The Cherry Orchard, Love for Love, A Member of the Wedding, Boy Meets Girl, Secret Service, Father's Day, Nest of the Wood Grouse, The Day Room, Secret Rapture, Othello,* Bdwy in *Crimes of the Heart* (1981), *The Misanthrope, Benefactors.*

**HUTCHISON, CHAD M.** Born April 28, 1980 in Indianapolis, IN. Bdwy debut 1990 in *Peter Pan*, also 1991.

**HUTTON, TIMOTHY.** Born August 16, 1961 in Malibu, CA. Bdwy debut 1989 in *Love Letters*, followed by *Prelude to a Kiss,* OB in *Babylon Gardens.*

**HYMAN, EARLE.** Born October 11, 1926 in Rocky Mount, NC. Attended New School, Am. Th. Wing. Bdwy debut 1943 in *Run Little Chillun*, followed by *Anna Lucasta, Climate of Eden, Merchant of Venice, Othello, Julius Caesar, The Tempest, No Time for Sergeants, Mr. Johnson*, for which he received a Theatre World Award, *St. Joan, Hamlet, Waiting for Godot, The Duchess of Malfi, Les Blancs, The Lady from Dubuque, Execution of Justice, Death of the King's Horseman, The Master Builder,* OB in *The White Rose and the Red, Worlds of Shakespeare, Jonah, Life and Times of J. Walter Smithneus, Orrin, The Cherry Orchard, House Party, Carnival Dreams, Agamemnon, Othello, Julius Caesar, Coriolanus, Pygmalion.*

**INGRAM, TAD.** Born September 11, 1948 in Pittsburgh, Pa. Graduate Temple U., LAMDA. Debut 1979 OB in *Biography: A Game*, followed by *The Possessed, Gospel according to Al, The Death of Von Richthofen,* Bdwy in *The Most Happy Fella* (1992).

**INNES, LAURA.** Born August 16, 1957 in Pontiac, Mi. Graduate Northwestern U. Debut 1982 OB in *Edmond*, followed by *My Uncle Sam, Life Is a Dream, Alice and Fred, A Country Doctor, Vienna Lusthaus, Stella, Prison Made Tuxedos, American Notes, In Perpetuity throughout the Universe, Paradise for the Worried,* Bdwy in *Two Shakespearean Actors* (1992).

**IVANEK, ZELJKO.** Born August 15, 1957 in Lujubljana, Yugo. Graduate Yale U., LAMDA. Bdwy debut 1981 in *The Survivor* followed by *Brighton Beach Memoirs, Loot, Two Shakespearean Actors,* OB in *Cloud 9, A Map of the World, The Cherry Orchard.*

**IVEY, DANA.** Born August 12 in Atlanta, GA. Graduate Rollins Col., LAMDA. Bdwy debut 1981 in *Macbeth* (LC), followed by *Present Laughter, Heartbreak House, Sunday in the Park with George, Pack of Lies, Marriage of Figaro,* OB in *A Call from the East, Vivien, Candida in Concert, Major Barbara in Concert, Quartermaine's Terms, Baby with the Bathwater, Driving Miss Daisy, Wenceslas Square, Love Letters, Hamlet, The Subject Was Roses, Beggars in the House of Plenty.*

**IVEY, JUDITH.** Born September 4, 1951 in El Paso, Tx. Bdwy debut 1979 in *Bedroom Farce*, followed by *Steaming, Hurlyburly, Blithe Spirit, Park Your Car in Harvard Yard,* OB in *Dulsa Fish Stas and Vi, Sunday Runners, Second Lady, Hurlyburly, Mrs. Dally Has a Lover.*

**JACKEL, PAUL.** Born June 30 in Winchester, MA. Graduate Harvard. Debut 1983 OB in *The Robber Bridegroom*, followed by *Side by Side by Sondheim, Gifts of the Magi,* Bdwy in *The Secret Garden* (1991).

**JACKSON, ANNE.** Born September 3, 1926 in Allegheny, Pa. Attended Neighborhood Playhouse. Bdwy debut 1945 in *Signature*, followed by *Yellow Jack, John Gabriel Borkman, The Last Dance, Summer and Smoke, Magnolia Alley, Love Me Long, Lady from the Sea, Never Say Never, Oh Men! Oh Women!, Rhinoceros, Luv, The Exercise, Inquest, Promenade All, Waltz of the Toreadors, Twice around the Park, Cafe Crown, Lost in Yonkers,* OB in *The Tiger and the Typist, Marco Polo Sings a Solo, Diary of Anne Frank, Nest of the Wood Grouse, Madwoman of Chaillot, Cafe Crown.*

**JACKSON, DAVID.** Born December 4, 1948 in Philadelphia, PA. Bdwy debut 1980 in *Eubie!*, followed by *My One and Only, La Cage aux Folles, Grand Hotel,* OB in *Blackamoor.*

**JACKSON, ERNESTINE.** Born September 18 in Corpus Christie, TX. Graduate Del Mar Col., Juilliard. Debut 1966 in *Show Boat* (LC), followed by *Finian's Rainbow, Hello Dolly!, Applause, Jesus Christ Superstar, Tricks, Raisin* for which she received a Theatre World Award, *Guys and Dolls, Bacchae,* OB in *Louis, Some Enchanted Evening, Money Notes, Jack and Jill, Black Girl, Brownstone, Sophie, Broadway Jukebox, Island Memories.*

**JACOBY, MARK.** Born May 21, 1947 in Johnson City, TN. Graduate GA Stat FL State U., St. John's U. Debut 1984 OB in *Bells Are Ringing*, Bdwy in *S Charity* for which he received a Theatre World Award, *Grand Hotel, The Phantc the Opera.*

**JAFFE, JOAN.** Born December 23 in Wilmington, DE. Attended Boston Co NYU. Debut 1960 OB in *Carousel*, followed by *The Boys from Syracuse, Once a Mattress, Stage Door, Professionally Speaking, Young Rube, Charge It Please, World,* Bdwy in *Bajour* (1964), *Much Ado About Nothing.*

**JAMES, KELLI.** Born March 18, 1959 in Council Bluffs, IA. Bdwy debut 19 *Les Miserables.*

**JAMES, LAWRENCE.** Born January 8, 1935 in Gadsden, AL. Graduate Ford U. Debut 1977 OB in *Cages*, followed by *Let Me Live, Black Eagles, A Tempest.*

**JAMROG, JOSEPH.** Born September 21, 1932 in Flushing, NY. Graduate CC Debut 1970 OB in *Nobody Hears a Broken Drum*, followed by *Tango, And W Little Boy Are You?, When You Comin' Back Red Ryder?, Drums at Yale, The Friend, Love, Death Plays, Too Much Johnson, A Stitch in Time, Pantaglieze, F Hours, Returnings, Brass Birds Don't Sing, And Things That Go Bump in the N Fun, Henry Lumpur, I Am a Winner, Little Lies,* Bdwy in *The Miser* (1990) *Borrowed Time* (1991).

**JARRETT, JERRY.** Born September 9, 1918 in Brooklyn, NY. Attended New Schl. Bdwy debut 1948 in *At War with the Army*, followed by *Gentlemen P Blonds, Stalag 17, Fiorello!, Fiddler on the Roof,* OB in *Waiting for Lefty, Nat Me Candido, That 5 A.M. Jazz, Valentines Day, Tickles by Tucholsky, Jazzbo Brov*

**JASON, JOHN.** Born August 25, 1962 in Middletown, Ct. Attended East Conn. Mesa Col. Debut 1991 OB in *Body and Soul*, followed by *Wyoming Blizzard, Bo, the Back Room,* Bdwy in *The Visit* (1992).

**JASON, MITCHELL.** Born in Philadelphia, Pa. Graduate Temple U. Debut OB in *Twelfth Night*, followed by *Merchant of Venice, Romeo and Juliet, Macl Hamlet, A House Remembered, 3 Penny Opera, Androcles and the Lion, On the Te Telemachus Clay, A View from the Bridge, The Man with a Flower in His Mo Show Me Where the Good Times Are, Steambath, Yanks 3, Detroit, Rubbers, Wha Babe Said, Easy Money, The Gentle People, World of Sholem Aleichem, Promen Cafe Crown,* Bdwy in *Gideon* (1961), *Seidman & Son, Fade-Out-Fade In, Darli the Day, Fiddler on the Roof, Tricks, Molly, So Long 174th Street, Heazl, A View j the Bridge, Cafe Crown, Grand Hotel.*

**JBARA, GREGORY.** Born September 28, 1961 in Wayne Mi.Graduate U. Juilliard. Debut 1986 OB in *Have I Got a Girl for You, Serious Money, Private Parade, Forever Plaid,* Bdwy in *Serious Money* (1988), *Born Yesterday.*

**JENNINGS, KEN.** Born October 10, 1947 in Jersey City, NJ. Graduate St. P Col. Bdwy debut 1975 in *All God's Chillun Got Wings*, followed by *Sweeney Todc* which he received a Theatre World Award, *Present Laughter, Grand Hotel, O Once on a Summer's Day, Mayor, Rabboni, Gifts of the Magi, Carmilla.*

**JEPSON, J.J.** Born in Richmond, Va. Graduate U. Richmond. Bdwy debut 197 *Lovely Ladies King Gentlemen*, followed by *Love Match, Frank Merriwell, Sno Irene, Music Man, The Tap Dance Kid, Grand Hotel,* OB in *One of Eight.*

**JEROME, TIMOTHY.** Born December 29, 1943 in Los Angeles, CA. Grad Ithaca Col. Bdwy debut 1969 in *Man of La Mancha*, followed by the *Rothsch Creation of the World..., Moony Shapiro Songbook, Cats, Me and My Girl, Gr Hotel, OB in Beggar's Opera, Pretzels, Civilization and Its Discontents, The L Prince, Colette Collage, Room Service, Romance in Hard Times.*

**JETER, MICHAEL.** Born August 26, 1952 in Lawrenceburg, TN. Gradu Memphis State U. Bdwy debut 1978 in *Once in a Lifetime*, followed by *Grand Ho OB in The Master and Margarita, G.R. Point* for which he received a Theatre W Award, *Alice in Concert, El Bravo, Cloud 9, Greater Tuna, The Boys Next Door, C Kidding.*

**JILLETTE, PENN.** Born in 1955 in Greenfield, MA. Debut 1985 OB in *Penn Teller*, Bdwy 1987, 1991, OB in *Rot in Hell.*

**JOHANSON, DON.** Born October 19, 1952 in Rock Hill, SC. Graduate USC. Bc debut 1976 in *Rex*, followed by *Cats, Jelly's Last Jam,* OB in *The American Da Machine.*

**JOHN, TAYLOR.** Born November 25, 1981 in NYC. Bdwy debut 1991 in *Miserables.*

**JOHNSON, PAGE.** Born August 25, 1930 in Welch, WV. Graduate Ithaca C Bdwy bow 1951 in *Romeo and Juliet*, followed by *Electra, Oedipus, Camino Real April Once* for which he received a Theatre World Award, *Red Roses for Me, Lovers, Equus, You Can't Take It with You, Brush Arbor Revival,* OB in Enchanted Guitar, 4 in 1, Journey of the Fifth Horse, APA's School for Scandal, Tavern, and The Seagull, Odd Couple, Boys in the Band, Medea, Deathtrap, Best L Whorehouse in Texas, Fool for Love, East Texas.*

**JOHNSTON, NANCY.** Born January 15, 1949 in Statesville, NC. Graduate Car Newman Col., UNC/Greensboro. Debut 1987 OB in *Olympus on My Mind*, follov by *Nunsense, Living Color, White Lies,* Bdwy in *The Secret Garden.*

**JOHNSTON, SAMME.** Born January 11, 1956 in Needham, Ma. Gradu Wellesley Col. Debut 1985 OB in *A Flash of Lightning*, followed by *Thea Olympics, Time and the Conways, Hedda Gabler, Three Sisters.*

**JONES, CHERRY.** Born November 21, 1956 in Paris, TN. Graduate Carneg Mellon. Debut 1983 OB in *The Philanthropist*, followed by *He and She, The Balla Soapy Smith, The Importance of Being Earnest, I Am a Camera, Claptrap, Big L Light Shining in Buckinghamshire, The Baltimore Waltz,* Bdwy in*Stepping Out* (198 *Our Country's Good.*

Julia Glander     Laurence Guittard     Cordelia Gonzalez     Allen Hidalgo     Helen Greenberg     Tommy Hollis

Carol Halstead     Earle Hyman     Annette Helde     Željko Ivanek     Sally Ann Howes     Lawrence James

Cady Huffman     Ken Jennings     Annette Hunt     Page Johnson     Laura Innes     Stephen Joseph

Dana Ivey     Robert Joy     Anne Jackson     Joe Joyce     Cherry Jones     Jeffrey Kearney

Jessie Jones     Robert Kerbeck     Jane Kaczmarek     Brian Kerwin     Lisa Kirchner     Erik King

**JONES, JAY AUBREY.** Born March 30, 1954 in Atlantic City, NJ. Graduate Syracuse U. Debut 1981 OB in *Sea Dream*, followed by *Divine Hysteria, Inacent Black and the Brothers, La Belle Helene*, Bdwy in *Cats* (1986).

**JONES, JESSIE.** Born August 21, 1950 in Texas. Attended U. Tx. Debut 1988 OB in *Saved from Obscurity*, followed by *Life on the Third Rail, Eden Court, The Poker Session, Dearly Departed.*

**JONES, NEAL.** Born January 2, 1960 in Wichita, Ks. Attended Weber Col. Debut 1981 OB in *The Dear Love of Comrades*, followed by *The Tavern, Spring's Awakening, Billy Liar, Groves of Academe, A Darker Purpose*, Bdwy in *Macbeth* (1982), *The Corn Is Green* (1983).

**JONES, SIMON.** Born July 27, 1950 in Wiltshire, Eng. Attended Trinity Hall. NY debut 1984 OB in *Terra Nova*, followed by *Magdalena in Concert, Woman in Mind, Privates on Parade*, Bdwy in *The Real Thing* (1984), *Benefactors, Getting Married, Private Lives.*

**JOSEPH, STEPHEN.** Born August 27, 1952 in Shaker Heights, Oh. Graduate Carnegie-Mellon U., Fla. State U. Debut 1978 OB in *Oklahoma!*, followed by *Is Paris Flaming?, Innuendo, Little Me.*

**JOY, ROBERT.** Born August 17, 1951 in Montreal, Can. Graduate Oxford U. Debut 1978 OB in *The Diary of Anne Frank*, followed by *Fables for Friends, Lydie Breeze, Sister Mary Ignatius Explains It All, Actor's Nightmare, What I Did Last Summer, The Death of von Ricthofen, Lenny and the Heartbreakers, Found a Peanut, Field Day, Life and Limb, Hyde in Hollywood, The Taming of the Shrew*, Bdwy in *Hay Fever* (1985), *The Nerd, Shimada.*

**JOYCE, JOE.** Born November 22, 1957 in Pittsburgh, PA. Graduate Boston U. Debut 1981 OB in *Close Enough for Jazz*, followed by *Oh Johnny!, They Came from Planet Mirth, Encore!, You Die at Recess, Forever Plaid, Pageant.*

**JUDD, REBECCA.** Born in Fresno, CA. Graduate U. Nev. Debut 1988 OB in *Dutchman*, followed by *Lost in the Stars, The Golden Apple*, Bdwy 1989 in *Sweeney Todd, The Secret Garden.*

**JUDE, PATRICK.** Born February 25, 1951 in Jersey City, NJ. Bdwy debut 1972 in *Jesus Christ Superstar* (also in 1977 revival) followed by *Got Tu Go Disco, Charlie and Algernon, Marlowe, The News*, OB in *The Haggadah, Dementos, Chess.*

**JULIA, RAUL.** Born March 9, 1940 in San Juan, PR. Graduate UPR. OB debut 1964 in *Life Is A Dream, Macbeth, Titus Andronicus, Theatre in the Streets, Blood Wedding, The Ox Cart, No Exit, Memorandum, Frank Gagliano's City Scene, Your Own Thing, Persians, The Castro Complex, Pinkviloe, Hamlet, King Lear, As You Like It, Emperor of Late Night Radio, Three Penny Opera, The Cherry Orchard* (1968), *Taming of the shrew,Tempest, Othello, Christmas Carol, Indians, Two Gentlemen of Verona, Via Galactica, Where's Charley?, Dracula, Betrayal, Nine, Design for Living, Arms and the Man, Man of LaMancha* (1992), Bdwy in *The Cuban Thing.*

**KACZMAREK, JANE.** Born December 21, 1955 in Milwaukee, Wi. Graduate U. Wisc. Yale U. Debut 1986 OB in *Hands of Its Enemy*, followed by *Loose Ends, Ice Cream/Hot Fudge, Eve's Diary*, Bdwy in *Lost in Yonkers* (1991).

**KADEN, EILEEN.** Born February 25, 1968 in Rahway, NJ. Graduate Carnegie-Mellon U. Debut 1991 OB in *Company.*

**KAHN, GARY.** Born February 22, 1956 in the Bronx, NY Graduate U. Miami, U. Tex. Debut OB 1982 in *All of the Above*, followed by Bdwy in *City of Angels* (1989).

**KANDEL, PAUL.** Born February 15, 1951 in Queens, NY. Graduate Harpur Col. Debut 1977 OB in *Nightclub Cantata*, followed by *Two Grown Men, Scrambled Feet, The Taming of the Shrew, Lucky Stiff, 20 Fingers 20 Toes, Earth and Sky*, Bdwy in *The Visit* (1992).

**KANTOR, KENNETH.** Born April 6, 1949 in the Bronx, NY. Graduate SUNY, Boston U. Debut 1974 OB in *Zorba*, followed by *Kiss Me Kate, A Little Night Music, Buried Treasure, Sounds of Rodgers and Hammerstein, Shop on Main Street, Kismet, The Fantasticks, Colette Collage, Philemon*, Bdwy in *The Grand Tour* (1979), *Brigadoon* (1980), *Mame* (1983), *The New Moon* (NYCO), *Me and My Girl, Guys and Dolls* (1992).

**KAPLAN, JONATHAN.** Born July 5, 1980 in Detroit, Mi. Debut 1991 OB in *Rags*, Bdwy in *Falsettos* (1992) for which he received a Theatre World Award.

**KATZMAN, BRUCE.** Born December 19, 1951 in NYC. Graduate Ithaca Col., Yale U. Debut 1984 OB in *Richard III*, followed by *Othello*, Bdwy in *The Crucible* (1991), *A Little Hotel on the Side.*

**KAYE, JUDY.** Born October 11, 1948 in Phoenix, AZ. Attended UCLA, Ariz. State U. Bdwy debut 1977 in *Grease*, followed by *On the 20th Century* for which she received a Theatre World Award, *Moony Shapiro Songbook, Oh Brother!, Phantom of the Opera, The Pajama Game* (LC), OB in *Eileen in Concert, Can't Help Singing, Four to Make Two, Sweethearts in Concert, Love, No No Nanette in Concert, Magdalena in Concert, Babes in Arms, Desire Under the Elms, The Cat and the Fiddle, What about Luv?*

**KEARNEY, JEFFREY.** Born June 30, 1963 in Lexington, Ky. Attended U. London, AADA. Debut 1988 OB in *Cave Life* followed by *Raft of the Medusa.*

**KEARNS, MICHAEL.** Born January 8 in St. Louis, Mo. Attended AADA, Goodman Theatre. Debut 1974 OB in *Tubstrip*, followed by *Dream Man, Intimacies.*

**KEATS, STEVEN.** Born February 6, 1945 in New York City. Attended Montclair State Col., Yale U. Debut 1970 OB in *One Flew over the Cuckoo's Nest*, followed by *We Bombed in New Haven, Awake and Sing, The Rose Tattoo, I'm Getting My Act Together ..., Sunday Runners in the Rain, Who They Are and How It Is with Them, Other People's Money, Raft of the Medusa, Rags*, Bdwy in *Oh! Calcutta!* (1971).

**KEITH, LAWRENCE/LARRY.** Born March 4, 1931 in Brooklyn, NY. Graduate Brooklyn Col., Ind. U. Bdwy debut 1960 in *My Fair Lady* followed by *High Spirits, I Had a Ball, Best Laid Plans, Mother Lover*, OB in *The Homecoming, Conflict of Interest, The Brownsville Raid, M. Amilcar, The Rise of David Levinsky, Miami, for a Saturday, Rose Quartet.*

**KELLY, CHARLES.** Born October 22, 1964 in New Orleans, La. Graduate Bc U. Debut 1988 OB in *Vampire Lesbians of Sodom*, followed by *The Decaying Me of Crescent City, I Can't Stop Screaming.*

**KERBECK, ROBERT.** Born July 30, 1963 in Philadelphia, Pa. Graduate U. Debut 1990 OB in *Bovver Boys*, followed by *Lloyd and Lee, Night Dance.*

**KERNER, NORBERTO.** Born July 19, 1929 in Valparaiso, Chile. Attended Pise Workshop, Goodman Theatre. Debut 1971 OB in *Yerma*, followed by *I Took Pan The F.M. Safe, My Old Friends, Sharon Shashanovah, Blood Wedding, Crisp, Great Confession, Cold Air, Don Juan of Seville, The Human Voice, The Ox Cart.*

**KERR, PATRICK.** Born January 23, 1956 in Wilmington, Del. Graduate Temp Debut 1988 OB in *Jerry*, followed by *Romeo and Juliet, The Warrior Ar Midsummer Night's Dream.*

**KERR, PHILIP.** Born April 9, 1940 in NYC. Attended Harvard, LAMDA. B debut 1969 in *Tiny Alice*, followed by *A Flea in Her Ear, Three Sisters, Jockey Stakes, Macbeth* (1988), OB in *Hamlet, The Rehearsal, Cuchlain, Mistress of End of the Day.*

**KERSHAW, WHITNEY.** Born April 10, 1962 in Orlando, FL. Atter Harkness/Joffrey Ballet Schools. Debut 1981 OB in *Francis*, Bdwy in *Cats.*

**KERWIN, BRIAN.** Born October 25, 1949 in Chicago, Il. Graduate U. S. Cal. D 1988 OB in *Emily* for which he received a Theatre World Award, followed by *Together Teeth Apart.*

**KILMER, VAL.** Born December 31, 1959 in Los Angeles, Ca. Attended Juill Appeared OB in *'Tis Pity She's a Whore* (1992).

**KING, ERIK.** Born August 18 in Washington, DC. Graduate Towson State U. D 1985 OB in *Balm in Gilead*, followed by *Streamers, Wasted, Servy 'n' Bernice 4ev*

**KINSEY, RICHARD.** Born March 22, 1954. Attended Cal. State U./Fullerton. B debut 1991 in *Les Miserables.*

**KIRBY, BRUNO.** Born in 1949 in NYC. Bdwy debut 1991 in *Lost in Yonkers.*

**KIRCHNER, LISA.** Born June 10, 1953 in Los Angeles, Ca. Graduate S Lawrence Col. Debut 1974 OB in *Hotel for Criminals* followed by *Amer Imagination, Threepenny Opera, Red Eye, Plagues for Our Time, The Radiant* Bdwy in *The Human Comedy* (1984).

**KLAVAN, SCOTT.** Born June 5, 1959 in Manhasset, NY. Graduate Kenyon Debut 1982 OB in *War and Peace*, followed by *Williwaw, The Homesteaders, The Gull, Marie and Bruce.*

**KLIBAN, KEN.** Born July 26, 1943 in Norwalk, Ct. Graduate U. Miami, N Bdwy debut 1967 in *War and Peace*, followed by *As Is*, OB in *War and Peace, P Dog Tails, Istanbul, Persians, Home, Elizabeth the Queen, Judith, Man Superman,Boom Boom Room, Ulysses in Traction, Lulu, The Beaver Coat, Troilus Cressida, Richard II, The Great Grandson of Jedediah Kohler, It's Only a Play, Framed, Love's Labour's Lost, Wild Blue, Lips Together Teeth Apart.*

**KNAPP, DAVE.** Born December 6, 1963 in Paterson, NJ. Attended Fordha Debut 1985 OB in *Animals*, followed by *As You Like It, The Hot 1 Baltimore, Back in Anger, Zoo Story, Winter Chimes, The Philosopher's Stone.*

**KNAPP, SARAH.** Born January 20, 1959 in Kansas City, MO. Graduate AA Debut OB 1986 in *Gifts of the Magi*, followed by *The No Frills Revue, Nuns Manhattan Class One-Acts, Opal.*

**KOCH, OSCAR.** Born in Boston, Ma. Attended Hofstra U. Debut 1989 OB in *Dick Dies*, followed by *Perpetrator, Not Enough Rope, Chess.*

**KOLINSKI, JOSEPH.** Born June 26 1953 in Detroit, MI. Attended U. De Bdwy debut 1980 in *Brigadoon* followed by *Dance a Little Closer, The T Musketeers, Les Miserables*, OB in *Hijinks!, The Human Comedy* (also Bdwy).

**KONG, PHILIP.** Born September 23, 1986 in Lattingtown, NY. Bdwy debut 19 *Miss Saigon.*

**KORBICH, EDDIE.** Born November 6, 1960 in Washington, DC. Graduate Bc Consv. Debut 1985 OB in *A Little Night Music*, followed by *Flora the Red Mer No Frills Revue, The Last Musical Comedy, Godspell, Sweeney Todd* (also B 1989), *Assassins, Eating Raoul*, Bdwy in *Singin' in the Rain* (1985).

**KOREY, ALIX** (formerly Alexandra). Born May 14 in Brooklyn, NY. Grad Columbia U. Debut 1976 OB in *Fiorello!*, followed by *Annie Get Your Gun, Je Girls, Rosalie in Concert, America Kicks Up Its Heels, Gallery, Feather Bittersuite, Romance in Hard Times, Songs You Might Have Missed, Forbi Broadway 10th Anniversary*, Bdwy in *Hello Dolly!* (1978), *Show Boat* (1983).

**KRAKOWSKI, JANE.** Born October 11, 1968 in New Jersey. Debut 1984 O *American Passion*, followed by *Miami, A Little Night Music*, Bdwy in *Star Express* (1987), *Grand Hotel.*

**KRISTIEN, DALE.** Born May 18 in Washington, DC. Graduate Ithaca Col. B debut 1981 in *Camelot*, followed by *Show Boat, Radio City Music Specials, Pha of the Opera.*

**KUBALA, MICHAEL.** Born February 4, 1958 in Reading, Pa. Attended N Bdwy debut 1978 in *A Broadway Musical*, followed by *Dancin', Woman of the Marilyn, Jerome Robbins' Broadway, Crazy for You*, OB in *Double Feature* (1981

**KUHN, BRUCE W.** Born December 7, 1955 in Davenport, IA. Graduate U. W. U. Wash. Bdwy debut 1987 in *Les Miserables.*

**KUHN, JUDY.** Born May 20, 1958 in NYC. Graduate Oberlin Col. Debut 1985 in *Pearls* followed by *The Mystery of Edwin Drood, Rodgers and Hart Revue, Bdw Edwin Drood* (1985), *Rags, Les Miserables, Chess, Two Shakespearean Actors.*

**KUROWSKI, RON.** Born March 14, 1953 in Philadelphia, Pa. Attended Templ RADA. Bdwy debut 1977 in *A Chorus Line*, OB in *Prom Queens Unchained* (199

**RTH, WALLY.** Born July 31, 1958 in Billings, Mt. Attended Loretto Hts. Col., L.A. Bdwy debut 1982 in *Pirates of Penzance,* OB in *Hurry! Hurry! Hollywood!* 91).

**RTZ, SWOOSIE.** Born September 6 in Omaha, NE. Attended U.S. Cal., MDA. Debut 1968 OB in *The Firebugs,* followed by *The Effect of Gamma Rays...,* er a *Free Man, Children, Museum, Uncommon Women and Others, Wine ouched, Summer, The Beach House, Six Degrees of Separation, Lips Together th Apart,* Bdwy in *Ah Wilderness!* (1975), *Tartuffe, A History of the American n, 5th of July, House of Blue Leaves.*

**CHANZE.** Born December 16, 1961 in St. Augustine, FL. Attended Morgan State Philadelphia Col. Bdwy debut 1986 in *Uptown It's Hot,* followed by *Dreamgirls* 87), *Once Upon This Island* for which she received a 1991 Theatre World Award, in *Once Upon This Island.*

**CHOW, STAN.** Born December 20, 1931 in Brooklyn, NY. Graduate Roger liams Col. Debut 1977 OB in *Come Back, Little Sheba,* followed by *The Diary of e Frank, Time of the Cuckoo, Angelus, The Middleman, Charley Bacon and nily, Crossing the Bar, Today I Am a Fountain Pen, The Substance of Fire,* Bdwy *On Golden Pond* (1979).

**COY, DEBORAH.** Born October 20, 1963 in Worcester, Ma. Graduate Boston U. ut 1988 OB in *What about Love,* followed by *Insatiable/Temporary People,* Bdwy *a Streetcar Named Desire* (1992).

**CY, TOM.** Born August 30, 1933 in NYC. Debut 1965 OB in *The Fourth Pig,* owed by *The Fantasticks, Shoemakers Holiday, Love and Let Love, The ionairess, Crimes of Passion, The Real Inspector Hound, Enemies, Flying Blind, el & Bela/Archtruc,* Bdwy in *Last of the Red Hot Lovers* (1971), *Two kespearean Actors.*

**GE, JORDAN.** Born February 17, 1963 in Palo Alto, CA. Graduate NYU. Debut 8 OB in *Boy's Life,* followed by *Three Sisters, The Virgin Molly, Distant Fires, vy* in *Our Town* (1989).

**GERFELT, CAROLINE.** Born September 23 in Paris. Graduate AADA. Bdwy ut 1971 in *The Philanthropist,* followed by *4 on a Garden, Jockey Club Stakes, The istant Wife, Otherwise Engaged, Betrayal, The Real Thing, A Small Family iness,* OB in *Look Back in Anger, Close of Play, Sea Anchor, Quartermaine's ms, Other Places, Phaedra Britanica, Swim Visit, Creditors.*

**GIOIA, JOHN.** Born November 24, 1937 in Philadelphia, Pa. Graduate Temple U. in *Keyhole, Lovers in the Metro, The Cherry Orchard, Titus Andronicus, Henry V, hard III, A Little Madness, Rubbers, Right You Are, Pavlo Hummel,* Bdwy in *Henry* 969), *Gemini, Doubles, On Borrowed Time* (1991).

**MBERT, BEVERLY.** Born May 20, 1956 in Stamford, CT. Graduate U. NH. ut 1980 OB in *Plain and Fancy,* followed by *Sitting Pretty in Concert, The tasticks, A Little Night Music* (NYCO).

**MBERT, ROBERT.** Born July 28, 1960 in Ypsilanti, MI. Graduate Wayne State Bdwy debut 1989 in *Gypsy* for which he received a Theatre World Award and rn in 1991, OB in *Unfinished Song, Forever Plaid.*

**ND, MARK EDWARD.** Born May 2 in NYC. Graduate Vassar Col. Debut 1986 in *In Their Own Words* followed by *Initiation Rites, Milestones, A Midsummer ht's Dream, Julius Caesar, The Tempest, Radical Roots, Mary Stuart, Dark of the n, Rutherford & Son, The Rover, As You Like It.*

**NDER, JOHN-MICHAEL.** Born January 17 in Hamilton, OH. Attended U. /Irvine, Wright State U. Debut 1989 OB in *Adam and the Experts,* followed by *tody.*

**NDIS, JEANETTE.** Born April 4 in England. Attended Nat. Theatre Schl. Bdwy ut 1966 in *Marat/deSade,* followed by *There's One in Every Marriage, Elizabeth I, e for Love, Rules of the Game, Member of the Wedding* (1976), OB in *Cowardly tard.*

**NDON, SOFIA.** Born January 24, 1949 in Montreal, Can. Attended Norhtwestern Debut 1971 OB in *Red, White and Black,* followed by *Gypsy, Missouri Legend, artbreak House, Peg O' My Heart, Scenes and Revelations, The Hasty Heart, Blue adow, Flatbush Faithful, Selling Off.*

**NDON, SOFIA.** Born January 24, 1949 in Montreal, Can. Attended Northwestern Debut 1971 OB in *Red White and Black,* followed by *Gypsy, Missouri Legend, artbreak House, Peg O' My Heart, Scenes and Revelations, The Hasty Heart, Blue adow, Flatbush Faithful, The Mud Angel.*

**NDRON, JACK.** Born June 2, 1938 in San Juan, PR. Graduate Emerson Col. ut 1970 OB in *Ododo* followed by *Mother Courage and Her Children, If You mise Not to Learn, What's a Nice Country Like You ..., Spell?, Mondongo, Ballet the Bridge, The Garden, Don Juan in NYC, I Am a Winner, The Chinese rade, Capitol Walk, The Hills of Massabielle,* Bdwy in *Hurry Harry* (1972), *Dr. z, Tough to Get Help, Murderous Angels.*

**NE, LAURA.** Born October 13 in Pittsburgh, Pa. Graduate U. Mi. Debut 1988 OB the *Good and Faithful Servant,* followed by *Morningsong.*

**NE, NATHAN.** Born February 3, 1956 in Jersey City, NJ. Debut 1978 OB in *A dsummer Night's Dream,* followed by *Love, Measure for Measure, Claptrap, The mmon Pursuit, In a Pig's Valise, Uncounted Blessings, The Film Society, The on Traviata, Bad Habits, Lips Tothether Teeth Apart,* Bdwy in *Present Laughter 82), Merlin, Wind in the Willows, Some Americans Abroad, On Borrowed Time, ys and Dolls.*

**NG, STEPHEN.** Born July 11, 1952 in New York City. Graduate Swarthmore . Debut 1975 OB in *Hamlet,* followed by *Henry V, Shadow of a Gunman, A ter's Tale, Johnny on a Spot, Barbarians, Ah Men, Clownmaker, Hannah, encrantz and Guildenstern Are Dead,* Bdwy in *St. Joan* (1977), *Death of a*

*Salesman* (1984), *A Few Good Men, The Speed of Darkness, Hamlet.*

**LANGE, ANN.** Born June 24, 1953 in Pipestone, MN. Attended Carnegie-Mellon U. Debut 1979 OB in *Rat's Nest,* followed by *Hunting Scenes from Lower Bavaria, Crossfire, Linda Her and the Fairy Garden, Little Footsteps, 10th Young Playwrights Festival,* Bdwy in *The Survivor* (1981), *The Heidi Chronicles.*

**LANGE, JESSICA.** Born in Cloquet, Mn. on April 20, 1949. Attended U. Min. Bdwy debut 1992 in *A Streetcar Named Desire* for which she received a Theatre World Award.

**LANK, ANNA BESS.** Born November 22 in Rochester, NY.Graduate UCLA. Debut 1989 OB in *The Witch,* followed by *The Hideaway Hilton.*

**LANNING, NILE.** Born February 21, 1967 in NYC. Graduate Cornell U. Debut 1988 OB in *A Shayna Maidel* followed by *First Is Supper.*

**LANSING, ROBERT.** Born June 5, 1929 in San Diego, CA. Bdwy debut 1951 in *Stalag 17,* followed by *Cyrano de Bergerac, Richard III, Charley's Aunt, The Lovers, Cue for Passion, The Great God Brown, Cut of the Axe, Finishing Touches,* OB in *The Father, The Cost of Living, The Line, Phaedra, Mi Vida Loca, The Sum of Us.*

**LARSEN, LIZ.** Born January 16, 1959 in Philadelphia, PA. Attended Hofstra U., SUNY/Purchase. Bdwy debut 1981 in *Fiddler on the Roof,* followed by *Starmites, A Little Night Music* (NYCO), *The Most Happy Fella,* OB in *Kuni Leml, Hamlin, Personals, Starmites, Company, After These Messages, One Act Festival.*

**LARSON, JILL.** Born October 7, 1947 in Minneapolis, Mn. Graduate Hunter Col. Debut 1980 OB in *These Men,* followed by *Peep, Serious Business, It's Only a Play, Red Rover, Enter a Free Man, Scooncat, Dearly Departed,* Bdwy in *Romantic Comedy* (1980), *Death and the King's Horseman* (LC).

**LASKY, ZANE.** Born April 23, 1953 in NYC. Attended Manhattan Col. Debut 1973 OB in *The Hot 1 Baltimore,* followed by *The Prodigal, Innocent Thoughts, Harmless Intentions, Time Framed, Balm in Gilead, Shlemiel the First, Caligula, The Mound Builders, Quiet in the Land, El Salvador,* Bdwy in *All Over Town* (1974), *A Little Hotel on the Side.*

**LAUB, SANDRA.** Born December 15, 1956 in Bryn Mawr, PA. Graduate Northwestern U. Debut 1983 OB in *Richard III,* followed by *Young Playwrights Festival, Domestic Issues, Say Goodnight Gracie, Les Mouches, Three Sisters, Edward II, Intricate Acquaintances, The Relapse, Blossom, Peacetime.*

**LAURIA, DAN.** Born April 12, 1947 in Brooklyn, NY. Graduate S. Conn. State, U. Conn. Debut 1978 OB in *Game Plan,* followed by *All My Sons, Marlon Brando Sat Here, Home of the Brave, Collective Portraits, Dustoff, Niagara Falls, Punchy, Americans, Other People's Money.*

**LAWLESS, WENDY.** Born May 8, 1960 in Kansas City, MO. Attended Boston U., NYU. Debut 1989 OB in *Cymbeline,* followed by *La Vie en Rose, Midnight Rodeo, Pagan Day, Dearly Departed, The Matchmaker,* Bdwy in *The Heidi Chronicles* (1990).

**LAWRENCE, MAL Z.** Born September 2, 1937 in NYC. Attended CCNY. Bdwy debut 1991 in *Catskills on Broadway.*

**LAWRENCE, SHARON.** Born June 29, 1961 in Charlotte, NC. Attended UNC/Chapel Hill. Debut 1984 OB in *Panache,* followed by *Berlin in Light,* Bdwy in *Cabaret* (1987), *Fiddler on the Roof.*

**LAWRENCE, TASHA.** Born January 31, 1967 in Alberta, Can. Graduate U. of Guelph. 1992 OB in *Loose Ends,* followed by *Cowboy in His Underwear, Ten Blocks on the Camino Real.*

**LAWRENCE, YVETTE.** Born March 3, 1964 in NYC. Graduate Mt. St. Vincent Col., AADA. Bdwy debut 1991 in *Nick & Nora.*

**LAYNE, MARY.** Born June 20, 1950 in Colorado, TX. Attended Houston Baptist Col., U. Houston. Bdwy debut 1975 in *The Royal Family,* followed by *The Misanthrope, Shadowlands, Private Lives,*OB in *The Fox.*

**LEAVEL, BETH.** Born November 1, 1955 in Raleigh, NC. Graduate Meredith Col., UNC/Greensboro. Debut 1982 OB in *Applause,* followed by *Promises Promises, Broadway Jukebox, Unfinished Song,* Bdwy in *42nd Street* (1984), *Crazy for You.*

**LEE, DARREN.** Born June 8, 1972 in Long Beach, CA. Bdwy debut 1990 in *Shogun,* followed by *Miss Saigon.*

**LEE, KATHRYN.** Born September 1, 1926 in Denison, Tx. Bdwy credits include *Helen Goes to Troy, Laffing Room Only, Are You with It?, Allegro, As the Girls Go.* OB in *Tartuffe.*

**LEE, MARY.** (Formerly Lee-Aranas) Born September 23, 1959 in Taipei, Taiwan. Graduate U. Ottawa. Debut 1984 OB in *Empress of China,* followed by *A State without Grace, Return of the Phoenix, Yellow is My Favorite Color, The Man Who Turned into a Stick, The Impostor, Rosie's Cafe, Three Sisters, Noiresque, Song of Shim Chung, The Dressing Room.*

**LEE, SHERYL.** Born in Augsburg, Ger. in 1969. Attended AADA. Bdwy debut 1992 in *Salome.*

**LEEDS, ANDREW HARRISON.** Born September 24, 1978 in Clearwater, Fl. Bdwy debut 1987 in *Teddy and Alice,* followed by *Falsettos.*

**LEGGETT, PAULA.** Born September 2, 1961 in Evansville, In. Graduate Ind. U. Bdwy debut 1989 in *A Chorus Line,* followed by *Crazy for You.*

**LEIBMAN, RON.** Born October 11, 1937 in NYC. Attended Ohio Wesleyan, Actors Studio. Bdwy debut 1963 in *Dear Me the Sky Is Falling,* followed by *Bicycle Ride to Nevada, The Deputy, We Bombed in New Haven* for which he received a Theatre World Award, *Cop-Out, I Ought to Be in Pictures, Doubles, Rumors,* OB in *The Academy, John Brown's Body, Scapin, The Premise, Legend of Lovers, Dead End, Poker Session, Fransfers, Room Service, Love Two, Rich and Famous, Children of Darkness, Non Pasquale, Give the Bishop My Faint Regards.*

**LEO, MELISSA.** Born September 14, 1960 in NYC. Attended SUNY/Purchase. Debut 1984 in *Cinders* followed by *Out of Gas in Lover's Leap, Today I Am a Fountain Pen, The White Rose.*

**LEONE, JOHN.** Born April 7, 1964 in Weymouth, Ma. Graduate Hofstra U. Bdwy debut 1991 in *Les Miserables.*

**LESHEIM, LOLITA.** Born January 25, 1960 in Rocky River, Oh. Graduate Boston U., Harvard U. Bdwy debut 1989 in *M. Butterfly*, OB in *The Hour of the Lynx.*

**LESSNER, JOANNE.** Born September 23, 1965 in NYC. Graduate Yale U. Debut 1990 OB in *Romeo and Juliet*, followed by *You're Gonna Love Tomorrow, Company.*

**LeSTRANGE, PHILIP.** Born May 9, 1942 in the Bronx, NY. Graduate Catholic U., Fordham U. Debut 1970 OB in *Getting Married*, followed by *Erogenous Zones, The Quilling of Prue, The Front Page, Six Degrees of Separation*, Bdwy in *A Small Family Business* (1992).

**LEVERETT, T. DOYLE.** Born January 19, 1954 in Kankakee, Il. Attended Ill. State U., Vienna Music Academy. Bdwy debut 1992 in *The Most Happy Fella.*

**LEVIN, MICHAEL.** Born December 8, 1932 in Minneapolis, Mn. Graduate U. Minn. Bdwy debut 1965 in *Royal Hunt of the Sun*, OB in *Ghosts, End of All Things Natural, LC's Camino Real 7, Operation Sidewinder and Good Woman of Setzuan.*

**LEVINE, EARL AARON.** Born December 1, 1952 in Tallahassee, FL. Attended Temple U., Westchester State U. Bdwy debut 1982 in *Little Johnny Jones*, OB in *The Fantasticks.*

**LEVINE, ILANA.** Born December 5, 1963 in New Jersey. Graduate Fordham U. OB in *The Agreement, Shmulnik's Waltz, Forgetting Frankie.* Bdwy 1992 in *Jake's Women.*

**LEVINE, RICHARD S.** Born July 16, 1954 in Boston, MA. Graduate Juilliard. Debut 1978 OB in *Family Business*, followed by *Magic Time, It's Better with a Band, Emma, Mistress of the Inn, I Can Get It for You Wholesale*, Bdwy in *Dracula, Rock 'n' Roll: First 5000 Years, Rumors, Gypsy* (1991), *The Visit.*

**LEWIS, MATTHEW.** Born January 12, 1937 in Elizabeth, NJ. Graduate Harvard U. Debut 1970 OB in *Chicago '70*, followed by *Fathers and Sons, The Freak, Happy Days Are Here Again, Levitation, The Sea Gull, My Papa's Wine, Apocalyptic Butterflies, White Collar, Group*, Bdwy in *Angels Fall* (1983).

**LEWIS, VICKI.** Born March 17, 1969 in Cincinnati, OH. Graduate Cinn. Consv. Bdwy debut 1982 in *Do Black Patent Leather Shoes Really Reflect Up?*, followed by *Wind in the Willows*, OB in *Snoopy, Angry Housewives, 1-2-3-4-5, One Act Festival, The Love Talker, Buzzsaw Berkeley, Marathon '90, The Crucible, I Can Get It for You Wholesale, Don Juan and the Non Don Juan.*

**LICATO, FRANK.** Born April 20, 1952 in Brooklyn, NY. Attended Emerson Col. Debut 1974 OB in *Deathwatch*, followed by *Fever, American Music, Angel City, Killer's Head, Haunted Lives, The Taming of the Shrew, New Voice Festival, Jekyll in Chamber.*

**LEYDENFROST, ALEX.** Born September 14, 1965 in Nyack, NY. Graduate Franklin & Marshall Col., New Actors Workshop. Debut 1990 OB in *Measure for Measure*, followed by *Tartuffe, As You Like It.*

**LI, LISA ANN.** Born August 6, 1966 in Dayton, Oh. Graduate Boston U. Bdwy debut 1992 in *A Little Hotel on the Side.*

**LIBERATORE, LOU.** Born August 4, 1959 in Jersey City, NJ. Graduate Fordham U. Debut 1982 OB in *The Great Grandson of Jeddiah Kohler* followed by *Threads, Black Angel, Richard II, Thymus Vulgaris, As Is, Burn This, Unidentified Human Remains, One of the All-Time Greats, Sight Unseen*, Bdwy in *As Is* (1985), *Burn This.*

**LIDE, MILLER.** Born August 10, 1935 in Columbia, SC. Graduate USC, AmThWing. Debut 1961 OB in *3 Modern Japanese Plays* followed by *The Trial at Rouen, Street Scene, Joan of Arc at the Stake, The Heiress, The Doctor's Dilemma, School for Wives, Rutherford & Son*, Bdwy in *Ivanov* (1966), *Halfway Up the Tree, Who's Who in Hell, We Interrupt This Program, The Royal Family, 84 Charing Cross Road.*

**LIGON, KEVIN.** Born May 17, 1961 in Dallas, Tx. Graduate SMU. Debut 1988 OB in *The Chosen*, followed by *Forbidden Broadway*, Bdwy in *The Secret Garden* (1991).

**LINDFORS, VIVECA.** Born December 29, 1920 in Upsala, Swed. Attended Stockholm Royal Academy. Bdwy debut 1952 in *I've Got Sixpence*, followed by *Anastasia, King Lear, Postmark Zero*, OB in *Miss Julie, Pal Joey* (CC), *Cuba Si, Guns of Carrar, Dance of Death, I Am a Woman, The Gypsy Swede.*

**LINNEY, LAURA.** Born February 5, 1964 in NYC. Graduate Brown U., Juilliard. Debut 1990 OB in *Six Degrees of Separation*, followed by *Beggars in the House of Plenty, The Seagull: The Hamptons 1990, Sight Unseen* for which she received a Theatre World Award, Bdwy in *Six Degrees of Separation.*

**LIPMAN, DAVID.** Born May 12, 1938 in Brooklyn, NY. Graduate LIU, Brooklyn Col. Debut 1973 OB in *Moonchildren*, followed by *The Devil's Disciple, Don Juan In Hell, Isn't It Romantic?, Kiss Me Quick, Iron Bars*, Bdwy in *Fools* (1981).

**LITTLE, DAVID.** Born March 21, 1937 in Wadesboro, NC. Graduate Wm & Mary Col., Catholic U. Debut 1967 OB in *Macbird* followed by *Iphigenia in Aulis, Antony and Cleopatra, Antigone, An Enemy of the People, Three Sons, Almost in Vegas, 6 Degrees of Separation.*

**LLOYD BEDFORD, JOHN.** January 2, 1956 in New Haven, Ct. Graduate Williams Col., Yale. Debut 1983 OB in *Vieux Carre*, followed by *She Stoops to Conquer, The Incredibly Famous Willy Rivers, Digby, Rum and Coke, Trinity Site, Richard II, Some Americans Abroad, Lambert's Latest*, Bdwy in *Some Americans Abroad* (1990).

**LOBENHOFER, LEE.** Born June 25, 1955 in Chicago, IL. Graduate U. Ill. Debut 1986 OB in *Rainbow*, followed by *I Married an Angel in Concert, Hans Christian Andersen, Bittersweet, Robin Hood, Lost in the Stars*, Bdwy in *Shogun* (1990), *G[...] Hotel, Cats.*

**LOCKWOOD, LISA.** Born February 13, 1958 in San Francisco, CA. Bdwy d[...] 1988 in *Phantom of the Opera.*

**LOMBARD, MICHAEL.** Born August 8, 1934 in Brooklyn, NY. Graduate Broo[...] Col., Boston U. OB in *King Lear, Merchant of Venice, Cages, Pinter Plays[...] Turista, Elizabeth the Queen, Room Service, Mert and Phil, Side Street Sce[...] Angelo's Wedding, Friends in High Places, What's Wrong with This Picture?, B[...] in *Poor Bitos* (1964), *The Devils, Gingerbread Lady, Bad Habits, Otherwise Enga[...] Awake and Sing, Nick & Nora.*

**LOPEZ, CARLOS.** Born May 14, 1963 in Sunnyvale, Ca. Attended Cal. S[...] U./Hayward. Debut 1987 OB in *Wish You Were Here*, followed by Bdwy in *[...] Pajama Game* (1989), *A Chorus Line, Grand Hotel, Guys and Dolls.*

**LOR, DENISE.** Born May 3, 1929 in Los Angeles, Ca. Debut 1968 OB in *To B[...] Not to Be*, followed by *Alias Jimmy Valentine, Ruthless!* Bdwy in *42nd St.*

**LOUDEN, DADE.** Born November 2, 1948 in La Harpe, IL. Graduate Pasac[...] Playhouse, Northwestern U. Debut 1991 OB in *Raft of the Medusa.*

**LOUDON, DOROTHY.** Born September 17, 1933 in Boston, MA. Atter[...] Emerson Col., Syracuse U. Debut 1961 OB in *World of Jules Feiffer*, followed by *Matchmaker*, Bdwy 1963 in *Nowhere to Go but Up* for which she received a The[...] World Award, followed by *Noel Coward's Sweet Potato, Fig Leaves Are Fal[...] Three Men on a Horse, The Women, Annie, Ballroom, West Side Waltz, Noises[...] Jerry's Girls.*

**LOVEJOY, DEIRDRE.** Born June 30, 1962 in Abilene, Tx. Graduate U.Evansv[...] NYU. Debut 1988 OB in *A Midsummer Night's Dream* followed by *Henry IV Pa[...] Hannah 1939, Machinal, Alice in Wonderland, Don Juan*, Bdwy in *Six Degree[...] Separation* (1991).

**LOWE, FRANK.** Born June 28, 1927 in Appalachia, Va. Attended Sorbonne. De[...] 1952 OB in *Macbeth* followed by *Hotel De Breney, The Lady's Not for Burning, Trot on Gardiner's Bay, As You Like It, A Sleep of Prisoners, Cymbeline, Did E[...] Cry?, Man with a Raincoat, Donkey's Years, Ring Round the Moon.*

**LOWE, ROB.** Born March 17, 1964 in Charlottesville, Va. Bdwy debut 1992 [...] *Little Hotel on the Side.*

**LOWERY, MARCELLA.** Born April 27, 1945 in Jamaica, NY. Graduate Hu[...] Col. American Pastoral, Debut 1967 OB in *Day of Absence*, followed by *Amer[...] Pastoral, Ballet behind the Bridge, Jamima, Recent Killing, Miracle Play, Welcom[...] Black River, Anna Lucasta, Baseball Wives, Louie, Bless Me Father, Ladies, Su[...] Hill, Before It Hits Home*, Bdwy in *A Member of the Wedding* (1975), *Lolita.*

**LUM, ALVIN.** Born May 28, 1931 in Honolulu, HI. Attended U. HI. Debut 1[...] OB in *In the Bar of a Tokyo Hotel*, followed by *Pursuit of Happiness, Monkey Mi[...] Flowers and Household Gods, Station J, Double Dutch, Teahouse, Song for a N[...] Fisherman, Empress of China, Manos Valley, Hot Sake, Chu Chem* (also Bdv[...] Bdwy in *Lovely Ladies Kind Gentlemen* (1970), *Two Gentlemen of Verona, Cit[...] Angels.*

**LUZ, FRANC** (a.k.a. Frank C.). Born December 22 in Cambridge, MA. Atten[...] New Mex. State U. Debut 1974 OB in *The Rivals*, followed by *Fiorello!, Little S[...] of Horrors*, Bdwy in *Whoopee!* (1979), *City of Angels.*

**LYLES, LESLIE.** Born in Plainfield, NJ. Graduate Monmouth Col., Rutgers[...] Debut 1981 OB in *Sea Marks*, followed by *Highest Standard of Living, Vanishing[...] I Am Who I Am, The Arbor, Terry by Terry, Marathon '88, Sleeping Dogs, Marat[...] '90, Young Playwrights '90, Nebraska, The My House Play, Life During Wart[...] Angel of Death, Sam I Am.*

**MA, JASON.** Born in Palo Alto, CA. Graduate UCLA. Bdwy debut 1989 in *[...] Chem*, followed by *Prince of Central Park, Shogun: The Musical, Miss Saigon.*

**MACKAY, LIZBETH.** Born March 7 in Buffalo, NY. Graduate Adelphi U., Y[...] Bdwy debut 1981 in *Crimes of the Heart* for which she received a Theatre W[...] Award, followed by *Death and the Maiden*, OB in *Kate's Diary, Tales of the [...] Formicans, Price of Fame, The Old Boy.*

**MacPHERSON, LORI.** Born July 23 in Albany, NY. Attended Skidmore C[...] Bdwy debut 1988 in *The Phantom of the Opera.*

**MacRAE, HEATHER.** Born in New York City. Attended Colo. Women's C[...] Bdwy debut 1968 in *Here's Where I Belong*, followed by *Hair, Coastal Disturban[...] Falsettos*, OB in *The Hot 1 Baltimore, Coastal Disturbances, Falsettoland.*

**MacVITTIE, BRUCE.** Born October 14, 1956 in Providence, RI. Graduate Bos[...] U. Bdwy debut 1983 in *American Buffalo*, followed by OB in *California Dog Fi[...] The Worker's Life, Cleveland and Half Way Back, Marathon '87, One of[...] Guys, Young Playwrights '90, A Darker Purpose.*

**MAGUIRE, MICHAEL.** Born February 20, 1955 in Newport News, Va. Gradu[...] Oberlin Col., U. Mich. Bdwy debut 1987 in *Les Miserables* for which he receive[...] Theatre World Award, followed by *A Little Night Music* (NYCO).

**MAHOWALD, JOSEPH.** Born in Huron, SD. Attended U. SD, U. TX., U. Ca[...] Debut 1990 OB in *Antigone*, followed by Bdwy in *Les Miserables* (1992).

**MAILER, STEPHEN.** Born March 10, 1966 in New York City. Attend[...] Middlebury Col., NYU. Debut OB 1989 in *For Dear Life*, followed by *What's Wro[...] with This Picture?, Peacetime.*

**MANTELLO, JOE.** Born December 27, 1962 in Rockford, IL. Debut 1986 OB[...] *Crackwalker*, followed by *Progress, Walking the Dead, The Baltimore Waltz.*

**MANZI, WARREN.** Born July 1, 1955 in Laurence, MA. Graduate Holy Cro[...] Yale. Bdwy debut 1980 in *Amadeus*, OB in *Perfect Crime*, followed by *The Aw[...] and Other Plays.*

**RCEAU, YVONNE.** Born July 13, 1950 in Chicago, IL. Graduate U. Utah. y debut 1989 in *Grand Hotel.*

**RCHAND, NANCY.** Born June 19, 1928 in Buffalo, NY. Graduate Carnegie . Debut 1951 in CC's *Taming of the Shrew,* followed by *Merchant of Venice, h Ado About Nothing, Three Bags Full, After the Rain, The Alchemist, Yerma, no de Bergerac, Mary Stuart, Enemies, The Plough and the Stars, 40 Carats, And Reardon Drinks a Little, Veronica's Room, Awake and Sing, Mornings at Seven, Octette Bridge Club,* OB in *The Balcony, Children, Taken in Marriage, Sister y Ignatius Explains It All, Electra, The Cocktail Hour, Love Letters, The End of )ay, A Darker Purpose.*

**RCUS, DANIEL.** Born May 26, 1955 in Redwood City, Ca. Graduate Boston U. y debut 1981 in *The Pirates of Penzance,* OB in *La Boheme, Kuni Leml, A Flash ghtning, The Pajama Game, Gunmetal Blues.*

**RGOLIES, DAVID.** Born February 19, 1937 in NYC. Graduate CCNY. Debut OB in *Golden Six,* followed by *Six Characters in Search of an Author, Tragical orie of Dr. Faustus, Tango, Little Murders, Seven Days of Mourning, La Analysis, vening with the Poet Senator, Kid Champion, The Man with the Flower in His th, 'Old Tune, David and Paula, Cabal of Hypocrites, The Perfect Party, Just Say George Washington Dances,* Bdwy in *The Iceman Cometh* (1973), *Zalmen or the ness of God, Comedians, Break a Leg, West Side Waltz, Brighton Beach Memoirs, versations with My Father.*

**RIE, JEAN.** Born December 14, 1968 in Mountainside, NJ. Attended Fordham dwy debut 1992 in *Crazy for You.*

**RINOS, PETER.** Born October 2, 1951 in Pontiac, MI. Graduate Mich. State U. y debut 1976 in *Chicago,* followed by *Evita, Zorba, The Secret Garden.*

**RKELL, JODIE.** Born April 13, 1959 in Memphis, TN. Attended Northwestern Debut 1984 OB in *Balm in Gilead,* followed by *Carrying School Children, UBU, ning Dogs, Machinal.*

**RKS, KENNETH.** Born February 17, 1954 in Harwick, PA. Graduate U. Penn., gh U. Debut 1978 OB in *Clara Bow Loves Gary Cooper,* followed by *Canadian hic, Time and the Conways, Savoury Meringue, Thrombo, Fun, 1-2-3-4-5, hattan Class 1 Acts, A Bright Room Called Day,* Bdwy in *Dancing at Lughnasa* 2).

**RSH, JAMIE.** Born September 17, 1966 in New York City. Attended HB Studio. y debut 1991 in *Lost in Yonkers.*

**RTEL, BILLY ARTHUR.** Born March 3, 1962 in Providence, RI. Graduate rson College. Debut 1989 OB in *Sadie Thompson,* followed by *Wonderful Town, Awakening of Spring.*

**RTELLS, CYNTHIA.** Born September 8, 1960 in London, Eng. Attended gers U. Debut 1983 OB in *Under Heaven's Eye,* followed by *Lightening, Rules of , Thornwood, No No Nanette, Caucasian Chalk Circle, Young Playwrights '90, ylon Gardens,* Bdwy in *Two Trains Running.*

**RTIN, GEORGE N.** Born August 15, 1929 in NYC. Bdwy debut 1970 in on in the Promise Land,* followed by *The Hothouse, Plenty, Total Abandon, Pack ies, The Mystery of Edwin Drood, The Crucible, A Little Hotel on the Side,* OB in ating Churches, Henry V, Springtime for Henry.*

**RTIN, LEILA.** Born August 22, 1932 in New York City. Bdwy debut 1944 in oshow,* followed by *Two on the Aisle, Wish You Were Here, Guys and Dolls, Best use in Naples, Henry Sweet Henry, The Wall, Visit to a Small Planet, The schilds, 42nd Street, The Phantom of the Opera,* OB in *Ernest in Love, Beggar's ra, King of the U.S., Philemon, Jerry's Girls.*

**RTIN, LUCY.** Born February 8, 1942 in NYC. Graduate Sweet Briar College. ut 1962 OB in *Electra,* followed by *Happy as Larry, The Trojan Women, genia in Aulis, Wives, The Cost of Living, The Substance of Fire,* Bdwy in *Shelter 3), Children of a Lesser God, Pygmalion.*

**RTINEZ, TONY.** Born January 27, 1920 in Santurce, PR. Attended UPR. Bdwy it 1967 in *Man of La Mancha* and in 1972, 1977, 1992 revivals.

**RTINI, LOU, JR.** Born December 7, 1960 in NYC. Graduate U. Houston. ut 1989 OB in *Tony 'n' Tina's Wedding.*

**SCOLO, JOSEPH.** Born March 13, 1935 in Hartford, Ct. Bdwy in *Night Life, A v from the Bridge, Dinner at 8,* LCRep's *The Time of Your Life, Camino Real and d Woman of Setuzan, That Championship Season,* OB in *To Clothe the Naked, rderous Angels, Breaking Legs.*

**SSEY, MARISOL.** Born in San Juan, PR. Graduate Emerson Col. Debut 1991 in *The Have Little,* followed by *Whitestones.*

**STRONE, FRANK.** Born November 1, 1960 in Bridgeport, CT. Graduate tral State U. Bdwy debut 1988 in *The Phantom of the Opera.*

**STROTOTARO, MICHAEL.** Born May 17, 1962 in Albany, NY. Graduate U. OB in *The Myth Project* followed by *A Darker Purpose.*

**TTHIESSEN, JOAN.** Born February 27, 1930 in Orange, NJ. Graduate egheny Col. Debut 1979 OB in *The Art of Dining,* followed by *The Cocktail Party, oll House, Summer, The Oil Well, Rutherford & Son.*

**TZ, JERRY.** Born November 15, 1935 in New York City. Graduate Syracuse U. ut 1965 OB in *The Old Glory,* followed by *Hefetz, A Day Out of Time, A Mad ld My Masters, The Rise of David Levinsky, The Last Danceman, Madrid Madrid, trude Queen of Denmark, Schmulnick's Waltz,* Bdwy in *Ghetto* (1989), *Fiddler on Roof* (1989).

**XWELL, JAN** Born November 20, 1956 in Fargo, ND. Graduate Moorhead State Bdwy debut 1990 in *City of Angels,* followed by *Dancing at Lughnasa,* OB in rybody Everybody, Hot Feet, Light Years to Chicago, Ladies of the Fortnight, Two tlemen of Verona, The Marriage Fool.*

**ZZIE, MARIN.** Born October 9, 1960 in Rockford, IL. Graduate W. Mi. U. ut 1983 OB in *Where's Charley?, And The World Goes Round,* Bdwy in *Big River*

(1986).

**McALLEN, KATHLEEN ROWE.** Born November 30 in the Bay area, CA. Attended UCB, UCLA. Debut 1981 OB in *Joseph and the Amazing Technicolor Dreamcoat,* followed by *Chess,* Bdwy in *Joseph and...* (1982), followed by *Aspects of Love* for which she received a Theatre World Award.

**McBRIDE, TOM.** Born October 7, 1952 in Charleston, W Va. Graduate Xavier U. Debut 1980 OB in *Plain and Fancy* followed by *Fast Women, House, Honor Bright, Going Down, Hollywood Scheherazade, Night Dance,* Bdwy in *5th of July* (1981).

**McCAMBRIDGE, MERCEDES.** Born March 17, 1918 in Joliet, IL. Graduate Mundelein Col. Bdwy debut 1945 in *A Place of Our Own* followed by *Woman Bites Dog, The Young and the Fair, Who's Afraid of Virginia Woolf?, The Love Suicide at Schofield Barracks, Lost in Yonkers,* OB in *Cages.*

**McCANN, CHRISTOPHER.** Born September 29, 1952 in New York City. Graduate NYU. Debut 1975 OB in *The Measures Taken,* followed by *Ghosts, Woyzeck, St. Joan of the Stockyards, Buried Child, Dwelling in Milk, Tongues, 3 Acts of Recognition, Don Juan, Michi's Blood, Five of Us, Richard III, The Golem, Kafka Father and Son, Flatbush Faithful, Black Market, King Lear, The Virgin Molly, Mad Forest.*

**McCONNELL, DAVID.** Born February 12, 1962 in Los Alamos, NM. Graduate AADA. OB in *You Never Can Tell, The Hot 1 Baltimore, Cloud 9, Working, The Normal Heart, The Winter's Tale, This One Thing I Do, The Rivers and Ravines, Anima Mundi.*

**McCORD, LISA MERRILL.** Born March 3, 1962 in Louisville, KY. Graduate Syracuse U. Debut 1986 OB in *Two Gentlemen of Verona,* followed by *As You Like It, No No Nanette,* Bdwy in *Grand Hotel* (1990).

**McCORMICK, CAROLYN.** Born September 19, 1959 in Texas. Graduate Williams Col. Debut 1988 OB in *In Perpetuity throughout the Universe,* followed by *Lips Together Teeth Apart.*

**McCRANE, PAUL.** Born January 19, 1961 in Philadelphia, PA. Debut 1977 OB in *Landscape of the Body,* followed by *Dispatches, Split, Hunting Scenes, Crossing Niagara, Hooters, Fables for Friends, Moonchildren, Right Behind the Flag, Human Nature, Six Degrees of Separation, The Country Girl, Group,* Bdwy in *Runaways* (1978), *Curse of an Aching Heart, The Iceman Cometh* (1985).

**McDANIEL, JAMES.** Born March 25, 1958 in Washington, DC. Attended U. Pa. Debut 1982 OB in *A Soldier's Play* followed by *E.S.T. Marathon, The Harvesting, Caligula, The Mound Builders, Incredibly Famous Willy Rivers, Diamonds, Balm in Gilead, Before It Hits Home,* Bdwy in *Joe Turner's Come and Gone, Six Degrees of Separation* (also OB).

**McDONALD, TANNY.** Born February 13 in Princeton, NJ. Graduate Vassar Col. Debut 1961 OB in *American Savoyards* followed by *All in Love, To Broadway with Love, Carricknabauna, The Beggar's Opera, Brand, Goodbye, Dan Bailey, Total Eclipse, Gorky, Don Juan Comes Back from the War, Vera with Kate, Francis, On Approval, A Definite Maybe, Temptation, Titus Andronicus, Hamlet,* Bdwy in *Fiddler on the Roof, Come Summer, The Lincoln Mask, Clothes for a Summer Hotel, Macbeth, Man of La Mancha.*

**McGANN, MICHAEL JOHN.** Born February 2, 1952 in Cleveland, Oh. Debut 1975 OB in *Three Musketeers,* followed by *Panama Hattie, A Winter's Tale, Johnny-on-a-Spot, Barbarians, A Midsummer Night's Dream, The Wild Duck, Jungle of Cities, The Tempest, Hamlet.*

**McGEE, TIM.** Born October 14, 1962. Graduate U. Min., Rutgers U. Debut 1990 OB in *Find the Felt Please,* Bdwy in *Hamlet* (1992).

**McGILLIN, HOWARD.** Born November 5, 1953 in Los Angeles, CA. Graduate U. Cal./Santa Barbara. Debut 1984 OB in *La Boheme,* followed by Bdwy in *The Mystery of Edwin Drood* for which he received a Theatre World Award, *Sunday in the Park with George, Anything Goes, 50 Million Frenchmen in Concert, The Secret Garden.*

**McGOVERN, ELIZABETH.** Born July 18, 1961 in Evanston, IL. Attended Juilliard. Debut 1981 OB in *To Be Young Gifted and Black,* followed by *Hotel Play, My Sister in This House* for which she received a Theatre World Award, *Painting Churches, Hitch-Hikers, Map of the World, Two Gentlemen of Verona, Maids of Honor,* Bdwy in *Love Letters* (1989), *Hamlet* (1992).

**McGOWAN, TOM.** Born July 26, 1959 in Neptune, NJ. Graduate Yale, Hofstra U. Debut 1988 OB in *Coriolanus,* followed by *A Winter's Tale, One of the All-Time Greats,* Bdwy in *La Bete* (1991).

**McGUIRE, BIFF.** Born October 25, 1926 in New Haven, CT. Attended Mass. State Col. Bdwy in *Make Mine Manhattan, South Pacific, Dance Me a Song, The Time of Your Life, A View from the Bridge, The Greatest Man Alive, The Egghead, Triple Play, Happy Town, Beg Borrow or Steal, Finian's Rainbow, Beggar on Horseback, Father's Day, Trial of the Catonsville 9, A Streetcar Named Desire, Conversations with My Father,* OB in *Present Tense, Marathon '91.*

**McHATTIE, STEPHEN** (formerly Stephen Smith) Born February 3 in Antigosh, NS. Graduate Arcadia U, AADA. Bdwy debut 1969 in *The American Dream,* followed by *The Misanthrope, Heartbreak House, You Never Can Tell, Ghetto, Twelfth Night, Pictures in the Hallway, Mourning Becomes Electra, The Iceman Cometh, Search and Destroy,* OB in *Henry IV, Richard III, The Persians, Now There's Just the Three of Us, Anna K, Alive and Well in Argentina, Winter Dancers, Casualties, Three Sisters, Mensch Meier, Haven, A Perfect Diamond, Macbeth.*

**McINERNEY, BERNIE.** Born December 4, 1936 in Wilmington, De. Graduate U. Del., Catholic U. Bdwy debut 1972 in *The Championship Season* followed by *Curse of an Aching Heart, The Front Page* (LC), OB in *Life of Galileo, Losing Time, Three Friends, American Clock, Father Dreams, Winners, Digby, A Woman without a Name.*

**McKERRACHER, MARK.** Born February 21, 1956 in Pasadena, Ca. Graduate Santa Barbara U. Bdwy debut 1991 in *Les Miserables.*

**McMANUS, DON R**. Born in 1960 in Sylacauga, AL. Graduate Yale U. Debut 1987 OB in *Holy Ghosts* followed by *Titus Andronicus, One of the Guys, Neddy, The Art of Success, Pericles*.

**McNABB, BARRY**. Born August 26, 1960 in Toronto, Can. Graduate U. Ore. Bdwy debut 1986 in *Me and My Girl*, followed by *The Phantom of the Opera*.

**McNAMARA, DERMOT**. Born August 24, 195 in Dublin, Ire. Bdwy debut 1959 in *A Touch of the Poet*, followed by *Philadelphia Here I Come!, Donnybrook, Taming of the Shrew*, OB in *The Wise Have Not Spoken, 3 by Synge, Playboy of the Western World, Shadow and Substance, Happy as Larry, Sharon's Grave, A Whistle in the Dark, Red Roses for Me, The Plough and the Stars, Shadow of a Gunman, No Exit, Stephen D., Hothouse, Home Is the Hero, Sunday Morning Bright and Early, Birthday Party, All the Nice People, Roots, Philadelphia Here I Come!, Grandchild of Kings*.

**McNIGHT, SHARON**. Born December 18 in Modesto, Ca. Graduate San Fran. State Col. Debut 1987 OB in *Murder at the Rutherford House* followed by *A Looney Experience*, Bdwy 1989 in *Starmites* for which she received a Theatre World Award.

**McROBBIE, PETER**. Born January 31, 1943 in Hawick, Scotland. Graduate Yale U. Debut 1976 OB in *The Wobblies*, followed by *The Devil's Disciple, Cinders, The Ballad of Soapy Smith, Rosmersholm, American Bagpipes, Richard III*, Bdwy in *Whose Life Is It Anyway?* (1979), *Macbeth* (1981), *The Mystery of Edwin Drood, The Master Builder* (1992).

**McVETY, DREW**. Born April 16, 1965 in Port Huron, Mi. Graduate NYU. Debut/OB 1988 in *The Heidi Chronicles* followed by *The Substance of Fire*, Bdwy 1989 in *The Heidi Chronicles*.

**McVEY, J. MARK**. Born January 6, 1958 in Huntington, W Va. Graduate Marshall U. Bdwy debut 1991 in *Les Miserables*, OB in *Cafe A Go-Go, Chess*.

**McWILLIAMS, RICHARD**. Born June 27, 1950 in Baytown, Tx. Graduate Sam Houston State U. Debut 1983 OB in *Except in My Memory*, followed by *Why Marry?, Get Any Guy, The Night Hank Williams Died, Macbeth*, Bdwy in *Orpheus Descending*.

**MEADE, JULIA**. Born December 17, 1928 in Boston, Ma. Attended Yale U. Bdwy debut 1954 in *The Tender Trap followed by Double in Hearts, Roman Candle, Mary Mary, The Front Page (1969)*, OB in *Harvest of Strangers, Isn't It Romantic?, Sublime Lives*.

**MEISLE, KATHRYN**. Born June 7 in Appleton, WI. Graduate Smith Col., UNC/Chapel Hill. Debut 1988 OB in *Dandy Dick* followed by *Cahoots, Othello*.

**MEISNER, VICKI**. Born August 2, 1935 in New York City. Graduate Adelphi Col. Debut 1958 OB in *Blood Wedding*, followed by *The Prodigal, Shakuntala, Nathan the Wise, Decathlon, Afternoon in Las Vegas, The Beauty Part, Trelawny of 'he Wells*.

**MEISTER, FREDERICA**. Born August 18, 1951 in San Francisco, CA. Graduate NYU. Debut 1978 OB in *Museum*, followed by *Dolphin Position, Waiting for the Parade, Dream of a Blacklisted Actor, No Damn Good, The Magic Act, Subfertile, Naked Rights*.

**MELLOR, STEPHEN**. Born October 17, 1954 in New Haven, CT. Graduate Boston U. Debut 1980 OB in *Paris Lights*, followed by *Coming Attractions, Plenty, Tooth of Crime, Shepard Sets, A Country Doctor, Harm's Way, Brightness Falling, Terminal Hip, Dead Mother, A Murder of Crows, Seven Blowjobs, Pericles*, Bdwy in *Big River*.

**MENDILLO, STEPHEN**. Born October 9, 1942 in New Haven, CT. Graduate Colo. Col, Yale. Debut 1973 OB in *Nourish the Beast*, followed by *Gorky, Time Steps, The Marriage, Loot, Subject to Fits, Wedding Band, As You Like It, Fool for Love, Twelfth Night, Grotesque Lovesongs, Nowhere*, Bdwy in *National Health* (1974), *Ah Wilderness, A View from the Bridge, Wild Honey, Orpheus Descending*.

**MENENDEZ, HENRY**. Born August 14, 1965 in Atlantic City, NJ. Graduate Boston Consv. Bdwy debut 1991 in *Miss Saigon*.

**MEREDIZ, OLGA**. Born February 15, 1956 in Guantanamo, Cuba. Graduate Tulane U. Bdwy debut 1984 in *The Human Comedy*, OB in *El Bravo!, Women without Men, El Grande de Coca-Cola, The Blessing, The Lady from Havana, 10th Young Playwrights Festival*.

**MERKERSON, S. EPATHA**. Born November 28, 1952 in Saginaw, MI. Graduate Wayne State U. Debut 1979 OB in *Spell #7*, followed by *Home, Puppetplay, Tintypes, Every Goodbye Ain't Gone, Hospice, The Harvesting, Moms, Lady Day at Emerson's Bar and Grill, 10th Young Playwrights Festival*, Bdwy in *Tintypes* (1982), *The Piano Lesson*.

**MERLIN, JOANNA**. Born July 15 in Chicago, Il. Attended UCLA. Debut 1958 OB in *The Breaking Wall*, followed by *Six Characters in Search of an Author, Rules of the Game, A Thistle in My Bed, Canadian Gothic/American Modern, Family Portrait*, Bdwy in *Becket* (1961), *A Far Country, Fiddler on the Roof, Shelter, Uncle Vanya, The Survivor, Solomon's Child*.

**MERRYMAN, MONICA**. Born June 2, 1950 in Sao Paulo, Brazil. Graduate E.Mich U. Debut 1975 OB in *East Lynne*, followed by *A Night in the Black Pig, Vanities, The Voice of the Turtle, Rhapsody Tachiste, Jacques and His Master, The Sum of Us*.

**MICHAELA, GENIA**. Born August 21, 1976 in Louisiana. Attended NC Sch. of the Art. Bdwy debut 1991 in *The Crucible* followed by *Jake's Women*.

**MICHENNER, ADAM**. Born March 12, 1931 in London, Eng. Graduate CCNY, NYU. Debut 1988 OB in *Revenge of the Space Pandas* followed by *Troilus and Cressida, King John, The Walk, Merry Wives of Windsor, The Illusionists, Dorian, Baked Meats, The Joneses, River Moves, Danton's Death, A Different Kind of Dog, Three Sisters, Trelawny of The Wells*.

**MILANI, LINDA**. Born October 28, 1946 in Boston, Ma. Attended Boston Cons. Bdwy debut 1983 in *Show Boat*, OB in *Bells Are Ringing, Princess Ida*.

**MILLER, BARRY**. Born February 6, 1958 in Los Angeles, Ca. Debut 1981 OB in *Forty Deuce* followed by *The Tempest, One Act Festival*, Bdwy in *Biloxi Blues* (1985) for which he received a Theatre World Award, followed by *Crazy He Calls Me*.

**MINOFF, TAMMY**. Born October 4, 1979 in New York City. Debut 1988 OB in

*The Traveling Man*, followed by *1-2-3-4-5*, Bdwy in *The Will Rogers Follies* (1991)

**MINOT, ANNA**. Born in Boston, Ma. Attended Vassar Col. Bdwy debut 194? *The Strings My Lord Are False*, followed by *The Russian People, The Visitor, Iceman Cometh, An Enemy of the People, Love of Four Colonels, The Tri? Bountiful, Tunnel of Love, Ivanov*, OB in *Sands of the Niger, Gettin Out, Vieux Ca State of the Union, Her Great Match, Rivals, Hedda Gabler, All's Well That E Well, Tarfuffe*.

**MITCHELL, ALETA**. Born in Chicago. Graduate U. Iowa. Yale Bdwy debut 1 in *Ma Rainey's Black Bottom*, OB in *Approaching Zanzibar*, followed by *Night ? Marvin's Room*.

**MITCHELL, BRIAN**. Born October 31, 1957 in Seattle, WA. Bdwy debut 198? *Mail* for which he received a Theatre World Award, followed by *Oh Kay!*

**MITCHELL, GREGORY**. Born December 9, 1951 in Brooklyn, NY. Gradu Juilliard. Principle with Eliot Feld Ballet before Bdwy debut 1983 in *Merlin*, follo by *Song and Dance, Phantom of the Opera, Dangerous Games, Aspects of Love, N of La Mancha* (1992), OB in *One More Song One More Dance, Tango Apasionado*.

**MITCHELL, JOHN CAMERON**. Born April 21, 1963 in El Paso, TX. Atten Northwestern U. Bdwy debut 1985 in *Big River*, followed by *Six Degrees? Separation, The Secret Garden*, OB in *Six Degrees of Separation*.

**MIXON, CHRISTOPHER**. Born in Orlando, FL. Graduate Warren Wilson C Rutgers U. Debut 1991 OB in *Candida*, followed by *Iron Bars*.

**MONTEVECCHI, LILIANE**. Born October 12, 1933 in Paris, France. W Rowland Petit's Ballet, and Folies Bergère before her Bdwy debut in *Nine* (19? followed by *Grand Hotel*, OB in her one-woman show *On the Boulevard*.

**MOONEY, DEBRA**. Born in Aberdeen SD. Graduate Auburn, U. Mn. Debut 1 OB in *Battle of Angels*, followed by *The Farm, Summer and Smoke, Stargaz? Childe Byron, Wonderland, A Think Piece, What I Did Last Summer, The Din Room, The Perfect Party, Another Antigone*, Bdwy in *Chapter 2* (1978), *Talle Folly, The Odd Couple* (1985), *The Price*.

**MOOR, BILL**. Born July 13, 1931 in Toledo, OH. Attended Northwestern, Deni U. Bdwy debut 1964 in *Blues for Mr. Charlie*, followed by *Great God Brown, L Juan, The Visit, Chemin de Fer, Holiday, P.S. Your Cat is Dead, Night of the Tribac Water Engine, Plenty, Heartbreak House, The Iceman Cometh, Two Shakespear Actors*, OB in *Dandy Dick, Love Nest, Days and Nights of Beebee Fenstermaker, Collection, The Owl Answers, Long Christmas Dinner, Fortune and Men's Eyes, K Lear, Cry of Players, Boys in the Band, Alive and Well in Argentina, Rosmersho The Biko Inquest, A Winter's Tale, Johnny on a Spot, Barbarians, The Purgi Potsdam Quartet, Zones of the Spirit, The Marriage of Bette and Boo, Tempat? Devil's Disciple, Happy Days*.

**MOORE, CRISTA**. Born September 17 in Washington, DC. Attended Am. Ba Th. Schl. Debut 1987 OB in *Birds of Paridise, Rags*, followed by Bdwy in *Gy (1989)* for which she received a Theatre World Award, *110 in the Shade* (LC/NYC C

**MOORE, DANA**. Born in Sewickley, PA. Bdwy debut 1982 in *Sugar Bab* followed by *Dancin', Copperfield, On Your Toes, Singin' in the Rain, Sweet Char Dangerous Games, A Chorus Line, The Will Rogers Follies*.

**MOORE, MAUREEN**. Born August 12, 1951 in Wallingford, CT. Bdwy debut 1 in *Gypsy*, followed by *The Moonie Shapiro Songbook, Do Black Patent Leather Sh Really Reflect Up?, Amadeus, Big River, I Love My Wife, Song and Dance, A Misérables, Amadeus, Jerome Robbins' Broadway, A Little Night Music* (NYC Falsettos, OB in *Godspell, Unsung Cole, By Strouse*.

**MORALES, ESAI**. Born in 1963 in Brooklyn. Graduate HS of Performing A Bdwy debut 1992 in *Salome*, OB in *El Hermano, The Tempest, Short Eyes*.

**MORAN, DANIEL**. Born July 31, 1953 in Corcoran, CA. Graduate NYU. De 1980 OB in *True West*, followed by *The Vampires, Tongues and Savage Love, Life a Dream, The Filthy Rich, The Return of Pinocchio, Merchant of Venice, Festival o Act Comedies, Pericles*.

**MORATH, KATHRYN** (Kathy). Born March 23, 1955 in Colorado Springs, C Graduate Brown U. Debut 1980 OB in *The Fantasticks*, followed by *Dulcy, Snapsh Alice in Concert, A Little Night Music, The Little Prince, Professionally Speaking, ? Apple Tree, Prom Queens Unchained*, Bdwy in *Pirates of Penzance* (1982), *Nick a Nora*.

**MORFOGEN, GEORGE**. Born March 30, 1933 in New York City. Graduate Bro U., Yale. Debut 1957 OB in *The Trial of D. Karamazov*, followed by *Christm Oratorio, Othello, Good Soldier Schweik, Cave Dwellers, Once in a Lifetime, T Eclipse, Ice Age, Prince of Homburg, Biography: A Game, Mrs. Warren's Professi Principia Scriptoriae, Tamara, Maggie and Misha, The Country Girl, Othello, Bd in *The Fun Couple* (1962), *Kingdoms, Arms and the Man*.

**MORIN, MICHAEL**. Born August 4, 1950 in Vineland, NJ. Graduate Vilanova Debut 1976 OB in *Rio Grande* followed by *La Ronde, Album, The Guitrtton, Gene El Grande de Coca-Cola, Creeps, Trelawny of The Wells*.

**MORSE, PETER G**. Born October 9, 1958 in Hanover, NH. Graduate Dartmo Col., U. Cal/San Diego. Debut 1983 OB in *That's It, Folks*, followed by *The Weeke The Merchant of Venice, The Racket, The Foundation, A Woman without a Name*.

**MORSE, ROBIN**. Born July 8, 1963 in New York City. Bdwy debut 1981 in *Br Back Birdie*, followed by *Brighton Beach Memoirs, Six Degrees of Separation*, OB Green Fields, December7th, Class I Acts, Eleemosynary, One Act Festival, Degrees of Separation*.

**MOSS, KATHI**. Born October 22, 1945 in Dallas, TX. Graduate Barat Col, U. Orleans. Debut 1972 OB in *Grease*, followed by *Country Cabaret, Hot Grog, Jack Ripper Revue, The Perils of Pericles, Dr. Selavy's Magic Theatre, Walk on the W Side*, Bdwy in *Grease* (1972), *Nine, Grand Hotel*.

**UENZ, RICHARD.** Born in 1948 in Hartford, CT. Attended Eastern Baptist Col. Bdwy debut 1976 in *1600 Pennsylvania Avenue*, followed by *The Most Happy Fella*, *Camelot*, *Rosalie in Concert*, *Chess*, *The Pajama Game* (LC), *Nick and Nora*, *110 in the Shade* (LC).

**ULLINS, MELINDA.** Born April 20, 1958 in Clanton, AL. Graduate Mt. Holyoke Col. Juilliard. Bdwy debut 1987 in *Sherlock's Last Case*, followed by *Serious Money*, *Mastergate*, OB in *Macbeth*, *The Hideaway Hilton*.

**URPHY, DONNA.** Born March 7, 1959 in Corona, NY. Attended NYU. Bdwy debut 1979 in *They're Playing Our Song*, followed by *The Human Comedy*, *The Mystery of Edwin Drood*, OB in *Francis*, *Portable Pioneer and Prairie Show*, *Little Shop of Horrors*, *A ... My Name is Alice*, *Showing Off*, *Privates on Parade*, *Song of Singapore*.

**URRAY, BRIAN.** Born October 9, 1939 in Johannesburg, SA. Debut 1964 OB in *The Knack* followed by *King Lear*, *Ashes*, *The Jail Diary of Albie Sachs*, *A Winter's Tale*, *Barbarians*, *The Purging*, *A Midsummer Night's Dream*, *The Recruiting Officer*, *The Arcata Promise*, *Candide in Concert*, *Much Ado about Nothing*, *Hamlet*, Bdwy in *All in Good Time* (1965), *Rosencrantz and Guildenstern Are Dead*, *Sleuth*, *Da*, *Noises Off*, *A Small Family Business*.

**URTAUGH, JAMES.** Born October 28, 1942 in Chicago, IL. Debut OB in *The Firebugs* followed by *Highest Standard of Living*, *Marathon '87*, *Other People's Money*, *Marathon '88*, Bdwy in *Two Shakespearean Actors* (1991).

**YDELL, JOSEPH.** Born June 30, 1945 in Savannah, GA. Graduate NYU. Debut 1969 OB in *The Ofay Watcher*, followed by *Volpone*, *Henry IV*, *Please Don't Cry and Say No*, *Love's Labour's Lost*, *Lyrics of the Hearthside*.

**AGY, KEN.** Born December 7, 1963 in Bucks County, PA. Bdwy debut 1992 in *The Most Happy Fella*.

**AUGHTON, JAMES.** Born December 6, 1945 in Middletown, CT. Graduate Brown U., Yale. Debut 1971 OB in *Long Day's Journey into Night* for which he received a Theatre World Award, followed by *Drinks before Dinner*, *Losing Time*, Bdwy in *I Love My Wife*, *Whose Life Is It Anyway?*, *City of Angels*, *Four Baboons Adoring the Sun*.

**EIDEN, DANIEL.** Born July 9, 1958 in Lincoln, NE. Graduate Drake U. Debut 1980 in *City of Life* followed by *Ratman and Wilbur*, *Nuclear Follies*, *Pearls*, *Sophie*, *The Witch*, *Groundhog*, *Job: A Circus*.

**EIPRIS, DAVID.** Born July 21, 1969 in Brookline, MA. Gradate NYU. Bdwy debut 1991 in *Lost in Yonkers*, OB in *The Mud Angel*, *Prometheus Bound*, *Endgame*.

**ELSON, MARI.** Born July 27, 1963 in Tacoma, WA. Graduate U. Washington, Juilliard. Debut 1989 OB in *Up Against It*, followed by *Twelfth Night*, Bdwy in *Six Degrees of Separation* (1990).

**ELSON, MARK.** Born September 26, 1955 in Hackensack, NJ. Graduate Princeton U. Debut 1977 OB in *The Dybbuk*, followed by *Green Fields*, *The Keymaker*, *The Common Pursuit*, *Flaubert's Latest*, Bdwy in *Amadeus* (1981), *Brighton Beach Memoirs*, *Biloxi Blues*, *Broadway Bound*, *Rumors*, *A Few Good Men*.

**EUBERGER, JAN.** Born January 21, 1953 in Amityville, NY. Attended NYU. Bdwy debut 1975 in *Gypsy*, followed by *A Change in the Heir*, OB in *Silk Stockings*, *Chase a Rainbow*, *Anything Goes*, *A Little Madness*, *Forbidden Broadway*, *After These Messages*, *Ad Hock*, *Rags*.

**EWLON, KATHERINE.** Born February 27, 1960 in Knoxville, TN. Graduate U. Tenn., Rutgers U. Debut 1985 OB in *The Lesson* followed by *The Vagabond King*, *Company*.

**EWTON, JOHN.** Born November 2, 1925 in Grand Junction, CO. Graduate U. Washington. Debut 1951 OB in *Othello*, followed by *As You Like It*, *Candida*, *Candaules Commissioner*, *Sextet*, LCRep's *The Crucible* and *A Streetcar Named Desire*, *The Rivals*, *The Subject Was Roses*, *The Brass Ring*, *Hadrian VII*, *The Best Little Whorehouse in Texas*, *A Midsummer Night's Dream*, *Night Games*, *A Frog in His Throat*, *Max and Maxie*, *The Lark*, *Measure for Measure*, Bdwy in *Weekend*, *First Monday in October*, *Present Laughter*, *Hamlet* (1992).

**NICHOLAW, CASEY.** Born October 6, 1992. Attended UCLA. Debut 1986 in *The Pajama Game*, Bdwy in *Crazy for You* (1992).

**IVEN, KIP.** Born May 27, 1945 in Kansas City, MO. Graduate Kan. U. Debut 1987 OB in *Company*, followed by *The Golden Apple*, *Two by Two*, Bdwy in *Chess* (1988).

**IXON, CYNTHIA.** Born April 9, 1966 in New York City. Debut 1980 in *The Philadelphia Story* (LC) for which she received a Theatre World Award, OB in *Lydie Breeze*, *Hurlyburly*, *Sally's Gone She Left Her Name*, *Lemon Sky*, *Cleveland and Half-Way Back*, *Alterations*, *Young Playwrights*, *Moonchildren*, *Romeo and Juliet*, *The Cherry Orchard*, *The Balcony Scene*, *Servy-n-Bernice 4Ever*, Bdwy in *The Real Thing* (1983), *Hurlyburly*, *The Heidi Chronicles*.

**IXON, MARNI.** Born February 22 in Altadena, CA. Attended LACC, U.S. Cal, Pasadena Playhouse. Bdwy debut 1952 in *The Girl in Pink Tights* followed by *My Fair Lady* (1964), OB in *Thank Heaven for Lerner and Loewe*, *Taking My Turn*, *Opal*.

**OAH, JAMES.** Born March 1, 1935 in Perry, IO. Graduate U. Denver, U. Mn. Bdwy debut 1990 in *The Grapes of Wrath* followed by *On Borrowed Time*, OB in *Casanova*.

**OLEN, TIMOTHY.** Born July 9, 1941 in Rotan, TX. Graduate Trenton State, Col., Manhattan School of Music. Debut in *Sweeney Todd* (1984) with NYC Opera. Bdwy in *Grind* (1985) followed by *Phantom of the Opera*.

**NORMAN, JOHN.** Born May 13, 1961 in Detroit, MI. Graduate Cinn. Consv. Bdwy debut 1987 in *Les Misérables*.

**'HARE, MICHAEL.** Born May 6, 1952 in Chicago, IL. Debut 1978 OB in *Galileo*, followed by *Shades of Brown*, *Farther West*, Bdwy in *Players* (1978), *Man and Superman*, *A Few Good Men*, *The Crucible*.

**O'KEEFE, MICHAEL.** Born April 24, 1955 in Larchmont, NY. Attended NYU. Debut 1974 OB in *The Killdeer* followed by *Christmas on Mars*, *Short Eyes*, *Uncle Vanya*, Bdwy in *5th of July*, *Mass Appeal* for which he received a 1982 Theatre World Award.

**O'KEEFE, PAUL C.** Born April 27, 1951 in Boston, MA. Graduate Columbia U. Bdwy debut 1958 in *The Music Man* followed by *Sail Away*, *Oliver!*, *A Texas Trilogy*, OB in *Passing Game*, *The Baker's Wife*, *Job: A Circus*.

**O'LEARY, THOMAS JAMES.** Born June 21, 1956 in Windsor Locks, CT. Graduate U. Conn. Bdwy debut 1991 in *Miss Saigon*.

**O'MARA, MOLLIE.** Born September 5, 1960 in Pittsburgh, PA. Attended Catholic U. Debut 1989 OB in *Rodents and Radios*, followed by *Crowbar*, *Famine Plays*, *Homo Sapien Shuffle*.

**O'REILLY, CIARAN.** Born March 13, 1959 in Ireland. Attended Carmelite Col., Juilliard. Debut 1978 OB in *Playboy of the Western World*, followed by *Summer*, *Freedom of the City*, *Fannie*, *The Interrogation of Ambrose Fogarty*, *King Lear*, *Shadow of a Gunman*, *The Marry Month of May*, *I Do Not Like Thee Dr. Fell*, *The Plough and the Stars*, *Yeats: A Celebration!*, *Philadelphia Here I Come!*, *Playboy of the Western World*, *Making History*, *Grandchild of Kings*.

**O'STEEN, MICHELLE.** Born May 7, 1964 in Pittsburgh, PA. Bdwy debut 1986 in *Sweet Charity*, followed OB in *Little Me*, *After the Dancing in Jericho*.

**O'SULLIVAN, ANNE.** Born February 6, 1952 in Limerick City, Ire. Debut 1977 OB in *Kid Champion*, followed by *Hello Out There*, *Fly Away Home*, *The Drunkard*, *Dennis*, *Three Sisters*, *Another Paradise*, *Living Quarters*, *Welcome to the Noon*, *The Dreamer Examines His Pillow*, *Mama Drama*, *Free Fall*, *The Magic Act*, *The Plough and the Stars*, *Marathon '88*, *Bobo's Guns*, *Marathon '90*, *Festival of I Acts*, *Marathon '91*, *A Murder of Crows*.

**OBERLANDER, MICHAEL.** Born August 25, 1960 in Newark, NJ. Graduate Carnegie-Melon U. Debut 1985 OB in *The Crows* followed by *The Misanthrope*, *Dracula*, *Georgy*, *Paradise Re-Lost*, *Promised Land*, *Family Obligations*.

**OLIENSIS, ADAM.** Born March 22, 1960 in Passaic, NJ. Graduate U. Wis. Debut 1985 OB in *Inside-Out* followed by *Little Blood Brother*, *Macbeth*.

**OSBURN, ALAN.** Born November 18, 1956 in Tulsa, OK. Graduate Grand Canyon Col., U. Houston. Debut 1988 OB in *Side by Side by Sondheim* followed by *The Wonder Years*, *Company*.

**OVERBEY, KELLIE.** Born November 21, 1964 in Cincinnati, OH. Graduate Northwestern U. Debut 1988 OB in *The Debutante Ball*, followed by *The Second Coming*, *Face Divided*.

**OWENS, GORDON.** Born February 23, 1959 in Washington, DC. Attended UNC. Schl of Arts. Bdwy debut 1984 in *Dreamgirls*, followed by *A Chorus Line*, *Starlight Express*, *Miss Saigon*.

**PACINO, AL.** Born April 25, 1940 in NYC. Attended Actors Studio. Bdwy debut 1969 in *Does a Tiger Wear a Necktie?* for which he received a Theatre World Award, followed by *The Basic Training of Pavlo Hummel*, *Richard III*, *American Buffalo*, *Salome*, *Chinese Coffee*, OB in *Why Is a Crooked Letter?*, *Peace Creeps*, *The Indian Wants the Bronx*, *Local Stigmatic*, *Camino Real*, *Jungle of Cities*, *American Buffalo*, *Julius Caesar*.

**PANARO, HUGH.** Born February 19, 1964 in Philadelphia, PA. Graduate Temple U. Debut 1985 OB in *What's a Nice Country Like you Doing in a State Like This*, followed by *I Have Found Home*, *Juba*, *Splendora*, Bdwy in *Phantom of the Opera* (1990).

**PANKOW, JOHN.** Born 1955 in St. Louis, MO. Attended St. Nichols Sch. of Arts. Debut 1980 OB in *Merton of the Movies* followed by *Slab Boys*, *Forty Deuce*, *Hunting Scenes from Lower Bavaria*, *Cloud 9*, *Jazz Poets at the Grotto*, *Henry V*, *North Shore Fish*, *Two Gentlemen of Verona*, *Italian American Reconciliation Aristocrats*, *Ice Cream with Hot Fudge*, *EST Marathon '92*, Bdwy in *Amadeus* (1981), *The Iceman Cometh*, *Serious Money*.

**PARKER, MARY-LOUISE.** Born August 2, 1964 in Ft. Jackson, SC. Graduate NC Schl. of Arts. Debut 1989 OB in *The Art of Success*, followed by *Prelude to a Kiss*, *Babylon Gardens*, *EST Marathon '92*, Bdwy in *Prelude to a Kiss* for which she received a 1990 Theatre World Award.

**PARKER, SARAH JESSICA.** Born March 25, 1965. Bdwy debut 1978 in *Annie*, OB in *The Innocents*, *One-Act Festival*, *To Gillian on Her 37th Birthday*, *Broadway Scandals of 1928*, *The Heidi Chronicles*, *Substance of Fire*.

**PARKS, KATHERINE.** Born May 11, 1946 in Louisville, KY. Graduate Stephens Col., U. Mo. Debut 1978 OB in *Old Man Joseph and his Family* followed by *Moliere in spite of Himself*, *Feelers*, *The Mask*.

**PASEKOFF, MARILYN.** Born November 7, 1949 in Pittsburgh, PA. Graduate Boston U. Debut 1975 OB in *Godspell*, followed by *Maybe I'm Doing It Wrong*, *Professionally Speaking*, *Forbidden Broadway*, *Showing Off*, *Forbidden Broadway 1990*, *Forbidden Broadway 1991_*, *Shmulnik's Waltz*, Bdwy in *Godspell* (1976), *The Odd Couple* (1985)

**PASQUALONE, RICK.** Born March 30, 1966 in Queens/NYC. Graduate Boston Col. Debut 1990 OB in *Tony 'n' Tina's Wedding*.

**PATINKIN, MANDY.** Born November 30, 1952 in Chicago, IL. Attended Juilliard. OB in *Henry IV*, followed by *Leave It to Beaver Is Dead*, *Rebel Women*, *Hamlet*, *Trelawny of the Wells*, *Savages*, *The Split*, *The Knife*, *Winter's Tale*, Bdwy in *The Shadow Box*, *Evita*, *Sunday in the Park with George*, *Mandy Patinkin in Concert*, *The Secret Garden*.

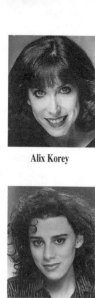

Alix Korey

Richard Kinsey

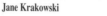

Jane Krakowski

Ken Kliban

Dale Kristien

Oscar Koch

Judy Kuhn

Philip Kong

Deborah LaCoy

Bruce Kuhn

Jeanette Landis

Robert Lambert

Jill Larson

Stephen Lang

Sandra Laub

Kevin Ligon

Lisa Ann Li

Michael Maguire

Lucy Martin

Joseph Mahowald

Carolyn McCormick

Stephen Mailer

Robin Morse

Peter Marinos

Mari Nelson

Rick Pasqualone

Kellie Overbey

Stephen Pearlman

Susan Pellegrino

Chris Peterson

224

**ATTON, LUCILLE.** Born in New York City. Attended Neighborhood Playhouse. .dwy debut 1946 in *Winter's Tale*, followed by *Topaze, Arms and the Man, Joy to the orld, All You Need is One Good Break, Fifth Season, Heavenly Twins, Rhinoceros, arathon 33, The Last Analysis, Dinner at 8, La Strada, Unlikely Heroes, Love uicide at Schofield Barracks, The Crucible, A Little Hotel on the Side*, OB in *Ulysses Nighttown, Failures, Three Sisters, Yes Yes No No, Tango, Mme. de Sade, Apple ie, Follies, Yesterday is Over, My Prince My King, I Am Who I Am, Double Game, ove in a Village, 1984, A Little Night Music, Cheri, Till the Eagle Hollers, Money alks, EST Marathon '92.*

**AUL, GUY.** Born September 12, 1949 in Milwaukee, WI. Attended U. Minn. Debut 984 OB in *Flight of the Earls*, followed by *Frankenstein, The Underpants, Oresteia, ver Afters, Oh Baby Oh Baby, Of Blessed Memory, Candida*, Bdwy in *Arms and the an* (1985), *Wild Honey, Rumors, Private Lives.*

**AWK, MICHELE.** Born November 16, 1961 in Pittsburgh, PA. Graduate incinnati Cons. Bdwy debut 1988 in *Mail* followed by *Crazy for You.*

**AYAN, ILKA TANYA.** Born January 7, 1943 in Santo Domingo, DR. Attended :oples Col. of Law. Debut 1969 OB in *The Respectful Prostitute* followed by rancesco Cenci, The Effect of Gamma Rays..., Blood Wedding, Miss Margarida's ay, The Bitter Tears of Petra von Kant, The Servant, Parting Gestures, Our Lady of e Tortilla.*

**EARLMAN, STEPHEN.** Born February 26, 1935 in New York City. Graduate artmouth Col. Bdwy debut 1964 in *Barefoot in the Park*, followed by *La Strada, Six egrees of Separation*, OB in *Threepenny Opera, Time of the Key, Pimpernel, In 'hite America, Viet Rock, Chocolates, Bloomers, Richie, Isn't It Romantic, 'oodletters, Light Up the Sky, Perfect Party, Come Blow Your Horn, A Shayna adel, Value of Names, Hyde in Hollywood, Six Degrees of Separation.*

**EDERSEN, MATTHEW.** Born March 28, 1966 in Austin, TX. Bdwy debut 1990 A Chorus Line*, followed by *Miss Saigon.*

**ELLEGRINO, SUSAN.** Born June 3, 1950 in Baltimore, Md. Attended CC anFrancisco, Cal. State U. Debut 1982 OB in *The Wisteria Trees*, followed by *Steel 1 Steel, The Master Builder, Equal Wrights, Come as You Are, Painting Churches, arvin's Room.*

**EN, POLLY.** Born March 11, 1954 in Chicago, IL. Graduate Ithaca Col. Debut 978 OB in *The Taming of the Shrew* followed by *The Guilded Cage, Charlotte Sweet, ..My Name Is Alice, Once on a Summer's Day, Don Juan and the Non Don Juan*, .dwy in *The Utter Glory of Morrissey Hall.*

**ENA, ELIZABETH.** Born September 23, 1959 in New Jersey. Debut 1969 OB in *inderella* followed by *Rice and Beans, Shattered Image, La Morena, Romeo and diet, Night of the Assassins, Act One and Only, The Cuban Swimmer, Blood 'edding.*

**ENDLETON, AUSTIN.** Born March 27, 1940 in Warren, OH. Debut 1962 OB in *h Dad Poor Dad...*, followed by *The Last Sweet Days of Isaac, Three Sisters, Say 'oodnight Gracie, Office Murders, Up from Paradise, The Overcoat, Two Character lay, Master Class, Educating Rita, Uncle Vanya, Serious Company, Philotetes, 'amlet, Richard III, What about Luv?, The Sorrows of Frederick*, Bdwy in *Fiddler on e Roof, Hail Scrawdyke, Little Foxes, American Millionaire, The Runner Stumbles, 'oubles.*

**ENNINGTON, GAIL.** Born October 2, 1957 in Kansas City, MO. Graduate SMU. .dwy debut 1980 in *The Music Man* followed by *Can-Can, America, Little Me* (1982), 2nd Street, The Most Happy Fella*, OB in *The Baker's Wife.*

**EPE, NEIL.** Born June 23, 1963 in Bloomington, IN. Graduate Kenyon Col. Debut 988 OB in *Boys' Life* followed by *Three Sisters, Virgin Molly, Return to Sender, Five ery Live.*

**EREZ, LAZARO.** Born December 12, 1945 in Havana, Cuba. Bdwy debut 1969 in 'oes A Tiger Wear a Necktie?*, followed by *Animals, A Streetcar Named Desire 992)*, OB in *Romeo and Juliet, 12 Angry Men, Wonderful Years, Alive, G.R. Point, rimary English Class, Man and the Fly, Last Latin Lover, Cabal of Hypocrites, Balm Gilead, Enrico IV.*

**EREZ, LUIS.** Born July 28, 1959 in Atlanta, GA. With Jeffrey Ballet before 1986 .dwy debut in *Brigadoon* followed by *Phantom of the Opera, Jerome Robbin's roadway, Dangerous Games, Grand Hotel, Man of La Mancha* (1992), OB in *The 'onderful Ice Cream Suit, Tango Apassionado.*

**ERKINS, CAROL.** Born December 29, 1957 in Sarasota, FL. Bdwy debut 1991 *enn & Teller Refrigerator Tour*, OB in *Penn & Teller Rot in Hell.*

**ERLMAN, RON.** Born April 13, 1950 in NYC. Graduate Lehman Col., U. Minn. .ebut 1976 OB in *The Architect and the Emperor of Assyria*, followed by *Tartuffe, :hool for Buffoons, Measure for Measure, Hedda Gabler*, Bdwy in *Teibele and Her .emon* (1979), *A Few Good Men.*

**ERRY, JOHN BENNETT.** Born January 4, 1941 in Williamston, MA. Graduate :. Lawrence U. Debut 1967 OB in *Is Now the Time for All Good Men* followed by *A Ionth of Sundays, Ballad of Johnny Pot, The Baby Dance*, Bdwy in *Mother Earth.*

**ERRY, KEITH.** Born October 29, 1931 in Des Moines, Iowa. Graduate Rice U. .dwy debut 1965 in *Pickwick*, followed by *I'm Solomon, Copperfield, City of Angels*, 'B in *Epicene, the Silent Woman, Hope and Feathers, Ten Little Indians.*

**ERRY, LYNETTE.** Born September 29, 1963 in Bowling Green, OH. Graduate inn. Consv. Debut 1987 OB in *The Chosen*, followed by *Lucy's Lapses*, Bdwy in 'rand Hotel* (1989).

**ETERS, MARK.** Born November 20, 1952 in Council Bluffs, IA. Yale graduate. .ebut 1977 OB in *The Crazy Locomotive* followed by *The Legend of Sleepy Hollow, ismet, The Awakening of Spring.*

**ETERSON, CHRIS.** Born November 19, 1962 in Malden, MA. Bdwy debut 1983 On Your Toes*, followed by *Crazy for You.*

**ETTIT, DODIE.** Born December 29, in Princeton, NJ. Attended Westminster Choir

Col. Bdwy debut 1984 in *Cats*, followed by *The Phantom of the Opera.*

**PEVSNER, DAVID.** Born December 31, 1958 in Skokie, IL. Graduate Carnegie-Mellon U. Debut 1985 OB in *A Flash of Lightning*, followed by *Rags*, Bdwy in *Fiddler on the Roof* (1990).

**PHILLIPS, ARTE.** Born February 13, 1959 in Astoria, Queens, NYC. Attended Baruch Col. Bdwy debut 1990 in *Grand Hotel.*

**PHILLIPS, BARY.** Born November 29, 1954 in Indianapolis, In. Graduate Ind. U. Debut 1981 OB in *Raisin* followed by *While We're Young, Cries and Whispers, Casanova, The 15th Ward.*

**PHILLIPS, ETHAN.** Born February 8, 1950 in Rockville Center, NY. Graduate Boston U. Cornell U. Debut 1979 OB in *Modigliani*, followed by *Eccentricities of a Nightingale, Nature and Purpose of the Universe, The Beasts, Dumb Waiter, The Indian Wants the Bronx, Last of the Red Hot Lovers, Only Kidding, Almost Perfect, Theme and Variations, Marathon '91, Lips Together Teeth Apart, Young Playwrights Festival.*

**PHILLIPS, GARRISON.** Born Oct. 8, 1929 in Tallahasee, FL. Graduated U. W.Va. Debut 1956 OB in *Eastward in Eden* followed by *Romeo and Juliet, Time of the Cuckoo, Triptych, After the Fall, Two Gentlemen of Verona, Ambrosio, The Sorrows of Frederick, La Ronde*, Bdwy in *Clothes for a Summer Hotel* (1980).

**PHILLIPS, KRIS.** Born in China on December 24, 1960. Attended Stanford U. Neighborhood Playhouse. Bdwy debut 1991 in *Miss Saigon*, followed by *Nick & Nora.*

**PIEHL, MICHAEL.** Born June 25, 1967 in Seattle, Wa. Bdwy debut 1991 in *Grand Hotel.*

**PINKINS, TONYA.** Born May 30, 1962 in Chicago Il. Attended Carnegie-Mellon U. Bdwy debut 1981 in *Merrily We Roll Along*, followed by *Jelly's Last Jam*, OB in *Five Points, A Winter's Tale, An Ounce of Prevention, Just Say No, Mexican Hayride, Young Playwrights '90, Approximating Mother.*

**PIONTEK, MICHAEL E..** Born July 31, 1956 in Canoga Park, CA. Graduate FSU. Bdwy debut 1987 in *Into the Woods*, followed by *3 Penny Opera, Grand Hotel*, OB in *Reckless, Florida Crackers.*

**PIRO, JACQUELYN.** Born January 8, 1965 in Boston, MA. Graduate Boston U. Debut 1987 OB in *Company*, followed by Bdwy in *Les Misérables* (1990).

**PITONIAK, ANNE.** Born March 30, 1922 in Westfield, MA. Attended UNC Women's Col. Debut 1982 OB in *Talking With*, followed by *Young Playwrights Festival, Phaedra, Steel Magnolias, Pygmalion, The Rose Quartet*, Bdwy in *Night, Mother* (1983) for which she received a Theatre World Award, *The Octette Bridge Club.*

**PITTU, DAVID.** Born April 4, 1967 in Fairfield, CT. Graduate NYU. Debut 1987 OB in *Film Is Evil: Radio Is Good* followed by *Five Very Live*, Bdwy in *The Tenth Man* (LC/89).

**PLAYTEN, ALICE.** Born August 28, 1947 in New York City. Bdwy debut 1960 in *Gypsy*, followed by *Oliver!, Hello Dolly!, Henry Sweet Henry* for which she received a Theatre World Award, *George M.!, Spoils of War, Rumors*, OB in *Promenade, The Last Sweet Days of Isaac, National Lampoon's Lemmings, Valentine's Day, Pirates of Penzance, Up from Paradise, A Visit, Sister Mary Ignatius Explains It All, An Actor's Nightmare, That's It Folks, 1-2-3-4-5, Spoils of War, Marathon '90.*

**PLUNKETT, MARYANN.** Born in 1953 in Lowell, MA. Attended U. NH. Bdwy debut 1983 in *Agnes of God* followed by *Sunday in the Park with George, Me and My Girl, The Crucible, The Master Builder, A Little Hotel on the Side*, OB in *Aristocrats.*

**POE, RICHARD.** Born January 25, 1946 in Portola, CA. Graduate U. San Francisco, U. Cal./Davis Debut 1971 OB in *Hamlet*, followed by *Seasons Greetings, Twelfth Night, Naked Rights, Approximating Mother*, Bdwy in *Broadway* (1987), *M. Butterfly, Our Country's Good.*

**POGGI, JACK.** Born June 14, 1928 in Oakland, CA. Graduate Harvard, Columbia U. Debut 1962 OB in *This Side of Paradise* followed by *The Tavern, Dear Janet Rosenberg, House Music, The Closed Door, Ghosts, Uncle Vanya, Tiger at the Gates, Wars of Roses, The Pajama Game, Two by Horton Foote.*

**POLEY, ROBIN.** Born in NYC. Graduate Oberlin Col. Debut 1988 OB in *Crystal Clear* followed by *Love's Labour's Lost, Marie and Bruce, Trelawny of the Wells.*

**POLIS, JOEL.** Born October 3, 1951 in Philadelphia, PA. Graduate USC, Yale. Debut 1976 OB in *Marco Polo* followed by *Family Business, Just Like the Night, Claptrap, The Baby Dance.*

**PONAZECKI, JOE.** Born January 7, 1934 in Rochester, NY. Attended Rochester U., Columbia U. Bdwy debut 1959 in *Much Ado about Nothing*, followed by *Send Me No Flowers, A Call on Kuprin, Take Her She's Mine, Fiddler on the Roof, Xmas in Las Vegas, 3 bags Full, Love in E. Flat, 90 Day Mistress, Harvey, Trial of the Catonsville 9, The Country Girl, Freedom of the City, Summer Brave, Music Is, The Little Foxes, Prelude to a Kiss*, OB in *The Dragon, Muzeeka, Witness, All is Bright, The Dog Ran Away, Dream of a Blacklisted Actor, Innocent Pleasures, The Dark at the Top of the Stairs, 36, After the Revolution, The Raspberry Picker, A Raisin in the Sun, Light Up the Sky, Marathon '80, OneAct Festival, EST Marathon '92.*

**POPE, STEPHANIE.** Born April 8, 1964 in NYC. Debut 1983 OB in *The Buck Stops Here* followed by *Shades of Harlem*, Bdwy in *Big Deal* (1986), *Jelly's Last Jam.*

**PORAC, MATTHEW.** Born March 10, 1981 in Hagerstown, MD. Bdwy debut 1991 in *On Borrowed Time.*

**PORTER, W. ELLIS.** Graduate Carnegie-Mellon U. Debut 1989 OB in *Romance in Hard Times*, Bdwy in *Miss Saigon* (1991), followed by *5 Guys Named Moe.*

**POTTER, DON.** Born August 15, 1932 in Philadelphia, PA. Debut 1961 OB in *What a Killing*, followed by *Sunset, You're a Good Man Charlie Brown, One Cent Plain, The Ritz*, Bdwy in *Gypsy* (1974), *Snow White, Moose Murders, 42nd Street, Peter Pan.*

**POWELL, JILL.** Born October 12, 1965 in Jacksonville, FL. Debut 1988 in *The Music Man* (LC), Bdwy in *Grand Hotel* (1991).

**POWELL, MICHAEL WARREN**. Born January 22, 1937 in Martinsville, VA. Attended Goodman Theatre Schl. Debut 1954 OB in *Home Free!*, followed by *This is the Rill Speaking, Balm in Gilead, The Gingham Dog, Thank You Miss Victoria, Futz, Tom Paine, Amulets Against the Dragon Force, Dirty Talk, On the Wing, The Weather Outside, Prelude to a Kiss.*

**PRENTICE, AMELIA**. Born September 14 in Toronto, Can. Graduate AADA, LAMDA, Bdwy debut 1987 in *Starlight Express*, OB in *Hooray for Hollywood, Lenny Bruce Revue, Broadway Jukebox, Little Me.*

**PRESTON, CORLISS**. Born February 3 in East Chicago, IND. Graduate Ind. U., Bristol Old Vic. Debut 1988 OB in *Hired Man*, followed by *The Cherry Orchard, Alive by Night, A Piece of My Heart.*

**PRESTON, WILLIAM**. Born August 26, 1921 in Columbia, PA. Graduate Penn State U. Debut 1972 OB in *We Bombed in New Haven*, followed by *Hedda Gabler, Whisper into My Good Ear, A Nestless Bird, Friends of Mine, Iphegenia in Aulis, Midsummer, The Fantasticks, Frozen Assets, The Golem, The Taming of the Shrew, His Master's Voice, Much Ado About Nothing, Hamlet, Winter Dreams, Palpitations, Rumor of Glory, Killers, Not Partners, Rumor of Glory*, Bdwy in *Our Town.*

**PRINCE, FAITH**. Born August 5, 1957 in Augusta, GA. Graduate U. Cinn. Debut OB 1981 in *Scrambled Feet*, followed by *Olympus on My Mind, Groucho, Living Color, Bad Habits, Falsettoland*, Bdwy in *Jerome Robbins Broadway* (1989), *Nick & Nora, Guys and Dolls* (1992).

**PRINCE, GINGER**. Born June 3, 1945 in Stuart, Fl. Attended Stephens Col Debut 1987 OB in *Steel Magnolias*, followed by *After the Dancing in Jericho*, Bdwy in *Gypsy* (1989/91).

**PUGH, RICHARD WARREN**. Born October 20, 1950 in New York City. Graduate Tarkio Col. Bdwy debut 1979 in *Sweeney Todd*, followed by *The Music Man, The Five O'Clock Girl, Copperfield, Zorba* (1983), *Phantom of the Opera*, OB in *Chase a Rainbow.*

**QUINN, PATRICK**. Born February 12, 1950 in Philadelphia, PA. Graduate Temple U. Bdwy Debut 1976 in *Fiddler on the Roof* followed by *A Day in Hollywood/A Night in the Ukraine, Oh, Coward!, Lend Me a Tenor*, OB in *It's Better with a Band, By Strouse, Forbidden Broadway, The Best of Forbidden Broadway,Raft of Medusa, Forbidden Broadway's 10th Anniversary.*

**RAIDER-WEXLER, VICTOR**. Born December 31, 1943 in Toledo, OH. Attended U. Toledo. Debut 1976 OB in *The Prince of Homburg*, followed by *The Passion of Dracula, Ivanov, Brandy Before Breakfast, The Country Girl, Dream of a Blacklisted Actor, One Act Festival, Loveplay, Our Own Family, Candide, Macbeth*, Bdwy in *Best Friend* (1976), *Ma Rainey's Black Bottom, Gypsy* (1990).

**RAITER, FRANK**. Born January 17, 1932 in Cloquet, MN. Yale graduate. Bdwy debut 1958 in *Cranks*, followed by *Dark at the Top of the Stairs, J.B., Camelot, Salome*, OB in *Soft Core Pornographer, The Winter's Tale, Twelfth Night, Tower of Evil, Endangered Species, A Bright Room Called Day, Learned Ladies, 'Tis Pity She's A Whore, Othello.*

**RAMOS, RAMON**. Born November 17, 1948 in Bayamon, PR. Graduate Brooklyn Col., LAMDA. Bdwy debut 1983 in *A View from the Bridge* followed by *A Comedy of Errors.*

**RAMSAY, REMAK**. Born February 2, 1937 in Baltimore, MD. Graduate Princeton U. Debut 1964 OB in *Hang Down Your Head and Die*, followed by *The Real Inspector Hound, Landscape of the Body, All's Well That Ends Well* (CP), *Rear Column, The Winslow Boy, The Dining Room, Save Grand Central, Quartermaine's Terms*, Bdwy in *Half a Sixpence, Sheep on the Runway, Lovely Ladies Kind Gentlemen, On the Town, Jumpers, Private Lives, Dirty Linen, Every Good Boy Deserves Favor, The Devil's Disciple, Woman in Mind, Nick and Nora.*

**RAMSEY, BARRY**. Born September 5, 1963 in Birmingham, AL. Attended U. Ala. Bdwy debut 1990 in *Peter Pan* (also 1991).

**RAMSEY, KEVIN**. Born September 24, 1959 in New Orleans, LA. Graduate NYU. Bdwy debut in *Black and Blue* (1989), followed by *Oh Kay!* for which he received a Theatre World Award, *5 Guys Named Moe*, OB in *Liberation Suite, Sweet Dreams, Prison Made Tuxedos, Staggerlee, Juba.*

**RANDALL, TONY**. Born February 26, 1920 in Tulsa, OK. Attended Northwestern, Columbia. Neighborhood Playhouse. Bdwy debut 1947 in *Antony and Cleopatra* followed by *To Tell You the Truth, Caesar and Cleopatra, Oh Men! Oh Women!, Inherit the Wind, Oh! Captain!, UTBU, M. Butterfly, A Little Hotel on the Side.*

**RANDELL, RON**. Born October 8, 1920 in Sydney, Aus. Attended St. Mary's Col. Bdwy debut 1949 in *The Browning Version* followed by *Harlequinade, Candide, World of Suzie Wong, Sherlock Holmes, Mrs. Warren's Profession, Measure for Measure, Bent, Brigadoon* (CC), OB in *Holy Places, After You've Gone, Patrick Pearse Motel, Maneuvers, Swan Song, A Man for All Seasons, Rosencrantz and Guildenstern Are Dead, M. Amilcar.*

**RASHOVICH, GORDANA**. Born September 18 in Chicago, IL. Graduate Roosevelt U., RADA. Debut 1977 OB in *Fefu and Her Friends* (for which she received a Theatre World Award) followed by *Selma, Couple of the Year, Mink Sonata, Class One-Acts, Morocco, A Shayna Maidel, The Misanthrope*, Bdwy in *Conversations with My Father* (1992).

**RATHGEB, LAURA**. Born September 5, 1962 in Burlington, VT. Graduate St. Michael's Col. Debut 1987 OB in *Deep Swimmer*, followed by *The Imaginary Invalid, Electra, All's Well That Ends Well, She Stoops to Conquer, The Philanderer, Three Sisters, Midsummer Night's Dream, Importance of Being Earnest, Medea,The Fine Art of Finesse, Major Barbara, As You Like It.*

**REDGRAVE, LYNN**. Born March 8, 1943 in London, Eng. Attended Central School. Bdwy debut 1967 in *Black Comedy* followed by *My Fat Friend, Mrs. Warren's Profession, Knock Knock, St. Joan, Aren't We All?, Love Letters, The Master Builder, A Little Hotel on the Side.*

**REED, VIVIAN**. Born June 6, 1947 in Pittsburgh, PA. Attended Juilliard. Bdw debut 1971 in *That's Entertainment* followed by *Don't Bother Me I Can't Cope, Bubbling Brown Sugar* (for which she received a Theatre World Award), *It's So Nic to Be Civilized, High Rollers.*

**REES, ROGER**. Born May 5, 1944 in Wales, Graduate Glade School of Fine Ar Bdwy debut 1975 in *London Assurance* followed by *Nicholas Nickleby* (1981), OB *The End of the Day.*

**REGAN, MOLLY**. Born October 8 in Mankato, MN. Graduate Northwestern U Debut 1979 OB in *Say Goodnight, Gracie* followed by *Personals, Etiquette*, Bdwy *Stepping Out* (1987), *The Crucible* (1991).

**REINGOLD, JACQUELYNE**. Born March 13, 1959 in New York City. Gradua Oberlin Col. Debut 1978 OB in *A Wrinkle in Time*, followed by *Marat/Sad Unfettered Letters, Working One Acts, Mortality Project, Group.*

**RENDERER, SCOTT**. Born in Palo Alto, CA. Graduate Whitman Col. Bdwy deb 1983 in *Teaneck Tanzi*, OB in *And Things That Go Bump in the Night, Crossfire, Ju Like the Lions, The Dreamer Examines His Pillow, Nasty Little Secrets, Unidentifie Human Remains.*

**RESNIK, REGINA**. Born August 30, 1924 in New York City. Graduate Hunter C After a career as an internationally acclaimed operatic singer, she made her debut c Bdwy in *Cabaret* (1987), followed by *A Little Night Music* (NYCO/LC).

**RICHARD, JEAN-PAUL**. Born January 13, 1950 in Montreal, Can. Attended O Dominion U., AADA, Neighborhood Playhouse. Debut 1983 OB in *I've Still Got Th Song*, followed by Bdwy in *Man of La Mancha* (1992).

**RICHARDS, ARLEIGH**. Born November 28, 1949 in Gary, In. Gradua Swarthmore Col., Neighborhood Playhouse. Debut 1977 OB in *The Crucible* followe by *Fefu and her Friends, Romeo and Juliet, Her Friends, Death and Life of Sherloc Holmes.*

**RICHARDS, CAROL**. Born December 26 in Aurora, IL. Graduate Northwestern U Columbia U. Bdwy debut 1965 in *Half a Sixpence*, followed by *Mame, Last of the Re Hot Lovers, Company, Cats.*

**RICHARDSON, LEE**. Born September 11, 1926 in Chicago, IL. Graduate Goodma Theatre. Debut 1952 OB in *Summer and Smoke* followed by *St. Joan, Volpone, Th American Dream, Bartleby, Plays for Bleecker Street, The Merchant of Venice, Kin Lear, Thieves Carnival, Waltz of the Toreadors, Talented Tenth*, Bdwy in *The Legen of Lizzie* (1959), *Lord Pengo, House of Atreus, Find Your Way Home, Othello, Th Jockey Club Stakes, The Devil's Disciple, Getting Married.*

**RICKMAN, ALLEN L**. Born February 4, 1960 in Far Rockaway, NY. Attende Brooklyn Col. Debut 1988 OB in *Faithful Brethren of Pitt Street* followed by D Dietrich's Process, The Big Winner, Tony 'n' Tina's Wedding.*

**RIFKIN, RON**. Born October 31, 1939 in New York City. Graduate NYU. Bdwy debut 1960 in *Come Blow Your Horn*, followed by *The Goodbye People, The Tenth Man*, OB in *Rosebloom, The Art of Dining, Temple, Substance of Fire.*

**RIGOL, JOEY**. Born January 6, 1979 in Miami, FL. Debut 1988 OB in *The Chosen* followed by *The Voyage of the Beagle, The Music Man, Stop the World, Sympathy, Radio City Christmas Spectacular*, Bdwy in *Les Misérables* (1989).

**RILEY, ERIC**. Born March 22, 1955 in Albion, MI. Graduate U. Mich. Bdwy debu 1979 in *Ain't Misbehavin'*, followed by *Dream Girls, Ain't Misbehavin'* (1988), *Once on This Island*, OB in *Once on This Island, Weird Romance.*

**RINEHART, ELAINE**. Born August 16, 1958 in San Antonio, TX. Graduate NC Schl. Arts. Debut 1975 OB in *Tenderloin*, followed by *Native Son, Joan of Lorraine, Dumping Ground, Fairweather Friends, The Color of the Evening Sky, The Best Little Whorehouse in Texas, The Wedding of the Siamese Twins, Festival of I Acts, Up 'n' Under, Crystal Clear, Black Market, Festival of 1 Act Comedies, Raft of the Medusa, Can't Stop Screaming.*

**RINGHAM, NANCY**. Born November 16, 1954 in Minneapolis, MN. Graduate St. Olaf Col, Oxford U. Bdwy debut in *My Fair Lady* (1981), *3 Penny Opera, The Will Rogers Follies, Oh That Jones Boy, Bugles at Dawn, Not-so-new Faces of 1982, Trouble in Tahiti, Lenny and the Heartbreakers, 4 one-act Musicals, Esther: A Vaudeville Megillah.*

**RITCHIE, MARGARET**. Born May 31 in Madison, WI. Graduate U. Wis, NYU Debut 1981 OB in *Last Summer at Bluefish Cove* followed by *Who's There?, All Sou Day, Days and nights of an Ice Cream Princess, Two by Horton Foote.*

**ROBARDS, JASON**. Born July 26, 1922 in Chicago, IL. Attended AADA. Bdw debut 1947 with *D'Oyly Carte Co.*, followed by *Stalag 17, The Chase, Long Day Journey into Night* for which he received a Theatre World Award, *The Disenchante Toys in the Attic, Big Fish Little Fish, A Thousand Clowns, Hughie, The Devils, W Bombed in New Haven, The Country Girl, Moon for the Misbegotten, A Touch of t Poet, You Can't Take It With You, The Iceman Cometh, A Month of Sundays, A Wilderness!, Long Day's Journey into Night* (1988), *A Christmas Carol, Park Yo Car in Harvard Yard*, OB in *American Gothic, The Iceman Cometh, After the Fall, B for Whom Charlie, Long Day's Journey into Night.*

**ROBB, R.D**. Born March 31, 1972 in Philadelphia, PA Bdwy debut 1980 in *Charl and Algernon*, followed by *Oliver!, Les Misérables.*

**ROBBINS, REX**. Born in Pierre, SD. Bdwy debut 1964 in *One Flew over th Cucko's Nest* followed by *Scratch, The Changing Room, Gypsy, Comecians, A Almost Perfect Person, Richard III, You Can't Take It with You, Play Memory, S Degrees of Separation*, OB in *Servant of Two Masters, The Alchemist, Arms and t Man, Boys in the Band, A Memory of Two Mondays, They Knew What They Wante Secret Service, Boy Meets Girl, Three Sisters, The Play's the Thing, Julius Caesa Henry IV Part I, The Dining Room, Urban Blight.*

**OBERTS, MARILYN**. Born October 30, 1939 in San Francisco, Ca. Graduate San Fran State U. Debut 1963 OB in *Telemachus Clay* followed by *The Maids, The Class, Gabriella, Tom Paine, Futz, Candaules Commissioner, Persia, Masque of St. George and the Dragon, Split Lip, Mert and Phil, The Blonde Leading the Blind, 3 by Colette, Heather McKay, Futz* (1991).

**OBERTS, TONY**. Born October 22, 1939 in New York City. Graduate Northwestern U. Bdwy debut 1962 in *Something about a Soldier*, followed by *Take Her She's Mine, Last Analysis, Never Too Late, Barefoot in the Park, Don't Drink the Water, How Now Dow Jones, Play It Again Sam, Promises Promises, Sugar, Absurd Doubles, Brigadoon* (LC), *South Pacific* (LC), *Love Letters, Jerome Robbins' Broadway*, OB in *The Cradle Will Rock, Losing Time, The Good Parts, Time Framed*.

**OBINS, LAILA**. Born March 14, 1959 in St. Paul, MN. Graduate U. Wis., Yale. Bdwy debut 1984 in *The Real Thing*, OB in *Bloody Poetry, The Film Society, For Dear Life, Maids of Honor, The Extra Man*.

**OBINSON, HAL**. Born in Bedford, IN. Graduate Ind. U. Debut 1972 OB in *Memphis Store Bought Teeth* followed by *From Berlin to Broadway, The Fantasticks, Promenade, The Baker's Wife, Yours Anne, Personals, And a Nightingale Sang*, Bdwy *On Your Toes* (1983), *Broadway, Grand Hotel, Nick & Nora*.

**OBINSON, LANCE**. Born June 21, 1979 in Salisbury, MD. Bdwy debut 1989 in *Gypsy*, followed by *Shadowlands, The Will Rogers Follies*.

**OBINSON, ROGER**. Born May 2 1941 in Seattle, WA. Attended U.S. Cal. Bdwy debut 1969 in *Does a Tiger Wear a Necktie?*, followed by *Amen Corner, The Iceman Cometh*, OB in *Walk in Darkness, Jericho-Jim Crow, Who's Got His Own, Trials of Brother Jero, The Miser, The Interrogation of Havana, Lady Day, Do Lord Remember Me, Of Mice and Men, The Middle of Nowhere, Measure for Measure, The Tempest*.

**ODGERS, SHEV**. Born April 9, 1928 in Holister, Ca. Attended San Fran State Col. Bdwy debut 1959 in *Redhead* followed by *The Music Man, Man of La Mancha* (also LC & 1992), *Home Sweet Homer, Legend*, OB in *Get Thee to Canterbury, War Games, Moonchildren, Marco Polo Sings a Solo*.

**OGERS, KEN LEIGH**. Born August 2 in NYC. Graduate S. Ill. U. Bdwy debut 1975 in *Hello, Dolly!*, followed by *A Chorus Line, My One and Only, Oh, Kay!, Grand Hotel*.

**ODRIGUEZ, AL**. Born May 29, 1960 in NYC. Graduate Syracuse U. Debut 1983 OB in *The Senorita from Tacna*, followed by *Savings, The Merchant of Venice, Death of Garcia Lorca, Don Juan of Seville, The English-Only Restaurant, Born to Rumba! The Right to Play*, Bdwy in *Open Admissions* (1984).

**OSENTHAL, MARK**. Born July 24, 1966 in Kettering, OH. Attended DePaul U./Goodman School. Debut 1991 OB in *Marvin's Room* for which he received a Theatre World Award.

**OSS, STEVEN TRACY**. Born July 24, 1958 in Houston, Tx. Attended U. Tx./Austin, Neighborhood Playhouse, RADA. Debut 1991 OB in *Company*, followed by *Edward II*.

**OSSETTER, KATHRYN** (a.k.a. Kathy). Born July 31 in Abington, PA. Graduate Gettysburg Col. Debut 1982 OB in *After the Fall*, followed by *The Incredibly Famous Will Rivers, A Midsummer Night's Dream, How to Say Goodbye, The Good Coach, Love Lemmings, The White Bear*, Bdwy in *Death of a Salesman* (1984).

**OTHMAN, JOHN**. Born June 3, 1949 in Baltimore, MD. Graduate Wesleyan U., Yale. Debut 1978 OB in *Rats Nest* followed by *The Impossible H. I. Mencken, The Buddy System, Rosario and the Gypsies, The Italian Straw Hat, Modern Ladies of Guanabacoa, Faith Hope and Charity, Some Americans Abroad, EST Marathon '92, Bdwy End of the World...* (1984), *Some Americans Abroad*.

**OUTMAN, STEVE**. Born August 28, 1962 in Washington, DC. Graduate Northwestern U. Bdwy debut 1987 in *Broadway*, OB in *Love's Labour's Lost, Much Ado about Nothing, Shmulnik's Waltz*.

**UBINSTEIN, JOHN**. Born December 8, 1946 in Los Angeles. Attended UCLA. Bdwy debut 1972 in *Pippin*, for which he received a Theatre World Award, followed by *Children of a Lesser God, Fools, The Soldier's Tale, The Caine Mutiny Court-Martial, Hurlyburly, M. Butterfly*, OB in *Rosencrantz and Guildenstern Are Dead, Urban Blight, Love Letters, Princess Ida*.

**UCK, PATRICIA**. Born September 11, 1963 in Washington, DC. Attended Goucher Col. Bdwy debut 1986 in *Cats*.

**UCKER, BO**. Born August 17, 1948 in Tampa, Fl. Debut 1978 OB in *Native Son* for which he received a Theatre World Award, followed by *Blues for Mr. Charlie, Streamers, Forty Deuce, Dustoff, Rosetta Street*, Bdwy in *Joe Turner's Come and Gone* (1988).

**UDY, MARTIN**. Born December 5, 1915 in Hartford, CT. Attended RADA. Bdwy *Joan of Lorraine, To Dorothy A Son, The Man in the Glass Booth, The Crucible, A Little Hotel on the Side*, OB in *Modigliani*.

**UIVIVAR, FRANCIS**. Born December 21, 1960 in Hong Kong, China. Graduate Loretto Heights Col. Bdwy debut 1988 in *Chess*, followed by *Starlight Express, Shogun: The Musical* for which he received a Theatre World Award, *Miss Saigon*, OB *A Promised Land*.

**UIZ, ANTHONY**. Born October 17, 1956 in New York City. Attended NYCC. Debut 1987 OB in *The Wonderful Ice Cream Suit*, followed by *Danny and the Deep Blue Sea, Born to Rumba!*.

**ULE, CHARLES**. Born August 4, 1928 in Springfield, MO. Bdwy debut 1951 in *Courtin' Time*, followed by *Happy Hunting, Oh Captain!, The Conquering Hero, Donnybrook, Bye Bye Birdie, Fiddler on the Roof, Henry Sweet Henry, Maggie Flynn, 776, Cry for Us All, Gypsy, Goodtime Charley, On the 20th Century, Phantom of the Opera*, OB in *Family Portrait*.

**RUPERT, MICHAEL**. Born October 23, 1951 in Denver, CO. Attended Pasadena Playhouse. Bdwy debut 1968 in *The Happy Time* for which he received a Theatre World Award, followed by *Pippin, Sweet Charity* (1986), *Mail, City of Angels, Falsettos*, OB in *Festival, Shakespeare's Cabaret, March of the Falsettos, Falsettoland*.

**RYALL, WILLIAM**. Born September 18, 1954 in Binghamton, NY. Graduate AADA. Debut 1979 OB in *Canterbury Tales*, followed by *Elizabeth and Essex. He Who Gets Slapped, The Seagull, Tartuffe*, Bdwy in *Me and My Girl* (1986), *Grand Hotel*.

**RYAN, STEVEN**. Born June 19, 1947 in New York City. Graduate Boston U., U. Minn. Debut 1978 OB in *Winning Isn't Everything*, followed by *The Beethoven, September in the Rain, Romance Language, Love's Labour's Last, Love and Anger, Approximating Mother*. Bdwy in *I'm Not Rappaport* (1986), *Guys and Dolls* (1992).

**RYDER, RIC**. Born March 31 in Baltimore, MD. Graduate U. Md,. Peabody Cons. Bdwy debut in *Starmites* (1989), OB in *The Gifts of the Magi, Chess*.

**RYNN, MARGIE**. Born in Princeton, NJ. Graduate U. Cal/Berkeley, UCLA. Debut 1988 OB in *Autobahn* followed by *The Bed Experiment, Suite Sixteen, Les*

**SALINGER, MATT**. Born February 13, 1960 in Windsor, VT. Attended Princeton, Columbia U. Graduate. Bdwy debut 1985 in *Dancing in the End Zone*, OB in *The Sum of Us* (1991).

**SALLOWS, TRACY**. Born April 27, 1963 in Valley Stream, NY. Graduate SUNY/Purchase, Bdwy debut 1986 in *You Never Can Tell*, followed by *The Miser, Shimada*.

**SALONGO, LEA**. Born February 22, 1971 in Manila, PI. Attended Manila U. Bdwy debut 1991 in *Miss Saigon* for which she received a Theatre World Award.

**SALVATORE, JOHN**. Born November 3, 1961 in Rockville Center, NY. Attended Adelphi U. Bdwy debut 1986 in *A Chorus Line*, OB in *Pageant*.

**SANDERS, ABIGAIL**. Born December 9, 1965 in NYC. Debut 1990 OB in *New York 1937* followed by *Raft of the Medusa*, Bdwy in *The Speed of Darkness* (1991).

**SANTELL, MARIE**. Born July 8 in Brooklyn, NY. Bdwy debut 1957 in *The Music Man* followed by *A Funny Thing Happened on the Way.., Flora the Red Menace, Pajama Game, Mack and Mabel, La Cage aux Folles*, OB in *Hi, Paisano!, The Boys from Syracuse, Peace, Promenade, The Drunkard, Sensations, The Castaways, Fathers and Sons, Dear World*.

**SANTIAGO, SAUNDRA**. Born April 14, 1957 in New York City, Graduate U. Miami, SMU. Bdwy debut 1983 in *A View from the Bridge* followed by OB's *Road to Nirvana* (1991), *Spike Heels*.

**SARANDON, CHRIS**. Born July 24, 1942 in Beckley, W. Va. Graduate U.W.VA., Catholic U. Bdwy debut 1970 in *The Rothschilds* followed by *Two Gentlemen of Verona, Censored Scenes from King Kong, Nick & Nora*, OB in *Marco Polo Sings a Solo, The Devil's Disciple, The Woods, Voice of the Turtle*.

**SATTA, STEVEN**. Born December 25, 1964 in The Bronx, NYC. Graduate NYU. Debut 1991 OB in *Macbeth* followed by *Chekhov Very Funny*, Bdwy in *A Little Hotel on the Side* (1992).

**SCHARFMAN, WENDY**. Born December 13, 1950 in Albany, NY. Graduate Wheeler Col. UNC Chapel Hill, Asolo Consv. Debut 1991 OB in *The Dropper* followed by *Betrayal, A Kind of Alaska, A Midsummer Night's Dream, Last Chance Texaco, Tides*.

**SCHECTER, DAVID**. Born April 12, 1956 in NYC. Graduate Bard Col., Neighborhood Playhouse. Debut 1976 OB in *Nightclub Cantata* followed by *Dispatches, The Haggadah, Temptation, The Balcony, Groundhog*, Bdwy in *Runaways* (1978), *3 Penny Opera*.

**SCHLARTH, SHARON**. Born January 19 in Buffalo, NY. Graduate SUNY/Fredonia. Debut 1983 OB in *Full Hookup*, followed by *Fool for Love, Love's Labour's Lost, Caligula, The Mound Builders, Quiet in the Land, The Early Girl, Borderlines, Making Movies, A Piece of My Heart*, Bdwy in *Sleight of Hand* (1987).

**SCHMITZ, PETER** Born August 20, 1962 in St. Louis Mo.Graduate Yale, NYU. Debut 1987 OB in *Henry IV Part 1*, followed by *We the People, Blitzstein Project, Imperceptible Mutabilities, Henry IV Parts 1 and 2, Comedy of Errors*.

**SCHNEIDER, HELEN**. Born December 23 in NYC. Bdwy debut 1989 in *Ghetto*, OB in *What a Swell Party!*

**SCHNEIDER, JOHN**. Born April 8, 1960 in Mt. Kisco, NY. Bdwy debut 1991 in *Grand Hotel*.

**SCHULL, REBECCA**. Born February 22 in NYC. Graduate NYU. Bdwy debut 1976 in *Herzl* followed by *Golda*, OB in *Mother's Day, Fefu and Her Friends, On Mt. Chimborazo, Mary Stuart, Balzamov's Wedding, Before She Is Ever Born, Exiles, Nest of the Wood Grouse, Green Fields, Panache!, Journey into the Whirlwind, Candide*.

**SCHULMAN, CRAIG**. Born March 1, 1956 in Weisbaden, W. Ger. Graduate SUNY/Oswego. Debut 1980 OB in *Pirates of Penzance, Light Opera of Manhattan, Gilbert & Sullivan Players*, Bdwy in *Les Misérables* (1990).

**SCOTT, CAMPBELL**. Born July 19, 1962 in NYC. Attended Lawrence U. Bdwy debut 1985 in *Hay Fever* followed by *The Real Thing, Long Day's Journey into Night, Ah Wilderness!*, OB in *Measure for Measure, Copperhead, A Man for All Seasons, The Last Outpost, Pericles*.

**SCOTT, GEORGE C**. Born October 18, 1927 in Wise, VA. Attended U. Mo. Debut 1957 OB in *Richard III* for which he received a Theatre World Award, followed by *As You Like It, Merchant of Venice, Children of Darkness, Desire under the Elms*, Bdwy in *Comes a Day, The Andersonville Trial, The Wall, General Seegar, The Little Foxes, Plaza Suite, All God's Chillun Got Wings, Uncle Vanya, Death of a Salesman, Sly Fox, Tricks of the Trade, Present Laughter, Boys in Autumn, On Borrowed Time*.

**SCOTT, MARTHA**. Born September 22, 1914 in Jamesport, MO. Graduate U. Mich. Bdwy debut 1938 in *Our Town*, followed by *Foreigners, The Willow and I, Soldiers Wife, Voice of the Turtle, It Takes Two, Design for a Stained Glass Window, Gramercy Ghost, The Number, Male Animal, The Remarkable Mr. Pennypacker, The Male Animal, Cloud 7, A Distant Bell, Tumbler, 49th Cousin, Never Too Late, The Subject Was Roses, The Skin of Our Teeth, The Crucible.*

**SEAMON, EDWARD**. Born April 15, 1937 in San Diego, CA. Attended San Diego State Col. Debut 1971 OB in *The Contractor*, followed by *The Family, Fishing, Feedlot, Cabin 12, Rear Column, Devour the Snow, Buried Child, Friends, Extenuating Circumstances, Confluence, Richard II, Great Grandson of Jedediah Kohler, Marvelous Gray, Time Framed, The Master Builder, Full Hookup, Fool for Love, The Harvesting, A Country for Old Men, Love's Labour's Lost, Caligula, The Mound Builders, Quiet in the Land, Talley and Son, Tomorrow's Monday, Ghosts, Of Mice and Men, Beside Herself, You Can't Think of Everything, Tales of the Lost Formicans, Love Diatribe, Empty Hearts, Ghosts*, Bdwy in *The Trip Back Down* (1977), *Devour the Snow, American Clock.*

**SERBAGI, ROGER**. Born July 26, 1937 in Waltham, Ma. Attended AmThWing, Bdwy debut 1969 in *Henry V* followed by *Gemini*, OB in *A Certain Young Man, Awake and Sing, The Partnership, Monsters, The Transfiguration of Benno, Blimpie, Family Snapshots, Till Jason Comes, 1984, Henry Lampur, Working One-Acts '91.*

**SERRANO, NESTOR**. Born November 5, 1955 in the Bronx, NY. Attended Queens Col. Debut 1983 OB in *Union City Thanksgiving*, followed by *Diamonds, Cuba and His Teddy Bear, Learned Ladies, The Creditors.*

**SESMA, THOM**. Born June 1, 1955 in Sasebo, Japan, Graduate U. Cal. Bdwy debut 1983 in *La Cage aux Folles* followed by *Chu Chem, Search and Destroy, Nick and Nora*, OB in *In a Pig's Valise, Baba Goya, Chu Chem.*

**SEVERS, WILLIAM**. Born January 8, 1932 in Britton, OK. Attended Pasadena Playhouse, Columbia Col. Bdwy debut 1960 in *Cut of the Axe* followed by *On Borrowed Time* (1991), OB in *The Moon is Blue, Lulu, Big Maggie, Mixed Doubles, The Rivals, The Beaver Coat, Twister, Midnight Mass, Gas Station, Firebugs, Fellow Travelers, The Iowa Boys.*

**SHALHOUB, TONY**. Born October 9, 1953 in Green Bay, WI. Graduate Yale U. Bdwy debut 1985 in *The Odd Couple*, followed by *The Heidi Chronicles, Conversations with My Father*, OB in *Richard II, One Act Festival, Zero Positive, Rameau's Nephew, For Dear Life.*

**SHANNON, MARK**. Born December 13, 1948 in Indianapolis, In. Attended U. Cin. Debut 1969 OB in *Fortune and Men's Eyes*, followed by *Brotherhood, Nothing to Report, When You Comin' Back, Red Ryder?, Serenading Louie, Three Sisters, K2, Spare Parts, Lips Together Teeth Apart.*

**SHAVER, HELEN**. Born February 24, 1952 in St. Thomas, Ont., Can. Bdwy debut 1992 in *Jakes Women*, for which she received a Theatre World Award.

**SHAWHAN, APRIL**. Born April 10, 1940 in Chicago, IL. Debut 1964 OB in *Jo* followed by *Hamlet, Oklahoma!, Mod Donna, Journey to Gdansk, Almost in Vegas, Bosoms and Neglect, Stella, The Vinegar Tree, Ghosts*, Bdwy in *Race of Hairy Men, 3 Bags Full* for which she received a Theatre World Award, *Dinner at 8, Cop-Out, Much Ado about Nothing, Over Here, Rex, A History of the American Film.*

**SHEEHAN, CIARAN**. Born October 23, 1961 in Dublin, Ire. Debut 1992 OB in *Grandchild of Kings.*

**SHEEN, MARTIN**. Born August 3, 1940 in Dayton, OH. Bdwy debut 1964 in *Never Live over a Pretzel Factory*, followed by *The Subject Was Roses, Death of a Salesman, The Crucible*, OB in *The Connection, Many Loves, Jungle of Cities, Wicked Cooks, Hamlet, Romeo and Juliet, Hello and Goodbye, Julius Caesar.*

**SHELL, CLAUDIA**. Born September 11, 1959 in Passaic, NJ. Debut 1980 OB in *Jam*. Bdwy in *Merlin*, followed by *Cats.*

**SHELTON, SLOANE**. Born March 17, 1934 in Asheville, NC. Attended Bates Col, RADA. Bdwy debut 1967 in *The Imaginary Invalid*, followed by *A Touch of the Poet, Tonight at 8:30, I Never Sang for My Father, Sticks and Bones, The Runner Stumbles, Shadow Box, Passione, Open Admission, Orpheus Descending*, OB in *Androcles and the Lion, The Maids, Basic Training of Pavlo Hummel, Play and Other Plays, Julius Caesar, Chieftans, Passione, The Chinese Viewing Pavilion, Blood Relations, The Great Divide, Highest Standard of Living, The Flower Palace, April Snow, Nightingale, Dearly Departed.*

**SHEPARD, SUZANNE**. Born October 31, 1934 in Elizabeth, NJ. Graduate Bennington Col. Debut 1977 OB in *The World of Sholem Aleichem* followed by *End Game, House Arrest, Appointment with a High Wire Lady*, Bdwy in *Awake and Sing* (1984).

**SHEW, TIMOTHY**. Born February 7, 1959 in Grad Forks, ND. Graduate Millikin U., U. Mich. Debut 1987 OB in *The Knife*, Bdwy in *Les Misérables.*

**SHIMIZU, KEENAN**. Born October 22, 1956 in New York City. Bdwy debut 1965 in *South Pacific*, followed by *The King and I*, OB in *Rashomon, The Year of the Dragon, The Catch, Peking Man, Flowers and Household Gods, Behind Enemy Lines, Station J. Rosie's Café, Boutique Living, Gonza and Lancer, Letters to a Student Revolutionary, Fairy Bones.*

**SHULL, RICHARD B**. Born February 24, 1929 in Evanston, IL. Graduate State U. Iowa. Debut 1953 OB in *Coriolanus*, followed by *Purple Dust, Journey to the Day, American Hamburger League, Frimbo, Fade the Game, Desire under the Elms, The Marriage of Betty and Boo, The Front Page* (LC), *One of the All-Time Greats*, Bdwy in *Black-eyed Susan* (1954), *Wake Up Darling, Red Roses for Me, I Knock at the Door, Pictures in the Hallway, Have I Got a Girl for You, Minnie's Boys, Goodtime Charley, Fools, Oh, Brother!*

**SHULMAN, MICHAEL**. Born December 31, 1981 in New York City. Debut 1989

OB in *Gardenia*, followed by *Assassins, The House That Goes on Forever*, Bdwy Four Baboons Adoring the Sun (1992).

**SILLIMAN, MAUREEN**. Born December 3 in New York City. Attended Hofstra Bdwy debut 1975 in *Shenandoah*, followed by *I Remember Mama, Is There Life Afte High School?*, OB in *Umbrellas of Cherbourg, Two Rooms, Macbeth, Blue Windo Three Postcards, Pictures in the Hall, The Voice of the Prairie.*

**SILVERS, LOUIS**. Born July 7, 1959 in Miami, FL. Attended Northwestern U Bdwy debut 1987 in *Oh! Calcutta!*, OB in *High Strung Quartet, The Bar, I Can't Sto Screaming.*

**SIMMONS, J.K.** (formerly Jonathan) Born January 9, 1955 in Detroit, MI. Gradua U. Mont. Debut 1987 OB in *Birds of Paradise*, followed by *Dirty Dick*, Bdwy in *A Change in the Heir* (1990), *A Few Good Men, Peter Pan* (1990/1991), *Guys and Doll.*

**SISTO, ROCCO**. Born February 8, 1953 in Bari, Italy. Graduate U. Ill, NYU. Deb 1982 OB in *Hamlet*, followed by *The Country Doctor, Times and Appetites Toulouse-Lautrec, The Merchant of Venice, What Did He See, A Winter's Tale, Th Tempest, Dream of a Common Language, 'Tis Pity She's a Whore.*

**SLAFF, JONATHAN**. Born October 29, 1950 in Wilkes-Barre, PA. Graduate Ya U., Columbia. Debut 1988 OB in *One Director against His Cast*, followed by *Futz!*

**SLEZAK, VICTOR**. Born July 7, 1957 in Youngstown, OH. Debut 1979 OB in *Electra Myth*, followed by *Hasty Heart, Ghosts, Alice and Fred, Widow Clair Miracle Worker, Talk Radio, Marathon '88, One Act Festival, Briar Patch, Maratho '90, Young Playwrights, Marathon '91, Appointment with a High Wire Lady, Sam Am, The White Rose.*

**SLOMAN, JOHN**. Born June 23, 1954 in Rochester, NY. Graduate SUNY/Genasc Debut 1977 OB in *Unsung Cole* followed by *Apple Tree, Romance in Hard Times, Th Waves, An Elephant Never Forgets*, Bdwy in *Whoopee!, 1940's Radio Hour, A Day Hollywood/A Night in the Ukraine, Mayor.*

**SMILEY, BRENDA**. Born in 1947 in Indiana. Attended Ind. U., NY U. Debut 196 OB in *America Hurrah* followed by *Scuba Duba* for which she received a Theatr World Award, *The Wedding Portrait.*

**SMITH, ANNA DEAVERE**. Born September 18, 1950 in Baltimore, MD. Gradua Beaver Col, AmConsvTheatre. Debut 1980 OB in *Mother Courage* followed b *Mercenaries, Fires in the Mirror.*

**SMITH, COTTER**. Born May 29, 1949 in Washington, DC. Graduate Trinity Co Debut 1980 OB in *The Blood Knot*, followed by *Death of a Miner, A Soldier's Play, I Savador, Borderlines, Walking the Dead, Empty Hearts.*

**SMITH, JENNIFER**. Born March 9, 1956 in Lubbock, TX. Graduate Tex. Tech. U Debut 1981 OB in *Seesaw*, followed by *Suffragette, Henry the 8th and the Grand O Opry, No Frills Revue, Whatnot, 1-2-3-4-5, Once at Recess, White Lies*, Bdwy in *L Cage aux Folles* (1981), *A Change in the Heir, The Secret Garden.*

**SMITH, LOIS**. Born November 3, 1930 in Toepeka, KS. Attended U.W.Va. Bdw debut 1952 in *Time Out for Ginger*, followed by *The Young and the Beautiful, Th Wisteria Trees, The Glass Menagerie, Orpheus Descending, Stages, The Grapes Wrath*, OB in *A Midsummer Night's Dearm, Non Pasquale, Promenade, La Bohem Bodies Rest and Motion, Marathon '87, Gus and Al, Marathon '88, Measure fo Measure, Spring Thing, Beside Herself, Sam I Am.*

**SMITH, SHEILA**. Born April 3, 1933 in Coneaut, OH. Attended Kent State U Cleveland Play House. Bdwy debut 1963 in *Hot Spot* followed by *Mame* for which sh received a Theatre World Award, *Follies, Company, Sugar, Five O'Clock Girl, 42n Street*, OB in *Taboo, Revue, Anything Goes, Best Foot Forward, Sweet Miam Fiorello!, Taking My Turn, Jack and Jill, M. Amilcar, The Sunset Gang.*

**SMITH-CAMERON, J.** Born September 7 in Louisville, KY. Attended Fla. State U Bdwy debut 1982 in *Crimes of the Heart*, followed by *Wild Honey, Lend Me A Teno Our Country's Good*, OB in *Asian Shade, The Knack, Second Prize: 2 Weeks Leningrad, Great Divide, Voice of the Turtle, Women of Manhattan, Alice and Fre Mi Vida Loca, Little Egypt.*

**SOBOL, ALEX**. Born December 7, 1984 in Teaneck, NJ. Bdwy debut 1992 in *Fou Baboons Adoring the Sun.*

**SOLO, WILLIAM**. Born March 16, 1948 in Worcester, Ma. Graduate U. Mass Bdwy debut 1987 in *Les Misérables.*

**SPIELBERG, ROBIN**. Born November 20, 1962 in New Jersey. Attended Mich State U., NYU. Debut 1988 OB in *Boys' Life*, followed by *Marathon '90, Thre Sisters, 5 Very Live, Cocktails and Camp.*

**SOREL, THEODORE/TED**. Born November 14, 1936 in San Francisco, CA Graduate Col. of the Pacific. Bdwy debut 1977 in *Sly Fox*, followed by *Horowitz an Mrs. Washington, A Little Family Business*, OB in *Arms and the Man, Moo Mysteries, A Call from the East, Hedda Gabler, Drinks before Dinner, Tamara, Th Matchmaker.*

**SOUHRADA, TOM**. Born May 27, 1962 in Bay Shore, NY. Graduate NU U. Deb 1985 OB in *The Second Hurricane*, followed by *Bugout, Take Me Along, Th Awakening of Spring, Oedipus Texas.*

**SPANO, JOE**. Born July 7, 1946 in San Francisco, CA. Graduate U. Cal./Berkeley Bdwy debut 1992 in *The Price.*

**SPECHT, PATTI**. Born August 13, 1954 in San Diego, CA. Graduate Ohio State U Debut 1979 OB in *Svengali*, followed by *A Pearl of Great Price, Two by Horton Foot.*

**SPIEWAK, TAMARA ROBIN**. Born February 20, 1980 in Bridgeport, CT. Bdw debut 1990 in *Les Misérables.*

**SPIVEY, TOM**. Born January 28, 1951 in Richmond, VA. Graduate Wm & Mary Penn State. Debut 1989 OB in *The Thirteenth Chair*, followed by *The Rover.*

**SPOLAN, JEFFREY**. Born July 14, 1947 in New York City. Graduate Adelphi U Debut 1982 OB in *Yellow Fever*, followed by *Savage in Limbo, Three Sisters.*

**PORE, RICHARD.** Born March 23, 1948 in Chicago, IL. Debut 1982 OB in *The Frances Farmer Story*, followed by *Counselor-at-Law, Troilus and Cressida, Motions of History, Henry IV, Comedy of Errors.*

**TAHL, MARY LEIGH.** Born August 29, 1946 in Madison, WI. Graduate Jacksonville State U. Debut 1974 OB in *Circus*, followed by *Dragons, Sullivan and Gilbert, The World of Sholem Aleichem*, Bdwy in *The Phantom of the Opera* (1988).

**TANNARD, NICK.** Born December 2, 1948 in Cohasset, MA. Attended Carnegie-Mellon U. Debut 1975 OB in *Wings*, followed by *Beyond Therapy, I Am Who I Am, Verdict, Currents Turned Awry*, Bdwy in *Dracula* (1979).

**TATTEL, ROBERT.** Born November 20, 1937 in Floral Park, NY. Graduate Manhattan Col. Debut 1958 in *Heloise* followed by *When I Was a Child, Man and Superman, The Storm, Don Carlos, The Taming of the Shrew, Titus Andronicus, Henry V, Peer Gynt, Hamlet, Danton's Death, The Country Wife, The Caucasian Chalk Circle, King Lear, Iphigenia in Aulis, Ergo, The Persians, Blue Boys, The Minister's Black Veil, Four Friends, Two Character Play, The Merchant of Venice, Cuchulain, Oedipus Cycle, Guilles de Rais, Woyzeck, The Feuhrer Bunker, Learned Ladies, Domestic Issues, Great Days, The Tempest, Brand, A Man for All Seasons, Bunker Reveries, Enrico IV, Selling Off*, Bdwy in *Zoya's Apartment* (1990).

**STANTON, ROBERT.** Born March 8, 1963 in San Antonio, TX. Graduate George Mason U., NYU. Debut 1985 OB in *Measure for Measure*, followed by *Rum and Coke, Cheapside, Highest Standard of Living, One Act Festival, Best Half-Foot Forward, Sure Thing, Emily, Ubu, Casanova*, Bdwy in *A Small Family Business* 1992).

**STEBER, JOHN.** Born April 10, 1955 in Queens, NYC. Graduate Wesleyan U. Debut 1988 OB in *Welcome Back to Salamanca* followed by *New Living Newspaper, Black Medea, The Death of the Last Black Man in the Whole Entire World, St. Joan, The Boxing Day Parade.*

**STEINER, STEVE.** Born November 30, 1951 in Chicago, IL. Graduate Webster U. Debut 1986 OB in *Two Blind Mice*, followed by *Hot Sake, Return to the Forbidden Planet*, Bdwy in *Anything Goes.*

**STENDER, DOUG.** Born September 14, 1942 in Nanticoke, PA. Graduate Princeton U. RADA Bdwy debut 1973 in *The Changing Room* followed by *Run for Your Wife, The Visit*, OB in *New England Eclectic, Hamlet, The Second Man, How He Lied to Her Husband, Bhutan.*

**STEPHENS, MARK EDGAR.** Born March 20, 1968 in Polk County, FL. Graduate Fla. State U. Debut 1991 OB in *Prom Queens Unchained.*

**STERN, CHERYL.** Born July 1, 1956 in Buffalo, NY. Graduate Northwestern U. Debut 1984 OB in *Daydreams* followed by *WhiteLies.*

**STEVENS, FISHER.** Born November 27, 1963 in Chicago, IL. Attended NYU. Bdwy debut 1982 in *Torch Song Trilogy* followed by *Brighton Beach Memoirs*, OB in *A Darker Purpose.*

**STEWART, PATRICK.** Born July 13, 1940 in Mirfield, Eng. Attended Bristol Old Vic School. Bdwy debut 1971 with RSC in *A Midsummer Night's Dream* followed by *A Christmas Carol* (1991).

**STILLMAN, ROBERT.** Born December 2, 1954 in NYC. Graduate Princeton U. Debut 1981 OB in *The Haggadah*, followed by *Street Scene, Lola, No Frills Revue*, Bdwy in *Grand Hotel* (1989).

**STOLTZ, ERIC.** Born in 1961 in California. Attended U.S. Cal. Debut 1987 OB in *The Widow Claire* followed by *The American Plan*, Bdwy in *Our Town* (for which he received a 1989 Theatre World Award), *Two Shakespearean Actors.*

**STONEBURNER, SAM.** Born February 24, 1934 in Fairfax, VA. Graduate Georgetown U., AADA. Debut 1960 OB in *Ernest in Love*, followed by *Foreplay, Anyone Can Whistle, Twilight Cantata, Six Degrees of Separation, Flaubert's Latest*, Bdwy in *Different Times* (1972), *Bent, Macbeth* (1981), *The First, Six Degrees of Separation.*

**STORCH, LARRY.** Born January 8, 1923 in New York City. Bdwy debut 1958 in *Who Was That Lady I Saw You With?*, followed by *Porgy and Bess* (1983), *Arsenic and Old Lace*, OB in *The Littlest Revue* (1956), *Breaking Legs.*

**STRAM, HENRY.** Born September 10, 1954 in Layfayette, IN. Attended Juilliard. Debut 1978 OB in *King Lear*, followed by *Shout and Twist, The Cradle Will Rock, Prison-made Tuxedos, Cinderella/Cendrillon, The Making of Americans, Black Sea Follies, Eddie Goes to Poetry City, A Bright Room Called Day, The Mind King.*

**STRAYHORN, DANNY.** Bdwy debut 1975 in *Dr. Jazz* followed by *It's So Nice to Be Civilized, Honky Tonk Nights, Starlight Express, Grand Hotel*, OB in *Sancocho, Opening Night, A Broadway Musical.*

**STRITCH, ELAINE.** Born February 2, 1925 in Detroit, MI. Bdwy debut 1946 in *Loco*, followed by *Made in Heaven, Angel in the Wings, Call Me Madam, Pal Joey, On Your Toes, Bus Stop, The Sin of Pat Muldoon, Goldilocks, Sail Away, Who's Afraid of Virginia Woolf?, Wonderful Town (CC), Company, Love Letters*, OB in *Private Lives, Rodgers and Hart Revue.*

**SULLIVAN, IAN.** Born April 1, 1933 in NYC. Attended Boston U. Bdwy debut 1970 in *Man of La Mancha* (also 1977 and 1992), followed by *Vivat! Vivat Regina!, My Fair Lady* (1976), *Home Sweet Homer.*

**SULLIVAN, KIM.** Born July 21, 1952 in Philadelphia, PA. Graduate NYU. Debut 1972 OB in *The Black Terror*, followed by *Legend of the West, Deadwood Dick, Big Apple Messenger, Dreams Deferred, A Raisin in the Sun, The Tempest, Ground People, Celebration.*

**SWANSEN, LARRY.** Born November 10, 1930 in Roosevelt, OK. Graduate U. Ok. Bdwy debut 1966 in *Those That Play the Clowns*, followed by *The Great White Hope, The King and I*, OB in *Dr. Faustus Lights the Lights, Thistle in My Bed, A Darker Flower, Vincent, MacBird, The Unknown Soldier and His Wife, The Sound of Music,*

*The Conditioning of Charlie One, Ice Age, Prince of Homburg, Who's There?, Heart of a Dog, Grandma Pray for Me,Frankenstein.*

**SZARABAJKA, KEITH.** Born December 2, 1952 in Oak Park, IL. Attended Trinity U., Chicago U. Bdwy debut 1973 in *Warp!*, followed by *Doonesbury, Search and Destroy*, OB in *Bleacher Bums, Class Enemy, Digby, Rich Relations, Women of Manhattan, Class One-Acts.*

**TAFFEL, STAN.** Born December 6, 1962 in NYC. Graduate Boston U. Debut 1987 OB in *Lenny Bruce Revue* followed by *Speakeasy, Noo Yawk Tawk.*

**TAFLER, JEAN.** Born November 18, 1957 in Schenectady, NY. Graduate Hofstra U. Debut 1981 OB in *Mandragola*, followed by *Lady Windermere's Fan, Richard II, Towards Zero, The Cotton Web, A Lady Named Joe, Guadeloupe, Brass Jackal, Philemon, Frankenstein.*

**TAHMIN, MARY.** Born December 28, 1937 in the Bronx, NYC. Bdwy debut 1959 *Two for the Seesaw*, OB in *Walk-Up, Balm in Gilead, The Oxcart, Valentine's Day, The Sticker Tree, The Damaging Effects of Love.*

**TALEPOROS, ZOE.** Born October 23, 1979 in NYC. Debut 1989 OB in *Rasputin* followed by *The Trojan Women*, Bdwy in *The Grapes of Wrath* (1990), *Four Baboons Adoring the Sun.*

**TALYN, OLGA.** Born December 5 in West Ger. Attended Syracuse U., U. Buffalo. Debut 1973 OB in *The Proposition*, followed by *Corral, Tales of Tinseltown, Shop on Main Street*, Bdwy in *A Doll's House, The Phantom of the Opera.*

**TARANTINA, BRIAN.** Born March 27, 1959 in NYC. Debut 1980 OB in *Innocent Thoughts and Harmless Intentions* followed by *Time Framed, Fables for Friends, Balm in Gilead, V & V Only*, Bdwy in *Angels Fall* for which he received a 1983 Theatre World Award, *Biloxi Blues, Boys of Winter, EST Marathon '92.*

**TARANTO, GLENN.** Born January 27, 1959 in Hackensack, NJ. Graduate Pace U. Bdwy debut 1981 in *Animals*, OB in *Tony 'n' Tina's Wedding* (1991).

**TASSIN, CHRISTEN.** Born January 2, 1979 in Spartanburg, SC. Bdwy debut 1989 in *Gypsy*, followed by *Radio City Christmas Spectacular.*

**TATE, ROBERT.** Born April 30, 1964 in Albuquerque, N. Mx. Graduate Yale U. Debut OB 1988 in *Ten Percent Revue*, followed by *Harold and the Purple Dragon, Nefertiti, Rags.*

**TATUM, MARIANNE.** Born February 18, 1951 in Houston, TX. Attended Manhattan Schl. of Music. Debut 1971 OB in *Ruddigore*, followed by *The Gilded Cage, Charley's Tale, Passionate Extremes.* Bdwy in *Barnum* (1980) for which she received a Theatre World Award, *The Three Musketeers, The Sound of Music* (NYCO/LC).

**TAVERNA, PATRICK.** Born January 16, 1954 in Ft. Monmouth, NJ. Graduate Northwestern Ct. Col. Bdwy debut 1990 in *Grand Hotel.*

**TAYLOR, DREW.** Born March 9, 1955 in Milwaukee, WI. Attended AADA. Debut 1985 OB in *She Loves Me*, followed by *Kiss Me Kate*, Bdwy in *The Secret Garden* (1991).

**TAYLOR, GEORGE.** Born September 18, 1930 in London, Eng. Attended AADA. Debut 1972 OB in *Hamlet*, followed by *Enemies, The Contractor, Scribes, Says I Says He, Teeth 'n' Smiles, Viaduct, Translations, Last of the Knucklemen, The Accrington Pals, Ragged Trousered Philanthropists, Brightness Falling.* Bdwy in *Emperor Henry IV* (1973), *The National Health, Loot, City of Angels.*

**TAYLOR, SCOTT.** Born June 29, 1962 in Milan, TN. AttendedMiss State U. Bdwy in *Wind in the Willows* (1985), followed by *Cats.*

**TELLER.** Born in 1948 in Philadelphia, PA. Graduate Amherst Col. Debut 1985 OB in *Penn & Teller*, Bdwy in same (1987), followed by *Refrigerator Tour*, OB in *Penn & Teller Rot in Hell.*

**TEMPERLEY, STEPHEN.** Born July 29, 1949 in London, Eng. Attended AADA. Debut 1968 OB in *Invitation to a Beheading*, followed by *Henry IV Parts I & II, Up Against It*, Bdwy in *Crazy for You* (1992).

**TERRY SUSAN.** Born May 30, 1953 in New Haven, CT. Graduate U. NH. Bdwy debut 1979 in *Evita*, followed by *Zorba*, OB in *Insert Foot, Follies in Concert, Forbidden Broadway, A Little Night Music* (NYCO/LC).

**TESTA, MARY.** Born June 4, 1955 in Philadelphia, PA. Attended URI. Debut 1979 OB in *In Trousers* followed by *Company, Life Is Not a Doris Day Movie, Not-So-New Faces of 1982, American Princess, Mandrake, 4 One-Act Musicals, Next, Please!, Daughters, One-Act Festival, The Knife, Young Playwrights Festival, Tiny Mommy, Finnegan's Funeral and Ice Cream Shop, Peter Breaks Through, Lucky Stiff, 1-2-3-4-5*, Bdwy in *Barnum* (1980), *Marilyn The Rink.*

**THACKER, RUSS.** Born June 23, 1946 in Washington, DC. Attended Montgomery Col. Bdwy debut 1967 in *Life with Father* followed by *Music! Music!, The Grass Harp, Heathen, Home Sweet Homer, Me Jack You Jill, Do Black Patent Leather Shoes Really Reflect Up?*, OB in *Your Own Thing* (for which he received a Theatre World Award), *Dear Oscar, Once I Saw a Boy Laughing, Tip-Toes, Oh, Coward!, New Moon in Concert, The Firefly in Concert, Rosalie in Concert, Some Enchanted Evening, Roberta in Concert, Ilio, Genesis, Little Me.*

**THIGPEN, LYNNE.** Born in 1940 in Joliet, IL. Graduate U. Ill. Bdwy debut 1975 in *The Night that made America Famous*, followed by *The Magic Show, Timbuktu!, Working, But Never Jam Today, Tintypes, A Month of Sundays, Fences*, OB in *Tintypes, Balm in Gilead, Boesman and Lena.*

**THOLE, CYNTHIA.** Born September 21, 1957 in Silver Springs, Md. Graduate Butler U. Debut 1982 OB in *Nymph Errant* followed by Bdwy in *42nd Street* (1985), *Me and My Girl, Meet Me in St. Louis, Nick & Nora.*

**THOMAS, JOHN NORMAN.** Born May 13, 1961 in Detroit, MI. Graduate Cinn. Consv. Bdwy debut 1987 in *Les Misérables*, followed by *The Merchant of Venice.*

**THOMAS, RAYMOND ANTHONY** Born December 19, 1956 in Kentwood, LA. Graduate U. Tex/El Paso. Debut 1981 OB in *Escape to Freedom*, followed by *The Sun Gets Blue, Blues for Mr. Charlie, The Hunchback of Notre Dame, Ground People, The Weather Outside, One Act Festival, Caucasian Chalk Circle, The Virgin Molly, Black Eagles, Distant Fires.*

**THOME, DAVID.** Born July 24, 1951 in Salt Lake City, UT. Bdwy debut 1971 in *No No Nanette*, followed by *Different Times, Good News, Rodgers and Hart, A Chorus Line, Dancin', Dreamgirls* (1981/1987), *Peter Pan* (1990/1992).

**THOMPSON, JENN.** Born December 13, 1967 in New York City. Debut 1975 OB in *The Wooing of Lady Sunday*, followed by *Cowboy Jack Street, The Wobblies, Looice, One Time One Place, You're a Good Man Charlie Brown, I Ought to Be in Pictures, Frankenstein*, (1990/1991), OB in *The Wedding of the SiameseTwins.*

**THOMPSON, RICHARD.** Born September 25, 1963 in Kinshsa, Zaire. Graduate Georgetown U., Catholic U. Debut 1992 OB in *The Baltimore Waltz.*

**THORSON, LINDA.** Born June 18, 1947 in Toronto, Can. Graduate RADA. Bdwy debut 1982 in *Steaming* for which she received a Theatre World Award, followed by *Noises Off, Zoya's Apartment, Getting Married, City of Angels.*

**TIMMERMAN, ALEC.** Born August 23, 1963 in Philadelphia, PA. Attended Temple U. Bdwy debut 1987 in *Anything Goes*, followed by *Gypsy, The Secret Garden*, OB in *Oy Mama Am I in Love, Rags.*

**TIMMS, REBECCA.** Born September 25 in Omaha, NE. Graduate Point Park Col. Bdwy debut 1987 in *Cats* followed by *Chess* (1992).

**TIMPANARO, NANCY.** Born December 30, 1952 in Patterson, NJ. Attended SUNY/Albany. Debut 1991 OB in *Tony 'n' Tina's Wedding.*

**TIRRELL, BARBARA.** Born November 24, 1953 in Nahant, MA. Graduate Temple U., Webber-Douglas Acad. Debut 1977 OB in *Six Characters in Search of an Author*, followed by *Cyrano, Romeo and Juliet, Louis Quinse, A Day Out of Time, King Lear, Oedipus Texas, Farther West.*

**TITONE, THOMAS.** Born March 24, 1959 in Secaucus, NJ. Attended NCar School of Arts. With AmBallet Theatre before Bdwy debut in *The Most Happy Fella* (1992).

**TOIGO, ALFRED.** Born September 17, 1934 in Chicago, IL. Graduate U. Pa., AmThWing. Debut 1958 OB in *Valmouth* followed by *The Sunset Gang*, Bdwy in *Hidden Stranger* (1963), *Those That Play the Clowns, Keane, Cabaret, Kismet, I'm Solomon, Zorba.*

**TOLIN, MEG.** Born November 11, 1966 in Wheatridge, CO. Attended Ind. U. Bdwy debut 1990 in *Grand Hotel.*

**TOMEI, MARISA.** Born December 4, 1964 in Brooklyn, NY. Attended Boston U., NYU. Debut 1986 OB in *Daughters* for which she received a Theatre World Award, followed by *Class I Act, Evening Star, What the Butler Saw, Marathon '88, Sharon and Billy, Chelsea Walls, The Summer Winds, Comedy of Errors.*

**TOMPOS, DOUG.** Born January 27, 1962 in Columbus, OH. Graduate Syracuse U., LAMDA. Debut 1985 OB in *Very Warm for May*, followed by *A Midsummer Night's Dream, Mighty Fine Music, Muzeeka, Wish You Were Here, Vampire Lesbians of Sodom*, Bdwy in *City of Angels.*

**TONER, THOMAS.** Born May 25, 1928 in Homestead, PA. Graduate UCLA. Bdwy debut 1973 in *Tricks*, followed by *The Good Doctor, All Over Town, The Elephant Man, California Suite, A Texas Trilogy, The Inspector General, Me and My Girl, The Secret Garden*, OB in *Pericles, The Merry Wives of Windsor, A Midsummer Night's Dream, Richard III, My Early Years, Life and Limb, Measure for Measure, Little Footsteps.*

**TOUSSAINT, ALLEN R.** Born January 14, 1938 in New Orleans, LA. Debut 1986 OB in *Staggerlee*, Bdwy in *High Rollers* (1992).

**TRAXLER, MARK.** Born July 13, 1964 in Centerville, Io. Graduate Point Park Col. Debut 1989 OB in *She Loves Me* followed by *Velveteen Rabbit, Don't Touch That Dial, Prom Queens Unchained.*

**TRIGGER, IAN.** Born September 30, 1942 in England. Graduate RADA. Debut 1973 OB in *The Taming of the Shrew* followed by *Scapino, True History of Squire Jonathan, Slab Boys, Cloud 9, Terra Nova, The Foreigner, The Misanthrope*, Bdwy in *Scapino* (1974).

**TRIPICIAN, BILL.** Born December 20, 1947 in Atlantic City, NJ. Graduate Catholic U. Debut 1991 in *I Can't Stop Screaming.*

**TRUE, BETSY.** Born April 19, 1960 in Cincinnati, OH. Graduate Boston Conv. Bdwy debut 1989 in *Les Misérables.*

**TSOUTSOUVAS, SAM.** Born August 20, 1948 in Santa Barbara, CA. Attended U. Cal., Juilliard. Debut 1969 OB in *Peer Gynt*, followed by *Twelfth Night, Timon of Athens, Cymbeline, School for Scandal, The Hostage, Women Beware Women, Lower Depths, Emigre, Hello Dali, The Merchant of Venice, The Leader, The Bald Soprano, The Taming of the Shrew, Gus & Al, Tamara, The Man Who Shot Lincoln, Puppetmaster of Lodz, Richard III, Three Sisters, Measure for Measure, Beggar's Opera, Scapin, Dracula, Our Country's Good, The Misanthrope.*

**TUCCI, LOUIS.** Born May 16, 1962 in Toronto, Can. Graduate Hunter Col. Bdwy debut 1990 in *The Buddy Holly Story*, OB in *Return of the Forbidden Planet.*

**TUCCI, MARIA.** Born June 19, 1941 in Florence, It. Attended Actors Studio. Bdwy debut 1963 in *The Milk Train Doesn't Stop Here Anymore*, followed by *The Rose Tattoo, The Little Foxes, The Cuban Thing, The Great White Hope, School for Wives, Lesson from Aloes, Kingdoms, Requiem for a Heavyweight, The Night of the Iguana*, OB in *Corruption in the Palace of Justice, Five Evenings, Trojan Women, White Devil, Horseman Pass By, Yerma, Shepherd of Avenue B., The Gathering, A Man for All Seasons, Love Letters, Substance of Fire.*

**TUCKER, SHONA.** Born in Louisville, KY. Graduate Northwestern U., NYU. Debut 1989 OB in *The Investigation of the Murder of El Salvador* followed by *A Light from the East, Diary of an African American, A Light Shining in Buckinghamshire,*

*Caucasian Chalk Circle, Greeks, Marvin's Room, From the Mississippi Delta.*

**TULL, PATRICK.** Born July 28, 1941 in Sussex, Eng. Attended LAMDA. Bdwy debut 1967 in *The Astrakhan Coat* followed by *The Crucible, The Master Builder, Getting Married, A Little Hotel on the Side*, OB in *Ten Little Indians, The Tame Tamed, Brand, Frankenstein, What the Butler Saw, She Stoops to Conquer, The Art of Success.*

**TURNBULL, LAURA.** Born September 9, 1956 in Denver, CO. Attended U. Denver. Debut 1986 OB in *Sex Tips for Modern Girls*, followed by *Showing Off Finkel's Follies*, Bdwy in *Sid Caesar and Company* (1989).

**TURNER, GLENN.** Born September 21, 1957 in Atlanta, GA. Bdwy debut 1984 in *My One and Only*, followed by *A Chorus Line, Grand Hotel.*

**TURNER, PATRICK.** Born December 2, 1952 in Seattle, WA. Attended U. Wa. AmConsTh. Debut 1984 OB in *The Merchant of Venice* followed by *Double Inconstancy, The Taming of the Shrew, Lady from the Sea, Two Gentlemen of Verona, The Contrast, Pericles, The Rivals, Rosaline, Much Ado about Nothing, You Never Can Tell, The Winter's Tale, Domino Courts, After the Rain, Rivers and Ravines, Cinema Mundi.*

**TURQUE, MIMI.** Born September 30, 1939 in Brooklyn, NYC. Graduate Brooklyn Col. Bdwy debut 1945 in *Carousel* followed by *Seeds in the Wind, The Enchanted, Cry of the Peacock, Anniversary Waltz, Carnival, Man of La Mancha, The Infernal Summit, The Dybbuk, Romeo and Juliet, The Happy Journey, God Bless You Mr Rosewater, 13, Tale of Two Toms.*

**TURTURO, AIDA.** Born September 25, 1962 in NYC. Graduate SUNY/New Paltz. Debut 1989 OB in *Tony 'n' Tina's Wedding*, followed by *Cavalleria Rusticana*, Bdwy in *A Streetcar Named Desire* (1992).

**TUTHILL, CHARLES.** Born November 11, 1961 in Cleveland, OH. Graduate NYU. Debut 1992 OB in *Ten Blocks on the Camino Real.*

**UBACH, ALANNA.** Born October 3, 1975 in Downey, CA. Debut 1991 OB in *Club Soda.*

**UBARRY, HECHTER.** Born September 5, 1946 in NYC. Bdwy debut 1965 in *Royal Hunt of the Sun* followed by *Man of La Mancha* (1970/'72/'77/'92), OB in *Romance Language, Chu Chem.*

**UNBERGER, ANDY.** Born February 21, 1957 in Portsmouth, VA. Graduate VaComU. Debut 1986 OB in *Rainbow* followed by *The Man of the Nineties, What Do They Want from Me*, Bdwy in *City of Angels* (1991).

**VACCARO, BRENDA.** Born November 18, 1939 in Brooklyn, NYC. Attended Neighborhood Playhouse. Bdwy debut 1961 in *Everybody Loves Opal* (for which she received a Theatre World Award) followed by *The Affair, Children from Their Games, Cactus Flower, The Natural Look, How Now Dow Jones, The Goodbye People, Father's Day, The Odd Couple, Jake's Women.*

**VAJTAY, NICOLETTE.** Born April 1, 1965 in New Brunswick, NJ. Graduate Montclair State Col. Debut 1991 OB in *Of Blessed Memory* followed by *The White Bear.*

**VAN DYCK, JENNIFER.** Born December 23, 1962 in St. Andrews, Scotland. Graduate Brown U. Debut OB 1977 in *Gus and Al*, followed by *Marathon '88, Secret Rapture, Earth and Sky*, Bdwy in *Secret Rapture, Two Shakespearean Actors, Dancing at Lughnasa.*

**VAN PATTEN, JOYCE.** Born March 9 in Kew Gardens, NY. Bdwy debut 1941 in *Popsy* followed by *This Rock, Tomorrow the World, The Perfect Marriage, The Wind Is 90, Desk Set, A Hole in the Head, Murder at the Howard Johnson's, I Ought to Be in Pictures, Supporting Cast, Brighton Beach Memoirs, Rumors, Jake's Women.* OB in *Between Two Thieves, Spoon River Anthology, The Seagull.*

**VANCE, COURTNEY B.** Born March 12, 1960 in Detroit, MI. Harvard graduate. Bdwy debut 1987 in *Fences* for which he received a Theatre World Award, followed by *Six Degrees of Separation*, OB in *Temptation, Six Degrees of Separation.*

**VARGAS, OVIDIO.** Born November 30, 1959 in Brooklyn, NY. Graduate Boston Conv. Debut OB in *Yes Dear* followed by *Wonderful Town, Salon, Blood on Blood, Greed, Eastern Standard, The Elephant Piece, The Rover.*

**VARRONE, GENE.** Born October 30, 1929 in Brooklyn, NYC. Graduate LIU. Bdwy in *Damn Yankees, Take Me Along, Ziegfeld Follies, Goldilocks, Wildcat, Fade-Out Fade-In, Subways Are For Sleeping, Bravo Giovanni, Drat! The Cat!, Don't Drink the Water, Dear World, Coco, A Little Night Music, So Long 174t Street, Knickerbocker Holiday, The Grand Tour, The Most Happy Fella* (1979), OB in *Promenade, Kuni Leml, The Sunset Gang.*

**VAUGHAN, MELANIE.** Born September 18 in Yazoo City, MS. Graduate LaStateU. Bdwy debut 1976 in *Rex* followed by *Sunday in the Park with George, On the 20th Century, Music Is, Starlight Express, The Most Happy Fella* (1992), OB in *Canterbury Tales.*

**VENNEMA, JOHN C.** Born August 24, 1948 in Houston, TX. Graduate Princeton U., LAMDA, Bdwy debut 1976 in *The Royal Family*, followed by *The Elephant Man, Otherwise Engaged*, OB in *Loot, Statements after an Arrest, The Biko Inquest, No End of Blame, In Celebration, Custom of the Country, The Basement, A Slight Ache, Young Playwrights Festival, Dandy Dick, Nasty Little Secrets, Mountain, Light Up the Sky, Selling Off.*

**VENNER, TRACY.** Born in 1968 in Boulder, CO. Attended Stephens Col. Bdwy debut 1989 in *Gypsy*, OB in *Rodgers & Hart: A Celebration.*

**VENTRISS, JENNIE.** Born August 7, 1935 in Chicago, IL. Graduate DePaul U. Debut 1954 OB in *Ludlow Fair* followed by *I Can't Keep Running in Place, Lautree, The Contest, Warren G., Mirage, Look after Lulu, Between Daylight and Boonville*, Bdwy in *Luv* (1966), *Prisoner of Second Avenue, Gemini, Sherlock's Last Case, On Borrowed Time* (1991).

| | | |
|---|---|---|
| Tonya Pinkins | Scott Renderer | Stephanie Pope |
| Nestor Serrano | Faith Prince | Thom Sesma |

| | | | | | |
|---|---|---|---|---|---|
| Gordana Rashovich | Victor Slezak | Kathryn Rossetter | Jonathan Slaff | Abigail Sanders | Robert Stanton |

| | | | | | |
|---|---|---|---|---|---|
| Helen Schneider | Robert Tate | Robin Spielberg | Courtney B. Vance | Cheryl Stern | Sal Viviano |

| | | | | | |
|---|---|---|---|---|---|
| Linda Thorson | Eli Wallach | Susan Terry | Lee Wilkof | Mary Testa | Walter Willison |
| Rebecca Timms | Ray Wills | Nicolette Vajtay | Jason Workman | Daisy White | Pippa Winslow |

**VINOVICH, STEPHEN.** Born January 22, 1945 in Peoria, IL. Graduate U. Ill. UCLA, Juilliard. Debut 1974 OB in *The Robber Bridegroom* followed by *King John, Father Usbridge Wants to Marry, Hard to Sell, Ross, Double Feature, Tender Places, A Private View, Love, Poker Session, Paradise, Secret Rapture,* Bdwy in *The Robber Bridegroom* (1976), *The Magic Show, The Grand Tour, Loose Ends, A Midsummer Nights Dream, Lost in Yonkers.*

**VIVIANO, SAL.** Born July 12, 1960 in Detroit, MI. Graduate E. Ill. U. Bdwy Debut 1984 in *The Three Musketeers,* followed by *Romance/Romance, Falsettos,* OB in *Miami* (1986), *Hot Times and Suicide, Romance/Romance, Broadway Jukebox, Catch Me If I Fall, Weird Romance.*

**VOGEL, DAVID.** Born October 19, 1922 in Canton, OH. Attended U. Pa. Bdwy debut 1984 in *Ballet Ballads* followed by *Gentlemen Prefer Blondes, Make a Wish, Desert Song,* OB in *How to Get Rid of It, The Fantasticks, Miss Stanwyck Is Still in Hiding, Marya, She Loves Me, The Male Animal.*

**VON BARGEN, DANIEL.** Born June 5, 1950 in Cincinnati, OH. Graduate Purdue U. Debut 1981 OB in *Missing Persons,* followed by *Macbeth, Beggars in the House of Plenty, Angel of Death,* Bdwy debut in *Mastergate* (1989) for which he received a Theatre World Award.

**WAGNER, HANK.** Born March 12, 1969 in New York City. Graduate London Central Schl. Debut 1990 OB in *Measure for Measure,* followed by *Cork, The Fine Art of Finesse, Two Schnitzler One-Acts, As You Like It, Tartuffe.*

**WAITES, THOMAS G.** Born in 1954; attended Juilliard. OB in *American Buffalo, Awake and Sing, Forty Deuce, Extremities, North Shore Fish,* Bdwy in *Richard III* (1979), *Teaneck Tanzie, Search and Destroy.*

**WALKER, RAY.** Born August 13, 1963 in St. Johnsbury, VT. Graduate NYU. Debut 1985 OB in *Christmas Spectacular,* followed by *Merrily We Roll Along, Chess,* Bdwy 1977 in *Les Misérables.*

**WALKER, SYBIL.** Born April 30 in Chicago, IL. Graduate SMU. Debut 1991 OB in *From the Mississippi Delta.*

**WALLACH, ELI.** Born December 7, 1915 in Brooklyn, NYC. Graduate U.Tx., CCNY. Bdwy debut 1945 in *Skydrift* followed by *Henry VIII, Androcles and the Lion, Alice in Wonderland, Yellow Jack, What Every Woman Knows, Antony and Cleopatra, Mr. Roberts, Lady from the Sea, The Rose Tattoo* (for which he received a 1951 Theatre World Award), *Mlle. Colombe, Teahouse of the August Moon, Major Barbara, The Cold Wind and the Warm, Rhinoceros, Luv, Staircase, Promenade All, Waltz of the Toreadors, Saturday Sunday Monday, Every Good Boy Deserves Favor, Twice around the Park, Cafe Crown, The Price,* OB in *The Diary of Anne Frank, Next of the Wood Grouse, Cafe Crown.*

**WALLER, KENNETH.** Born April 12, 1945 in Atlanta, GA. Graduate Piedmont Col. Debut 1976 in *Boys from Syracuse,* Bdwy in *Sarava* (1979), *Onward Victoria, Me and My Girl, Phantom of the Opera.*

**WALSH, BARBARA.** Born June 3, 1955 in Washington, DC. Attended Mongomery Col. Bdwy debut 1982 in *Rock 'n' Roll: The First 5000 Years,* followed by *Nine, Falsettos,* OB in *Forbidden Broadway.*

**WALSH, TENNEY.** Born October 18, 1963 in New Haven, CT. Attended Yale U. Debut 1981 OB in *The Wild Duck,* followed by *A Think Piece, Joe Egg, Even in Laughter, Breaking the Prairie Wolf Code, Tomorrow's Monday, A Tapestry of Dreams, The White Rose of Memphis, Julie Johnson,* Bdwy in *Joe Egg* (1985).

**WALTERS, KELLY.** Born May 28, 1950 in Amarillo, TX. Graduate U. Wash. Debut 1973 OB in *Look We've Come Through* followed by *The Tempest, The Taming of the Shrew,* Bdwy in *Candide* (1975), *Canterbury Tales, Barnum, Grind, The Visit.*

**WALTHER, GRETCHEN.** Born March 8, 1938 in NYC. Attended Northwestern U. Bdwy debut 1962 in *Something about a Soldier,* OB in *Innocent Pleasures,* followed by *The Novelist.*

**WALTON, JIM.** Born July 31, 1955 in Tachikawa, Japan. Graduate U. Cinn. Debut 1979 OB in *Big Bad Burlesque,* followed by *Scrambled Feet, Stardust, Sweeney Todd, Closer Than Ever, Life on the Third Rail, And The World Goes Round,* Bdwy in *Perfectly Frank* (1980), *Merrily We Roll Along, 42nd Street, Stardust, Sweeney Todd.*

**WARD, ELIZABETH.** Born November 16, 1962 in Denver, CO. Graduate U. Pacific, U. Cal. Bdwy debut 1990 in *City of Angels.*

**WARING, WENDY.** Born December 7, 1960 in Melrose, MA. Attended Emerson Col., Debut 1987 OB in *Wish You Were Here,* Bdwy in *Legs Diamond* (1988), *The Will Rogers Follies.*

**WARMFLASH, STUART.** Born June 27, 1949 in New York City, Graduate NYU. Debut 1970 OB in *The Lady from Maxim's,* followed by *Secret Service, Boy Meets Girl, Let Me Finish!, A Map and a Cap.*

**WARRA, SCOTT.** Born June 5, 1957 in Chicago, IL. Graduate SMU. Debut 1982 OB in *The Rise of Daniel Rocket,* followed by *The Dining Room, Johnny Pye and the Foolkiller, Gifts of the Magi, Falsettoland, 50 Million Frenchmen,* Bdwy in *The Wind in the Willows* (1985), *Welcome to the Club, City of Angels, The Most Happy Fella.*

**WASHINGTON, DENZEL.** Born December 28, 1954 in Mt. Vernon, NY. Graduate Fordham U. Debut 1975 OB in *The Emperor Jones,* followed by *Othello, Coriolanus, Mighty Gents, Becket, Spell #7, Ceremonies in Dark Old Men, One Tiger to a Hill, A Soldier's Play, Every Goodbye Ain't Gone, Richard III,* Bdwy 1988 in *Checkmates.*

**WASHINGTON, SHARON.** Born September 12, 1959 in New York City. Graduate Dartmouth Col, Yale U. Debut 1988 OB in *Coriolanus* followed by *Cymbeline, Richard III, The Balcony, Caucasian Chalk Circle, Before It Hit Home.*

**WASSON, CRAIG.** Born March 15, 1954 in Ontario, OR. Attended LaneComCol, U. Ore., Bdwy debut 1975 in *All God's Chillun Got Wings,* OB in *The Ballad of Soapy Smith* (1984), followed by *For Sale, Jock.*

**WATERBURY, MARSHA** (formerly Marsha Skaggs). Born August 23, 1949 in

Bedford, OH. Attended Purdue U., AADA. Bdwy debut 1981 in *They're Playing Our Song,* followed by *Einstein and the Polar Bear, Smile, Jake's Women,* OB in *Little Shop of Horrors.*

**WEAVER, FRITZ.** Born January 19, 1926 in Pittsburgh, PA. Graduate U. Chicago Bdwy debut 1955 in *The Chalk Garden* (for which he received a Theatre World Award) followed by *Protective Custody, Miss Lonelyhearts, All American, Lorenzo, The White House, Baker Street, Child's Play, Absurd Person Singular, Angels Fall, The Crucible* (1991), *A Christmas Carol,* OB in *The Way of the World, White Devil, The Doctor's Dilemma, Family Reunion, The Power and the Glory, The Great Goe Brown, Peer Gynt, Henry IV, My Fair Lady* (CC), *Lincoln, The Biko Inquest, The Price, Dialogue for Lovers, A Tale Told, Time Framed.*

**WEBB, ALEXANDER.** Born August 25, 1962 in Valentine, NE. Graduate U. Cal Debut 1987 OB in *The Tavern* followed by *More Fun Than Bowling.*

**WEBER, JAKE.** Born March 12, 1963 in London, Eng. Graduate Middlebury Col Juilliard Debut 1988 OB in *Road,* followed by *Twelfth Night, Maids of Honor, Richard III, The Big Funk, Othello, Mad Forest,* Bdwy in *A Small Family Business* (1992).

**WEISS, GORDON JOSEPH.** Born June 16, 1949 in Bismarck, ND. Attended Moorhead State Col. Bdwy debut 1974 in *Jumpers* followed by *Goodtime Charley, King of Hearts, Raggedy Ann, Ghetto, Jelly's Last Jam,* OB in *A Walk on the Wild Side.*

**WEISSMAN, CLIFF.** Born April 3, 1957 in Brooklyn, NYC. Graduate Brooklyn Col. Debut 1991 OB in *But There Are Fires* followed by *Raft of the Medusa.*

**WELBY, DONNAH.** Born May 4, 1952 in Scranton, PA. Graduate Catholic U. Debut 1981 OB in *Between Friends,* followed by *Double Inconstancy, The Taming of the Shrew, The Contrast, Macbeth, Electra, All's Well That Ends Well, Hot/Baltimore, The Philanderer, Three Sisters, The Importance of Being Earnest, A Midsummer Night's Dream, Between Friends, The Fine Art of Finesse, As You Like It.*

**WELLER, FREDERICK.** Born April 18, 1966 in New Orleans, LA. Graduate UNC Chapel Hill, Juilliard. Bdwy debut 1991 in *Six Degrees of Separation.*

**WESTENBERG, ROBERT.** Born October 26, 1953 in Miami Beach, FL. Graduate U. Cal/Fresno. Debut 1981 OB in *Henry IV Part I,* followed by *Hamlet, The Death of von Richthofen,* Bdwy in *Zorba* (1983) for which he received a Theatre World Award *Sunday in the Park with George, Into the Woods, Les Misérables, The Secret Garden.*

**WHITE, AL.** Born May 17, 1942 in Houston, TX. Graduate San Fran CC. Bdwy debut 1992 in *Two Trains Running* for which he received a Theatre World Award.

**WHITE, ALICE.** Born January 6, 1945 in Washington, DC. Graduate Oberlin Col .Debut 1977 OB in *The Passion of Dracula,* followed by *La Belle au Bois, Zoology, Snow Leopards, Fridays, Candida.*

**WHITE, AMELIA.** Born September 14, 1954 in Nottingham, Eng. Attended London Central School. Debut 1984 OB in *The Accrington Pals* (for which she received a Theatre World Award), followed by *American Bagpipes,* Bdwy in *Crazy for You* (1992).

**WHITE, DAISY.** Born January 7, 1966 in Paris, Fr. Graduate Bennington Col., RADA. Debut 1991 OB in *The Christmas Rules,* followed by *A Shayna Maidel,* Bdwy in *A Little Hotel on the Side* (1992).

**WHITE, JULIE.** Born June 4, 1962 in San Diego, CA. Attended Fordham U. Debut 1988 OB in *Lucky Stiff,* followed by *Just Say No, Early One Evening at the Rainbow Bar and Grill, The Stick Wife, Marathon '91, Spike Heels.*

**WHITE, LILLIAS D.** Born July 21, 1951 in Brooklyn, NYC. Graduate NYCC. Debut 1975 OB in *Solidad Tetrad* followed by *The Life, Romance in Hard Times,* Bdwy in *Barnum* (1981), *Dreamgirls, Rock In' Roll: The First 5000 Years, Once on This Island, Carrie.*

**WHITE, PATRICK.** Born September 9, 1963 in Albany, NY. Graduate AADA. Debut 1988 OB in *Male Animal,* followed by *After the Rain, Take the Waking Slow, Anima Mundi.*

**WHITEHEAD, PAXTON.** Born in Kent, Eng. Attended Webber-Douglas Acad. Bdwy debut 1962 in *The Affair* followed by *Beyond the Fringe, Candida, Habeas Corpus, Crucifer of Blood, Camelot, Noises Off, Run for Your Wife, Artist Descending a Staircase, Lettice and Lovage, A Little Hotel on the Side,* OB in *Gallows Humor, One Way Pendulum, A Doll's House, Rondelay.*

**WIDDOES, KATHLEEN.** Born March 21, 1939 in Wilmington, DE. Attended Paris Theatre de Nations. Bdwy debut 1958 in *The Firstborn* followed by *The World of Suzy Wong, Much Ado about Nothing, The Importance of Being Earnest, Brighton Beach Memoirs, Hamlet,* OB in *The Three Sisters, The Maids, You Can't Take It with You, To Clothe the Naked, World War 2, Beggar's Opera, As You Like It, A Midsummer Night's Dream, One-Act Festival, Hamlet, The Tower of Evil.*

**WILKOF, LEE.** Born June 25, 1951 in Canton, OH. Graduate U. Cinn. Debut 1977 OB in *Present Tense,* followed by *Little Shop of Horrors, Holding Patterns, Angry Housewives, Assassins,* Bdwy in *Sweet Charity* (1986), *The Front Page.*

**WILLIAMS, ALLISON.** Born September 26, 1958 in NYC. Debut 1977 OB in *Guys and Dolls* followed by *Young Gifted and Broke, Thrill a Moment,* Bdwy in *The Wiz* (1977), *Dreamgirls, Sweet Charity, Jelly's Last Jam.*

**WILLIAMS, ELLIS.** Born June 28, 1951 in Brunswick, GA. Graduate Boston U. Debut 1977 OB in *Intimation,* followed by *Spell #7, Mother Courage, Ties That Bind, Kid Purple, The Boys Next Door,* Bdwy in *The Basic Training of Pavlo Hummel, Pirates of Penzance, Solomon's Child, Trio, Requiem for a Heavyweight,Once on This Island.*

**WILLIFORD, LOU.** Born August 14, 1957 in Dallas, TX. Graduate Trinity U. Debut 1990 OB in *The Brass Jackal,* followed by *Lips Together Teeth Apart,* Bdwy in *Fiddler on the Roof* (1990).

**WILLISON, WALTER.** Born June 24, 1947 in Monterey Park, CA. Bdwy debut 1970 in *Norman Is That You?*, followed by *Two by Two* for which he received a Theatre World Award, *Wild and Wonderful, A Celebration of Richard Rodgers, Pippin, A Tribute to Joshua Logan, A Tribute to George Abbott, Grand Hotel,* OB in *South Pacific in Concert, They Say It's Wonderful, Broadway Scandals of 1928 and Options,* both of which he wrote, *Aldersgate 88.*

**WILLIAMS, GARRY D.** Born February 14, 1964 in Macon, GA. Graduate U. Ga, UCLA. Debut 1990 OB in *Texaco Star* followed by *The Monkey's Wedding, Young Abe Lincoln,* Bdwy in *The Visit* (1992).

**WILLIAMSON, RUTH.** Born January 25, 1954 in Baltimore, MD. Graduate U. Md. Bdwy debut 1981 in *Annie,* followed by *Smile, Guys and Dolls,* OB in *Preppies, Bodo.*

**WILLIS, RICHARD.** Born in Dallas, TX. Graduate Cornell U., Northwestern U. Debut 1986 OB in *Three Sisters* followed by *Nothing to Report, The Rivalry of Dolls.*

**WILLS, RAY.** Born September 14, 1960 in Santa Monica, CA. Graduate Wichita St. U. Brandeis U. Debut 1988 OB in *Side by Side* by Sondheim, followed by *Kiss Me Quick, The Grand Tour, The Cardigans, The Rothschilds, Little Me.*

**WILSON, CHANDRA.** Born August 27, 1969 in Houston, TX. Graduate NYU. Debut 1991 OB in *The Good Times Are Killing Me* for which she received a Theatre World Award.

**WILSON, JULIE.** Born in 1925 in Omaha, NE. Bdwy debut 1946 in *Three to Make Ready* followed by *Kiss Me Kate, Kismet, Pajama Game, Jimmy, Park, Legs Diamond,* OB in *From Weill to Sondheim, Hannah 1939, Cole and Coward.*

**WILSON, MARY LOUISE.** Born November 12, 1936 in New Haven, CT. Graduate Northwestern U. Bdwy debut 1963 in *Hot Spot,* followed by *Flora the Red Menace, Criss-Crossing, Promises Promises, The Women, The Gypsy, The Royal Family, The Importance of Being Earnest, Philadelphia Story, Fools, Alice in Wonderland, The Odd Couple, Prelude to a Kiss,* OB in *Our Town, Upstairs at the Downstairs, Threepenny Opera, A Great Career, Whispers on the Wind, Beggar's Opera, Buried Child, Sister Mary Ignatius Explains It All, Actor's Nightmare, Baby with the Bathwater, Musical Comedy Murders of 1940, Macbeth, Flaubert's Latest.*

**WINANT, BRUCE.** Born April 9, 1957 in Santa Monica, CA. Graduate U.S. Intl. U. Bdwy debut 1991 in *Miss Saigon.*

**WINSLOW, PIPPA.** Born July 25 in Syracuse, NY. Graduate U. Cal./Irvine, AmConsvTh. Debut 1992 OB in *Opal.*

**WINSON, SUZI.** Born February 28, 1962 in New York City. Bdwy debut 1980 in *Brigadoon,* followed by OB in *Moondance, Nunsense.*

**WINSTON, LEE.** Born March 14, 1941 in Great Bend. KS. Graduate U. Kan, Debut 1966 OB in *The Drunkard,* followed by *Little Mahagony, The Good Soldier Schweik, Adopted Moon, Miss Waters to You, Christmas Bride, The Elephant Piece,* Bdwy in *Showboat* (1966), *1600 Pennsylvania Avenue.*

**WINTERS, SCOTT.** Born December 5, 1959 in Newark, NJ.Graduate Northwestern U. Debut 1986 OB in *Three Sisters,* followed by *Trelawny of The Wells!*

**WISBART, STEVEN.** Born May 11, 1962 in NYC. Graduate Berklee Col. Bdwy debut 1991 in *City of Angels.*

**WOJDA, JOHN.** Born February 19, 1957 in Detroit, MI. Attended U. Mich. Bdwy debut 1982 in *Macbeth,* followed by *The Merchant of Venice, Two Shakespearean Actors,* OB in *The Merchant of Venice, Natural Disasters, The Coming of Mr. Pine, Henry IV Parts 1 and 2.*

**WOLF, KELLY.** Born January 9, 1964 in Nashville, TN. Graduate Interlochen Arts Acad. Debut 1983 in *Ah Wilderness,* followed by *Marathon '86, Young Playwrights Festival, Bloody Poetry, The Summer Winds, Peacetime.*

**WOODS, CAROL.** Born November 13, 1943 in Jamaica, NY. Graduate Ithaca Col. Debut 1980 OB in *One Mo' Time* followed by *Blues in the Night,* Bdwy in *Gring* (1985), *Big River, Stepping Out, The Crucible, A Little Hotel on the Side.*

**WOODS, RICHARD.** Born May 9, 1923 in Buffalo, NY. Graduate Ithaca Col. Bdwy in *Beg Borrow or Steal, Capt. Brassbound's Conversion, Sail Away, Coco, Last of Mrs. Lincoln, Gigi, Sherlock Holmes, Murder Among Friends, Royal Family, Deathtrap, Man and Superman, Man Who Came to Dinner, The Father, Present Laughter, Alice in Wonderland, You Can't Take It with You, Design for Living, Smile,* OB in *The Crucible, Summer and Smoke, American Gothic, Four-in-One, My Heart's in the Highlands, Eastward in Eden, Long Gallery, Year Boston Won the Pennant, In the Matter of J. Robert Oppenheimer,* with APA in *You Can't Take It with You, War and Peace, School for Scandal, Right You Are, Wild Duck, Pantagleize, Exit the King, Cherry Orchard, Cock-a-doodle Dandy,* and *Hamlet, Crimes and Dreams, Marathon '84, Much Ado about Nothing, Sitting Pretty in Concert, The Cat and the Fiddle, The Old Boy.*

**WOODSON, JOHN.** Born May 12, 1950 in Des Moines, IA. Attended NC Schl. of Arts. Debut 1990 OB in *King Lear,* followed by *The Sorrows of Frederick.*

**WOPAT, TOM.** Born in 1950 in Lodi, WI. Attended U. Wis. Debut 1978 OB in *A Bistro Car on the CNR,* followed by *Oklahoma!, The Robber Bridegroom, Olympus on My Mind,* Bdwy in *I Love My Wife* (1979), *City of Angels.*

**WORKMAN, JASON.** Born October 9, 1962 in Omaha, Neb. Attended U. Ky., Goodman School. Bdwy debut 1989 in *Meet Me in St. Louis* for which he received a Theatre World Award. OB in *Haunted Host, Safe Sex.*

**WORKMAN, SHANELLE.** Born August 3, 1978 in Fairfax, VA. Bdwy debut 1988

in *Les Misérables.*

**WORTH, PENNY.** Born March 2, 1950 in London, Eng. Attended Sorbonne/Paris. Bdwy debut 1970 in *Coco,* followed by *Irene, Annie, Grand Hotel.*

**WRIGHT, TERESA.** Born October 27, 1918 in NYC. Bdwy debut 1938 in *Our Town,* followed by *Life with Father, The Dark at the Top of the Stairs, Mary Mary, I Never Sang for My Father, Death of a Salesman, Ah Wilderness!, Morning's at 7, On Borrowed Time,* OB in *Who's Happy Now, A Passage to E.M. Forster.*

**WYATT, MONA.** Born January 31 in Ft. Monmouth, NJ. Attended Shenandoah Consv. Debut 1984 in *Radio City Christmas Spectacular,* followed OB in *Manhattan Serenade,* Bdwy in *Oh Kay!* (1990), *High Rollers.*

**WYCHE, MIMI.** Born December 2, 1955 in Greenville, SC. Graduate Stanford U. Debut 1986 OB in *Once on a Summer's Day,* followed by *Senor Discretion, Juan Darien, The Golden Apple,* Bdwy in *Cats* (1988).

**WYLIE, JOHN.** Born December 14, 1925 in Peacock, TX. Graduate No. Tex. St. U. Debut 1987 OB in *Lucky Spot,* followed by Bdwy in *Born Yesterday* (1989), *Grand Hotel.*

**WYMAN, NICHOLAS.** Born May 18, 1950 in Portland, ME. Graduate Harvard U. Bdwy debut 1975 in *Very Good Eddie,* followed by *Grease, The Magic Show, On the 20th Century, Whoopee!, My Fair Lady* (1981), *Doubles, Musical Comedy Murders of 1940, Phantom of the Opera,* OB in *Paris Lights, When We Dead Awaken, Charlotte Sweet, Kennedy at Colonus, Once on a Summer's Day, Angry Housewives.*

**WYN, COURTNEY.** Born April 27, 1969 in Ft. Worth, TX. Attended Southwestern U. Bdwy debut 1990 in *Peter Pan,* also 1991.

**WYNKOOP, CHRISTOPHER.** Born December 7, 1943 in Long Branch, NJ. Graduate AADA. Debut 1970 OB in *Under the Gaslight,* followed by *And So to Bed, Cartoons for a Lunch Hour, Telecast, Fiorello!, The Aunts,* Bdwy in *Whoopee!* (1979), *City of Angels.*

**XIFO, RAY.** Born September 3, 1942 in Newark, NJ. Graduate Don Bosco Col. Debut 1974 OB in *The Tempest,* followed by *Frogs, My Uncle Sam, Shlemiel the First, A Murder of Crows,* Bdwy in *City of Angels* (1989).

**YEOMAN, JO ANN.** Born March 19, 1948 in Phoenix, AZ. Graduate Ariz. St. U., Purdue U. Debut 1974 OB in *The Boy Friend,* followed by *Texas Starlight, Ba Ta Clan, A Christmas Carol.*

**YORK, MICHAEL.** Born March 27, 1942 in Fulmer, Eng. Attended Oxford U. Bdwy debut 1973 in *Outcry* followed by *Bent* (1980), *The Little Prince and the Aviator, The Crucible.*

**YOUNGMAN, CHRISTINA.** Born September 14, 1963 in Philadelphia, PA. Attended Point Park Col. Debut 1983 OB in *Emperor of My Baby's Heart,* followed by *Carouselle des Folles,* Bdwy in *Starlight Express* (1987), *Largely New York, The Will Rogers Follies.*

**YULIN, HARRIS.** Born November 5, 1937 in Calif. Attended US Cal. Debut 1963 OB in *Next Time I'll Sing to You,* followed by *A Midsummer Night's Dream, Troubled Waters, Richard III, King John, The Cannibals, A Lesson from Aloes, Hedda Gabler, Barnum's Last Life, Hamlet, Mrs. Warren's Profession, Marathon '86, Marathon '87,* Bdwy in *Watch on the Rhine* (1980), *The Visit.*

**ZARISH, JANET.** Born April 21, 1954 in Chicago, IL. Graduate Juilliard. Debut 1981 OB in *The Villager,* followed by *Playing with Fire, Royal Bob, An Enemy of the People, A Midsummer Night's Dream, Festival of 1-Acts, Other People's Money, Human Nature, Selling Off.*

**ZAY, TIM.** Born August 13, 1952 in Cleveland, OH. Graduate U. Cincinnati. Debut 1988 OB in *Moby Dick* followed by *This One Thing I Do, The Rover.*

**ZEMON, TOM.** Born January 13, 1964 in Hartford, CT. Graduate U. Hartford, Bdwy debut 1988 in *Les Misérables.*

**ZERLE, GREG.** Born August 19, 1957 in Wisconsin, Graduate U. Wis., U. Wash. Debut 1986 OB in *Sherlock Holmes and The Redheaded League,* followed by *Bittersuite, Juba,* Bdwy in *Into TheWoods* (1988), *Grand Hotel.*

**ZIEMBA, KAREN.** Born November 12 in St. Joseph, MO. Graduate U. Akron, Debut 1981 OB in *Seesaw,* followed by *I Married an Angel, Sing for Your Supper, 50 Million Frenchmen, And the World Goes Round, 110 In The Shade* (NYCO/LC).

**ZIEN, CHIP.** Born March 20, 1947 in Milwaukee, WI. Attended U. Penn. OB in *You're a Good Man Charlie Brown,* followed by *Kadish, How to Succeed ..., Dear Mr. G., Tuscaloosa's Calling, Hot/Baltimore, El Grande de Coca Cola, Split, Real Life Funnies, March of the Falsettos, Isn't It Romantic, Diamonds, Falsettoland,* Bdwy in *All Over Town* (1974), *The Suicide, Into the Woods, Grand Hotel, Falsettos.*

**ZIMMERMAN, K.** Born April 19, 1952 in Harrisburg, PA. Graduate U. Pa. Debut 1976 OB in *Fiorello!* followed by *Silk Stockings, On a Clear Day You Can See Forever, 110 in the Shade, Fellow Travelers, Frankie, First Is Supper,* Bdwy in *Brigadoon* (1981).

**ZINDEL, LIZABETH.** Born October 30, 1976 in New York City. Debut 1989 OB in *Essence of Margrovia,* followed by *Last Night, Come Again, Common Clay, David's Mother, Night Sky, EST Marathon '92.*

**ZISKIE, KURT.** Born April 16, 1956 in Oakland, CA. Graduate Stanford U., Neighborhood Playhouse. Debut 1985 OB in *A Flash of Lightning* followed by *Ulysses in Nighttown, Three Sisters, EST Marathon '92,* Bdwy in *Broadway* (1987).

| Judith Anderson | Erma Campbell | Ralph Bellamy | Yvonne Bryceland |

# OBITUARIES
## (June 1, 1991-May 31, 1992)

**DAME JUDITH ANDERSON** (Frances Anderson-Anderson), 94, Australia-born stage, screen and TV actress, who had her greatest acting triumph in the 1947 Broadway production of *Medea*, died on January 3, 1992 in Santa Barbara, CA, of pneumonia. Following her Broadway debut in *Peter Weston* in 1923 she appeared in *Cobra, The Dove, Strange Interlude, As You Desire Me, Firebird, The Mask and the Face, Come of Age, The Old Maid, Family Portrait, Hamlet, Macbeth, The Three Sisters, Tower Beyond Tragedy, John Brown's Body, In the Summer House, Chalk Garden, Comes a Day, Elizabeth the Queen, Hamlet* (title role), and *Medea* (revival). Survived by a niece.

**A.J. ANTOON** (Alfred Joseph Antoon, Jr.), 47, Massachusetts-born NY theatre director, died on January 22, 1992 in New York of AIDS. His stage work, most of it for the NY Shakespeare Festival, includes *That Championship Season* (for which he won a Tony Award), *Much Ado About Nothing, Cymbeline, Trelawney of the Wells, Dance of Death, The Art of Dining, The Rink, The Good Doctor,* and *The Taming of the Shrew.* Survived by his companion, his brother, and two sisters.

**JEAN ARTHUR**, 90, born Gladys Georgianna Greene in New York City, one of Hollywood's leading female stars of the 1930s and 1940s, died on June 19, 1991 in Carmel, CA. Broadway debut 1932 in *Foreign Affairs* followed by *The Curtain Rises, The Bride of Torozko,* the out of town tryout of *Born Yesterday,* and *Peter Pan* (1950). She attempted returns in *Saint Joan* (1954) and *The Freaking Out Of Stephanie Blake* (1967), but left both productions before they opened. She taught drama at Vassar in the 1970's. There were no survivors.

**PEGGY ASHCROFT**, 83, born Edith Margaret Emily Ashcroft, Croydon, England-born stage and film actress, died on June 14, 1991 in London. For more than half a century a leading English actress, she was made a Dame of the British empire in 1956. Known for her Shakespearean heroines, her only New York appearances were in *High Tor* (1937) and *Edward, My Son* (1948). In recent years she became widely known for her television work in *Jewel in the Crown,* and film work highlighted by her Oscar-winning performance in *A Passage To India* (1984). She is survived by a son and daughter.

**MARTIN ASHE**, 80, Illinois-born stage, film and TV actor, died April 15, 1991 in Woodland Hills, CA. His Broadway credits included *Bathsheba* and *The Happiest Millionaire.* No survivors.

**PHILIP ASTOR**, 47, stage actor died of AIDS on October 19, 1991. He appeared on Broadway in *1776, Nuts, All Over Town,* and *Torch Song Trilogy* (in the leading role). Survived by his parents, and a sister.

**JACQUES AUBUCHON**, 67, Massachusetts-born stage, screen and TV actor, died of heart failure in Woodland Hills, CA, on December 28, 1991. He appeared on Broadway in *The Madwoman of Chaillot, The Happy Time, Mr. Pickwick,* and City Center productions of *Charley's Aunt, Cyrano de Bergerac,* and *The Shrike.* He is survived by his wife, two sons, a daughter, a grandson, a brother, and three sisters.

**ELEANOR AUDLEY**, 86, stage and TV actress, died on November 25, 1991 of respiratory failure in North Hollywood. Her Broadway credits include *Pigeons and People,* and *Susan and God.* No reported survivors.

**WILLIAM BALL**, 60, Chicago-born founder of the American Conservatory Theatre and director, died, possibly a suicide, on July 30, 1991 in Los Angles. He acted and directed with regional companies across the country before making his New York directing debut Off Broadway with *Ivanov* in 1958, for which he won Obie and Drama Desk awards. Other Off Broadway work included *Under Milk Wood, Six Characters in Search of an Author, Tartuffe* and *Homage To Shakespeare.* In 1979 he accepted A.C.T.'s Tony Award. During his career, he directed 87 productions and produced more than 300. Survived by his mother, two brothers, and a sister.

**MARGARET BARKER**, 83, Baltimore-born stage, screen and TV actress, died on April 3, 1992 in New York of lung cancer. Following her 1928 Broadway debut in *The Age of Innocence* she appeared in *The Barretts of Wimpole Street, The House of Connelly, Men in White, Gold Eagle Guy, Leading Lady, Member of the Wedding, Autumn Garden, See the Jaguar, Ladies of the Corridor, The Master Builder,* and Off Broadway in *Wayside Motor Inn, The Loves of Cass McGuire, Three Sisters, Detail Without a Map, The Inheritors, Caligula, The Mound Builders, Quiet in the Land, Uncle Vanya,* and *Ladies.* No immediate survivors.

**RALPH BELLAMY**, 87, Chicago-born stage, screen and TV actor, perhaps best remembered for his Tony Award winning role as Franklin Roosevelt in the 195- Broadway drama *Sunrise at Campobello,* died on November 29, 1991 in Sant- Monica, CA, after a long illness. His other Broadway appearances include *Town Boy* (his debut in 1929), *Roadside, Tomorrow the World, Stage of the Union, Detective Story.* His more than 100 movies include the film version of *Campobello* and *The Awful Truth* (for which he received an Oscar nomination). Survived by his fourth wife, his adopted son, a daughter, and a sister.

**DEHL BERTI**, 70, Colorado-born stage, screen and TV character actor, died of a heart attack on November 26, 1992 in Los Angeles. His Broadway credits include *Thank You Svoboda, Richard III, Broadway Nocturne, Hickory Stick,* and *The Strong Are Lonely.* Survived by 2 sons, a daughter and 2 grandchildren.

**JULIE BOVASSO**, 61, Brooklyn-born actress and playwright, died of cancer on September 14, 1991 in NYC. In the mid-50s she established the experimental Tempo Playhouse in Manhattan, which introduced the Theatre of the Absurd to NYC audiences. Her Broadway roles included *Monique, Minor Miracle, and Gloria and Esperanza.* The Off-Broadway staging of that work won her 3 Obies Off-Broadway credits included *Naked, The Maids, The Lesson, The Typewriter, Screens, Henry IV Part I, What I Did Last Summer,* and *Italian American Reconciliation.* Work as playwright included *Moon Dreamers, Schubert's Last Serenade, Monday On The Way To Mercury Island, The Nothing Kid,* and *Angelo's Wedding.* She directed the latter play along with 1973's *In The Boom Boom Room,* but was replaced amid dissention in both cases. She became well known also for film and tv. Survived by her mother and a brother.

**L. SLADE BROWN**, 68, died of cancer on June 29, 1991 in Hartwell, GA. He produced the Broadway shows *Bye Bye Birdie, Entertaining Mr. Sloane, All American, A Joyful Noise,* and *The Rink.* Survived by two daughters, a son, a brother and six grandchildren.

**ANTHONY BRUNO**, 46, playwright and critic, died of AIDS on June 14, 1991 in Los Angeles. His play *Soul Survivor* was produced Off-Broadway and in many cities. He was theatre critic for *Frontiers* magazine. Survived by his father and two sisters.

**HOWARD BRUNNER**, 51, stage, screen and TV actor, whose Broadway appearance included *Children of a Lesser God,* died on November 12, 1991 in Marietta, GA of AIDS. No reported survivors.

**YVONNE BRYCELAND** (Yvonne Heilbluth), 66, South African stage actress, who acted in several works by Athol Fugard, died on January 13, 1992 in London of cancer. In addition to her many roles in London and South Africa she made her sole New York stage appearance in *The Road to Mecca,* winning a Theatre World and Obie Award. Survived by her husband and three daughters.

**BRENDAN BURKE**, 63, stage actor and teacher, died in New York on October 1- 1991 after a long illness. His NY theatre credits include *Purple Dust, Red Roses for Me, Beyond the Fringe,* and *Camelot.*

234

**David Carroll**  **Brad Davis**

**ERMA CAMPELL**, 49, NYC-born actress, died of cancer July 30, 1991 in New York City. She received a Theatre World Award in 1990 for her debut Off-Broadway in *Ground People,* followed by *The Goat.* She is survived by her mother, two sons, a daughter, and three grandchildren.

**ROBERT CAREY**, 32, New Jersey-born actor and founding member of Theater-in-Limbo, died of AIDS on June 27, 1991 in New York. he made his debut Off-Broadway in 1985's *Vampire Lesbians of Sodom,* followed by *Times Square Angel, Psycho Beach Party* and *The Lady in Question.* Survived by his parents, a brother, and a sister.

**JOAN CAULFIELD**, 69, New Jersey-born actress, died of cancer on June 18, 1991 in Los Angeles. Best known for television and film work, she also appeared on Broadway in *Kiss And Tell* (1943). Survived by two sons, two sisters, and a grandson.

**DAVID (Formerly David-James) CARROLL**, 41, Rockville Centre, NY-born actor and singer, died of AIDS on March 11, 1992 at the BMG/RCA Recording Studio in Manhattan where he was recording the *Grand Hotel* album. Widely considered one of the best musical leading men on or Off-Broadway, he made his debut in 1975's *Matter of Time* Off-Broadway. Broadway debut the same year in *Rodgers and Hart.* Broadway included *Where's Charley, Oh Brother!, 7 Brides for 7 Brothers, Roberta in Concert, Wind in the Willows,* in *Chess* where he memorably sang *Anthem,* and his last Broadway role as the Baron in *Grand Hotel.* OB included *Joseph and the Technicolor Dreamcoat, New Tunes, La Boheme, Company and Cafe Crown* which transferred to Broadway. Although he did not live to finish the *Grand Hotel* recording, he can be heard on the New York *Chess, Oh Brother!* and studio recordings of *Girl Crazy, Lola* and others. Survived by his companion, parents, two brothers and two sisters.

**PANOS CHRISTI**, 54, actor and director, died April 25, 1992 of AIDS in LA. He was one of the pioneers of theatre in LA where he performed in *View From the Bridge, Caligula,* and numerous others. His directorial credits included LA's *Cabaret.*

**MAE CLARKE**, 81, actress died of cancer April 29, 1992 in CA. Best known for films, especially *Public Enemy,* her Broadway work included *Manhattan Mary.*

**BERT CONVY**, 58, St. Louis-born Actor and TV host, died of cancer on July 15, 1991 in Los Angeles. He made his Broadway debut in 1959 in *The Billy Barnes Revue,* followed by *Nowhere To Go But Up, Morning Sun, Love and Kisses, Fiddler On The Roof, Impossible Years, Cabaret* (creating the part of Cliff), *Shoot Anything With Hair That Moves* (OB), *Front Page,* and *Nine.* Survived by his second wife and three children from his first marriage.

**OLGA COOK**, 100, musical comedy actress, died December 15, 1991 in NY. Big success was achieved in 1921's *Blossom Time,* Broadway work included *Student Prince, Rio Rita,* and *My Maryland.* No survivors.

**ANN SORG COSTON**, 62, actress and casting director, died in NY state December 6, 1991. She appeared in NY productions of *The Young and Fair* and *Springtime Folly.* She was in many tours before becoming an agent and casting director. Survived by her husband, a daughter and a son.

**BRAD DAVIS**, 41, Florida-born stage, screen and TV actor, died on September 8, 1991 of AIDS at his home in Studio City, CA. Perhaps best known for his role in the 1978 film *Midnight Express,* he appeared on the New York stage in *Crystal and Fox, The Elusive Angel, Entertaining Mr. Sloane,* and *The Normal Heart.* Survived by his wife, daughter, brother, and parents.

**JOHN DEHNER** (John Forkum), 76, stage, screen and TV actor, died on February 4, 1992 in Santa Barbara, CA of emphysema and diabetes. In addition to his many film and television roles he acted on the Broadway stage in *Bridal Crown* and directed *Alien Summer.* Survived by his wife, 2 daughters, a stepdaughter, 3 stepsons, 2 grandchildren, and 3 stepgrandchildren.

**GERALDINE DELANEY**, 67, Broadway dancer-singer, died on May 29, 1992 at her home in Pomona, NY following a short illness. Her Broadway credits include *Where's Charley?, Guys and Dolls, Wonderful Town,* and *Silk Stockings.* Survivors include her husband, 3 sons, and a daughter.

**SANDY DENNIS**, 54, Nebraska-born stage, screen and TV actress died on March 2, 1992 of ovarian cancer at her home in Westport, CT. Following her 1957 Broadway debut in *The Dark at the Top of the Stairs,* she appeared in *Face of a Hero, The Complaisant Lover, A Thousand Clowns* (for which she won a Theatre World and Tony Award), *Any Wednesday* (Tony Award), *Daphne in Cottage D., How the Other Half Loves, Let Me Hear You Smile, Absurd Person Singular, Same Time Next Year, Supporting Cast,* and *Come Back to the Five and Dime Jimmy Dean,* and Off-Broadway in *Burning Bright,* and *Buried Inside Extra.* She received an Oscar for playing Honey in the film version of *Who's Afraid of Virginia Woolf?* Survived by her mother and a brother.

**Sandy Dennis**  **Richard Derr**

**Colleen Dewhurst**

**Marlene Dietrich**

**Mildred Dunnock**

**Jose Ferrer**

**RICHARD DERR**, 74, Pennsylvania-born stage, film and TV actor, died May 8, 1992 in Santa Monica, CA of heart failure. He received a *Theatre World* Award for his role in *The Traitor*. Other stage credits included *Dial M. for Murder, Plain and Fancy, Dream Girl, Grand Tour, Closing Door, A Phoenix Too Frequent, Maybe Tuesday* and *Invitation to a March.* Survived by his brother.

**COLLEEN DEWHURST**, 67, Montreal-born stage, screen and TV actress, one of the great actresses of her generation, died August 22, 1991 in South Salem, NY of cancer. Broadway debut in 1952 with *Desire Under the Elms,* followed by *Tamburlaine the Great, Country Wife, Caligula, All the Way Home, Great Day in the Morning, Ballad of the Sad Cafe, More Stately Mansions, All Over, Mourning Becomes Electra, Moon for the Misbegotten, An Almost Perfect Person, Queen and the Rebels, You Can't Take it With You, Ah! Wilderness, Long Day's Journey into Night* (1988) and OB in *Taming of the Shrew, Eagle Has Two Heads, Camille, Macbeth, Children of Darkness* for which she received a 1958 *Theatre World* Award, *Antony and Cleopatra, Hello and Goodbye, Good Woman of Setzuan, Hamlet, Are You Now or Have You Ever Been?, Taken in Marriage, My Gene* and *Reassurance* (in April, 1991). She toured widely in *My Gene* and *Love Letters.* In 1985 Dewhurst was elected president of Actors' Equity and was a passionate supporter of a variety of issues including nontraditional casting and support for AIDS victims. She often appeared with second husband George C. Scott and also appeared on Broadway with her son Campbell Scott in *Long Day's Journey* and *Ah Wilderness.* She is also survived by another son, Alexander, a stage manager, and two grandchildren.

**MARLENE DIETRICH**, 90, screen legend, died May 6, 1992 in Paris. Though best known for her film work, she performed a concert act for many years, most notably on Broadway in 1967 at the Lunt-Fontanne Theatre. Survived by her daughter, Maria Riva and four grandchildren.

**DONALD GENE DUBBINS**, 63, actor, died of cancer on August 17, 1991. His stage work included *Tea and Sympathy.*

**DIXIE DUNBAR**, 72, actress, died August 29, 1991 in Miami after a series of heart attacks. She made many films in the 1930s, but started in the Broadway production of *Life Begins at 8:40* (1934) followed by *Yokel Boy.*

**MILDRED DUNNOCK**, 90, Baltimore-born stage, film and TV actress, died July 5, 1991 in Massachusetts. She created the role of Linda Loman in *Death of a Salesman* in 1949. She made her Broadway debut in 1932's *Life Begins,* followed by *Corn is Green, Richard III, Only the Heart, Foolish Notion, Lute Song, Another Part of the Forest, The Hallams, Pride's Crossing, Wild Duck, In the Summer House, Cat on a Hot Tin Roof, Child of Fortune, Milk Train Doesn't Stop Here Anymore, Traveller without Luggage, Days in the Trees, Tartuffe,* OB in *Trojan Women, Phaedra, Willie Doesn't Live Here Anymore, Colette* and a *Place without Doors.* Survived by her husband, a daughter and three grandchildren.

**DAVID EISLER**, 36, singer and actor, died February 16, 1992 in Houston of pneumonia. He was best known for playing the title role in the City Opera productions of *Candide.* Other NYCO credits included *Barber of Seville, Mikado* and *Brigadoon.* Survived by longtime companion, parents and a sister.

**RICK EMERY**, 39, actor, singer and dancer, died April 7, 1992 in NY. He appeared on Broadway and in tours of *Tap Dance Kid, Chorus Line, Musical Chairs, Chicago* and *Girl Crazy.* Survived by his mother and sister.

**JOHN MORGAN EVANS**, 49, actor and writer, died December 27, 1991 in LA after lengthy illness. Broadway included *Jimmy Shine, Our Town* and *Mike Downstairs.* Survived by his companion, father and brother.

**STEPHEN J. FALAT**, 34, actor and teacher, died after a long illness on October 10, 1991 in NY. He was one of the founders of Equity Fights AIDS and coordinated the annual Shubert Alley flea market. Theatre work included *Fire in the Basement* and other Off-Broadway plays. Survived by longtime companion and parents.

**JOSÉ FERRER**, 80, stage and screen actor and director, died January 26, 1992 in Coral Gables, FL. He twice won Tony awards for acting, *Cyrano de Bergerac* (1947) and *The Shrike* (1952), and another for direction of *The Fourposter, Stalag 17* and *The Shrike,* all in the 1951-52 season. Broadway debut in *A Slight Case of Murder* (1935) was followed by *Charley's Aunt,* opposite Paul Robeson in *Othello* (1943). *Silver Whistle, Twentieth Century, The Girl Who Came to Supper,* and many City Center revivals including *Volpone, Angel Street, Chekhov One-Acts,* and *The Alchemist.* Other Broadway acting credits included *Lets Face It* and *Man of La Mancha.* In 1990 he appeared in the London musical *Born Again* and was due to return to Broadway in *Conversations With My Father* prior to his illness. His marriages to Uta Hagen, Phyllis Hill and Rosemary Clooney ended in divorce. Survived by fourth wife, three sons, including actor Miguel Ferrer, three daughters, two sisters, a half-brother and eight grandchildren.

**VIRGINIA FIELD**, 74, British stage and screen actress died January 2, 1992 in CA of cancer. She came to America to appear with Helen Hayes in *Victoria Regina* but due to film roles ended up debuting on Broadway in *Panama Hattie* followed by *The Doughgirls* and *Light Up the Sky* in the 1940s. Survived by her husband, Willard Parker and a daughter.

**SYLVIA FINE (KAYE)**, 78, songwriter and producer, died October 28, 1991 in NY of emphysema. Her collection of sketches, *Straw Hat Revue* hit Broadway in 1940. She wrote special material for husband Danny Kaye's stage acts and produced PBS TV specials on the American Musical Theatre in recent years. Survived by a daughter, sister and brother.

**FREDERICK FOX**, 81, theatre and opera set designer, died September 11, 1991 in Englewood, NJ of a stroke. He designed over 200 Broadway shows including *Darkness at Noon, Seven Year Itch, King of Hearts, John Loves Mary* and *Anniversary Waltz*. Survived by wife, three sons, a daughter, and four grandchildren.

**WILLIAM T. GARDNER**, 57, director and producer, died April 24, 1992 in Pittsburgh of a heart attack. He produced the 1973 production of *A Moon for the Misbegotten* with Colleen Dewhurst and Jason Robards. He was the producing director of the Pittsburgh Public Theatre for eight years. Survived by a sister.

**MICHAEL SCOTT GREGORY**, 29, died of AIDS on February 25, 1992 in Ft. Lauderdale, FL. He sang and danced in the original casts of *Sophisticated Ladies, Starlight Express* and *Jerome Robbins' Broadway*. He also appeared in *Cats* and *Stardust* on Broadway. Survived by his mother, stepfather, two brothers and three sisters.

**RODNEY GRIFFIN**, 46, dancer and choreographer, died December 26, 1991 in NY of AIDS. Broadway work as a performer included *A Time for Singing, Promises Promises* and *Molly*. He acted in a NYSF production of *Peer Gynt*. He co-founded the Theatre Dance collection company. His survivors include his companion, parents and a brother.

**BRYON Q. GRIFFITH**, 73, actor, acting teacher, agent and producer, died December 23, 1991 of cancer in CA. Broadway debut in *Follow the Boys* was followed by *Arsenic and Old Lace, The Streets Are Guarded* and *Family Affair*.

**PATRICK HAMILTON**, 45, actor, died November 8, 1991 of respiratory failure in Lubbock, TX. Broadway credits included *Best Little Whorehouse in Texas, Singin' in the Rain* and *Late Night Comic*. Off-Broadway he acted in *Hamelin, Romantic Detachment* and *All's Fair*. Survived by his parents and a daughter.

**CHET LEAMING**, 66, Des Moines-born actor, died February 19, 1992 in NY. Off-Broadway included *In April Once, From Morn to Midnight, Entertain a Ghost, Pantagleize*. He toured with *Inherit the Wind, Long Day's Journey into Night* and *Dear Me the Sky is Falling*. He also worked as a stage manager on and off-broadway. Survived by a longtime companion, three children, a brother and 10 grandchildren.

**EVA LE GALLIENNE**, 92, much honored actress, director, author and translator, died June 3, 1991 in CT of heart failure. Born in London, she made her debut there in 1914 and came to Broadway in 1915 in *Mrs. Boltay's Daughters*. This was followed by *Bunny, Melody of Youth, Mr. Lazarus, Saturday to Monday, Lord and Lady Algy, Off Chance, Lusmore, Elsie Janis and Her Gang, Not So Long Ago, Lillion, Sandro Botticelli, The Rivals, The Swan, Assumption of Hannele, LaVierge Folle, Call of Life, Master Builder, John Gabriel Borkman, Saturday Night, Cradle Song, Inheritors, Good Hope, First Stone, Improvisations in June, Hedda Gabler, Would-Be-Gentleman, Cherry Orchard, Peter Pan, Sunny Morning, Sea Gull, Living Corpse, Romeo and Juliet, Siegfried, Alison's House, Camille, Dear Jane, Alice in Wonderland* (1932/1947/1982), *L'Aiglon, Rosmersholm, Women Have Their Way, Prelude to Exile, Mme. Capet, Frank Fay's Music Hall, Uncle Harry, Therese, Henry VIII, What Every Woman Knows, Ghosts, Corn Is Green, Starcross Story, Southwest Corner, Mary Stuart, Exit the King, Royal Family* (1975), *To Grandmother's House We Go*. No immediate survivors.

**FRANKLIN R. LEVY**, 43, theatre, film and TV producer, died on March 17, 1992 of a brain hemorrhage. Mr. Levy was a consultant to LA's Center Theatre Group and produced *Hasty Heart, Journey's End, Child's Play* and *A Lovely Way to Spend an Evening* in LA theatres. Survived by companion Bill Hutton, three brothers and his parents.

**KAY LORING**, 79, actress, died February 24, 1992 in Palm Beach, FL after a long illness. Broadway debut in *Three Men On a Horse* followed by *Having a Wonderful Time, What a Life, Spring Again, Ask My Friend Sandy* and *Rugged Path*. She later acted in various Florida theatres. Survived by her brother and three stepsons.

**EDWARD LOVE**, 43, Toledo-born actor, dancer and choreographer died December 27, 1991 of AIDS in NY. Debut 1972 Off-Broadway in *Ti-Jean and His Brothers* followed by *Spell #7*. Broadway credits included *Raisin, Chorus Line, Dancin', Censored Scenes from King Kong*. He also danced with the Alvin Ailey company. Survived by two sisters.

Virginia Field

Edward Love

John Lund

Leueen MacGrath

237

Marisa Mell

George Murphy

**JOHN LUND**, 81, Rochester-born screen leading man, died May 1[ 1992 in Coldwater Canyon, CA. He won a *Theatre World* award for hi Broadway role in *The Hasty Heart*. Other stage work included *As Yo Like It* (1941), *New Faces of 1942* and *Early to Bed*. Survived by a sister

**LEUEEN MacGRATH**, 77, London-born Actress and playwright, die March 27, 1992 in London. Broadway debut in *Edward My Son* (1948 followed by *The Enchanted, High Ground, Fancy Meeting You Agair Love of 4 Colonels, Tiger at the Gates, Potting Shed* and Off-Broadwa in *The Seagull* and *Tribute to Lili Lamont*. As a playwright, sh collaborated with third husband George S. Kaufman on *Small Hour: Fancy Meeting You Again*, and *Silk Stockings*. Survived by a sister an stepdaughter.

**FRED MacMURRAY**, 83, popular film and TV actor, died November ! 1991 in Santa Monica of pneumonia. While best known for films lik *Double Indemnity* and the TV series *My Three Sons*, his Broadway wor included *Three's a Crowd* (1930), *The Third Little Show*, and the origina *Roberta*. Survived by his wife, June Haver, a son and three daughters.

**DANIEL MANN**, 79, stage and film director, died November 21, 199 in LA of heart failure. He directed the Broadway plays *Come Back Littl Sheba, The Rose Tattoo* and Uta Hagen in *Streetcar Named Desire* Survived by three children.

**RALPH MARRERO**, 33, stage, film and TV actor, died in car acciden in Albuquerque November 16, 1991. He appeared in *Miriam's Flower: Bad Habits, Ubu*, and *Machinal* Off-Broadway. Survived by his paren: and a sister.

**JAMES McCALLION**, 72, stage, film and TV actor, died July 11, 199 of a heart attack in Van Nuys, CA. As a child actor he appeared o Broadway in *Yours Truly* (1927), *Roosty* and *But For The Grace of Goc* Survived by a son, daughter, sister and two grandchildren.

**MARISA MELL**, 53, stage and film actress died May 16, 1992 i Vienna of cancer. She starred in the troubled 1967 musical *Mata-Har* which closed prior to in's Broadway opening.

**BRIAN MOORE**, 59, stage and film actor, died May 8, 1992 of hear failure in Hollywood. He starred in a NYSF production of *As You Like* and worked many regional theatres. Survived by his mother and a sister.

**GEORGE MURPHY**, 89, stage and film actor and politician, died Ma 3, 1992 in Palm Beach, FL of leukemia. Although best known for hi musical films and later career as a U.S. senator for California, he mad his stage debut in 1927 in the chorus of Broadway's *Good News*. Othe shows included *Hold Everything!, Off Thee I Sing* and *Roberta*. Survive by his second wife, son and four grandchildren.

**JOHN MYHERS**, 70, stage and film actor, screen writer and director died May 27, 1992 in LA of pneumonia. His credits included *Golde Fleecing, Chic, Good Soup*, and tours of *Kiss Me Kate* and *Sound o Music*. Survived by his wife Joan Benedict and a daughter.

**LAURENCE NAISMITH** (Laurence Johnson), 83, British stage, scree and TV character actor died on June 5, 1992 in Southport, Australia afte a brief illness. Following his Broadway debut in the 1963 production o *School for Scandal* he appeared in *Here's Love, A Time for Singing*, anc *Billy*. He is survived by his son and several grandchildren.

**BILL NAUGHTON**, 81, British playwright who wrote the 1964 play *Alfie*, died on January 9, 1992 at his home on the Isle of Man o undisclosed causes. His other works for the stage include *Spring anc Port Wine, Keep It in the Family*, and *All in Good Time* (which late became the film *The Family Way*). Survived by his wife, son anc daughter.

**MERVYN NELSON**, 76, theatre actor, director, writer and produce died on August 17, 1991 of cancer in Manhattan. He directed *Babes ir Arms, The Secret Life of Walter Mitty*, and *Tickets Please;* acted in *'Tis o Thee* and *The Snark Was a Boojum;* wrote *The Ivy Green* and wrote anc produced *The Jazz Train*. He is survived by two sisters.

**ROBERT NEMIROFF**, 61, New York City-born theatre producer, diec on July 18, 1991 in New York of cancer. His credits include *The Sign ir Sidney Brustein's Window, To Be Young Gifted and Black*, and *Raisin fo* which he won the Tony Award. He is survived by his wife, a daughter, brother, and two grandchildren.

**DON NUTE**, 56, Pennsylvania-born actor, died August 25, 1991 in NY of AIDS. He made his debut Off-Broadway in *Trojan Women* (1965) followed by *Boys in the Band, Mad Theatre for Madmen, Eleventl Dynasty, About Time, The Urban Crisis, Christmas Rappings, Life of Man, A Look at the Fifties* and *Aunt Millie*. He also appeared in many films and the TV version of *My Sister Eileen*.

**DANIEL OCKO**, 78, stage, screen and TV actor, died on August 29 1991 in Argentina of a respiratory condition. His Broadway appearances include *Cafe Crown, What a Life, First Lady, Hopes for a Harvest*, anc *Horse Fever*. He is survived by his wife and a sister.

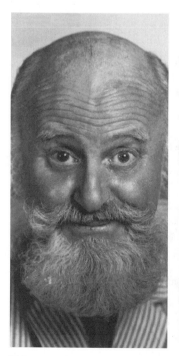

238    Laurence Naismith

Don Nute

**Joseph Papp**

**Molly Picon**

**KEVIN O'CONNOR**, 56, Hawaii-born stage actor, director and teacher, died of cancer on June 22, 1991 in New York City. After his 1964 debut Off-Broadway in *Up to Thursday,* he appeared in *Six from La Mama, Rimers of Eldritch, Tom Paine, Boy on the Straightback Chair, Dear Janet Roseberg, Eyes of Chalk, Alive and Well in Argentina, Duet, Trio, The Contractor, Kool Aid, The Frequency, Chucky's Hutch, Birdbath, The Breakers, Crossing the Crab Nebula, Jane Avril, Inserts, 3 by Beckett, The Dicks, A Kiss is Just a Kiss, Last of the Knucklemen, Thrombo, The Dark and Mr. Stone, The Miser, The Heart Outright* and *By and for Havel.* On Broadway he was featured in *Gloria and Esperanza, The Morning After Optimum, Figures in the Sand, Devour the Snow,* and *The Lady from Debuque.* He is survived by two brothers, his mother, two step-brothers and a stepsister.

**HECTOR OREZZOLI**, 38, Argentine director, designer, writer, died on December 5, 1991 at his Manhattan home of cardiopulmonary arrest. With his partner Claudio Segovia he created the Broadway revues *Tango Argentina, Falmenco Puro,* and *Black and Blue.* Survived by his mother, father, and a brother.

**JOSEPH PAPP** (Joseph Papirofsky), 70, legendary New York theatre producer, founder of the NY Shakespeare Festival and free Shakespeare in Central Park, died on October 31, 1991 in New York of prostate cancer. As head of the Public Theatre he was responsible for some of the most significant Off-Broadway and Broadway productions of the past thirty years including *Hair, A Chorus Line* (Broadway's longest running show), *I'm Getting My Act Together* and *Taking It on the Road, Runaways, Two Gentlemen of Verona, The Pirates of Penzance, The Human Comedy, The Mystery of Edwin Drood, Short Eyes, The Basic Training of Pavlo Hummel, That Championship Season, No Place to Be Somebody, Sticks and Bones, For Colored Girls Who Have Considered Suicide when the Rainbow is Enuf, The Water Engine, Plenty, Streamers, The Normal Heart, Rum and Coke, Aunt Dan and Lemon,* and *Serious Money.* He is survived by his wife, three daughters, a son, two sisters, and a brother.

**BERT PARKS**, 77, TV host best known as the announcer for the Miss America Pageant, died February 2, 1992 in La Jolla, CA. During the 1960-61 Broadway season he assumed the role of Prof. Harold Hill in the long running *Music Man.*

**WENDELL K. PHILLIPS**, 83, Illinois-born stage and screen actor died on October 6, 1991 at his home in Berkeley, CA, of undisclosed causes. Following his 1931 Broadway debut in *Incubator* he appeared in *Mother Signs, Many Mansions, Abe Lincoln in Illinois, Fifth Column, Anne of the Thousand Days, The Solid Gold Cadillac,* and *The Investigation,* and Off-Broadway in *Death of J.K.* and *The Birds.* No reported survivors.

**BEN PIAZZA**, 58, Arkansas-born stage, screen and TV actor, died of cancer on September 7, 1991 in Sherman Oaks, CA. he made his Broadway debut in 1958 in *Winesburg Ohio,* followed by *Kataki,* for which he received a *Theatre World* Award, *A Second String, Fun Couple, Who's Afraid of Virgina Woolf?, Song of the Grasshopper,* and *The Death of Bessie Smith.* Off-Broadway he was seen in *American Dream, Deathwatch, Zoo Story,* and *Endgame.* He is survived by his companion, two sisters and six brothers.

**JANE PICKENS-HOVING**, 83, stage and TV actress-singer, former member of the Pickens Sisters, died on February 21, 1992 in Newport, RI, of heart failure. On Broadway she appeared in *Thumbs Up, Boys and Girls Together,* and *Regina* in the title role. Survived by her daughter, and a sister.

**MOLLY PICON**, 94, New York City-born stage, screen and TV actress, one of the most famous and beloved figures of the Yiddish theatre, died on April 5, 1992 in Lancaster, PA. On Broadway she appeared in *Morning Star, For Heaven's Sake Mother, Milk and Honey, How to Be a Jewish Mother, The Front Page, Paris Is Out, Something Old Something New,* and Off-Broadway in *Abi Gezunt.* She is survived by a sister.

**TENO POLLICK**, 62, stage, screen and TV actor, died at his Los Angeles home of September 7, 1991 after a long illness. He appeared on Broadway in *Peter Pan,* with Mary Martin, and *Much Ado About Nothing,* with John Gielgud, and Off-Broadway in *Steambath.* Survived by his sister.

**SAL PROVENZA**, 45, Brooklyn-born stage and TV actor-singer, died on December 25, 1991 in New York City of lymphoma. On Broadway he appeared in *Oh! Brother!,* and *The King and I* (1984), and Off-Broadway in *The Fantasticks* and *A Matter of Tone.* Survived by his mother, brother and sister.

**GEROME RAGNI**, 48, Pittsburgh-born author, lyricist and actor, who helped create the 1967 musical *Hair,* died of cancer July 10, 1991 in New York City. In addition to appearing in *Hair* he also was seen on Broadway in *Hamlet* (1964), and the Off-Broadway productions *Viet Rock, Hang Down Your Head and Die,* and *The Knack.* He also co-wrote *Dude* and *Jack Sound and His Dog Stage Blowing His Final Trumpet on the Day of Doom.* He is survived by his wife, son, mother, five sisters, and two brothers.

**Jane Pickens-Hoving**

**Sal Provenza**

**239**

**Robert Reed**

**Lee Remick**

**THALMUS RASULALA (Jack Crowder)**, 55, stage, film and TV actor died October 9, 1991 in Albequerque, NM of a leukemia related heart attack. He received a *Theatre World* award for his Broadway debut in the Pearl Bailey *Hello Dolly* (1967). He also appeared in New York productions of *Fly Blackbird, Fantasticks, Roar of the Greasepaint, Damn Yankees, Merchant of Venice, No Time For Sergeants, Orpheus Descending* and *Zulu and The Zoyde*. Survived by his wife and four children.

**BERTICE READING**, 54, American singer-actress died on June 8, 1991 in London following a stroke. She received a 1959 Tony Award nomination for her role in *Requiem for a Nun*. She is survived by her son and her fourth husband.

**ROBERT REED** (John Robert Rietz, Jr.), 59, Illinois-born stage, screen and TV actor, died on May 12, 1992 in Pasadena, CA of AIDS. He appeared on Broadway in such plays as *Barefoot in the Park, Avanti!, Deathtrap,* and *Doubles*. On television he achieved his greatest fame in the series *The Defenders* and *The Brady Bunch*. Survived by his mother, daughter, and grandson.

**LEE REMICK**, 55, Massachusetts-born stage, screen, and TV actress, died on July 2, 1991 at her home in Brentwood, CA, of cancer. She acted on Broadway in *Be Your Age, Anyone Can Whistle,* and *Wait Until Dark,* for which she received a Tony Award nomination. Her successful motion picture career include an Oscar nomination for *Days of Wine and Roses*. She is survived by her husband, producer Kip Gowans, a daughter, a son, two stepdaughters, and her mother.

**JOHN REMME**, 56, North Dakota-born stage and TV actor-singer, died on January 18, 1992 in New York City of AIDS. On Broadway he appeared in such productions as *The Ritz, The Royal Family, Can-Can, Alice in Wonderland, Teddy and Alice,* and the 1989 revival of *Gypsy*. Survived by his sister.

**TONY RICHARDSON**, 63, British stage, screen, and TV director, died on November 14, 1991 in Los Angeles of complications from AIDS. He directed the original 1957 Broadway production of John Osborne's classic drama *Look Back in Anger*. On screen he was best known for directing the 1963 comedy *Tom Jones* for which he won an Academy Award. He is survived by three daughters including actresses Natasha and Joely Richardson.

**LARRY RILEY**, 39, Memphis-born stage, film and TV actor, died June 6, 1991 of AIDS in California. After Broadway bow in *A Broadway Musical* (1978) he appeared in *I Love My Wife, Night and Day, Shakespeare's Cabaret* and *Big River*. Off-Broadway included *Street Songs, Amerika, Plane Down, Sidewalkin', Frimbo, A Soldier's Play, Maybe I'm Doing It Wrong, Diamonds* and *The Leader*. Survived by his wife, a son, his mother and two sisters.

**BITTMAN RIVAS**, 51, stage actor who appeared in the Broadway production of *Short Eyes,* died on May 21, 1992 of a heart attack at the Brooklyn school where he taught. No reported survivors.

**PAUL REID ROMAN**, 55, stage, screen and TV actor, died on November 17, 1991 in Los Angeles of cancer. His New York stage credits include *On a Clear Day You Can See Forever, Over Here, The Girl Who Came to Supper, Fiorello!, Hallelujah Baby* and *American Roulette*. No reported survivors.

**JERRY SCHLOSSBERG** (Gerald W. Schlossberg), 55, New York-born theatrical producer, died on October 10, 1991 in Englewood, NJ, of cancer. Among productions were *Voices, On the Town* revival, *Line/Acrobats, Gantry,* and *Charley's Aunt,* with Louis Nye. Survived by his mother, sister, and five children.

**ALLAN SOBEK**, 46, dancer and stage manager died on September 16, 1991 in New York of AIDS. He appeared on Broadway in *Cabaret, Georgy, Seesaw, The Little Prince and the Aviator,* and *La Cage aux Folles*. Survived by his mother and three brothers.

**HELENE STANLEY** (Dolores Diane Freymouth), 62, stage, screen and TV actress, died on December 27, 1990 of undisclosed causes. In addition to acting in the 1950 Broadway production *Pardon My French,* she served as a model for several Disney animation characters. She is survived by her husband and son.

**FRAN STEVENS**, 72, Washington D.C.-born stage, screen and TV actress, died of cancer on November 2, 1991 in Bronx, NY. On Broadway she appeared in *Pousse Cafe, The Most Happy Fella, A Funny Thing Happened on the Way to the Forum, How Now Dow Jones, Her First Roman, Cry for Us All, On the Town,* and *Mame* (1983), and Off-Broadway in *Frank Gagiano's City Scene, Debris,* and *Polly*. Survived by a daughter and brother.

**SYLVIA SYMS**, 74, Brooklyn-born stage actress-singer, one of New York's most noted nightclub performers, died on May 10, 1992 in New York City of a heart attack following a show at the Algonquin Hotel. Following her 1949 Broadway debut in *Diamond Lil* she appeared in *Dream Girl, South Pacific, Whoop Up,* and *Camino Real*. Survived by her brother and sister.

**John Remme**

**Larry Riley**

**Sylvia Syms**                    **Florence Tarlow**

**Nancy Walker**                    **Dick York**

**FLORENCE TARLOW**, 70, Obie award winning actress died of cancer February 10, 1992 in New York. Off-Broadway included *Red Cross, Istanbul, A Beautiful Day, Gorilla Queen, Dracula Sabbat.* Broadway included *Man in the Glass Booth, Promenade, Inner City* and *Good Woman of Sechzuan* (LC).

**DOROTHY THREE** (Dorothy Estelle Triebitz), 85, Brooklyn-born actress and voice teacher died February 12, 1992 in Englewood, NJ of heart failure. Her Broadway credits included 1928's *Holiday* and *Clear All Wires.* Survived by her son and a sister.

**GENE TIERNEY**, 70, Brooklyn-born actress and film star died November 6, 1991 in Houston of emphysema. Prior to Hollywood, she appeared on Broadway in 1939 in *Mrs. O'Brian Entertains, The MaleAnimal* and *Ring Two.*

**THOMAS TRYON**, 65, Connecticut-born author and actor died September 4, 1991 in Los Angeles of cancer. Prior to his writing career he worked on Broadway as an understudy in the 1952 musical *Wish You Were Here,* followed by TV and film work.

**HEIDI VOSSELER**, 74, dancer died March 9, 1992 in Woodstock, NY of lung cancer. She danced in *The Boys From Syracuse* and *Louisiana Purchase* in the 1940s.

**BILL WALKER**, 95, stage and film actor, died January 27, 1992 in Woodland Hills, California of cancer. His Broadway credits include *Harlem, Solid South, White Man, The Big Fight* and *Golden Dawn.*

**NANCY WALKER** (Anna Myrtle Swoyer), 69, Philadelphia-born stage, screen and TV actress and director, died of lung cancer March 25, 1992 in Studio City, Calif. Her stage appearances included *Best Foot Forward, On the Town, Barefoot Boy with Cheek, Look Ma I'm Dancin', Along Fifth Ave., Phoenix '55, Fallen Angels, Copper and Brass, Wonderful Town* (CC), *Boys Against the Girls, Do Re Mi, Cherry Orchard, The Show-Off,* and *The Cocktail Party.* Her comic style made her a TV favorite in later years. Survived by composer/vocal coach David Craig, a daughter and a sister. Her legit directing credits include *Pushcart Affair* and *Utbu.*

**CASEY WALTERS**, 75, Boston-born stage, film and TV actor, died of a stroke December 3, 1991 in Montana. He debuted on Broadway in *Mister Roberts* (1946) followed by *First Love, Red Roses For Me,* OB in *First Week in Bogata* along with many national companies.

**THORLEY WALTERS**, 78, British stage, film and TV actor, died July 6, 1991 in London. His Broadway credits included *Under the Counter.*

**KEN WARD**, 37, actor and choreographer, died in a German train accident April 10, 1992. He appeared in Broadway's *Pirates of Penzance* and *La Cage Aux Folles.* He played Seymour in the first national tour of *Little Shop of Horrors* and recently was in *The Music of Andrew Lloyd Webber* in Chicago.

**JACK WASHBURN**, 64, Illinois-born stage actor, died March 15, 1992 after a long illness in New Hope., PA. Debuted on Broadway in 1955's *Fanny* followed by *Paradise Island* and *Mr. President.* In the 1960's and 70's he appeared in many Bucks County Playhouse productions. Survived by his wife, a son and daughter, and a grandson.

**BYRON WEBSTER**, 58, London-born stage, screen and TV actor, died of AIDS December 1, 1991 in Sherman Oaks, California. Broadway roles included *Camelot, Ben Franklin in Paris, My Fair Lady* (CC), *On a Clear Day, Abelard and Heloise,* and *Sherry.* OB included *Feast of Panthers* (1960) followed by *Ticket of Leave Man.* Survivors are his longtime companion and two sisters.

**WINIFRED WELLINGTON** (Grice), 97, Massachusetts-born actress died May 10, 1992 in Maryland of cardiac arrest. She appeared in Broadway productions from 1912-26 including *The Show Off.* Survived by a son, a sister, seven grandchildren and five great-grandchildren.

**JOHN OGEN WHEDON**, 86, writer died November 21, 1991 in Oregon of pneumonia. His Broadway plays included *Life's Too Short* (1933) and the musical *Texas Li'l Darlin'* (1950). Survived by six children, 12 grandchildren, a sister and a brother.

**CHARLES WILLARD**, 48, New York City-born producer and manager died August 11, 1991 in a boating accident. He managed *Lucifer's Child, Belle of Amherst, Driving Miss Daisy* for Julie Harris, *Pirates of Penzance, Anna Christie, I Remember Mama, Comedians,* and *Hollywood/Ukrane.* Survived by his mother and a sister.

**DICK YORK**, 63, Ft. Wayne, Indiana-born stage, television and film actor died of emphysema on February 20, 1992 in Grand Rapids, Mich. Best known for the TV series *Bewitched,* he appeared on Broadway in *Tea and Sympathy* (1953) and *Night of the Auk* (1956).

# INDEX

Forbes, Kate, 149, 190
Forbes-Kelly, Carla, 121
*Forbidden Broadway*, 66
*Forbidden Christmas*, 66
Ford, Clebert, 83, 91, 212
Ford, Jennifer, 178
Ford, John, 125
Ford, Linda, 186
Ford, Lonnie, 181
Ford, Robert, 76
Ford, Rodney, 82
Ford, Sarah, 92, 101
Ford, T. Cat, 108
Ford, Timothy, 189
*Foreigner, The, 143*
Forem, Wendy, 77
Foreman, Richard, 96
*Forever Plaid, 67, 137, 143, 154, 172*
Forlow, Ted, 47
Fornes, Maria Irene, 181, 190
Forrest, George, 57
Forrest, Michael L., 146
Forrester, Bill, 141, 185
Forston, Don, 133
Forsyth, Jerold R., 132
Fort, Audrey, 88
Forton, Ray, 162
Foss, Eliza, 119
Foster, Angela, 96
Foster, Ellis, 159
Foster, Gloria, 125, 200, 212
Foster, Joan, 170, 181
Foster, Karen, 96
Foster, Rick, 79
Fountain, Suzanne, 157
Fouquet, Paul, 46, 168
*Four Baboons Adoring The Sun, 32, 120*
*Four Play, 84*
*Four Short Operas, 128*
Foust, Kathryn, 163
Foust, Susie, 174
Foust, Thomas, 174
Fowler, Beth, 148, 158, 189
Fowler, Monique, 150, 158, 164
Fowler, Scott, 13, 212
Fox, Frederick, 237
Fox, Alan, 132
Fox, David, 194
Fox, Elliot, 85
Fox, Kevin Edward, 156
Fox, Lydia J., 88
Fox, Stephen, 13
Foxworth, Bo, 172
Foxworth, Robert, 161, 163, 201
Foy, Cathy, 71
Foy, Harriet D., 146
Fraboni, Angelo, 174
Frame, Donald M., 126
*Fran And Jane, 84*
Franca, Duca, 124
França, Ary, 124
Franciosa, Christopher, 142
Francis, Alice, 192
Francis, Genie, 104
Francis, Giuliana, 100

Francis, Kim, 192
Francis, Stephan, 100
Franck, Sandra M., 104
Frandsen, Erik, 71
Frank, David, 86, 183
Frank, Jeffrey, 49
Frank, Marilyn Dodds, 179
Frank, Richard, 190
Frankel, Mark, 111
Frankel, Richard, 71, 78, 102
Frankel, Scott, 53
Frankenfield, Kim, 134
*Frankenstein, 80*
Franklin, Bonnie, 183, 201
Franklin, Kim, 188
Franklyn-Robbins, John, 163, 194
Frano, Carl J., 95
Franz, Elizabeth, 6, 174, 212
Franz, Robert, 76
Franzblau, Bill, 13
Fraser, Alison, 62, 212
Fraser, Brad, 80
Fratantoni, Diane, 143
Fratti, Mario, 105
Frayn, Michael, 178
Frazier, Michael, 80
Frederick, Rebecca G., 156
Fredericks, Joel, 175
*Free Speech In America, 114*
Freed, Donald, 183
Freed, Morris, 134
Freedman, Bob, 160
Freedman, Gerald, 13, 161
Freedman, Glenna, 10, 14, 16-17, 24, 66-67, 69-70
Freedman, Harris W., 73
Freedman, Katherine, 187
Freeman, Heidi C., 160
Freeman, John Joseph, 55
Freeman, Stan, 83-84, 212
Freidrichs, Hans, 80
Freistadt, Louise, 97
French, Arthur, 80, 83, 91, 99, 212
French, David, 99
French, Rai, 176
French, Timothy, 194
Freschi, Bob, 25, 151, 160
*Fresh Of Breath Air, A, 112*
Fretts, Christopher, 187
Frey, Matthew, 83
Frezza, Christine, 194
Friday, Betsy, 62, 212
Fried, Jonathan, 149, 187
Friedman, Barry Craig, 80
Friedman, David, 173
Friedman, Doug, 134, 189
Friedman, Gene Emerson, 161
Friedman, Jonathan, 99, 103
Friedman, Leah Kornfeld, 131
Friedman, Warren, 81
Friedmann, Joyce, 151
Friel, Brian, 5, 10
Frierson, Andrea, 163
Frilles, Anky, 103
Frimark, Merle, 37, 58, 60-61, 88
Frisch, Bob, 97
Frisch, Max, 193

Frish, Alexander "Sasha", 13
Frkonja, Jeff, 185
Froeyland, Oeyvind, 106
*From The Mississippi Delta, 5, 88, 150*
Frost, Richard J., 143
Frost, Sue, 151, 160
Fry, Ray, 142
Fry, Stephen, 178, 189
Frye, David, 7
Fucile, Steven, 74
Fudge, Deidre, 161
Fuertes, Amparo, 79
Fugard, Athol, 108, 123, 141, 149, 190, 234
Fujiii, Timm, 138
Fulbright, Peter, 26, 43, 62
Fuller, Charles, 94
Fuller, David, 7
Fuller, Elizabeth, 180
Fuller, Nat, 162
Fuller, Susie, 101
Fulton, Barbara, 194
Fulton, James, 150
Funicello, Ralph, 152, 172-173
Funkhouser, Debra, 193
Funking, Bob, 189
Fuqua, Joseph, 142
Furber, Douglas, 178, 189
Furr, Teri, 166
Furth, George, 89
Fusco, Anthony, 118
Futterman, Dan, 95, 131
*Futz, 119*
Fyfe, Jim, 130, 212
Gabay, Roy, 83
Gabis, Stephen, 93
Gable, June, 149, 172
Gable, Tim, 127
Gabler, Linda, 178
Gabler, Milton, 37
Gabriel, Norma, 124
Gaeto, Jeffrey, 150
Gaffney, Lauren, 78, 133
Gaines, Boyd, 123, 190, 201, 212
Gaines, James E. "Sonny Jim", 81
Gaipa, Amy, 99
Galan, Esperanza, 7
Galante, Michael, 95
Galardi, Michael, 36
Galati, Frank, 159
Galbraith, Philip, 77, 212
Galbreath, Robert, Jr., 150
Gale, Andy, 140
Galica, Katarzyna, 44
Galindo, Ramon, 151, 160, 212
Gallagher, Colleen, 119, 142
Gallagher, Damond, 92
Gallagher, Fiona, 103
Gallagher, Helen, 76, 119
Gallagher, Peter, 5, 42-43, 201, 213
Gallagher, Terence, 159
Le Gallienne, Eva, 237
Gallin, Susan Quint, 88
Gallo, David, 148
Gallo, Paul, 26, 43, 135

Galloway, Pat, 194
Galloway, Shawn, 193
Galndo, Ramon, 25
Galvez, Georgia, 105
Galvin, Tara M., 146
Galvin-Lewis, Jane, 77
Gamble, Julian, 172
Gambrell, Gary, 178
Gamburg, Yevegeny, 115
Ganakas, Greg, 112
Gandolfini, James, 39
Gandy, Irene, 73, 76, 102, 112, 117
Ganio, Michael, 157, 192
Gannon, Liam, 10
Gantenbein, Peter, 190
Ganun, John, 63, 213
Ganzer, Lee James, 93
Garber, Victor, 5, 20-21, 201, 213
Garcia, Ann, 78
Garcia, Elaine, 124
Garcia, Kimberly Leslie, 176
Garcia, Vincent, 157
Garcilazo, Tomas, 63
Gardali, Glen, 19, 23, 33
Gardella, Elizabeth, 124
Gardenia, Vincent, 64, 213
Gardiner, John, 148
Gardner, C.R., 185
Gardner, Dean, 64, 70
Gardner, Gary, 78
Gardner, Herb, 35, 165
Gardner, Jerry, 163
Gardner, Josie, 185
Gardner, Kelly, 185
Gardner, Rita, 150, 164
Gardner, Tom, 187
Gardner, William T., 177, 237
Gardner, Worth, 113
Garfinkle, Tiffany, 103
Gari, Angela, 26, 32
Garin, Michael, 71
Garito, Ken, 72, 131, 148, 213
Garlin, Jeff, 179
Garman, Bob, 103
Garner, Bill, 177
Garner, Jay, 140
Garner, Patrick, 163
Garren, Joseph, 85
Garrett, Becky, 189
Garrett, James R., 73
Garrett, Lillian, 193
Garrett, Melody J., 190
Garrett, Russell, 70, 213
Garrett-Groag, Lillian, 131, 152, 172
Garrick, Barbara, 50
Garrick, Kathy, 135
Garrison, Angela, 174
Garrity, J. Robert, 143
Garsson, Keith, 81, 91
Garst, Samuel A., 170
Gartelos, Teria, 159
Gartlan, Nancy, 95
Garvanne, Kelvin, 81
Garvey, Thom, 84
Garza, Julian, 143
Gash, Kent, 117, 191

Hodgson, Colin, 96
Hodgson, Michael, 92
Hodson, Ed, 144
Hoebee, Mark, 18, 174, 215
Hoesl, Joseph, 69
Hoffenberg, Julianne, 85, 94
Hofflund, Mark, 172
Hoffman, Avi Ber, 77, 79, 111, 215
Hoffman, Constance, 93
Hoffman, Dustin, 118, 200
Hoffman, Miriam, 77
Hoffman, Philip, 53, 113, 215
Hoffmann, Cecil, 112
Hoffmann, E.T.A., 178
Hofmaier, Mark, 177
Hofmann, Robert, 187
Hofsiss, Jack, 158
Hofvendahl, Steve, 128, 215
Hogan, Chris, 179
Hogan, Harold, Sr., 157
Hogan, Jonathan, 5, 12, 193, 215
Hogan, Luke, 140
Hogan, Robert, 36
Hogan, Tessie, 142, 157
Hoge, John, 125
Hogle, Richard, 141
Hoiby, Lee, 117
Holbrook, Hal, 161, 172
Holbrook, Priscilla, 100
Holbrook, Ruby, 116, 215
Holden, Sarah J., 179
Holder, Donald, 8, 73-74, 78, 111, 123, 130, 152, 158, 165
Holder, Geoffrey, 76
Holder, Laurence, 114
Holderness, Rebecca, 101
Holdgrive, David, 150
Holeva, Linda, 178
Holgate, Danny, 186
Holgate, Ron, 164
Hollaender, Friederick, 117
Holland, Dorothy, 177
Holland, Dr. Endesha Ida Mae, 88, 150
Holland, Jan, 91
Holland, Leslie, 161
Hollander, Anita, 76
Holleman, John, 112
Holliday, David, 47, 201, 215
Hollis, Marnee, 160
Hollis, Stephen, 191
Hollman, Heidi, 101
Holman, Equiano, 78
Holman, Terry Tittle, 186
Holmes, Jake, 50
Holmes, Jennifer, 174
Holmes, Marti, 166
Holmes, Michael, 171
Holmes, Paul Mills, 168
Holmes, Richard, 91, 93, 124
Holmes, Violet, 15
Holmquist, Anders, 121
Holms, John Pynchon, 148
Holof, Georgia, 173
Holt, Lorri, 144
Holt, Monique, 170

Holt, Rebecca, 176
Holt, Stacy Todd, 176
Holten, Michael, 35, 150
Holton, Melody, 156
Holton, Tim, 157
Holtzman, Merrill, 85, 215
Homa-Rocchio, Catherine, 168
*Home And Away, 130, 159*
*Home Show Pieces, The, 125*
*Home, 10*
*Homecoming, The, 12*
Homer, Jeanne M., 194
Homes, Denis, 160
*Homesick, 99*
*Homeward Bound, 186, 194*
*Homo Sapien Shuffle, 125*
Homuth, Richard, 124
Honan, Mark, 127
Honda, Carol A., 88, 125, 215
Honegger, Gitta, 190
Honeywell, Roger, 194
Hood, Daniel, 150
Hook, Cora, 114
Hooker, Brian W., 180
Hooper, Jeff, 142
Hoover, Teressa Lynne, 77
Hopkins, Bill, 113
Hopkins, Billy, 39, 84
Hopkins, Karen Brooks, 115
Hopper, Paul, 169
Horaitis, Ellen R., 78
Horan, James, 75
Horchow, Roger, 26
Horen, Bob, 87, 105, 215
Horgan, Mike, 168
Horitz, Murray, 147
Hormann, Nicholas, 164-165
Horn, Andrew M., 175
Horne, Gretchen Van, 141
Horne, J.R., 129-130
Horne, Larry, 81
Horne, Marjorie, 95
Horneff, Wil, 32
Horovitz, Israel, 14
Horowitz, Jeffrey, 96
Horowitz, Murray, 175
Horrigan, Patrick, 47
Horst, Ellen, 194
Horton, Jamie, 157
Horton, John, 12, 138
Horton, Vaughn, 37
Horvath, Jan, 97, 116, 215
Horvath, Odon Von, 142
Horwath, Anita, 103
Hoshi, Shizuko, 88
Hoskins, Raymond, 176
Hosney, Doug, 161
Hostetter, Curt, 163
*Hot'n Cole, 150*
*Hotel Paradiso, 23*
Hotopp, Michael J., 16
Hoty, Dee, 63, 215
Hoty, Tony, 110, 158, 180
Houdyshell, Jayne, 183
Hough, Paul, 146
Houghton, James, 85, 93, 109
Hould-Ward, Ann, 53, 163

*Hour Of The Lynx, 106*
*House Of Bernarda Alba, The, 170*
*House Of Blue Leaves, The, 148*
Houser, David, 156
Houston, Gary, 179
Houston, Velina Hasu, 172, 184
Hoven, Bryant, 92
Hovland, Carroll, 185
*How I Got That Story, 148*
*How The Other Half Loves, 188*
*How To Succeed In Business
    Without Really Trying, 110*
Howard, Andrew, 84, 118
Howard, Celia, 93, 216
Howard, David S., 150
Howard, Ed, 170, 175, 188
Howard, Gay, 92
Howard, M.A., 85, 129
Howard, Mel, 9
Howard, Noel, 37
Howard, Peter, 26
Howard, Richard, 193
Howard, Sidney, 7, 25, 151
Howard, Steven C., Jr., 142
Howard, Stuart, 18, 134, 154, 168
Howard, Susan, 53
Howard, Tim, 166
Howarth, Roger, 131
Howe, Brian, 108, 165
Howell, Jeff, 178
Howell, John, 174
Howell, Michael W., 146
Howells, Greg, 154
Hower, Nancy, 124
Howes, Sally Ann, 7, 76, 216-217
Hoxie, Richmond, 158
Hoyes, R. Stephen, 99, 152
Hoyle, Kalen, 186
Hoyt, Lon, 71
Hreben, Ty, 140
Hu, Jia Lu, 109
Huang, Helen Q., 183
Hubatsek, Andrew, 19, 23
Hubbard, Dana S., 102
Hubbard, Philip, 193
Hubbell, Lawrence, 78
Huber, David, 172
Hubner, Kathi Jo, 91
*Huck Finn's Story, 165*
Hudson, Carl R., 190
Hudson, Chuck, 168
Hudson, Gayle, 109
Hudson, Richard, 159
Huey, Susan, 156
Huffman, Cady, 63, 216-217
Huffman, Eric, 179
Huffman, Mike, 79
Huggins, Cheryl, 103
Huggins, Dennis P., 55
Hughes, Allen Lee, 88, 107-108, 139, 146
Hughes, Allen, 146
Hughes, Douglas, 182
Hughes, Julie, 26, 63
Hughes, Jurian, 146
Hughes, Langston, 125
Hughes, Liam, 149

Hughes, Lisa, 95
Hugo, Tara, 148
Hugo, Victor, 58
Hugot, Marceline, 174
Hui, Alyson, 91
*Huipil, 98*
Hull, Mindy, 134
Hume, Michael J., 148
Humes, Linda H., 77
Hummel, Mark, 43
Hummert, James, 157
Humphrey, Nina, 124
Humphreys, John, 77
Humphreys, Polly, 96
*120 Seconds, 86*
Hunley, C.L., 184
Hunold, Michael, 95
Hunt, Annette, 100
Hunt, Gordon, 118
Hunt, LaShonda, 139
Hunt, Linda, 168
Hunt, Lois Kelso, 183
Hunt, Pamela, 170, 180
Hunt, William E., 80
Hunter, Dawn, 98
Hunter, JoAnn M., 43, 60
Hunter, Kathryn, 104
Hunter, Kim, 39, 177
Hunter, Timothy, 70, 168, 174
Hunter, Todd, 15
*Hunting Of The Snark, 171*
Huntington, Burr, 157
Huntington, Crystal, 99, 117, 130
Huntington, John, 125
Huntley, Paul, 167
Hurd, Bruce, 15
Hurd, Derek Harrison, 172
Hurd, Michelle, 104, 155
Hurko, Roman, 119
*Hurray!Hurray!Hollywood, 80*
Hurst, Gregory S., 158
Hurst, Lillian, 105
Hurst, Melissa, 111
Hurston, Zora Neale, 114, 152, 159
Hurt, Mary Beth, 124, 216
Hurt, William, 144, 201
Hurwitz, Nathan, 177-178
Huse, Cynthia, 165
Husmann, Andrew, 135
Husovsky, Peter, 192
Hussey, Nathanial, 95
Hutchinson, Jeffrey, 159
Hutchinson, Fiona, 108
Hutchison, Christopher R., 177
Hutchison, Mark, 184
Hutnik, Andrea, 168
Hutsell, Melanie, 81
Huttar, Shaun, 77
Hutton, Bill, 116, 237
Hutton, John, 157
Hutton, Timothy, 116, 216
Hwang, David Henry, 128, 142, 182
*Hyaena, 142*
Hyatt, Jeffrey, 70
Hyatt, Lani, 171
Hyatt, Pam, 80